Advances in Manufacturing Technology - XX

Acknowledgements

The editors wish to thank Ms. Helen Pottle for her assistance in the coordinating of the conference and its proceedings, and to thank the Conference International Scientific Committee (below) for their assistance with the paper review process.

Dr. D. Allanson	Liverpool John Moores University, UK
Professor B. Hon	University of Liverpool, UK
Professor A. Torrance	Trinity College, Dublin, ROI
Professor P. Maropoulos	University of Bath, UK
Dr. Xun Chen	University of Nottingham, UK
Professor W. B. Rowe	Rowe Consulting, UK
Professor K. Cheng	Brunel University, UK
Dr. J. Webster	Cool Grind Technologies, USA
Professor P. Shore	Cranfield University, UK
Professor R. Baines	De Montfort University, UK
Professor Lin Bin	Tianjin University, China,
Professor G. Byrne	University College, Dublin, ROI
Professor K. Case	Loughborough University, UK
Dr. D. Ford	University of Cambridge, UK
Professor D. Ford	University of Huddersfield, UK
Dr. J. Gao	Cranfield University, UK
Professor Yongsheng Gao	Hong Kong UST
Professor N. Gindy	University of Nottingham, UK
Professor F. Holevosky	J.E. Purkynê, Czech Republic
Professor W. Knight	University of Rhode Island, USA
Professor B. Kruszynski	Technical University of Lodz, Poland
Professor T. Kuriyagawa	Tohoku University, Japan
Professor G. Levy	FHS St. Gallen, Switzerland
Professor Guo Li	Hunan University, China
Professor Y. C. Liang	Harbin Institute of Technology, China
Professor Grier Lin	University of South Australia, Australia
Dr. L. Newnes	University of Bath, UK
Dr. T. Pearce	University of the West of England, UK
Professor T. Perera	Sheffield Hallam University, UK
Professor D. T. Pham	Cardiff University, UK
Dr. Qin Yi	University of Strathclyde, UK
Professor Cai Quangqi	NEUT, China
Dr. J. Ren	Liverpool John Moores University, UK
Dr. S. Saad	Sheffield Hallam University, UK
Dr. M. Saadat	University of Birmingham, UK
Professor P. Sackett	Cranfield University, UK
Professor D. Smyth	University of Paisley, UK
Professor D. Stephenson	Cranfield University, UK
Professor D. Stockton	De Montfort University, UK
Professor Jun'ichi Tamaki	Kitami Institute of Technology, Japan
Dr. N. Woodfine	Southampton Solent University, UK

Books   turned o

Advances in
Manufacturing
Technology - XX

**Proceedings of the 4th International Conference on Manufacturing Research
(ICMR2006)**

Liverpool John Moores University, UK

5th - 7th September 2006

Edited by
M. N. Morgan and I. D. Jenkinson

Liverpool John Moores University

First Published 2006

Liverpool John Moores University
Faculty of Technology and Environment
Byrom Street Annexe
Byrom Street
Liverpool, L3 3AF
United Kingdom

t: +44 (0) 151 231 2590   f: +44 (0) 151 231 2590   e: m.n.morgan@ljmu.ac.uk

© 2006 Liverpool John Moores University and the Institution of Mechanical Engineers

ISBN 0-9553215-0-6

Design and production: Ron Jones Associates

Printed in Great Britain

About the Editors

Dr. Michael Morgan is Research Manager for the Advanced Manufacturing Technology Research Laboratory (AMTReL, GERI) and Reader in Manufacturing Technology. He has over 17 years experience in manufacturing research and has contributed to key developments and innovations in grinding process technology through major collaborative research contracts leading to award winning products in the grinding machine tool industry. He is a founder member of the International Committee for Abrasive Technology (ICAT), a member of the Consortium of Manufacturing Engineering Heads (COMEH), member of the EPSRC College of Peers, member of the Steering committees of the UK Precision Engineering Network and LamdaMap and member of the IMechE. He has published over 50 research papers including an influential Royal Society paper and is a member of the editorial boards and reviewing committees of a number of international journals. He has managed a large number of recent successfully completed EPSRC / Industry projects, EU and other UK Council / industry projects. The detail of current and recently concluded research is available at: http://www.ljmu.ac.uk/geri/.

Dr. Ian Jenkinson is Director of the School of Engineering at Liverpool John Moores University. On graduating from the University of Newcastle he worked as a project engineer with a number of major companies before joining the University in 1991 as a senior lecturer in mechanical and manufacturing. Dr. Jenkinson is active in the development of engineering education, technology transfer and enterprise. His major research interests are in manufacturing engineering and in the development of decision support tools for operations management. He is a member of the Institute of Electrical and Electronic Engineers, and the Institution of Engineering and Technology.

Contents

Session - Virtual Reality and Process Selection

DAY TWO

Keynote Speaker (2)

Invited speaker from Industry (2)

Session - Advanced Manufacturing Technology: Grinding

Session - Production Systems and Process Optimisation

Session - Intelligent Design and Simulation

DAY THREE

Keynote Speaker (3)

Invited Speaker From Industry (3)

Special Session - Micro-Manufacturing

Session - Intelligent Manufacturing Systems

Authors' Index

Preface

The Consortium of UK University Manufacturing Engineering. (COMEH)

The Consortium is an independent body and was established at a meeting held at Loughborough University on 17 February 1978. Its main aim is to promote manufacturing engineering, education, training and research. To achieve this the consortium maintains a close liaison with those government departments and other bodies concerned with the initial/continuing education and training of professional engineers, while also responding to appropriate consultative and discussion documents and other initiatives. It organises and supports national manufacturing engineering education research conferences and symposia. COMEH is represented on the Engineering Professors' Council (EPC) and it organizes and supports national manufacturing engineering education research conferences and symposia. The key event in the COMEH calendar is the annual 'International Conference on Manufacturing Research' (ICMR).

The ICMR is normally held in the early part of September. For many years, it was a UK National Conference that had successfully brought academics and industrialists together to share their knowledge and experiences. The conference has developed as a major international event with a growing number of international delegates participating to exchange their research findings with UK researchers and practitioners. The first NCMR was held at the University of Nottingham in 1985. The subsequent NCMR and ICMR conferences have been held as follows:

1986		Napier
1987		Nottingham
1988		Sheffield
1989		Huddersfield
1990		Strathclyde
1991		Hatfield
1992		University of Central England
1993		Bath
1994		Loughborough
1995		De Montfort
1996		Bath
1997		Glasgow Caledonian
1998		Derby
1999		Bath
2000		University of East London
2001		Cardiff
2002		Leeds Metropolitan
ICMR	2003	Strathclyde
ICMR	2004	Sheffield Hallam University
ICMR	2005	Cranfield
ICMR	2006	Liverpool John Moores

Conference Timetable

	DAY ONE	DAY TWO	DAY THREE
Morning	5th September 2006 **Keynote Speaker** Professor Nam P Suh, MIT, USA	6th September 2006 **Keynote Speaker** Dr Gareth M Williams, Airbus UK	7th September 2006 **Keynote Speaker** Professor Neil Barlow, Northwest Automotive Alliance
Morning	**Invited Speaker From Industry** Andrea Guidotti- Balance Systems	**Invited Speaker From Industry** Bob Willey, Mike Hitchiner- Saint Gobain Abrasives	**Invited Speaker From Industry** Mr. Rahul Sharma- Infosys Technologies Limited, India
Morning Session 1A	**Special Session - Design Information Management** Six papers are scheduled for presentation	**Session - Advanced Manufacturing Technology, Grinding** Six papers are scheduled for presentation	**Special Session - Micro Manufacturing** Six papers are scheduled for presentation
Morning Session 1B	**Session - Intelligent Planning and Scheduling Systems** Five papers are scheduled for presentation	**Session - Innovative Manufacturing Processes** Six papers are scheduled for presentation	**Session - Intelligent Manufacturing Systems** COMEH Meeting
Afternoon Session 2A	**Session - E-Manufacturing and Supply Chain Management** Five papers are scheduled for presentation.	**Session - Materials Processing Technology** Four papers are scheduled for presentation	
Afternoon Session 2B	**Session - Precision Manufacturing** Five papers are scheduled for presentation.	**Session - Advanced Manufacturing Technology, Cutting** Five papers are scheduled for presentation	
Afternoon Session 3A	**Session - Operations Management** Four papers are scheduled for presentation	**Session - Production Systems and Process Optimisation** Four papers are scheduled for presentation	
Afternoon Session 3B	**Session - Virtual Reality and Process Selection** Four papers are scheduled for presentation	**Session - Intelligent Design and Simulation** Four papers are scheduled for presentation	

Keynote Paper

● **The Effect of Coupling of Functional Requirements of Products, Processes, and Systems on Manufacturing Competitiveness**
Professor Nam P. Suh, MIT, USA

The Effect of Coupling of Functional Requirements of Products, Processes, and Systems on Manufacturing Competitiveness

Professor Nam P. Suh

M.I.T., Cambridge, MA 02139, U. S. A.
npsuh@mit.edu

Abstract.

The choice of manufacturing processes and systems determines the required capital investment and the productivity of industrial operations. They in turn determine the quality, functionality, dimensional accuracy, and cost of products that can be manufactured by an industrial firm. Consequently, many different manufacturing processes and systems are employed to maximize the productivity with minimum capital investment. In an ideal situation, manufacturing processes and systems should be so flexible and robust that they can make a large variety of products to the desired degree of accuracy and functionality without major new capital investment. To approach the ideal situation, products, processes, and systems must be designed based on basic principles.

In this presentation, the importance of maintaining the independence of functional requirements (FRs) of products and processes for flexibility, quality, accuracy, functionality, and productivity will be illustrated using the manufacture of traditional and new products as examples.

3

Invited Speaker
from Industry

● **Balance Systems- An introduction to application based technologies in mechanical manufacturing processes**
Dr. Ing Andrea Guidotti, Product Marketing Manager, Balance Systems

BALANCE SYSTEMS – An Introduction to Application Based Technologies in Mechanical Manufacturing Processes

Dr. Ing. Andrea Guidotti[1] - Product Marketing Manager.

Balance Systems s.r.l. – 20060 Pessano con Bornago, Milan, Italy – www.balancesystems.com
Auxiliary Measuring and Control Systems for Machine Tools.Testing and Balancing Systems for the Production of Rotary Components.

[1] guidotti@balancesystems.it

Abstract. Product quality, economy and productivity of manufacturing industry relies heavily on suitable automatic process control and inspection systems applied at all the stages of the production process.
Balance Systems, drawing on the most advanced technologies and investing 15% of its turnover in R&D, designs, sells and assists a global market in balancing machines, production inspection equipment and grinding cycle control systems that effectively fit into production architectures.
Examples of Balance Systems' technological solutions, aimed at satisfying present and future trends in customer demand within different industries, are presented. Focus is given to the following applied research projects:

- BVK, a family of vertical balancing machines which introduces high dynamic measuring range to drastically reduce the re-tooling time for parts such as crank-shafts where precise virtual balancing is achieved in the presence of high physical unbalance. Unbalance correction is automatically effected by milling, where the material removal and the efficiency of the cutting tool are monitored by acoustic emission analysis.
- VTM, an inspection bench for the assessment of the noise and the electrical characteristics of assembled electrical motors of domestic appliances (i.e. washing machines, vacuum cleaner, etc.) The system reproduces the skill of an expert operator in the judgement of acceptable acoustic emission. It also provides tools to evaluate the impact on the past production by changing the acceptance criteria levels.
- PR4, an inspection bench based on contact and vision technology to check the dimensional, geometrical and assembly defects of armatures.
- VM20, a modular multi-function equipment for grinding cycles control that provides for automatic balancing, acoustic emission and power sensing, and in-process gauging. Examples of new applications, made possible due to the enhanced performances of the system, will be presented.

Design Information Management

Developing a Framework for Affordability Engineering

Anil Ray[1, a], Paul Baguley[1, b] and Rajkumar Roy[3, c]

[1]Decision Engineering Centre, Cranfield University, Cranfield, Bedford, MK43 0AL, UK.

[a]a.ray@cranfield.ac.uk, [b]p.baguley@cranfield.ac.uk, [c]r.roy@cranfield.ac.uk

Abstract. Affordability Engineering is a process which enables companies to reduce costs and improve value throughout the whole life cycle of a product. This is specifically achieved through the use of cost estimating and risk information, especially at the conceptual design stage. Costs generated at the conceptual design stage easily account for the greatest percentage of the whole life cycle costs of a product. Reducing these costs will enable the development of new products that are more affordable to the customer. Research into Affordability Engineering has progressed through a Network of Excellence, incorporating industrial and academic partners. The network output to date has been in the form of a framework capturing the essential aspects found so far, of Affordability Engineering. The framework is motivated by the creation of a new formal definition of Affordability Engineering.

Keywords: Affordability Engineering, Affordability Definition, Affordability Framework

Introduction

Cost Engineering research at Cranfield University is being further developed through a Network of Excellence in Affordability Engineering. The purpose of the network is to create a new interdisciplinary research community, consisting of academic and industrial groups, with a desire to develop and promote the concept of Affordability Engineering. The objectives of the network include providing opportunities for information exchange and debate, generating new research topics, developing roadmaps, developing a framework that helps to attract funding for future projects in Affordability Engineering, encouraging industry to utilise academic-based expertise, and disseminating best practices and procedures within the Aerospace and Automotive industries. These objectives are being achieved through various activities, including workshops and newsletters, research seminars and conferences, and the development of a Web Portal.

Affordability has been scoped through regular events, presentations, a literature review, and the presence of main stakeholders from within the aerospace, automobile and Cost Engineering software industry sectors. Their observations are complemented through academic rigour and state-of-the-art knowledge from university academics, and the support of the sponsoring British Association of Cost Engineers (AcostE) and the Society of Cost Estimating and Analysts (SCEA).

Research Methodology

The research methodology has a number of building blocks within its structure, peculiar to network type projects. An important generator of concepts and a source of validation has been the Focus Group of the network's members. A number of brain storming sessions have been conducted in order to scope the concept of Affordability. The following are examples of some of the main issues which were discovered:

- The maintenance of Affordability from the perspective of multiple stakeholders.
- The factors involved in engineering Affordability, for example (1) cost, price and economic factors, (2) performance, for example through functionality and quality, and (3) schedule.
- Requirements change from the perspective of (1) the market, (2) evolution of requirements, and (3) from the "voice of the customer".
- Development of technology as influenced from previous product developments and also from the needs of the product development phases.
- The need and requirements of an index of Affordability.

In summary a number of factors have been considered important for Affordability, these being represented in Figure 2, in the spider diagram. They are: economic criteria, Whole Life Cycle Cost, possible impact of regulations, technology innovation, perceived quality, probability of value chain, probability of requirement chain, customer ability to pay, global competition, performance related measure, and probability of such configuration. Research shall determine whether these are wholly complete. The spider diagram itself is a prototype tool for measuring Affordability.

The network has further demonstrated the concept of Affordability through the consideration of the deviation of the quantity of Whole Life Cycle Cost and the quantity of investment cost, as shown in Figure 1. These considerations are finally captured via the development of an Affordability Engineering definition stated in a later Section. The definition has been previously disseminated at a recent meeting of the European Aerospace Working Group on Cost Engineering (EACE) at the Ministry of Defence (MOD) in Abbey Wood, Bristol.

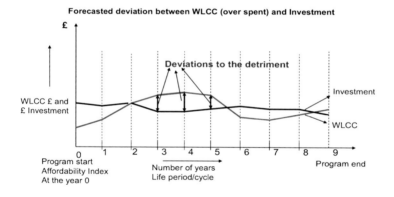

Figure 1: The Deviation Between Whole Life Cycle Costs and Investment Costs

Concepts Found Through the Network

The focus group of industry and academia has motivated multi-directional discussion around Affordability Engineering. The following text indicates some of these ideas. Increasing globalisation has made price and cost competition of product and services more intensive. Besides the growing cost competition criteria which are price, quality and early delivery, an added criterion is being embodied in the competition. The literature terms this the philosophy of "cost effectiveness". The philosophy entails, the requirements to deliver cost effective products with value added services through knowledge creation and knowledge application [1].

The shift in competitiveness in the market can now be exemplified by the introduction of new economic models, for example a model termed the: "demand pull economic model". This is creating a paradigm shift and emphasising how much the market for new products, processes and services is willing to pay. And not just how much to pay, but also the concerns of proportional functional worth and a price within the customer Affordability range [2].

Affordability concerns the objectives of all stakeholders within the full life cycle. Affordability for the supplier is an environment where highly synthesized products fulfil customer requirements in the three dimensions of performance, availability or cost; matching respectively the improvements termed, "better", "faster" "cheaper" [3]. Engineering the "Affordability" is carried out at an early concept design stage where selling the cost of effective functionality of product and / or program by added service value, as a package, can be prepared in order to trade-off against customer wants and requirements.

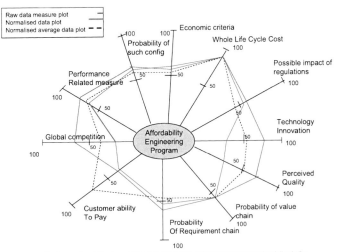

Note: The diagram is only for demonstration and not to scale. Space vector are drawn in relation to the perspective of the major criteria. Criteria are interrelated, hence each criterion are placed in relation to the next space vector and not on any space vector.

Figure 2: A Proposed System of Measures for Affordability Engineering

Further observations from the network sponsors direct that at the early concept stage, trade-offs of the program strategy are more widely related to systems feasibility and Affordability. This is in terms of capability, support and the actual process of buying and running the manufactured product. This might be understood through the examples of running an aircraft engine, or running a car. However the systems flow down requirements from higher level specification is often a challenge for the systems developers at the concept stage which can be expressed through the illustration in Figure 3. It shows that for developers there is a need to answer the requirements of the users in terms of want, needs, Affordability and willingness to pay. As they move towards substantiating how much the user is willing to pay, the degree of uncertainty reduces.

Capability Based Contracting

Significant discussion has been enacted around a principle which can be termed, "capability based contracting". For example a contract which would provide a number of flying hours of performance from an aero engine, rather than providing the physical engine itself. Or the capability to provide a radar image of the United Kingdom without the need for a full product specification of how that image can be delivered physically. This emphasis on capability provides further degrees of freedom around Affordability Engineering concepts for all stakeholders. Hence it is found that a shift to capability based contracting, as a competitive advantage for the supplier, is delivered through an Affordability strategy.

Delivering Affordability

Supplier, and or producer, should implement a systems approach to Affordability strategy by instigating Whole Life cycle Costing (WLC) over a program or project time which could stretch for 20, 30 or even 40 years. This is a length of time which is often observed in the aerospace industry. It is thought that implementing Affordability strategy through WLC would improve future systems parameters and conditions. In addition it would provide competitive advantages and allocate resources more efficiently to where they are needed at a particular point in the full life cycle. The lack of this scenario is often observed in industry after the program / project contract is awarded. Literature based sources concur with the observation [1].

Therefore, Affordability, in essence becomes an ability to "afford" a project / program, not only from the perspective of supplier but also the acquirer. The meaning of "Affordability", it could be argued, does not lie in the ability to afford, but in the attitude to be fully proactive in participation in the evaluation of the trade space exploration process through systems engineering. This is, not per se, evaluating an engineering optimization solution, which is rather carried out after facts gathering on the project are known. In essence the concept embraces "Design for Cost and Quality" at the concept stage and not after a product hits the production floor or indeed worse, after it gets to the customer. The concept, therefore, focuses on cost effectiveness in evaluating the "trade space" through applying multi-criteria decision making [4] in terms of cost, performance and schedule; namely how much systems effectiveness can we acquire per unit of Whole Life Cycle Cost [1].

In the Multi-Criteria Decision Making method (MCDM), the analysis is often applied in a situation where customer and supplier objectives conflict during the development of the product. In practice, the Preliminary Design Review (PDR) is an example. Here, the first screening of conceptual design alternatives is short listed; and a compromise solution [5] is reached between the customer and the supplier, based on the defined goals at the managerial level. MCDM, then defines the alternatives identifying a design "Trade Space" and points out one alternative examining the established criteria. The chosen alternative generates detailed evaluation to undertake Critical Design Review (CDR) and to set a target cost of the product. This is often termed as Designing for "Target Cost".

Affordability Definition

A significant output of the network thus far has been a definition of Affordability. The definition has been developed through consensus of the network members. The consensus was generated by the events and communication encouraged by the network type project. The definition of Affordability has been synthesised from the perspective of the network's members. The definition was to capture the main aspects brought forth through brain storming, information dissemination, experience and expectations of the stakeholders. The final definition was stated as being:

"Affordability is the degree to which Whole Life Cycle Cost (WLCC) of an individual project/ program is in consonance with long range investment capability and evolving customer requirements. Affordability Engineering therefore aims to engineer Affordability early at the concept stage, aligning customer requirements and willingness to pay in a project/program through innovative design and cost management".

Consonance is a term from music and is defined by the Hutchinson Encyclopaedia on the 22nd of September as: "in music, a combination of two or more notes that "agree" with each other (due to their relationship within the naturally occurring harmonic series) and thus sound pleasing to the ear". Consonance is the opposite of dissonance.

Affordability Engineering Framework

The research methodology which contributed to the preceding discussion has thus identified a number of related concepts able to fulfil the requirements set out by the definition of Affordability Engineering. These concepts have been assembled into an Affordability Framework shown in Figure 4. This diagrammatic framework indicates the stages in which to assess an Affordability measure throughout the full life cycle of a product. The framework shall generate major criteria and so examine those constituents which are applicable to measure the Affordability of the program. A significant extra concept to the framework has been the notion of an Affordability Index to be developed at an early stage. This early stage index will thus be carried forward to reconcile Affordability with the supportable committed budget for the Whole Life Cycle Cost. The six major identified phases of Whole Life Cost in this context are: (1) need of recognition, (2) design development, (3) production, (4) distribution, (5) use, and (6) disposal.

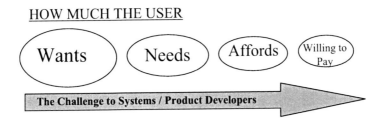

Figure 3: Reducing Uncertainty Under Affordability

Affordability Engineering Framework

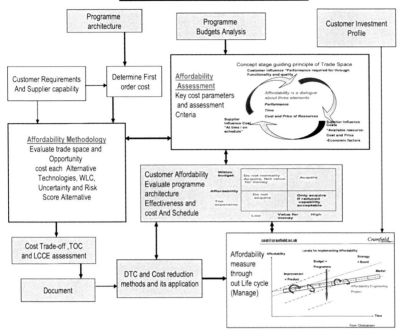

Figure 4: Affordability Engineering Framework

Conclusion

A new concept of Affordability Engineering is being considered at Cranfield University though a Network of Excellence. A definition of Affordability Engineering has been developed, and methods of measuring Affordability investigated. The concept has been defined and scoped so to produce a prototype Affordability Engineering framework. The framework will form the basis of an Affordability Assessment task and a new Affordability Index.

References

[1]   Wasson, C.S.: *Systems Analysis Design and Development* (John Wiley and Sons, 2006).

[2]   Curran, R., Raghunathan, S., and Price, Review of Aerospace Engineering Cost Modelling: the Genetic Causal Approach, Progress in Aerospace Science, Vol. 40, No. 8 (2004), pp. 487-534.

[3]   Bradberry, R.: *Development of a Descriptive Framework for Affordability Engineering* (MSc Thesis, Cranfield University 2005).

[4]   Kirkpatrick, D.: *Conquering Complexity* (Lessons for Defence Systems Acquisition, 2005)

[5]   Belton, V., and Stewart, F,Y.: *Multi-Criteria Decision Analysis, an Integrated Approach* (Kluwer, 2002).

Product-Service Systems: Issues and Challenges

E. M. Shehab and R. Roy

Decision Engineering Centre
Cranfield University, Cranfield, Bedford MK43 0AL, UK
{e.shehab / r.roy}@cranfield.ac.uk

Abstract

Most western economies are shifting their focus from a product-based economy to a product-service based economy in which companies are selling functions instead of products to satisfy customers' needs. In other words the customers purchase the service provided by products rather than the traditional way of owning the products themselves. The product-service system (PSS) strategy has great impacts on both the product life cycle and companies strategies. Therefore an attempt has been made in this paper to review several issues and challenges that are critical to the success of developing product-service systems. This will aid to identify areas where further research is needed. During the last decade, PSS have received a significant amount of attention from researchers and practitioners from business-to-customers perspectives. Sustainability was one of the main areas that attracts their attention. The paper presents also a comprehensive review of the recent research literature concerning PSS.

Keywords: Technical Product-Service Systems, Service and Design Processes, Cost Engineering

Introduction

Nowadays manufacturing companies are moving their attention away from old business strategy of selling products to a new business model of selling functions and results that effectively fulfill the final-users' needs. This business model is referred to product-service system (PSS). The PSS model means that the companies are paid per unit of functions delivered, not per physical product unit sold. In these circumstances customers become more interested in having an integrated-solution for their needs rather than in owning the product, which is supposed to provide the function. As a result of this business model, companies will have the ownership of a product which will force the companies to make more high quality and efficient products. Consequently this approach can have significant environmental benefits due to reducing waste generation since this business model can decouple the business success of companies from the volume of products sold.

A product-service system has been defined as a system of products, services, supporting networks and infrastructure that is designed to be: competitive, satisfy customer needs and have a lower environmental impact than traditional business models [1]. In other words, the goal of the PSS concept is to provide a system of products and services that would be able to fulfill customer needs as efficiently as possible from an economic, operational and environmental point of views. The infrastructure represents existing structures and systems within society, such as, (recycling) technologies, waste collection points and incineration plants, the existence and suitability of which should be considered when a product and services are developed.

Technical product-service system can be defined as formulation and evaluation of alternative architectures of both material artefact and its associated services of a PSS that provide the end users with integrated solution throughout its lifecycle. The objective of this paper is to describe the major technical challenges of realising the product service systems. It also presents an integrative review and discussion of the recent literature in areas relevant to the PSS. Finally, conclusions and the implication for future research are explored.

An Overview of the State-of-the-Art Research

In the last decade, product-service systems (PSS) have attracted the interests of many researchers and governments. One area has received much attention which is sustainability. In this context, the majority of the research papers within a recent special issue on PSS, the Journal of Cleaner Production [2] present methods, methodologies and tools for companies to design scenarios of new business models to shift towards PSS in environmentally sound ways and evaluate the outcomes of the shift [3-6].

An appropriate methodology to transfer the PSS concept from UK academic circles to industry has been discussed in reference [3]. Additionally they identified the factors which impact upon, and importantly lead to, the successful completion of this process. Morelli [4] proposed methods for mapping the actors that are or should be involved in developing and delivering PSS, methods to define the requirements and structure of a PSS and methods to represent and blueprint a PSS. He identified tools that exist in other than design disciplines, which may help to incorporate cultural and social norms into product-service design. Krucken and Meroni [5] presented an approach to develop a communication tool that aims to stimulate the building of stakeholder networks and delivering product-service systems. Roy [7] stated that sustainable PSS attempt to create designs that are sustainable in terms of environmental burden and resource use, whilst developing product concepts as parts of sustainable whole systems, which provide a service or function to meet essential needs.

Williams [8] suggested that the concept of micro-factory retailing (MFR) offers an opportunity for the introduction of the PSS concept at a practical level within the automotive industry. MFR is based on novel approaches to vehicle design that facilitate the economic viability of small-scale localised manufacturing sites. In addition, the logic of localization facilitates a greater degree of interaction between producer and consumer, and allows many of the possible shortcomings of PSS to be overcome. These sites provide a means of facilitating many of the components of PSS, such as upgrading, repair and end-of- life management. Ling et al [9] developed a 3-point cost estimating model to predicate costs of railway maintenance and renewal projects at the early stages of the project life cycle. The practical implications of their developed model were its ability to estimate maintenance and renewal project costs when there is a lack of qualitative data and detailed project definition. Roy and Sackett [10] indicated that cost is a factor of success in the product/service of many industries. Companies unable to provide detailed, meaningful cost estimates at the early development phases have a significantly higher percentage of programs behind schedule with higher development costs than those that can provide completed cost estimates. Their work was focused on aerospace, automotive and defense industries.

There are three main uncertainties regarding the applicability and feasibility of PSS: the readiness of companies to adopt them, the readiness of consumers to accept them, and their environmental implications [11]. Additionally Mont [11] indicated that successful PSS requires different societal infrastructure, human structures and organisational layouts in order to function in a sustainable manner.

Very little effort was made in technical product-service systems. In this respect, Aurich et al [6] introduced a process for the systematic design of product related technical services that upon its modularization represents a promising starting point for linkage with corresponding product design processes. Additionally they discussed a modular approach for integrating existing product and service design processes. Life cycle oriented design of technical Product-Service Systems is also presented. Furthermore the authors indicated that the allocation of specific service design tasks to the regional and local service providers in the extended value creation network must be systematically supported in order to flexibly meet changing customer requirements.

Issues and Challenges

The PSS concept encompasses challenges in different ways and levels within an organisation. From the business management perspective, it requires a substantial change in the way companies see themselves and their businesses. The companies have to adapt their business strategy with this business model. Almost all company functions, including design, purchasing, accounting, management, marketing, etc might encounter extensive changes as shown in Figure (1). Organisational changes required by the concept will depend on the initial status of the company. An investigation is needed in order to study the impacts of the PSS concepts and identify which functions might be affected, to what extent, how can companies ease the transition and what new skills are required for that shift and for making the product-service system competitive. The new environment might involve financial risks in the initial stages for establishing contacts, education of personnel and chain actors, informing stakeholders, etc.

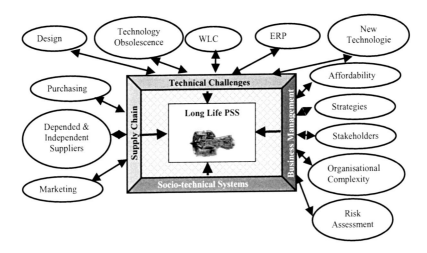

Figure (1) Challenges with long life product-service systems

The product-service systems are currently extended to long life products such as air engine and military products. For these product categories, the function provider needs to develop product support services and systems for monitoring products' working condition to manage producer-owned products at customer sites. This means entering customers' facilities and processes, and getting access to the information about some of the performance parameters of the customers' processes. This might be a sensitive issue for customers and a strong sense of trust should be present in such relations, which might be costly to establish.

19

In the product-service environment, the OEM (original equipment manufacturer) relies on a network of depended and independent suppliers and service to provide an integrated solution to the customers. The OEM is typically responsible for the design of both product as well as services. While the physical product is designed and developed at a certain time, the associated services are realized successfully throughout the product life cycle based on the customers' demands [6]. An optimum solution is required to achieve balance between product lead time, cost and quality.

In the case of functional products, the competition of product prices is shifting towards competition of functions, which means that product price, and thus raw materials price, does not play such as decisive a role. Historically, design efforts were directed towards product and production which lead to an increased productivity and corresponding decrease of production costs. Cost reductions of services, associated with the product provision to the customer are expected from companies. Designers should consider the entire system to identify what would be required to provide an efficient system and the needed function to consumers in the least costly manner [6]. Thus producers need to improve productivity of services in order to minimise the total cost of the product-service.

A trade-off analysis of a product-service system between cost, time and quality is representing a big challenge for this business model. The reason is that the analysis requires companies to predict the whole life cost and costs of alternative technologies with high confidence at the early stages of product development especially with economical changes such as oil prices. The designers are responsible to generate alternative architectures for the product-service systems to meet customer functional requirements and expectations. Furthermore companies have an incentive to optimise the function and to reduce associated costs of delivering the function, i.e. costs of consumables, labour, maintenance and disposal/refurbishment.

However systematic methods of product design have been well-established in industry. There is a need to develop new methodologies and tools to integrate physical product design with their associated services design at the early design of the product development cycle to meet the customers' expectations. Additionally a new approach is necessary to assess the impact of the changing customer requirements and technological development on the PSS design.

The PSS environment creates a challenge for designers within a company who have traditionally focused their activities on material artefact. They now need to stretch their knowledge and competence to encompass both physical and non-physical components of such systems [12]. Understanding the difference between both components requires major attention. They need to acquire special skills of working closely with product-service providers and customers. Within PSS concepts, the companies are responsible on the whole life cycle of their product including manufacturing, maintenance and upgrading service and end of life. Additionally companies have to broaden scope of design from product design to systems design including products, services, infrastructure and networks. There is a need, however, to incorporate continuous improvement element to improve efficiency of the whole systems. These issues should be in the focus of the PSS design at the conceptual stage. Closing product cycles allows companies to use recycled materials and re-use components from impaired products. This should be considered during the design stage.

The treatment of uncertainty in information and data is crucial to a successful implementation of PSS. Since this business model deals with the future and the future is unknown. It also requires new approaches to tackle uncertainties and risk assessment. There might be a risk of increased time-to-market due to increased information requirements for designing a product-service system.

Introduction and development of the PSS concept will probably have a considerable impact on the supply chain structure. There may be a need to consider not only the product chain in the design phase, but also networks of companies. The PSS approach requires closer collaboration of manufacturers, retailers and end-users, who become involved in the process of function extraction from products or directly purchase results of the product use. Moreover, the company gets a direct feedback from the customers about whether they are satisfied with the service, and what can be improved. Manufacturers can also design and develop new products with their customers. Besides, there is also a possibility to not only meet, but even to create new customer demands for function provision, which may give a competitive advantage. Within the PSS concept, the companies have to establish closer and longer relationships with customers, to provide feedback from the sale and use phase back to the design phase, to apply system approach that widens the scope from one company to a chain of companies collaborating on providing a function to the customer, and to incorporate environmental considerations into the system design. This direct feedback ensures continues improvement of the product-service system.

Conclusions

This paper discussed the challenges that may affect the implementation of business-to-business product-service systems (PSS) in different ways and levels within an organisation. It has focused on long life products such as air engine and military products. In terms of business management, companies have to change their business strategy to accommodate this business model. Companies' strategy within this new environment is a new topic that needs to be addressed.

Future research work is necessary in technical PSS since few researchers have directed their attention to this area of research. Traditionally designers within a company have focused their activities on material artefact. They now need to acquire new knowledge and competence to understand both the product and the various types of functions within the PSS concept. They have to generate alternative architectures for the product-service systems to meet customer functional requirements and expectations. Furthermore companies have an incentive to optimise the function and to reduce associated costs of delivering the function. A trade-off analysis of a product-service system between cost, time and quality is representing a big challenge for this business model.

References

1. O. Mont "Introducing and developing a Product-Service System (PSS) concept in Sweden" *IIIEE* *Reports* *2001:6* *(www.iiiee.lu.se/Publication.nsf/$webAll/71B8996A95A245B1C1256BE9003C2F62/$FILE/N UTEK.PDF) (Accessed on 31 May 2006)*
2. O. Mont and A. Tukker "Product-Service Systems: reviewing achievements and refining the research agenda" *Journal of Cleaner Production*, 2006, In Press
3. M.B. Cook, T.A. Bhamra and M. Lemon "The transfer and application of Product Service Systems: from academia to UK manufacturing firms" *Journal of Cleaner Production, 2006,* In Press
4. N. Morelli "Developing new product service systems (PSS): methodologies and operational tools" *Journal of Cleaner Production,* 2006, In Press
5. Krucken L. and Meroni A. "Building stakeholder networks to develop and deliver product-service-systems: practical experiences on elaborating pro-active materials for communication" *Journal of Cleaner Production, 2006,* In Press
6. J.C. Aurich; C. Fuchs and C. Wagenknecht "Life cycle oriented design of technical Product-Service Systems" *Journal of Cleaner Production, 2006,* In Press
7. R. Roy "Sustainable product-service systems" *Futures*, Vol 32, 2000, pp. 289 – 299.

8. A. Williams "Product-service systems in the automotive industry: the case of micro-factory retailing" *Journal of Cleaner Production*, Vol **14**, 2006, pp. 172 – 184.
9. D. Ling, R. Roy, E. Shehab, J. Jaiswal "Modelling the Cost of Railway Asset Renewal Projects Using Pairwise Comparisons" *Proceedings of Instn Mech Engrs (IMechE), Part F: Journal of Rail and Rapid Transit, 2006,* In Press.
10. R. Roy and P. Sackett "Cost Engineering: The Practice and the Future" *Blue book Series, Society of Manufacturing Engineers* (SME), USA, ISSN 0895-5085, 2003
11. Mont O. "Clarifying the concept of product–service system" *Journal of Cleaner Production*, Vol **10**, 2002, pp. 237 – 245.
12. N. Morelli "Product-service systems, a perspective shift for designers: A case study: the design of a telecentre" *Design Studies* Vol **24,** 2003, pp. 73–99.

An Automatic Mark-up Approach for Structured Document Retrieval in Engineering Design

S. Liu [a], C.A. McMahon [b], M.J. Darlington [c], S.J. Culley [d], P.J. Wild [e]

Innovative Manufacturing Research Centre, Department of Mechanical Engineering,

University of Bath, BA2 7AY, UK

[a]enssl@bath.ac.uk, [b]enscam@bath.ac.uk, [c]ensmjd@bath.ac.uk, [d]enssjc@bath.ac.uk, [e]enspjw@bath.ac.uk,

Abstract. Information and knowledge retrieval has been recognized as a key issue in engineering design. A huge amount of information and knowledge are formally recorded in huge numbers of documents. Those documents become more useful if they are structured in a consistent way so that they can be accessed and retrieved more effectively and the integrity of communication between business partners can be maintained at all times. This paper proposes a Knowledge Engineering approach for document automatic mark-up. XML (eXtensible Mark-up Language) has been employed to explicitly identify the structural information, with a focus on long and complex engineering documents. A three layer model is explored to fulfil the automatic semantic mark-up with document decomposition schemes: a strategic layer to study document features: style based, inference based, or template based, etc; a tactical layer to define the rules to realize semantic mark-up according to document features; an operational layer to perform the computational implementation of the mark-up rules. By doing so, information retrieval can return: (1) the most relevant *document components* that are most interested by engineering designers, other than return whole documents; (2) information relevant to the designer's need both with respect to document *structure and content*, not *content-only*; (3) Implicit interpretation obtained by human can be hardwired into documents, which allows us move closer to semantic retrieval level.

Keywords: knowledge engineering, automatic mark-up, structured document retrieval, engineering design, document decomposition, XML, DTD

1. Introduction

Engineering design is an information and knowledge intensive process that comprises many tasks as conceptual design, detailed design, engineering analysis, process design and performance evaluation etc. In each of these tasks, engineering designers often record their own design ideas, solutions and results in documents. In the meantime, they access and retrieve information from numerous documents to make decisions. Survey shows that engineering designers spend as much as thirty percent of their working time on searching and accessing information [1]. Documents have become an important source of information and knowledge that lie in the heart of engineers' work. The value of the documents can be greatly increased by mark-up to make the information more accessible [2]. Because from a computer system's point of view, a document without mark-up is just a long sequence of strings, and the operations that can be performed on such a document are rather limited. Once the documents are marked up (for example with XML, and thus called structured documents), however, the computer system is able to exploit the implicit semantics of the mark-up tags, thus allowing for operations that are closer to the semantic level, which allows engineers find the most "meaningful" information for their design tasks.

Document mark-up can take place with paper or electronic documents. In terms of paper documents, mark-up usually comprises three important stages: scanning, recognizing, and tagging. In many cases, a paper document is converted to its electronic form either by keyed-entry or Optical Character Recognition (OCR) technology [3]. Document mark-up can be at macro-level (dealing with the global visual and logical structure of a document), micro-level (used for marking single words or word groups), or symbol-level [2]. Mark-up practice is usually done manually, semi-automatically or automatically according to how much human effort is involved. Manual mark-up is the most popular, most accurate but most labour-intensive effort, where human read the document, interpret the values of existing fields embedded within the documents, and tag the document accordingly. Where there are a lot of documents involved in a task such as engineering design process, the manual method is clearly inadequate, and automatic mark-up should be considered as the first choice. Automatic mark-up not only reduces manual intervention but also gives a more integral representation of the documents. There have been limited publications concerning with automatic mark-up. For example, [4] and [5] both explored automatic mark-up with different methods and targeting on different types of documents, but by the knowledge of the authors of this paper, there has been so far no existing publication targeting on engineering documents.

To better meet the challenges of structured document retrieval and access, advance in automatic semantic mark-up, especially with a specific DTD or vocabulary targeting particular scenario, are highly desired. This paper addresses the automatic mark-up of logical content elements as well as physical structural elements that comply with a specified vocabulary for engineering documents, based on document decomposition schemes. The final target of the automatic mark-up is to support engineers to extract the most relevant document fragments that meet their information needs, rather than to return the whole documents. The remaining of this paper is organized as follows: Section 2 introduces the document decomposition and vocabulary development. Section 3 presents the process of automatic mark-up. A three level model of automatic mark-up with XML is discussed in Section 4. Section 5 investigates the application of the automatic mark-up system to a fragment retrieval web service. Finally, Section 6 draws some conclusions.

2. Vocabulary Development by Document Decomposition
It's well understood that engineering documents cover such wide a variety: technical manuals, product brochures, sketches and drawings, let alone countless books and files on the local computer, on internal network and most vastly on the Internet. Because of the complexity of engineering documents, it is non-trivial work to develop a DTD or vocabulary that takes into most engineering documents. Based on an analysis of the characteristics of engineering documents [1] and an empirical study on how engineers use documents [6], the authors took a decomposition approach by looking into a document from multiple viewpoints.

Document decomposition has been seen as a difficult task because decomposition can be made not only across different dimensions but also within those dimensions at different levels of granularity and abstraction. Decomposition can take place not only based on what a document says, but also what is said about it. Closely connected with this is decomposition according to explicit and implicit content. Based on the above consideration, a number of decomposition schemes have been defined and six of them are illustrated in Fig. 1, accordingly a vocabulary is developed that contains the elements and their definitions within the decomposition schemes. The result from empirical study of engineers' behaviour in using documents has also been taken into account to make sure that the vocabulary will meet engineers' requirements. Once we have the vocabulary, we have the foundation to define a DTD for semantic mark-up. The creation of DTDs for the decomposition schemes has been discussed elsewhere [7].

24

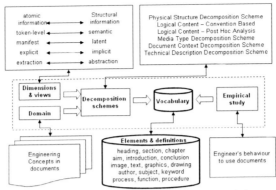

Figure 1 Document decomposition and the vocabulary

3. Process of Automatic Mark-up and Key Controls

The automatic mark-up of legacy documents in other formats such as in Word and PDF with XML includes three main steps: format conversion, semantic mark-up and creation of output hierarchy. Fig. 2 is the process model represented in IDEF0, which shows the information flow (input I, output O, control C and mechanism M) in the process. Format conversion (activity A1) takes in legacy documents in Word, PDF, Excel etc. and generates a pre-processed ppXML documents (with non-interpreted tags). The importance of conversion other document formats into XML has been addressed in [8]. At the semantic mark-up stage, ppXML documents will be annotated by computers according to the two significant controls: mark-up *rules* (C1) and the *DTD* (C3). Meaningful tags compliant with the *vocabulary* will be placed for corresponding elements. It is essential that an XML document conforms to its special syntax, for example, all elements must be nested properly in the hierarchy. The final output of the automatic mark-up process should be well formed with meaningful tags. The success of the process will be greatly dependent on the mark-up rules that instruct the computers to interpret the document content. How to develop and implement mark-up rules is discussed in the following section.

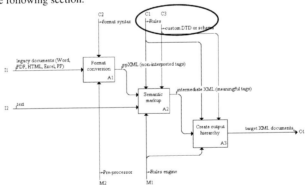

Figure 2 Process of automatic mark-up

4. A Knowledge Engineering Approach to Automatic Mark-up

Generally, there are two types of approaches to develop mark-up systems: a *knowledge engineering* approach and a *machine learning* approach. In machine learning, annotated corpora are needed. System learns rules from the training data and applies them to mark up documents. On the other hand, mark-up rules to be applied by the system can also be constructed by knowledge engineers. In this case, experienced knowledge engineers' implicit expertise can be transferred to the system by "hardwiring" rules to achieve better results. Especially when appropriate knowledge (e.g. lexicons) and human resources (i.e. knowledge engineers/ rule writers) are available, knowledge engineering approach should be preferred. We took this approach because we intended to make use of our knowledge in understanding of engineering document decompositions and engineers' behaviour in using documents, and we also have developed an XML DTD for the vocabulary of engineering documents. A three level model including a strategic level, a tactical level and an operational level, as shown in Fig. 3, summarizes the idea of development and implementation of mark-up rules. At the high level, decisions are made on strategies to trigger the provenance that mark-up rules may be based on. For example, style based, template based, or inference based. Fig. 3 illustrates some typical style information embedded in a common Word document. For example, a document title may be written in Arial with bolded font size 14 pt. When the Word document is converted into a ppXML document, the style information are captured and represented as attributes/values pairs when we use CanbridgeDocs software xDoc XML Converter [9].

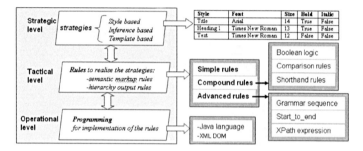

Figure 3 The three level model for automatic mark-up

At the tactical level, specific mark-up rules are developed to realize the strategies set at the high level. Three types of semantic mark-up rules have been defined: simple rules, compound rules and advanced rules. By simple rules we mean by using a single element. When these simple rules are used together, we define it as compound rules such as Boolean logic (AND, OR, NOT), comparison rules (contains, equals, less than, greater than, true, false) and shorthand rules (element name with attributes). The advanced rules make use of sequence of elements, for example, grammar sequence, start-to-end sequence and XPath expressions. Programming for implementation of these rules is undertaken at the operational level. The authors employed Java coding and XML DOM (Document Object Model) to develop a software system, named *AutoMarker*, including two modules to fulfil the automatic mark-up functionality with four chosen decomposition schemes, as illustrated in Fig. 4. In module 1, automatic mark-up has been undertaken against three decomposition schemes: Physical Structure Decomposition Scheme (PSDS), Document Context Decomposition Scheme (DCDS) and Media Types Decomposition Scheme (MTDS). Once we have those document elements marked up with vocabulary from the above three decomposition schemes, module 2 uses these information to detect and tag the elements against the Logical Content Decomposition Scheme – Convention Based

(LCDS-CB), for example to mark a *section* as an *introduction*, a *case study*, or a *conclusion*. If the document users are not happy with the final output of the marked up documents, amendment requirements should be identified and mark-up rules should be refined, or maybe some correction rules should be added to direct the programming coding. It is an advantage of the knowledge engineering approach that effective rule sets can be constructed iteratively and transparently. Knowledge engineers can always start with relatively simpler rule sets, evaluate the results and refine them stepwise when they have better and better understanding of the documents.

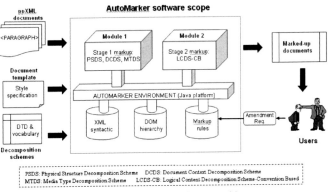

Figure 4   Automatic mark-up software architecture

5. Application of the Automatic Mark-up System to a Document Fragment Retrieval Web Service

In authors' earlier study of engineering document management, a fragment retrieval web service has been developed and used to organise information for engineers [7]. Fig. 5 illustrates the application of the automatic mark-up system, i.e. the *AutoMarker*, to the web-based document fragment retrieval system to automate the structured document management process. In the existing fragment retrieval web service, there are four modules to fulfil the functions of document mark-up, fragment extraction, fragment classification and fragment retrieval (navigation and presentation). The other three functions are performed automatically either by programming or legacy system (i.e. Waypoint [10]) while document mark-up, however, is done manually, which unfortunately impediments the automation of the whole information management process. Integrating the automatic mark-up system, i.e. the AutoMarker, solves this issue.

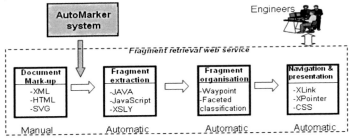

Figure 5 Application of the AutoMarker to the fragment retrieval web service

6. Conclusions

This paper has introduced a knowledge engineering approach for document automatic mark-up so that more focused information retrieval can be realised to facilitate design process. A three level model of automatic mark-up with XML has been discussed and applied to a number of decomposition schemes. The significance of decomposition of engineering documents into pre-defined elements and study of structured document retrieval arises with ever increasing importance of collaborative design and information support co-ordinated decision making. It is well recognised that the co-operation and co-ordination between design team members relies heavily on the consistent communication and information access. This paper makes a first attempt to automatic mark-up system compliant with decomposition schemes to support structured document retrieval in the engineering design domain.

Further work on automatic mark-up with all eleven decomposition schemes will be using a combination approach, i.e. a knowledge engineering and machine learning approach, maybe supported by Natural Language Processing (NLP) technology.

Acknowledgement

The research reported in this paper was undertaken at the Engineering Innovative Manufacturing Research Centre (EIMRC) at the University of Bath. It was funded by the UK Engineering and Physical Sciences Research Council (EPSRC) under grant GR/R67507/01.

References

[1] A. Lowe, C.A. McMahon and S.J. Culley: Characterising the requirements of engineering information systems. International Journal of Information Management 24 (2004), pp. 401-422

[2] M. Abolhassani, N. Fuhr and N. Govert: Information extraction and automatic mark-up for XML documents, Intelligent Search on XML Data, Lecture Notes in Computer Science, 2818 (2003), pp. 159-174.

[3] K. Taghva, R. Beckley and J. Cooms: The effects of OCR on the extraction of private information. Document Analysis Systems VII, Proceedings Lecture Notes in Computer Science 3872 (2006), pp. 348-357

[4] R. Feldman, B. Rosenfeld and M. Fresko: TEG - a hybrid approach to information extraction. Knowledge and Information Systems 9(1) (2006), pp. 1-18

[5] S. Akhtar, R.G. Reilly and J. Dunnion: Auto-tagging of text documents into XML. Text, Speech and Dialogue, Proceedings Lecture Notes in Artificial Intelligent 2807 (2003), pp.20-26

[6] P.J. Wild, C.A. McMahon, S.J. Culley, M.J. Darlington and S. Liu: Towards a method for profiling engineering documentation. Proceeding of the 9th International Conference of Design, Dubrovnik, May 15-18th (2006)

[7] S. Liu, C.A. McMahon, M.J. Darlington, S.J. Culley and P J. Wild: A computational framework for retrieval of document fragments based on decomposition schemes in engineering information management. (International Journal of) Advanced Engineering Informatics (accepted) (2006)

[8] S. Liu, C.A. McMahon, M.J. Darlington, S.J. Culley and P J. Wild: An approach for document fragment retrieval and its formatting issues in engineering information management. Lecture Notes in Computer Science 3981 (2006), pp.279-287

[9] CambridgeDocs (USA) http://www.cambridgedocs.com/index.htm

[10] C.A. McMahon, A. Lowe, S.J. Culley, M. Corderoy, R. Crossland, T. Shan and D. Stewart: Waypoint – an integrated search and retrieval system for engineering documents. Journal of Computing and Information Science in Engineering 4(4) (2004), pp.329-338

Benchmarking Engineering Efficiency within the Premium Automotive Industry

Rajkumar Roy, Johannes R. Bayer, Shyam Durai, Arij Hammad, Manuel Lopez, Sergio Lopez, Miguel Molto, David Peinador

Decision Engineering Centre, Cranfield University, Cranfield, Bedfordshire, MK43 0AL, UK
Email: r.roy@cranfield.ac.uk

Abstract
Due to the rising demand for premium automobiles, manufacturers aim to meet demand by ramping up production and at the same time achieve efficient engineering processes in terms of reduced costs and time while improving quality. Until today, a study which compares levels of engineering efficiency in the premium automotive industry does not exist.
The aim of this research was to compare engineering efficiency in new product development of the premium automotive industry. Efficiency metrics were developed based on comprehensive literature review with a focus on time, cost and quality perspectives. Primary data was collected through questionnaire-based semi structured interviews with engineering process stakeholders in 5 participating companies to cover design, design release and change process, concern management process, engineering process, cost estimating and engineering organisation.
Results have indicated substantial differences in the areas of communication in projects, platforms, prototypes built, application of cost engineering practices, level and timing of supplier involvement as well as the level of application and integration of virtual engineering and testing tools.
To improve engineering efficiency suppliers need to be involved at the concept stage. Improved exploitation of lessons learned from past and current development projects as well as integration of CAD-CAM as basis for enhancing virtual prototyping to reduce number of physical prototypes are key practices to be considered. Shifting engineering work to the beginning of projects is required for right-first-time initiatives.

Keywords
Automotive industry, Benchmarking, Engineering efficiency, Metrics, New Product Development, Performance measurement

Introduction
With rising demand for premium automobiles and new models coming out on a regular basis manufacturers slightly increase production. One of the key characteristics of the premium sector is exclusivity. Therefore, overall production volume still remains low. At the same time development costs are substantial and have to be covered by sales of a relatively low number of cars. Consequently, efficient engineering processes with reduced costs and time are sought, while improving quality. Within the scope of this study engineering processes for new car development from start of the design phase until start of production were covered. Until today, a study which compares levels of efficiency in engineering processes in the premium automobile industry does not exist. Therefore, there was a need to study this area and develop performance metrics that cover the new product development process comprehensively.
There is no unique definition for engineering efficiency. Thus, to develop performance metrics a generic efficiency definition was chosen and combined with performance description from an industrial point of view. "Efficiency is the ratio of the effective or useful output to the total input in any system." [1]

Performance is related to quality, delivery speed, delivery reliability, cost and flexibility [2]. For this study the authors decided to compare participating companies from three key points of view to assess engineering efficiency: time, cost and quality.

Focus of this study is the new product development (NPD) process that comprises main stages of product concept, product plan, product design and process design [3]. NPD processes must adapt continuously to the emerging or rapid changes of the environment to remain flexible to exploit opportunities for improvement and innovation. Moreover, the majority of project cost is committed in the design stage within the NPD cycle, i.e. between 60% and 80% of the future incurred costs [4]. Cost, time and quality are drivers of the NPD process [3]. In order to manage these drivers as well as internal and external constraints, uncertainty and multiple objectives, concurrent engineering (CE) should be applied [3]. This can have a major influence on cost, time and quality improvements. The number of studies about product development metrics is very limited. However, some metrics applied in industry were described by [5]. Examples from cost, time and quality perspective are: Cost performance, number and speed of design changes, lead times, meeting gateway targets, schedule performance, meeting customer requirements.

Methodology

The aims of this research were to compare engineering efficiency in new product development projects of the premium automotive industry and establish current processes, their advantages, disadvantages and possible means of improvement. Engineering efficiency in this study means to research engineering processes for new car development from start of the design phase until start of production from key perspectives of time, cost and quality.

Therefore, a questionnaire was developed that covers main stages of the NPD process from design to start of production; namely, design release and change process, project concern management process, engineering process, cost estimating and engineering organisation, which were divided into 20 separate topics. A comprehensive literature review was carried out to establish current state of product development, product development metrics and product development in the automotive industry. Based on the available information a questionnaire was developed, including a set of metrics for each of the above described areas. Metrics available in existing literature cover only some parts of the NPD process, mainly; design, project management, cost and suppliers. Therefore, the authors combined metrics available from existing research and developed new ones for areas where no literature was available or where existing metrics were too general in order to cover the whole NPD process. Metrics were defined from three key points of view in terms of engineering efficiency: time, cost and quality. These metrics were validated with industry to ensure feasibility for the purpose of the study. Questionnaire-based semi-structured interviews with engineering process stakeholders were conducted to cover all 20 topics. Next, metrics were analysed to assess and compare engineering efficiency in five participating companies: four UK based companies and one from Italy. As several metrics were used for each topic the same weighting was assigned for any metric within each topic to obtain a single final score – between 0 and 100. Within each question, scores are defined according to the different proposed answers by giving the highest score to those answers more successful for engineering efficiency from the three key points: time, cost, quality. The methodology allows changing weights to adapt them to relevant importance as perceived by each company.

The full study as well as a list of all used performance metrics is available as Cranfield University publication in the Decision Engineering Report Series [6].

Results

Results will be divided into three main areas of organisational issues, process issues as well as tools and techniques. Main commonalities and differences will be highlighted from this study.

Organisational issues

Major differences are observed regarding project duration of new car development, including platform, and number of engineers involved in these projects.

Project duration varies between 32 and 48 months. The number of engineers engaged in these projects, including permanent employees and contractors, shows that 3 companies require the same number of total heads, which is around 240. One company requires significantly more engineers. If project duration is related to the number of heads required it could be observed that 2 companies require 12-14 months less time to complete the project with the same number of engineers. This might indicate a substantially higher degree of engineering efficiency.

Different approaches in terms of contractors used have been disclosed. One company defines a strategy of maximum 10% of contractors as a business rule. The other companies have significantly more contractors (maximum 20%). The challenge is to identify areas that are core to the company and product and employ permanent staff here to keep critical knowledge within the business.

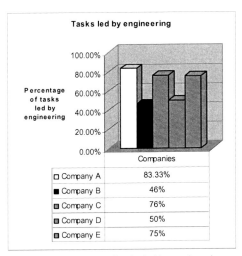

The number of engineers required for a project and time to complete it could also depend on the scope of engineering roles. A list of 24 tasks were split into technical tasks (e.g. vehicle and component development and validation) and non-technical areas (e.g. benchmarking, supplier selection and concept creation), investigating whether engineering takes the lead responsibility. It can be observed that three companies suggest a very engineering-centred working practice (Fig. 1) by defining 75% or more tasks as engineering responsibilities. In contrast, two firms have specific teams which support engineering especially in non-technical tasks, which results in a low percentage of non-technical tasks led by engineering.

Figure 1 – Extent of tasks led by engineering

The challenge here is to review task leadership and shift responsibility for non-technical tasks from engineers to other departments to free engineering resources, concentrating on real engineering work.

All companies show a low employee turnover with a maximum of 5%. Despite a loyalty factor of working for a company that builds exclusive premium cars, geographical aspects of few employment alternatives in the surrounding area were identified as reasons for low turnover.

One company does not promote rewards or actively encourage employees at all. The common way is to reward managers based on company achievements while employee's rewards are based on company achievements and/or a bonus strategy based on individual performance.

There is a common approach among companies to develop one flexible platform that is the basis for all models. Use of only one platform allows sharing components between different models. Consequently, savings are achieved due to the complexity reduction of the new product development project. Two companies have this platform already developed and are currently using it. Other companies will follow this trend but might not decide to use only one flexible platform.

Process issues

Process issues include technical, quality and manufacturing concern management processes as well as design, design release and change processes, amongst others.

Process bottlenecks and problems found in these areas were different, non-integrated processes and IT systems for different stages of the product life cycle. Moreover, lengthy decision making and approval processes of several weeks for design changes as well as poor knowledge transfer and re-use from past projects were observed. Although all companies can find past problems and concerns of past projects, no one has an automatic computer based system or a set process to consider compulsory checking of past problems for avoidance in future projects. It is the responsibility of the engineer to look for past project data and develop new components avoiding past mistakes.

In terms of concern management, firms use mainly teams to lead concern solving for production line and each engineering department by defining and tracking resolution progress. All participants have a computer based system at their disposal to communicate with different technical areas and share information for concern solving. Only two companies use the same approach and process for all concerns, i.e. technical, quality or manufacturing, without distinguishing stages of product life cycle where concerns are raised. It permits integration between all technical areas and work with one defined method including all required stakeholders. Integration of all project stakeholders is achieved by conducting daily or weekly meetings. Other companies have one concern management system for quality and after-sales and separate one for production and design. In this solution integration problems are evident and arise constantly. Due to the lack of clear leadership to handle manufacturing concerns, the engineers and designers are overwhelmed with a great number of concerns.

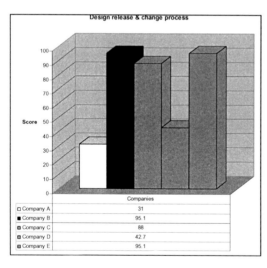

Companies	
☐ Company A	31
■ Company B	95.1
▣ Company C	88
▣ Company D	42.7
▣ Company E	95.1

The companies that score highest for design release and change process (Fig. 2) involve suppliers at development stage. Moreover, they tend to overlap between product design and process design by making sure that production process and product fit each other. That avoids future problems and design changes at manufacturing stages. This collaborative approach between suppliers and manufacturing results in achieving "right first time". This way, attempts are made to use prototypes for validation purposes rather than problem finding or car integration. These practices result in significantly lower no. of prototypes, costs and project time

Figure 2 – Design release and change process

Companies which got higher scores use the same change management system for the whole product life cycle and ensure by means of business rules that impact analysis is agreed by any involved stakeholder. These firms need no more than 4 weeks to get changes approved. In contrast, other companies use different change management systems by distinguishing different product life cycle stages. These firms need 5 weeks or more to get change approval.

Tools and techniques

This section describes the application of virtual engineering tools, cost estimation, project timing and suppliers.

The big opportunity in using virtual tools is to reduce lead time and cost at the development stage. Out of a list of 23 virtual tools identified by the authors, three companies use around 15 internally. One company stands out and uses tolerance management and PLM software to facilitate data transfer with suppliers and include any functional area in product data management (finance, purchase, quality, and manufacturing). Trust in virtual testing of components and prototypes vary significantly. However, this field is advancing in the premium sector.

With regard to project timing all companies would like to involve the majority of stakeholders and engineers in early stages of project and solve engineering problems up-front, i.e. practice front-loading. Main differences found were effort applied until the first physical prototype is built (around 50% of project time has passed) and when suppliers are involved in the project. Some participants involve suppliers after between 25%-45% of the project has gone by and apply between 40%-55% of the total engineering resources before first prototype build. It is remarkable that two companies have an independent timing department that defines project timing plans, critical paths and detailed schedules. The number of long-term suppliers, early involvement in development projects and close collaboration seem to be key in reducing project completion time, cost and right-first-time efforts.

Only one of the companies tries to deal exclusively with long-term suppliers since they consider it the best way for making profit from the knowledge and expertise shared with them. The majority of companies have a specific technical support team for suppliers to help them to achieve quality levels desired. All companies except for one run formal learning lessons involving suppliers after each project in order to detect potential areas for improvement.

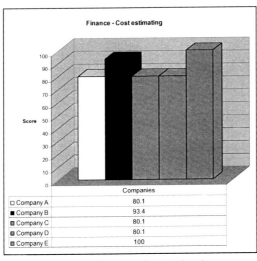

Figure 3 – Finance and cost estimating

The study revealed that cost estimating as a tool for project cost control is applied differently in participating firms (Fig.3). There is no consistent method or policy followed by all the companies. Cost estimating is carried out by dedicated teams in 2 companies. In other firms engineering teams and finance staff participate to undertake this task. All firms now implement cost estimation during the design stage and achieve varying degrees of accuracy. In 3 companies cost estimation is conducted between 20%-60% of the design process. The time at which suppliers get involved in the project can also dictate the timing of a cost estimation exercise. 3 companies conduct a cost estimating exercise during the supplier selection process.

There is no common trend with regards to the employees who conduct the cost estimating exercise. They can be specialists in either finance or engineering. The challenge here is to implement a company wide process that is followed consistently to improve project cost control.

Concluding Remarks

This benchmarking exercise helped to present the current state of the premium automotive industry. It can be concluded that the traditional business strategy based on craftsmanship is moving towards a more contemporary and technological approach while maintaining the luxury and image. Thus, front loading practices and early problems solving in the new product development process are becoming key points in the current policies. Companies are reducing costs and time by applying advanced technologies such as product life cycle data management tools (PLM); a complete CAD integration and virtual testing tools. In this respect they are narrowing the gap with mass market producers, where these practices are more common to integrate development and build physical prototypes for validation, not testing. However, participating companies in this study develop cutting edge technology to be launched in luxury and performance cars. Thus, failure mode and effect analysis (FMEA) might not reveal critical areas of new developments, which makes testing with physical prototypes crucial. An optimum mixture of technology and tradition is being implemented which will ensure a successful future for these companies.

Five key areas for improvement were identified in order to reduce project costs, project time, no. of physical prototypes, enhance right first-time and front-loading initiatives, avoid past mistakes and re-work as well as improve project cost and timing control.
1. Increased use of virtual tools for testing (crash simulation, aerodynamics), manufacturing process simulation at product design stage, communication between technical and other areas (PLM).
2. Improve knowledge re-use through transfer of problem and solution-specific information from past projects as a set process to include problem checking as embedded step for future projects.
3. Reduce overall number of suppliers and increase no. of long term relationships as well as involvement of suppliers from day one of the development stage.
4. Development of a formal cost estimating team composed of engineering, manufacturing, supply chain, finance to do detailed estimations for key components. Use of parametric cost estimating as an easy and quick technique for other components.
5. Develop a formal project timing department to co-ordinate timing with authority.

References

[1]   Anon.: *The American Heritage Dictionary of the English Language Fourth Edition* (Houghton Mifflin Company 2000) http://www.thefreedictionary.com (accessed April 2006).

[2]   A. Neely, M. Gregory and K. Platts: Performance measurement system design: A literature review and research agenda. *International journal of operations & production management,* Vol. 25(12) (2005), pp. 1228-1263.

[3]   K. Clark and T. Fujimoto: *Product Development Performance: Strategy, Organisation and Management in the World Auto Industry* (Harvard Business School Press, USA 1991)

[4]   J.V. Farr and D.M. Buede: Systems Engineering and Engineering Management: Keys to the Efficient Development of Products and Services. *Engineering Management Journal* Vol 15(3) (2003), pp. 3-9.

[5]   B. Haque and M.J. Moore: Measures of performance for lean product introduction in the aerospace industry. *Proceedings of the Institution of Mechanical Engineers, Part B: Journal of Engineering Manufacture Vol.* 218(10) (2004), pp. 1387-1398.

[6]   R. Roy et al., (2006). Benchmarking Engineering Efficiency within the Premium Automotive Industry. Submitted to Decision Engineering Report Series. Cranfield University (Cranfield, UK 2006)

Industrial Requirements for FMEA Knowledge in the New Product Development Process

Modupeola Ajayi [1, a]**, and Dr James Gao**[2, b]
[1, 2] Decision Engineering Centre, Department of Manufacturing, Cranfield University, Bedfordshire, MK43 0AL, UK
Email: [a]m.o.ajayi@cranfield.ac.uk, [b]j.gao@cranfield.ac.uk
Tel: +44 (0)1234 754271,
Fax: +44 (0)1234 750852

Abstract. New product development is a knowledge intensive process and its success depends on effective technique such as Failure Mode Effect Analysis (FMEA) to manage risk. This paper presents the findings from an investigation of industrial requirements for FMEA knowledge in the product development process. The project is sponsored by a medium sized, multi-national domestic product manufacturer in Europe. An extensive exploratory study was conducted within the sponsoring company and the problems identified are: (i) Incomplete and vague description of components, functions and failure modes, (ii) Lack of reusability of FMEA Knowledge and (iii) Time consuming and complicated. This paper proposes a knowledge engineering approach to model the knowledge intensive task within the FMEA process so that it can be reused in new projects and also to aid in the decision making process in order to reduce repetitive task and duplication of effort.

Keywords: Knowledge Management, New Product Development, Failure Mode and Effect Analysis

1. Introduction

The challenges of meeting customer requirements, shorter development cycle and competitive product innovation that meets customer satisfaction are driving manufacturing organisations to depend on information or knowledge in order to develop their core competency and improve the effectiveness and quality of their business operations [1]. Successful new product development is vital for the survival of manufacturing organisations. Hence, the success of a new product development depends on the effective strategy for risk reduction [2]. A variety of quality tool and techniques are used during the new product development process to achieve quality assurance, which are often applied at an early stage of the development process in order to detect and prevent failures from occurring. Knowledge embedded in quality process during product development process requires the use of both tacit and explicit knowledge. Tacit knowledge resides in people's heads and refers to the experience and expertise of a person in a particular domain. In contrast explicit knowledge refers to structured information, which is articulated through documentation, tools and procedures [3].

New product development is a knowledge intensive process and its success depends on effective technique such as Failure Mode Effect Analysis (FMEA) to manage risk. The concept of knowledge management can help in the reduction of risk through capturing and processing of relevant information from various sources [2]. One of the major challenges encountered during product development project is how to acquire knowledge and manage sources of uncertainty in order to reduce the risk of failure of the resulting product.

The manufacturing sector for instance, is experiencing fierce competition where design, manufacture, procurement, assembly and delivery of products are geographically dispersed. To this effect, there is an existence of tremendous pressures for product quality and speed to the market. Recent contributions have been directed toward how organisations could best improve product quality. The improvement of quality of design and the reduction of cost relating to design failures is critical to the survival of manufacturing organisations. Consequently manufacturing organisations are adopting quality assurance techniques, which are integrated into the stages of the product development process in order to improve product quality [4]. The importance of quality in manufacturing cannot be understated, since quality as a function has played a pivotal role in the highly competitive manufacturing environment. Manufacturing companies have adopted quality management techniques such as FMEA, to improve product quality and reliability.

This research paper presents the findings from the exploratory study conducted to investigate the requirements for a knowledge based FMEA process. The second section gives a background introduction to FMEA technique, how it is applied and existing research on the technique. The third section describes the methodology used for data collection. The fourth section presents the finding from the interviews and defines the identified problems with performing FMEA. In the fifth section a proposed solution is described to address the problems identified. The final section concludes that integrating knowledge-base system with the FMEA process will aid engineers in decision-making and hence improve the quality of result generated from the process, which as a result encourages reusability in similar projects.

2. Failure Mode Effect Analysis
Failure modes effect analysis is a technique used for identifying potential causes of failure before they reach the customer. Originally FMEA was developed by the US military to evaluate the impact of system and equipment failure. However it was then adopted by the automotive industry and eventually adopted by manufacturing industry for assessing risk in produt design and improving product quality. FMEA as a tool is an effective low risk technique for predicting problems and identifying the cost effective solutions for preventing these problems [5]. FMEA technique is applied during the early phase of the development process of a product or service to avoid complicated and costly changes to the design at a later stage. In reality FMEA is performed too late in the design process and would have no positive effect on the overall product design.

There are three main types of FMEA which can be conducted at various stages of the product development process. They are: i) System FMEA, which involves the evaluation of functions and interactions between systems, ii) Design FMEA involves the evalutaion of products or parts before they are released for production and finally, iii) Process FMEA involves the evaluation of manufacturing and assembly processes. Each of these categories of FMEA has separate objectives. However causes identified in each category can influence one another. For example causes identified in system FMEA can influence design FMEA. The report produced from an FMEA process is only as good as the team that conducted the process. To be successful it is essential that the FMEA team is well experienced and includes experts from cross functional team within the organisation, who have thorough knowledge of the system's design and application. For example it should include people from all functions of the product development process such as quality engineers, productional engineers, service, sales and marketing, manufacturing engineers etc.

2.1. Existing research on FMEA
Various research has been conducted in the area of using FMEA to conduct risk assessment in product development. Kmenta *et al.* (1999) for instance, proposed an advance FMEA based on behaviour model that relates process functionality and physical entities to early process design [7]. Cooper (2003) discussed the research agenda to reduce risk in new product development through knowledge management [2]. Teng *et al.* (2006) demonstrated an example of inconsistency in ranking of severity, occurrence and detection to show that the inconsistency may delay FMEA implementation in a supply chain [6]. Wirth et al (1996) identified

the problems with conventional ways of carrying out FMEA and proposed an approach that provides information model to build functions and structure taxonomies of library for knowledge based FMEA [8]. Dittmann *et al.* (2004) presented an approach that integrates Ontology technique with performing FMEA [9]. Research into the area of FMEA has undertaken two diverse approaches, the first approach is an attempt to improve the traditional method of performing FMEA and the second approach is the integrating of knowledge-based system with the methodology. However there are still some limitations within the failure analysis of FMEA, these include lack of well defined vocabulary, difficulty in identifying key failures and failure analysis is subjective to user experience.

3. Research Methodology

An exploratory study was conducted to understand the quality management processes undertaken in the new product development process, in particular to investigate the requirements for FMEA knowledge. The data collected for this research was through literature and company visits in order to observe and conduct interviews with process experts. The author developed a questionnaire that was aimed at collecting data to achieve the set objectives. A pilot test of the questionnaire was conducted with two academics to ensure that the questions were suitable, covered the relevant areas or issues and were capable of achieving the set objectives. The pilot test was also used to modify the questions till it reached a final satisfactory stage. A semi-structured interview was conducted with quality engineers from the R&D function of the collaborating company, to capture requirements and to elicit data on how FMEA technique is applied during the product development process. Several company visits were made to the company. The objectives were to understand the process of conducting FMEA during the early phase of the product development and identify the current problems with the methodology. The observation approach was to understand the "what" and "how" of performing FMEA, for example, to identify the tasks involved, the knowledge inputs and outputs of the process, and to identify the knowledge sharing and how to reuse problems. During the visit, documentation for FMEA process was also obtained. The result of the data collection was analysed using qualitative techniques and validated by experts to confirm accuracy of the data. The combination of data collected from literature and industrial company was used for this research paper.

4. Results and Problem Definition

The research is part of the on-going research embarked by Cranfield University with the collaborating company since 2003. The knowledge management initiative originated within the industrial division of the collaborating company with the aim to improve communication, collaboration and integration of business processes, so that lead-times, duplication of effort and defects in process could be reduced and product quality improved.

The manufacturing operation of the company is located in UK, France and Germany. The company developed a business process describing all the activities involved in new product development ranging from marketing to product launch. The business innovation process is used as a step by step guide in every product development project carried out within the organisation. As innovation is critical to the business operation of this organisation, the business process was developed to improve quality of product and customer satisfaction experience. The aim of this research and methodology used for collecting data have already been discussed in a previous section. This section presents the findings from the exploratory study. A number of problems were identified through the cause of the interviews and observation carried out. The key problems are:

  a. FMEA Process is not favoured by project teams because it is a time consuming and complicated process. Although a cross-functional teams input is utilised during an FMEA session, however not enough effort is put into recognising the benefits of the process. An FMEA is only as good as the team involved. Not done properly, valuable information will not be generated which would affect the product quality improvement. The resulted generated from an FMEA session varies depending on the experience and knowledge applied by the quality engineers.

b. No explicit description of the knowledge required for inputs and outputs of the tasks involved in the FMEA process and the FMEA report does not explain the decision rationale of the process. The description of components, functions, and failure modes are vague and incomplete.

c. Lack of reusability of FMEA knowledge as a consequence of problems A & B mentioned above. Also the use of natural language in the FMEA process often results to inconsistent description of systems and function, which makes it difficult for FMEA knowledge to be reused. As it is subjected to different interpretations by the FMEA team, it is difficult to elicit relevant knowledge from existing FMEA knowledge base. As a result efforts are duplicated when performing FMEA in project with similar product.

5. Proposed research solutions

A knowledge engineering approach to knowledge management will be used to model knowledge intensive task in the FMEA process, so that the knowledge can be clearly represented and reused in other projects. The goal is to provide knowledge based decision support for quality engineers when performing FMEA during the early phase of product development. The diagram shown in (figure 1) illustrates the high-level model of current FMEA process; it is proposed that the processes contained in box will be modelled into a detailed level process to illustrate the knowledge inputs, outputs, constraints and mechanism. By doing this, the researcher would be able to identify bottlenecks and knowledge intensive task within the process, so that this knowledge can be reused in similar projects, therefore cutting down FMEA development time. To model this process a method to elicit relevant knowledge would have to be developed, this will be done by assessing existing knowledge capture method to identify there usefulness.

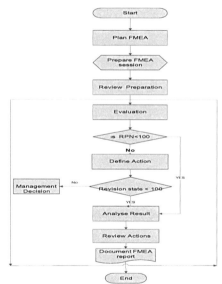

Figure 1: FMEA Process Model

To improve the explicit definition and to facilitate the reuse of FMEA knowledge base, the knowledge base FMEA model will be integrated with Ontology technique based on the approach presented in Dittmann *et al.* (2004) [8] and further development on the approach would be also be carried out. Ontology is an explicit specification of a conceptualisation [10]. More research will also be conducted to examine how Ontology has been used in the development of a knowledge base system. Ontology of libraries of terminologies will be developed to standardise the language used in an FMEA process. The ontology will provide a structured knowledge base that is easy to reuse and updated during other product development project. The knowledge contained in the knowledge base would aid in decision-making when performing FMEA at the early phase of the product development.

Team motivation problems are often difficult to solve but it is hoped that by resolving the technical issues identified in the FMEA process, the project team would be more receptive towards the methodology, hence recognise the benefits of the knowledge base FMEA.

6. Conclusions

This research has identified some industrial problems with the application of FMEA technique in new product development process. As a result we propose the development of a methodology to capture FMEA process knowledge in order to develop a detailed model of the knowledge intensive task in the FMEA process. A prototype of the FMEA knowledge model will be developed to demonstrate the feasibility of the proposed knowledge model within the context of its use during the product development process. Once the technical issues are resolved, the FMEA team will be motivated and more receptive towards the methodology, recognising the benefits of the knowledge base FMEA. Successful new product development and the ability to produce quality product that satisfies customer requirements is critical to the survival of manufacturing companies. Therefore FMEA technique has been adopted in the manufacturing industry to manage risks. FMEA is an assessment of potential failures and analysis of effects failure modes could have during a product lifecycle. The major benefit of this technique is it ensures all risks are identified and effective actions are taken to reduce risks. Adopting a knowledge management approach to FMEA can increase the likelihood of success in reducing risk during new product development process.

Acknowledgements

The authors would like to thank the collaborating company and EPSRC for their support.

References

[1]   Browne. J. et al, Innovation Management for Product and Process Development, CIMRU, National University of Ireland, Galway, Ireland.

[2]   Cooper Lynne .P. (2003), A research agenda to reduce risk in new product development through knowledge management: a practitioner perspective, Journal of Engineering technology management, vol 20, pp. 117-140

[3]   Nonaka, I. (1991), "The knowledge-creating company", Harvard Business Review, Vol. November/December pp.96-104.

[4]   Booker Julian D. (2003), Industrial practice in designing for quality, international journal of quality & reliability management, vol 20, no 3, pp 288-303

[5]   Palady, P. (1988), FMEA: Risk analysis risk management, authors edition, Pal publication, pp2-11

[6]   Teng S.G et al. (2006), Implementing FMEA in a collaborative Supply chain environment, International Journal of quality & reliability management,vol23,no 2, 2006, pp179-196.

[7]   Kmeta et al. (1999), Advanced failure modes and effects analysis of complex processes, Proceedings of the 1999 ASME Design Engineering Technical Conferences, September 12 - 15, Las Vegas, Nevada

[8] Wirth *et al.* (1996), Knowledge based support of system analysis for the analysis of failure modes and effects, Engineering application of artificial intelligence. vol 9, no 3, pp219-229.

[9] Dittmann, L., Rademacher, T., Zelewski, S., (2004) Performing FMEA Using Ontologies. 18th International Workshop on Qualitative Reasoning, 02.-04.08.2004 in Evanston, USA, Proceedings, Evanston, pp 209-216.

[10] Gruber T.R, (1993). A translation approach to portable ontology specifications. Knowledge Acquisition, no 5, 199-220

An Investigation of Knowledge and Information Sharing in the New Product Development Process

Bradfield, D. J.[1, a], Ajayi, M. O.[2, b], Jian, A. G.[3, c] and Gao, J. X.[4, d]

[1, 2,3,4] Centre for Decision Engineering, Department of Manufacturing, Cranfield University, Bedfordshire, MK43 0AL, UK.

[a] d.j.bradfield@cranfield.ac.uk, [b] m.o.ajayi@cranfield.ac.uk, [c] g.jian@cranfield.ac.uk, [d] j.gao@cranfield.ac.uk

Abstract. Information and knowledge sharing are critical to the success of the new product development process. In multinational organisations, product development involves teams of people from many disciplines and backgrounds each of whom may speak a different language, a scenario that gives rise to various knowledge-sharing challenges. This paper presents the findings of an exploratory study to investigate knowledge and information sharing in the new product development process of a multinational electromechanical goods manufacturer. These findings include the identification of ten types of information and knowledge and four categories of problems encountered while searching for knowledge. The findings served as a focus for the development and implementation of a knowledge management strategy at the company.

Keywords: Knowledge sharing, information, product development.

Introduction

As new products become the focus of competition for many manufacturers, the new product development process becomes increasingly important to these businesses [1; 2]. Furthermore, a growing need by manufacturing companies to compete on quality and time to market has made the effective sharing and transfer of product development process knowledge into a means of achieving a competitive advantage [2]. Consequently, great attention has been focused in recent years on the application of knowledge management to new product development [3]. Ulrich and Eppinger propose that the product development process is comprised of: 'a sequence of steps or activities which an enterprise employs to conceive, design, and commercialize a product' [4]. According to Browning and Eppinger [5], these activities are linked by an exchange of information. In this way, the sharing of information and knowledge plays a crucial role in the product development process.

Product development demands the cooperation of people from different parts of the organization with different expertise and varying levels of experience. As a result, effective communication is required to manage the activities in the New Product Development (NPD) process, as argued by Effendi et al [6]. The emergence of the multinational corporation with a network of geographically dispersed operations, as described by Ghoshal and Bartlett, has complicated this issue still further [7]. Product development project teams often consist of members located in different countries and they face various communication challenges, among them differences in language and culture, as discussed by Desouza and Evaristo [8]. Previous studies, such as that by Zahay at al [3],examined the role that managing information and knowledge played in the NPD process, but focused on business-to-business physical goods and software industries. This study presents the key findings of an exploratory study to investigate the sharing of information and knowledge in the new product development process of a medium-sized, multinational manufacturer of electromechanical goods. It differs from earlier research by focusing on a single manufacturer producing business-to-consumer goods, and by considering the impact of a multilingual product development environment on knowledge sharing.

Background to Industrial Study

Cranfield University embarked upon a project with a medium-sized, market-leading manufacturer of electromechanical goods. The aim of the collaboration was to develop and implement a long-term knowledge management strategy for the company. New product development projects undertaken by the company are mostly of two types: technological changes to existing product ranges in order to accommodate environmental legislation, and minor upgrades to existing products. The manufacturing and research and development (R&D) operations in the company are located on sites in Germany, France and the UK. A major component of this project was an exploratory study of information and knowledge sharing in the company's new product development process conducted in early 2006. The main aims of this study were (1) to identify the information and knowledge shared among members of R&D organization and the challenges these members encountered finding and accessing this knowledge and (2) to recommend improvements to current knowledge sharing practices to improve the capitalization of knowledge within the company. This paper presents the findings related to the first aim.

Methodology

Elicitation of information about knowledge and information sharing was achieved by conducting semi-constructed interviews with personnel from R&D functions in the company. Selection of personnel for the interviews was based on four criteria. The first criterion was that collectively, the interviewees must represent all of the competences that play a major role in the R&D function, which were. Hydraulics, Electronics and Control, Thermodynamics and Certification. The second criterion was that the interviewees must include the key roles involved in product development: Managers and Engineers. The third criterion was that collectively, the interviewees must represent each of the sites where product development activities take place i.e. Germany, France and the UK. The final criterion was that all of the candidates must be willing and available to be interviewed. An interview protocol served as the data collection tool. Questions posed in the interview addressed the following issues: the types and format of knowledge used in the NPD process, the storage of knowledge, and the process of searching for knowledge

Results and Discussion

Findings from the study were broken down into six areas: the interviewee's understanding of the term 'knowledge', the types of knowledge used in a product development project, the media used to communicate and deliver the knowledge, sources of knowledge, storage of knowledge, and issues related to the act of searching for knowledge.

    Understanding of 'Knowledge'. In order to avoid a misunderstanding of what was meant by the term 'knowledge' in the course of the interviews, each interviewee was asked to explain their understanding of the term knowledge in the context of the product development process. Responses provided by the interviewees were broken down into four definitions. These definitions are shown in Fig. 1, accompanied by supporting quotations from the interviews. It would seem that knowledge used in the new product development process resides in people, documents or information systems. Two examples of knowledge residing in people are the skill of a person to do something and their understanding of the distribution of knowledge in the organization, which might include knowing who possesses the experience or expertise necessary to solve a problem. Examples of knowledge encoded in documents included design rules and the scientific methods used to test a product.

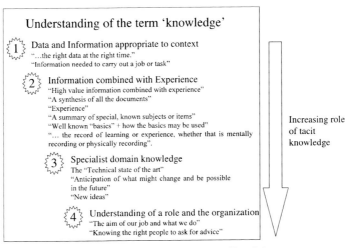

Figure 1: Interviewees' understanding of knowledge.

Types of Knowledge. Ten types of information were identified by the study. These were: technical information about a product (e.g. test reports and technical reports), information related to Quality processes (e.g. Failure Mode Effect Analysis or FMEA reports), financial information (e.g. costs and business plan), information about competitors (e.g. product brochures and data sheets), knowledge about customer requirements, regulatory knowledge (e.g. environmental legislation), information about the product development process, knowledge about previous projects, and information about knowledge (e.g. the location of the knowledge, its medium and the tasks that create it).

Media. Media used to store and deliver knowledge in the new product development process consisted of paper-based or 'hard copy' documents, digital documents, digital data files generated by software tools and verbal discourse. Some examples of the knowledge items available in each medium are given in Table 1.

Main Sources of Knowledge. Knowledge required to execute tasks in the NPD process is taken from a broad range of internal sources (within the company) and external sources (outside the company). The main internal sources used by the R&D engineering specialists were reports, including product, part and material test reports. Other reports included quality reports (such as FMEA reports), summaries of environmental legislation, safety laws, and norms relevant to the design of a product. Company NPD business process documentation was also consulted to obtain information about project management issues. In instances where knowledge cannot be found in reports or documents, colleagues may be contacted to find a source of the required expert advice. Project leaders and managers exploited the same sources as the engineering specialists, with the addition of business reports from finance functions to understand product and project cost requirements. Reports, presentations and advice from the marketing functions were used to communicate and explain customer requirements.

External sources consisted of technology exhibitions, university research departments and newsletters from part suppliers, which are used to gain knowledge of new technologies which may be incorporated into product design. Additionally, the websites of market competitors are examined to gain product information and actual products are purchased from competitors for testing by research engineers and assessment by cost analysts. Examples of sources for knowledge concerning product certification in different markets included personal contacts on legislative committees (e.g. the European Commission), the relevant notified bodies and certification organisations for each country. Occasionally direct contact with competitors is established to discuss changes that affect the industry as whole. An example of such an issue might be a significant change in environmental legislation.

Knowledge Medium	Example drawn from interviews
Paper-based document	Brochures and data sheets Journals and periodicals
Digital document	Project documentation, business reports, test reports (Microsoft Office file formats, Portable Document Format (PDF)) Emails exchanged among project team members
Digital data filed generated by Special Software Tools	Simulation software (simulation data from previous projects and simulation histories) Drawings (Mentor Graphics® files) Data and Information in SAP Company Intranet Portal External Internet 'Web sites'
Databases	Various specialist databases: Quality, Certification and Regulation
Verbal discourse	Advice from experienced colleagues • Telephone calls • Face-to-face contact in meetings

Table 1: Media used to deliver knowledge in the NPD process.

Storage of Knowledge. Knowledge generated during the product development process was stored in five types of repository. The first type was a folder on a network drive accessible to all personnel involved in the product development process. This folder stores all information pertaining to the NPD business process itself, such as project audit documentation and project reports. The second type was a project folder on a network server shared by personnel in the R&D function. Knowledge and information stored on this drive includes various technical reports and design data generated during the development process. The structures of these folders varied between sites and projects. The third type is a collection of knowledge management systems (including product quality management knowledge), databases (containing product drawings) and Enterprise Resource Planning (ERP) applications, such as SAP® (containing data about parts, suppliers and financial data). The fourth type is an archive of paper documents stored on each site. An example of this is information relating to the conformance of a product to various regulations, such as test reports. Information is kept in this format for each product so that it may be quickly handed over to a regulatory body, should it be requested. Finally, the fifth type of repository is the personnel in the NPD teams. These members retain knowledge that cannot be or is not encoded in any of the documentation, like the context in which a decision was taken or the reasoning behind it.

Searching for Knowledge. R&D personnel engaged in product development process activities often need to search for knowledge created in earlier stages of the current project or even knowledge created in previous projects. The interviewees were questioned about three issues related to searching for knowledge, namely the search methods they employ, which search tools they use and the challenges they face in this process. A summary of the main findings for each of these issues follows. Table 2 presents a summary of the three main methods used to search for knowledge. Explicit knowledge, such as test reports or information about environmental legislation in a market is usually found using a software search tool. Sources of implicit knowledge on the other hand, are located by communicating with a network of colleagues to track down an expert with the required technical competence or experience.

Method	Examples
Use an Internet search engine	Regulations and standards
Use an existing network of contacts (both Internal and External) to find somebody with the required expertise and experience (typically members of teams engaged in previous projects)	Phone calls Video conferences Can help directly or point in right direction Meetings with other project teams and suppliers
Search for documentation in project server drive / Database/ Email	Relevant documents, E-mail, design drawings for old products, project reports outlining proceedings in previous projects

Table 2: Methods used to search for knowledge.

Each of the interviewees claimed to use at least one software tool to search for knowledge. Four of the most common tools were Microsoft Windows Explorer® to search for documents on the R&D organization project server, a search engine on the company Intranet portal (mostly used to find contact details for people), the SAP® Enterprise Resource Planning software (used to store part drawings and part lists for products currently in production) and web-based search engines such as Google®. Other tools included specialist databases such as a tool by APIS® used to generate FMEA reports, and Open Text Livelink®, which is used to find and access certification information.

Finally, the challenges encountered by the interviewees while executing these searches will be considered. Four problem categories were identified: (1) the time required to search for knowledge, (2) difficulties finding the knowledge, (3) missing knowledge and (4) language. A more detailed explanation of each of these categories follows.

In the case of category 1, interviewees reported that they spent significant amounts of time searching for knowledge and indicated that they spent between ten minutes and a few hours a week on this activity. An additional burden was that the knowledge required to execute a task was obtained by compiling information from many different sources. In the case of category 2, interviewees indicated that explicit knowledge (such as that contained in reports) could usually be found without significant difficulty. Problems arose, however attempting to find knowledge located on another site. An example of this scenario was a component drawing located in a database of part drawings for old products that was not accessible via the company network. Furthermore, it was remarked that identifying sources of tacit knowledge (such as experience possessed by experts) was often problematic. Consequently, it could be difficult to understand the 'history' behind a decision made in an earlier project.

Now consider problem category 3. The type of knowledge most frequently identified as missing or unavailable while searching for knowledge was the experience or expertise possessed by employees. For example, knowledge might be required to establish the relevance of information and knowledge contained in an archived technical report to the current project or to explain the rationale behind a decision taken on a previous project, as mentioned in the explanation of the previous category. This may be best achieved by the contacting author of the report, since they are likely to possess detailed, tacit knowledge of the project history. However, it was emphasised by many of the interviewees that the person with the relevant experience might have changed roles within the organization or may even have left the company. Lastly, consider category 4. As already alluded to, activities in the product development process are carried out by multinational, multilingual teams. While NPD projects at the company use English as a working language, the documentation generated could be in any one of three languages. Consequently, knowledge encoded in documents may be available in theory, but inaccessible in practice to employees who are unable to read the language in which the document is published. This problem appeared to be exacerbated by the use of special abbreviations and terminology on each manufacturing site. Furthermore, some technical terms have multiple synonyms in each language. An example of such a term is 'nozzle holder', which is known as both 'Kammerträger' and 'Düsenstock' in German.

Conclusions

An exploratory study has been conducted to investigate information and knowledge sharing in the new product development process by the R&D personnel at a multinational electromechanical goods manufacturer. The key findings from the study included the identification of ten types of information and knowledge, the media used to store and deliver knowledge, sources of knowledge inside and outside of the company and repositories used to store knowledge. Additionally the methods and tools used to search for knowledge have been described, as well as the challenges encountered during the search process. The findings of the study will serve as the focus for future knowledge management activities at the case study company. Furthermore, they should provide an insight into knowledge sharing issues for manufacturers with similar multilingual, multinational product development environments.

Acknowledgements

The authors would like to acknowledge the support of the EPSRC in conducting this research.

References

[1] Brown, S.L. and Eisenhardt, K.M. (1995) Product development: Past research, present findings, and future directions. *Academy of Management Review* **20**, 343-378.

[2] Ramesh, B. and Tiwana, A. (1999) Supporting collaborative process knowledge management in new product development teams. *Decision Support Systems* **27**, 213-235.

[3] Zahay, D. et al (2004) Sources, uses and forms of data in the new product development process. *Industrial Marketing Management* **33**, 657-666.

[4] Ulrich, K.T. and Eppinger, S.D. (2003) *Product Design and Development*, 3rd edn. New York: McGraw-Hill.

[5] Browning, T.R. and Eppinger, S.D. (2002) Modeling Impacts of Process Architecture on Cost and Schedule Risk in Product Development. *IEEE Transactions on Engineering Management* **49**, 428-442.

[6] Effendi, I., Henson, B., Agouridas, V., and de Pennington, A. Methods and tools for requirements engineering of made-to-order mechanical products. 2002)

[7] Ghoshal, S. and Bartlett, C.A. (1990) The multinational corporation as an interorganizational network. *The Academy of Management Review* **15**, 603-623 .

[8] Desouza, K. and Evaristo, R. (2003) Global knowledge management strategies. *European Management Journal* **21**, 62-67.

Intelligent Planning and Scheduling Systems

Simulation-Model-Based Process Control of Discontinuous Production Processes

Martin Kremp[1,2,a], Thorsten Pawletta[2,b], Gary J. Colquhoun[1,c]

[1]Liverpool John Moores University, School of Engineering, UK

[2]Wismar University, RG Computational Engineering and Automation, Germany

[a]m.kremp@mb.hs-wismar.de, [b]pawel@mb.hs-wismar.de, [c]G.J.Colquhoun@livjm.ac.uk

Abstract. In cost-intensive, automated manufacturing systems, such as automotive and aircraft industries, simulation is used to support system design and development. In this context simulation techniques are used for system performance analysis and to develop optimum control strategies. In the subsequent process control development the control strategies are re-implemented into specific process control software. This paper proposes a novel holistic approach using a simulation model for process control after the simulation model has been used to design the process. The paper shows the necessary structuring of the simulation model, its extension by a process interface and the real-time synchronisation of the model execution to control the process.

Keywords: Process control, real-time event-based control, discrete event simulation, model re-use, simulation-model-based process control

1 Introduction

To be successful in today's global market the development and operation of manufacturing and material flow systems must be flexible, dynamic, precise, rapid and cost effective. However, these features often conflict for system designers. With *Mass Customisation* a new level of requirements is defined for manufacturing systems and its design and development. It demands process flexibility to manufacture customised products with the efficiency of mass production. The process control system as one of the most important elements of a manufacturing system has to deal with this flexibility. Today's industrial solutions providing this flexibility for process control systems are usually custom written for the given system configuration and manufacturing tasks. Anderson [1] summarises that this may consume up to 40 percent of total system costs. Re-use of software from the preceding development phases is one approach to reduce the development and implementation costs.

Simulation models are widely used in the *process design phase* to support the design and development of processes. *Discrete event simulation* (DES) is used in the design phase of complex *discontinuous production processes* [2] to compare different system structures, layouts and control strategies. During a DES project the system model and control strategies are implemented in a simulation model using one kind of simulation software. Simulation in such an application can prove the required system performance before the system is built.

With completion of the design phase the subsequent *automation phase* starts. It aims to develop and implement the process control system. Usually, the outcome of a DES project is a text document with a description of the best structure, layout and control strategies for given planning tasks and the expected system performance. The conventional procedure re-implements control strategies into a specific process control software system. The results are increased programming effort, a high probability of hidden programming errors and communication problems between system engineers and control engineers. Other research has also clearly identified this gap, for example in container terminal automation [3] and in real-time embedded systems [4].

49

This paper proposes a *simulation-model-based process control* approach. The basis is a simulation model developed, validated and used in the design phase of manufacturing and material flow systems. Section two gives a state of the art overview of research dealing with the identified gap between design and automation phase. Two important approaches are: (i) automatic code generation and (ii) direct use of a simulation model for process control. This research, introduced in section three, is based on the second approach. A detailed discussion of (i) a hierarchically structuring of the simulation model, (ii) the proposed process interfaces and (iii) the real-time synchronisation of the model execution to control the process is provided. Section four discusses the integration of an optimisation module in the simulation-model-based process control approach. A complex application of the approach is presented by Maletzki et al [5] demonstrating its relevance for industrial use.

2 Model-based Process Control Approaches

Current approaches dealing with the identified gap are driven by the design phase where detailed simulation models have been developed and implemented to analyse process control strategies. A prerequisite for efficient control strategy analysis and model re-use for process control is appropriate structuring of the simulation model. This research prefers the separation of a simulation model into two sub-models, a *system model* and *control model*. The system model maps the elements of a real or planned manufacturing system and their material flow connections. The control model contains the control strategies to describe the material flow between the elements of the system model. There are different approaches to realise an entire simulation model or parts of it for process control.

Automatic Code Generation. This approach is known from feedback control applications and embedded systems. The software system Matlab/Simulink [6] provides an automatic code generation toolbox (compiler) for several target systems. A compiler is used to translate the software code of a program into another programming language or into executable code. The advantage of using a compiler is a reduction of implementation time and costs. A consequence is that traceability and verification of compiler-generated code is hard to achieve [4]. However, today there is no commercial code generation system for discrete event systems available, reasons could be the following:

- compilers are custom written software systems,
- development is cost and time consuming,
- a large number of different compilers would be necessary for each combination of simulation and process control language and their updates.

Simulation-Model-Based Process Control. The term has been defined in this research. It describes the direct use of simulation models or parts of it for process control after the simulation model has been used to design the process.

A theoretical approach to extend a simulation model for process control has been published by Zeigler and Kim [7]. The approach is based on the DEVS-theory (Discrete Event System Specification) developed in the 1970s to describe a discrete event system formally. In [4] an application is presented using the real-time extension of DEVS to develop a controller for an embedded system. In [8] DEVS is used in the context of manufacturing systems. Even though DEVS is a formal approach it has not been applied for system dynamic analysis outside the small DEVS community.

Other research is based on a more intuitive approach based on the characteristic of simulation systems. In [9] an approach is proposed using the simulation software *Arena* to link simulation software with a physical process. An other approach is initiated in [3] using the simulation software *Simple++* to develop control strategies for a container terminal application. *Simple++* is used to implement the control model, the system model is provided by the transport equipment manufacturer as a software module. Both control and system model are linked by a custom written C++ interface. When the design phase is completed, the system model is replaced by the real physical system and the control model acts as a process controller. The effort to develop, to test and to validate the system model is not described.

This research proposes the re-use of the entire simulation model. Both control and system model are used for process control in the operation phase of the process. In contrast to the above approach the potential advantage of this research is the exclusive use of a simulation system during the design phase without any additional interfaces or data transfer protocols. Until a process interface has to be integrated with the automation phase in the simulation model. During process operation all software features (such as visualisation, data recording and evaluation, etc.) provided by the simulation system are usable in the context of a process control system.

3   The Simulation-Model-Based Process Control Approach

During the design phase a process is modelled using a strict separation of material flow (system model) and information flow (control model). The system model contains elements (e.g. buffer, server, etc.) representing real process devices. The elements are connected as the real material flow. Each element has internal variables to save the current state, such as number of jobs in a buffer, processing progress, etc. State information is used in the control model and for additional features, such as visualisation or data recording. The control model generates control signals, used in the system model to control activities and the job flow between elements. This general structure is presented in Figure 1a.

Two significant extensions on the simulation model and simulation software are necessary to act directly as a process control system. The changes are highlighted with a grey background in figure 1b.

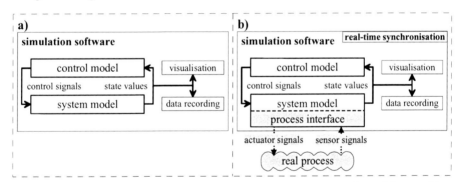

Figure 1.   From a Design Phase simulation model (a) to a Process Control System (b)

At first the simulation model is extended by a process interface. It is used to receive sensor signals from and to send actuator signals to the real world process. A distributed structure of the process interface has been selected. Each system model element has its own adapted process interface to link the corresponding material flow devices of the physical process. During the design phase a simulation model with its internal time delays is executed as fast as possible. Thus the second extension synchronises the simulation engine with real-time. That means a real-time clock drives the simulation model. A prerequisite for a successful synchronisation is that the execution of the simulation model is faster than real-time.

Figure 2 shows in detail the extension of a single-server design simulation model to a simulation-model-based process control system.

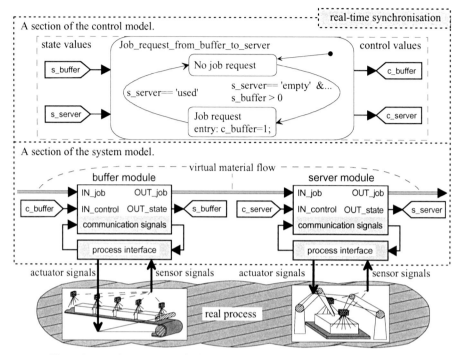

Figure 2.   Simulation-model-based process control of a single-server system

The system model contains two elements: buffer and server module. Both are implemented using the finite state machine methodology. They are coupled by the virtual material flow on system model level. The system model communicates with the control model using the signals: *c_buffer*, *s_buffer*, *c_server*, *s_server* (*c_* indicates control signals and *s_* indicates state values). The control model defines the job scheduling strategy from buffer to server. Its initial state is *No_job_request*. If server is empty and there are jobs in buffer the control model receives this information from the system model evaluating *s_buffer* and *s_server* state values. The result is a state transition in the control model from *No_job_request* to *Job_request*. This induces a *c_buffer* control signal for the buffer module. The control signal is evaluated and an actuator signal is sent to the real buffer device. The buffer module is now waiting for a sensor signal confirming a job departure from the real buffer device. Receiving this signal the buffer module sends a job object over the virtual material flow to the server module. This event updates the internal states of the buffer and server module. The new server state *s_server=='used'* transits the control model to the *No_job_request* state. When the server process interface receives the expected sensor signal, the job arrival is confirmed and the server starts its operation.

Figure 2 is used as a demonstration example. The system and control model have a more complex structure in real applications. Research has been done on structuring process models. All these concepts can be applied unmodified to the simulation-model-based process control approach. A complex application is presented in [5] using a simulation-model-based robot control application.

4 Optimising Simulation-Model-Based Process Control

In automated and customer-oriented manufacturing processes situations change frequently because of process disturbances, rush orders or other uncertain events. An important task is to find best-fit control strategies including optimal parameters for each process situation. Short term planning based on *online optimisation* could be a flexible and successful approach. The core task is to select the most appropriate control strategy and to optimise its parameters. Hence, it is necessary to keep production schedule and systems state information up to date. The simulation-model-based process control approach provides this characteristic. The system model always contains all current state information of the real process. Figure 3 outlines the integration of an optimisation module into a simulation-model-based process control system.

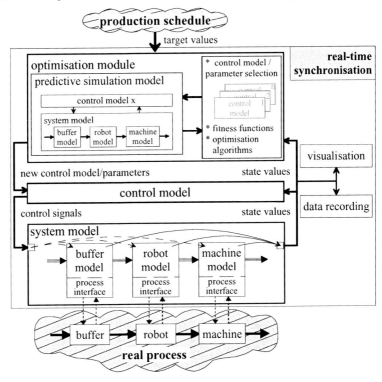

Figure 3.   Optimising simulation-model-based process control

The optimisation module is wholly executed in parallel to process control. It observes *production schedule target values* and system *state values* in real-time. When process disturbances occur and the demanded target values cannot be achieved or current target values change a new optimisation cycle has to be started. An optimisation cycle consists of three phases. (i) The initialisation phase saves the current target values and state values to guarantee a fair comparison of all calculations in the current optimisation cycle. Depending on the optimisation problem a suitable optimisation algorithm, the fitness function and specific optimisation parameters are selected. (ii) The actual optimisation starts. The performance values of each parameter set are determined by predictive simulations for a defined planning horizon. The execution of predictive simulations do not require complex interfaces because the process control system itself is based on a simulation software. The predictive simulation models are developed from design phase simulation models. (iii) When the optimisation algorithm has finished the results must be assessed. If the optimisation was successful individual controller parameters will be changed or the complete control model will be replaced. Because of time restrictions it could be possible that only a limited amount of variants can be investigated. With the integration of an optimisation module in the simulation-model-based process control the process control system is able to react immediately and nearly optimally to process disturbances. These aspects are discussed in detail in [10].

5 Conclusion

A prototype of the simulation-model-based process control approach was developed with Matlab and its toolboxes for a miniaturised laboratory plant. The laboratory plant reflects a real manufacturing application. The relevance of this approach is demonstrated in a second application controlling an industrial robot cell.

An important advantage of the approach is its complete implementation with a uniform methodology within a homogeneous engineering software environment. Thus, the software development effort could be significantly reduced, not least because of multiple re-use of software components from the early system design phase in its real operation phase.

References

[1] Anderson, C. (2000): Tomorrow's ideas at work today - scalable flexible manufacturing. Advanced Manufacturing Magazine, Research Report 2000. Available online at: www.advancedmanufacturing.com/March00/research.htm.

[2] Robinson, S. (2005): Discrete-event simulation: from the pioneers to the present, what next?, Journal of the Operation Research Society 56, pp. 619-629.

[3] Saanen, Y.A., A. Verbraeck, J.C. Rijsenbrij (2000): The application of advanced simulations for the engineering of logistic control systems, In Proc. of the 9th ASIM Dedicated Conference on Simulation in Production and Logistics, eds. K. Mertins, M. Rabe (pp. 217-231). Berlin.

[4] Hu, Xiaolin (2004): A simulation-based software development methodology for distributed real-time systems. Dissertation, University of Arizona.

[5] Maletzki, G., T. Pawletta, P. Dünow, S. Pawletta, B. Lampe (2006): A model-based robot programming approach in the MATLAB/Simulink environment, 4th International Conference on Manufacturing Research, Liverpool, 6 pages.

[6] Robot Car (2000): An embedded target example, The MathWorks, http://www.mathworks.com/products/rtwembedded/demos.html

[7] Zeigler, B., J. Kim (1993): Extending the DEVS-scheme knowledge-based simulation environment for real-time event-based control. IEEE Transactions on Robotics and Automation 9 (3), pp. 351-356.

[8] Praehofer, H., G. Jahn, W. Jacak, G. Haider (1994): Supervising manufacturing system operation by DEVS-based intelligent control. IEEE Computer Society Press, 221-228.

[9] Peters, B.A., J.S. Smith (1998): Real-time simulation-based shop floor control. In Proc. of ArenaSphere '98, Pittsburgh, PA, pp. 188-194.

[10] Kremp, M., T. Pawletta, G. Colquhoun (2004): Optimisation of manufacturing control strategies using on-line simulation, In Proc. of EUROSIM Congress 2004 Paris, 6 pages, France.

Integrated optimal planning of product family and manufacturing technology of its components

R. Kyttner[a], K. Karjust[b] and M. Pohlak[c]

Tallinn University of Technology, Ehitajate tee 5, Tallinn, 19086, Estonia

[a] rein.kyttner@ttu.ee, [b] kristo@staff.ttu.ee, [c] meelisp@staff.ttu.ee

Abstract. The objective of the study was to investigate how to optimize the family of products and its manufacturing processes, and to take the full advantage of the computer-based optimal engineering decision making process.

The simultaneous design of multiple products and collaborative multidisciplinary optimization are earning much attention in the engineering research community in the last years. The main problems are the decomposition of initial complex design tasks, identification links between different engineering tasks while maintaining effective coordination. For each considered sub-problem a multi-criteria optimization task is formulated. The attempt to integrate different subtasks so that they would support the complex optimization in the whole lifecycle of the product has been made.

Keywords: Multidisciplinary Optimization, Product Family Planning, Simulation

1 Introduction

Current trends in engineering design indicate the transformation of emphasis from product-level optimality to optimality for the portfolio of products, from one company to the network of cooperating companies. Today's typical engineering design decision making is a process with many iterations of synthesis and analysis. Challenges to design simultaneously multiple products, have led to the collaborative multidisciplinary optimization [1, 2, 3, 4]. It is supposed that the initial design task has to be decomposed due to its complexity. The decomposition will lead to the better understanding of the whole problem and to the realization of the design in different teams considering that there already exist models that can provide useful information.

The objective of the study was to investigate how to optimize the family of products considering its manufacturing processes, and to take the full advantage of the computer-based optimal engineering decision making process. As an example of the proposed approach, there was developed a high volume plastic parts product family in cooperation with hydro-spa producing company.

2 Outline of optimization method

As the result of decomposition, two design (planning) tasks, corresponding to product family optimal design and technological process optimal planning, are introduced. If there is no coordination among these tasks, the overall optimum could not be achieved because the different tasks (different designers) are pursuing their own goals without paying attention to global objectives and interactions. Consequently, a coordinator has to be introduced. The task of the coordinator is to prepare the necessary relations between the design parameters and performance attributes, to choose the suitable values of design parameters, such as the planning and design activities on the lower level, would yield results consistent with the optimality for the overall task.

To coordinate and to eliminate step-by-step possible discrepancies between different tasks, the coordinator provides [4, 5]:

- The prognosis of "design parameters", typical and recommendable solutions, and response models for main performance attributes of product family.
- Specification of the constraints to design parameters and performance attributes.
- Specification of the objective functions for the subtasks.

Each derivative product ($p_i \in P$) of product family is associated with the vector of design parameters ($x_j^{p_i}$). To start the design process concurrently, the coordinator has to propose the initial "guesses" for vector (x_0^p) and distribute parameters between different tasks. The objective of the coordinator is to improve these estimations iteratively ($j = 0,1,...,n$).

Adding constraints and focus on constraints satisfaction is one of the major approach for coordinating design sub-systems [4]. The process of adding and processing constraints, for instance, in the form of manufacturability constraints, is traditional for engineering design practice. The constraint-based reasoning approach changes the design process from one of selecting the best alternatives to one aimed at rejecting alternatives that would not meet the specified constraints.

To measure performance, evaluate decisions and coordinate the objective functions of subtasks, optimization with multiple objectives is proposed as a general framework. Two methods for handling multiple criteria in current case were considered:
- Goal programming approach [6];
- Physical optimization approach [7].

In goal programming, the objective function minimizes the weighted sum of deviational variables of objective functions. Unfortunately, it is difficult to specify the relative weights of deviational variables in practical cases. A defining characteristic of the physical optimization approach is that the coordinating subsystem knows the physical meaning of the objectives and the preference levels for the performance attributes.

For optimization it is necessary to establish appropriate models of system performance, cost, profit, etc for examining product family feasibility and optimality. Rather than directly linking CAD, CAE and process planning tasks with numerical optimization tools, the basic approach involves the design performance attribute propagation through the response surface equations (RSE). That will define the variation of key responses of product family with respect to the design parameters of interest. The key approach was to base the generation of the RSE on a classical design of experiments (DOE) approach.

In Fig. 1 is brought out one possible response surface. It was prepared using finite element analysis (software: ANSYS) of a hydro-spa equipment product family.

For generating appropriable optimization models, finite element analysis was made. Part consists of two plies: an acrylic polymer material ply and glass fibre reinforcement ply. Depending on the acrylic material sheet thickness changes in vacuum forming process and physical parameters of the composite material, the recommendations for the composite reinforcement (minimal required ply thickness) were proposed for designing of reinforcement operations. Fig. 2 a) shows the deformation plot of the composite structure; Fig. 2 b) shows diagram indicating deformation - reinforcement thickness relationship in some critical nodes (areas). The diagram is illustrating the selection of reinforcement ply thickness depending on maximum deformation allowed.

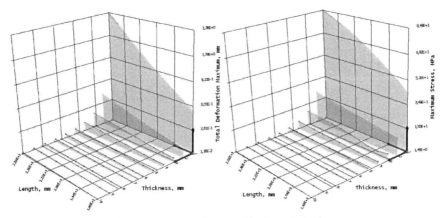

Fig. 1. Response surfaces used in the optimization

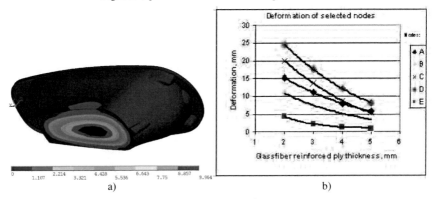

a)   b)

Fig. 2. Deformation of composite structure

Using the simulation, it is possible to optimize the reinforcement ply thickness specially for that part. It will also help to examine the product family in the point of the cost, profit, material usage etc. In Fig. 3 is shown the equivalent stress plot for the model, which indicates the stress concentrators and helps to determine the optimal glass-fibre reinforcement thickness in the certain areas.

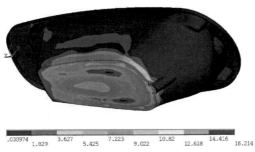

Fig. 3. Equivalent stress plot

3 Product family planning and optimal design

The product family design helps to resolve issues related to the markets, the types of the products and the resources of the company.

It is recommended to split the product family design process into two layers: a product family planning layer, and the layer for optimization (for each fixed combination of functional features) the design parameters of derivative products (product attributes optimization task). Under the introduction of these two layers, the product family design process is a hierarchical system of mixed-integer programming model for family planning and a constrained nonlinear programming model for product attribute optimization tasks.

The objective of product family planning is to optimize the sales volumes and module combination pattern for each derivative product. The constraints of effective use of resources and fulfillment of market demands must be satisfied. For optimal planning volumes of product family and module combination, the model was developed that maximizes net profit minus all investment costs and is subject to upper and lower bounds of demand on the market and capacity constraints used on workstations and materials. The following optimal planning task formulation can be expressed. Find the optimal volumes of the production X_i and use of the additional features $F_{j,i}$ that provides the results as follows: maximum profit and minimum manufacturing/purchasing times; and subject to constraints of:

- upper and lower bounds of demand on the market for all product variants and market segments;
- the capacity constraints for all used workstations;
- the available resources for all materials and purchased components.

As an example, the proposed approach is used to develop a family of products for hydro-spa equipment in Wellspa Inc. (Estonia). The examples of functional features for the proposed product family are, the existence of: translucent shell; far infrared heat; vibratory massage bed; Vichy shower; underbody shower; foot massage shower; vitamin/mineral diffusion system, etc. For optimization the standard integer and non-linear programming tools were used. For analysis CAE (ANSYS) and CAD (Unigraphics) systems were used. Fig. 4 shows examples of the derivative members of a product family of hydro-spa equipment.

Fig. 4. Examples of the derivative products

For illustration, some results of optimal product family planning are represented in Table 1. In spite of different input parameters, we could see an effective set, the profit is maximal, when the first, second and third product is produced and optimal when the additional functions for the second product are added.

Using the optimization model, new additional functions depending on the market needs; required investments; possible market growth; and production cost for each product were found out. After that it was considerably easier to see the direction where to invest and what modifications and changes are profitable to do. It allowed to reduce the delivery time and lead-time. Based on these results, the company developed two additional functions and the present sale figures show that the decisions made, were right.

Table 1. Optimization results

Parameters	p_1	p_2	p_3	p_4	
X_1, X_2, X_3, X_4	30	65	25	0	Production volumes
$F_{1,j}$	0	1	0	0	2G LCD display system
$F_{2,j}$	0	0	0	0	Additional aroma system
$F_{3,j}$	0	1	0	0	New material and design arch
$F_{4,j}$	0	0	0	0	Randomized vibration system

4 Planning of manufacturing technology

The manufacturing technology planning can be defined as the process of identifying a manufacturing operation plan, which defines either a complete or partial order in which the manufacturing tasks can be performed. The two layers for manufacturing technology planning are: the technology (route) planning model (the combinatorial 0-1 integer programming model is used) and optimal design of manufacturing (and assembly) operations (a constrained nonlinear programming model is used).

The generalized structure of technological route for the whole product family is represented in Fig. 5.

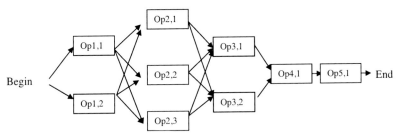

Fig. 5. The structure of the technology process

In Fig. 5 $Op_{1,1}$ represents reverse draw forming with two heaters; $Op_{1,2}$ represents straight vacuum forming; $Op_{2,1}$ represents automatic cutting; $Op_{2,2}$ represents automatic complied with manual cutting; $Op_{2,3}$ represents manual cutting; $Op_{3,1}$ represents manual reinforcement; $Op_{3,2}$ represents automatic reinforcement; $Op_{4,1}$ represents sub-assembling; $Op_{5,1}$ represents assembling.

The technology planning model for the product family is based on the maximization of the total profit and minimization of the manufacturing time and is subject to all constraints of operation establishment (operation necessity and operation precedence constraints), workstation time capacities, material availability, etc. Production cost is assumed to be composed of material cost and manufacturing/assembly cost (e.g. labour cost).

We can give the following formulation of the task:

Find the feasible operation sequences for a product family that gives us: maximum profit and minimize the manufacturing time; and is subject to the following constraints:
- capacity constraints for all workstations;
- use of materials;
- use of technologies.

The results of the technology planning optimization task, represent the list of operations used to manufacture the proposed family together with the data of the used resources.

59

Applying abovementioned methodology, it is possible to find out the optimal set of technologies, which maximizes the profit, minimizes the production times and production costs.

Conclusions

The objective of the study was to investigate how to optimize the family of products and their manufacturing processes. The accepted basic approach was the "evolutionary multidisciplinary product and process development". It was supposed that the initial task has to be decomposed because of its complexity. For measuring performance, evaluating decisions and coordinating the objective functions of subtasks, optimization with multi-objectives is proposed as a general framework. The proposed approach is exemplified by the development of a family of products in Wellspa Inc. The demonstrated examples ascertain the validity and effectiveness of the proposed method.

It has been analyzed how a company can adopt the concepts of optimal product family planning in their product development and technology planning processes, considering the whole product lifecycle process. Using partitioning by subtasks reduces the complexity of the overall planning problem and allows more systematic concurrent planning of the product family. To estimate the bottlenecks as net profit, lead time and other important characteristics, the simulation as a numerical technique for conducting experiment on computer is realized on basis of proposed models.

Acknowledgements

The research was supported by the Estonian Science Foundation (Grant ETF5883).

References

[1]   K. Fujita and H. Yoshida. Product variety optimization: Simultaneous optimization of module combination and module attributes. Proceedings of DETC'01 ASME 2001 Design Engineering Technical Conferences and Computers and Information in Engineering Conference. Pennsylvania, September 2001, 14 pp.

[2]   X. Gu and J.E. Renaud. Decision Based Collaborative Optimization. 8th ASCE Speciality Conference on Probabilistic Mechanics and Structural Reliability. PMC2000-217. 2000, 6 pp.

[3]   R. Küttner. A Framework of collaborative Product and Production Development System. Proceedings of the 3rd International Conference "Industrial Engineering – New Challenges to SME". April 2002, Tallinn, Estonia. TTU, pp. 34-37.

[4]   L. Zhu and D. Kazmer. A Performance-based representation of constraint-based reasoning and decision-based design. DETC'2000/DTM-14556 Proceedings of 12th International Conference on Design theory and Methodology, Design Engineering Technical Conferences. Baltimore, Maryland, 2000, 10 pp.

[5]   M. D. Mesarovic and Y. Takahara. Abstract System Theory. Lecture Notes in Control and Information Sciences, 116. Ed. by M. Thoma and A. Wyner. Springer Verlag. Berlin, Heidelberg. 1989. 439 pp.

[6]   A. Ravindran, D. Phillips and J. Solberg. Operation Research Principles and Practice, 2.edition. John Wiley & Sons, NY, 1987, 637 pp.

[7]   A. Messac, S.M. Gupta, and B. Akbulut. Linear Physical Programming: A new Approach to multiple Objective Optimization. Transactions on Operational Research, Vol. 8, Oct 1996, pp. 39-59.

Research on Job-shop Scheduling Optimized Method With Limited Resource

Liu Yongxian, Liu Xiaotian, Zhao Jinfu
Northeastern University, Shenyang, Liaoning, P.R China

Abstract

Job-shop scheduling is an important subject in the fields of production management and combinatorial optimization; it is also a problem to be solved urgently in actual production. It is usually hard to achieve an optimal solution with classical methods due to its high computational complexity (NP-Hard). According to the character of job-shop scheduling problems, a solution for job-shop scheduling problems based on PSO is presented in the dissertation. A Job-shop scheduling model based on PSO is established, the coding and optimized operation of PSO is researched, and more suitable methods of coding and operation about job-shop scheduling have been thought out, as well as the target function and calculation of the proper figure. The software system of the job-shop scheduling is developed according to the PSO algorithm. Simulation tests illustrate that the PSO algorithm is an available and effective approach to solve the Job-shop scheduling problem.

Key words:

Production scheduling; Particle Swarm Optimizer (PSO); Coding

1. Introduction

In today's economic society, how to improve the availability ratio of enterprises resources, adapt to the changes of market demands, and improve the benefits of running businesses accordingly, is the most concerning issue for modern enterprises. Job-shop scheduling- that is arranging fore-and-aft order of all processing tasks in all machines, making the total processing time the shortest time possible, delivering tasks with the least delay, the best utilization ratio of equipment, satisfying the conditions being restricted as well, making some performances optimization. Consequently Job-shop scheduling has become a key task in the operation of enterprises. Its aim is to use resources efficiently; react to demands promptly; according with the last time limit.

Production scheduling is the typical issue of combinatorial optimization, and the most part is NP-hard problems, it is difficult to get the best solution. So far, many kinds of algorithms have been designed in order to get to the nearest optimization solution, for example, neural network algorithm, genetic algorithm etc. But these algorithms mostly exist the interactional problems of contradiction one another between searching efficiency and results. When encountering the scheduling problems of more quantities of the machines and workpieces, using above mentioned algorithms take longer running time and the result of practical application is not quite ideal. In comparison with the other algorithms, the advantage of Particle Swarm Optimizer (PSO) is its simple and easy operation, convergence with speed, needing less knowledge of the field, simultaneity with profound intelligent background. It adapts not only to science research but also to engineering application. PSO is an optimizing technology based on swarm, which have many searching orbits, shows stronger

61

parallel, don't need grads information, only need using information of target function value, have very strong universal characteristic. The principle of PSO is very simple and needs less parameters. Therefore, from the beginning of its birth, POS algorithm attracts a lot of attention from scholars both domestic and abroad, and has been applied successfully in many fields. In this paper, the PSO algorithm is applied to job-shop scheduling. A feasible and efficient method is put forward to solve the job-shop schedule problem by PSO algorithm. Through setting proper parameters and applying it repeatedly it shows that the algorithm can get very good scheduling results quickly

2. Particle Swarm Optimizer Algorithm

The Particle Swarm Optimizer, PSO algorithm is put forward by Dr. Eberhart and Dr. Kennedy. It is a kind of intelligent optimization algorithm, developed from swarm intelligence and the study process of human being knowing. A new evolving calculation technology, it uses mass-less and volume-less particle as the individual, and stipulates a simple behavior rule for each particle, thereby making whole particle swarm showing the complex character, which can be used to solve the complicated optimization problems.

The PSO algorithm searches for the best solution over the complex space through cooperation and competition. First of all, the PSO algorithm creates the initial particle swarm, namely, initializing a swarm of particle randomly in the available solution space, each particle is an available solution of optimization problem, and it is determined fitness value through the target function. Each particle will move in the space of the solution, its direction and distance determined by speed. A general particle will move following the best current particle, obtaining the best solution through searching for generation by generation. In each generation, particle will trace two limited value, one of them is the best solution *pbest* which is found so far by particle itself, the other is the best solution *gbest* which is found so far by general group swarm.

The standard PSO algorithm is described as: suppose in searching spaces of n dimensions, swarm particles composed by m particles $x = (x_1,.....,x_i,...,x_m)$, where the position of particle i is $x_i = (x_{i1}, x_{i2}, ..., x_{in})^T$, where velocity is $V_i = (v_{i1}, v_{i2}, ..., v_{in})^T$. Its limited value is $P_i = (p_{i1}, p_{i2}, ..., p_{in})^T$, whole limited value of the swarm is $P_g = (p_{g1}, p_{g2}, ..., p_{gn})^T$. According to the principle of current best particle, the speed and the position of the particle x_i will be changed according to formula (2-1) and formula (2-2).

$$v_{id}^{(t+1)} = wv_{id}^t + c_1 r_1 \left(p_{id}^{(t)} - x_{id}^{(t)} \right) + c_2 r_2 \left(p_{gd}^{(t)} - x_{id}^{(t)} \right) \qquad (2\text{-}1)$$
$$x_{id}^{(t+1)} = x_{id}^{(t)} + v_{id}^{(t+1)} \qquad (2\text{-}2)$$

where $d = 1, 2, ..., n$, $i = 1, 2, ..., m$, m is the scale of swarm, t is current number of evolution generation, r_1 and r_2 are random number distributing between [0,1]; c_1 and c_2 are acceleration constant; w is inertial-weight [4], which can balance searching ability both whole and part. The first part of formula (2-1) is previous speed of particle; the second part is "Knowing", which indicate the thought of the particle itself; the third part is "society", indicating shared information and cooperation among particles. The first part acts as searching ability of balancing both whole and part. The second part makes particle with whole searching ability strongly enough in order to avoid appearing a minimum value in part. The third part indicates that information share among the particles.

3. Job- Shop Scheduling Algorithm

3.1. Description of Job- shop Scheduling

Job-shop scheduling can be described as: Suppose that there are n pieces, machining in m sets of equipment, workpieces concourse $P = \{p_1, p_2, ..., p_n\}$, variable p_i is the *ith* workpiece $(1 \leq i \leq n)$, every workpiece p_i needs to pass through J_i processes, the aggregation of working processes $OP = \{op_1, op_2, ..., op_n\}$, variable op_i belong to working processes aggregation of p_i, $op_i = \{op_{i1}, op_{i2}, ..., op_{iJ_i}\}$ is the sequence of working processes of workpiece p_i, machine aggregation $M = \{m_1, m_2, ..., m_m\}$, m_j is the jth machine $(1 \leq j \leq m)$. The time matrix which machine is used for each workpiece $T = \{t_{ij}\}$, t_{ij} is time that m_j machine is used for p_i workpiece.

Furthermore job-shop scheduling should meet the following restricted condition;
(a) Restricting the process sequences, the working processes sequences of every workpiece cannot be changed.
(b) Restricting resources; one set of machine should not be machining more than one part at the same time.
(c) Working processes restriction can not be intermitted: Once every part begins to be produced in an equipment, the working process can not be intermitted, not until the process of the part is finished can the equipment be used for another kind of part.
(d) The same part can be machined in a machine only for one process at a time.
(e) The working process time must be obeyed strictly

The target function in the paper is minimizing maximal finished time, it is determined by the formula (3-1)

$$T = \min\left(\max_{1 \leq j \leq m} c_j\right) \qquad (3-1)$$

where c_j denotes finished working time of the jth machine

3.2. Parameter Setting

PSO parameters include: swarm scale m, inertia weight, acceleration constant c_1 and c_2, maximal velocity V_{max}, maximal number of generation c_{max}[2]. What parameters are chosen in algorithm have great effect on the searching ability of the algorithm.
(a) Maximal velocity V_{max}
V_{max} determined resolving power (or precision) between the current position and the best position. If the V_{max} is too large, particles may fly over the best solution; if V_{max} is too small, particles cannot conduct enough searching outside the best area in part, which can result best value in part. In this paper, the value of v_{id} and x_{id} in the expressions (2-1) and (2-2) are restricted in a certain scope, which are $[-v_{max}, v_{max}]$ and $[-x_{max}, x_{max}]$ respectively, suppose that v_{max} is 1, x_{max} is 5.

(b) Weight factor

Inertia weight w keep the particles moving inertia, and have the tendency of extending searching space, and the ability of searching new areas. If the value of the inertia weight (w) is bigger, the ability of searching best in whole is strong, and the ability of searching best in part is weak; whereas the ability of searching the best in part is increased and the ability of searching the best in whole is reduced. The value of dynamic inertia weight is adopted in the paper, that is, linearity change of the value of inertia weight (w) during the PSO searching process, calculating formula is expression (3-2):

$$w = w_{min} + \frac{w_{max} - w_{min}}{n} \times i \qquad (3\text{-}2)$$

where n is the maximal generation number, i is current generation number, w_{max} is the maximal value of inertia weight, w_{min} is minimum value of inertia weight, which are 1.2 and 0.4 respectively in the paper.

(c) Acceleration constant C_1 and C_2

Acceleration constant C_1 and C_2 represent statistical acceleration item weight which can put the particles towards the position of *pbest* and *gbest* .The low value allows particles to wander outside the target area before they are put back, whereas a high value can result in particles rushing towards or across the target area suddenly. According to the experience in the paper, C_1 and C_2 are set as 2, that is $C_1=C_2=2$

3.3. Coding

Due to job-shop scheduling problem have variety attributes of discrete, dynamic and many variable, PSO algorithm coding which is aimed at job-shop scheduling has certain difficulties, since it is restricted by the process route, it is not easy determining an expression like such as traveling shop problems (TSP) flow-shop scheduling. The expression method based on working process is adopted for coding in the paper. This expression method use scheduling code as sequence of working process, each particle represents a scheduling project. All working processes of the same part is specified as workpiece label p_j, therefore what every element correspond to in the particle is workpiece label, then the working process of the workpiece is determined according to the order of the workpiece number which appear in the sequence, which is expressed by vector K, k (i) is the part number of the *ith* working process, code is made according to the operation order of working processes which occur randomly. The *ith* working process is set as p_j, k (i) $=j$, which meets the restriction (1) spontaneously. Corresponding each particle produce a vector y_i, which express the position weight of various working processes, y_i (j)= $w_{k(j)}$. the vector y_i contains integrally the position information of various working process in the original particle. After operation the vector we get vector y_i^1, scheduling the position information of y_i^1 can get a new scheduling project.

It can be seen that we can operate this sequence of working process through this new vector, and make sure that the particles that got from each operation are reasonable, which can represent a scheduling project.

3.4. Calculation of target function and its proper value

In the job-shop scheduling problem, minimizing the maximal finished time needs calculating, the target function is given in formula (3-1). Having known that working time t_{ij} is used for each workpiece in each working process on the machine, vector $T_M = [t_{M1}, t_{M2}, ... t_{Mm}]$, where t_{Mj} represents accumulative total processing time of workpiece on the jth machine, vector $T_P = [t_{P1}, t_{P2}, ..., t_{Pn}]$, where t_{Pi} represents accumulative total processing time of the ith workpiece, Each ponderance of initialization vector T_M and T_P is 0. Workpieces are assigned corresponding machines according to the order determined by the code, while during this time of assigning, restriction (2) and restriction (4) must be considered, adding the processing time t_{ij} to the vector T_M and vector T_P correspondingly and respectively. Vector T_M obtained from the above-mentioned method, its maximal ponderance value is finished time of processing

For example, the process of each workpiece is corresponding to the number of machine and processing time, which is shown in table 3.1, the processing time on each machine is given in the parentheses.

Table 3.1 Time of processing

No. of workpiece	Working procedure 1	Working procedure 2	Working procedure 3
p_1	m_1 (4)	m_2 (7)	m_3 (6)
p_2	m_2 (3)	m_1 (5)	m_3 (7)
p_3	m_3 (2)	m_2 (6)	m_1 (7)

Setting as particle $K = [3\ 2\ 2\ 1\ 1\ 2\ 3\ 1\ 3]$, initialization vector $T_M = [0,0,0]$, $T_P = [0,0,0]$. Referring to the code described above, first of all, the first working process of p_3 is done on the m_3, $t_{33} = 2$, so $T_M = [0,0,2]$, $T_P = [0,0,2]$; and the first working process of p_2 is done on the m_2, $t_{22} = 3$, so $T_M = [0,3,2]$, $T_P = [0,3,2]$; and then the second working process of p_2 is done on the m_1, $t_{21} = 5$, so $T_P = [0,8,2]$, $T_M = [5,3,2]$, but considering the process principle that the same part can not be machined on two machines at the same time, vector T_M should be set as $T_M = [8,3,2]$, which can meet the restriction (2) that more than one kind of part can not be machined on one machine at the same time, and the restriction (4) that a certain part can be machined for only one working process on a certain machine at a certain time.. The rest may be deduced by analogy, the maximal ponderance value of the vector T_M which is obtained finally is process finished time T, namely, target function value mentioned in the paper.

4. Application paradigm

The task which is given in the reference literature [1] is scheduled according to the above model and algorithm. The Gantt of scheduling result is shown in figure 4.1. The task of example use neural network algorithm, genetic algorithm and scheduling algorithm of improved process efficiency function. After scheduling using these algorithms, maximal finished times are 465, 560 and 450 respectively, After scheduling using the algorithms method in this paper, the maximal finished time is

440. The result of the researching proved the feasibility and advantage of the algorithm.

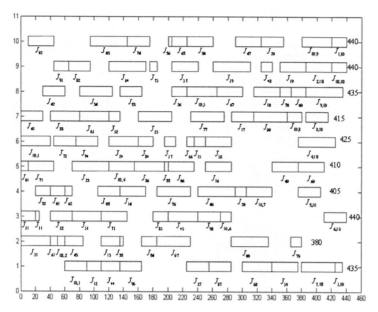

Figure 4.1 Gantt of scheduling result

5. Conclusion

The theory of Job-shop scheduling is an important researching subject in the fields of production management and combinatorial optimization, and it has been widely applied in the practice production. Due to its inherent calculation complicacy, it cannot get the best solution by means of typical method currently, The paper Fig. 4.1 The Gantt of scheduling introduced how to apply the Particle Swarm Optimizer (PSO) algorithm to Job- Shop scheduling, and how to solve the problem of job-shop scheduling in complicated shop by means of the advantage of particle swarm algorithm itself. The result of the study shows that setting proper parameters can assure astringency of algorithm, and avoid involving in the best in part, get the best result of scheduling.

References

[1] Xie Xiaofeng, Zhang Wenjun, Yangzhiqian Summarizing PSO [J].Control and Decision-making, ,18(2):129-134. 2003
[2] R C Eberhart, J Kennedy. A New Optimizer Using Particle Swarm Theory[C]. In: Proc Sixth International Symposium on Micro Machine and Human Science, Nagoya, Japan, 1995.
[3] R C Eberhart, J Kennedy. Particles Swarm Optimization[C]. In: IEEE International Conference on Neural Network, Perth, Australia, 1995.
[4] Shi, Y and Eberhart, R.C.Empirical study of particle swarm optimization. Proceedings of the World Multiconference on Systemics, Cybernetics and Informatics, Orlando,FL,2000,1945-1950.

ERP selection for small and medium-sized manufactures

Lin, I[1] and Ford.D.W.[1,a]

[1]Instutute for Manufacturing, University of Cambridge, United Kingdom

[a]dwf21@eng.cam.ac.uk

Abstract

This paper presents the findings of an investigation which sought to provide a solution for small and medium-sized manufactures who are about to invest in business software. The paper presents a short literature review of different selection models and the results of a practitioner survey and a questionnaire. A new model and workbook are presented that have the potential to assist small and medium-sized manufactures make more informed choices when selecting new business software.

Introduction

Today's competitive market has forced many small and medium-sized manufacturers (SMM) to adopt leading-edge technology to reduce cost and lead time and improve communication with external stake holders. Within manufacturing businesses there is an increasing demand to upgrade their IT infrastructure to generate a single stream of information flow in real time. Arguably, an Enterprise Resource Planning (ERP) system is a suitable solution to accomplish this objective. Selection and implementation of an effective information ERP system is a critical business activity that has been recognised and emphasised by many researchers and enterprises. As Davenport states in an interview by Gable [1] 'enterprise systems have become the primary way that companies re-engineer themselves'. However, a decision to deploy one is not a mere technical decision; it can impact on an organisation in every aspect and engage it in long-term commitments. Sarkis and Sundarraj [2]; Teltumbde [3] and Hong & Kim [4], argue that no single ERP software package can meet every different company's functionality or all special business requirements. Thus selecting a suitable ERP system and a supportive vendor is a challenging task facing many enterprises. All too often, SMMs do not use a systematic evaluation framework to assist evaluating ERP systems and vendors. As a result, decision-makers often rely solely on frivolous justifications such as gut-feel or executive mandate, without the ability to discern the best solution [5]. In addition, a poorly structured selection process will run over time and budget, and once selected, could potentially lead to buying an unsuitable ERP software package and an uncooperative vendor, all leading to poor future business performance.

Selection frameworks

A number of frameworks were reviewed. Langenwalter, G. *et al* [6] recommended a thirteen-step selection process. Using all the data collected to make a final go, no-go decision on the implementation. In extreme cases, if necessary, reverse the decision to implement ERP, change vendors, or renegotiate the contract. Arguably this model is more of a descriptive model of the stages that companies go through when selecting the software in the real world. However, it lacks sufficient scientific structure to give advice to improve future ERP system selection decision. Verville, J. and Halingten, A. [7] have proposed a six-stage model of the acquisition process for ERP software, which reflected the findings from the four cases examined in their study. The model depicts the principal processes and many of the constituent activities, issues, dynamics, and complexities that pertain to the acquisition of ERP software. Verville and Halington recognised that the buying process is non-linear and that some of the stages are embedded or done concurrently. All of the activities, with the exception of "choice," are iterative; each process is causal and results in deliverables that are used by another process. However, at certain points in the model, there is a sequential "next process" progression that takes the teams from the planning process to the information search, selection, evaluation, and choice processes, ending finally with the negotiations process. Arguably, this model is limited in the sense that it does not provide practical guidance on the issue of how to select the appropriate system. The four case studies were all based on multinational giant

67

companies, the value of the purchased ERP systems all exceeded 5 million dollars, thus may not be scaleable for SMMs. The concept of AHP (analytic hierarchy process) was proposed by Saaty in 1980 [8] as a method to determine the priority of a set of alternatives and the relative importance of attributes in a multiple criteria decision-making problem. Thus it is commonly used in solving socio-economic problems. Wei *et al.* (2005) [9] adopted this framework to establish an AHP-based approach to ERP system selection. In their study, a systematic procedure is proposed to construct the objective structure taking into account company strategies and thus extract the associated attributes for evaluating ERP systems. The core part of the model is the four level hierarchy. The weighted detailed attributes of each criteria were then listed. The following table presents the detailed description of the attributes in the AHP model with the associated means extracted from a means-objective network. Finally, the result of the AHP analysis is obtained from the multi-criteria attribute scoring system. In summary, this model addresses the issue of objective structures for evaluating ERP systems to promote logical judgement in the evaluation process. The model is flexible enough to add or delete attributes according to each firm's goals and strategic development. This suggests the methodology embedded in this model may be useful for designing a refined model for SMMs' ERP selection. J. Strub (2003) [10] proposed the following approach that is dubbed the probe approach. The feature of this approach was that it attempts to identify quickly the potential best package solution firstly on paper. When the firm is satisfied through a demonstration and reference visit that it is the best solution, or the selected solution fails to meet the needs of the business, the firm moves on to the next promising candidate. Accordingly, one company does not drill down to the same depth for all package candidates at the same time. Strub claims that if this method is used appropriately, the selection process can be cost and time-effective. A similar method named R^2ISC was developed by Hollander [11] on the ERP system selection criteria and process. R^2ISC is an acronym for the five key criteria: 1) ability of the package to meet your current business needs, 2) ability to modify the package to meet your new business needs, 3) ease of implementing the package, 4) ease of supporting the package in the future, and 5) total cost of the implementation of the package and ongoing maintenance. Then a four step R^2ISC process is deployed to analyse the R^2ISC criteria: 1) set the goal which includes determining the ratings for each of the R^2ISC criteria and the detailed requirements that make up each of the criteria, 2) narrow the field to four finalists, 3) select the winner by scripted demonstration, technical review and background checks, and 4. negotiate and sign the contract. The methodology described by Hollander appears to be intuitive. Its purpose is to analyse and quickly determine whether a software package can meet one company's need.

Summary of selection processes. The literature confirms the fact that ERP selection has a significant impact on the manufacturer's future performance. However, researchers appear to focus more on describing the acquisition process rather identifying any pros or cons of the process involved. Although the AHP model does provide a framework for how to choose software based on the objectives evaluation on software attributes, it does not provide a complete practical guidance which SMMs can utilise immediately. The applicability of some of the above models is weakened by over sophistication or absence of relevance to real-world applications. In addition to the academic research, there are many reports published by research institutes and consulting companies on ERP market share, vendor size, system performance and so on. Arguably these reports are dispersed and difficult to access and often biased in favour of the author. As a consequence decision-makers need to spend time and effort to extract the important attributes from these reports. It is evident that the current literature fails to consider the case of the SMM with finite financial and human resources, and with limited competence to carry out a large scale ERP selection process. Therefore, the aim of this research was to develop a methodology which is easy to understand and well structured, and produce a guide to assist SMMs through the selection process.

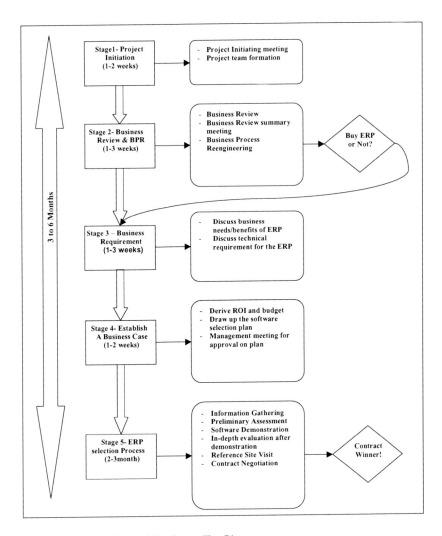

Figure 1 – ERP Acquisition Process Flow Diagram

Research methodology, data gathering and analysis

The two primary techniques for data collection were surveys and interviews. An Online survey was chosen because of popularity of 1) internet, 2) email and 3) access to data analysis tools. The link was posted to 20 companies of which 12 responded. The findings are presented below:

- 75% claim that it took too much management time and effort to compare and decide the appropriate software
- 67% said that it is difficult to put money value on the potential benefit of the MRP/ERP software to justify the cost

- 50% admitted that the large numbers of MRP/ERP software available in the market leads to difficulty in comparison
- 50% admitted that they did not have established criteria on selecting an MRP/ERP system
- 50% stated that they did not have a handbook/guidebook on this subject to assist them
- 42% claim that some modules bought were never utilised within the company
- 42% admitted a lack of knowledge about MRP/ERP system
- 33% tend to agree that the delivered system was "not bug free"

Concurrent with the sending out of questionnaires, interviews were arranged with a software vendor and SMMs. The selection of manufacturers was based on three criteria. Firstly, these companies had just chosen or implemented a MRP/ERP system, so they had fresh experience of the selection process. Secondly, the company manufactured a product. Thirdly, they were classified as SMMs, PLCs were excluded from the research. The purpose of applying these criteria was to facilitate identifying common problems in the selection process across different fields of manufacturing. The primary findings are summarised below

1. Nearly all interviewees confirmed that they had several stand-alone systems resulting in duplication and inefficiency, and inconsistent and untimely information within the organisation.
2. In other cases, decision-makers admitted that investment decisions were made without reaching a comfortable confidence level.
3. Due to the fact that most SMMs cannot afford to resource cross-discipline ERP selection teams to carry out a formal assessment process, Company A had only one person in charge for a decision to spend over £200,000. Only one company interviewed actually kept documents related to system selection, others have them in the minds of the decision-makers.
4. Interestingly, and surprisingly, all the firms interviewed seem to have sufficient budget set aside for the ERP system. They estimated that a typical ERP system for their size would range from £100,000 to £250,000.
5. Most of the ERP acquisition projects are initiated by the Managing Director, and for most of the time, the process is carried out by management level in the organisation. So most of the SMMs consider that a justification for investment was made earlier than indicated in most of the selection models and there is often no need to present the case to management at the end of selection. However, they did point out that insufficient involvement by the end users during the selection process has triggered a lot of resistance later on in the implementation stage. Change management issues should be addressed to improve employee morale once a decision to purchase an ERP system was made, not after the purchase of a specific ERP system.
6. All the respondents claim that companies should keep the customisation to the minimum.
7. Given the level of investment and length of time needed to implement ERP systems, none of the companies interviewed made any formal return on investment (ROI) calculations before the acquisition. The primary justification was that they need a single information flow system to integrate diverse business units and support the growth of the company: they invested in an ERP because they can afford it. However, they also all expressed the willingness to carry out ROI if there is a simple and practical way available.
8. None of the interviewed companies has a tight control on the selection time span. But all of them consider it would be more efficient to do so, but difficult to manage due to limited human resource dedicated to this project.
9. Three out of five companies did not define their business requirements or identify the critical vendor and software criteria prior to initiating the evaluation process.

The interviewees in this sample indicated that they obtained information from software events. They suggested it was impractical and time consuming to read published academic literature or even articles online because of limited access and disparate nature. The interviewees expressed demand for a decision-making tool, which can keep a balance between very detailed assessment and rough assessment, best practice, and contains templates, checklists and case studies. The feedback from the interviewees and the questionnaires suggests there is a need for a solution which is able to establish 'how to do things' rather than simply 'what to do'. As a result, it was decided to structure a practical workbook as the primary decision-making technique. The completed workbook contains flowcharts, decision trees, checklists, and case studies to provide a comprehensive understanding by the decision-makers.

Acquisition Process and workbook structure

The structure of the workbook assumes that users have little or no previous experience with IT investment. For each step in the process (see figure 1) the company needs to understand the aim of the step and how this step is executed. As identified in the literature review, most of the ERP selection processes are non-linear and iterative, with information going forwards and backwards. The workbook aims to provide a rounded consideration at each stage in order to reduce the iterative work to the minimum. The new workbook is not designed to replace, but to support, the experienced decision-making within the targeted SMMs, it does intend to reduce the time and effort within SMMs trying to build selection methodology from scratch. A workbook was designed to assist SMMs to investigate their requirement for ERP software then guide them through the process of selecting an appropriate software and service provider for its specific business environment. It has been designed to provide an easy to follow route through the ERP procurement lifecycle. It sets out a clear agenda for action to provide an element of control over the entire process. In essence it has been structured to help SMMs carry out the following steps:

a) understanding their medium to long term vision and business requirements
b) assess their current business process
c) assess their legacy information systems
d) guide the selection of a cross-functional team to ensure the right balance between technical and business expertise
e) assist to establish a business case for ERP investment, including ROI analysis and realistic budget setting
f) and so on

The workbook aims to provide a solid base for the overall structure and assistance in the decision-making process by providing practical templates, decision-trees and checklists. The workbook provides a guide which can be adapted to individual applications. Each stage of the process is broken down into individual elements. Where appropriate questionnaires and templates have been developed to help assist the user in navigating through to the next stage of the process.

Limitation of the study

The time limitation of research prevented the developed workbook being piloted and evaluated in an industrial setting. The sample companies involved in the study had some connection with the Institute for Manufacturing (IfM), Cambridge University. Therefore the source of information is not random or independent and might be biased in the way that they could be better informed than the average manufacturer. However, the authors suggest that this does not invalidate the study. The research has made two primary contributions to the body of knowledge. Firstly, it contains an up to date investigation of SMMs' difficulties and concerns in ERP software selection. Secondly, the research provides a review of a number of the available selection models.

Conclusion

It is clear from the study that those SMMs who were interviewed suffer from lack of integration between systems and poor information sharing between departments. This has led to problems such as high inventory levels, shortages, multiple data entry and conflict data which prolongs decision-making. However, the highly competitive nature of the manufacturing industry in the UK requires SMMs to continually identify ways of reducing cost while developing high quality products to meet increasingly enhanced customer requirements. In addition, buying an ERP system means much more than purchasing a piece of software. It actually means buying into the software vendor's view of best business practice.

The investment in ERP is a strategic and long term investment. However, the difficulty facing SMMs is that the rapid development of new technology in manufacturing management leads to an increasing number of options for ERP systems, which makes the decision-making process very complicated and painful. In response to the above situation, a simple and systematically structured workbook was developed for SMMs on how to organise and conduct the selection process. The methodology is phase based and takes into consideration control of time and project management. It is envisaged that the new workbook will provide SMMs with a methodology that has the potential to improve their current ERP acquisition process. The workbook is currently being tested by a number of SMMs and early indications suggest it is aiding their decision-making process.

References

[1] Gable, G. (1999) 'A conversation with Tom Davenport', *Journal of Global Information Management*, April-June, 8:2

[2] Sarkis J. and Sundarraj, R.P., (2000). Factors for strategic evaluation of enterprise information technologies. *International Journal of Physical Distribution & Logistics Management* **30** 3/4, pp. 196–220.

[3] Teltumbde A. (2000) A framework of evaluating ERP projects. *International Journal of Production Research* **38**, pp. 4507–4520.

[4] Hong K.K. and Kim, Y.G., 2002. The critical success factors for ERP implementation: An organizational fit perspective. *Information & Management* **40**, pp. 25–40.

[5] P.J. Jakovljevic, (2002) 'The 'Joy' Of Enterprise Systems Implementations' http://www.technologyevaluation.com/research/researchhighlights/erp/2002/07/research_notes/

[6] Langenwalter, G. (2000) 'Enterprise Resources Planning and Beyond: Integrating Your Entire Organization' Boca Raton, FL: St. Lucie Press.

[7] Verville, J. and Halingten, A. (2003) 'A six-stage model of the buying process for ERP software', *Industrial Marketing Management, Volume 32, Issue 7* , October, Pages 585-594

[8] Saaty, L. (1980) *The Analytic Hierarchy Process*: McGraw-Hill, New York.

[9] Wei, C.C., Chien, C-F., and Wang, M-J. J. (2005) 'An AHP-based approach to ERP system selection', *International Journal of Production Economics* , Volume 96, Issue 1 , April Pages 47-62

[10] Strub, J.J. (2003) 'Software Selection: An Approach', June 25 2003, http://www.technologyevaluation.com/Research/ResearchHighlights/TechnologySelections/2003/06/research_notes/

[11] Hollander. H. (nd) 'A Guide to Software Package Evaluation & Selection', American Management Association. http://www.r2isc.com/Process.htm

Optimising PCB part placement and routing

Crispin A J[1] and Holland J[2]

[1]Innovation North,
Faculty of Information and Technology,
Leeds Metropolitan University,
LS1 3HE
UK.
a.crispin@leedsmet.ac.uk

[2]Atkins Rail Telecommunications
Holgate Villa,
22 Holgate Road,
York,
YO24 4AB
john.holland@atkinsglobal.com

Abstract. The design of modern printed circuit boards (PCB's) requires that components are densely packed to reduce board area and manufacturing cost. Currently most PCB's are fabricated using copper clad boards and mask based chemical etching methods although PCB milling machines are used for small batch runs. The increasing requirement that circuits are highly compact means that designers must rely on computer-aided design tools for placement and routing. This paper describes a method for optimising PCB layout and routing. A software tool has been developed which uses the Lee-Moore algorithm for track auto-routing and a heuristic algorithm for optimising part position and routing order. Experimental results for a PCB circuit layout problem are presented.

Keywords: Optimisation, PCB Routing and Placement, Design Automation

Introduction

Electronic design automation is concerned with the physical design and manufacture of printed circuit boards (PCBs). The demand for miniaturisation has resulted in new fabrication methods (e.g. surface mount technology) and the need to compact circuit layout. This paper describes automatic placement and routing techniques for producing a compact PCB layout.

The PCB layout problem can be defined as follows. Given a set of N components and a component connection list (called a net-list) find an optimal placement and routing configuration which minimises layout area given constraint requirements. The constraint requirements are often dependent on the circuit design and can include electromagnetic constraints e.g. avoiding the creation of dipole radiating tracks in high frequency design and manufacturability constraints e.g. track and grid size constraints.

PCB Design and Manufacture

Electronic designers use CAD tools for producing a PCB layout. The first stage involves converting a circuit schematic into a net list. The net list describes how component pins are connected to each other. The net list is then imported into a PCB layout program where automated routing can be used to find a path between a set of connecting pins on the PCB which does not overlap other tracks. The placement of the components on the PCB is often done manually by the designer using placement strategies based on experience.

The major steps in a typical PCB design process are shown in Fig.1. The focus of this paper is on PCB layout which involves automated component placement and track routing. The work is developing a design tool for optimising a PCB layout given a set of components and a routing net list. The general philosophy is to place components on the board in an order arrangement and route pins using a routing algorithm. An optimum layout can then be found by changing the order in which components are placed on the board.

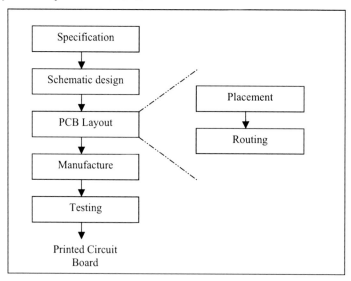

Fig. 1. The PCB design process

Routing

The track router is based on the Lee algorithm [1]. The Lee method is a maze routing technique for connecting two points in a matrix grid and is widely used in electronic CAD [2]. A maze router first searches the grid cells that are closest to the starting terminal and then proceeds in a breadth first manner by searching the cells adjacent to those that have already been searched. Maze routers will always find a minimum length path, if one exists, at the time the net is being routed.

Fig. 2 shows how the Lee algorithm works. The routing layer is represented as grid points used to route a track between a start and destination point. The algorithm works in two phases; wave propagation (expansion phase) and re-tracing. The wave propagation phase labels each grid point with it's Manhattan distance from the start point and will reach the destination point if a path exists. The re-tracing phase then forms the connection by following a path with decreasing labels.

■	■	■	■	■	■	■	■
■	■	■	■	■	■	■	■
4	3	2	1	2	3	4	■
3	2	1	S	1	2	3	■
4	3	2	1	2	3	4	■
5	4	3	2	■	■	5	■
	■	■	3	4	■	D	
	■	■	■	■	■		

■ =Obstruction (blocked grid point)

Fig. 2. Lee-Moore maze routing algorithm

Net Ordering and Optimisation

The main issue with PCB routing is the order in which routes should be placed on the PCB as this determines the quality of the result. Some route order combinations result in tracks that can not be routed as previously laid tracks block possible paths. If the number of routes to be placed is N then the number of different combinations of routes is N factorial or N! For example, routing 15 tracks can be done in one of 1,307,674,368,000 combinations (15!). The best combination could be measured by calculating the overall routing length for each combination which routes all tracks and choosing the routing order which yields the minimum value.

As the number of routes to be placed increases, the size of the net ordering search space increases and it is not feasible to search all route order combinations with an exhaustive (brute force) search approach as this would take an excessive amount of processing time [3]. In this case a heuristic search can be used. The basic idea of a heuristic search is to focus on order combinations that seem to be getting closer to the goal state rather than search all possible order combinations. Heuristics are used to make an educated guess at the next best combination and require that a fitness function (also called the objective function) be calculated. The fitness function should provide a score value according to how close to the target goal the result appears to be.

In the net ordering problem [4] it is required to minimise the number of route failures and the overall track length. This means that the fitness function needs to calculate the number of failed routes and the overall track length of the tracks laid for a particular routing order. Consequently it is required to optimise two objective parameters making this a multi-objective optimisation problem. One way of dealing with multiple objectives is to combine (aggregate) all the objective parameters into one scalar value using weighting values to establish preferences between objectives. In this work the fitness value F is calculated as;

$$F = 500 \, f_1 + f_2 \tag{1}$$

where f_1 is the number of route failures and f_2 is the total track length of all possible routes. The heavy weighting of f_1 makes this the dominant factor when minimising the fitness value. Further terms can be included in the fitness function such as a term that prevents the parallel routing of two tracks where crosstalk could be a problem [4].

The simple hill climbing method [5] has been used as the optimisation method. The basic idea of the hill climbing algorithm is as follows. An initial current route combination is chosen at random and evaluated using the fitness function. Within an iteration loop the order of the current route combination is changed at random and the new combination is evaluated with the objective function. If the new combination yields a better goal value than the current combination then it is assigned as the best route order found so far and is used as the current solution (hill climbing always works from the current best solution). This process continues for a fixed number of iterations or until a preset goal value is achieved. The best route order obtained is used for routing the circuit.

Layout Optimisation

Automatic placement is a challenging task as it requires developing a coding strategy for component layout and creating new evaluation methods for determining what is a good layout. This work is investigating a constraint based approach for component placement where the placement of a component relies on where the previous part has been placed. An automatic placement algorithm has been developed that calculates the routability of a given placement pattern. The order in which components are placed in the pattern is optimised using a hill climbing search algorithm.

With the inclusion of the automatic placement algorithm, the size of the search space increases significantly and further emphasises the need of a heuristic strategy for optimisation. Even for the relatively simple instrumentation amplifier below, examining each component layout (for 9 components) and all combinations of routes for that layout (15 routes), the search space increases to 9!*15!, or 474,528,874,659,840,000 solutions. The enormity of the search space dictates the use of heuristic optimisers.

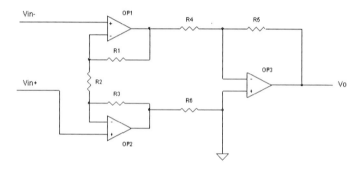

Fig. 3. Instrumentation amplifier

Experiments and Results

Experiments have been performed on the automatic placement and routing of a three operational amplifier (op-amp) instrumentation amplifier circuit. This is a relatively simple circuit but incorporates important features to enable the optimisation of placement and routing to be evaluated. An instrumentation amplifier is widely used to condition small signals in the presence of large common-mode voltages and DC potentials (e.g. ECG sensing). A schematic of a three op-amp instrumentation amplifier is shown in Fig. 3. It is made up of two stages; a buffered amplifier based on op-amps OP1 and OP2, and a differential amplifier based on op-amp OP3.

A typical resulting PCB layout generated by the placement and routing algorithm is shown in Fig. 4. Components are initially placed in a horizontal alignment pattern so that component placement order and routing can be optimised. Routing of tracks inside the components is prohibited so that the power lines can be subsequently routed through the centre of the op-amp components. The optimisation algorithm changes the order in which components are placed and for each case finds the best routing combination. The fitness value can be exported as an Excel file for plotting purposes (see Fig.5). The application allows a Gerber file output to be generated from the optimised layout which can be used for producing a mask for manufacturing purposes.

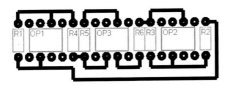

Fig. 4. Automatic placement and routing of the instrumentation amplifier PCB

The placement and routing hill climbing algorithm produces a high quality solution as shown in Fig. 4. However hill climbing is a non-deterministic algorithm and so different runs can result in different layout solutions even when the main objective (i.e. failed routes=0) is met. The objective function attempts to balance the layout as this produces the shortest track length. An experienced designer would attempt to produce a PCB which keeps the track lengths as short as possible and balance the PCB design by placing op-amp OP3 between op-amps OP1 and OP2. Keeping the layout symmetrically balanced helps to balance track resistance and parasitic capacitance maximising common mode rejection. The routing algorithm does not consider crosstalk. Crosstalk is generally not a problem when the input to an instrumentation amplifier is a low frequency sensor signal and the purpose of the amplifier is to reject 50 Hz noise.

Fig. 5 shows how the fitness value changes during the optimisation process leading to the resulting layout shown in Fig. 4. It shows that the fitness value reduces towards a situation where the number of failed routes is zero and the track length is minimised. The plot shows plateau regions where the number of failed routes has not changed but a better overall wire length has been found.

In this work the hill climbing algorithm is thread coded so that component order and route order are changed simultaneously. This was found to be superior to coding the problem with an inner loop for routing and an outer loop for component placement. The hill climbing algorithm works from a single best solution and so a large number of iterations are normally required to obtain a good layout solution. Other optimisers such as a population based genetic algorithm [6] are better suited to searching wider ranging search spaces and will be studied as future work.

Conclusions

The paper has presented strategies for the automatic placement and routing of a PCB layout. This involves optimising the component placement order and the net list routing order. A PCB layout and routing software application has been developed and layout experiments performed on an instrumentation amplifier design. This is a multi-objective optimisation problem and a fitness function is defined which aggregates the number of routing failures and track length. A hill climbing algorithm is used as the optimiser. Results have been obtained using a one dimensional layout pattern and show that a high quality solution can be obtained. The authors intend to extend the work by investigating complex circuit designs requiring two dimensional placement strategies and by investigating population based optimisers such as a genetic algorithm.

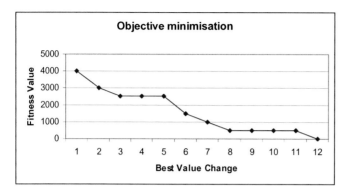

Fig. 5. Objective minimisation

References

[1] Lee, C. Y. An algorithm for path connections and its applications, IRE Transactions on Electronic Computers, EC-10, 1961, pp. 346-365.

[2] Sarrafzadeh M. and Wong C.K., An introduction to VLSI design, McGraw-Hill, 1996.

[3] S. Arya, D. M. Mount, N. S. Netanyahu, R. Silverman, and A. Wu. An optimal algorithm for approximate nearest neighbour searching. In Proc. 5th ACM-SIAM Sympos. Discrete Algorithms, pages 1994, pp. 573-582.

[4] Hai Zhou and D.F. Wong. Global routing with crosstalk constraints. In 35th Design Automation Conference, 1998, pp. 374-377.

[5] V. Kvasnicka, M. Pelikan, and J. Pospichal. Hill-climbing with learning. Technical report, Slovak Technical University, Bratislava, 1995.

[6] Crispin, A. J., Clay, P., Taylor, G. E., Bayes, T., Reedman, D., Genetic algorithm coding methods for leather nesting, International Journal of Applied Intelligence, 2005, Vol. 23, pp. 9-20.

Acknowledgements

The authors would like to thank Atkins Rail Telecommunications for funding research conference costs.

E-Manufacturing and
Supply Chain Management

Achieving Cultural Change in an SMM – Balancing Growth and Control

Mauleverer, C.M.D. [1, a], Ford, D.W. [2, b]

[1]Briton EMS Ltd, Bedford, UK

[2]Institute for Manufacturing, University of Cambridge, UK

[a]marcus.mauleverer@britonems.co.uk, [b]dwf21@cam.ac.uk

Abstract. This paper presents the findings following eighteen months of a two-year Knowledge Transfer Partnership (KTP) between the Institute for Manufacturing (IfM), University of Cambridge and the small and medium sized manufacturer (SMM) Briton EMS (Electronic Manufacturing Services) Ltd. The objective of the KTP is to develop and implement new business processes leading to improved productivity and business growth. This paper continues from a previous study where success mapping techniques were developed to define those areas of the company which were strategically important and in need of improvement. The use of this methodology provided an indication of the route to achieve success, and aligned the KTP objectives with the output from the success mapping exercise. During the study period the company has exceeded its growth targets which has necessitated significant internal change due to the increase in number and complexity of customer orders. However, it was recognised that although the KTP resource was dedicated to managing critical parts of the change process, neither the company nor the associate had experience in change management and therefore a number of proven change management processes were researched. Amendments to the selected process were made to ensure success in a SMM environment. Three areas of targeted improvement are described in this paper: sales order processing, purchasing and the new product introduction process.

Keywords: Change management, Cultural change, KTP case study, SME research

Introduction

Briton EMS is a 25 year old company and has incrementally grown to around £4M and provides stable employment for around 80 employees. In order to continue in a market where competition is ever increasing the company set out a five year growth plan to double turnover and treble net profit; the company is now in the third year of this plan. The KTP was established with the specific aim of preparing the internal business processes for growth. However it is not necessarily evident to employees that change is also required to sustain a business. As markets become increasingly complex and competitive, a company must develop its internal processes to satisfy increasing customer demands. The methods by which these changes have been effected within the KTP project are the main findings of this paper.

Diagnostic and Success Mapping

The first deliverable was to process map the primary business processes. A diagnostic and action planning technique was developed to identify the strategic process that required mapping [1]. The primary finding from this process was that the administrative processes rather than the value adding processes required improvement. A prioritised list of areas requiring attention was formed and the KTP plan amended to meet them:

- Sales Order Processing – uniting information systems for improved data reliability.
- Purchasing – reduce known shortages at manufacture; MRP implementation.
- Engineering – introduce improved new product introduction process for better control.

Preparation for Cultural Change

First the associate spent time to understand the company, its employees as individuals and the relationships between them, and to determine their readiness for change. As part of this process the associate integrated himself into the business.

Understanding and becoming part of the company Deploying the diagnostic, creating the success maps, and developing the initial process maps helped to develop the associate's understanding of the relationships between the various departments in the business. As the process progressed Maslow's [2] hierarchy of needs was informally deployed. It was found that employees were satisfied by their safety and security needs and most had a sense of belonging. However, the self esteem and actualisation needs were rarely met. It was found that although many employees suggested they were motivated by the "higher" needs, in reality the day to day issues often took priority. Different individuals and team members needed different motivations to change.

Before the change process was formally initiated three areas of preparatory work were completed. First a mini project was established to reduce the number of unknown component shortages at manufacture. This enabled cross functional working between members of the shop floor and administrative processes, resulting in a 60% decrease in shortages and a boost in confidence. Second, the stock control system was updated to a windows version which greatly increased usability for new users (of which there would be many). Finally, a new telephone system and an array of workstations were installed across the shop floor to enable inter-site communication from the individual build bays and give a sense of control to the team leaders.

Change Method

Before the changes recommended from the success mapping exercise were initiated, two management skills were researched: First, the process by which each of the individual changes could be realised was specified. Second, the appropriate leadership styles to effect these changes in real time were understood.

Change Management Process The concept of change management is not new, many methodologies have been developed in a variety of situations. Caldwell and Platts [3] suggest that the most popular of these are broadly the same, based on three steps: unfreeze behaviour, change behaviour, then refreeze behaviour. To achieve this, Demming's Plan-Do-Check-Act process [4] underpins each methodology. Rather than follow this basic process, further research was performed to better understand the SMM environment, and specifically to achieve the KTP's objectives. Although each area identified for improvement seemed to be individual, each had the potential to affect other areas of the company. Goldratt's five focusing steps [5] were considered to direct work towards individual objectives whilst ensuring that the implications of each change were understood before implementation began. At every stage it was important to have a multi-disciplinary mix of staff involved (or at least informed) to ensure successful cultural change. This enabled a better understanding of the means and ability [6] required by the employees involved in each change, and supported the communication chain to create a link between the changes and improvements [7]. A new simple methodology was developed suitable for an SMM environment:

1. Understand the objective and explore possibilities and "knock on" with main stakeholders
2. Justify the change and prepare all stakeholders, eliminate confusion
3. Implementation
4. Keep communicating, ask questions and report results
5. Re-start from stage 1 if appropriate

6. Update and document understanding

Leadership From the beginning of the KTP it was evident that encouraging the employees to change in line with the process changes would probably be the most challenging aspect of the programme. The previous preparatory projects developed an understanding for the company's day to day workings and validated the associate's role in the business. Goleman [8] identified six distinct styles of leadership and argues that the most effective leaders are capable of adapting their style to the most appropriate for the current situation in standard projects. It is arguable that in change projects the continuously varying environment requires an even greater degree of this skill. Therefore, the associate identified his preferred style and learnt to adapt it to the situation. This helped to minimise the effects of personal and emotional issues relating to each change. In the SMM environment, general friendliness and informality worked well at most levels. However, it was important to recognise the potential danger of delayed decision-making and actions.

Examples of Change

Kotter [6] states that "empowerment implies an incremental suspension of control", for this reason the areas targeted for improvement were addressed individually with some overlap. This reduced confusion, minimising incidental effects, and simplified the management of the change.

Process Integration & Assembly Booking Historically, the sales order process from receipt of a customer order to the creation of a delivery note had been controlled by a standalone database. The results of this are the potential for mismatched information, increased processing time, keying errors, and increased throughput times. The objective was to implement the unused sales order module within the stock control system, which would be capable of filling this gap.

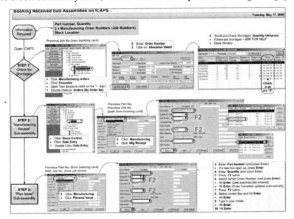

Figure 1.   Assembly booking process chart

The first planning stage developed an understanding of the stakeholders and how their daily activities and the process would change. It was concluded that the administrative data entry and reporting functions required training in the use of the new system. Implementation went ahead in parallel with the old system. However, it soon became apparent that, due to the use of multilevelled bill of materials (BOM), it would be necessary to book subassemblies through the system from one BOM level to the next in order to ship a final product to the customer. Due to resource constraints it was decided that the team leaders would perform the booking. This was an entirely new concept to the company. It is arguable that the team leaders were ideally placed to perform this task, however the "over the wall mentality" hid the fundamental knowledge of which job an assembly had come from and where it needed to go. Therefore, a booking card system was set up to encapsulate this information with all moving assemblies. During implementation it became apparent that the booking was not working correctly, the team leaders did not understand the process. Therefore, Knowledge was transferred from another KTP with similar experience, the result of this was an A3 poster (Fig. 1) explaining the process. This was distributed to all workshop PC areas, improving interaction and therefore learning. Prior to the project, the principal users of the stock control system had a very protective attitude towards data entry. A very diplomatic leadership style was required to develop this successfully across the shop floor.

Process improvement As stated above, the first deliverable was a set of primary process maps to drive the project's change process. This identified the need to improve the New Product Introduction (NPI) process shown on the left of figure 2. This showed the current state and highlighted areas for improvement but few actions were taken. A new engineering manager was appointed to lead the change process. The first step was to understand and procedurise the NPI process so that it could be managed. A series of meetings with all the engineers, quality manager and KTP associate was arranged during which the process was split into four distinct areas. Maps were drawn and improved with suggestions from all sides (Fig. 2 right) and procedures linked to each item on the maps. One key factor was the translation of loops into distinct inputs and outputs, the aim being to reduce delayed decisions due to lack of information. The increase in business and therefore engineering workload hampered the new engineering manager's ability to perform the final check phase of the change management process. Unfortunately, a coercive leadership style may be required to ensure the engineers follow the new procedures.

Figure 2.   NPI process maps – old and new

System's implementation – Purchasing (MRP) As the volume of work has grown, complexity has grown with it, there has been little shift along Hayes and Wheelwright's natural diagonal [9] and the manufacturing and engineering teams have grown roughly in line with requirements. Briton's supply chain is very supplier heavy; over the last three years around 10,000 different components have been bought from 430 suppliers, contrasted with just 28 customers. The effect of this is an exponential increase of purchasing work as new customers and products are developed. However, throughout this growth, purchasing capacity has remained constant.

The planning phase of this part of the programme was led by two postgraduate student projects. A Pareto analysis showed that 75% of spend was with 12% of the supplier base and that the remainder could be located on the leverage or non-critical quadrants of the Kraljic matrix [10]. It was also found that the company's lack of a dedicated planner was making it increasingly difficult to balance customer requirements with materials and capacity, this role being informally distributed between the Manufacturing Director and Purchasing Manager. This finding led to the decision to fully implement MRP. The education phase identified the system's requirements and limitations; similar companies were visited to understand potential problems and solutions. A plan was drawn up and implemented. As most areas of the company would be affected in some way the PDCA process was cycled a number of times. Although the management team understood the potential benefits, change decisions often took a considerable length of time as they were thought to be strategic and therefore circled the team before an action could be taken. From a leadership perspective it was sometimes difficult to "sell" the idea to employees: Middle management saw a drastic and potentially uncomfortable change in how they would use the system and the shop floor had to clock on jobs. It was found that a variety of leadership styles were required to keep the project moving. This work is ongoing and has been found to be particularly challenging due to the mindset change required in key management roles. The company is now looking to employ two new staff as part of its migration towards systemised purchasing and planning.

Aggregated Findings & Implications

This KTP project has enabled the improvement of Briton EMS's business processes at all levels of the business. It was found that changes often complemented and occasionally confronted others. It is arguable that although most change management methodologies cover the requirements and psychology of the company, teams and individuals, there is little explanation as to how to balance these. Briton's business plan and the success maps clearly specified the company's requirements for development. This then enabled the associate to concentrate on managing the team and individuals for each change through the adapted PDCA process. The decision to make the changes incrementally not only reduced confusion on those to which the changes applied, but also enabled a better understanding of impact as they happened, thus easing the associate's management task. One key finding was that later changes were made much easier by those which had happened before. For example, once assembly booking was continuous on the shop floor, the staff took to job clocking much more easily; this in turn will simplify the implantation of MRPII (Fig. 3).

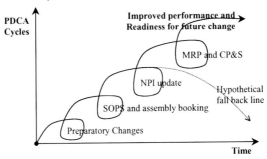

Figure 3.   The helical path of cultural change

It was not recognised until well into the implementation stage of the new sales order module that sub-assemblies would have to be booked through the system. Fortunately there was little negative impact and the lesson was learnt to prioritise the planning stage for the following changes. The most prominent advantage and disadvantage of the PDCA process was that, by definition, it is a cycle. Whilst this enabled good feedback and continuous improvement, many decision points were created; if these were considered strategic then they became delayed in the management process.

There is also evidence that, once a change has been made successfully and the culture has developed, there is a danger of complacency. Unless people are continually ready for change they can revert to the previous methods of working. The hypothetical dotted line on figure 3 shows the potential effects of this on the NPI process. This is most likely to occur when the "Check" segment of the PDCA process is not properly carried out.

Understanding the feelings and motivation of all stakeholders was considerably more challenging than the technical aspects of each change. Goleman [8] is not alone in recognising the imbalance towards EQ in the IQ:EQ ratio for leadership. Rather than leading by example, the associate adapted his style to bring out the employee's individual skills. The best method found to instil cultural change at the lower levels was to involve the key stakeholders by asking for help. At a management level the meeting-based mechanism to ensure progress often failed. The associate had to balance the planning and real time issues, focus on the appropriate ones and actively pursue them.

Conclusions

This paper has presented the findings of a KTP designed to prepare Briton EMS for significant growth. The success mapping technique identified four areas for improvement and four related changes are described alongside the change management and leadership methods deployed. Although the associate had no official control over the company staff he was able to gain their respect and instigate productive changes. Excellent companies are not only good at manufacturing product, but are extremely capable of responding to any change in their environment as a direct result of their cultural attributes. The work of this KTP has not only developed the internal processes of Briton EMS to operate more efficiently, but has also improved the culture to one that is much more accepting of and ready for future change. Direct improvements have been seen in company-wide communication and an enhanced keenness to think. This has helped Briton to exceed its growth targets without incurring excessive costs.

References

[1]   Mauleverer, C. M. D. et al. (2005) The Success Map – Deployment of decision-making tools in a Small and Medium sized Manufacturing Environment. Working paper, Institute for Manufacturing, University of Cambridge.

[2]   Maslow, A. (1954) Motivation and Personality. Harper and Row, New York.

[3]   Caldwell, P. and Platts, K. (2005) From Prescription to Treatment: How can diagnostic tools be improved to increase take-up of the recommendations? Proceedings of SMESME Conference 2005, UK, Glasgow.

[4]   Ishikawa, K. (1985) What is Total Quality Control? Prentice Hall Inc., New Jersey.

[5]   Goldratt, E. M. (1984) The Goal. The North River Press, Great Barington, MA.

[6]   Kotter, J. P. (1996) Leading Change. Harvard Business School Press, Boston.

[7]   Schuitema, E. (2004) Leadership – the Care and Growth Model. Ampersand Press, Kenilworth, South Africa.

[8]   Goleman, D. (2000) Leadership That Gets Results. Harvard Business Review. March-April: pp. – 78-90

[9]   Hayes, R. H. and Wheelwright S, C (1979) The dynamics of process-product life cycles. Harvard Business Review. March-April: pp – 172-136.

[10]   Kraljic P (1983) Purchasing must become supply management. Harvard Business Review 61(5): pp. – 109-117.

The Development of an Agent Sourcing Methodology for UK SMMs Wishing to Purchase from China

Patrick, J[1,], and Ford, D.W[1,a].

[1]Instutute for Manufacturing, University of Cambridge, United Kingdom

[a]dwf21@eng.cam.ac.uk

Abstract. This paper presents the findings of an investigation into solutions for making a rational agent partner decision for component sourcing from China. The paper presents a new agent sourcing process that has been developed specifically for small and medium-sized manufacturers (SMMs) who may have limited competence in managing an international supply-chain. The new model provides SMMs with a simple methodology that enables them to assess potential agents, and provide evidence to their customers that procuring China sourced components will not impair product quality and lead-time. The paper discusses the advantages and disadvantages of the different type of agent based in China.

Keywords: China, supply-chain, small and medium-sized manufacturers

Introduction

The methodology presented is intended for UK small and medium sized manufacturers (SMMs) that are considering sourcing from suppliers based in China. It is aimed at companies who have no or very limited experience at sourcing from China. The focus is on the role that agents play in the relationship between UK SMMs and Chinese suppliers. A simple methodology has been devised to enable UK companies to choose a suitable agency. The new methodology considers the issues of make-or-buy, general advantages and disadvantages about choosing China, Chinese business etiquette and export information is also included. The technique has been developed to provide background knowledge and to show the other decisions that must be made before beginning to source from China. China is a new business area and although some literature exists about how to do business in China, the topic of agents selection is a new phenomenon and only very limited research exists.

Why source from China?

Statistics from UK SMMs regarding China imports provide a background to the current situation. These data illustrate the proportion of UK firms already using China as an area to source from and to show the real opportunity that exists. There appears to be limited literature on current UK outsourcing practises because it is such a new area of investigation. It has only been recently that SMMs have started to source from places like China. Research carried out by Han, *et al* [1] was an attempt to structure the sourcing process. This work has been built upon and adapted, particularly the concept of an assessment form sent out to prospective companies. Slaight, *et al* [2] and Cheng [3] both offered general pros and cons for using China as a country to use for supplier sourcing. The quoted values of labour costs, shipping frequency and so on provided an excellent background for the situation in China.

Agent definition

The research identified two primary ways of approaching sourcing from China. If the UK firm has limited experience of importing from or doing business in China then using an agent can be helpful to find suitable suppliers for the required product/parts. Two main types of agent were identified: managed outsourcing agents (MOA) and market place agents. The paper will focuses on the role of MOAs because the suggested methodology presented in this document refers to the sourcing of them rather than market place agents. A MOA acts as a third party between the sourcing of foreign suppliers by buyers and manages the relationship between the two. In this case the MOA sources suppliers from China suitable for a UK SMM. The SMM will discuss with the MOA the exact specification, technical drawings, engineering details and so on of the required part or product that they wish to outsource. Reputable and experienced MOAs will have an extensive network of Chinese suppliers that it has already built up a business relationship with. Distribution responsibilities will rest with either the MOA or the supplier depending on what has been agreed. Usually the MOA will manage the on-going relationship between the Chinese supplier and the UK firm. The advantages of using a MOA include 1) if the agency uses a supplier already within its network for the required part then further discounts and negotiations can be entered into easier than if the supplier had been newly sourced specifically for the required part, 2) the agency will manage the different supplier relationships so saving the UK company valuable management time. It is unlikely that a UK company will be able to speak fluent Chinese to a technical level, and so on. Disadvantages of using a MOA include: 1) the agency will charge commission on orders or a flat rate and will probably charge the UK company initially for the supplier sourcing depending on the number of suppliers or complexity of the operation. 2) As the UK company grows in confidence with sourcing from China the partnership may be restrictive. 3) If the agency is managing all relationships it will be hard for the UK firm to change suppliers or agencies because of the dependence on them.

Managed Outsourcing Agent Attributes. The following attributes, having been identified as being important for a MOA are summerised below. For each attribute a measure has been identified that can show the ability of the MOA at that attribute. 1) Bilingual – the agency must have staff with the ability to communicate with the UK company and Chinese suppliers. 2) Operational Experience – the agency should have extensive operational experience within their specialist industry sector. 3) Business Etiquette – the Chinese perform business communication in a different way to western countries. 4) Reputation – the reputation of the agency amongst others in the industry, UK firms already sourcing from China and Chinese suppliers, is a good gauge of opinion and should be considered. 5) Links to Chinese Firms – the agency should have an already well-established network of Chinese suppliers which they are already sourcing regularly from for other clients. 6) Quality – many suppliers will have quality certificates and accreditation's e.g. CE, CCC, ISO9000. 7) Cost – although cost should not be the main aspect of how the agencies are compared it is still worth considering if costs vary greatly. 8) Regulations Awareness – regulations in China vary greatly between different areas so the agency must be aware of these so that they can check and inspect their suppliers are keeping to them.

Market Place Agents

Market place agents act as a forum (usually on the internet) for buyers and suppliers to meet. This classification of agent typically has suppliers signed up and they register the products they produce on the site. The buyer is then able to search online for a particular product they require usually in a variety of ways e.g. product type or supplier name. This requires the part to already be in existence.

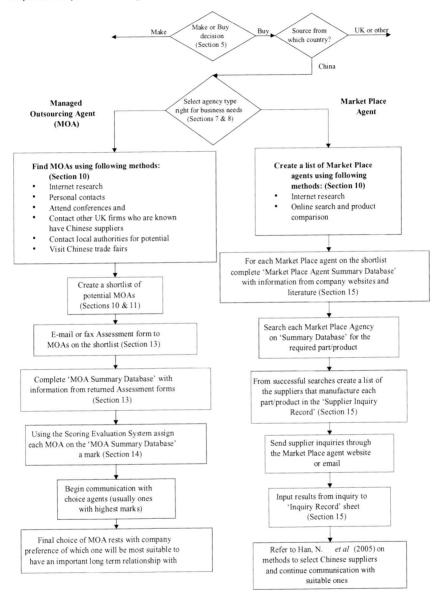

Figure 1 – The Agent Sourcing Process

If the required product is found then the supplier details are shown and the buyer contacts the supplier direct. There is usually an online supplier inquiry form that links direct from the market place website. The advantages of using market placed agents include, 1) they are quick and easy to register and buy from, especially for first time UK importers, 2) minimum cost involved with using the agency, 3) allows a direct relationship with the supplier to evolve, and so on. Disadvantages of market place agents include, 1) typically the market place agents will not manage the supplier relationship so leaving the UK company to arrange minimum order quantities, shipping, quality checks with the supplier, 2) there is no guarantee of the standard of the supplier, 3) the agency may not have the exact part or part specification that the SMM requires, and so on. Figure 1 provides flow diagram of processes involved with each type of agency.

Market Place Agent Attributes.

The import attributes for market place agents are summarised as: 1) Website Language – these agencies rely on the internet as the medium of communication with their clients, 2) Website Usability – to be effective the website should be easy to navigate around and self-explanatory to use, 3) Supplier Choice – the number of suppliers that produce the required part is very important to give the SMM the most choice, 4) General/Specialised – some agencies specialise in certain product types e.g. electrical, textiles. General agencies will have a wider scope of products to chose from. However, specialised ones are more likely to be able to source a rare product, and 5) Agency Supplier Standards – as previously mentioned some agencies have their own set standards for suppliers. If they reach a certain pre-set standard with certificates, facility checks and so on, they will then be recognised for that on the agencies website. This will give the UK firm a better idea on how competent the supplier is. The choice of a MOA is more critical to the success of the UK SMM as usually only one or two are used regularly and on a long term basis to manage the relationship between the UK firm and the Chinese supplier. With a market place agent many are used simultaneously and only facilitate the introduction between buyers and suppliers.

The Agent Sourcing Process

The flow diagram seen in figure 1 provides a summary of a step-by-step process undertaken by the SMM. Initially the issues that need to be considered before deciding to source from China include whether to make or buy the product and from which country to source components. A brief discussion on the make-or-buy process for companies is included here to emphasis some of the prior decisions that need to be made before sourcing a supplier from China should begin. For a more detailed discussion and to view a structured approach of the make-or-buy process refer to Platts. *et al* [4] framework. Make-or-buy is the choice companies have between making a product themselves in-house or to outsource and buy it from another company. UK SMMs have been experiencing an increase in the amount of outsourcing compared to other industry sectors such as finance or catering. Deciding whether to make a product or outsource it is not just a cost issue. There are many other trade-offs that need to be considered. The trigger for a make-or-buy analysis is often the external environment, which is usually uncontrollable to the individual business. For example, increased competition pushing sale prices down will require cost cutting: new government imposed regulations increasing costs (WEEE directive or lead-free solder legislation) will mean implementing new manufacturing processes. However the areas that need to be reviewed to make the make-or-buy decision are internal and company specific. The internal areas recommended to focus on are the manufacturing processes, costs, supply chain management and support systems. These decisions are not static and need to be reviewed as conditions change. Each area can be split into different factors that affect it as in figure 1. These areas and then factors in turn can be analysed by ranking the importance of each one to the success of the product under review. The factors can then be rated within their areas as to how well the company currently performs them and an estimate of how well an external company would also perform them.

How to choose the right type of agent

The choice of which agency type to use depends on many different variables including: 1) the type of product/parts the SMM requires, 2) the specification of the product/part i.e. are they standard or specialised, 3) volume and variety of product/parts required, 4) import experience of the SMM, 5) how the SMM prefers to do business, and 6) knowledge of Chinese and culture. Table 1 provides an example of how certain combinations of the above variables can point to using one agency type over another.

	MOA	Market Place
Specialised product	√	×
Standard product	×	√
High volume	×	√
Low volume	√	×
High variety	√	×
Low variety	×	√
Extensive Chinese import experience	×	√
Limited Chinese import experience	√	×
Chinese language skills	×	√
No Chinese language skills	√	×
Time available to manage multiple supplier relationships	×	√
Limited time available to manage relationships	√	×

Table 1 – UK Company characteristics corresponding to agency types

The research suggests that if most of the MOA favourable variables apply to the SMM then it is recommended that the company uses an MOA and vice versa. However there is no set method for assessing which will be most suitable and it will require the UK firm's judgement. As a general rule if the SMM has not sourced from China before then a MOA can potentially provide the easiest, safest and a hassle-free method.

The MOA Assessment form

To assess how effective different MOAs will be at working with a UK SMM and to help assist the selection process an Assessment form was developed. Each question on the Assessment form is based upon a different measurable attribute. The results from the Assessment forms can then be entered into the MOA Summary Database scored according to the Scoring Evaluation System. The responses can then be analysed, scored and weighted. This methodology allows comparisons of each MOA and documented evidence for the future. A scoring evaluation system is proposed to enable a total mark to be awarded to each analysed MOA. The higher the score the more likely that MOA is going to be suitable for the UK SMM. As previously mentioned each question on the Assessment form corresponds to an attribute identified that should be present in the MOA. The system consists of each Assessment form question being assigned a *weighting* depending on its importance and a *score* depending on what the answer suggests is the MOA's ability to perform or provide the attribute. A weighting system was developed to show which attributes are most important though these may alter depending on the SMM's needs and circumstances. The weighting assigned to each attribute is judged by the authors as being suitable for most businesses. However, each business is different and may judge the attributes to have differing importance to those that have been suggested here. If this is the case then the weightings can be changed and this will not alter the validity of the results. The MOA's ability of being able to perform or provide each attribute should be assessed and rated as being good (3), average (2) or poor (1) i.e. how well the MOA answered each question on the Assessment form. Each ability level is assigned a score. As the questions vary and are a mixture of quantitative and qualitative it is up to the judgement of the individual SMMs as to what represents good, average and poor abilities. For example, the MOA only speaking Chinese may gain an ability rating of poor, only the sales staff speaking English and Chinese may gain an ability rating of average and engineering staff speaking English and Chinese may gain an ability rating of good. If the assessment form is returned within 48 hours score good, within one week score average and over a week score poor. The weighting and the score are multiplied together to obtain the *mark* for that attribute for the MOA. By adding all the marks for each question the final *total* for the MOA is gained. The marks are then added together to gain the final total for the MOA. The higher the mark the more likely the MOA is going to be suitable for having a successful business relationship with the UK SMM. If the suggested weightings are used and all the attributes are given a score then the highest mark possible to achieve is 114.

Conclusion

The paper presents the outline aimed at UK SMMs considering sourcing from China for the first time. It focuses on the role of managed outsourcing agents in the relationship between UK companies and Chinese suppliers. The paper highlights that strategic decisions need to be made prior to foreign sourcing commencing including whether to make or buy the considered product. The two main types of agents are discussed including their roles, services they offer, and advantages and disadvantages of each. Early indication of practitioner deployment is that the methodology is robust for SMMs to deploy successfully.

References

[1] Han, N., Wang, & Ford, D. W., (2005) *'The Development of a Supply Chain for Electrical Component Sourcing from China for Small and Medium-Sized Manufactures'*, Institute for Manufacturing, University of Cambridge

[2] Slaight, T., Naramore, T. & Bouchet, G. (2004) *'China's Role in a Global Supply Strategy'*, Business Briefings – Global Purchasing and Supply Chain Strategies

[3] Cheng, I. (2005) *'Sourcing Goods from China: The Mass Migration'*, The China Business Review -

[4] Platts, K., Probert, D. & Canez, L. (2001) *'Make or Buy - A Practical Guide to Industrial Sourcing Decisions'*, Institute for Manufacturing

ORDERING PROBLEMS FOR E-MANUFACTURING

A.S.White[1, a], M.Censlive[2, b]

[1] School of Computing Science
Middlesex University
Bramley Rd
Trent Park
London N14 4YZ
United Kingdom

[2]ditto

Abstract. This paper reviews the current major issues in the implementation of e-manufacturing, particularly the dynamic aspects. It will examine the progress in the last few years, drawing out particular issues that need to be addressed.
A simulation, using SIMULINK/MATLAB®, of the effect on the inventory, WIP and order rate caused by changing the effective smoothing of demand shows in graphical form how it is possible to allow more effective response to e-ordering by customers.
Keywords: e-manufacture, order problems, lean manufacturing, SIMULINK®, input-output models.

Introduction

What is meant by e-manufacture? The one used here is from AMR research [1]:
" The core of [a] manufacturing strategy is the technology roadmap for information transparency between customer, manufacturing operations and suppliers. An e-manufacturing strategy takes e-business processes, such as build-to-order and reliability-centred maintenance, and generates guidelines for implementing plant systems. The e-manufacturing strategy takes e-business and manufacturing strategies and creates a roadmap for system development and implementation in the plant."

This definition is primarily about information, secondly it is about a systems wide approach, while the final important point is that products are built to order not for stock. The availability of near instant recall of plant and system wide data is not itself a panacea. Effective use has to be made of this data.
The current theme of business is 'mass customerization'. Joseph Pine II [2] in his book talks about *'mass* production of individually *customized* goods and services'. This is the biggest challenge is the speed at which modern customers expect to be supplied with goods and services, since their loyalty is fickle they change their supplier without hesitation. One of the prime features of e-shock [3] is that the important clients who use Internet ordering at present are amongst the most articulate customers and will be the first to complain about faulty service.

Who are the customers? They will be the same individuals and companies as at present but they will behave in new ways as new possibilities open up to them. They may intervene in the supply chain to insist on getting what they want . What are the relationships that will govern the market.

We have **B2B** or business to business or more commonly **B2C or** business to customers. Here it is the B2C transactions that will require the greatest speed.

What do customers want? Ayres and Miller [6] state that they want delivery, quality and variety, Wright [5] goes on to jibe that they want pizza, eyeglasses and their vacation photographs in 1 hour or less or their money back! This may be cynical but the potential for demand should not be underestimated in an electronic environment as the Dot.com pioneers did. Even Amazon was overwhelmed initially by the demand they generated and they have only just reached a satisfactory financial position.

The scale of the design/production time problem is outlined by Table 1. Here Ulrich and Eppinger [7] contrast the scale of the problems in different product sectors.

	Stanley Tools Jobmaster screwdriver	Rollerblade in line skates	Hewlett Packard DeskJet 500 printer	Chrysler Concorde automobile	Boeing 777 aeroplane
Annual production volume	100000 units/yr	100000 units/yr	1.5 million units/yr	250000 units/yr	50 units/yr
Sales lifetime	40 yrs	3 yrs	3 yrs	6 yrs	30 yrs
Sales price	$3	$200	$365	$19000	$130 M
Number of unique parts	3	35	200	10000	130000
Development time	1 yr	2 yrs	1.5 yrs	3.5 yrs	4.5 yrs
Internal development team	3	5	100	850	6800
External development team	3	10	100	1400	10000
Development cost	$150000	$750000	$50 M	$1 B	$ 3 B
Development/sales cost	50000	3750	136985	52632	23
Price/design personyear	1	20	2.4	6.4	4248
Production investment	$150000	$1 M	$25 M	$600 M	$3 B

Table 1 Product Development Times for common products from [7]

Although most of the products illustrated in the table were built to stock, aircraft were never built in this way and were always built to order due to the complexity and expense of the product
It would not be prudent to respond to single customers for cash outlays as large as this so to promise to do so would lead to failure to satisfy the customer. As the costs of production come down due to lean production and new manufacturing technology the costs of inventory relative to the other costs are a higher proportion. The effects of maintenance scheduling will again represent a higher proportion than hitherto.

Review Of E-Manufacturing Progress

There are three review papers that describe the current state of the art very well. A review of agile manufacturing systems was undertaken by Sanchez and Nagi [8], for one-of-a-kind product development over the Internet by Xie, Tu, Fung and Zhous [9] and an evaluation of virtual production by Qui, Wysk and Xu [10].

What are the prime conclusions from these reviews? In 2001 Sanchez and Nagi complained that few solutions to enable agile production were described in the literature. The majority of papers were in process and manufacturing planning. Most papers were about information systems, this is the area that IT companies know best and it is not surprising that these are the first products to be proposed. Xie *et al.* [10] in 2003 found a much improved picture but a completely chaotic world view with many competing ideas and no fully proven solutions.

E-Order Rate Effects on Manufacturing

The previous sections should make it clear that rapid delivery is being facilitated by the e-networks and improvements in design/manufacturing. This paper looks at one aspect that of the ordering system used in the process. Current systems involving Vendor Managed Inventory have used the practice of WalMart and other retailers. Is this the pattern we expect or will the customer drive industry to consider build to order? The simple examination given later will look at how the effects of order rate are affected by this prospect. Current practice uses some smoothing of orders to allow a rational production schedule. The model used by Towills' group as a basis for current industrial systems is the Automatic Pipeline and Order Based Production Control System [11]. This model is shown in Figure 1. Orders are filtered by a simple exponential function approximating to statistical averaging techniques used in companies surveyed. The response of such a system to a simple step increase in sales is given in Figure 2. The results show a deficit in inventory with a rise in the level of WIP above the steady demand of 4 units and an order rate that exceeds the steady value initially.

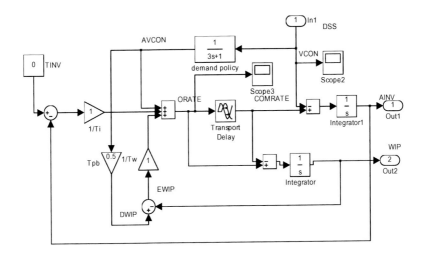

Figure 1 APIOBPCS Simulink model

95

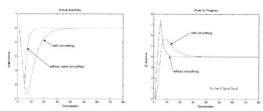

Figure 2 Inventory and WIP with and without sales smoothing

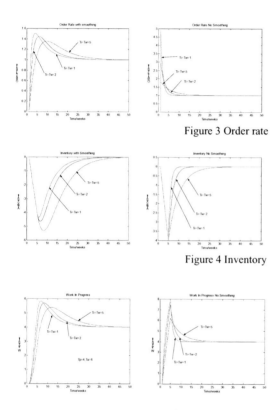

Figure 3 Order rate

Figure 4 Inventory

Figure 5 Work In Progress

Choice of Simulation

The models used in this work can be solved analytically [11] or by simulation. In order to demonstrate the results of policy changes graphical output makes the results clearer and it is quicker to use simulation from the outset. SIMULINK® was chosen because it is widely used and easy to set up the equations describing the system with a wide range of built in functions. It can also allow the use of both discrete and continuous models. The model can be built from scratch by an experienced user of SIMULINK® in less than 20 minutes and by a novice in a few hours. A wide range of tools to perform analysis of the results is available and different system inputs, deterministic and random, can be shown. The models here use a continuous solution of the equations as it is felt that for rapid changes this will be a better description of the problem.

Conclusions

- Complete electronic integration of the order to manufacturing in e-manufacturing has not yet been achieved
- The main areas of deficiency are not in data management but in aids to decision making
- In the Inventory system modelled here, using a block simulator SIMULINK® using a continuous system dscription, show the effect of eliminating the filter on sales has the benefit of shortening the time that the system is in stockout and drastically reducing the time to steady state. The penalty is in a higher peak order rate and WIP
- Reducing production time with new processes is clearly seen to be reducing WIP and inventory. This with the shortened order response time would give a better system e-response.

Symbols

AINV	Current Inventory level
AVCON	Average sales rate
CONS	consumption or market demand
EINV	Error in inventory level
DWIP	Desired work in progress
DINV	Distributor inventory
G	Distributor estimate gain
ORATE	Outstanding level of orders placed with the supplier
COMRATE	Rate of production
TINV	Target inventory
T_a	Smoothing time constant (8 weeks)
T_i	Order constant time. (4 weeks)
T_P	Production delay time (4 weeks)

VMI-APIOBPCS Vendor Managed Inventory, Automatic Pipeline Inventory and Order Based Production Control System

VCON   virtual consumption

References

[1] "How and Why You Will Use e-Manufacturing Systems" AMR Research Inc January 2000
[2] Pine II, B J. Mass Customerization, Harvard Business School Press, 1999
[3] De Kare-Silver, M. e-shock, Macmillan Business Press, 1998
[4] Sharma, A & Moody, P E. The Perfect Engine, The Free Press, 2001.
[5] Wright, p K. 21st Century Manufacturing, Prentice-Hall, 2001.
[6] Ayres, R U. & Miller, S M. Robotics: applications and social implications, Ballinger Press, 1983.
[7] Ulrich, K T. & Eppinger, S D. Product Design and Development, McGraw-Hill, 1995.

[8] Sanchez, L M & Nagi, R A review of agile manufacturing systems, Int. J. Prod. Res., vol. 39, no. 15, pp3561-3600, 2001

[9] Xie, S Q, Tu, Y L, Fung, R Y K & Zhou, Z D, Rapid one-of-a-kind product development via the Internet: a literature review of the state-of-the-art and a proposed platform, Int. J. Prod. Res., vol. 41, no. 18, pp 4257-4298, 2003.

[10] Qiu, R, Wysk, R & Xu, Q, Extended structured adaptive supervisory control model of shop floor controls for an e-manufacturing system, Int. J. Prod. Res., vol. 41, no. 8, pp 1605-1620, 2003.

[11] Disney, S M, Towill, D R, A discrete transfer function model to determine the dynamic stability of a vendor managed inventory supply chain, Int. J. Prod. Res., vol. 40, no.1, pp.179-204, 2002

Value Added Services – Driving Value Delivery in the Electronic Distribution Industry

Rahul Sharma, Infosys Technologies Limited, 44, Electronics City, Hosur Road, Bangalore - 560100, India. Rahul_Sharma09@infosys.com

Andy Jones, VAS Specialist, Arrow Electronics, Edinburgh Way, Harlow, Essex- CM20 2DF, United Kingdom. ajones@arrowuk.com

Abstract

This paper will focus on the Value Added Services (VAS) offerings provided by Electronic Distributors & the associated value proposition. The significance of VAS for Electronic Distribution industry stems from:

➢ Differentiation Strategy – Increasingly sophisticated value added services like kitting, programming, bar coding, labeling and more are positioned by distributors as unique & valuable. The distributors who can provide service in these areas will have an advantage.

➢ High Margin Business Opportunity – Some of the value added services like Programming, Assembly provide handsome returns. Once prototyped, these operations are not so difficult to perform & provide a stable revenue stream. Design services are also a big source of revenue.

➢ Customer Acquisition & Retention Strategy - There is demand for supply chain and design services as more OEMs and customers are looking for lean inventories & need help managing their supply chains. Also operating strategically from a distributor point of view, once a customer decides to do a given value added service e.g. Forecasting & hence shares the future requirement data, it is less likely that this customers will move away to any competitor.

Globally the electronic distributors continue to seek new ways to extend the range of services they offer, into a wide spread of activities that generally compliment their core component distribution businesses. Evidently, the distributors are focusing more & more on creative Value Added Services and justifying their place in Hi-tech value chain.

Keywords: OEM – Original Equipment Manufacturers; VAS – Value Added Services, KPI – Key Performance Indices, EMS – Electronic Manufacturing Services, CEM – Contract Electronic Manufacturers, JIT – Just In Time, VMI – Vendor Managed Inventory

Introduction

In the post-war era, the commercial electronics distribution industry grew from simply supplying radio parts to supplying the emerging television industry of the 1950s and 1960s. It grew even further with the advent of computers and electronic office equipment in the 1970s. Still, distributors merely acted like middlemen between part producers and OEMs – taking orders and shipping parts. In the 1980s, global competition placed increasing design & production strains on OEMs. Also the economy changed from an industrial one to a service economy & distributors moved to a demand-creation model in this era. Distributors started working with customers to help incorporate their needs into designs and get customers to production and market quicker. In response, the role of distributor saw an increasing focus on value-added services.

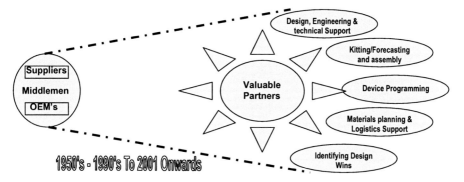

Increasing competitive pressures also forced distribution industry to seek additional ways of 'proving & enhancing their value' to both OEM customers and the component manufacturers they represent. By the 1990s, distributors discovered new design & supply chain opportunities which evolved the electronic distribution industry.

Electronics Distribution Industry – Products, Service areas & Challenges involved

Electronic Component Distributors provide a range of products, services & logistics solutions to industrial & commercial users of electronic components & computer products.

The global electronic components market is huge & is segmented by products that are categorized as:

➤ **Semiconductors** ("silicon chips") are electronic devices created on very small pieces of silicon and used in most electronic devices. Examples include diodes, rectifiers, transistors, IC etc
➤ **Passives** are electronic components that transfer, store, or dispose of energy but do not consume power. Examples include capacitors, resistors, electronic filters etc
➤ **Component Assemblies** include CRT, LCD, LED, plasma, modems, motors etc
➤ **Electromechanical** devices connect the mechanical world with the electrical world.
➤ **Connectors** are devices that make an electrical or fiber optic connection between one part of a circuit and another. Examples include IC sockets, terminal strips etc
➤ **Computer Products** include monitors, disk drives, modems, printers, software, and other components used in the manufacture and operation of PC's.

Whether an electronics distributor is broad range, buying and selling a vast range of electronic component and computer products, or niche, targeting a specific area of the marketplace, they support their customers by providing specialized services:

➤ Serve as **"supply chain partners"** by providing customers with expertise to maximize productivity of their manufacturing process.
➤ Serve as **"design specialists"** by providing customers engineering expertise in product development.

- Serve as an **"electronics supermarket"** providing a wide variety of product lines to customers at one time from a single, knowledgeable source.
- Serve as a **"service organization"** by providing flexible, reliable services and value-added solutions to a wide range of customers of varying sizes and needs world-wide.
- Serve as **"intermediaries"** by purchasing electronic products and computer products from many suppliers and selling them to many customers.
- Serve as a **"financial institution"** by offering the customers credit and other financial arrangements customized to their situations which suppliers may not provide.

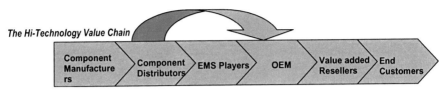

In this context of Electronic & Hi-tech distribution industry, companies are facing challenges to differentiate themselves from competition, get locked in to existing customers and provide long term revenue prospects through greater value delivery. The critical issues facing the Hi-tech & Electronic Companies are:

- **Configurable Supply Chain Execution** - Producing Hi-Tech finished goods is unlike any other industry. From the use of contract manufacturing and components suppliers to postponement strategies, perhaps done by a third party provider, the production process has a lot more variables than other manufacturing. In addition, the composition of these supply chain partners is continually changing. At the same time, customer requirements are also changing. Customers are demanding more product configuration and value-added services (VAS). The emergence of e-business has added new customers who tend to place smaller, more frequent orders. Customers also want visibility to their orders and fast delivery.

- **Postponement Strategies** - Many Hi-Tech & Electronics companies are pushing final manufacturing steps down to distribution centers, either to provide customers required VAS or to support more flexible inventory deployment plans. This helps keep SKUs generic as long as possible, reducing inventory and handling costs, while increasing flexibility for assemble to order / configure to order mass customization strategies and other customer requests.

- **Global Marketplace** - Increasingly, Electronic products are designed and prototyped in one geography, manufactured in another, and sold worldwide. This places huge demands not only for physical flexibility in the Supply Chain, and for communications support both up and down the inventory pipeline, but also for control of the IP inherent in electronics design.

- **High Velocity Flow of Goods** - Perhaps more than any other industry, Hi-Tech / Electronics requires a high velocity flow of goods. Not only is Hi-Tech inventory extremely expensive to maintain, the rapid technological obsolescence and downward price spiral puts it at great risk if product is not shipped immediately. Smaller window of opportunity necessitates Hi-tech companies to quickly en-cash new product introductions.

- **Variable Component Availability** – The electronics industry has a history of cyclical over- and under-supply. The basis of silicon technology is that the crystal has to be grown, and that constrains the flexibility of supply. Manufacturers have historically responded to increased demand by developing additional "fabs", but these take time to come on stream, during which phase products will go on allocation. The inherent inaccuracy in forecasting demand later creates a glut in the marketplace, with associated downward pressure on prices and margins.

Business Challenge	Configurable Supply Chain	Postponement Strategy	Global manufacturing	High Velocity of Goods	Variable Component Availability
VAS Offering	Assembly, Kitting, De-kitting	Consignment (VMI), Manufacturing	3P Manufacturing	Bar - coding, Labeling, Kanban, Product Design	Forecasting

Role played by Value Added Services in the industry & the associated value proposition

VAS provides the customers with a level of engineering or technical expertise more sophisticated than they could support in-house. The increasing importance of Value added services stems from following propositions:

1. Process Efficiency Related

➢ Barcodes (and eventually no doubt RFID tags) for use at Goods In, Warehousing, and automated product identification on Surface Mount machines.
➢ Kanban for line side & fixed quantity inventory availability.
➢ Kitting, Programming, Customizing (cropping, pre-forming) - both can sometimes be done more quickly and at lower cost by Distributor due to economies of scale.
➢ All the electronic messaging support - EDI, Rosetta net, File import from e-mail etc and E-Commerce.
➢ Provide real-time inventory updates at point of transaction using RF equipment and other state-of-the-art automation, which ensures that the right product is stocked at the right place, resulting in fewer pick errors.

2. Manufacturing Flexibility

➢ Kanban, Buffer Stocks, Forecast sharing. All about making product available to support variable build plans and build-to-order.
➢ Consignment (VMI) – customers take ownership of the components only when they are released from the inventory hub to their product lines. This enables them to operate them in a JIT environment & not take actual ownership of the goods until they are ready for manufacture.
➢ Kitting can support outsourced production.
➢ Forecast pipeline held at Distributor means actual production can quickly be redirected to lower cost service providers, CEMs (Contract Electronics Manufacturers) in lower cost economies etc.

3. **Total Cost of Ownership** This covers actual Inventory reductions due to more efficient procurement models or better sharing of information, as well as Consignment or special payment terms that improve the Customer's return on working capital by reducing their cash-to-cash cycle times.

4. The other Value added service that a Distributor provides is **Product Design, Engineering & Support information**.

➤ The Distributor works with Customers to help them optimize their designs for the latest (procurable) technology, and also provide PCN/EOL information, supporting end of life redesign and diminishing manufacturing resources.

➤ Additionally through a variety of engineering & design-support programs, distributors are seeking to help fill the void of tier – two & three accounts which suppliers do not have resources to directly cover themselves. By bolstering their technical offerings & resources, distributors are better able to represent suppliers to wider range of customers.

➤ At the same time they're providing OEMs with information and support that the suppliers cannot afford to cover. It's in this area that the web provides other opportunities to share information with Customers in a way they can use.

5. Distributors also work with those Customers who need global manufacturing flexibility, to ensure that relationships established between Manufacturers & Customers in one location, (and the cost-benefit of that relationship) are transferable worldwide.

Value Added Services – Is it delivering on the promise & does it command differential pricing

Evidently VAS is not very new, but they remain an important part of electronics distribution business. According to a purchasing survey, about 17% of revenue of the top 75 distributors is derived from VA sales. Nearly all top 75 distributors offer value-added services. The survey shows that 16 distributors derive 50% or more of their sales from value-added services & 17 distributors say 20-49% of their sales are derived from VAS. The remaining distributors say value-added services account for 19% or less of their sales. In Europe, the percentage of sales with "Value-Added" content is increasing steadily & in certain markets is as high as 70%. Industry leaders Arrow & Avnet are projecting that nearly two-thirds of annual revenues will soon be derived from specialized products and value-added services.

As the role of distributors has expanded into design, programming and other value added services, structuring ways to quickly recover costs has became a challenge. There are significant investments that the distributors make in IT, warehousing, asset management and materials logistics that broadens the company's base. To that end, some of the distributors employ hundreds of field application engineers to help with design and thousands of people to physically alter products to customer specifications.

The old pricing system – the broker or "parts for dollars" financial model is changing to a demand creation model that reflects the importance of distributors in the new industrial age. In this demand creation model, the distributor works with customer to help incorporate their needs into designs and get customer to production & market quicker. While the company will still make catalogue-style information for free, the value-added services like bar coding, kitting, programming, assembly etc must be priced into a customer's bill. To recover the cost of any new services, some of the methods adopted include:

➤ Value based pricing or custom 'a la carte' pricing based on type of service
➤ On-line access fee to services like product and technical info
➤ Contractual bonus paid by Customer, subject to meeting agreed KPIs (on-time delivery, quality etc)
➤ Management fees on slow moving consigned inventory

This new pricing model is slow in coming, but the industry is moving away from averages and starting to separate the product from the service.

Value Added Services – Emerging Demands from the Customers

In terms of primary business issues customers are trying to solve, where various value added services can offer support are:

- JIT & Lean Manufacturing initiatives
- Process Change (BPR, CPI experience)
- Make or Buy analysis
- Total Inventory deals – sole supplier
- Self Billing
- NPI Service model analysis & update
- Global Alignment – global toolset – standardizing global tool wherever possible so that the customer experience of the distributor is mirrored across the world
- Web presence, rather than fragmented approach along with www based Order Handling (Portals)
- Electronic Catalog
  - Parametric Part Search
  - Show Catalog Data in Web e.g. Export catalog
  - Multi Currency Functionality
  - Local & multi-language websites

Conclusion

The role of electronic distributors is expanding – the major challenge is to be sensitive to the emerging needs of both customers and suppliers and even predict their needs. Now Distributors must become experts in all aspects of demand forecasting requirements and be "knowledge centers" for markets & products, providing the information manufacturers and retailers will be eager to obtain. Evidently value added service is the emerging area of focus for all the electronic distributor relationships as it provides:

- Better positioning against competitors
- Directly addresses issues customers are facing
- Improved Customer loyalty
- Meets customer's growing appetite for advanced supply chain solutions

References

[1]   Electronic Component Distribution Report 2004.

[2]   Dissecting the Distribution Business Model (October 2001 edition) Cahners Electronics Group.

[3]   www.purchasing.com

Knowledge Sharing within both Make-to-Order and Engineer-to-Order Manufacturing Enterprises

I Reid[1, a], H. Ismail[2, b] and C. Cockerham[3, c]

[1]Iain Reid Sheffield Hallam University, Sheffield, UK

[2]Hossam Ismail, University of Liverpool, Liverpool UK

[3]Graham Cockerham Sheffield Hallam University, Sheffield, UK

[a]reidi@liv.ac.uk, [b] hsismail@liverpool.ac.uk, [c]g.cockerham@shu.ac.uk

Abstract. One of the main problems associated with Make-to-order (MTO) is how MTO manufacturers learn from what are essentially "one-off" projects. This paper proposes a framework that supports knowledge sharing across the MTO projects. The framework focuses on assessing the critical phases of the new product development (NPD) process, as well as providing a knowledge base for embedding, managing and disseminating the aspects of the learning curve in order to support future projects. The paper highlights the importance of knowledge sharing and the on-going frustrations of NPD-MTO and is supported by a complex industrial case study within a Small Medium Enterprise (SME) MTO manufacturing enterprise.

Keywords: knowledge sharing, make-to-order, NPD, SME, IDEF, enterprise modeling

1 Introduction

Make-to-Order (MTO) companies mainly produce customize products, for the purpose of this paper MTO includes (oil platforms to steam generators) and can be identified as of the following:

- High value, low volume (often one-offs);
- High levels of uncertainty (product, process product mix & volume);
- At least customised, and often unique to the customers need;
- Both produced by and sold to, large industrial users (hence the better name industry to industry)

The products can have high levels of customization and complexity, which gives rise to many levels of decision making. Certain items are highly customised, whilst others are standardised and need to be coordinated and controlled. Each customer order is at least partly unique, this means that MTO companies are in a very specific product development process. Therefore, the process of MTO warrants a separate product development approach compared to Make-to-Stock (MTS) companies. [1, 3] illustrated some of the defining characteristics of MTO compared to mass-produced goods (or made-to-stock) and the high level of uncertainty associated with the MTO product development process [2].

2 Literature Review

From the previous findings there is an apparent need to support future projects in terms of uncertainties with lessons learnt across previous projects [1]. Bartezzaghi [4] suggested that project reviews provide knowledge and information that can be shared across projects, however, they also note firms where more forthcoming with the information when the project was complete. However, the key decision makers record their actions on a regular basis during the event or projects life cycle [5]. Therefore there is a need for a framework and methodology knowledge sharing to address those critical decision making points within the NPD-MTO process. The framework also needs address the variations between what has been sold and what has been designed and manufactured.

3 Research Methodology

There is a limit amount of research data that exists about the NPD-MTO from both a practical and theoretical sense. Therefore a multi-case study method was used that provided an empirical method of inquiry which enabled the researcher to investigate NPD within a real life context using multiple resources of evidence. This paper presents the findings within one particular MTO manufacturer which was a small medium enterprise (SME).

Within the case study company five projects were 'live' or on-going which allowed the researcher to focus on different aspects on the NPD-MTO process e.g. quotation, order review, engineering, manufacturing, testing, despatch & other (project management). Between 7 interviews were conducted for data gathering and process mapping purposes. In addition project related documentation was made available to the researcher. The investigation was designed to identify the critical decision making points within the NPD-MTO process. Particular attention was given to the mechanisms of transferring project related information and knowledge gained as the projects evolved.

4 Proposed Methodology for assessing the decision making process: 'Points of Commitment'

We define a 'Point of Commitment' is when somebody is committing the organisation to a course of action that will cost significantly to change. During the course of the live projects the PoCs occurred more frequently through the non-physical stages (sales, tendering and engineering) of the NPD-MTO. According to the case studies, the PoCs were of significant importance because the critical decision making points appear to be loaded towards the 'front-end' compared to the more traditional NPD process within MTS. Table 2 compares the PoC between MTO and MTS industry sectors, within MTS process the PoCs seemed to occur further downstream, thus allowing MTS organisations more flexibility within their critical decision making in terms of price, delivery, quality and specification.

Table 1: The PoC impact across the two main types of manufacturing enterprises

Manufacturing Strategy	Sales	Design Engineering	Manufacturing & Assembly	Despatch
Make-to-Stock	-------------	-------------	------------→	POC →
Engineer-to-Order	POC ---→			─────────→

4.1 The Points of Commitment Calculation

The success of NPD-MTO depends on a wide variety of NPD methods, control, influences factors, uncertainties, fuzziness that have different effects on the NPD-MTO activities. Therefore a framework is desirable to organise, identify and measure the effect of the uncertainties, ambiguities and fuzziness on the NPD-MTO process. This requirement highlights the need for a tool that is, universally applicable to all activities identified under the NPD process, which can model the whole process and yet provide the opportunity to focus on specific detailed activity and its' elements when required. It has been well documented that the IDEF modeling is one such approach was used to represent the NPD process and represents both the activities of the NPD-MTO process and the required support tools. Figure 1 shows the first level of the IDEF0 model that contains the main activities of the NPD–MTO process. These activities determine the general structure of the MTO process.

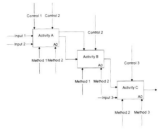

Figure 1 IDEF "Pont of Commitment" Assessment

As shown in Figure 1, in a single IDEF activity box, the transformation of input to output is carried out by the tool(s), which are also referred to as means or mechanism, following certain instructions or operating within certain conditions and monitors referred to as "Controls". The quality of each output is derived from the 'Methods Effectiveness' function and the 'Control Confidence' function to generate the 'Output Quality' of the Activity. The PoC assessment matrix is presented in Figure 2. The calculation is based on the Failure Mode and Effects Analysis (FMEA) [6] which is a methodology for analysing potential reliability problems early in the product development cycle. The PoC assessment matrix is an analytical tool that supports the IDEF diagrams in terms of assessing process reliability and will be used to assess a NPD-MTO case study.

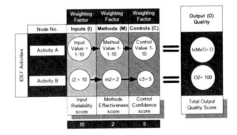

Figure 2 Pont of Commitment Assessment Matrix

5 Case Study:

The case study company is small medium enterprise (SME) MTO manufacturer of pipework, vessels, sheet metalwork and steelwork. Their NPD-MTO process starts by a customer requesting a response from a contractor to a project specification (varying in detail from a detailed design through to a functional or cardinal point specification). In accordance with the customer requirements, the sales and estimating department produces a quotation defining the time, costs and specification for the product or service delivered. This quotation is submitted to the customer via a bidding process and if successful with the bid, the sales and estimating function issues the specifications to the engineering function control via the project management function. Production planning then provides the purchasing with the specifications and purchasing manages the supply of material and parts for the order. Once these parts and materials have been supplied, the production function carries out the manufacturing process as seen in Fig 3.

Should implementation problems occur the project management function is asked to change the product specification, in many cases, this triggers repetitive processes which significantly effects the logistics, planning, and which has direct impact on the firm's ability to satisfy the commercial requirements laid down by the customer. This happens because the necessary inter-functional coordination between the individual functions is lacking and therefore the NPD-MTO process is carried out sequentially, thus causing both project lead-times and costs to increase.

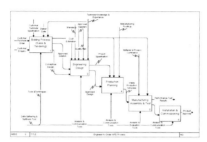

Figure 3 IDEF NPD-MTO Process

To avoid some of these problems, the integration of project management tools (work breakdown structure, overall master plan) and typical manufacturing management tools (master production schedule, material requirements planning and enterprise resource planning) have resulted in companies making new products better and faster. However, there is usually very little information available to managers to guide them through the decision making process, and assist them with uncertainties in the NPD-ETO. This is largely because of the difficulties associated with knowing what has been sold at the 'front-end' of the process. According to the case studies, the PoCs were of significant importance because the critical decision making points appear to be loaded towards the 'front-end' compared to the more traditional NPD process within MTS. Table 2 compares the PoC between ETO and MTS industry sectors, within MTS process the PoCs seemed to occur further downstream, thus allowing MTS organisations more flexibility within their critical decision making in terms of price, delivery, quality and specification.

6 Conclusions and Further Work

Due to the 'uncertainty factors' within the NPD-ETO process the proposed PoC methodology will assist both MTO and ETO organisations with repetition and project-based learning of customer orders through the monitoring, review and examination of past projects via the PoC assessment. This paper has discussed the need and presented the requirements for a knowledge sharing framework. Our sample case study has highlighted the need for project-based learning and the general problem areas (each of which contains a number of PoC) which kept coming up include:

- Requirements Capturing (customer specification) via Enquiry Review
- Order Review: both Technical Commitments & Contractual/Commercial Commitments

Future work will attempt to develop a PoC knowledge-base system that will support project managers that will include the features as mentioned above. The framework could be modified to suit weighting factors including any other key performance indicators (KPIs) associated to the NPD including the assessment of the existing methods and controls e.g. project budget and quality of resources e.g. suitable NPD tools and techniques

References

[1]. Reid, I., Cockerham G., Pickford C., (2004) A Methodology for Project–Based Learning within Engineer-to-Order (ETO) Product Development, International Conference Manufacturing Research (*ICMR, 2004*) Sheffield Hallam University, Sheffield UK.

[2]. Muntslag, D., (1994) Profit and risk evaluation in customer driven manufacturing International Journal of Production Economics, volume 36 pp97-107

[3]. Rahem, A., Rahim, A., Baksh M,. (2003) The need for a new product development framework for engineer-to-order products. European Journal for Innovation Management Volume 6 No. 3, pp.182-196.

[4]. Bartezzaghi, E., Corso, M. & Verganti, R. (1996) 'Continuous Improvement and Inter-project learning in New Product Development' International Journal of Technology Management, Volume 14, Number 1.

[5]. Kransdorff, A. (1996), 'Using the benefits of Hindsight' The Role of Post Project Analysis ' The Learning Organization, Volume 3, Number 1, pp11-15.

[6]. Teng Sheng-Hsien, Ho Shin-Yann, Failure mode and effects analysis—an integrated approach for product design and process control, Int. J. Qual. Reliab. Manag. 13 (5) (1996) 8–26, MCB University Press.

Precision
Manufacturing

CNC manufacturing to improve hip and knee joint replacement lifetimes

Phillip Charlton[1, a], Liam Blunt[2, b] and Philip Harrison[3, c]

[1] Centre for Precision Technologies, University of Huddersfield, UK

[2] Taylor Hobson Chair of Metrology, University of Huddersfield, UK

[3] Centre for Precision Technologies, University of Huddersfield, UK

[a] p.charlton@hud.ac.uk, [b] l.a.blunt@hud.ac.uk, [c] p.harrison@hud.ac.uk

Abstract

Oesteo-arthritis is defined as progressive degeneration of the natural cartilage tissue which is a critical part of the load bearing function of the human hip and knee joints and is particularly problematic in ageing persons and those who indulged in extreme sporting activities. The tissue breakdown problem can be alleviated by the administration of anti-inflammatory drugs but in most advanced cases the replacement of part or all of the knee or hip joint is required In the UK alone, over 25,000 hips and 22,000 knees are replaced each year at a cost of approximately £175 million per annum [1]. Worldwide, the total number of implants is around 800,000. Considerable amounts of research have been conducted in the field of design and functionality of these partial and total knee and hip replacements and as of today the life expectancy of such systems is 5-15 years.

Material wear occurs during the rubbing of the mating surfaces consisting of a femoral component running on a polymeric bearing surface. This wear is acceptable although not desirable throughout the current lifetimes. However in a considerable portion (10-15%) a process of aesthetic loosening causes premature failure. This failure is caused by considerable wear at the interface of the mating components which generates wear particles which in turn trigger an immune response which attacks and loosens the joint and hence the joint is replaced prematurely. Hard on hard bearings have been researched and are the thrust forwards in increasing the lifetime of prosthetic joint replacements by reducing wear using either metal on metal or ceramic on ceramic load bearing surfaces. To enable this combination extremely low surface roughness' and excellent conformances of the part is necessary.

This is currently achievable in the case of hip joints but it is the freeform surface of the hard on hard knee components that has proven difficult to achieve the conformance and roughness constraints. This paper outlines techniques which have the ability to bridge this gap. The manufacturing route utilizes a 7 axis CNC Zeeko polishing machine to polish knee joint surfaces to the required form and finish. The paper discusses the machine constraints, optimal settings and surface generation process.

Keywords: CNC, Manufacture, Hips, Knees, Medical engineering, Wear test simulation.

1. Introduction to the Zeeko IRP200 7-axis CNC Polishing Machine

The machine uniquely uses an inflated bulged polymer polishing head as the lap medium in combination with water based polishing slurries. The inflated head can be adjusted to vary the polished spot size. Novell precessions control software allows the polishing head to polish off axis whilst maintaining close form control. For free form surfaces the head is driven by a new generation of intelligent software and is capable of moving in multiple axes, the adaptive polishing head allows components to be manufactured to a precision of $\lambda/4$ [2].

Fig. 1 Zeeko 7-axis IRP200 Polishing Machine

The seven axes of motion consist of two sections the workpiece holder, which consists of horizontal, vertical movement and clockwise / anti-clockwise workpiece rotation (X-Y and C Axis rotation respectively) together with a forward and reverse motion of the holder (Z Axis). The second section consists of the tool which is split into a virtual pivot (A and B axis) where the centre of the two axis intersect at the same point giving a know position of contact on the workpiece surface. This is combined with a rotation of the adaptive pressure tool (H-Axis).

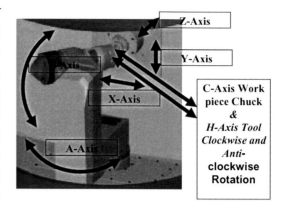

Figure 2: 7-axis of movement of the CNC polisher

The key features of the Zeeko polishing Machine are; an adaptive pressure-tool tuned automatically to local surface errors. Precession ability allows multi-directional lapping for excellent texture where the resulting tool footprint is Gaussian-like with no sharp central zero velocity artefacts. The result is a polished surface corrected form, and excellent texture demonstrating no directional properties. The machine has several variable parameters (Fig. 3) which are H-axis head pressure and speed, precess angle, (angle between polishing head and perpendicular to the workpiece surface), X-Y spacing (control of the polishing tool movement across the workpiece) and spot size (contact area of the polishing media to the workpiece).

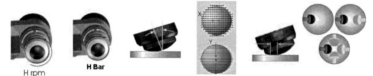

Fig. 3: (Left to Right) H-axis head speed, H-axis pressure, precess angle, X-Y spacing, spot size and precess positions

2 Initial Trials

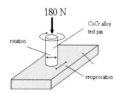

Prior to clinical testing in the design or manufacture of a Total Hip Replacement (THR) or Total Knee Replacement (TKR), the material to be used needs stringently tested for bio-compatibility and wear properties. A pin on plate wear test rig (Fig 4) is usually the beginning of the preliminary wear screening. This test piece is used an initial demonstrator for the present polishing technology.

Fig. 4: Schematic setup of pin on plate wear rig

2.1   Results of Initial Trails

Seven stages of polishing were required together with the knowledge obtained from Taguchi testing [3] to complete the cobalt chrome pins ready for pin on plate wear testing. The first of the seven stages was a 120 grit roughing stage with a nickel bonded diamond polishing pad and ranged up to a final polishing stage using a 3000 grit resin bonded diamond cloth in progressive grit size steps. Recycled tap water was used as the polishing medium throughout all stages. Figure 5 shows and optical image of the cobalt chrome pin along with interferometer images of first and final stages.

| (a) | (b) | (c) |

Fig 5 Optical image of CoCr pin (a), interferometer image after 1st stage (b) interferometer image after final pole down polish stage (c)

Table 1 shows a summary of repeatability machine polish tests (MP) and a comparison with hand polished pins (HP). It is considered the variation in the machine polished results is caused by edge effects on the pins. The results show that for the machine polished pins the roughness obtained was within the bounds considered acceptable for these types of surfaces [4].

Interferometric Surface Measurement, Surface Roughness Sa/nm					
Pin Number	A	B	Crown	C	D	Average
HP1	20.1	27.1	17.2	36.3	24.1	25.19
HP2	17.8	13.6	19.2	36.8	24.1	22.27
HP3	12.6	40.4	15.1	16.5	18.1	20.54
MP1	3.2	3.8	2.8	3.3	4.6	3.54
MP2	17.7	5.8	10.0	10.7	11.2	11.08
MP3	23.1	7.8	10.3	11.7	15.5	13.68

Table 1 : Repeatability results of pin polishing for wear tests

2.2 CoCr pin on plate wear test results

The results of the machine polished and hand polished pins outlined in Table 1 of section 2.1 are compared through a predefined methodology. A series of pin-on-disc tests where carried on in which the wear of polyethylene discs articulated against cobalt chrome pins were measured and analysed.

2.2.1 Cobalt chrome pin on disc test methodology

The pins were made from wrought cobalt chrome and were CNC ground to a spherical radius as seen in Fig 5 (a). These were finished either by hand polishing or by the Zeeko IRP200 7-axis CNC polishing machine, the hypothesis being that the wear of the polyethylene would be greater on the pins that were hand polished.

A constant load of 2.3kN (equivalent to three times body weight) was applied throughout the pin on disc testing. With this constant load applied to the pins the discs were reciprocated with a 10mm total travel and a radial motion of +/-5°. A 30% serum solution was used as lubrication throughout the articulation of the bearing surfaces. At every million cycles the test was broken down and the following measured:

1. Surface profile of the pin surface. This included measurements of Ra, Rz and Rm.
2. Weight loss of the plastic.
3. Penetration depth into the plastic.
4. Volumetric change in the wear track.

A blank disc of polyethylene was used as a soak test left in the 30% serum solution to compensate for the fluid absorption properties into the plastic polymer in a capillary action.

2.2.2 Cobalt chrome pin on disc simulator test results

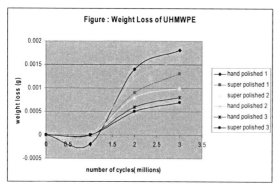

Figure 6: Weight Loss of UHMWPE (Plastic) during CoCr Pin on Disc Simulator Testing

The surface finish of the hand polished versus the CNC polished pins at time 0 are shown in Figure 13 in Section 5.1. The average Ra for the CNC polished pins is lower than that for the hand polished pins (Table 3, Section 5.1). After two million cycles, both the hand polished and the CNC polished pins had become rougher, but there was still a difference with the CNC polished pins having a lower Ra of 35nm compared to that 45nm of the hand polished pins.

There was no significant difference in the weight loss of the plastic after two million cycles for discs that articulated against the hand polished cobalt chrome pins compared with the plastic articulating against the CNC polished pins (Figure 6).

Gravimetric readings taken of the polyethylene discs at 2 million cycles showed that overall there is no statistical difference in the weight loss between polyethylene articulating with CNC polished cobalt chrome and hand polished cobalt chrome. Although it can be seen that there is a trend to a more uniform and lower weight loss with the CNC polished pins between the 2 million and 3 million cycle points. Examination of the graph in Figure 6 shows that two out of three of the polyethylene discs articulating against hand polished plastic showed the greatest wear.

116

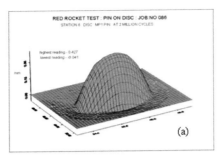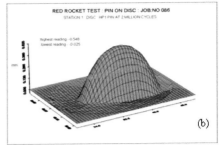

Figure 7: Wear track profile of the polyethelene plate caused by CNC polished (a) and hand polished (b) pins after 2 million cycles

To demonstrate the penetration of the plastic above the zero plane and also the effect of creep below the plane the profile of the wear tracks on the polyethylene discs were measured by a special CMM. Figures 7a and 7b show these measurements and indicate that a hand polished cobalt chrome articulating with a plastic disc showed a trend of overall greater penetration. The average penetration depth at 2 million cycles for the plastic articulating with the hand polished discs was 0.526mm (0.025SD) and the average penetration for the plastic articulating with the CNC polished discs was .485mm (0.052SD). All discs showed plastic creep (below zero plane) with material thrown up at the margins of the wear track.

The trend to increase wear may be associated with the increased roughness of the pin surfaces. Figures 8(a) and 8(b) show 2D diamond stylus surface profiles of the cobalt chrome pins demonstrating that in some instances there is a greater Ra value for hand polished pins than for CNC polished pins. Further analysis shows that not only Ra is larger in some instances for hand polished pins, Rz and Sm are also higher.

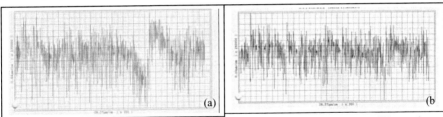

Figure 8 2D Stylus profile of CNC polished (a) and hand polished (b) pins after 2 million cycles

3   Development of Freeform Knee Joint Surface for 7-axis CNC Polishing

With positive results from the pin on disc wear testing (section 2.2), by utilizing RhinoCAD 3D a Non-Uniform Refined B-Spline (NURBS) surface was created . The generated NURBS surface was then fed into uniquely designed ZeeCAD software to create a CNC file for the polishing process of a freeform femoral knee component using the control points of the NURBS the CNC program allows the polsihing head to be precessed across the freeform knee joint surface.

3.1 Results of Freeform Knee Joint Surface Polishing

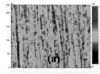

The surface of a part finished cobalt chrome knee component was prepared to a 1200 grit hand polish. Two stages of polishing were used. A roughing stage using a 600 grit nickel bonded diamond cloth and a polishing run using a 3000 grit resin bonded diamond cloth. Figure 2 shows (a) interferometer images of before the roughing stage with a surface roughness Sa = 175.8nm (0.25mm x 0.25mm) and Figure 4 (b) an image of the final pole down polish with a surface roughness Sa = 9.7nm (0.25mm x 0.25mm). This image shows distinctive peaks caused by hard and pronounced carbides in the matrix of the material. The slurry medium used was recycled tap water. It is considered that the use of colloidal silica as the slurry medium could aid in the reduction of these peaks by enhancing the chemical element of the polishing process. Figure 4(c) shows an optical image of the polished cobalt chrome knee component. The left of the component shows the dull 1200 grit pre polish surface and the on the right of the component shows the mirror finished machine polished condile on the Zeeko 7-axis CNC machine.

Fig. 2: Interferometer images of CoCr knee polishing process (a, b) and optical image of polished knee condile section (c)

Conclusions:

The present work has shown initial results as to the applicability of the Zeeko IRP 200 polishing system for the manufacture of orthopaedic "freeform" knee joints in particular the system has shown the ability to generate nanoscale surface topography. It is evident that the Zeeko IRP2000 polished femoral knee components have a slightly better surface roughness (Sa) to that of results of those that are hand polished. In addition the machine seems capable of manufacturing freeform surfaces as defined to be biologically compatible with knee joint movement requiring high levels of conformance which could facilitate the development of hard on hard knee joints.

Acknowledgements:

Prof. Gordon Blunn at Centre for Biomedical Engineering, University College London for his assistance in the conduction of the pin on plate wear trials and the ongoing knee simulator tests as well as the financial support of the EPSRC.

References:

[1] National Joint Registry for England and Wales, 1st Annual Report, September 2004
[2] D. Walker, D, Brookes "The First Aspheric Form and Texture Results from a Production Machine Embodying the Precession Process", SPIE 46th Annual Meeting, the International Symposium on Optical Science and Technology, San Diego, July 2001
[3] P Charlton, Progress Report "From Optical Surfaces to Prosthetic Joint Lifetime" EPSRC Grant Ref GR/S10216/01.
[4] L. Blunt X.Q. Jiang and K.J.Stout "3D measurement of the surface topography of ceramic and metallic orthopaedic joint prostheses" Journal of Materials Science: Materials in Medicine, pp235-246 11(2000).

NURBS approximation method for tool path generation in a new free-form grinding machine

X. Luo[1a], P. Morantz [1b], P. Shore [1] and I. Baird[2]

[1] School of Industrial & Manufacturing Science, Cranfield University, Bedfordshire MK43 0AL, UK

[2] GE Fanuc Automation CNC UK Ltd, Northampton, NN4 5EZ, UK

[a] x.luo@cranfield.ac.uk [b] p.morantz@cranfield.ac.uk

Abstract: A 3-axis ultra precision free-form grinder - BOX®, is under development to generate large optics with high form accuracy at high material removal rate. High machining accuracy and machining efficiency are critical requirements in the motion control for this grinding machine. This paper presents a Non-Uniform Rational B-Splines (NURBS) approximation method which is used for tool path generation. NURBS provides a unified mathematical basis for representing free-form entities with remarkably little data. The path between points at which the grinding wheel contacts the workpiece is constructed by a NURBS curve, which precisely follows the demanded optic height variation. Changes in surface local slope cause a change in contact point on the grinding wheel; therefore a point fixed relative to the grinding spindle axis has been chosen as the command point for part programming which is distinct from the contact point. The tool control path of the command point is also represented by a NURBS curve to compensate its deviation relative to the corresponding contact point. A third order NURBS function is applied to maintain the continuity of the first and second derivative of tool control path. A case study on tool path generation for an off-axis aspheric mirror shows that the NURBS curve results in a smooth and continuous tool path with a short NC program. As a result, a NURBS approximation approach can help to achieve high machining accuracy and machining efficiency at the same time.

Keywords: NURBS, ultra precision grinding, large optics, free-form, aspherics, off-axis

Introduction

Growing interest is seen in the fabrication of large off-axis aspheric optics for astronomical research, remote sensing, and military surveillance applications [1]. For instance, in some telescope projects, such as Keck and Euro50, large off-axis aspheric segments have been adopted or proposed as the mirror segments [2]. Free-form optics have not entered the mainstream of optical products, but it is anticipated that their adoption will be widespread [3]. Consequently a new ultra-precision grinding machine - BOX® is under development which aims to generate large optics with high form accuracy at high material removal rate [4].

For large optics with aspheric, off-axis aspheric and free-form shapes, a large number of linear/circular segments have to be used to approximate the required optic surface in order to satisfy the 1 um form accuracy requirement of this grinding machine, if a conventional interpolation approach is adopted. This in turn demands a large part program and data transmission time. It also causes discontinuities of machine axis motion derivatives at the intersections of linear or circular segments. Non-Uniform Rational B-Splines, commonly referred as NURBS, have become the de facto industry standard for the representation, design, and data exchange of geometric information processed by computers [5]. However, the use of NURBS is not yet widespread in large optics manufacturing industry. To decrease the size of the NC file and keep a continuous tool path, NURBS is used in the NC program for the BOX® machine. Using NURBS, only a few parameters are needed to describe a complex surface shape with the same interpolation accuracy as a much larger number of linear/circular interpolation parameters. This paper presents a NURBS

119

approximation method which represents complex surface data and explains its application to tool path generation.

Sampling surface data on a spiral curve

The BOX® machine utilizes an r-theta grinding mode, in which a tilted toric grinding wheel is used. Two linear motions (X and Z axes) and one rotational motion (C axis) are applied to generate aspheric, off-axis aspheric and free-form surfaces [6]. As shown in Fig. 1 the path of workpiece/wheel contact points will follow a spiral curve, so grinding contact points on the surface can be sampled in Cartesian coordinates by a parametric function along the spiral curve in the form of:

$$\begin{cases} x_{i,j} = f_1(r_{i,j}, \theta_{i,j}) = r_{i,j} \cdot \cos(\theta_{i,j}) \\ y_{i,j} = f_2(r_{i,j}, \theta_{i,j}) = r_{i,j} \cdot \sin(\theta_{i,j}) \\ z_{i,j} = Z_{optic-height} \end{cases} \tag{1}$$

$$i = 1, 2, \ldots, N_i, j = 1, 2, \ldots, N_j$$

where r is the distance from point $A(x_{i,j}, y_{i,j}, z_{i,j})$ to Z axis, θ is the angle between X axis and OA. i and j are the polar distributions of grinding contact points. N_i and N_j are the number of sampling grid points.

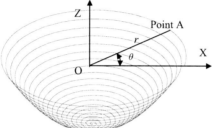

Fig. 1 Illustration of grinding contact points.

Non-Uniform B-Splines approximation method

The purpose of NURBS curve fitting is to find a NURBS curve that can follow the shape of the given data polygon with a minimum number of control points and still satisfy a prescribed value of error tolerance. There are two types of NURBS curve fitting methods. One is an interpolation method and the other is an approximation method. In the interpolation method, a curve is constructed which satisfies the given data precisely, e.g. the curve passes through the given points and matches the given data precisely at the prescribed points. In the approximation method, a curve is constructed which does not necessarily match the given data precisely, but only approximately. In the part program for the BOX® machine, the NURBS approximation method is adopted for two reasons:

- A large quantity of surface data is needed to describe a free-form surface. If the NURBS interpolation method is used, the resultant number of control points will be equal to the number of given data points, which will not reduce the size of the NC file. Therefore it is not desirable to fit a curve by using the interpolation method for such a large number of data points.
- When part error compensation is applied to the optic surface, measurement data is acquired by use of a probe, which may contribute measurement noise. It is logical for the fitted compensated

curve to capture the "shape" of the data and not to "snake" its way through every point. To reduce the effects of measurement noise, the NURBS approximation method is more suitable for curve fitting than the interpolation method.

Once the surface data are obtained, the NURBS approximation method is used to fit those surface data. A pth-degree NURBS curve is defined by:

$$C(u) = \frac{\sum_{i=0}^{n} N_{i,p}(u)w_i P_i}{\sum_{i=0}^{n} N_{i,p}(u)w_i} \qquad\qquad 0 \leq u \leq 1 \qquad\qquad (2)$$

where $C(u)$ represents $C_x(u)$, $C_y(u)$ and $C_z(u)$and u is the interpolation parameter. P_i and w_i are control points and their corresponding weights. $N_{i,p}(u)$ is the pth-degree basis function defined on the non-uniform knot vector:

$$U = \{0,...,0, u_{p+1},..., u_{m-p-1}, 1,...,1\} \qquad\qquad (3)$$

where $m+1$ is the number of data points.

Basis functions are calculated by the de Boor-Cox recursive function [5]. They are expressed as:

$$N_{i,1}(u) = \begin{cases} 1 & \text{for } u_i \leq u \leq u_{i+1} \\ 0 & \text{otherwise} \end{cases} \qquad\qquad (4)$$

$$N_{i,p}(u) = \frac{u - u_i}{u_{i+p-1} - u_i} \cdot N_{i,p-1}(u) + \frac{u_{i+p} - u}{u_{i+p} - u_{i+1}} \cdot N_{i+1,p-1}(u) \qquad\qquad (5)$$

The basis functions determine how strongly control points influence the curve.

The NURBS curve approximation method is then used for acquiring the NURBS parameters. Here, the degree (p) of the basis function is chosen as 3 in order to maintain continuity of the first and second derivatives of the NURBS curve. In the NURBS approximation processes, the curve fitting error tolerance, E is set at 50 nm, on the basis that this is well below the target form error. An initial number (n) of control points is set as one fifth of the number of known data points, to produce a significant scale of data reduction. If the maximum curve error is higher than E, n will be increased and curve fitting reiterated until curve error is lower than the limit E. The details of obtaining control points, knot vector, and weights of the NURBS curve are described in the following procedure.

(1) In order to simplify computation, the weights are set to 1 in this algorithm.

(2) Precomputed parameters are needed to get the knot vector. The precomputed parameters are obtained from the known data points by the chord length method.

Let d be the total chord length of the given data point,

$$d = \sum_{k=1}^{m} |Q_k - Q_{k-1}| \qquad\qquad (6)$$

where Q_k and Q_{k-1} are the known data points. The precomputed parameters are then described as:

$$\bar{u}_0 = 0, \qquad \bar{u}_m = 1 \qquad\qquad (7)$$

$$\bar{u}_k = \bar{u}_{k-1} + \frac{|Q_k - Q_{k-1}|}{d} \qquad k = 1, ..., m\text{-}1 \qquad\qquad (8)$$

(3) An averaging technique [5] is used to obtain the knot vector U.

$$u_0 = ... = u_p = 0 \quad u_{n+1} = ... = u_{n+p+1} = 1 \qquad\qquad (9)$$

$$u_{j+p} = \frac{1}{p} \sum_{i=j}^{j+p-1} \bar{u}_i \qquad j = 1, ..., n\text{-}p \qquad\qquad (10)$$

(4) Once the precomputed parameters and knot vector are determined, the basis function can be calculated based on Eq. 3 and Eq. 4. An algorithm which only calculates the non-vanishing terms of the basis function is used to improve the calculation efficiency.

(5) A least squares curve approximation method is used to acquire the control points.

Setting $R_{i,p}(u) = \dfrac{N_{i,p}(u)w_i}{\sum\limits_{j=0}^{n} N_{j,p}(u)w_j}$, the NURBS function Eq. 2 can be rewritten as:

$$C(u) = \sum_{i=0}^{n} R_{i,p}(u)P_i \quad u \in [0,1] \tag{11}$$

Let $C(0) = Q_0$ and $C(1) = Q_m$, the remaining Q_k are approximated in the least square sense, i. e.

$$f = \sum_{k=1}^{m-1} \left| Q_k - C(\overline{u}_k) \right|^2 \tag{12}$$

To minimize f the derivatives of f with respect to the n-1 control point P_l, equal to zero, and it can be further simplified as:

$$\sum_{i=1}^{n-1} \left(\sum_{k=1}^{m-1} N_{l,p}(\overline{u}_k)N_{i,p}(\overline{u}_k)P_i \right) = \sum_{k=1}^{m-1} N_{l,p}(\overline{u}_k)R_k \tag{13}$$

Where $R_k = Q_k - N_{0,p}(\overline{u}_k)Q_0 - N_{n,p}(\overline{u}_k)Q_m$ and $k = 1, \ldots, m$-1.

Eq. 13 is a single linear equation in the unknowns P_1, P_2, ..., P_{n-1}, Letting l=1, 2, ..., n-1 yields the system of n-1 equations in n-1 unknowns

$$(N^T N)P = R \tag{14}$$

The control point matrix can be solved as:

$$P = (N^T N)^{-1}R \tag{15}$$

where N is the (m-1) by (n-1) matrix of scalars

$$N = \begin{bmatrix} N_{1,p}(u_1) & \ldots & N_{n-1,p}(u_1) \\ \cdot & \cdot & \cdot \\ \cdot & \cdot & \cdot \\ \cdot & \cdot & \cdot \\ N_{1,p}(u_{m-1}) & \ldots & N_{n-1,p}(u_{m-1}) \end{bmatrix} \tag{16}$$

$$R = \begin{bmatrix} N_{1,p}(u_1)R_1 + \ldots + N_{1,p}(u_{m-1})R_{m-1} \\ \cdot \\ \cdot \\ \cdot \\ N_{n-1,p}(u_1)R_1 + \ldots + N_{n-1,p}(u_{m-1})R_{m-1} \end{bmatrix} \tag{17}$$

and the control point matrix

$$P = [P_1 \quad \cdot \quad \cdot \quad \cdot P_{n-1}]^T \tag{18}$$

Setting $P_0 = Q_0$ and $P_n = Q_m$, satisfies the condition that the first and last control points coincide with the first and last data points respectively.

(6) If the fitting error is higher than 50 nm, n is increased by 1 and the curve fitting procedure from step (3) to (5) will be is reiterated until it meets the 50 nm fitting accuracy requirement. A number of iterations may be required; computational efficiency could be improved with larger

iterative increases of n, although the current procedure ensures the minimum knot vector size consistent with uniform weights.

Tool path generation

By applying the NURBS approximation method, the path linking (close to) the contact points can be generated. However it is not the required tool control path to be used by the CNC controller. As the local slope changes across spherical, aspheric, off-axis and free-form surfaces, the grinding contact region changes around the sectional and circumferential profile of the toric grinding wheel. A point fixed relative to the grinding spindle axis has to be used as the control command point for part programming. An algorithm has been developed and implemented for compensation for the precession of the grinding contact region [7], by which the displacements between contact point locus and NC tool control path are obtained. The tool control path is also constructed by a NURBS

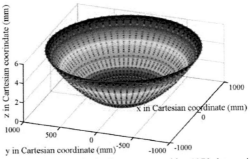

Fig. 2 An off-axis aspherical mirror presented by 4079 data points.

curve by applying the NURBS approximation method.

Case study

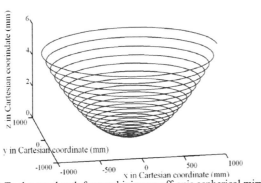

Fig. 3 Tool control path for machining an off-axis aspherical mirror.

Tool path generation for rough machining an off-axis aspheric mirror is taken as a case study. The diameter of this mirror is 2 m. Its surface data is taken from the surface data of the farthest off-axis primary mirror segment of Euro50 telescope, which is at a 28 meter radius from the centre of primary mirror[8]. Fig. 2 shows the mirror surface which is represented by 4079 data points. The generated tool control path constructed by a NURBS curve is shown in Fig. 3. It only contains 714 control points while maintaining 50 nm curve fitting tolerance. It can be seen that the NURBS curve results in a continuous tool path and a relatively short NC program. A novel feed rate control algorithm has been applied in the motion control of the BOX® machine [7]. The feed rate of the machine motions is shown in Fig. 4. It can be seen that the vector speed between grinding wheel and workpiece is constant until the grinding wheel approaches the centre of rotary table. The continuous tool control path and constant feed rate will help to achieve an optical surface of high form accuracy.

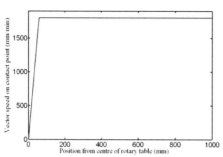

Fig. 4 Feed rate diagram of the machine motion.

Conclusions

A NURBS approximation method has been developed for representing complex free-form surface data and the corresponding tool control path. The case study on an off-axis aspheric mirror shows that the NURBS curve results in a smooth and continuous tool path with a short NC program compared with conventional linear or circular segments. Therefore the machined surface accuracy will not be affected by any discontinuity due to linear or circular segmentation. The burden of data transmission to the NC machine is reduced. As a result, a NURBS approximation approach can help to achieve high machining accuracy and machining efficiency at the same time on the BOX® grinding machine.

References:

[1]   I. F. Stowers, R. Komanduri and E. D. Baird: Proc. SPIE 966 (1988), pp. 62-73.
[2]   D. D. Walker, A. T. H. Beaucamp, R. G. Bingham, D. Brooks, R. Freeman, S.W. Kim, A. King, G. McCavana, R. Morton, D. Riley and J. Simms: Proc. SPIE 4842 (2003), pp. 73-84.
[3]   C. Brecher, M. Weck, M. Winterschladen, S. Lange, O. Wetter, T. Pfeifer, D. Dörner, E. Brinksmeier and L. Autschbach: Proc. ASPE 2004 Winter Topical Meeting (2004), pp. 88-93.
[4]   P. Shore, P. Morantz, X. Luo, X. Tonnellier, R. Collins, A. Roberts, R. May-Miller and R. Read: Proc. SPIE 5965 (2005), pp. 241-248.
[5]   L. Piegl and W. Tiller: *The NURBS Book* (Springer-Verlag, Berlin 1997).
[6]   P. Shore, X. Luo, T. Jin, X. Tonnellier, P. Morantz and D. Stephenson, R. Collins, A. Roberts, R. May-Miller and R. Read, Proc. 2005 ASPE Annual Meeting (Norfolk, USA 2005), pp. 114-117.
[7]   P. Morantz, P. Shore, X. Luo and I. Baird: Proc. Euspen 6th International Conference (Austria 2006) (Accepted for publication)
[8]   A. Gontcharov: Optical design for the Euro50, (http://www.astro.lu.se/~torben/euro50) (Accessed on 13th April 2006).

A Proposed Data-cloud Reduction Method for Laser Scanned and CMM Data Integration

Jafar Jamshidi[1, a], Antony Roy Mileham[2, b] and Geraint Wyn Owen[3, c]

IMRC, Department of Mechanical Engineering, The University of Bath, BA2 7AY, Bath, UK

Tel: [1] (+44)1225385366   [2] (+44)1225826462   [3] (+44)1225826826(4033)

Fax: (+44) 1225386928

[a]J.Jamshidi@bath.ac.uk, [b]A.R.Mileham@bath.ac.uk, [c]G.W.Owen@bath.ac.uk

Abstract. In the Reverse Engineering of a component, Laser scanning, as a fast digitizing tool can generate thousands of data-points in a short time. Accurate scanning is achieved by setting the laser scanner optical constraints to fine adjustments. This inevitably results in higher levels of noise and redundant points. Filtering such a data-cloud can help reduce the number of redundant points. However, it may not be desirable when dealing with precision parts that have critical areas of geometry in which the dimensional tolerance is normally tighter. Therefore it is necessary to have control over the data reduction process in order to comply with the various dimensional tolerances. In this paper a method of data-cloud reduction for laser scanned models, based on the integration of scanned data-points from a CMM, is proposed. Highly accurate CMM digitised data guides the process of data-cloud reduction by recognition of the critical features. Different sections of the data-cloud can be filtered according to the tolerance of their neighbouring CMM created features. If the CMM generated features are used as filling features, the neighbouring data-cloud can be eliminated fully, due to its replacement by such features. Furthermore other areas of the model can be filtered to any desirable level within the overall tolerance of the part. Experimental results of the data-cloud reduction are presented.

Keywords: Reverse Engineering, Laser Scanning, CMM, Data-cloud, CAD Modelling, Measurement

Introduction

In Reverse Engineering (RE), the design information is obtained from an existing prototype or actual component by full digitisation of the part. In order to undertake this, various scanning and measurement systems are available in industry. In fact any measurement device can be regarded as a tool for scanning. Scanning systems are divided into two main groups of non-contact or vision systems, like Laser Scanner (LS), and contact or touch systems, like Coordinate Measurement Machine (CMM) with touch probes.

CMM, as one of the most common scanning systems, can generate high accuracy digitised data-points of the part geometry. They are fast and reliable in routine inspection applications, but when the number of scanning points is too large due to the complexity of the component, they tend to be costly and time-consuming systems. On the other hand, LS as a fast digitising scanning tool can generate thousands of data-points (data-cloud), from the component surface in a short time. But they tend to be inefficient in precision engineering due to the low data resolution. Also, there are technical problems in the models they generate such as missing information and unreal surfaces that are the result of occlusions on the component.

More accurate scanning can be achieved by the appropriate setting of the laser scanner variables. This inevitably results in higher level of noise and a larger number of redundant points. Filtering such a data-cloud can help reduce the number of redundant points. However, this may not be desirable when dealing with precise geometric features.

In a typical component there are critical areas of geometry in which the dimensional tolerance is normally tighter. Control over the data reduction in such areas, as described in this paper, can be achieved by regional filtering of the data-cloud. For this purpose, data-points captured by a CMM can give guidance on critical area recognition. Highly accurate CMM digitised models guide the process of data-cloud reduction. Neighbouring areas of the laser scanned model can be filtered to a greater extent or even be completely eliminated from the data-cloud. Also other areas of the model can be filtered to any desirable level since the missing accuracy of such areas is not of concern due to their isolation from the critical areas.

Related Work

In RE of an existing component the ultimate goal is to realise a 3D digitised model with detailed design information [1]. This requires the digitisation of the component from different view angles to allow the inclusion of all the features in the scanned model. Such a process is straightforward for non-sensitive components with smooth and convex features, and can take place with any desired resolution. However, when the component includes complex features with various tolerances, a uniform resolution can produce excessive number of redundant points, for non-sensitive features, or a loss of accuracy, for sensitive features. In order to avoid the latter, higher resolution scanning can be used.

Higher resolution scanning would significantly increase the number of data points, most of which would be redundant. This makes working with the model problematic. The problem is more evident in merged models with overlapping regions that is typical in scanned views registered by using the ICT (Iterative Closest Point) algorithm [2].

It is important to reduce the amount of data points in the model and convert it into a usable format for manufacturing and other downstream processes while maintaining accuracy [3]. With triangulation meshing of flatter regions, the triangles of data-points need to be merged into a larger one. But in the curved areas triangles have to remain as they are, to prevent the risk of losing curvature data. In a typical component the tolerance varies for different features depending on their functionality. This brings further limitations in point reduction of the data-cloud. There is much research in this field mainly on data point reduction, which inevitably brings the risk of compromising surface detail.

Hur et al [4] developed a program for data reduction in STL files. In their software the user specifies the criteria for triangle selection by interference between triangles, the percentage of reduced triangles and the allowable area. This method can reduce the number of points in flat and smooth sections of the data-cloud to a great extend without reducing the accuracy. If the data-cloud includes sharp slopes or curvatures, data reduction would not occur. The main disadvantage of this method is its inability to distinguish the critical features, and treating all the features in the same way. Therefore it cannot be considered as an optimal data-reduction method.

Martin et al [5] proposed a method of data reduction using a median filtering approach. They used a uniform grid to which the data points were assigned accordingly. Then a median point is calculated to represent that grid. The data reduction is dependent on and influenced from the points' distribution in the scanned model. This approach is not appropriate for features with sharp edges. Furthermore it is not suitable for parts with various tolerance levels, due to its uniform approach.

In a reverse approach Johnson and Manduchi [6] have used different resolution during the scanning procedure. Although the focus of their work was based on high and low resolution data fusion, however this can potentially be a preventative approach for scanning features with various sensitivity levels. In other words if a feature includes a tighter tolerance, this feature should be scanned at higher resolution and vice versa. However, such an approach requires extensive data-processing that might be time consuming and inefficient with available systems.

Problems in the LS Models:

High Level of Noise in Data-cloud. This problem relates to the LS hardware and software settings where the low resolution settings can result in the loss of accuracy in scanned model, and the high resolution settings can result in a high level of noise in the model. The latter is one of the main causes of excessive redundant points in the scanned model, which can slow down data processing in the following stages. For instance, three separate points on a surface are sufficient for the identification of the plane to which such points belong, and the remaining points on that surface can be considered redundant. The initial data-cloud can be useful for precision purposes, i.e. when a mean value for points is required or for the view registration process. However they become redundant again after completion of the calculations.

Light Reflection. Laser beam reflection on the polished surfaces of the component or from the environmental objects in the fields of view can affect the scanning result. This occurrence can generate unreal features attached to the model as shown in Figure-1. In transparent material parts, light beam can pass through the features, resulting in unreal surface and missing information.

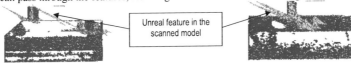

Figure 1 – Examples of unreal features

Appropriate surface spraying [7] on the object can reduce this type of scanning defect. However, the accuracy of the result can be affected due to the added thickness and possible uneven distribution of spray material. The scanning results on grit blasted or spark-eroded components were found to have fewer defects of this type, but not all parts have this type of surface finish.

Rough Features in the Scanned Model. The last scanning defects in this discussion are very rough faces in the scanned model (Figure-2), which do not correspond to the actual model. This type of imperfection can be the result of a combination of the previously discussed defects. The problems explained above could be solved to some extent, for example by considering the light reflection in the scanning planning. Also the missing information defect can be minimised by dimming the reflective material surfaces, for instance by anodizing the component, where possible.

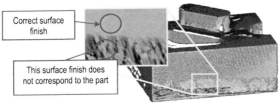

Figure 2 - Effect of Uneven reflection on scanned model surface

Method Description

The precision data-cloud reduction method is based on the sensitivity level of the feature in the part geometry. If the CAD model exists, the sensitivity level of a particular feature can be identified in relation to its dimensional tolerance and the data-reduction can be processed in a straightforward approach. However, in RE, which is the application purpose of this paper, no CAD model exists. Therefore the sensitive features are required to be identified using a combination of CMM and LS.

127

In this method the user selects the features that require accurate scanning and measurement. Such features include the machined faces with smooth surface finishes, the features that are in direct contact and close fitting to the neighbouring parts in their assembly. The sensitive features are touch-scanned, using the CMM touch probe. The CMM scanned model, which is in the form of tessellated geometric features (Figure-3), is then sent to a CAD environment after its translation into IGES (Initial Graphics Exchange Standard) file format.

Figure 3 - Stage-model scanned by CMM touching probe

In the CAD environment appropriate volumetric features are created using the CMM generated stage-model. Depending on the level of sensitivity, larger scales of the volumetric features are then created to form closure-envelopes. This stage is similar for inward and outward features. For instance a boss and a hole with the same size, have the shape of a similar size cylinder in their larger scale. The closure-envelopes are then used to select the 3D points that they contain for data-point reduction in the close neighbourhood of the sensitive features (For a fuller explanation of the large scale volumetric feature approach see [8]).

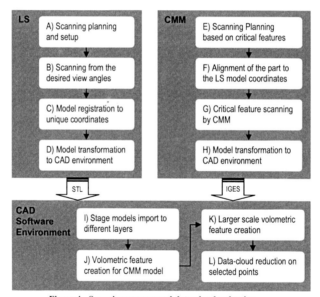

Figure 4 - Scanning process and data-cloud reduction

The stage-model scanned by LS is also imported into a CAD environment, preferably in a different layer, after its file translation into STL (Stereolithography) file format. Both of the stage-models from CMM and LS are expected to be in the same coordinate system due to the registration of the models during the scanning. In the next stage, the data-reduction process commences. The data-points trapped in the closure-envelope are treated as sensitive points and temporarily quarantined. The remaining points that are outside the envelopes are non-sensitive, and can therefore be reduced in number by one of the rapid data-cloud reduction methods, like the median value method [5], to the largest acceptable level.

The sensitive points of the data-cloud can also be reduced, but with more care and in isolation from one another according to their individual tolerance. More accurate data-reduction method can be used for the very sensitive features. This can take a longer time, however the overall processing time of data-reduction can be reduced due to the elimination of a large number of non-sensitive points in the previous stages. The data-cloud of a sensitive feature can be trapped and exchanged with a feature created by a CMM in a data fusion process [8].

Figure-4 shows the flow of information in the data reduction method. As can be seen in the diagram, the component is scanned using LS (stages A to D) and CMM (stages E to F) separately. The LS resolution level can be set to the desired resolution, preferably within the resolution level for the finest tolerance. Then the stage-models are registered to a unique coordinates system by one of the available methods such as ICT [2], or use of auxiliary devices like 3CB (3 Coordinate Balls) [9].

Experimental Results

In order to validate the data-reduction method, several components were investigated, one of which is presented here. The accuracy of registration between the scanned views of the stage-models depends on the accuracy and size of the 3CB set. In this experiment the registration accuracy was in the region of ±0.41mm in each principal axis.

Table 1 - Data-reduction in non-sensitive features of a simple cubic component

Cubic component	A) Complete LS model	B) Sensitive feature selected	C) Toggled selection	D) Data reduction on non-sensitive points
Number of points in blue	14,666	14,199	467	467
Number of points in red	0	467	14,199	2,496

The sample component is a simple cubic part with two orthogonal holes on two joints surfaces. It is assumed that a complete CAD model of the part is required and the two holes are the sensitive features. Therefore the hole features have to be modelled based on the features measured by the CMM touch probe. The closure envelope of the feature is made to be slightly larger than the actual volumetric values and its direction has to be transposed to its parent. Data-points inside closure envelopes are then recognised as sensitive and therefore reduced according to the tolerance required.

The data reduction results are shown in Table-1. As can be seen, stage *A* indicates the total number of points (14,666) in the data-cloud, which is gained after the digitisation, registration and merging of the scanned views. In stage *B* the data-cloud of the sensitive features (467 points) are selected using the CMM created features. In the next stage the selection is toggled in order to select points in non-sensitive features (stage *C*), which are then reduced in number by more than 80% to 2,496 points (stage *D*), yet the number of points in the sensitive sections has remained unchanged.

The resulting data-cloud can be used for the conventional modelling processes, including surface fitting, feature extraction, and surface smoothing, in order to generate a complete solid CAD model for downstream manufacturing processes.

Conclusion

A new method for data-cloud reduction of a model scanned by laser scanning has been introduced. This method can highlight and eliminate the noise and unreal data-points caused by light reflection that typically emerge in the neighbourhood of the real features. This is done by creating larger scale features from CMM scanned model to differentiate useful data-points from redundant ones. The method uses CMM scanned features as a guide to calculate the allowable level of reduction, which is a function of the feature sensitivity, in the data-cloud. Depending on the tolerances of the desired features, the data-cloud inside and in the neighbourhood of such features is reduced. This can vary from a minimal filtering of the data-cloud up to a complete elimination of the data-cloud and their replacement by CMM generated features. This method is therefore most suitable for scanning of the components that have different levels of accuracy on different features, such as machined casting parts used in the automotive industry. This method currently requires several stages of manipulation to complete the data reduction. Further development of this work, therefore includes the automation of the data-cloud reduction by its integration into a reverse engineering system.

Acknowledgments

The work has been carried out as part of the EPSRC E-IMRC at the University of Bath under grant No GR/R67597/01. The authors wish to thank Phil Williams of Renishaw, and Peter Smith from Konica Minolta Photo Imaging UK for their technical input.

References

[1] T. Varady, R. R. Martin and J. Cox: *Reverse Engineering of Geometric Models – An Introduction*, CAD, Vol. 29, No. 4, (1997), pp. 255-268

[2] P. J. Besl and N. D. McKay: *A Method for Registration of 3D Shapes*, IEEE Trans. Pattern Analysis and Machine Int., (Gen. Motors Lab., USA,1992), Vol. 14, No. 2, pp 239-256

[3] K. H. Lee, H. Woo and T. Suk: *Data Reduction Methods for Reverse Engineering*, Adv. Manuf. Tech., Vol. 17, No 10, (2001), pp 735-743

[4] S. Hur, H. C. Kim and S. H. Lee: *STL File Generation with Data Reduction by the Delaunay Triangulation Method in Reverse Eng*, Adv. Manuf. Tech., Vol. 19, No. 9, (2002), pp 669-678

[5] R. Martin, I. A. Stroud and A. D. Marshall: *Data Reduction for Reverse Engineering*, Proc. 6th IMA Conf. Math. Surfaces, Info. Geometers, (1997), pp 85-99

[6] A. E. Johnson and R. Manduchi: *Probabilistic 3D Data Fusion for Adaptive Resolution Surface Generation*, Proc. 1st Int. Sym. 3D Data Processing Visual. and Trans., (2002), pp 578-587

[7] S. Son, H. Park and K. H. Lee: *Automated laser scanning system for reverse engineering and inspection*, Machine Tools and Manuf., (South Korea, 2002), Vol. 42, pp 889-897

[8] J. Jamshidi, A. R. Mileham and G. W. Owen: *A New Data Fusion Method for Scanned Models*, JCISE Special Issue on 3D Computation Metrology, 2006, to appear

[9] J. Jamshidi, A. R. Mileham and G. W. Owen: *A Laser Scanning Registration Technique for Reverse Engineering Applications*, (3rd ICMR, Cranfield Uni., UK, 2005)

2D Freeform Component Fixture Design Optimisation Using Genetic Algorithm

Ka Yiu Yeung[1, a], Xun Chen[2, b]

[1,2]School of Mechanical, Materials and Manufacturing, Engineering, University of Nottingham, University Park, Nottingham, NG7 2RD, England

[a] epxkyy@nottingham.ac.uk, [b] xun.chen@nottingham.ac.uk

Abstract. This paper details an application of genetic algorithm (GA) developed for the optimisation of fixture locator positioning for 2D freeform component. The fitness function has been developed based on the location error functions. Various locating error occurs at the contact points were analysed for specified fixture configuration and error tolerance. Based on the information provided for the workpiece, a genetic algorithm based approach is applied to determine the most statically stable fixture configuration from a large number of possible candidates. The preliminary implementation is introduced to demonstrate the ability of GA under two different types of error definitions in automated fixture design.

Keywords: Genetic Algorithm, Fixture design optimisation

1   Introduction

Fixture arrangement optimisation is critical in the development of an automated fixture design (AFD) system [1]. When deriving the optimal layout of fixture elements, it is important to reduce the impact of fixture-workpiece error. The AFD is required to coordinate a set of locator points on workpiece surfaces such that the component is completely restrained during manufacturing procedures such as, machining, assembly and inspection etc. The designing of such fixture is complex and it relies significantly on the designer's expertise and experience, hence to ensure high quality fixture design is costly and there is no assurance that the results is optimal or near optimal.

A Number of literatures indicates a general consensus that genetic algorithm (GA) is capable of creating fixture design and thought to have the potential to improve existing fixture design. In addition, GA is able to reduce the dependency on human designer expertise to produce high quality fixture design [2]. Reasonable amount of computational time is required to execute GA search [3] but this mainly depended on the structure of the actual artificial chromosomes [4-6]. Since the GA deals with only the design variables and the objective function value (fitness function) for a particular fixture layout, no gradient to auxiliary information is needed, it allows implementation to be relatively straightforward and to provide easy manoeuvrability [1,4].

The fitness functions for GA applied in this study focusing on minimize errors in workpiece datum features, which are related to geometric variations that may exist in the physical datum features of the component before or after machining. The datum geometric variations will result in contact point errors between locators and workpiece. At present there are no standard ways to model a particular problem. This research compares two different types of errors that can occurs in workpiece datum features, in order to investigate which methods are more suitable for AFD, hence we developed two different approach to evaluate the same component using genetic algorithms.

2   Description of the Test Case

2D freeform component in the form of an aerofoil is chosen as test cases, users are allowed to input any monochrome photo or diagram as information source for the component. The component is to be restrained by three locators. The locating datum errors caused by workpiece errors may be analysed in two ways as illustrated in figures 1 and 2.

For the case 1 illustrated in figure 1, there are two distinctive types of localized errors in workpiece datum features, either the edge curved into the workpiece or bended out. For this research both types are modelled with semi-circle showed in fig 1.a. and fig 1.b. Black line is the original shape, grey semicircle represents the change of workpiece shape that would causes contact error. The amount of rotation required in order to adapt the errors in workpiece can be estimated by finding the rotational angle of workpiece around centre C, which can be obtained by finding point of interception for the normal line from the error free locator points L1 and L2. The rotational angle (α), which can represent the locating error, is the angle between the line C-L3 and tangential ray through centre C. Fig 1.d shows the change of position due to error in datum feature the component Black line is the original position before rotation and grey line represents the change of position due to error in datum feature, hence after rotation.

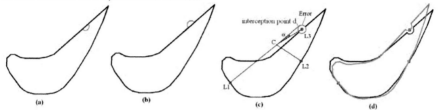

Fig. 1, Distinctive localized errors in workpiece datum features for investigation 1.

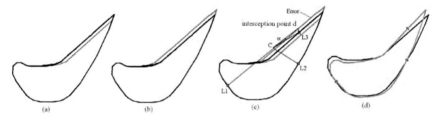

Fig. 2, Localized errors in workpiece datum features for investigation 2.

For the case 2 illustrated in figure 2,the localized errors in workpiece datum features are more close to real situations in manufacturing industry. Either the edge is lengthened or shortened then the expected length, both types are modelled with a grey line as showed in fig. 2.a. and fig2.b. Black outline is the original shape of the component; grey line represents the change of shape due to error in datum feature. The amount of rotation required in order to adapt the errors in workpiece can be estimated by finding the rotational angle of workpiece around centre C, which can be obtained by finding point of interception for the normal line from the error free locator points L1 and L2. The angle of intersection (α) is the angle between of line C – L3 and C – d, as illustrated in fig. 2.c. The next important posture is the interception point d, which is the interception point between normal of line C – L3 and error line. Fig. 2.d shows the component before and after rotation. Black outline is the original position, grey outline represents the change of position due the error.

For both cases, the aim is to derive the optimal layout of fixture elements to minimize the impact of fixture-workpiece errors using GA. In other word, the aim is to minimise the rotational angle caused by the workpiece shape errors. The effect of errors in component shape will only be considered if it occurs near or at any of locators points. Therefore some assumptions are made:

- The error occurs in the component are assumed to be relatively small, for investigation 1 the radius used is 0.02 mm and investigation 2 the distances with expected edge is ± 0.02 mm.
- Errors in the component can occur at any of the locators once at a time.

A feasible solution can be achieved by rotating the workpiece clockwise or anti clockwise.

3   Genetic Algorithm

Genetic algorithms are based on an analogy with biotic genetics and natural selection, it exploits the idea of the survival of the fittest and an interbreeding population abstracting the adaptation ability from nature to form a robust search mechanism to solve optimisation problems. It comprises a set of individual elements, which has known as the population and a set of biologically simulated operators to produces next generations. The fixture locator configuration optimisation was implemented using MATLAB® and genetic algorithm and direct search toolbox 1.0 [7]. The parameters used for this application was determined after trials with different combinations of mutation rate, crossover and selection methods.

Iterative process of GA start by creates the initial generations of solution (population size = 20). This process would continue until a predefined maximum number of generations are reached (100), or until there is no appreciable improvement in the fitness function after 40 consequent iterations. With each new generation, the populations are getting closer to an optimal layout. Once the search is complete, the best layout from the final general is taken as the optimal solution.

Constraint for solution:
(1) All three locators cannot be on the same side, or located one side with the same gradients.
(2) All three locators need to be in contact with the component before and after rotation to adapt localization error.

String representation and convert into solution: The string (artificial chromosomes) corresponds to locator positions based on ratio of the component perimeter from a reference point. Since there are only three locator points, the length of artificial chromosomes consists of three parameters. L1 meaning fixture locator number 1, L2 meaning fixture locator number 2 and L3 meaning fixture locator number 3. The encoded string for this research uses a real number between 0-1 to represent the locators' position in relation to the workpiece frame for the initial population as showed in fig. 3. In order to reduce the Hamming distances [8] of the coding structure some redundancy is introduced into the artificial chromosomes. The applied method adapted continuous looping search space technique. Although the initial population only uses a real number between 0-1 to represent the position of each locator, subsequence population could mutate to any real number, but it would still remain in the same problem space. Hence 1.34 would equal to 0.34 and –0.2 is equal to 0.8.

Constraint number 2 is already built into the individual solution this ensures all three locators are in contact with the component before and after rotation, hence locator position cannot be too close to the corner point. The minimum distance locator need to be away from the end of any side can be estimated by the degree of error deformation. Therefore feasible perimeter for positioning the locator is equal to perimeter subtracts the area that is too close to the edge.

| L1 | L2 | L3 |

(a)

| 0.4 | 0.04 | 0.9 |

(b)

. (a) Structure of the artificial chromosomes   (b) Example of artificial chromosomes.

Fig. 3. Artificial chromosomes used in genetic algorithm

Fitness function: The fixture layout evolution procedures has already briefly described in section 2. The fitness function would apply error to the locator one at a time until all three-locator points are checked. Three different assessments were used as the fitness value for each investigation:

- The smallest rotation for each individual from all locator point (MinMin)
- Maximum rotation for each individual from all locator point (MinMax)
- Average rotation for each individual from all locator point (MinAvg)

Selection: One of the issues often encountered with generic algorithm is premature convergence. A good solution found early in the search tends to grow in number exponentially over a few consecutive generations. As a result, the algorithm will limit the search space and unable to find better solution. To prevent this, a method of selection called roulette [7] was used. This method simulates roulette wheel, it chooses parents by corresponding an area in the wheel to an individual is proportional to the individual's fitness. The algorithm uses a random number to select one of the sections with a probability equal to its area.

Crossover: Crossover is the operator that creates next generation (offspring) of solution from parent locator configurations. In this application, intermediate operator, offspring parameters are obtained by taking a weighted average of the parents. The function creates the child from parent 1 and parent 2 using the following formula:

$$\text{child} = \text{parent1} + \text{rand} * \text{Ratio} * (\text{parent2} - \text{parent1}) \tag{1}$$

Ratio is weight represented by a single parameter. If all the entries of ratio lie in the range 0-1, the children produced are within the hypercube defined by placing the parents at opposite vertices. If ratio is not in that range, the children might lie outside the hypercube. If ratio is a scalar, then all the children lie on the line between the parents.

Mutation: Mutation is used to generate new parameters, thus it not only provides randomness and improvement to the search but also selects a parameter to altars the values, usually a very low probability. A new random number is generated from a uniform distribution with the range for that entry to replace the mutated parameter. Uniform mutation is applied for this research that consists of two-steps. First, the algorithm selects a fraction of the vector entries of an individual for mutation, where each entry has a probability of 0.4 being mutated. In the second step, the algorithm replaces each selected entry by a random number that selected uniformly from the range for 0-0.3.

4   Results and discussion

In order to compare and inspect the performance of GAs for different types of errors that occur in component datum features, 6 test cases were carried out each of which 10 trials were conducted. Table 1 and table 2 show summaries of the results for each test case, while fig. 5 and fig. 6 illustrated an example from each of the case. On average there is no significant improvement on the quality of the results yields after 80 generation. The result for investigation 1 is presented in table 1 and investigation 2 is presented in table 2. The fitness values yielded from all three assessments are very consistent, supported with the small value of standard deviation (SD).

There is a general consistence of yielding solutions in similar configurations for both of the methods of representing different types of error, as shown in fig. 5 and 6. Black dots in the diagram represent the positions of the locators, which suggest that the applied genetic algorithms are searching toward the optimal solution and are getting very close to finding the best possible fixture locator configuration for a specified component.

Comparing this research work with other known results it clearly shows the 'MinMax' assessment method in investigation 2 have the best match with the optimal solution, which is obtained by complete problem space search result [9]. The reason for investigation 2 performs better mainly due to the fact that the method applied in modelling component datum feature errors is similar to real situation.

Table 1, Summary results for investigation 1

	Investigation 1 (all units in radian)		
	MinMin	MinMax	MinAvg
Mean	0.0000104	0.0000141	0.0000102
SD	0.0000012	0.0000039	0.0000021

Table 2, Summary results for investigation 2

	Investigation 2 (all units in radian)		
	MinMin	MinMax	MinAvg
Mean	0.0000326	0.0000344	0.0000324
SD	0.0000005	0.0000044	0.0000005

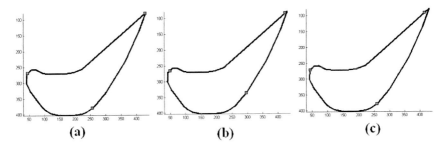

(a) (b) (c)

Fig. 4. Example result for investigation 1. (a) MinMin. (b) MinMax. (c) MinAvg.

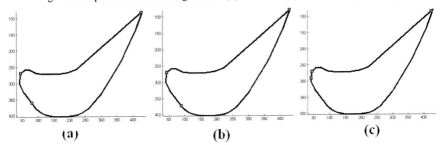

(a) (b) (c)

Fig. 5. Example result for investigation 2. (a) MinMin. (b) MinMax. (c) MinAvg.

At present this research only solves the locators configuration for 2D freeform component, the same evaluation methods can be extended to take into consideration of minimizing the clamping forces. In addition it could even be applied on optimisation for 3d component fixture design.

Further investigations can be carried out specifically in fine-tuning for the performance of GAs, by experiment with different GA parameters and different coding schemes for the artificial chromosomes. Performances are measured in terms of efficiency as well as quality of the final solution. Hence yield the most repeatable solution using least amount of computational time as well as reaches optimal solution with least amount of generation and population size.

5   Conclusion

The fixture optimisation using genetic algorithm has been proven effective at finding high quality solutions, which could be integrated into industry automated fixture design (AFD). The paper has discussed two variations of modelling component datum feature errors in application of GA, demonstrated the robustness of GA. However out of the two cases discussed, investigation case 2 was seen to be more promising in yielding an optimum solution that also satisfied the total constraint condition.

There are sufficient amount of studies confirm that genetic algorithms are capable of creating high quality fixture designs and have the potential to improve existing fixture designs. This will reduce the dependency on human designer expertise to produce high quality fixture designs even for complex components.

References

[1]   N. H. Wu, K.C. Chan: A genetic algorithm based approach to optimal fixture configuration. Computers & Industrial Engineering. Vol. 31 (1996) pp. 919-924

[2]   V. Subramaniam, A. Senthil Kumar, K.C. Seow: Conceptual Design of Fixtures using Genetic Algorithms. The International Journal of Advanced Manufacturing Technology. Volume 15 (1999) pp. 79-84

[3]   B. Li, B.W. Shiu: Principle and Simulation of Fixture Configuration Design for Sheet Metal Assembly with Laser Welding. Part 2: Optimal Configuration Design with the Genetic Algorithm. The International Journal of Advanced Manufacturing Technology. Volume 18 (2001) pp. 276-284

[4]   K. Krishnakumar, N. Melkote, N. Shreyes: Machining fixture layout optimization using the genetic algorithm. International Journal of Machine Tools and Manufacture. Volume 40 (1999) pp. 579-598

[5]   S. Vallapuzha, E. D. De Meter, S. Choudhuri, R.P. Khetan: An investigation of the effectiveness of fixture layout optimization methods. International Journal of Machine Tools and Manufacture. Volume 42 (2002) pp. 251-263

[6]   S. Vallapuzha, E. D. De Meter, S. Choudhuri, R. P. Khetan: An investigation into the use of spatial coordinates for the genetic algorithm based solution of the fixture layout optimization problem. International Journal of Machine Tools and Manufacture. Volume 42 (2002) pp. 265-275

[7]   Genetic Algorithms and Direct Search Toolbox

http://www.mathworks.com/access/helpdesk/help/toolbox/gads/index.html

Last check: 8 November 2005

[8]   R. Hillier: Genetic algorithms: AN investigation into Novel evolution methods with particulate reference to the De Jong test suite, Dissertations. University of Derby (1999)

[9]   X. Chen, Y. Wang, Q. Liu, N. Gindy: A method of clamping optimization for machining fixture. Proceedings of the 34th International MATADOR conference. (2004) pp. 51-56

Characterization of the surface functionality on precision machined engineering surfaces

Najmil Faiz Mohamed Aris and Kai Cheng

School of Engineering and Design, Brunel University, Uxbridge UB8 3PH, Middlesex, United Kingdom

Email: Najmil.Aris@brunel.ac.uk, Kai.Cheng@brunel.ac.uk

Abstract. The surfaces characterization of a component generated from the machining process is important as the surfaces have significant effects on the performance of the component and associated product. The work presented aims to investigate the surfaces functionality characterization of a component by using 3D surface parameters. The paper also investigates the surface generation related with machining process and the associated functionality formation. The corresponding surfaces characterization is investigated with two case studies on typical engineering components. The generation of the sample surfaces and associated surface functionalities are also studied by computer modelling and simulation. The relationship between surface characterization and surface functionality are further studied by computer simulations. The paper concludes with discussions on the applications and potential of this approach for the achievement of high quality surfaces, optimization and control of their functional performance at the manufacturing stage.

Keywords: Surface functionality, 3D Surface roughness, 3D Surface texture, Precision machining

Introduction

Surface characterization is becoming important for engineering surfaces because there is a high demand of components with precision surface within precision industry such as, precision ball screws, gears, bearings, etc. The invention and continuous development of 3D surface parameters made it possible to inspect and characterize the surfaces in a comprehensive manner. Parallel with the improvement of measurement instrument, whereas the manufacturing tools are continuously being improved, using the surface characterization parameters describes surface functionality becoming essential for miniature and micro precision components in particular.

The visualisation of surface texture and profile is still the common method to inspect workpieces and their surfaces for quality control. It also makes functional tests to ensure the functionality as required. Therefore, there is a strong need for the development of new surface parameters and for embedding the physical, chemical and machining related properties. There are only few researchers studying the effect of machining process variables on the surface functionality formation [1]. In this paper the characteristics of the surface functionality generated from precision turning processes is investigated with an integrated modelling approach. The functionality effects of surface generated are further studied by the simulation and machining trials

Surface functionality generated from the machining

The definition of the surface functionality is different from the operational performance of the surfaces. For instance, the tribogical functionality will become dominant when the translational surfaces are used such as the surfaces of the bearing inner and outer rings and slideways. The joint stiffness, contact and adhesion functionality will behave significantly for static contact surface, such as optical mirrors and precision lenses [2]. Therefore precision machining of the component/product surfaces must be conducted with close attention on their functionalities rather than just using tolerance and 2D surface roughness as in conventional machining process [3,5].

137

The amount of parameters for surface characterisation plays an important role in industrial metrology. Starting with the clear definition of functional surface from both metrology and machining process variables are selected, the measurement and machining will then be responsible for the structure of the parameter set, containing specific surface parameter and functionality. This approach ensures that the functionality and parameters optimally match the needs and functional demand of the component, as illustrated in Figure 1.

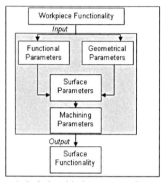

Figure 1. Relationship between surface functionality and process parameters

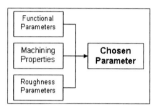

Figure 2. Classification of parameters

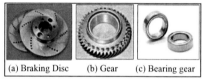

| (a) Braking Disc | (b) Gear | (c) Bearing gear |

Figure 3. Component generated from the machining

In the classification the surface parameters are categorized into three groups as listed in Figure 2. It is useful to use multiple parameters to describe the surface functionality of the sample, although in most cases only a few of them are really suitable.

Functional parameters refer to the specific demands on the functionality of the component. For instance, the surfaces on a braking disc, gear tooth or bearing rings have huge tribological indications on wear resistance, lubrication, friction, etc, in the light of the surface texture, topography and profile. The effects of the machining process show enormous variations in the surface of the sample component. It is obvious that each surface can be represented by a set of parameters that describe the particular nature of the machining process and tooling geometry. Modified 3D surface roughness parameters can be used for a general characterization of the surface topography and texture, particularly for the components as shown in Figure 3.

Characterization of the surface functionality

The complexity of surface functionalities characterization is obvious since the deflection of the machine tool and workpiece, vibration, chatter, the flexibility of the machine, the error in the slideway, etc, will all leave their signatory marks on the machined surfaces and will affect the surface functionality formation. Indeed, the surface conveys a vast amount of information, which can be used to identify the machining system dynamics and thus adaptively control the machining process as well. The characterization of surface functionality should clarify the information and the effects on the functional performance of the component [4, 6].

After defining the functional property of the component, having chosen the measurement tools and determining the parameter set, a minimum number of parameters is chosen which optimally describes the function of the component. Table 1 lists some surface functionalities in term of wear, friction, lubrication and fatigue in relation which significant 2D/3D surface parameters. Some of them are significant parameter linking to the functional performance of the component.

Functionalities	Parameters	Height	Distribution & Shape	Slope & Curvature	Length & Peak Space
Wear, Friction	2D	Ra, Rq, Rt	Rsk, Rku	$R\Delta a, R\Delta q$	$R\lambda a, R\lambda q$
Lubrication, Fatigue	3D	Sz, Sq	Ssk, Sku, Ssc	$S\Delta q, Ssc$	Sal, Sdr

Table 1. The functional performance and roughness parameters

Modelling approach and simulation

Modelling
Figure 4 illustrates the modelling approach, which includes tooling geometry, Sku 3D kurtosis modelling, machine parameter modelling, operation condition model and surface functionality modelling. The machining parameter and tooling geometry, such as tool rake angle and clearance angle, are inputs to the operation condition model. The 3D surfaces are generated in the interactions between the cutting tool and workpiece in the cutting zone. The effects of machining variables and tooling geometry on the surface generation can therefore be analytically studied to the extent of surface texture, topography, roughness and functionality. Proposed surface functionality modelling is a result of mixing the three main elements. The generated surface functionality heavily depends on tooling geometry and process variables described as follows:

$$Sfc \approx Ct + Mc \tag{1}$$

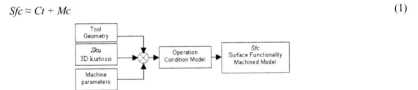

Figure 4. Modelling surface generation to control surface functionality

Sfc is straight forward Sku parameter to be used to describe and evaluate the machined surfaces in term of the surface contact functionality. It should be noted that the equation does not take account of any machining errors. So it is a surface generation model under the ideal conditions. Ct representing the cutting tool details include nose radius, initial side rake angle, side clearance angle, back rake angle and back clearance angle.

Sku is the mean for Kurtosis of Topography Height Distribution. This is a measure of the peakedness or sharpness of the surface height distribution. It is given by the formula:

$$S_{ku} = \frac{1}{MNS_q^4}\sum_{j=1}^{N}\sum_{i=1}^{M}\eta^4(x_i, y_j)$$ (2)

This parameter characterizes the spread of the height distribution. Referring to Figure 5, a Gaussian surface has a kurtosis value of 3. A centrally distributed surface has a kurtosis value larger than 3 whereas the kurtosis of a well spread distribution is smaller than 3. For some practical engineering surfaces, e.g. ground, honed and plateau honed surfaces, the existence of outliers (pits and troughs) may cause very large values of kurtosis, sometimes achieving a value of over 100.

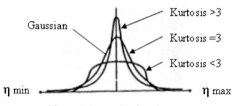

Figure 5. Kurtosis of surfaces

As explained, the illustrated model needs to identify the affecting factors and to model those factors which will contribute to the surface generation of functionality. Those factors will be the inputs to the investigation of the relationship between the three element models. The outputs will include 3D surface topography characterization parameters and surface functionality parameters.

Simulation

Simulation of the surface functionality simulates the relationship between tooling geometry, process variables and surface parameters generated from the process. Based on MATLAB and Simulink, the surface generation modelling can be implemented step by step. The whole simulation model of the surface generation implemented with MATLAB/Simulink programming as shown in Figure 6.

The green blocks represent affecting factors and the red blocks stand for indirect affecting factors. Those indirect affecting factors are connected with the machining process module by some Manual Switch which is light blue block. It is convenient to add or remove indirect affecting factor during the simulation process. The machining process module includes cutting force model (the dark blue blocks), vibration model (red block) and tool wear model (light blue block). The details of implementation of these models are hidden in the respective subsystems within the whole models hierarchy. Machining response pink block is constructed by using Transfer Function blocks in Simulink. The output is orange blocks consists of dynamic displacements for the tooling system and residual stress subsystem.

140

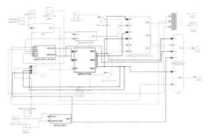

Figure 6. Modelling implementation in MATLAB/Simulink

Simulink provides an easy way to use Transfer Function Block. To implement the machining system response model, the user can only change the parameters in the Transfer Function Block according to the modal parameters of the machining system. The regenerative vibration is simulated by Variable Transport Delay function block since it results in the variation of feed rate and depth of cut in the real machining process. Acquiring inputs from material thermal properties and operation conditions, the temperature rise at the interface between tool flank face and machined surface can be simulated.

Machining trials

Experiments were conducted on a turning machine (Harrison M250). The machining trial setup is shown in Figure 7. The cutting process vibrations is measured by using Kistler Acoustic Emmission sensor, type 8152B, on which the carbide tool holder is mounted. The machined surfaces are measured with the surface profiler Zygo New View 5000 optical microscope, which is a general purpose three dimensional surface texture/topography analyzer. It provides non-contact, high resolution numerical measurement and analysis to accurately characterize the surface texture/topography of test parts. The steel sample components are machined in the experiments. The machining conditions are listed in Table 1. Machining trial results for Ra and RMS had shown in Table 2. Figure 8 shows the measurement results of 3D surface in the Zygo surface profiler.

Figure 7. Machining trial setup

Workpiece	Material	C50 steel
	Diameter (mm)	32
Cutting tool	Material	Carbide insert
	Nose radius(mm)	0.8
	Rake angle(°)	7
	Clearance angle(°)	0
Operation conditions	SpindleSpeed (rpm)	320-550
	Feedrate(mm/rev)	0.1
	Depth of cut (mm)	1,2,3,4

Table 1. Machining trial conditions

Work material: C50					Diameter: Ø32 mm	
Test No	Spindle speed (rpm)	Feed rate (mm/rev)	Depth of cut (mm)	Time (min)	Ra (µm)	RMS (mv)
1	320	0.1	1	2	0.3001	3.826
2	320	0.1	2	2	0.9430	8.168
3	320	0.1	2	2	0.2843	4.413
4	320	0.1	3	3.5	0.8087	9.671
5	320	0.1	3	5	0.2717	3.446
6	320	0.1	4	25sec	0.3707	4.594

Table 2. Surface roughness results by Zygo 3D surface profiler

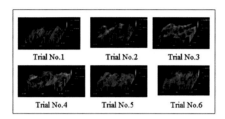

Figure 8. 3D surface results by Zygo 3D profiler

Conclusions

An integrated modeling approach is proposed to simulate the surface functionality generation in turning processes. The machined trials show the modelling approach can accurately present the machining process and the effects of machining process variables and surface generation. It is found that the depth of cut plays the significant role on the machined surfaces. Poor tooling structure can result in tool wear and poor surface as well as poor machined accuracy. The modelling approach and simulations are useful with particular references to the optimization of the machining process based on the product/component surfaces functionality requirements.

References

[1]   Y. Atlintas, (2000) Manufacturing Automation: Metal Cutting Mechanics, Machine Tool Vibrations and CNC Design. Cambridge University Press, Cambridge.

[2]   K. J. Stout and L. Blunt, (2000) Three Dimensional Surface Topography, Penton Press, London.

[3]   X. Luo, K. Cheng and R.Ward, The effect of machining process variables and tooling characterisation on the surface generation. Int J Adv Manuf Technol (2005) 25 : 1089-1097

[4]   X. K. Luo, K. Cheng, X. C. Luo and X.W. Liu, A simulated investigation on the machining instability and dynamic surface generation. Int J Adv Manuf Technol (2005) 25: 718-725

[5]   K. J. Stout and L. Blunt, (2000) Development of Method for the Characterisation of Roughness in three Dimensions. Penton Press, London.

[6]   C. Arcona and T. A. Dow, (1998) An empirical tool force model for precision machining. Trans ASME: J Manuf Sci Eng 120:700-707.

Operations
Management

Operational Schemes for Flexible Robotics

G. Schuh[1, a], F. Giehler [1, b], M. Schönung [1, c]

[1]Laboratory for Machine Tools and Production Engineering (WZL) at RWTH Aachen University
Steinbachstr. 19
D-52074 Aachen
Germany

[a]g.schuh@wzl.rwth-aachen.de, [b]f.giehler@wzl.rwth-aachen.de, [c]m.schoenung@wzl.rwth-aachen.de

Abstract. The combination of an increasing amount of variants and changing lot sizes provokes a lot of uncertainty and high initial costs for the users of automation technology. On the one hand the application of conventional automation solutions is not flexible enough for the processing of small lot sizes. On the other hand manual manufacturing is too expensive, especially in high-wage countries. This development demands new automation solutions. This article presents a technological and organisational concept that allows for the development of solutions for automation which is modular and flexible in space and can be rented by industrial users. By means of the concept presented in this paper it is possible to meet the increasing demands in the field of automation.

Keywords: Industrial Services, Cooperative Services, Flexible Assembly Systems.

Introduction

For companies, which are manually producing small series with a high variety of assembled parts such as gear boxes, clutches or electric motors, the main problem is to combine flexibility and efficiency. Especially German and European companies are characterised by flexibility in the worldwide market. The implementation of automatic systems would limit or even reduce this unique selling proposition (USP). Moreover, investment costs due to uncertain sales forecasts entail financial risks. Due to this small and medium-sized companies often are hesitant to use automation – they do not have the necessary lot-sizes to exploit the commercial advantages of the stationary robotic equipment. A quite paradoxical risk results from this: Sophisticated assembly with a lot of variants can only be processed in low wage countries, whereas assembly with little variation that can easily be automated remains in Europe.

Companies tend to recruit cheap temporary workers instead of using automation technologies. However, the problem here is that it is hard to find qualified workers and on-the-job training absorbs time and is no option for a short-term staff.

To keep their position in the global competition, the companies' dependency on staff that is available on short notice has to be reduced. Conventional systems of automation cannot solve this problem, because they are not flexible enough for small series. To compensate for variation of capacity, flexible automation is needed, which can be used temporarily. Today these systems are not used because the following problems can occur:

1. There are no operating schemes with an adequate infrastructure for the use of automated assembly systems for an economically efficient short-time application.
2. Today there are no adequate technical conditions for a highly flexible use of automation on the basis of conventional industrial robotics. The same is true for the integration of modular peripheral equipment such as grippers, separating units and automated supply.

Operational Schemes for Flexible Robotics

The fundamental relevance of operating schemes in mechanical and manufacturing systems engineering has been proven by successful realisation.

Important for the effective use of operating schemes are the organisational structures which should be subject to the operated product. The companies to be considered as users and customers are mainly small and medium-sized companies. A large number of these companies run a manual assembly and, therefore have no experience in the design, establishing and application of robotic systems. Therefore, a provider of such systems should offer most of these functions as services. The suppliers for technical systems have the competencies, but the majority do not possess enough capacity and organisational structures to offer these services. The traditional business model of these suppliers comprises that they produce and sell goods in order to promptly get paid. An application of these new operating schemes means that operation and utilisation is paid in stead of selling. This leads to later returns and makes it necessary to develop new ways of financing. [1, 2]

Considering operation schemes that are used for the utilisation and commercialisation of modular systems for production automation, one can deduce two dimensions: The dimension of the provision of benefit for the users (the vertical dimension in figure 1) and the financial dimension (horizontally displayed in figure 1).

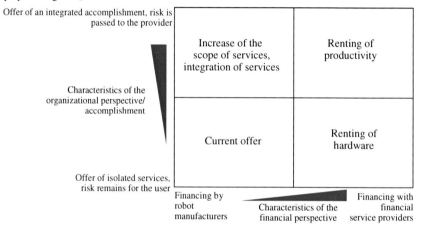

Fig. 1: Organisational and financial perspective as two dimensions of operating schemes

The dimension of the provision of benefit for the users shows how benefit can be generated. The organisational solutions are essential for the use of modular systems for automation of production. They are used to actualise the utilisation and to provide the related services. [3] The trend develops from the leasing of hardware and single services to the leasing of full systems including application on site with guaranteed availability and productivity. To meet individual demands, suppliers must be able to offer individual system bundles and services. Therefore, an architecture for the value-added chain is necessary, taking into account the creation of benefit, the relative processes and the internal and external organisation. Emphasis should be on how suppliers offer their services. A good example is an operating company that independently uses rental robots. This company can be a subsidiary of a manufacturer of robotics or a joint venture comprised of several manufacturers. For the configuration of the architecture both the planning and design of the product in the operating scheme and its use as a part of a fleet of robots has to be considered.

In figure 1 the financial dimension shows how the technical systems can be financed and commercialised and how prices for the utilisation can be estimated. The design of the earning-model includes the fleet management with the relevant mechanisms of earnings and the definition of prices and the cost structure of the operation scheme. In addition the providers (suppliers, manufacturers of robotics, service companies), the users and the financial realisation are integrated into the model. In this connection it is essential to consider the different abilities of potential providers. Most of the present business models such as manufacturers of robots and peripheral equipment depend on the payment after completion and on site installation of the system. Even for a temporary finance companies oftentimes need a financial service provider, in particular when the return flow for the produced system is received during the lifecycle of the product – For the realisation of this concept either the formation of an operating company as an element of the financial dimension or the sale-and-lease-back of technical systems is possible. The later is shown in figure 2.

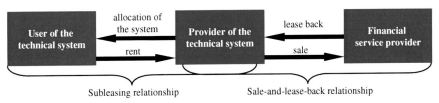

Fig. 2: relationships between users and providers of technical systems and financial service providers

In both cases the manufacturer of the automation system would sell his system, but ensure his returns. The operating company or alternatively the leasing company has to finance the system during its lifecycle. The leasing revenue must cover the costs of production, the costs of the temporary financing and the organisation costs of the leasing business. There are additional costs for services such as planning of an individual production of a user with such a system, the installation of the system, programming and maintenance. However, these costs can be balanced immediately with the user and need no temporary financing. Another aspect is pricing: Conventional models such as the leasing with payment which depends on the available time or innovative pay-per-piece models are possible. [4] These models have to take into account the individual demands of the users. Consequently, offers have to be customised that are optimal for both the user and the provider of the system. Moreover, the concept has to correspond with this consideration of user and provider and the definition of the optimal arrangement.

The previous offerings of automation system manufacturers consist of robots and additional services. The expenses for the production of robots are covered by their selling. Concerning this business model, there are two possible directions to develop a portfolio of offerings: On the one hand the selling can be replaced by a renting. This means an innovation of the financial dimension. On the other hand the amount of services and responsibility can be increased. This means an innovation of the organisational dimension. The combination of these dimensions results in the business model 'renting productive production capacity to the user'. According to this business model the provider can decide how to realise the productivity. The users are only qualified to the contractually guaranteed features of the manufacturing system. This includes that neither an insufficient construction results in less output nor that technical problems result in stoppages.

These characteristics entail a different allocation of risks between provider and user of the systems. If the provider takes the responsibility for a running system, he also takes the risk of production stoppages, and in case of stoppages he has to compensate the user. In this case the user is secured concerning risks that he cannot influence. The allocation of risks and the allocation of performance- and payment obligation have to be balanced. For this, methods to evaluate risks can be helpful tools. The balancing should be performed in such a way that the party being responsible for something can decide how much effort is sufficient to achieve the intended results. When a party did not manage a process, the other party is not disadvantaged, respectively will receive full compensation for the disadvantage. This is an important difference in comparison to conventional contracts, in which the client often defines long terms of safety without using the system at all.

3 MODULAR AUTOMATION IN ASSEMBLY

The assembly is the last step in product creation and can be considered as a kind of reservoir, where all of the product variants occur. [5] According to the industry sector, 20% - 70% of the total costs of production itself occur in assembly. An economical production needs an assembly that is adaptable to special situations. Consequentially, a mobile, modular and highly flexible robot system, which can be adapted to the requirements of certain tasks in assembly, is substantial.

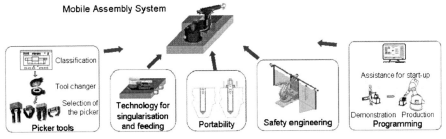

Fig. 3: Parts of a Mobile Assembly System

Figure 3 shows important aspects of such a system. Constitutive for such a system is an easy transport to the application location. It should be possible to transport the system within the production location and also to other locations outside of the company. [6] All parts must either be transported in a ready-for-operation status or allow a convenient and quick start-up procedure. If an in-ground fixture is necessary, it must be easily realisable to meet the demands on a mobile system. In this context an important aspect is safety devices, which do not physically separate robots and workers. A possible way to solve the conflict of safety requirements and mobility are safeguard systems that are scanning the local boundaries of the system with light or laser.

The gripper and feeding technology is an important component of an assembly system. According to recent studies, 60%-90% of the market share for grippers can be covered with standardised gripper systems. [7] These standard grippers can have different functions that improve flexibility such as devices for an easy change and fast setting-up or functions to control the modulation of the gripper. For an easy application of gripper technology, a method is needed, that supports the adjustment of conventional grippers to applications which can only be managed with individual grippers. A standardisation of grippers with a modular kit for the gripper elements would be first step. With such a kit it is possible to run a lot of different applications with a manageable amount of elements. To develop a standard-gripper, a classification of manufacturing tasks is helpful. Moreover, for an assembly tasks that requires different grippers, a station for changing tools should be integrated. Small parts such as screws and bolts are often delivered as bulk parts, which is a reason for the importance of the feeding system - these parts need to be isolated and fed to the assembly tool. The requirements of the feeding system are chiefly depending on the different applications, so that a modular design and adaptability is substantial.

For a fast start-up procedure it is essential to simplify the programming of the robotics. Using conventional software for online- or offline-programming would make this procedure long and complex. By means of one software tool that comprises both common and customised functions, the time for initial training for different software systems could be saved; therefore, all programming functions have to be made available to the operator by an intuitive user interface. For potential errors in implemented routines, assistance for detecting and fixing these has to be included.

To achieve this objective, a laboratory prototype of an assembly system will be designed and built, which is capable of performing sample assembly tasks. The results concerning robot, the gripper system, the feeding, the programming, and the technical support for the operator, will help to design a software system that will have the desired features. To validate the system, it will be implemented at the locations of potential users and field tested for real assembly tasks. Finally, in an evaluation of the conducted pilot tasks, a lot of important information on the quality, the calculation of costs, lead time, the starting up, the operation and the performance of the technical system will be gathered.

4   SUMMARY

The approach presented in this paper offers a chance for users to balance the short-term demand of capacity in assembly by means of modular, mobile and flexible robotics systems. Thus, automation will no longer be a solution for mass production only, but mean an increased flexibility of small and medium-sized companies. As a result, the presented concept opens up new markets for providers of robots and peripheral systems. Especially companies, which did not use robotics yet because of the inevitable reduction of flexibility, can be acquired as users.

This approach has been developed in the co-operative project "Rent-A-Robot". The project is guided by the Project Management Agency Forschungszentrum Karlsruhe – Production and Manufacturing Technologies Division (PTKA-PFT). It is financed by the German Federal Ministry of Education and Research (BMBF). The co-operation of the Laboratory for Machine Tools and Production Engineering (WZL) at RWTH Aachen University with small and medium-sized companies ensures a concentration of competencies concerning all relevant aspects. The co-operating companies benefit from the large scale advantages and economic profits of this approach. The successful implementation of the prototype is expected to have an enourmous impact on those companies, who did not use automation yet.

5   REFERENCES

[1]   Lay, G., 2003, Betreiben statt Verkaufen - Häufigkeit des Angebots von Betreibermodellen in der deutschen Investitionsgüterindustrie, ISI, Karlsruhe.
[2]   Michalas, N., 2003, Methodik zur Gestaltung von nachhaltigen Nutzungskonzepten im Maschinen- und Anlagenbau, Diss. RWTH Aachen.
[3]   Schuh, G., Friedli, T., Gebauer, H., 2004, Fit for Service, München.
[4]   Mast, W. 2004, Pay on Production - langfristige Partnerschaft mit Verantwortungstransfer. In: Meier, H. (ed.), 2004, Dienstleistungsorientierte Geschäftsmodelle im Maschinen- und Anlagenbau, Springer, Berlin.
[5]   Licha, A., 2003, Flexible Montageautomatisierung zur Komplettmontage flächenhafter Produktstrukturen durch kooperierende Roboter, Meisenbach, Erlangen.
[6]   Stopp, A., Baldauf, T., Hantsche, S., 2002, The Manufacturing Assistant: Safe, Interactive Teaching of Operation Sequences. In: Proceedings of the 11th IEEE Int. Workshop on Robot and Human interactive Communication, ROMAN2002, Berlin, 386-391.
[7]   Widmann, W., 2004, Trends im Bereich der Werkstückhandhabung, Produktion 32/33: 15-16.

Ramp-up time reduction in high volume production

B. Denkena, C. Ammermann and P. Kowalski

Institute of Production Engineering and Machine Tools,

Schoenebecker Allee 2, 30823 Garbsen, Germany

Phone: ++49 511 762 2533

Fax: ++49 511 762 5115

info@ifw.uni-hannover.de

Abstract. For many companies an important issue is the reduction of ramp-up time. Especially during the ramp-up phase in high volume production clear procedures and methods assigned to them are important factors. This paper presents results of the German research project "Ramp-Up/2", which aims at significantly reducing the time to the planned production output. As a part of this research several production and machine ramp-ups within different plants of the manufacturing industry were analyzed. Incidents such as failures, disturbances or delays during the ramp-up process have been acquired and assigned to different causes. The results validated the assumption that -among others- cooperation of many partners involved in the processes of construction, delivery and assembly of production-equipment offers enormous room for improvements.

Keywords: Production ramp-up, High-volume production, Analysis of delays

Introduction

A smooth and quick ramp-up of production equipment means reduced costs for all companies involved. Due to customer demands an increasing number of variants and product derivates has been developed and launched especially in the automotive industry. Thus manufacturers have to cope with an increasing number of production-ramp-ups in the last decade. Lost sales and the use of capital-intensive production equipment are only two facts indicating that companies have to minimize the time-to-market and therewith costs of production ramp-ups [1,2]. In addition production ramps-ups are typically characterized by the participation of one or more machine-manufacturers, suppliers of further production-equipment and of course the user of the production system. This paper presents results of the development of a new ramp-up solution. As a first step a survey on several production ramp-ups has been carried out. It reveals typical failures occurring during the ramp-up in high-volume production manufacturing. The causes of these failures point out potential for optimisation of several kinds.

State of the art

Yet only little effort has been spent to quantify ramp-up-problems for certain industrial branches. A qualitative comprehensive survey has been accomplished in German industry in the year 2002 [2]. Ramp-up scenarios are said to be dependent on the degree of novelty of both, product and dedicated production facilities. With the help of interviews and workshops areas for further improvements have been suggested. These are organization, ramp-up-robust production systems, change-management, cooperation as well as staff-qualification. Similar potentials are stated in [3]. With the exception of staff-qualification, they have been identified to be critical during the ramp-up of a single product on an existing labour-intensive assembly line in a medium-sized manufacturing company.

151

Project Overview

Attending and analyzing the production ramp-up represent the first step within the German research project "Ramp-Up/2". The upper part of Fig. 1 shows the current ramp-up process of production machines and machine-tools from development, assembly and commissioning in the machine manufacturer's plant, disassembly and delivery to the user, assembly and integration into the production environment, commissioning, start-up and production at last. The lower part shows the visionary ramp-up process with a virtual commissioning substituting the first assembly, commissioning and disassembly steps and reducing the time-need of commissioning and start-up.

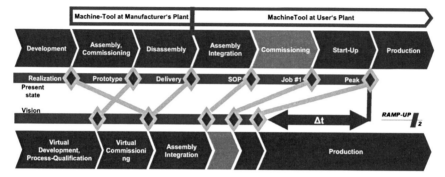

Figure 1: Incidents during production ramp-up

To realize this vision tools are developed that enable process-qualification, operator training, simulation of operating-modes and disturbance-scenarios on the one hand side. On the other hand methods for functional verification and the fast ramp-up of automated manufacturing systems are developed. With the help of these tools, the milestones of delivery to the costumer and realization of the machine will be consolidated. The following analysis, accomplished at the beginning of the project work, enables to estimate the impact of using virtual commissioning tools. In addition it points out important problems to bear in mind for the development of a reference scheme which integrates the new virtual tools into a new ramp-up process.

Survey

Investigation area and methodology. To identify typical failures occurring, the ramp-up processes of three new production lines have been attended in each machine-user's plant. Table 1 describes these lines, the machines they contain and the products manufactured. All production-facilities considered, manufacture new products on a different number of machines. In opposite to line number three, the lines number one and two are equipped with an interlinked material flow system.

To analyze the disturbances, a „Notice of Incident" has been used. A similar method has been already used successfully to check maintenance activities [4]. Whenever an incident causes a delay during the course of the ramp-up, the circumstances are logged into a single card. Besides the time and place of the disturbance the exact component of the machine or line affected is recorded. Possible causes of the incident (from the workers point of view) and the resulting clearance and delay times are requested. It is possible to enter additional information in textual format as well.

Line		Product	Machine types
1	Inter-linked	Spindle carrier	Rotary indexing machine, Measuring station, Washing station.
2	Inter-linked	Shaft	Vertical lathes, Inductive hardening station, Re-cooling station, Straightener, Cold-roll machine.
3	Non-inter-linked	Cylinder head	Machining centres.

Table 1: Machines examined

Incidents during the ramp up of line one have been logged from the end of the assembly in the user's plant to the beginning of the start-up (refer to Fig. 1). The assembly/integration and commissioning phases of lines two and three have been considered. In this way information on the core steps of the ramp-up process of different production machines and supporting equipment have been gathered. During the investigation time incidents have been reported by an overall number of thirteen machines.

Results. Additional interviews with ramp-up-staff verified that most of the failures occur during the commissioning phase in opposition to the start-up phase where the number of incidents is decreasing significantly. Simple machines or others that have been previously supplied by the same company reveal only little problems whereas complex or new developed equipment is responsible for the majority of cases. Different numbers of disturbances occurred which depend on the ramp-up progress and the type of machine. Figure 2 shows all incidents reported.

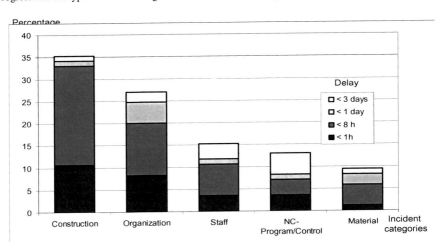

Figure 2: Incidents during production ramp-up

Most disturbances are issues of construction, organisation, staff and NC-programs. Considering the delay following each disturbance it turns out that the same order of issues is responsible for most small and medium delays of up to eight hours duration time. Contrary to this, most of the long-lasting delays are part of the categories NC-program/control followed by staff-related failures. Differentiation between machining centres and linked production lines shows that staff, organization and construction are main causes for disturbances of the latter equipment category whereas NC-programs and devices (these are members of the "construction"-group) cause the majority of problems during the ramp-up of machining centres.

To avoid disturbances in future ramp-up procedures, the causes of incidents have been contemplated further with a Failure-Methods-Effects-Analysis (FMEA). Based on the results of this analysis the causes of the incidents have been cumulated to groups: About 40% of all failures can be prevented by strengthened and continuous coordination and cooperation. 30 % are preventable by the use of planning, development and simulation tools. About 10 % of all incidents would not have been caused by better-trained staff. Thus an overall number of 85% of all disturbances is considered to be avoidable. The number of causes remaining is either caused by human errors (5 %) or can not be traced back (10 %).

Conclusion. Technical problems directly linked to the complex machines like construction issues of devices or other machine parts and the machine control are responsible for the majority of disturbances. The great number of participants - staff of different suppliers, service providers and the machine user – make a well-organized ramp-up procedure necessary. Due to the fact that the technicians and operators are not familiar with the new production equipment, the construction site in the user's plant represents an environment encouraging the appearance of human failures. According to the literature stated above and the recent survey represented in this paper, the recorded failure scheme for the ramp-up of new complex production equipment is considered to be typical for high-volume production.

Summary and Outlook

Several production ramp-up processes of different complex production lines have been analyzed. Failures have been logged and cumulated to the categories construction, organization, staff, NC-program and material. These causes have been identified to be representative for a failure scheme that typically delays production ramp-up processes in high-volume production.

Based on this scheme new tools and methods are currently developed to improve the future ramp-up procedure. In addition to the analysis present in this paper, critical processes have been monitored and a new guideline for the cooperated virtual production ramp-up is currently developed. It is based on the generic PEK-Process scheme developed at IFW [5] and will be extended for use in a cooperated virtual production ramp-up. A first prototype already has been integrated into a standard collaboration system. In this way it will be able to coordinate all participants of production ramp-ups. In combination with further virtual simulation tools up to 85% of the logged failures are expected to be avoided.

References

[1]   A. Roth (2005): Perspectives for the European automotive industry - Zukunftsperspektiven für die europäische Automobilindustrie. Automobile-Congress, Ruhr- University Bochum, Germany.

[2]   A. Kuhn, H.-P. Wiendahl, W. Eversheim and G. Schuh (2002,in German) Fast ramp up: Schneller Produktionsanlauf von Serienprodukten. Verlag Praxiswissen, Dortmund, Germany

[3]   M. Berg, S. Fjällström, J. Stahre, K. Säfsten (2005) Production ramp-up in the manufacturing industry – Findings from a case study. Proceedings of 3rd International Conference on Reconfigurable Manufacturing, Ann Arbor, MI, USA

[4]   H.-K. Tönshoff, A. Seufzer (1998) Planning and controlling of maintenance activities. Proceedings of 2nd International Conference on Engineering, Design and Automation, Hawaii, USA

[5]   B. Denkena, A. Brandes, R. Apitz (2004) Dimensioning technological interfaces regarding flow-oriented planning of manufacturing process chains, XV Workshop on Supervising and Diagnostics of Machining Systems,"Machine Tools and Factories of the Knowledge", Karpacz, Poland

Acknowledgements

The presented work is based on the "Ramp-Up/2" project which is funded as grant number 02PS2070 by the German Office for Education and Research (Bundesministerium für Bildung und Forschung - BMBF) and supervised by Forschungszentrum Karlsruhe. The authors would like to acknowledge these institutions for the offered support.
The Institute of Production Engineering and Machine Tools of Hannover University (IFW) is member of the I*PROMS Network of Excellence.

Enhancing New Process Introduction (NPI) within an SME manufacturer

I. Reid[1, a], H. Ismail[2, b] M. Rashid[3, c] S. MacLeod[4, d]

[1]Iain Reid Agility Centre, University of Liverpool, Liverpool, UK.

[2] Hossam Ismail Agility Centre, University of Liverpool, Liverpool, UK.

[3] Mustafa Rashid Agility Centre, University of Liverpool, Liverpool, UK.

[4]Stewart MacLeod Agility Centre, University of Liverpool, Liverpool, UK.

[a]reidi@liv.a.uk, [b]hsismail@liv.ac.uk, [c]mustafa.rashid2@virgin.net, [d]stewartmacleo20@hotmail.com

Abstract. This paper examines the issues related to the development and introduction of new manufacturing processes in SME's, specifically addressing two central questions. First, how can a Small Medium Enterprise (SME) introduce new manufacturing processes with rapid and effective implementation? Second, what are the fundamental project management steps necessary to enable SME's to respond successfully to the challenge of new technologies or process change? In order to overcome the problems associated with new product introduction (NPI), this paper describes some research work that has been carried out using the integrated definition method (IDEF) model to systematically integrate the NPI processes. Moreover, in order to illustrate the methodology, a SME case study company was invested to see how the NPI process is applied.

Keywords: Process, Introduction, IDEF, SME

1. Introduction

Manufacturers have continually been under pressure to adopt new processes and technologies, with shorter product life cycles, greater demands on manufacturing flexibility, and ever increasing intensity of global competition. This environment has driven firms to strive for more responsive manufacturing technologies and techniques. This paper introduces a model which supports the management of new process introduction (NPI) in terms of the resources available, the constraints on the organisation in order to satisfy the process requirements for the new system or process. First, the stages of NPI are examined by using IDEF methodologies. Second, project uncertainties when introducing new manufacturing processes are examined. The model thus provides both theoretical and managerial insights into the critical phases between manufacturing flexibility and process capability decisions. Finally, the implications of a specific NPI project within a Small Medium Enterprise (SME) will be explored.

2. Background

SME manufacturers are facing constant challenges in terms of process flexibility and manufacturing efficiency and ever changing supplier and demand patterns [1]. These demands often require companies to invest in new technologies in order to achieve flexibility and efficiency. There is always a degree of risk in the process of introducing new technologies and SME's by the nature of their size cannot afford to make mistakes. To minimise this risk a detailed review of the process as well as the selective technology is required. In some cases this process might entail a redesign of the required manufacturing equipment. The application of enterprise modelling tools can support this process as the technology's impact on the machine design can be assessed and managed without the need for costly prototypes and rework [3]. Furthermore, the NPI activities can be assessed in terms of reliability and uncertainty.

157

Due to the innovative nature are of a new process design, it is necessary that the NPI process starts with a clear of identification of the problem definition. This includes, in addition to requirements, the main technological and operational constraints that the process as to operate within. However, there is usually very little information available to managers to guide them through the decision-making process, and assist them with uncertainties of developing new processes or technologies. Therefore, a structured approach is one way of addressing such risks and uncertainties.

3. Research Methodology

There is a limited amount of research data that exists about NPI from both a practical and theoretical sense. In view of this, a case study approach was used that provides an empirical method of inquiry which enabled the researcher to investigate NPI process within a real life context using multiple resources of evidence. The researcher adopted an action research approach interacting with 'live' or on-going issues that allowed a focus on different aspects of the manufacturing process. The investigation was designed to identify the existing process characteristics. The action research approach also provided a unique perspective into all functions of company including sales and design prior to manufacturing process. Due to an expected surge in demand over the following 12 months it was also recognized, early in the project, that the introduction of the new process will require a structured approach in order to prevent costly delays due to maintenance and service reliability.

This project was coordinated via a 'knowledge transfer partnership' (KTP) programme between the University of Liverpool and Company partner. The programme is coordinated via a Department of Trade & Industry (DTI) grant for a period of two years.

4. Case Study: Company A

The company produces high quality sublimated mugs under license for a number of major retailers and organisations. The company's order winning criteria is achieved through the quality of the images on their products, achieved through the process of sublimation. The company has a graphic design department enabling the company to introduce new products with an extremely responsive lead time. However, this market is highly seasonal and the company is under pressure to respond quicker to customers during peak times as well as being restricted, due to process constraints, on a minimum order requirement. It can sell as much as it can make in high season, but the seasonality of the market imposes a constraint on how much the company can invest in new processes without fully utilising these facilities off peak. The introduction of the new technologies will have to adopt a 'step change' approach rather than incremental manufacturing change with new optimised manufacturing facilities.

4.1 The Approach for NPI:

Integration Definition for Function Modelling (IDEF) is a process mapping or modelling technique developed to facilitate process understanding, analysis, improvement, or reengineering processes [2, 3]. An IDEF approach was used to represent the NPI process and represents both the activities of the NPI and the required inputs, controls, outputs and methods. Figure 1 shows the first of several levels of the NPI model that contains the main activities.

The first step in IDEF modelling is thus concerned with establishing the objectives of the process from which a context and viewpoint can established. Moreover, this is a top-down method which starts from general activities and moves on to more specific issues, from a single page that represents an entire system to more detailed pages that explain how the subsections of the system work [4]. For this example these activities determine the general structure of the NPI process in terms of: process analysis, specification requirements, prototyping and testing, supplier selection manufacture, installation and commissioning.

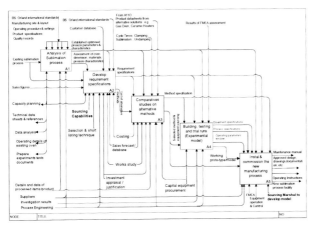

Figure 1 IDEF New Process Introduction model

4.2 Applicability of the technique

When dealing with the introduction of new processes with the company, the topic was to identify and monitor and analyse the process steps, the reliability of the outputs was key in terms of the front end activities in order to ensure the consecutive outputs were reliability and in accordance to the desired objectives of the specification and process parameters.

4.3 Analysis of the Process

The IDEF modeling approach was then extended by adding quantitative measures indicating the quality of each of the input entities (Input, Control, Tool) and the impact they have on the quality of the Output as shown in figure 2 below. The flowcharted activities were categorised as the following:

a. Robustness and risk assessment: The technique is a valuable tool to assess the robustness and sensitivity of the process to changes in the quality of inputs, controls and tools. The developed model can be used as a risk assessment tool whereby various scenarios are tested and the severity and impact of each on the success of the process is evaluated. Preventative action can then be identified and implemented.

b. Process improvement: The technique can also be used to monitor and control the process. Frequent evaluation of the process model throughout the project life can be carried out using current data to assess whether the quality of the outputs are achievable or not. Remedial actions can be identified and implemented. This avoids the ad hoc approach to process improvement when the numbers of factors to consider make it difficult to understand their interdependency.

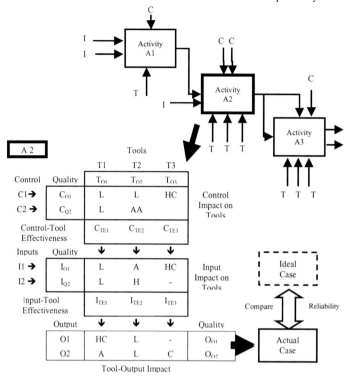

Figure 2 IDEF (A1): Analysis of the existing sublimation process

The robustness and risk assessment and conformance and process improvement were identified for each phase and the researcher recorded the characteristics of robustness and risk assessment and aspects to do with continuous improvement. The reliability of the tools and resources available was then used to calculate the reliability of the output. The four major processes which were identified for modelling are, comparison of alternative technologies, build & test prototype version, design and manufacture and installation & commissioning.

The four phases were chosen for several reasons; they were well defined, would provide an opportunity for clearer understanding of the NPI process, as well as improved understanding the of the projects requirements. They also included activities fundamental to the successfully coordinate the critical phases of the process. The installation and commissioning was considered as one due to the one-off nature of the sublimation project and the subsequent need to foster good working relations with the supplier and subcontractor. The use of this hybrid model gave a ready understanding to all levels of personnel of their own and other departments' activities. It also provided an easy visualisation of NPI activities and communication channels. It assisted in the identification of non-conformance activities and in reaching an agreed basis for prioritising the continuous improvement activities.

The Integrated or functional flowcharts were found to be the most effective process modelling tool. A high level of ownership and participation was achieved as a result of the use of the flowcharts and interactive workshops. The following results were achieve as seen in the table below.

Process Characteristics	Old Technology	New Technology (NPI)
Productivity (mugs / week)	12,000	20 – 24,000
tunnel length (metres)	12	7
Cycle Time (minutes)	17	7
Control System (+/- $^{\circ}$C)	5	0.1
Process/Equipment life Span	18 months	12 years
Worst Scrap Rate scenario	120 mugs	66mugs

Summary

In this paper, an enhanced sublimation line that incorporates the company's future growth strategy has been designed and implemented with the use of IDEF methodology. The result of this study demonstrates that the NPI should not be conducted without assessing the resources available as well as constraints of the process, design specification. By using appropriate modelling methods such as IDEF is invaluable to the integration of resources. Further research could be done using this approach to enhance its applicability to large scale projects.

References

[1]   I. Arokiam, H. Ismail, I. Reid, J. Poolton: The Application of Agile Techniques for Manufacturing Flexibility, International Conference on Agility, ICAM 2005, Helsinki, Finland.

[2]   V.D., Hunt "Process Mapping: How to Reengineer Your Business Processes", John Wiley, New York, 1996

[3]   G.M., Winch, B. Carr, "Processes, maps and protocols: understanding the shape of the construction process", Construction Management and Economics, Vol. 19 No.5, pp.519-31. (2001),

[4]   C. Goulden, L. Rawlins: "A hybrid model for process quality costing" International Journal of Quality & Reliability Management; Volume: 12   Issue: 8; 1995.

Initial review on Collaborations and the relevance in engineering design

John Paul Hayes[1], Louise Knight[2] and Linda Newnes[1]

[1]IMRC, Department of Mechanical Engineering, University of Bath, Claverton Down, Bath,BA2 7AY

[2]School of Management, University of Bath, Claverton Down, Bath,BA2 7AY

J.P.Hayes@bath.ac.uk

Abstract. Collaborations are widely proposed to create unique solutions but are often complex entities. This paper provides a summary of current literature connected to the study of collaborations extracting common values in collaborating and illustrating important links to emerging contemporary, international, cross cultural and inter disciplinary characteristics.

Keywords: Collaboration, Knowledge Transfer

1. Introduction

In the current engineering environment there is an increasing desire expressing a need for collaboration to achieve and deliver cutting edge and unique solutions. The evolution of companies and their restructuring to survive in today's economic climate has led many to create and form collaborations to ensure their continuing success and this is reflected in academia where there is increasingly interactions through collaborative efforts between both academic and industrial fields. Research has been completed studying collaboration from a number of perspectives (e.g. the gap between academics and industry, knowledge transfer, cultural impact) to enlighten and improve performance in collaborative endeavours. This paper aims to provide an initial review of some of the current literature connected to collaborations. The notion of collaboration is presented under the broad process of knowledge management and connections are shown to the topics of internationalism, culture, and discipline. These latter three topics represent characteristics in current emerging collaborations (international, cross cultural and inter disciplinary) and are used to illustrate the content and landscape of the current literature.

2. Knowledge management

The design process is highly dependent on knowledge and the management of it between individuals. Knowledge management is a broad topic itself and collaboration and its creation are shown as features that characterises the pursuit of knowledge [1] through its acquisition and dissemination [2]. The requirement and approach to a collaboration depends on the time, cost and specification for knowledge and all are dependant on individual and academic or organisational characteristics [3]. Consequently the transfer of knowledge is intrinsic to collaboration and of particular relevance to the design process. Within knowledge transfer two key topics are effective knowledge transfer and knowledge conversion.

2.1 Effective Knowledge Transfer Working in a design collaboration desires high efficacy in the transfer of knowledge between the individuals to achieve the requirements of the collaboration. The literature shows quantitatively that the effectiveness of technology transfer has been positively connected with research grants from industry [4] and in academic teaching [2]; hence logically social policies should reflect these findings [4]. A comprehensive "ecological framework for analysing effectiveness" is presented by Sundstrom et al [5] for "a work team" through four sets of variables this could be adapted for a collaboration by introducing a temporary life span.

The literature shows that transfer of knowledge can be hampered under a variety of conditions. Physical distance is a barrier to the success of knowledge transfer [6, 7]: increasing the distance is generally perceived to decrease the success. However Beise & Stahl [4] show quantitatively that proximity is not significantly important for technology transfer in Germany. Tacit knowledge, gained through socialisation and empathy is considered difficult without visual contact [3] and without it, the capacity of an effective collaboration to develop would be limited [2]. In contrast codified (or explicit) knowledge is easier to transfer [6, 3] where Cummings & Teng [6] test quantitatively factors that affect the success of knowledge transfer. They suggest further that codified knowledge is however less likely to be retained due to possible "incompatibilities with cultural beliefs or ways of conducting business"; that is present in both national and organisation cultures..

2.2 Knowledge conversion. The second set of variables from Sundstrom et al [5], work team boundaries, is redefined by Nonaka et al [8] in terms of knowledge conversion. They present four interactive methods of knowledge conversion that aim to illustrate steps to close the gap between parties collaborating: 1. Externalisation - tacit knowledge is made explicit, 2. Internalisation - explicit knowledge is converted to tacit through actively learning, 3. Socialisation - tacit to tacit and 4. Combination - explicit to explicit. Institutional theory expands knowledge internalisation into three aspects a. ownership, b. commitment and c. satisfaction. These three aspects emphasise important factors that are not explicit in collaborations but need to be retained in a collaboration's methodology and are revisited under collaboration in the sections on the dynamic, goal and success. It is not clear whether the logical assumption that knowledge needs to be articulated and recognised to be retained [9] where other research [6] shows that articulation is not be statistically important

3.   Collaboration

Collaboration in the design process is seen as a way to combine the potential of many to deliver creative solutions, to aim for successful outcomes using "collaborative advantage" [10] to obtain results that the endeavours of an individual alone could not achieve and "is required when a unique solution is required" [11]. This section is split into seven topics that reflect common important factors in the literature that are relevant to collaborations including engineering: definition, collaborators, management, goal, success, negotiation and evolution.

Definition. The term collaboration is used extensively in research to represent anything from a process that combines individual perspectives to derive a solution that goes beyond individual components [11] to "a pragmatic alliance" [12] and Katz & Martin [7] list a comprehensive guide based on the initial conditions, desires and requirements of the collaboration. Many choose to collaborate for a number of reasons that have shown to vary from expertise, equipment or resources, to cross-fertilisation across disciplines and for pleasure [2, 7]. Genuth et al [1] classify these collaborative motives further into types with each reflecting the desire or need to adapt to and step ahead of the surrounding environment (individual and organisational) through collaborative efforts. Above all it is important to recognise that the process does not end simply with cooperation - working together for individual ends; but working together for a common end - collaboration [12].

Collaborators. The choice of collaborators is often derived from the motivations of the collaboration and it has been reported [2] to be determined by: inter institutional structures, formal structures, informal research network alliances [noted in 13] and sharing rare knowledge. Evidently this can limit options but it must also not be underestimated that to collaborate is an attitude, a "mindset" [11] that needs to be fostered amongst the collaborators when requiring a unique solution and invoking a collaborative style involving a widespread participation in key decisions that affect the individual and collaborative future [14]. This latter point is often obscured or assumed during collaborations and is one area that is of interest within the design process.

Management. In the management of individuals there is a balance between leadership, delegation and participation to complete research in a collaboration [15, 16]. Furthermore the control of the leadership of a collaboration should consider and reflect the individual perspectives [17]. This needs to accept that traditional hierarchies, or those that the individuals are accustomed to, may no longer apply and as a consequence may create pressures (internal and external) from the structures and processes used. The role of communication [7, 11, 14, 15, 16, 17, 18, 19, 20, 21] and in addition that of vocabulary [12, 22] although often linked to culture must not be underestimated in their influence of the leadership of a collaboration and the trust it retains.

Goal. In the initial definition and management of the collaboration it is important to set clear objectives or goals [9, 10, 17, 18, 21, 23, 24] to allow for complexity in the network of relationships with multiple aims and reduce the risk of "collaborative fatigue" [17] that leads to an unproductive and difficult working group. The goals are an influential aspect within a collaboration and individuals need to understand the relation to their own goal and what the project is aiming to achieve [24]. This can often be a source of conflict within the collaboration particularly where goals are polarised or obscured. O'Connor et al [25] suggest that "given a set of desired objectives, variation in methodological requirements must occur". A "synergy" of the individuals' goals is recognised to aid the success of the collaboration [26] and where there is synthesis in relationships harmony is not required simply that a whole can be constructed from "fragmentary parts" [9].

Success. The success of achieving and recognising the goals of collaboration are often a "multi party problem" [11] and are significant for all involved. Three topics are identified as precursors for the success of a collaboration [26]: Firstly,. social purpose synergy in the goals of the partners, secondly. individual personal traits matched to form effective teams and finally. emotional connection important in cross-sector collaboration. Easterby-Smith & Malina [27] create a synergy over these three points and show that in a cross cultural collaboration the quality of the inter personal relationships between researchers and those researched and their management [16] is vital for success. A number of measures to categorise if a collaboration is successful are noted [23, [7] where the latter illustrate important individual and organisational benefits. Similarities to defining knowledge transfer are noted with a dependency on the initial arrangements and goals of the collaboration, hence preparation and forethought are crucial [15, 16], that is aided by a flexible structure [3, 24] "to respond to rather than control the environment" [9].

Negotiation. Questions are asked and compromises are made hence an important concept within a collaboration is negotiation. This "conflict resolution" [20] needs to become an accepted part of the process from the initial configuration of the collaboration. It is important that everybody is aware of each compromise to give justification, satisfaction and unity in the outcome. Often it is suggested that this "creative tension" should be sought [3] and a number of different contexts are reported where creative tension has been observed:eg inter discipline and between planning and prototyping. This "tension" in a group can also occur in initial stages between the "need for trust and the methods to build trust and the initial lack of trust" [21]. Trust is an important factor [18, 21, 23, 24] and relationships improve through experience and repeat collaborations [28, 9] though it can be "particularly problematic" to engender trust as both power and control are closely related to each other [21, 24]. Unfortunately if negotiations are difficult in "establishing common aims" this can lead to a "collaborative inertia" [10] where the rate of work output is much lower than expected.

Evolution. A group can move through various steps over time and Corey & Corey [18] have defined five stages for groups applicable to collaborations: (1) Formation , (2) Initial, (3) Transition, (4) Working and (5) Ending stage. Each stage relates to the groups progress and change in status from beginning, to orientation to the structure and leadership of the group, through anxiety to the ideal of group cohesion before finishing. Awareness of these stages, the development of acronyms support the idea that the design of a collaboration is important [20, 23, 24]. Pitsis et al [9] take this a step further and define "ten building blocks" in the synthesis of design of inter-organisational relations. A factor that is often not considered is that the collaboration itself is a dynamic entity and a simple plan of the dynamics of collaboration is provided by Gray [11]. "Collaborative structures need to be understood as ambiguous, complex and dynamic"[10] and this reflects a trend towards the study of the "conceptualist and dynamic view of knowing" [29].

4. Internationalism

As economic markets are becoming international it is inevitable that collaborations will be formed crossing national limits. Increasingly collaborations are becoming international [6, 12, 15, 16, 22, 24, 27, 30] due to their nature and goals. Penny et al [24] show three factors that feature in their cross national study from practical issues (ownership trust and power) to theoretical ones (theorising the research) and the complexities of working across national limits (crossing boarders).

The first factor is also noted in Vangen & Huxham [21] where "a high level of mutual trust between the partners could lead to both partners' needs being satisfied, even if one partner is dominant" in comparative case studies of four US–China collaborations.

The physical distance, previous noted in *effective knowledge transfer*, is an obvious major barrier to the free flow of information internationally, though "virtual collaborations" [20] aim to overcome this but need to be aware of the possible "tension" created. The next two topics on culture and disciplines develop further other aspects related to internationalism.

5   Culture

During the last 50 years there has been significant movement of populations through the world crossing national and cultural boundaries that has developed the term globalisation. This has led to many societies developing to represent their populations and reflect their multi cultural heritage that is mirrored in academia and industry. Culture defined by Hofstede [30] consists of shared mental programs that condition individuals' responses to their environment. This is key to individual recognition and understanding that can facilitate interaction; two parts explored under "culture" are: organisational culture and national culture.

5.1   Organisational culture. The definitions of an organisational culture have "initially focused on distinguishing levels of organizational culture" [31], or multiple layers [32], where a number of definitions are suggested using "cognitive components" that are visible: assumptions, beliefs, and values; and those that are hidden: behaviours and artefacts [31]. The culture of an organisation is recognised as an influential factor to achieving a competitive advantage [19, 33, 34] but can encourage defensive routines [34]. The culture and career ladders of academia are remarked to "endorse a defensive kind of disciplinary closure that inhibits critical self reflection" [35] and reward individual performance or accountability almost exclusively [14, 25] providing a barrier to overcome to encourage successful collaborations. Some cultures are more embedded in organisations than others (strong rather than weak), though having a strong culture does not automatically lead to an effective organisation [36].

The relationships between different organisations have an impact on a collaboration and is highlighted by the interface between academia and industry [2, 3, 23, 37]. A simple outline for the interface process is given by Bloedon & Stokes [23] requiring a balanced structure [38] that does not impede professional, organisational and institutional success [3] or restrict creativity [39]. There are present beliefs that companies and academics have mutually exclusive ideals of quality and relevance. The knowledge produced by academia is not always consistent with that required by industry [3]; however Baldrige et al [37] suggest that there is an area where they overlap, reiterated and categorised as a "double hurdle" [29] that academics have to overcome by building "an intellectual, social and political platform" to carry out research that is of high quality and relevant.

5.2   National culture. The national culture depicts the history, background, traditions encompassing the language and context of individuals. Adler [40] notes five steps that are fundamental problems to be considered in comparative cross cultural research; that are reiterated in research [16, 27] including the notion of reflexivity [27] reinforced by Knights & Willmott [35] "as human beings we are the object as well as the subject of our actions". Other studies have noted that the existence of cultural differences aid the development of trust in a collaboration [28] (differences in knowledge are often sought after in collaborations), and differing levels of success for academics in different countries [3] crossing into the interests of industry. On an individual level a new term to classify awareness, appreciation and capability to interact across cultures: Cultural Intelligence (CQ) [22] is being introduced, and practically "multicultural research within a multidisciplinary framework" is suggested [15] to recognise and incorporate cultural differences.

6   Disciplines

Each individual within a collaboration has a discipline: a training and methodological approach that is supported through structured and fundamental theory and research. These disciplines may or

166

may not share a common knowledge, but often the motives to collaborate are a combination of knowledge to provide a unique solution [7]. The present climate of "complex dynamic realities of management research" suggest a single discipline is too narrow to capture the required ideas [35] and the permanent structure of one discipline can be restrictive to individual intellectual needs [39]. This has led to shift to cross/inter/multi disciplined research [2, 7, 9, 12, 16, 20, 24 , 26] to challenge individuals to "overcome discipline identity" [35], for a project to be cross functional [14] to solve a problem and communicate it to a wider audience. This recognises that many stakeholders themselves are "inter multi or non disciplinary" [39] but there are few reviewed papers [25, 35, 39] that study or note the process of combining disciplines in a collaboration.

The initial idea that combining disciplines provides research that has a larger possible audience and will offer new insights has produced a number of concerns in the literature; Knights and Willmott [35] question whether these results will be automatic and relevant or their application to new fields will not dilute or misuse the "original"? concepts or disciplines. O'Connor et al [25] recognise increased requirements and considerations in project management from combining different disciplines noting in their framework that the composition of the group is critical and multiple "interim steps" help facilitate the interpretation in accordance with the goals of the project.

There are concerns over future research and teaching under the term "inter discipline" as "there are major social/psychological/institutional barriers to be overcome" and the success or "proof will eventually be in the use of the theory in practice" [35].

5.   Concluding remarks and further research

The engineering design process uses collaborations to increase the resources, capabilities and ideas individuals produce through interaction and cross fertilisation. The literature records a mixture of observations related to collaborations as factual or interpretations of meanings people place on experiences; the former tend to be derived from quantitative models that can show statistical relevance to the questions posed, and the latter from qualitative surveys and or interviews.

This paper presents collaboration as a form of knowledge management and illustrates connections to research in three further topics: internationalism, culture and discipline. Many of the topics and sub themes are inter related and can create a complex network leaving a number of gaps for future research. Seven sub themes are presented under the term collaboration to illustrate from a number of scientific perspectives that fundamental to working collaboratively is the understanding or appreciation of those that one is collaborating with. This paper does not want to suggest that there is an optimum balance between the involvement of different disciplines, cultures or nationalities though that may be relevant but wishes to show that there are benefits to be gained by understanding the context of the individuals and the collaboration.

6.   References

1   Genuth J., I. Chompalov, et al. (2000). "How experiments begin: The formation of scientific collaborations." Minerva 38(3): 311-348.

2   Bozeman B. & E. Corley (2004). "Scientists' collaboration strategies: implications for scientific and technical human capital" Research Policy 33(4): 599-616.

3   Rynes, S., J. Bartunek, et al. (2001). "Across the Great Divide: Knowledge Creation and Transfer between Practitioners and Academics." Academy of Management Journal 44(2): 340-355.

4   Beise M. & H. Stahl (1999). "Public research and industrial innovations in Germany." Research Policy 28(4): 397-422.

5   Sundstrom, E, De Muse K, & Futrell D, " Work Teams", American Psychologist, 1990, February, pp 120-33

6   Cummings, J. & B.-S. Teng (2003). "Transferring R&D Knowledge: the key factors affecting knowledge transfer success." Journal of Engineering and Technology Management 20: 39-68.

7   Katz, JS & BR Martin (1997). "What is research collaboration?" Research Policy 26(1): 1-18.

8   Nonaka, I, & Takeuchi, H (1995). "The knowledge-creating company: How Japanese companies create the dynamics of innovation". Oxford: Oxford University Press.

9   Pitsis, T., M. Kornberger, et al. (2004). "The Art of Managing Relationships in Interorganizational Collaboration." M@n@gement 7(3): 47-67.

10   Huxham, C & S. Vangen (2000). "Ambiguity, complexity and dynamics in the membership of collaboration." Human Relations 53(6): 771-806.

11   Gray, B. (1998). "Collaboration: The constructive management of differences" in G. R. Hickman (Ed.) "Leading Organizations", pp. 467-480.

12   Jeffrey, P. (2003). "Smoothing the waters: Observations on the process of cross- disciplinary research collaboration" Social Studies of Science 33(4): 539-562.

13   Hagstrom, WO (1980) "The scientific community", Ch I, III.

14   Huczynski, A & D Buchanan (2001), "Organizational behaviour: an introductory text, 4th ed, Ch 9, 12

15   Ettorre E. (2000). "Recognizing diversity and group processes in international, collaborative research work: A case study." Social Policy & Administration 34(4): 392-407.

16   Teagarden, MB., MA. Vonglinow, et al. (1995). "Toward a Theory of Comparative Management Research - an Idiographic Case-Study of the Best International Human- Resources Management Protect." Academy of Management Journal 38(5): 1261-1287.

17   Huxham, C & S. Vangen (2004). "Doing Things Collaboratively: Realizing the advantage or succumbing to inertia?" Organizational Dynamics 33(2): 190-201.

18   Corey MS & Corey G, "Groups process and practice" (1987), Brooks/Cole 3rd Ed, Ch 3, 4, 5, 6, 7.

19   Ouchi, WG. (1981), "Theory Z: How American Business Can Meet the Japanese Challenge". Addison-Wesley Publishing Co.Ch 6, 7

20   O'Sullivan, A. (2003). "Dispersed Collaboration in a Multi-firm, Multi-team Product-development Project." Journal of Engineering and Technology Management 20: 93-116.

21   Vangen, S. & C. Huxham (2003). "Nurturing Collaborative Relations: Building trust in interorganizational collaboration." The Journal of Applied Behavioral Science 39(1): 5-31.

22   Thomas, DC. & Inkson, K. (2003), " Cultural Intelligence". San Francisco, CA: Berrett-Koehler

23   Bloedon RV. & DR. Stokes (1994). "Making University-Industry Collaborative Research Succeed." Research Technology Management 37(2): 44-48.

24   Penny, A. J., M. A. Ali, et al. (2000). "A study of cross-national collaborative research: reflecting on experience in Pakistan." International Journal of Educational Development 20(6): 443-455.

25   O'Connor, G. C., M. P. Rice, et al. (2003). "Managing interdisciplinary, longitudinal research teams: Extending grounded theory-building methodologies." Organization Science 14(4): 353-373.

26   Barrett D, Austin J, and McCarthy S (2000). "Cross-Sector Collaboration: Lessons from the International Trachoma Initiative", HBS Working Paper.

27   Easterby-Smith, M. & Malina D. (1999). "Cross-cultural Collaborative Research: Toward reflexivity." Academy of Management Journal 42(1): 76-86.

28   Davenport, S., J. Davies, et al. (1999). "Collaborative research programmes: building trust from difference." Technovation 19(1): 31-40.

29   Pettigrew, A. (2001). "Management Research after Modernism." British Journal of Management 12(Special): S61-70.

30   Hofstede, G (1980). "Culture's consequences : international differences in work-related values", London Sage

31   Baker, KA. (2002), "Organizational Culture" in "Management Benchmarking Study", edited by the Washington Research Evaluation Network

32   Schein, EH. (1992). "Organizational Culture and Leadership". San Francisco: Jossey-Bass Publishers.Chapter 2

33   Pfeffer, J. (1995/2005). "Producing sustainable competitive advantage through the effective management of people" Academy of Management Executive, vol 19, Issue 4 pp. 95-108.

34   Senge, P. (1991). "Team learning", McKinsey Quarterly, Vol 2, pp. 82-93.

35   Knights, D. & H. Willmott (1997). "The Hype and Hope of Interdisciplinary Management Studies." British Journal of Management 8: 9-22

36   Schein, EH. (1989), "Conversation with Edgar H. Schein", interview conducted by F. Luthans, Organizational Dynamics, Vol. 17 No. 4, pp. 60-76.

37   Baldridge, D., S. Floyd, et al. (2004). "Are Managers from Mars and Academicians from Venus? Toward an understanding of the relationship between academic quality and practical relevance." Strategic Management Journal 25: 1063-1074.Background

38   Buisseret, T. J. and H. Caneron (1994). "Management of Collaborative Research: Collaboration and Exploitation under the UK's Information Engineering Advanced Technology Programme." Technology Analysis & Strategic Management 6(2): 215-230.

39   Katz, S. N. (1995). "Do Disciplines Matter - History and the Social-Sciences." Social Science Quarterly 76(4): 863-877.

40   Adler NJ, (1984), "Understanding the ways of understanding: Cross-cultural management methodology reviewed". In RN Farmer (Ed) "Advances in international comparative management, p31-67. Greenwich, CT: JAI Press

Virtual Reality and Process Selection

An Alternative Method for Evaluation of Design Alternatives in the Early Stage of Design Process

S.M.Ali Khatami Firouzabadi[1, a] and Brian Henson[2, b]

[1]Business School of Allameh Tabatabaie University, Nezami Gangavi Avenue, Tavanir Avenue, Vali Asr Street, Tehran, Iran

[2]School of Mechanical Engineering, University of Leeds, Leeds, LS2 9JT, U.K.

[a]s.m.ali.khatami.f@gmail.com, [b]b.henson@leeds.ac.uk

Abstract. One of the most important decisions which should be made at the early stage of the design process is to select the most appropriate alternative that can be competitive in the market. This decision which should satisfy the different objectives is a Multiple Criteria Decision Making (MCDM) problem. In this problem, there are often conflicting criteria and each single competitive alternative is the best from the point of view of some criteria and is not from the viewpoint of others. In this situation, the best alternative is that one for which the most important criteria are satisfied. In this paper, an alternative method for choosing the most suitable alternative is introduced by using the Analytical Hierarchy Process (AHP) and Mixed Integer Programming (MIP) programming. In this method, the alternatives are pairwise compared with regard to a criterion. After applying the process of the AHP method, each alternative will have a weight with regard to that criterion. This process is repeated for the remaining criteria. These weights are then used to establish the coefficients of the constraints in a MIP model in which, the decision variables are binary types: selection or non-selection. The target value for each constraint is the best weight of the left hand side coefficients because the aim is to choose the best alternative that satisfies the criteria as much as possible. The criteria also are compared to each other in a pairwise fashion to obtain the numerical relative importance of each criterion. These weights are then used to form the coefficients of the slack variables in the objective function in which slack variables are the difference between the left hand sides and target values of the constraints. The minimisation of added slack variables associated with their weights in the objective function allows the system of mathematical models to suggest that alternative which has the minimum of undesirable differences.

Keywords: Design process, multiple criteria decision making, analytical hierarchy process, mixed integer programming, concept selection

Introduction

The success of manufacturing companies depends on their ability to identify the needs of customers and to quickly create products that meet these needs and can be produced at low cost [1]. Achieving these goals is not solely a marketing problem, nor is it solely a design problem or manufacturing problem; it is a concept development problem involving all of these functions [2]. Concept development process is the set of activities beginning with the perception of a market opportunity and ending in the production and sale of a product [3]. The concept development entire process include 1) identifying customer needs, 2) establishing target specification, 3) concept generation, 4) concept screening, 5) concept selection, 6) concept setting, 7) setting final specification, 8) manufacturing, and 9) selling.

This paper focuses on fifth step; concept selection. Evaluating and selecting the most appropriate concept design alternative after screening phase is a critical step because all subsequent detailed design and process design is based on this decision [4,5]. Concept selection is the process of evaluation and selection from a range of competing alternatives with respect to customer needs and other tangible or intangible criteria, comparing their relative strengths and weaknesses, and selecting one or more concepts for further investigation, testing, or development [4]. Success of the complete design process depends on selecting the right alternative [4]. Changes made early in the design process are less costly than those made in detail design and later stages [6]. Concept selection is frequently iterative process and may not produce a dominant concept design immediately [7]. A dominant alternative can be found using decision making techniques, with comparing the alternatives, remained from concept screening step.

The available methods for concept design selection problems are categorized within two general approaches as concept-specification and concept-concept [4]. Concept-specification comparison involves direct comparison between the concept alternatives and the Product Design Specification (PDS), while concept-concept approach involves direct comparison between two competing concepts. Although both approaches to design evaluation are well known to designers and form the basis for many methods of evaluation, individual application of these two approaches are insufficient because they cannot consider the PDS and comparing the alternatives with each other simultaneously. In one hand, comparing the alternatives with each other is important because insignificant differences between alternatives can be detected [8]. On the other hand, PDS should be considered because it reflects how much an alternative has fulfilled its requirements.

To overcome the problem, this paper suggests combining these two approaches by using AHP and MIP; AHP from concept-concept approach and MIP from concept-specification approach. Since concept design selection is a problem that requires decomposition of elements (structuring), estimation of relative importance of elements (measurements of many tangible and intangible elements), and combining them (synthesizing), therefore AHP can be used because of consistency between concept design selection characteristics and AHP characteristics. Using MIP allows not only to take into account the binary variables, but also it can consider the effect of difference between left hand side and right hand side of a constraint (relates to a criterion) which is necessary for evaluation of a design alternative. It is obvious that the final selected alternative cannot be the best from point of view of all criteria or sub-criteria. If the final selected alternative is the best from a single criterion, then there is no distance between the final selected alternative and the best alternative from that criterion, but if the final selected alternative is not the best from another criterion, so there is a distance between the final selected alternative and that criterion. MIP is able to consider these distances with their relative importance, obtained through AHP, which will be appeared in its objective function.

Methodology

The basic idea in the methodology is to use problem decomposition and explicit value or preference tradeoffs from point of view of each criterion or sub-criterion. When there are multiple criteria for evaluating alternatives, the best alternative from point of view of each criterion is different. Therefore, there are distances between the final selected alternative and the best alternative from point of view of each single criterion. The methodology tries to select that alternative which has minimum total distances. The distances are minimised with their associated weights, which are the relative importance of each single criterion, obtained by global weights of the AHP.

In the methodology, each individual criterion has a constraint in the MIP model. The global weights of criteria (the relative importance of criteria when they are compared with each other), obtained from the AHP, become the objective function coefficients of MIP model. These coefficients associate with the distance from the left hand side (coefficients of each individual alternative which can be obtained by AHP, when each all alternatives are compared with regard to a single criterion)

172

and right hand side (target value) of a constraint. In the other words, these coefficients are the slack variables' coefficients (related to each constraint) in the objective function. Right hand side of each constraint is always the best coefficients of left hand sides' coefficients.

The model minimisation iterative process tries to eliminate those alternatives which related criterion coefficients in the objective function are more than others.

Case Study

In this section, the proposed methodology is evaluated by application of a real world problem. The selection of a swivel joint design used in an underwater marine environment as part of a current-metering system among available designs is this problem [9]. A previous design was considered unsuitable because of its high cost and poor performance (especially the high friction between adjacent moving parts).

Three different new designs have been developed by design department in order to make one of them by manufacturing department. These new designs have been shown in Figure 1. The problem is which of these alternatives should be selected as the most appropriate alternative.

Design A   Design B   Design C

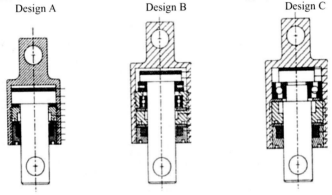

Figure 1 New swivel joint designs for selection

The hierarchy, criteria and sub-criteria for selection problem is shown in Figure 2. The criteria and sub-criteria include tangibles and intangibles. For example, cost, time, and strength are tangible, while sealing, smoothness and other criteria or sub-criteria are intangible.

To obtain the weights of each criterion or sub-criterion, the AHP requires answers to a sequence of questions that compare two criteria or two alternatives. The numerical answers are given using a fundamental 1-9 scale. Then using the eigenvalue method, the relative weights of elements can be determined. When applying the AHP, there will be two types of weights: global and local. The former measures the relative importance of each single criterion with considering all the criteria, while the latter measure the relative importance of sub-criterion with regard to its parent node. The result of applying AHP is shown in Figure 3.

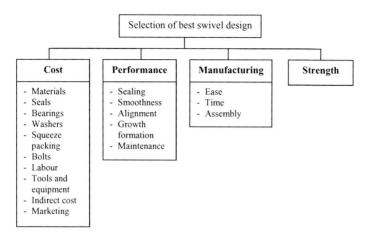

Figure 2 The hierarchy, criteria, and sub-criteria for selection of swivel design

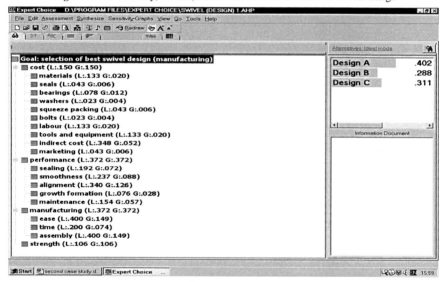

Figure 3 The result of applying AHP

Establishment of MIP model. Before making the MIP model, it is necessary to normalize the tangible data for criteria or sub-criteria (cost, manufacturing time, and strength) to make them comparable with intangible data. Since there are not available every part alternatives' costs, so the full cost of alternatives are considered. As mentioned before, each single criterion or sub-criterion is associated with a constraint. The target value of each criterion (right hand side of a constraint) is the best value of left hand side's coefficients because the aim of this model is to consider the minimum distance between the final selected alternative and the best alternative with regard to a criterion.

174

$$Min\ Z = 0.150\ s_{co} + 0.072\ s_{se} + 0.088\ s_{sm} + 0.126\ s_{al} + 0.028\ s_{gr} + 0.057\ s_{ma} + 0.149\ s_{ea} + 0.074\ s_{ti} + 0.149\ s_{as} + 0.106\ s_{st} \quad (1)$$

s.t.

$0.419A + 0.349B + 0.232C + s_{co} = 0.419$	(cost - tangible)	(2)
$0.500A + 0.250B + 0.250C + s_{se} = 0.500$	(sealing - intangible)	(3)
$0.140A + 0.528B + 0.332C + s_{sm} = 0.528$	(smoothness - intangible)	(4)
$0.169A + 0.387B + 0.444C + s_{al} = 0.444$	(alignment - intangible)	(5)
$0.200A + 0.400B + 0.400C + s_{gr} = 0.400$	(growth formation - intangible)	(6)
$0.500A + 0.250B + 0.250C + s_{ma} = 0.500$	(maintenance – intangible)	(7)
$0.600A + 0.200B + 0.200C + s_{ea} = 0.600$	(ease – intangible)	(8)
$0.429A + 0.214B + 0.357C + s_{ti} = 0.429$	(time – tangible)	(9)
$0.630A + 0.152B + 0.218C + s_{as} = 0.630$	(assembly – intangible)	(10)
$0.372A + 0.314B + 0.314C + s_{st} = 0.372$	(strength – tangible)	(11)
$A + B + C = 1$	(selection of just one alternative)	(12)
$A, B, C \in (0,1)\ ;\ s_j \geq 0\ \forall\ all\ j$	(binary selection of alternatives)	(13)

The coefficients of objective function (equation 1) are global weights of criteria or sub-criteria which are obtained from AHP directly. The coefficients of constraints in equations 3, 4, 5, 6, 7, 8, and 10 were obtained from application of the AHP when all available alternatives are compared with regard to a criterion. For example, when considering the sealing criterion (equation 2), then alternative A is 2 times better than alternative B and 2 times better than alternative C. These values were obtained by pairwise comparisons of the AHP. The coefficients of equations 2 and 9 were obtained from the real data after reverse normalisation (because the less is better) and the coefficients of equation 11 was obtained after normalisation of the real data (because the more is better). For example the 0.419 value related to the coefficient of alternative A, indicates that the cost of alternative A is 1.2 times more favourable than the cost of alternative B ($0.419/0.349 = 1.200$) and 1.806 times more favorable than the cost of alternative C ($0.419/0.232 = 1.806$). In other words, the value of 0.419 is the utility of alternative A when compared with two other alternatives. Selection of just one alternative is reflected in equation 12. Equation 13 shows that the alternative selection variables are binary and slack variables are non-negative.

MIP model solution. The solution of this model selects A, B, and C in order. This solution means when just one alternative should be selected, then the model suggests alternative A. Selection of this alternative has the minimum distance between the final selected alternative; i.e. alternative A, and the best alternative from each individual criterion. When two alternatives must be chosen, then the model suggests alternative A and B (the MIP model can be modified with putting A = 0 as a new constraint after selecting alternative A as a first ranking alternative).

Although this result reconcile with the result of the AHP, but the second ranking is different. AHP as a stand-alone methodology uses an additive function for synthesising the results from each single criterion, while this methodology uses distance function from the best final selected alternative with other alternatives.

Summary

This paper indicated using AHP as a stand-alone methodology for evaluation of design alternatives in the early stage of design process may not be sufficient because of AHP's additive synthesizing procedure. On the other hand, using available methods such as weighted method or controlled convergence method does not seem to be strong enough to guarantee the best alternative can be selected because these methods cannot consider the concept-concept and concept-specification approach simultaneously. The presented methodology with taking into account both approaches, can be an alternative approach for selection of design alternatives.

References

[1]   N. Slack and M. Lewis: *Operations Management* (Prentice Hall, New York 2003)

[2]   K.T. Ulrich and S.D. Eppinger: *Product Design and Development* (McGraw-Hill Higher Education, New York 2000)

[3]   S. Pugh: *Total Design: Integrated Methods for Successful Product Engineering* (Addison-Wesley, New York 1991)

[4]   G. Green: *Towards Integrated Evaluation: Validation of Models* (Journal of Engineering Design, 11(2): 2000)

[5]   L.C. Chen and L. Lin: *Optimisation of Product Configuration Design using Functional Requirements and Constraints* (Research in Engineering Design, 13: 2002)

[6]   P.R. Childs: *Mechanical Design* (Elsevier Butterworth-Heinemann, Oxford: 2004)

[7]   Y.C. Liu, T. Bligh and A. Chakrabarti: *Towards an "ideal" Approach for Concept Generation* (Journal of Design Studies, 24(4): 2003)

[8]   N.K. Malhotra and D.F. Birks: *Marketing Research: An Applied Approach* (Prentice Hall, Hamel Hapsted, United Kingdom 1999)

[9]   N. Cross: *Engineering Design Methods: Strategies for Product Design* (John Wiley & Sons, New York 2000)

Automated consideration of quality risks in inspection planning

Marcel Blank[1, a], Martin Haueis[2, b], Tobias L'Armée[1, c]

[1]Technical University of Darmstadt, Landgraf-Georg-Str. 4, 64283 Darmstadt, Germany

[2]DaimlerChrysler Research Böblingen, Hanns-Klemm-Str. 45, 71034 Böblingen Germany

[a]mblank@rtr.tu-darmstadt.de, [b]martin.haueis@daimlerchrysler.com, [c]tobias.talmon.larmee@gmx.de

Abstract. End of line inspection in production is a key element for assurance of shipment quality of a product. Inspection planning needs systematic consideration of quality risks in order to choose the most important tests and to keep the effort for the inspections within budget. A new fuzzy logic based method is proposed and demonstrated for prioritisation of test cases. The described method is capable to consider more quality risks than today's inspection planning and allows the automatic processing of a complete catalogue of quality criteria. Proposed new test planning method is demonstrated on a lawn mower tractor.

Keywords: automated consideration, inspection planning, production, quality risks, fuzzy logic, complex products.

Introduction

Motivation. In today's mass production of complex products with a high count of single variants, assurance of shipment quality is a growing challenge [1]. Classic ways of approaching this duty are doomed to failure because they require elementary assumptions such as for example existence of identical products and larger lot numbers.

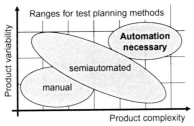

Figure 1. Classification and coverage of test planning methods in high volume production as function of product variability and product complexity.

Existing test planning methods only insufficiently cover high product variability and high product complexity. A good example for such product class is a passenger car, especially in the premium sector. The motivation is to lower the testing time and effort and also lower the possibility of errors slipping through testing by deploying a new method of automated inspection planning.

Inspection planning today. Especially in the area of mass production of complex products quality management is a key element to achieve stable processes and constant high quality levels. A typical flowchart for inline inspection is shown in Fig. 2. Assuming, during manufacturing a defect is built into the product, the testing at the end of line assures that the defect is found and a defect-free product is shipped. Product information and quality sensor data have to be considered to choose the right tests. Quality sensors can come from manufacturing itself or field data. Traditionally, test planning is done by analyzing the statistical occurrence of failures or the distribution of key attributes (e.g. dimensions). Normally those attributes change slowly with time, for example by wear of involved tools. When the products are all the same and only a small number of variants are built, using means of occurring defects for test planning is an appropriate way to measure and assure the overall quality.

To fulfil the task of choosing the right tests for each single product, today a planner takes several input variables into account and considers the right selection of tests by weighting and balancing the single values. After combining them with the experience of the past inspection plans, a test planner creates a list of tests to do. For simplicity, quality data is usually not related to single products but to defined lots. Such an approach does not hold for products with high product variability and product complexity as shown in figure 1. The result is a remaining risk that defects are not found during inspections.

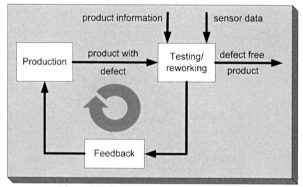

Figure 2. Inline inspection in mass production

Addressed Questions in this Paper. The paper presents an interdisciplinary approach on testing quality in mass production of individualized products. Key quality criteria are introduced, and their data sources explained. A quality function matrix (QFM) is introduced together with a fuzzy logic operator in order to prioritize a given list of tests.

The example of a lawn mover tractor has been chosen to demonstrate the automated consideration of quality risks. The result is a prioritized list of tests cases. Finally, approaches to a full automated consideration of quality risks are discussed.

The fuzzy solution to automated inspection planning

To overcome the fundamental restrictions in today's methods of end of line inspection planning, first an extended data base of sensor data and second, additional product information have to be incorporated into test planning (see Fig. 3). In difference to the process today (Fig. 2), development, production planning, production and service will provide detailed information about quality risks to the product. A PPFLO (pre-processing and fuzzy logic operator) module calculates a test plan for each single product. To make a prioritisation possible, the product information and the sensor data have to be pre-processed and transformed to so call quality criteria. The different types of criteria are described in the following chapter and details on the PPFLO stage are shown afterwards.

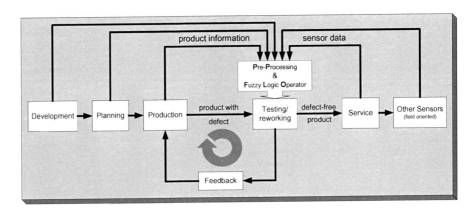

Figure 3. Extended inline inspection in mass production to enable the new planning method
(PPFLO – Pre-Processing and Fuzzy Logic Operator)

Details of used quality criteria. 13 different kinds of sources of information were identified, which have impact on the prioritisation of the associated functions. Two main categories can be distinguished (see table 1). The values of each criterion have a uniform range between 0 and 1. It stands for the applicability of the criteria to the function. The 'must do' criteria can only have two values, 1 or 0. For 1 the corresponding test has to be done on the product. 'Can do' criteria describe attributes which make a fuzzy logic prioritisation possible, because they can be set to values between 0 and 1.

Table 1. Quality criteria for prioritisation of functions (and corresponding tests)

Nr.	Description	Priority
1	Product liability law	'must do'
2	Road traffic licensing regulation (in Germany StVZO)	
3	Supplier or development recommendation	
4	Defect frequency	'Can do'
5	Feasibility of the test	
6	Time needed for the test	
7	Software/hardware changes	
8	Criticality of function for the product performance	
9	Complexity	
10	Repair costs	
11	Location of test action on product	
12	Function importance to customer	
13	Possible adverse effect on corporate image in case of failure	

The different criteria imply different ways of gathering and pre-processing to make them usable by an automated selection process. One requirement for the fuzzy logic operator is the normalized range of values (0..1). Numerical information (the occurrence rate of a single error can be measured in per cent) can easily be converted to values in the required format and range. Other quality criteria, however, have to be evaluated by experts (e.g. the engineer who developed a function) and then transformed to the required format and range. These criteria normally do not change in time, therefore this manual process of reviewing has to be done only once per major change of the product. The remaining criteria have to be pre-processed in a way to get the raw data usable by the following fuzzy logic prioritisation (in Fig. 5 conversion from r_{PKij} to x_{PKij}). For example a component of the product is changed because of a software or hardware update, the right test case can be chosen by the knowledge of the link of the feature to the involved components. The link between a feature and associated components can be taken from documentation databases [2, 3].

Each of the criteria of the quality criteria catalogue has to be assigned to each of the possible tests of the inspection catalogue. The result is the quality function matrix (see QFM in Fig. 4) which is used by the fuzzy logic prioritization stage. The quality risks (C_n) represent the columns and the features (test cases, F_n) of the product form the rows of the QFM.

Fuzzy Test selection. A transformation operator is applied to the QFM resulting in a prioritized list of tests. This operator is fuzzy logic because of its ability to reproduce human behaviour based on experience (e.g. see [4] for details on fuzzy logic and its application). It weights the single criteria to build up a resulting single priority value of each test. The whole list is sorted for convenience and shorted to fit a maximum given testing time for each product.

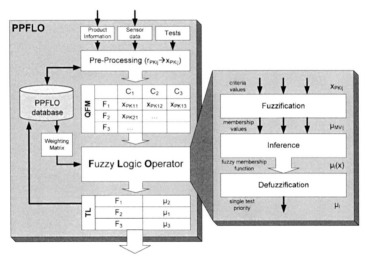

Figure 4. Detailed layout of the automated test planning using fuzzy logic and a QFM;
r_{PKij}: raw value for feature i and criteria j; x_{PKij}: pre-processed value for feature i and criteria j;
Kn: criteria n; Fn: Feature n; TL: Testinglist

The QFM is the main input for the first fuzzy logic stage: the fuzzification. It is the process of transforming crisp criteria values into grades of membership for the linguistic terms of a criteria (like for 'Complexity of the function' the linguistic variables are: 'very applicable', 'less applicable', etc.). The calculated membership values are fed into the operator of the inference step. Maximum operator, Hamacher, Einstein and the algebraic sum are validated. The defuzzyfication delivers the resulting priority value of the single test case (see Fig. 4). This is done by combining the fuzzy membership values into a crisp factor. The weighting matrix is used to adjust the base priority of the single criterions. Every test case is rated with a priority number. Tests with the highest prioritisation are selected so that total test time matches the requirements. The resulting list of tests has to be resorted a second time to match additional boundary conditions for production (e.g. the test location on the product). The resulting test plan defines tests performed on the product. The results are stored in a database and used as quality criteria for future test planning.

Lawn Mower Tractor - A product example. A lawnmower tractor is used to show the potential of automated consideration of quality risks in inspection planning. The demonstrated method is not constrained to chosen example but can be used for any product which has a high level of complexity and variability (see Fig. 1). The lawn mower in this fictive example can be customized with many features and functions (see Fig. 5 for samples of selectable parts).

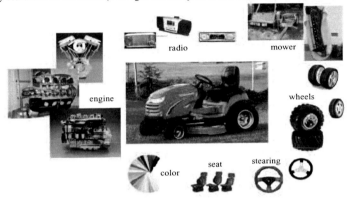

radio   mower

engine   wheels

color   seat   stearing

Figure 5. Lawn Mover Tractor and feature versions (engine, radio, mover, etc.)

A quality criteria catalogue consisting of 5 of the 13 possible criteria is defined (safety, complexity, supplier issues, test time and error costs). Interfaces between the criteria catalogue and quality sensors, the development and production organization are modelled. A set of fictive functions of the tractor is linked to the criteria resulting in a QFM. Next a fuzzy operator is applied to prioritize each function by its quality criteria.

Table 2: Detail of QFM for the mover tractor example, showing one function and its quality criteria

Nr.	Function	Quality critera				
		Safety	Complexity	Supplier issues	Test time	Repair costs
F1	servo steering	0,5	0,75	0,25	0,5	0,5

Results of Test selection

The applicability of an operator based on fuzzy logic is shown on a numerical example. The introduced method robustly converted a QFM of considerable complexity into a prioritized list of 50 tests matching a given maximum testing time. For the FLO (fuzzy logic operator) the algebraic sum is used because it delivers robust results and is the one with the least necessary calculation effort. An example result is shown in Fig. 6. Each test is represented by a square. The width stands for the time needed by the test and the height displays its priority. F_n is the number of the test and T_m is the given maximum testing time for each product. The left four test cases were selected for testing the product. The test sequence can be further optimized by considering the specific testing procedure, in particular the position where the test has to be executed on the product.

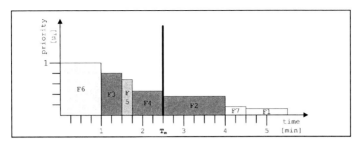

Figure 6. The list of tests (F_n) after prioritisation in time-importance diagram

Discussion

Fuzzy logic is successfully used to prioritise tests for inline inspection on products in mass production. The method introduces a solution to the difficulties in deciding the right tests for quality assurance of mass products with both a high level of complexity and product variability. It can react more flexible and selective than a human test planner on quality issues by regarding the most important quality criteria and map them to test cases of the product.

The knowledge of internal dependencies of the product determines the accuracy of the decision process. Any delays of quality sensor data will limit the responsiveness of the selection process to faster changing quality issues.

Using a test catalogue, the selection is limited to its coverage on the functions of the product. The method cannot introduce new tests. It chooses them from the given test case catalogue.

Future research has to investigate the data pre-processing stage. Neural networks are seen as promising improvement [5]. They should be considered to detect patterns of quality issues in, e.g. special product variants by combining information about the used components and the occurrence rates of defects by analyzing the real world sensor data.

Fuzzy Logic in combination of appropriate quality criteria pre-procession is seen as promising contribution to solve the challenges of quality assurance in mass production of many variants of complex products by automated consideration of quality risks.

References

[1] Wildemann H.: Teure Vielfalt – wie Komplexitätsmanagement auch Qualitätskosten reduziert. Qualität und Zuverlässigkeit 11/2005, pp. 33-36

[2] Falkner, O., Picard C.: Quo vadis Kfz-Elektronik? Optimierungsvorschläge für die Fahrzeugelektronik, Elektronik Automotive 01/2005, pp. 82-85

[3] Betschner, R., Bortolazzi, J., Freess J., Hettich G., Mroßko M.: Gesamtheitlicher Entwicklungsansatz für Entwurf, Dokumentation und Bewertung von E/E-Architekturen, Automotive Electronics II/2005, pp. 18-23

[4] Bandemer, H.: Einführung in Fuzzy-Methoden. Akademie Verlag 1993, Berlin

[5] Schmidberger E., Neher J.: Höchste Aufmerksamkeit – Zyklische Produktionsprozesse qualitätsorientiert regeln. Qualität und Zuverlässigkeit 2/2005, pp. 58-59

Effect of Training on Virtual Lifting Tasks

D. T. Pham[1], Faieza Abdul Aziz[1, a], Ieuan A. Nicholas[2, b]

[1] Manufacturing Engineering Centre, Cardiff University, Cardiff CF24 3AA, UK

[2] Welsh e-Science Centre, School of Computer Science, Cardiff University, Cardiff CF24 3AA, UK

[a] abdul_azizF@Cardiff.ac.uk, [b] i.a.nicholas@cs.cardiff.ac.uk

Abstract. This paper describes an investigation into the effect of training on virtual lifting that utilise visual display feedback to encourage users to adopt appropriate lifting methods. Subjects were required to perform two lifting phases. The first was a "Self-Training Phase", where the subject learnt to execute safe lifts while monitoring their own lifting performance in real-time. The second was a "Test Phase", where a subject was examined on the effectiveness of the learnt technique without any feedback. The objective was to evaluate the learning effect on lifting with feedback in terms of time taken to complete the tasks and the Lifting Index (LI) scores and to determine how quickly subjects learnt an appropriate lifting method. The learning curve/lifting trajectory during training and test was monitored throughout the trials. The results show that subjects learnt to use feedback information during the Self-Training Phase.

Keywords: Virtual Reality, ergonomics, manual lifting

Introduction

Virtual reality (VR) technology can be a powerful tool for training people to perform dangerous, inconvenient or expensive tasks. For example, simulators have been used to train pilots how to fly and to help surgeons practice new procedures before they operate on patients. Other examples of hazardous environments may be found in diverse fields such as automotive, defence, high voltage, marine, medical, nuclear and mining industries.

The potential for Virtual Environments (VEs) in disseminating knowledge about the ergonomic design of working systems has been investigated by many researchers. Studies have been conducted on factors which affect users' performance and on improving workplace design. Manual material handling (MMH) tasks of lifting, lowering, pushing, pulling and carrying are among hazardous activities considered for VE training. Ergonomic lifting can play an important role in minimising lower back pain (LBP) and other associated injuries. Studies have been carried out with the use of visual feedback in virtual environments by many researchers. Agruss [1] in his work proved that the feedback given during training on MMH can reduce the risk of lumbosacral compression. Other studies [2] also agree that visual feedback can enhance user performance.

The experimental hypothesis for this research was that differences would occur in task completion time and performance before and after a training session.

Virtual Lifting Simulation

Research has been conducted into lifting tasks simulated dynamically [3] and analysed in 3D using kinetic models [4]. An effort has been made by [5] to compare the results of an experiment performed in both virtual and real environments. The task was to move boxes between tables of varying heights. The results showed that Virtual Reality (VR) can be compared to a similar experimental task in the real environment if it involves measuring only a particular range of movements, with no velocities or acceleration. This is because the user moves more slowly in VR in comparison with the real environment.

In this work, VR is used as a tool to provide real-time feedback to the user on their lower back condition and to investigate requirements for user training. The Recommended Weight Limit (RWL) is the principal product of the revised NIOSH lifting equation, which is formulated to minimise the likelihood of back injuries. This formula can be used to define safe working limits for use in ergonomic analysis. RWL defines the maximum weight that should be lifted in a particular task by the following equation:

$$RWL = LC \times HM \times VM \times DM \times AM \times FM \times CM \qquad (1)$$

where:

RWL = Recommended Weight Limit
LC = Load Constant
HM = Horizontal Multiplier
VM = Vertical Multiplier
DM = Distance Multiplier
AM = Asymmetric Multiplier
FM = Frequency Multiplier
CM = Coupling Multiplier

The Lifting Index (LI) is defined by the following equation:

$$LI = \frac{LoadWeight}{RWL} = \frac{L}{RWL} \qquad (2)$$

Experimental Set-up

A SGI Onyx 300 visualisation server was used to generate the images on a Portico Workwall (a large scale display device manufactured by Fakespace). The VE software was a C-based application that was designed and programmed by the authors using CAVELib API (by VRCO). Stereoscopic 3D images were created with the use of CrystalEyes LCD shutter glasses from StereoGraphics, with a refresh rate of 120Hz (60Hz update for each eye). Tracking of head and hand position/orientation was performed using 6 degrees-of-freedom sensors together with Trackd software.

Ergonomic functions were used to calculate the NIOSH Lifting Index (LI) values, which indicate how safe the movement was (as in Eq. 1 & Eq. 2). The LI value varied between 0.00 and 0.99 for safe lifts, with values equal to or greater than 1.00 indicating harm to the user. In this experiment two thresholds were assigned, LI lower threshold and LI upper threshold. These two thresholds divide the LI values into three regions. LI values under the lower threshold represent safe situation. LI values between the lower threshold and the upper threshold define the risk area and LI values above the upper threshold indicate the danger zone. Participants were told to perform the task in a safe working zone throughout the lift.

Subjects were asked to lift a box from a lower shelf and place it on to an upper shelf guided by the visual display feedback. Vision was utilised to provide feedback about the stresses placed on the user's lower back during lifting tasks. Each subject was provided with feedback consisting of text and colour displays indicating the zone in which he or she is operating. Figure 1 and 2 show picture of user conducting the experiment with Colour and Text feedback (user received both Colour and Text Feedback simultaneously). The virtual box would change in Colour according to the LI values. Three colours have been chosen: Green represents Safe Lift, Yellow represents Risk Lift and Red represents Danger Lift. The user would also receive feedback in Text for their LI results.

Fig. 1: Subject lifting a box

Fig. 2: Colour and Text Feedback

Subjects were required to perform 2 lifting phases. The first was a Self-Training Phase, where the subjects monitored their own lifting performance in real time from the given visual display feedback. This was followed by a Test Phase, where the subjects were tested on the effectiveness of the learnt technique. No feedback was provided during the Test Phase. The learning effect was evaluated in terms of the time to complete the task (TCT), LI and the time taken for the subjects to adapt their lifting methods. The lifting trajectory during training and test was also observed throughout the trials. A virtual weight of 2kg was used for the experiment.

Experimental Procedure

Lifting experiments were performed by 17 male and 1 female adult participants, with a mean age of 29.2 years and a standard deviation of 5.6 years. The participants were in good health with no history of back injuries. Trials were carried out by each participant individually. Each participant conducted 10 trials for both the Training and Test Phases.

Self-Training Phase. Each subject learnt the feedback techniques on their own while performing the lifting task, as no instructions on lifting techniques were given before conducting the experiment in the Self-Training Phase. However, the subjects were informed that they needed to perform the lifting task in the Safe Lifting Zone throughout the trials. Therefore, participants would have to react to the real time feedback by changing the position and orientation of their hands. They were also told to keep the LI value as low as possible and were reminded to adapt their lifting technique according to the feedback provided during the Training Phase, as they were to be tested on completion of this Phase.

Test Phase. Participants were asked to conduct a Test Phase upon completion of the Self-Training Phase. In the Test Phase, they were examined on the effectiveness of the feedback. During this phase the subjects were not provided with feedback relating to potential lower back pain. They were told to perform the test to the best of their ability and to apply the lifting methods they had learnt beforehand.

Results

Comparison of the mean LI values for the Self-Training Phase and the Test Phase conducted by every subject is shown in Figure 3. During the trials the LI values reduced by 30.7% for the Training Phase, while for the Test Phase the value remained almost steady throughout the trials. It can be seen clearly that the value for LI in the Training Phase decrease dramatically for the first few lifts, because the subjects were actively learning and trying to respond to the feedback provided. After a few trials the LI values for the Training Phase were almost steady, only varying in a smaller range. The mean LI values for the Training Phase and the Test Phase were found to differ significantly (Student's $t = 8.23$, degrees-of-freedom $= 179$, probability value < 0.05).

Task Completion Time (TCT) is depicted in Figure 4. During the Training Phase, subjects took as long as 51.6 seconds to complete a lift, with a mean of 9.18 and standard deviation of 6.07. In the Test Phase the longest time taken to complete a lift was only 9.16 seconds. The mean TCT was 5.89 seconds and the standard deviation was 1.5 seconds. The mean TCT for the Training Phase and the Test Phase were found to differ (t = 7.47, df = 179, $\underline{p}$ < 0.05).

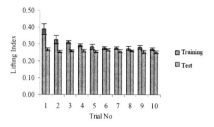

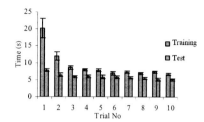

Fig. 3: LI values for Training and Test Phases

Fig. 4: Task Completion Times for Training and Test Phases

Examples of lifts carried out by one of the subjects are depicted in Figures 5. From this it can be seen clearly that the subjects were trying to learn lifting techniques during the first few trials because the LI values then reduced noticeably. In the first trial the LI index values exceeded both the lower LI threshold and the upper LI threshold, which means they reached the Dangerous Lifting Zone. However in the second trial the subject only exceeded the lower LI threshold as he started to reduce the LI according the feedback he was receiving. Trials number 3 onwards were conducted successfully in the Safe Lifting Zone and it was noticeable that after trial 5, the user performance varied within a smaller LI range.

It became noticeable that the LI values reduced with the number of trials. During the Test Phase all the lifts were conducted in the low LI region with variations over a small range. A subject took a longer time to perform a lifting task at the beginning of the Training Phase. Thereafter, the lifts were good as the subject could lift faster. In the Test Phase, all the lifts were conducted in similar times for the different trials.

Figures 6 shows in detail the lifting curves for every trial performed by one subject. In the Training Phase, the subject took 26 seconds to perform a lift for the first time (Trial 1). This was due to unfamiliarity with the feedback provided, as no training had been given beforehand. The graph of the first trial clearly shows that much time was spent on the placement of the box (24 seconds) rather than on the initial (starting) lifting phase, which only took 2 seconds. Then TCT reduced to 21 seconds and the lowest TCT was 4 seconds. In Test Phase, it shows that all the trials were completed between 3.3 and 5.4 seconds in the Test Phase, which meant that the subject learnt quickly from the feedback and managed to lift in a progressively shorter time.

Figure 7 shows details of various Lifting Zones with reference to vertical distance and LI values. Only one lift has been shown for the purpose of explanation. It can be seen that the subject entered the Risky Lifting Zone between 23 and 24 seconds. Then he reached the Dangerous Lifting Zone from 24 to 26 seconds. From the top graph, it can be seen that the learning curve, where the subject was trying to manoeuvre his hands and at the same time learn to assimilate the feedback provided by the virtual simulation technique. After 31 seconds the subject was back in the Safe Lifting Zone, but only arrived at the final destination in 37 seconds. It can be seen that the subject stayed still for a few seconds to indicate that he had finished the lifting task.

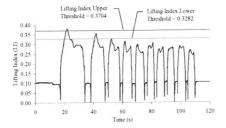 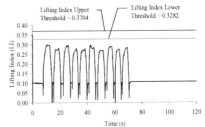

Fig. 5: An example of trials during the Training Phase (left) and Test Phase (right)

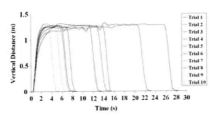

Fig. 6: An example of a learning curve for Training Phase (left) and Test Phase (right)

Discussion

Subjects learnt the feedback technique well during the Self-Training Phase. This was due to the fact that at this stage they were learning for the first time the nature of the feedback given and how to respond to it, i.e. they required some time to understand how their lifting movement and technique affected the feedback of the forces acting on their lower back pain. Comprehensive analysis was carried out on the first experiment, which was performed by all subjects.

On average subjects became familiar with the feedback technique supplied to them from trial 6 onwards. It can be seen from Figure 7, that following trial 5, where the learning stage took place, the LI reduced. The TCT also decreased dramatically when comparing trial numbers 1 and 2. It then reduced slowly until it became almost stable from trial number 6 onwards. From the results obtained, it was apparent that the subjects learnt correctly the feedback technique during the Training Phase. As for the learning curve, it can be seen from the plotted graph that the initial and lifting phases were carried out almost consistently for every subject, as they need only 2 seconds. In the Test Phase all subjects performed the trials well exhibiting almost the same LI values and speed to complete the lifting tasks. This outcome suggests that the learning technique can play an important role in conditioning people to use appropriate lifting methods in the real world. By having input in real time regarding their back condition while performing lifting activities, as well as learning the techniques

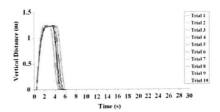

of lifting, lower back injury among workers could be minimised.

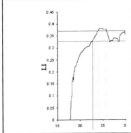

Fig. 7: Details of learning
curve for various lifting
zones

Conclusion and Future Work

This paper has presented an investigation of the effect of training on virtual lifting tasks. It has been found that 10 trials are sufficient for subjects to become familiar with the virtual feedback, which consists of LI values as well as the response required in order to minimise risk to their lower back. The information from this research can be used to enhance virtual training simulations in other MMH tasks, i.e. carrying, pulling, pushing and also to determine whether or not this outcome is consistent with other manual handling tasks. It could also increase the understanding of human reaction to the virtual environment.

References

[1]   C. D. Agruss, K. R. Williams, and F. A. Fathallah, "The effect of feedback training on lumbosacral compression during simulated occupational lifting," *Ergonomics*, vol. 47, pp. 1103-1115, 2004.

[2]   C. Lathan, K. Cleary, and L. Traynor, "Human-Centered Design of a Spine Biopsy Simulator and the Effects of Visual and Force Feedback on Path-Tracking Performance," *Presence*, vol. 9, pp. 337–349, 2000.

[3]   W. S. Marras, S. A. Ferguson, D. Burr, K. G. Davis, and P. Gupta, "Spine loading in patients with low back pain during asymmetric lifting exertions," *The Spine Journal*, vol. 4, pp. 64–75, 2004.

[4]   M. Nalgirkar and A. Mital, "A User-Friendly Three-Dimensional Kinetic Model for Analyzing Manual Lifting Tasks," *International Journal of Industrial Ergonomics*, vol. 23, pp. 255-268, 1999.

[5]   L. Whitman, M. J. Jorgensen, K. Hathiyari, and D. Malzahn, "Virtual reality: its usefulness for ergonomics experiments," presented at Proceedings of the 2004 Winter Simulation Conference, Washington, DC, 2004.

Product Design for Multi-Material Overmolding Technologies

YH Chen, SH Tong and Z Gao

Department of Mechanical Engineering

The University of Hong Kong, Hong Kong, China

yhchen@hku.hk, h0261975@hkusua.hku.hk, gaozhan@hkusua.hku.hk

Abstract. Injection molding is the most commercially important of all plastic processing methods. In recent years, multi-material over molding has become one of the fastest growing sectors of the injection molding industry mainly due to its in-mold assembly and in-mold decoration features. Unlike the rapid development of overmolding technologies, research in computer aided design of multi-material overmolding parts lags far behind. This paper reports initial thoughts and preliminary results about computer aided design for multi-material overmolding parts. Haptic modeling has been developed into the computer aided design system for quick and intuitive design concepts generation and evaluation. Some of the tedious and difficult tasks such as freeform surface painting, part decompositions, and stiffness evaluation can now be easily done in the proposed system.

Keywords: overmolding, haptics, part decomposition, multi-materials.

Introduction

Soft touch materials that have low modulus and high flexibility similar in a way to rubbers are increasingly used in today's product design. Thermoset rubber materials have been available for a long time, but currently many families of injection moldable thermo-plastic elastomers (TPE) are replacing traditional rubbers because TPE can be processed and recycled like thermoplastic materials. Typical applications of soft touch materials can now be found in the following categories [1,2]:

* Personal care products, tooth brushes, razors.
* Power-tool grips, handle and housings.
* Recreational and sporting products
* Water proof cameras
* Automotive instrument panels, consoles, etc.
* Medical devices, especially those used in ambulances such as the automated external defibrillator that needs to survive drop tests, cyclic loading test, and a water ingress test.
* Cell phones/portable digital products
* Cosmetic packaging. Overmolding soft touch materials to glass that are used for packaging of cosmetics such as perfume could make the package more durable, non-breakable, resistant to chips and marring, light weight and a pleasant color and touch.
* Overmolded intricate shapes present attractive decorative effects.

Figure 1 shows two samples of contemporary product design with soft touch materials. Figure 1(a) is a razor. The colored soft touch material is good for gripping with good aesthetic effect. The camera design with soft touch material is water proof. When accidentally dropped to a solid ground, it is not easily breakable.

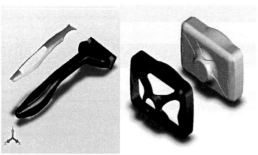

(a) a razor design   (b) a camera design
Figure 1 Sample design with soft touch materials

The widespread uses of multi-material overmolding technologies are mainly due to parts made by these technologies having the following advantages [1,2,3]:
Better Safety: improved grip in dry and wet environments, vibration damping and electric insulation.
Ergonomics: increased comfort and visual pleasure
Enhanced product performance: water-resistant seals, sound absorption, electric insulation and vibration damping.
Material optimization: material composition can be optimized to comply with the targeted applications.
Aesthetics: multiple colors, soft-touch effects;
Reduced cost: due to the in-mold assembly and in-mold decoration features of multi-materials overmolding, less factory floor space and shorter manufacturing cycle time can be achieved due to reduced assembly processes. By removing the need for the assembly processes or perhaps a further finishing stage, a single multi-material molding can offer a considerable unit cost reduction. Consider for example the case of toothbrush. Application of multi-material molding of this product has transformed this simple and standardized design. The proper combinations of hard and soft touch materials and a myriad of multiple color combinations have filled supermarkets shelves all over the world. Over molding technologies and the resulting design freedom have again helped the dominance of international brands in toothbrush business. Future product design composed of hybrids of many materials such as plastics, metals and ceramics can be molded as a single component in which the individual material properties are optimized.

Given the design freedom presented by the rapidly emerging manufacturing technologies, current computer aided design (CAD) systems can no longer meet the designers' need in designing multi-material parts. For example, the simple toothbrush shown in Figure 2 means different things to different people. The industrial designer would design the toothbrush as a single component. However the CAD engineer would design the toothbrush as an assembly. Both parties may have problems because if the toothbrush is designed as an assembly, the design must be decomposed. Current CAD systems do not support t h e easy decomposition operation required here. If the toothbrush is to be designed as an assembly of parts, it is extremely difficult because it is against the traditional wisdom that a design starts from conceptual stage instead of detailed parts. So far, information about overmolding process and part design is piecemeal. There are very few, if any, academic papers about these issues. This paper will mainly investigate the aspects of overmolding part design and related design assistive technologies such as haptic modeling.

The Multi-material part design methodologies

This paper showcases an experimental system that was developed based on haptic modeling with more intuitive user-computer interaction. Haptic is more intuitive in a way that it lets the user interact with a 3D computer model as if he is working on the real object [4,5]. The authors are in favor of the industrial designer's approach, that is, an overmolding part should be designed as a single part and then be decomposed. The proposed system setup is shown in Figure 3(a) where a six degree of freedom haptic device Phantom® is used.

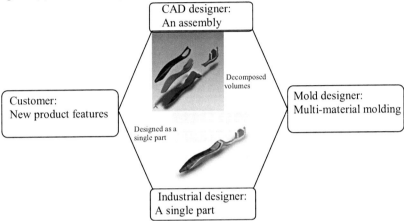

Figure 2 Different point of views

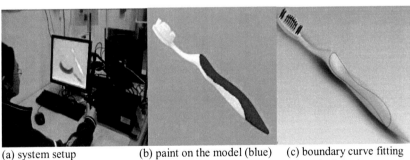

(a) system setup   (b) paint on the model (blue)   (c) boundary curve fitting
Figure 3 The proposed multi-material design system and methodologies.

When designing a multi-material part in the proposed system, the overall process flow is shown in Figure 4. In designing the overall part geometry, the task can be done either in a traditional CAD system or in a haptic system such as FreeForm®. Then the model is exported to the proposed system for colour painting. Haptic painting lets the user easily and quickly paint the region on a 3D model even without training [5]. Each painted area represents a volume of

191

specific material, and of course, the choice of colour for that volume by the designer. A sample painted region is shown in Figure 3(b) as blue colour. After the painting job is over, the designer may evaluate if the colour assignment is acceptable, if yes, the job continues to part decomposition. If not, the paints can be undone and painting can be started over again and again until a satisfactory result is achieved. When a painting is considered satisfactory, that means the color and material assignments are done. Now the part decomposition needs to be done. Part decomposition is a non-trivial job. It is recommended to do the decomposition by two ways. Firstly, the soft material part can be considered as an offset inside from the painted area. Secondly, it can be done by fitting a cutting surface based on the boundary curve as shown in Figure 3(c). The cutting surface cuts the volume into two parts, with each part composed of a different material.

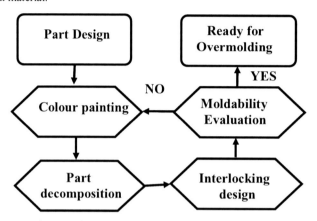

Figure 4 The multi-material part design flow chart

After the part is cut into different volumes, it is sometimes necessary to design interlock features to enhance the bond between different material volumes. Figure 5(a) shows some sample interlock design. Apart from interlock design, the decomposed volume should obey the general guidelines in overmolding. That is, the decomposed volume may be changed according the actual overmolding process.

To facilitate the moldability evaluation of the decomposed parts, a quick guideline together with 3D graphic illustration is implemented. Figure 6 shows a snap shot of the user interface. The user is prompted with questions related to moldability issues and asked to check if his/her part decomposition is moldable or not based on the guidelines. A database storing most features related to wall thickness, undercuts, warpage & shrinkage, shut-off, mechanical interlocks, and draft is developed. Figure 6 shows part of the features related to shut-off design. If the decomposition is not moldable, the decomposition has to be modified.

Discussions and further research

A complete computer aided design and manufacturing system need to support not only the part design but also tooling design. Selection of overmolding method and mold design should be supported too.

(a) Interlocking feature design   (b) Allowable undercut

Figure 5 Sample interlock design

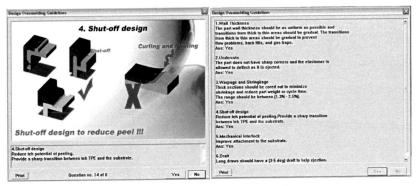

Figure 6 User assisted moldability evaluation

However, the mold design for overmolding has some different guidelines compared to traditional injection mold design as outlined in [6]. For example, under-cut is not allowed in traditional injection molding while it is possible for overmolding as shown in Figure 5(b) because the soft touch material portion on the part can be stretched and deformed while ejecting. However, sharp corners should be avoided in order not to cause any scratches while ejecting. Current mold design software packages are unable to handle such cases.

In overmolding part design, selection of compatible materials is very important as the bonding strength between materials directly affects the quality of end product. In addition to chemical bonding, mechanical bonding in terms of interlocks and special geometry design is also important. Apart from these, overmolding process control also affects the bonding strength. The timing of the injection of material, and the temperature of the first material when the second material is molded onto it are very tricky. Overmolding part problems such as incomplete filling and flashing are also affected by improper process control and mold design.

It is also important to simulate the overmolding process once a mold design is done, and an appropriate molding technology is chosen. Figure 7 shows the simulation of each shot for molding a sample part where three shots are needed to mold a multi-material toothbrush.

The above has briefly discussed the authors' ongoing research about issues related to multi-material part design for overmolding. It is expected that more research effort from academia will be put into this area as multi-material part design and heterogeneous material part design have been very hot in the CAD/CAM communities in recent years.

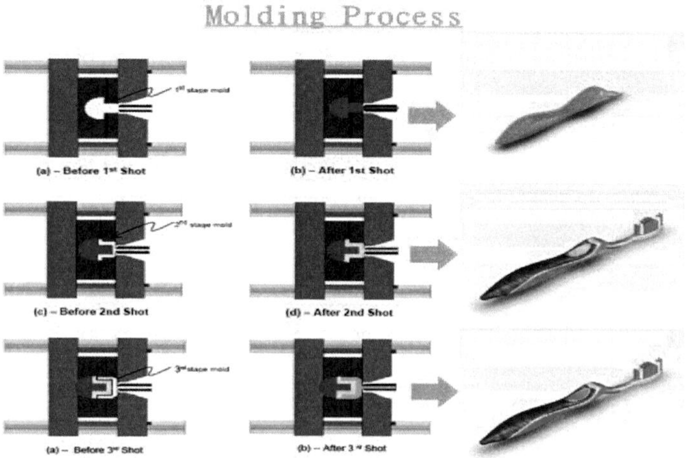

Molding Process

Figure 7 Overmolding simulation for a multi-material toothbrush design

Conclusions

This paper has presented a systematic approach to multi-material part design. Haptic painting has been proposed and demonstrated as an effective method for conceptual design of material and colour assignment. Preliminary research on part decomposition, overmolding process simulation and moldability evaluation is also reported.

Acknowledgement

This research is supported by a grant from Hong Kong Research Grants Council under the code HKU 7116/05E.

References

[1]   GLS Corporation: http://www.glscorporation.com/home.html. 2006.

[2]   V. Goodship and J.C. Love, Multi-Material Injection Moulding, Rapra Review Reports, Vol. 13, No. 1, (2002).

[3]   X. Li and S.K. Gupta, Geometric Algorithms for Automated Design of Rotary-platen multi-shots molds, Computer-Aided Design 36(12) (2004), pp. 1171-1187.

[4]   Z.Y. Yang, L, Lian and Y.H. Chen, Haptic Function Evaluation of Multi-material part design, Computer-Aided Design 37(7) (2005), pp.727-736.

[5]   D. Johnson, T.V. Thompson, et al. Painting textures with a haptic interface, IEEE Virtual Reality Conference 1999.

[6]   D.M. Bryce, Plastic injection molding: material selection and product design fundamentals, (Society of Manufacturing Engineers 1997).

Keynote Paper

● **Advances in Airframe Manufacture**
Dr Gareth M Williams, Airbus UK.

Keynote Lecture
International Conference on Manufacturing Research 2006 (ICMR 2006)
Liverpool John Moores University
England, United Kingdom

Advances in Airframe Manufacture

Mr. Andrew Levers
Technology Specialist, Manufacturing Systems, Airbus UK
Andrew.Levers@Airbus.com

Abstract.

The manufacture of commercial aircraft wings has traditionally been characterised by a combination of high complexity, high value added manufacturing processes coupled with heavy reliance on the manual skill base of assembly operators. Future product developments will see an increasing reliance on the use of Carbon Composites in primary structure, which in turn will require the development of new and alternative manufacturing processes, and a shift towards more automated assembly operations

In this presentation a basic outline of the manufacturing processes employed in the construction of the current generation of commercial aircraft wings are explained and contrasted against the likely processing route for emerging products that may feature large scale use of Carbon Composite in primary structure.

Invited Speaker from Industry

● **Developments in Micro Grinding with Planetary Kinematics**
Bob Willey, GPK Product Engineer, Saint-Gobain Abrasives
Mike Hitchiner, Product and Technology Manager, Saint Gobain Abrasives

Keynote Lecture
International Conference on Manufacturing Research 2006 (ICMR 2006)
Liverpool John Moores University
England, United Kingdom

Developments in Micro Grinding with Planetary Kinematics

Bob Willey – GPK Product Engineer – Saint-Gobain Abrasives

Mike Hitchiner – Product and Technology Manager – Saint Gobain Abrasives

Abstract.

The ever-growing demands on part flatness and machine capitalization are pushing the envelope for machine tools for flat grinding at the micron level. This has opened new markets for Grinding with Planetary Kinematics (GPK). This process has been developed and perfected by several, predominantly European; machine tool manufactures such Melchiorre, Peter Wolters and Stahli previously known for lapping machines.

GPK on dedicated machines provides order of magnitude improvement in productivity over lapping for parts with flatness requirements in the range of 0.1 to 3.0 microns. Initially grinders designed for GPK were limited to wheel speeds of less then 5m/s. This is now increasing rapidly with improved coolant delivery, superabrasive wheel design and formulations, in-process size gauging and force monitoring, and increased spindle power and machine stiffness. Wheel design advances include both the bond systems themselves and the surface distribution of the abrasive in the form of pie-shaped wedges or pellets. Vitrified, resin, epoxy and metal are all options depending on application

Applications for GPK for the precision steel markets such as fuel injection systems, pump, tool inserts and bearing are reviewed.

Advanced Manufacturing Technology: Grinding

Diamond resin bond wheel wear in precision grinding of optical materials

X. Tonnellier[1], P. Shore[1,a], P. Morantz[1], X. Luo[1] and A.Baldwin[1]

[1]School of Industrial & Manufacturing Science, Cranfield University, Bedfordshire MK43 0AL, UK.

[a]Paul.Shore@cranfield.ac.uk

Abstract. A new ultra precision large grinding machine - BoX® - has been developed at Cranfield University to machine large optical components. The form accuracy target is 1 μm p-v over a 1 metre part along with a surface finish of 50-150 nm RMS. Its maximum material removal rate of 200 mm³/s will permit a 1 metre piece to be machined in less then 10 hours with subsurface damage in the range of 2-5 μm.

This paper presents the analysis of wheel wear of diamond resin bond wheels that occurs when grinding optical materials. The materials chosen for these tests are ULE®, Zerodur® and SiC which are candidate materials for the new ELT telescope primary mirror segments.

Initial grinding experiments have been conducted on a Holroyd Edgetek machine using diamond resin bond wheels with grit sizes of 76 μm and 46 μm. In order to assess the wheel wear, 10 cm³, 40 cm³ and 125 cm³ were removed without intermediate dressing. An in-print technique on graphite was used to evaluate the wheel wear. The grinding forces, the spindle power and the acoustic emission levels were recorded during each cutting test.

These experiments point out the relationship between the wheel wear and the amount of material removed. They also show the influence of the volume of material removed and the grinding forces and spindle power. Data collected show that an error compensation methodology for large optics when using the BoX® grinding mode can be developed.

Keywords: wheel wear, ultra precision grinding, large optics, Zerodur, SiC, ULE.

Introduction

The next generation of large European ground based telescopes (ELT) is under study through different projects such as the Euro50 [1] or OWL [2] similar to, but much larger then the Keck hexagonal segmented mirror design. The number of large segments required for such projects range between 600 (Euro50) to 3000 (OWL). The segments' size is expected to be 1 to 2.5 metres and have a hexagonal shape. [3] The segments' candidate materials are glass (ULE®), glass ceramic (Zerodur®), ceramics (SiC, CVD SiC) and some other materials such as the Beryllium. [4]

To realise one of these telescopes in less than five years, the actual segment machining process must be shortened. A possible production improvement is to achieve a rapid grinding process with precise form accuracy and low subsurface damage. This will subsequently shorten the polishing process.

To achieve this production capability, a new ultra precision large optics grinder - BoX® - has been developed at Cranfield University. [5] Its form accuracy target is 1 μm p-v over a 1 metre part along with a surface finish of 50-150 nm RMS. Its maximum material removal rate of 200 mm³/s will enable a 1 metre piece to be machined in less than 10 hours with subsurface damage in the range of 2-5 μm.

The work reported in this paper has been performed on a 5 axis Holroyd Edgetek grinding machine with a fixture that reproduced the BoX® grinding mode. The purpose of the work has been to study the relation between the resin bond diamond wheel wear and the amount of material removed. These results will allow a "wheel wear compensation technique" to be developed for precision grinding of selected optical materials. Relations between the volume of material removed after

205

dressing and the grinding forces, the acoustic emission signal and the spindle power have been investigated. Additional results on surface form accuracy [6] and subsurface damage [7] results have been reported previously.

Experimental details

Specimens:
Specimens used in half scale grinding tests were Silicon carbide, ULE® and Zerodur®. (Table 1) The samples' dimensions were 100 x 100 mm square and 20 mm thick.

Material	Density	Elastic modulus E	Micro hardness H	Fracture toughness T	Thermal Conductivity k	Specific Heat Cp	CTE
	$[g/cm^3]$	[GPa]	[GPa]	$[MPa.m^{1/2}]$	[W/(m.K)]	[J/(Kg.K]	$[10^{-6}/K]$
Zerodur	2520	91	6.2	0.9	1.63	821	0.05
ULE	2205	70	4.6	1.8	1.35	745	0.025
SSiC	3150	420	27.4	3.5	190	700	2.1

Table 1: Materials properties

Zerodur® [8] is a glass-ceramic, manufactured by Schott in Germany and ULE® [9] is a glass made by Corning in USA. They have both ultra low thermal expansion coefficients. The sintered silicon carbide (SSiC) material [10] is made in France by Boostec. For optical purpose a CVD SiC coating is usually applied prior to final grinding and polishing.

Grinding equipment and grinding mode:
The grinding experiments were conducted on a Holroyd Edgetek 5 axis superabrasive grinding machine. A fixture was added on its grinding table so the material blank was tilted at 70°, recreating the 20° wheel tilt angle employed on the BoX® machine. [11] The test sample was held by a vacuum system mounted on a Kistler force dynamometer. (Figure 1a)

The BoX® grinding mode creates ground surfaces with cusps whose depth increases with the feedrate (f_w) per revolution of the workpiece. In the case of the grinding tests performed on the Holroyd machine, the feed per revolution of BoX® is simulated using an increment step of a linear axis (f). (Figure 1b)

Figure 1: a) Grinding set-up and b) Grinding mode

Two resin bond cup grinding wheels have been used to perform rough, semi finish and finish cuts. They had both a FEPA 6V5 cup wheel shape with a cutting layer radius of 300mm. The wheel used for the rough cuts employed 76 μm diamond grits at 75 concentration. Wheel diameter was 200mm. The wheel used for the semi finish and finish cuts was a 46 μm resin bonded diamond wheel at 50 concentration having a 150mm diameter.

A nickel electroplated wheel with 181 μm diamond size was employed to true and form the wheels cross section to a 300mm radius. The wheels were balanced in-situ using a Schenk dynamic balancing system. Before each cut, the wheel was dressed using a soft alumina white stick.

The coolant, a water based fluid (2% Dowel diluted), was delivered with a slot nozzle at a pressure of 2 Bar which provided a laminar flow.

Experimental conditions:

Three different machining conditions, which correspond to rough, semi finish and finish cuts for the BoX®, have been used on each material. (Table 2)

	MRR [mm³/s]	Depth of cut [μm]	Feedrate [mm/rev]	Velocity [mm/s]	Wheel speed [m/s]	Volume removed [cm³]
Rough	187.5	500	15	25	30	125
Semi finish	40	200	10	20	30	40
Finish	1.87	50	1.5	25	30	10

Table 2: Grinding conditions

The rough cut is used to remove a large amount of material. The semi finish cut reduces the cusps height value and removes most of the surface and subsurface damage left by the rough cut. The finish cut achieves the final form accuracy with low subsurface damage. The volume of material removed for the half scale wheel wear tests was 125 cm³, 40 cm³ and 10 cm³ respectively for the rough, semi finish and finish tests with no intermediate dressing.

For each test, the spindle power was monitored using the Edgetek in-situ power measurement and recorded using a NI Labview program developed at Cranfield. The grinding forces were recorded using a Kistler dynamometer. The acoustic sensor was mounted on the tilted fixture and the signal stored with a Dittel program.

 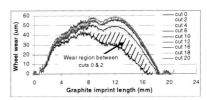

Figure 2: a) Wheel graphite imprint for finish grinding
and b) Graphite profile records for finish grinding of SiC

In order to record the wheel wear after repeated tests, the wheel was plunged into a graphite block. [12] This mark left an imprint of the wheel abrasive layer radius. (Figure 2a) Using the Talysurf profilometer to get a profile measurement of each graphite imprint, it was possible to compare differences of the wheel radius and calculate the amount of volumetric wheel wear. (Figure 2b) The stylus used was a 2μm radius conisphere diamond.

Results and analyses

Grinding performance:

The results obtained for the normal grinding forces and the spindle power for the rough and finish cuts for the three materials are presented in Graph 1.

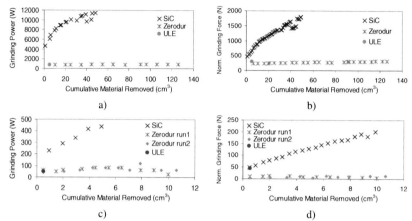

a)

b)

c)

d)

Graph 1: Rough cut (D76): a) Grinding power, b) Normal grinding force
and Finish cut (D46): c) Grinding power, d) Normal grinding force

The rough tests showed that the initial spindle power when grinding SiC is four times larger then Zerodur® and ULE®. The BoX® spindle power (10kW) is reached after removing 25 cm³ of SiC. The difference between SiC and Zerodur® increases to a factor of 10 after 48.4 cm³ of material is removed. The normal grinding force when rough cutting SiC shows an increase from 466 N to 1796 N after removing 48.4 cm³. For Zerodur®, the normal grinding force increases from 240 N to 320 N for Zerodur® after 126 cm³ has been removed.

As expected, the finish grinding tests revealed lower grinding forces and grinding power. For SiC, these parameters increase linearly to 199 N and 440 W. The total grinding tool deflection will attain 2 μm as the BoX® stiffness is over 100N/μm. The grinding power, for Zerodur® and ULE®, is considerably lower. The normal grinding force when finish grinding Zerodur® stays at 10 N.

Wheel wear:

As previously mentioned, the amount of wheel wear is recorded using a graphite imprint. Then it is measured with a profilometer and is computed using Microsoft Excel. The results showed that the amount of material worn from the wheel during the finish grinding of SiC is 133 mm³. For the finish cut of Zerodur®, 37mm³ to 65 mm³ are removed from the wheel. If the abrasive layer wear is considered uniformly distributed, the wheel radius modification is 40μm when grinding SiC and 11-20μm when grinding Zerodur®.

The cumulative material removed and the cumulative wheel wear during semi finish and finish grinding of Zerodur® and SiC can be compared using Graph 2.

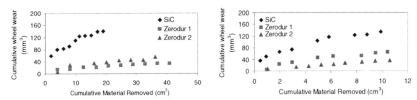

Graph 2: a) Cumulative wheel wear during semi finish grinding and b) finish grinding

The wheel wears quickly after the first cut for each material and grinding condition. The wheel wear during semi finish grinding is faster than for finish grinding. Once 5 cm^3 is removed during the semi finish grinding, the amount of wheel wear for Zerodur® and SiC follow a linear trend. This same behaviour appears for the finish grinding when 2 cm^3 is ground. As expected, the cumulative wheel wear follows a higher slope for SiC than for Zerodur®.

To analyze the influence of the wheel wear, the normal grinding force (Graph 3a) and the acoustic emission signal (Graph 3b) have been plotted against the cumulative wheel wear for the semi finish and finish grinding of SiC.

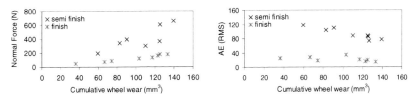

Graph 3: a) Normal grinding force with cumulative wheel wear and b) Acoustic emission response when cutting SiC

The normal grinding force during the semi finish cut increases more rapidly than for the finish cut when the same amount of wheel wear has occurred. The wheel wear is more critical when the material removal rate increases. The same appears when looking at the acoustic emission signal recorded. The linear trend decreases faster for the semi finish cut when the same amount of wheel wear is reached. A faster wear of the grits can explain these results.

Summary

The target of 200 mm^3/s material removal rate can be achieved on SiC, Zerodur® and ULE® with the BoX® 10 kW grinding spindle. However, the grinding power used for rough grinding of SiC shows that the actual wheel used needs to be dressed after removing 25 cm^3 of SiC.
The normal grinding forces are more important when grinding silicon carbide than Zerodur® or ULE®. During the finish grinding of SiC, with the BoX® high static loop stiffness (> 100N/μm), the wheel will need to be dressed after removing 3 cm^3 of SiC to keep the normal grinding force under 100N. It will be possible to keep the tool deflection under 1 μm with no need to compensate it.
These results show that Zerodur® and ULE® can be ground with the grinding wheels used during these tests on BoX®. Additional work is needed on wheel specifications to reduce the amount of dressing necessary when grinding silicon carbide.

The possibility of measuring the grinding power, grinding force and acoustic emission signal in BoX® will permit optimization of the dressing process to obtain an efficient grinding process. The investigation of the subsurface damage in silicon carbide will be reported in future papers.

Acknowledgements

The authors would like to acknowledge the project funding through the UK's Joint Research Councils – Basic Technologies programme and funding support from the McKeown Precision Engineering and Nanotechnology Foundation at Cranfield.

References

[1] Andersen, T.; Ardeberg, A.; Owner-Petersen, M.; "Euro50 Design Study of a 50 m Adaptive Optics Telescope"; Lund University, Sweden; 2003

[2] Dierickx, P.; Brunetto, E.T.; Comeron, F.; Gilmozzi, R.; Gonte, F.; Koch, F.; le Louarn, M.; Monnet, G.J.; Spyromilio, J.; Surdej, I.; Verinaud, C.; "OWL Phase: A status report"; In: Proceedings of SPIE, Vol.5489, pp.391-406; 2004

[3] Shore, P.; May-Miller, R.; "Production challenge of the optical segments for extra large telescopes"; In: International Workshop on EOS; 2003

[4] Gilmozzi, R.; "Science and technology drivers for future giant telescopes "; In: Proceedings of SPIE, Vol.5489, pp.1-10; 2004

[5] Shore, P.; Morantz, P.; Luo, X.; Tonnellier, X.; Read, R.; May-Miller, R.; "Design philosophy of the ultra precision big optix "BoX" machine"; In: Proceedings of Landamap Conference, pp.200-209, 2005

[6] Tonnellier, X.; Shore, P.; Luo, X.; Morantz, P.; Baldwin, A.; "High performance grinding studies on optical materials suitable for large optics", 2nd CIRP conference on High Performance cutting, Vancouver, 2006.

[7] Tonnellier, X.; Shore, P.; Luo, X.; Morantz, P.; Baldwin, A.; Evans, R.; Walker, D.; "Wheel wear and surface/subsurface qualities when precision grinding optical materials"; submitted to SPIE conference, Orlando, 2006.

[8] Schott AG; http://www.schott.com/optics_devices accessed 19/05/06

[9] VanBrocklin, R.R.; Hobbs, T.W.; Edwards, M.J.; "Corning's approach to segment blank manufacturing for an extremely large telescope"; In: Proceedings of SPIE, Vol. 5494, pp.1-8, 2004.

[10] Bougoin, M.; Deny, P.; "The SiC technology is ready for the next generation of extremely large telescopes"; In: Proceedings of SPIE, Vol.5494, pp.9-18, 2004.

[11] Shore, P.; Luo, X.; Jin, T.; Tonnellier, X.; Morantz, P.; Stephenson, D.; Collins, R.; Roberts, A.; May-Miller, R.; Read, R.; "Grinding mode of the "BOX" ultra precision free-form grinder"; In: Proceedings of ASPE, 2005.

[12] Li, Y.; Funkenbusch, P.D.; Gracewski, S.M.; Ruckman, J.; "Tool wear and profile development in contour grinding of optical components", In: International Journal of Machine Tools & Manufacture, Vol.44, pp.427-48, 2004

Development of Solid-Type Diamond Rotary Dresser Utilizing CVD Diamond Disc
- Application to High-Speed Rotary Dresser -

Akihiko Kubo[1, a] and Jun'ichi Tamaki[1, b]

[1]Dept. of Mechanical Engineering, Kitami Institute of Technology, 165 Koen-cho, Kitami, Hokkaido, 090-8507, Japan

[a]kuboak@mail.kitami-it.ac.jp, [b]tamaju@mail.kitami-it.ac.jp

Abstract. A solid-type diamond rotary dresser utilizing a CVD diamond disc is developed and applied to the dressing of a vitrified CBN grinding quill for internal grinding. This dresser has a feature not found in discrete-type diamond rotary dressers that have been used thus far, which have continuous contact with the grinding quill and exert static dressing force. The solid-type rotary diamond dresser was mounted on a high-speed spindle rotating at 33 m/sec, and basic dressing performance was investigated. It was found that the solid-type diamond rotary dresser has almost the same performance as the discrete-type diamond rotary dresser in terms of grinding force, ground roughness and grinding wheel wear.

Keywords: solid-type dresser, discrete-type dresser, CVD diamond disc, rotary diamond roll, vitrified CBN quill, high-speed rotary dresser, grinding performance.

Introduction

In the dressing of a vitrified CBN grinding wheel, a diamond roll on which surface diamond grits are arranged at random or diamond logs are arranged at regular intervals is generally used. The most effective dressing condition that results in a good grinding performance is when the speed of the dressing roll is almost equal to that of the grinding wheel. This condition can be realized independently of grinding wheel diameter by changing the rotational speed of the grinding wheel. However, note that the contact time of diamond grits or logs decreases as grinding wheel diameter decreases. In the case of a grinding quill that has a small diameter and a long shaft, the small number of diamond grit or log contacts per revolution of the grinding quill induces intermittent dressing force resulting in undesirable vibration.

In this study, a solid-type diamond rotary dresser that makes continuous contact with grinding quill without intermittent dressing force is developed and its applicability is investigated. To distinguish the solid-type diamond rotary dresser from those that have been used thus far, the rotary diamond roll on which surface diamond grits or logs are discretely arranged is, hereafter, called the discrete-type diamond rotary dresser.

Diamond Rotary Dresser

Figure 1 depicts the kinematics of rotary dressing and the traces left on the surface of a grinding quill in the cases of the discrete-type and solid-type dressers. D_d denotes the dressing roll diameter, D_q the grinding quill diameter, V_d the dresser rotational speed and V_q the quill rotational speed. In the case of the discrete-type dresser shown in Fig. 1(a), diamond logs are arranged at regular intervals of p.

The trace depicted in Fig. 1(a) is the result of a dressing simulation using the conditions listed in Table 1. In this case, the diamond logs make contact with the grinding quill intermittently; then, the nondressed and dressed parts appear alternately. The trace pattern is determined by the speed ratio V_d/V_q and the interval p.

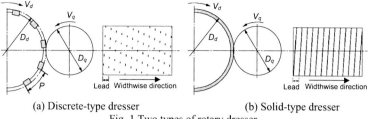

(a) Discrete-type dresser   (b) Solid-type dresser

Fig. 1 Two types of rotary dresser

The number of contacts per revolution of the grinding quill is expressed as

$$N_c = \pi (D_q/p)(V_d/V_q). \tag{1}$$

Figure 2 shows the calculated results of N_c against D_q for various p values. The number of contacts decreases with quill diameter and takes a value of less than 2 when a grinding quill of less than 1 mm diameter is dressed by the discrete-type dresser used in the experiment. This result suggests that the grinding quill vibrates because of the intermmittent dressing force under these conditions. The solid-type dresser shown in Fig. 1(b) is expected to eliminate undesirable vibration from the grinding quill because this dresser continuously contacts the grinding quill and leaves a spiral on the quill surface.

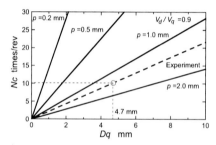

Fig. 2 Number of contact times of discrete-type dresser

Experimental Procedures

Solid-type Dresser and Discrete-type Dresser. Figure 3 shows a micrograph and the topography of the solid-type diamond dresser. An electroconductive CVD diamond disc 0.5 mm wide is fastened with a pair of screwed flanges to form the solid-type diamond dresser. The application of a CVD diamond disc to the rotary dresser was patented [1] 15 years ago, but the thickness was limited to within 0.1 mm owing to manufacturing difficulties. A CVD diamond plate 0.5 mm thick is now available, and it is possible to form the edge of this CVD diamond ring into any shape still with sufficient stiffness to prevent vibration. In this study, a flat-edged CVD diamond ring of 50 mm diameter was used, and the initial run-out of the dresser was removed by a mechanical method to achieve a roundness of 0.6 μm. In the examination of the micrograph, some crevicelike grooves perpendicular to the dresser travelling direction were found on the CVD diamond surface; however, the overall surface consists of asperities 1~2 μm high.

Figure 4 shows a micrograph and the topography of the discrete-type diamond dresser. Single-crystal-diamond logs 0.2 mm wide were set on the circumference of the dressing roll at regular intervals. The number of diamond logs was 120 and the roll diameter was 50 mm such that the interval between logs was 1.31 mm. In the examination of the 3-D topography, the front and back sides were dulled due to a severe contact with the grinding quill and the surface consists of asperities 3~5 μm high, which are higher than those for the solid-type diamond dresser.

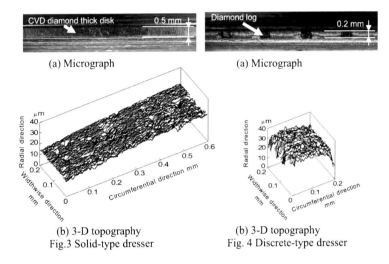

(a) Micrograph   (a) Micrograph

(b) 3-D topography   (b) 3-D topography
Fig.3 Solid-type dresser   Fig. 4 Discrete-type dresser

Experimental equipments. An internal grinding machine tool whose spindle rotates at 150,000 rpm with oil-mist lubrication was used for the experiments and a vitrified CBN grinding quill 4.7 mm diameter was dressed with two types of dresser: a solid-type dresser and a discrete-type dresser. Figure 5 illustrates the grinding force measuring system. A rotary-type dynamometer (Kistler 9123) was installed on the workpiece spindle and grinding forces F_n, F_t were measured by a telemetric method. Each dresser was fixed on the spindle shown in Fig.6, and rotated at 12,700 rpm. The touch of the dresser on the grinding quill surface was detected by an AE sensor fixed on the housing of the dressing spindle within a positioning accuracy of 0.1 μm.

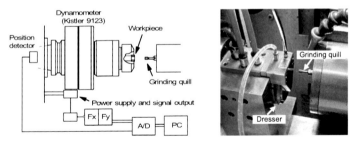

Fig.5 Grinding system   Fig.6 Dressing equipment

Experimental Conditions. The experimental conditions are listed in Table 1.The diamond rotary dressers rotate at 33 m/sec in the same direction as the grinding quill or in the down cut mode. Thus, the speed ratio of the dresser to the grinding quill is calculated to be +0.9. Two dressing depths of cut, 0.2 μm and 2.0 μm, were applied.

The grinding conditions are listed in Table 2. An internal plunge grinding of hardened SUJ2 steel was carried out with an infeed rate of 0.2 μm/rev. The grinding forces converged to a constant at an accumulated depth of cut greater than 0.5 mm. Thus, the grinding forces, the ground surface and the radial wear of the grinding quill were measured at the accumulated depth of cut, 0.5 mm.

Table 1 Dressing conditions

Grinding machine	Internal grinding machine, SG-25
Grinding quill	BZ140NM34V, ϕD_q =4.7 [mm], Width 5 [mm]
	Rotational speed of grinding quill V_q = 37 [m/sec] (N_q = 150,000 [rpm])
Dresser	Rotary dresser
	1) Solid-type
	CVD diamond, ϕD_d = [50] mm, t =0.5 [mm]
	2) Discrete-type
	Single crystal diamond log
	0.2 [mm] wide, 120 pieces, ϕD_d = 50 [mm]
	Rotational speed of dresser
	V_d = 33 [m/sec] (N_d = 12,700 [rpm])
	Speed ratio V_d/V_q = +0.9 (down cut)
Traverse speed	f_d = 6,000 [mm/min], Dressing Lead L_d = 40 [μm/rev]
Dressing depth of cut	Δ_d = 0.2 [μm]×50 pass, 2.0 [μm]×5 pass

Table 2 Grinding conditions

Grinding method	Internal plunge grinding (down cut)
Rotational speed of grinding quill	V_q = 37 [m/sec] (N_q = 150,000 [rpm])
Rotational speed of workpiece	V_w = 0.94 [m/sec] (N_w = 1,500 [rpm])
Infeed rate(plunge speed)	f_w = 0.2 [μm/rev]
Accumulated depth of cut	$\Sigma\Delta_w$ = 500 [μm]
Workpiece	SUJ2(Hrc58~63), ϕd_w = 9 [mm]
Coolant	Soluble type, 80% dilution

Experimental Results

Surface topography of grinding quill. Figure 7 shows SEM micrographs of CBN grit dressed by the solid-type diamond dresser. In the case of fine dressing (dressing depth of cut Δ_d = 0.2 μm), traces of small exfoliation can be observed on almost the entire grit surface, although a trace of brittle fracture can also be observed. In the case of rough dressing (dressing depth of cut Δ_d = 2.0 μm), the amount of small exfoliation is less and the degree of brittle fracture is greater than that for fine dressing.

Figure 8 shows SEM micrographs of CBN grit dressed by the discrete-type diamond dresser. There is no trace of exfoliation but traces of brittle fracture are left on the overall surface. From the examination of the effect of dressing depth of cut, the fracture seems to be larger for rough dressing (Δ_d = 2.0 μm) than for fine dressing (Δ_d = 0.2 μm).

Grinding performance. The grinding outputs are listed in Table 3. Form the examination of the effect of dressing depth of cut, grinding forces decrease, surface roughness deteriorates, and wheel wear increases; grinding forces remain constant for the solid-type dresser. This means that the solid-type dresser can control grinding performance by changing the dressing depth of cut, as the discrete-type dresser can.

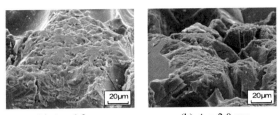

(a) $\Delta_d = 0.2$ μm (b) $\Delta_d = 2.0$ μm
Fig. 7 SEM micrographs of CBN grit dressed by solid-type dresser

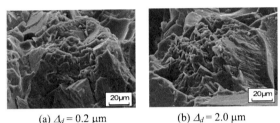

(a) $\Delta_d = 0.2$ μm (b) $\Delta_d = 2.0$ μm
Fig. 8 SEM micrographs of CBN grit dressed by discrete-type dresser

From the examination of the effect of difference in dresser type, the solid-type dresser has the same grinding performance as the discrete-type dresser at a dressing depth of cut of 0.2 μm. However, at a dressing depth of cut of 2.0 μm, the normal grinding force is slightly larger and the surface roughness is worse than those of the discrete-type dresser. This may be due to the differences in dressing parameters, namely, contact mode and the width, between the two dressers.

Table 3 Grinding performances

Dresser	Dressing Depth	Grinding Force		Roughness	Wheel wear
	Δ_d [μm]	F_n [N/mm]	F_t [N/mm]	Ra [μm]	W_r [μm]
Solid-type	0.2	0.80	0.27	1.04	4.1
	2.0	0.80	0.27	2.00	7.1
Discrete-type	0.2	0.90	0.32	1.02	4.6
	2.0	0.62	0.23	1.36	7.7

Conclusions

A solid-type diamond rotary dresser utilizing a CVD diamond disc was developed and applied to the dressing of a vitrified CBN grinding quill for internal grinding. It was found that this dresser has almost the same dressing ability as a discrete-type diamond rotary dresser and promises to useful for grinding quills with low stiffness.

References

[1]   Tsutsui, T. (1991) Rotary Diamond Tool for Truing Grinding Wheel, European Patent Application, Publication No. 0410481A2.6.

Classification of varying levels of ploughing, rubbing and cutting during Single Grit tests using Evolutionary Inspired Computer Techniques

James Griffin[1,a], Xun Chen[2,b]

School of Mechanical, Materials and Manufacturing
University of Nottingham, Nottingham NG7 2RD, UK[1,2]

Abstract

Grit interaction with workpiece materials is a key action of grinding. The process of single grit (SG) scratches allows the separation of the different grinding phenomenon namely that of rubbing, ploughing and cutting. Rubbing and ploughing usually occur before or after cutting. Out of the three phenomena the most difficult to separate is ploughing and cutting as they both cause plastic deformation. The energy effects which are measured by acoustic emission (AE) signal mimic the plastic material deformation whereas with rubbing, the AE would mimic elastic material deformation energy. It is therefore imperative to identify these different phenomenon using advanced signal processing techniques such as Wavelet Transforms and hybrid evolutionary computing classification techniques. With these fundamental investigations verified through repeated tests a high level of confidence is obtained. These results can then be applied to grinding and distinguish cutting, ploughing and rubbing phenomenon at the micro level. To validate the AE extracted signal, a Kistler force sensor would be used to obtain the force experienced in x, y and z axis of Makino A55 Machine Centre.

Keywords: Acoustic Emission, Single Grit, Short Time Fourier Transforms, Wavelet Transforms, Fuzzy Clustering, Neural Networks and Genetic Algorithms

1 Introduction

Varying levels of grinding phenomenon is particularly difficult to distinguish in terms of the energy differences through different signal extraction methods. One of the more successful signal extraction methods is that of Acoustic Emission. When an object is subjected to an external force, it will generate elastic waves due to material particle displacements and these waves can propagate in material media [1]. Acoustic Emission (AE) is released in the form of both elastic and plastic material energy footprints this is due to the material particle displacements under various stresses. When different external forces act on the same material or the same external force acts on different materials, the elastic waves will have different characteristics. This is an important consideration as elastic waves can be used for monitoring many machining processes and/or material non-destruction tests [2], [3], [4], [5].

When compared with other non destructive tests AE monitoring, grinding is considered a much more difficult task due to random interaction of grit and workpiece materials. Single Grit (SG) scratching experiments are important to the fundamental understanding of grinding of materials such as what energy footprints are made during the SG cutting process in terms of cutting, ploughing and rubbing. Once the fundamentals of SG have been investigated, these findings will be used to identify the similar energy footprints within a grinding pass. Aerospace alloys are used as

---

[a] Tel: +44 115 9514146. E-mail address: epxjmg@nottingham.ac.uk
[b] Tel: +44 115 9514015; fax +44 115 9513800. E-mail address: xun.chen@nottingham.ac.uk

workpiece materials this is due to their material properties being characteristically hard and withstanding high levels of prolonged temperature.

The AE wave is described as a non-stationary stochastic signal. Traditionally event driven analysis of AE was used. However due to SG producing short burst high frequency and long duration low frequency components simultaneously, continuous AE waveforms are extracted. Once the continuous waveform has been extracted a Digital Signal Processing (DSP) Techniques is required for representing the time signal in terms of frequency bands over time. Fast Fourier Transform (FFT) is a method of representing the frequency bands albeit they do not adequately describe the transient features in terms of frequency resolution over time [6].

An improvement to the FFT is that of Short Time Fourier Transforms (STFT) [13]. STFT is similar to FFT however it provides a much richer picture of the signal providing both frequency and time information. STFT suffers from a trade-off between frequency and time resolution. That said the technique can still provide a useful analysis just as long as an optimised approach is adapted between the two domain resolutions.

Wavelet Transforms (WT) [7] [12], a family of orthogonal basis functions, can overcome some of the limitations posed by both FFT and STFT in representing non-stationary signals through scaled time-frequency (TF) analysis. WT provides both an approximate and a detailed representation of scaled TF analysis. The scaled localised TF analysis characterises AE signals in terms of high frequency burst of short duration and low frequency components of longer duration [6] [7] at any point along the original time-frequency original signal [8]. To that end, the WT approximate and detailed representations provide both a rich picture in terms of useful and redundant information [11]. This redundant information requires another technique to represent this information without adding too much to information dimensionality (hinders the classification process) such as a statistical windowing technique. To calibrate the AE sensor and normalise the signals from day to day basis, the AE sensor is tested with a 2H pencil calibration method [9].

2 Single grit and grinding tests

The experiment of SG cutting interaction was carried out on a specially designed rig on Makino A55 Machine Centre. All the sample materials were polished to a very high quality finish to distinguish the SG cuts from other material markings. Roughness measurements (R_a) across all work pieces were measured between 0.0278µm and 0.0477µm.

To signify whether cutting, ploughing or rubbing occurred, the SG groove would be measured using a Fogale Photomap microscope and the groove area (using the Matlab Trapezoidal numerical integration method for calculating the area under the curve [14]) minus the total surface roughness would be divided into the material area left by two the sides of the groove also minus the total surface roughness. If the surface area above the groove was more than the groove then rubbing with plastic deformation occurred, if however they were approximately equal then ploughing occurred otherwise if the groove was more than the surface area above the groove then cutting occurred.

By simulating the grinding chip formation with a scratch test, the acoustic emission of grinding chip formation may be investigated. The scratch test can be carried out by feeding an Al_2O_3 grit towards the rotational flat sample. With a grit in-and-out stroke, a scratch groove will be formed on the flat sample surface. The maximum scratch depth is about 1.5µm, which is a typical value of grinding chip in high efficiency grinding. The scratching speed is 35 m/s. By using STFT and WT, the features of acoustic emission at both time-frequency domains are illustrated in Figure 1 Left. The AE frequency band of the SG Scratches were typically found in the range of 100 ~ 550 kHz, which are similar to the AE feature frequencies in grinding tests experienced in previous work [10]. A similar set-up for grinding is illustrated the right hand side of Figure 1.

3 Grinding Phenomenon Classifiers

The AE is converted into frequency bands over time using both STFT and WT. STFT representations can be windows to manageable levels however with WT it needs another stage to reduce this information into even richer summary descriptors. This is accomplished through the WT detailed data (Wavelet parameters set to level 4 decomposition and debauches 4th transform) being windowed in data segments of 50 data points and 1st to 4th order mechanics (kurtosis, standard deviation, mean and skew) are taken to extract and summarise this rich information for classification.

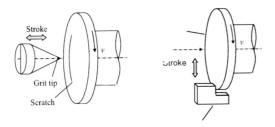

Figure 1. Sketch of a single grit scratch test rig and a grinding test rig.

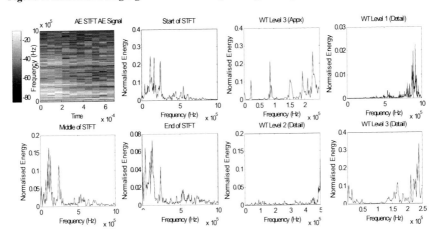

Figure 2. CMSX4 SG Cut (a) STFT and (b) WT

Looking at Figure 2 (a) the STFT is displayed by the greyscale map and the start, middle and end parts of the STFT can be found to the right of the greyscale map and the two below also within section 2 (a). In comparison Figure (2b) displays an approximate waveform with a third level WT decomposition (top left) and following on from that in a clock wise fashion the detailed WT coefficient levels from 1 to 3 respectively are displayed. From looking at the two DSP methods WT offers a much richer picture over the frequency and time domains.

219

A neural network (NN) was developed to identify different phenomena involved in SG scratch tests. The parameters used for the NN for different experiments are listed in Table 1. There were a total of 6 scratches made 2 mm apart for each material therefore a total of 24 scratches existed for all the materials. The materials used in the following tests consisted of EN8 steel, Inconel 718, CMSX4 and MAR-M002.

Table 1. NN parameters for experiments

NN Parameters	Value
hidden layers	2
Input size	(1) STFT: 256 Neurons (2) WT & Statistical window: 72 Neurons (8 windows with 6 values across the set of coefficients + 24 time constants (8 windows))
Transfer function for layer 1,2,3	Tan-Sigmoid
Transfer function for output layer	Pure-linear
Epochs	10000 for (1) Time: 25 minutes 10000 for (2) Time: 5 minutes
Learning Rule	Backpropagation
Learning rate	0.1^{-25}
Momentum	0.8
Training	60 different Cutting, Ploughing and Rubbing cases 60 different Cutting, Ploughing and Rubbing cases

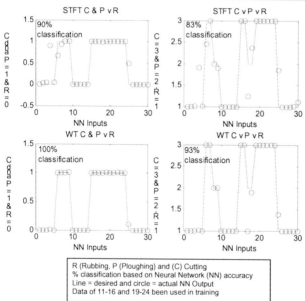

Figure 3. NN Results for STFT SG data (top) and WT data (bottom).

220

Figure 3 displays results that are very encouraging in regard to the classification of rubbing, ploughing and cutting phenomenon. With the dynamic scale and high resolution of frequency and time information, Wavelet Transform (WT) for both cases provided a 10% greater accuracy than that of the STFT representation. The next part of the paper looks at a different technique in using fuzzy clustering with Genetic Algorithm Optimisation (optimise cluster segregation and number of iterations) to segregate the WT data into different clusters to signify cutting and ploughing from rubbing phenomenon. This is a particularly useful technique when classifying grinding data that has an unknown state in how much of the signal contains rubbing, ploughing or cutting phenomenon.

Using a combination of WT and statistical windowing it was possible to get the salient principal components and obtain 100% and 93% classifications for identifying both the two phenomena (Figure 3 bottom left) and three phenomena (Figure 3 bottom right).

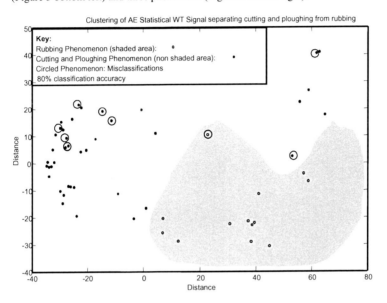

Figure 4. Fuzzy-GA Clustering for Statistical WT AE Signal for SG Cut.

Figure 4 displays a high confidence of classifications where 43 out 53 cases were segregated correctly. With more data the technique becomes more robust towards generalising the SG phenomenon and can be used to distinguish the features of cutting, ploughing and rubbing from that of an AE grinding signal. This technique uses fuzzy clustering along with a Genetic Algorithm (GA) to optimise the soft clusters giving an accurate segregation of unknown data. The GA optimises the Fuzzy clustering technique through the amount of iterations, cluster accuracy parameters and the numbers of clusters.

4 Conclusion

Single Grit tests were carried out with aerospace materials on A55 Machine Centre. After SG cuts it was possible to distinguish ploughing and cutting from the rubbing phenomenon. This is expected as ploughing and cutting have different energy signatures than that of rubbing (cutting and ploughing actually remove material and therefore has plastic material energy properties whereas rubbing does not and instead has only elastic material properties). The rubbing was very difficult to identify as there were some marks found during analysis which signified the rubbing had miniscule plastic deformation present and was not consistent with straight rubbing phenomenon. From looking at the results displayed in Figures 3 and 4 it can be seen that the cutting, ploughing and rubbing phenomenon can be separated with some high confidence. The DSP technique of Wavelet Transforms proved to be more successful than using STFTs. This is due to the dynamic resolution of the time and frequency components anywhere along the original time extracted signal. This initial work forms a sound basis for more in depth future work which bolster this fundamental work further of SG and grinding investigation.

References

[1]   **Royer, D., Dieulesaint, E.** (2000). Elastic Waves in Solids I, II. New York, Springer-Verlag Berlin Heidelberg.
[2]   **Webster, J., Marinescu, I. Bennett, R.,** (1994) Acoustic emission for process control and monitoring of surface integrity during grinding, Annals of the CIRP, 43(1), 299-304.
[3]   **Coman, R., Marinescu, I. D., et al.,** (1999) Acoustic emission signal - an effective tool for monitoring the grinding process, Abrasives Dec/Jan: 5.
[4]   **Chen, M. Xue, B. Y.** (1999). Study on acoustic emission in the grinding process automation. American Society of Mechanical Engineers, Manufacturing Engineering Division, MED Manufacturing Science and Engineering - 1999 (The ASME International Mechanical Engineering Congress and Exhibition), Nov 14-Nov 19 1999, Nashville, TN, USA, ASME, Fairfield, NJ, USA.
[5]   **Holford, K. M.** (2000) Acoustic Emission basic principles and future directions, Strain 36(2): 51-54.
[6]   **Li, X., Wu J.** (2000). "Wavelet analysis of acoustic emission signals in boring." Proceedings of the Institution of Mechanical Engineers, Part B: Journal of Engineering Manufacture 214(5): 421-424.
[7]   **Staszewski, W. J. and Holford, K. M.** (2001). Wavelet signal processing of acoustic emission data, Key Engineering Materials, v.204-205: 351-358.
[8]   **Chui K.C.,** 1992, "An Introduction to Wavelets," Academic Press, San Diego, ISBN 91-58831
[9]   **Barbezat M., Brunner, A.J. Flueler, P. Huber, C.** and **Kornmann, X.** (2004), "Acoustic emission sensor properties of active fibre composite elements compared with commercial acoustic emission sensors", Sensors and Actuators Volume: 114, pages: 13-20.
[10] **Chen, X., Griffin, J., Liu, Q.,** (2006) Mechanical and Thermal Behaviours of Grinding Acoustic Emission, International Journal of Manufacturing Technology and Management (IJMTM), Special Issue on: High Performance Grinding Processes.
[11] **Liu, Q., Chen, X., Gindy, N.** (2005) Fuzzy pattern recognition of AE signals for grinding burn, International Journal of Machine Tools and Manufacture, 2005, vol. 45/7-8, pp. 811-818.
[12] **Mallat, S. G.** (1999) A wavelet tour of Signal Processing, 2nd Ed, San Diego; London, Academic Press.
[13] **Smith S.W.,** (1997), "The Scientist and Engineer's Guide to Digital Signal Processing" California Technical Publishing, ISBN 0-9660176-3-3
[14] **Matlab** Function Reference Volume 3: P – Z, *Version 7, The Mathworks Inc, Trapezoidal function (trapz) Page 2-2286, 2004.*

Design of User Guidance Manual for Optimal Coolant Delivery in Grinding

R. Cai[1, a] and M. N. Morgan[1, b]

[1]AMTReL, General Engineering Research Institute, Faculty of Technology and Environment, Liverpool John Moores University, Byrom Street, Liverpool, L3 3AF, UK

[a] r.cai@ljmu.ac.uk

[b] m.n.morgan@ljmu.ac.uk

Abstract. Grinding fluid plays a vital role in achieving high removal rates and good workpiece quality. This paper provides a summary description of a software based User Guidance Manual which has been developed as an aid to the design of improved coolant delivery systems. The User Guidance Manual system includes a series of design procedures based on Case Based Reasoning (CBR) and Rule Based Reasoning (RBR). This paper also describes an intelligent database which has been designed as an integral feature. The User Guidance Manual is constructed in MS Access with Visual Basic support code. The system described may be subject to further refinement / modification dependent on the outcome of planned industrial evaluations.

Keywords: Grinding, Coolant delivery, Database, Artificial Intelligence methods

1   INTRODUCTION

Grinding fluid is a commonly expensive parameter to any grinding process. Approximately 7-17% of total machining costs are consumed by the use and disposal of the grinding fluid [1]. Coolant delivery system design remains an important activity that impacts significantly on production cost [2]. A User Guidance Manual (UGM) with accompanying software supported Design Procedures to assist a user in achieving optimum useful fluid delivery [3] is described. The UGM has been developed as an output of a current research council project. The Knowledge Base of the UGM was established from outcomes of published research, from industrial experience and from complementary research projects within the laboratory. Problems specific and/or common to the industries of collaborating partners are identified. The Design Procedures steer the user to a recommended fluid application system, based on inputs defining the process. A problem solving methodology has been established and initial work is based on simple algorithms and procedures. User inputs include: grinding operation, wheel specifications, process parameters, workpiece material, geometry and target quality. The Design Procedures output a recommended coolant type and useful flowrate, in addition to the nozzle profile and position and pump pressure required. Outputs from the Design Procedures are to be fully evaluated and compared with target workpiece quality criterion. The Design Procedures will be assessed for their ability to offer suitable coolant application methods leading to target workpiece quality. A further measure of improved and efficient coolant application will be reduced cycle time leading to lower total costs per part. The Design Procedures take account where necessary of production constraints for a specific coolant or maximum available pump pressure.

2   SYSTEM OVERVIEW

This User Guidance Manual is developed in MS Access / Visual Basic. 'Intelligence' embedded in the system includes: Rule based reasoning (RBR) and Case based reasoning. The UGM has a modular structure and modules include: Useful flow rate module, Coolant selection module, Nozzle design module and Pump and reservoir design module. The relationship between the User Guidance Manual and supported Artificial Intelligence is shown in Figure 1.

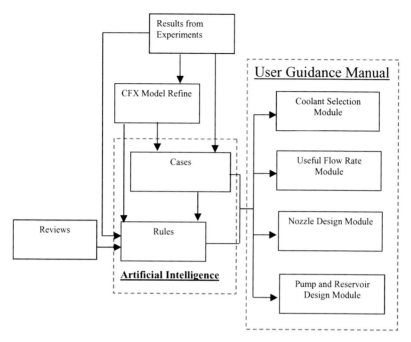

Figure 1 Relationship between User Guidance Manual and supported Artificial Intelligence

3   OPTIMISATION PROCEDURES

A flowchart of the overall User Guidance Manual system is shown in Figure 2. User inputs include: grinding operation, wheel specifications, process parameters, workpiece material, geometry and target quality. The Design Procedures will output a recommended coolant type, useful flowrate, nozzle profile, position and pump pressure required. The UGM has been designed to also allow for parameters to be input by the user based on his knowledge and the resources he has. The selection of Coolant type and properties is based on data obtained from experiments and reviews. The estimation of Useful flow rate is also based on data obtained from experiments and reviews. Delivery pressure and flow rate are calculated using data from experiments and CFX simulations, as are the Nozzle profile design, nozzle position and Pre-nozzle arrangement. Classical fluid dynamics relationships are used to calculate the pump requirement.

Three cutting fluids are categorized in this work based on their composition: Basic oils, basic oils with or without additives, coolant emulsion (concentrate: basic oil + emulsifier), coolant solutions (organic or inorganic). Table 1 shows the recommendation for Coolant selection.

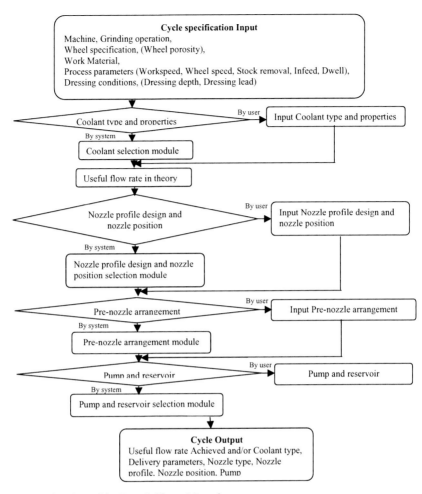

Figure 2 Flowchart of the User Guidance Manual

The aim of the User Guidance Manual is to steer the user to a recommended fluid application system based on inputs defining the process. The optimisation target is to achieve optimal useful flow. The optimal useful flow is that amount of fluid that passes through the grinding contact zone beyond which no further benefit to lubrication or cooling is achieved.

There are many ways to estimate the useful flow. In the approach of Rowe et al [4], the useful flow Q_u is estimated based on the assumption of making a comparison to a theoretical fluid layer [5].

$$Q_u = h_{uf} \times v_s \times b_s$$

Eq.(1)

Where h_{uf} = theoretical fluid layer, v_s = wheel speed, and b_s = wheel width

A porosity value and surface pore depth of the wheel are used to give the thickness of the theoretical fluid layer.

$$h_{uf} = \phi \times h_{pores}$$

Eq.(2)

Where h_{pores} = mean depth of pores and ϕ = wheel porosity

From Eq.(1) and Eq.(2), the optimal useful flow can be estimated. Based on this estimation, grinding conditions and coolant type, the nozzle profile and position, pre-nozzle delivery, pump and reservoir can be designed.

By way of example, the User Guidance Manual frontend access to the Nozzle Selection module are shown in Figures 3 and 4 respectively.

Table 1. The recommendation for Coolant [6]

Materials	Hardness	Fluid
Carbon steels	50Rc max	2,4
	Over 50Rc	1
Tool steels		3,5
High Speed Steels	50Rc max	3
	Over 50Rc	3
Super alloys		1
Stainless Steels & Ni Alloys		3
Cast Iron	50Rc max	2
	Over 50Rc	3
Aluminium Alloys		1
Copper Alloys		2
Ti Alloys, wrought		4

1. Oil
2. Coolant emulsion - light duty (general purpose)
3. Coolant emulsion - heavy duty
4. Coolant solutions - light duty (general purpose)
5. Coolant solutions - Heavy duty

4   STRUCTURE OF THE INTELLIGENT GRINDING DATABASE

The database was developed in Access 2000. The structure of the database was designed such that all the attributes that define a grinding cycle and its components are included. The database elements are:

machine – cycle – material – wheel – dress – coolant-coolant system-nozzle-individual record

Machine Data: This provides details of all Machine parameters.

Cycle Data: This provides details of Work Material, Work Size, Coolant, Wheel Type and Grinding Parameters for each part.

Material Data: This provides details of the mechanical and thermal properties of Work Material.

Wheel Data: This provides details of wheel type, size, mechanical and thermal properties of the Wheel.

Dress Data: This provides details of dressing parameters.

Coolant Data: This provides details of physical and thermal properties of the Coolant.

Coolant System Data: This provides details of pump and reservoir.

Nozzle Data: This provides details of nozzle profile and nozzle position.

Individual Part Record: This stored all agreed details of ground parts including Batch No, Part No. Cycle Data, Calculated Data including the maximum grinding temperature, Algorithm Data and Work Post Assessment Data. This 'Record' could be used to monitor the production of 'critical' parts.

The Database HMI is programmed in Visual Basic and enables the operator to read and edit data (password protected for data editing) from the database, the frontend is illustrated in Figure 3. Data validation routines are written to ensure data input is valid and within stated limits.

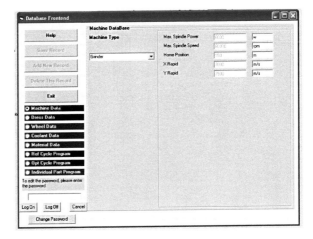

Figure 3 Database Front End

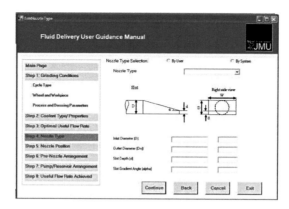

Figure 4 The Nozzle Selection module frontend of the User Guidance Manual

5   SUMMARY

The key features of a User Guidance Manual (UGM) developed for fluid delivery in grinding operation have briefly been described. The UGM includes modules for: Useful flow rate, Coolant selection, Nozzle design moule and Pump and reservoir design. The artificial intelligence techniques employed include: Case Based Reasoning (CBR) and Rule Based Reasoning (RBR). A fundamental characteristic of CBR systems is the requirement for sufficient cases to be resident in the database to cover the target Cycle Specification. If insufficient cases are available for a successful search the system will default to RBR procedures. A database designed as an integral part of the User Guidance Manual is also described. The structure of the database has been designed based on the following elements: Machine Tool Data, Grinding Cycle Data, Material Data, Wheel Data, Dressing Data, Coolant Data, Coolant System Data, Nozzle Data, Individual Part Record and other secondary elements. The Database interface (HMI) allows the operator to read and edit data. There is the potential to greatly reduce production cost and improve workpiece quality. Work on the UGM is continuing and the present system may be subject to further refinement / modification dependent on the outcomes of planned industrial evaluation.

References

[1]   K. Ramesh, H. Huang, L. Yin, Analytical and experimental investigation of coolant velocity in high speed grinding, Int. J. Machine Tools & Manufacture, Vol. 44 (10) (2004) pp. 1069-1076

[2]   Brinksmeier, E., Heinzel, C., Wittman, M. (1999) *Friction, cooling and lubrication in grinding*, CIRP Annals - Manufacturing Technology, v 48, n 2, 1999, p 581-598

[3]   Gviniashvili, V.K., Woolley, N.H., Rowe, W.B. (2004), *Useful flowrate in grinding*, International Journal of Machine Tool sand Manufacture, 44 pp 629-636.

[4]   W.B. Rowe, I. Inasaki, I.D. Marinescu, B. Dimitrov, Tribology of abrasive machining Processes, (2004) William Andrew Publishing. New York

[5]   Schumack, M.R., Chung, J.B., Schultz, W.W., Kannatey-Asibu Jnr, E. (1991), *Analysis of fluid flow under a grinding wheel*, Journal of engineering for industry-Transactions of the ASME 113 (2): 190-197 May

[6]   Machining Data Hand Book, Machinability Data Centre, (1980) 3rd Edition, Vol 2, Metcut Research Associates Inc., USA

Fibre Bragg Grating Temperature Sensors for Grinding Application.

F. A. Bezombes, D. R. Burton, M. J. Lalor
General Engineering Research Institute, Room 114, James Parsons building, Liverpool John Moores University, Byrom Street, Liverpool, L3 3AF, England.
Tel.: 0044 (0)151 2312018
Fax.: 0044 (0)151 2982447
F.Bezombes@livjm.ac.uk, D.R.Burton@livjm.ac.uk, M.J.Lalor@livjm.ac.uk.

Abstract. In high-speed grinding research it is required to measure temperature within the workpiece. Present techniques are thermocouple based, and often suffer from excessive electrical noise on the signal. This paper presents a number of novel fibre optic and existing sensing devices that overcome this limitation and also, in some cases, offer greater performance. The optical sensors are fibre Bragg grating based and the optical techniques used to interrogate that sensor include thin film dense WDM. Some optical fibre sensing devices offer faster response and greater sensitivity than was previously possible. Results are presented from grinding tests and the new devices are compared with each other and thermocouple techniques.

Keywords: Fibre Bragg Grating, temperature sensor, thin film dense WDM technique, high-speed grinding.

1. Machining Temperature Sensing Background.

To increase productivity of a machining process, it is essential to prevent tempering, re-hardening, surface cracking and residual stress levels, with the temperatures achieved during a machining process [1,2]. To achieve this theoretical models have been developed [3] validated by data obtained from sensors which have been developed to measure temperature during machining. Work undertaken by Rowe, Morgan, Black et al [1,3,5,6] has to date concentrated on the measurement of machining temperatures using thermocouple techniques. Extensive experience [4] has been gained in the application of thermocouples for temperature measurement during machining operations, however there are still problems with signal reliability. The effects of machining coolant on thermocouple junctions, thermocouple calibration and high noise levels limit the accuracy, repeatability and reliability of thermocouple techniques [5]. To avoid such undesirable effects, good insulation of the thermocouple is necessary and this makes the setting up of experiments, long and difficult. Another technique developed was the infrared radiation technique where an optical fibre is used to collect the infrared radiation being generated by the newly ground workpiece surface [7,8]. This method was first used to determine the temperature of cutting grains on a grinding wheel just after cutting [7]. The work was further extended to measure the inner temperature of the workpiece [8]. The optical systems described can detect brief heat pulses that cannot be detected by the thermocouple with its slower response time. The infrared radiation pyrometer was found to be the most suitable detection technique since it has a time response of the order of 1μs [8]. Other commercially available techniques used to measure temperature during machining processes include thermal imaging systems where a camera is used to detect and display the infrared radiation emitted by the machined surface. This technique is limited by the reaction time of the camera and also by the fact that the camera cannot detect the heat at the point of contact. Thermo sensitive painting can also be used but it is an approximate method and the workpiece temperature achieved during the machining can only be read after the event.

2. Fibre Bragg grating - background.

An increasingly used method of sensing temperature, strain etc. is the use of fibre Bragg gratings. Fibre Bragg techniques have been demonstrated by several research groups [9]. One of the benefits of using intrinsic optical fibre sensors such Bragg gratings or fluorescent emission is that the sensing element is intrinsic to the fibre. This is particularly important for the measurement of temperatures within a manufacturing, where the equipment will be subject to a relatively dirty environment.

The most common way of manufacturing a fibre Bragg grating is by laterally exposing the core of a single-mode fibre to ultraviolet (UV) radiation through a phase mask or an interferometer [10]. The UV exposure creates a fixed refractive index modulation of the core of the fibre producing a fibre Bragg grating [10]. Figure 1. illustrates the principle of the Bragg grating. The figure shows spectrum of light entering the grating, the spectrum of the light transmitted through the grating and the spectrum of the light reflected by the grating.

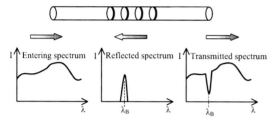

Figure 1.: Bragg grating properties.

The Bragg wavelength is defined by Bragg's law which states that:

$$\lambda_B = 2 \times n_{eff} \times \Lambda \qquad (1)$$

where n_{eff} is the effective refractive index of the core and Λ is the Bragg grating period [9].

The Bragg wavelength of a given fibre grating depends on the period of the grating and the refractive index of the material (Braggs Law). Both of these parameters are sensitive to mechanical strain and the temperature field within the grating [11] and any change in strain or temperature will modify the spacing between the gratings of a Bragg sensor and the refractive index of the core of the fibre. It is therefore necessary to develop methods of detecting a wavelength or a wavelength shift without using an expansive spectrum analyser or wavelength meter. The basic idea behind doing this detection is to relate the wavelength change caused by a measurand on the Bragg grating to an intensity change that is easily measurable using photodetectors. This lead to the design and development of the following system:

2.1. Thin film dense Wavelength Division Demultiplexer (DWDM) technique.

A broadband spectrum (C-Band) is launched in the optical system by an ASE light source. The light source power output is stabilised and its value is 13.7dBm. It is important to have a stabilised power since the wavelength change caused by the temperature field will ultimately be measured as an intensity change. The broadband light is then going through a circulator that makes the signal circulate without splitting it and also acts as an isolator preventing damage to the light source due to back reflection. The broadband spectrum then reaches a fibre Bragg grating that is used for the sensing. The Bragg grating will reflect just a narrow peak at the Bragg wavelength. That peak is reflected back toward the circulator which in turn directs it to the thin film dense WDM. DWDMs are commonly used in telecommunication systems to mutiplex (combine) or demultiplex (separate) an optical signal; this allows signals of different wavelengths to travel in one single fibre. In this particular case, the thin film dense WDM is used to link wavelength and intensity as explained below. Using a photodetector on each channel of the thin film dense DWDM would allow a temperature range of approximately 1200°C to be achieved. However this assumes that the sensing fibre could sustain such a temperature without permanent damage. A similar set-up was used to monitor temperature during milling [12].

Using the spectral specifications given by the manufacturer of the thin film dense WDM, it is possible to relate the optical power (transformed into voltage by the photodetectors) to the reflected wavelength and therefore the temperature. The layout is illustrated in figure 2..

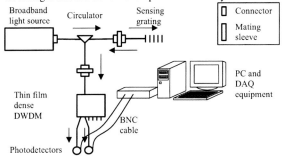

Figure 2.: Thin film dense DWDM system.

As the temperature sensed increases, the wavelength of the sensing grating increases. Since the spectrum of the thin film dense DWDM channel is steady, it results in a decrease in the intensity output on that channel (area between the two spectra). Figure 3. illustrates the principle.

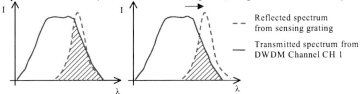

Figure 3.: Thin film dense DWDM principle (one channel).

The DWDM interrogation system allows for easy multiplexing [13].
The DWDM multiple sensing system (figure 4.) has the main advantage that it can differentiate each sensing grating. In other terms, using that technique it is possible to achieve the sensing of four gratings or more at the time if each grating is chosen so it is matching the various DWDM channels.

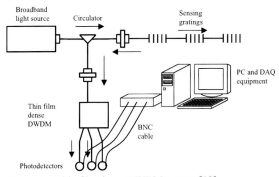

Figure 4.: Thin film dense DWDM system [13].

3. Experiments and results.

3.1. Workpiece design.

In order to allow comparison of the optical temperature measurement systems with the existing thermocouple based temperature measurements, a thermocouple was embedded in close proximity to the sensing Bragg grating. A groove was made in the workpiece to fit the fibre in. This grove allowed for insulating the FBG from strain without restraining it from thermal expansion so that the wavelength changes measured are due to thermal expansion and refractive index changes. The distributed sensing using the DWDM interrogation technique was used to monitor the heat penetration at different depths in the workpiece. This was achieved by inclining the groove of the sensing fibre and employing a fibre with multiple gratings.

3.2. Grinding experiments.

Since the depth of cut used during grinding were very small (a few μm), the workpiece cap was first machined so that the sensors were initially at a depth of 3mm below the grinding wheel. Then each of the optical systems thin film dense WDM was tested. The tests were undertaken with an applied 37.5μm depth of cut, however the real depth of cut was approximately 27μm on average. Following the tests at 3mm depth the cap was ground so that the sensors were at a depth of 2mm below the surface. The tests were then repeated using an applied cut of 37.5μm for each optical system in the same order as for the first test. The cap was then ground so that the sensors were at a depth of 1mm below the surface and the tests repeated using an applied 37.5μm depth of cut. This approach to testing allowed the tests to be carried out relatively quickly and without disturbing the sensing elements and the fibres. Although each applied cut was 37.5μm, the actual cut achieved was significantly less. The reduction in cut was caused by the deflection of the machine tool and grinding wheel. The material remaining due to deflection was then removed prior to testing the next measurement system.

3.3. Results.

3.3.1. Noise reduction.

Figure 5. illustrates the typical noise level associated with a running electric motor. During recording of test data, another machine tool in the laboratory was inadvertently switched on and then switched off after a further 8 seconds of recording. The noise of the thermocouple signal dramatically increased when the other machine was running, the peak-to-peak noise level increasing from 0.0146V to 0.2685V. During the same time, the peak-to-peak noise level of the optical systems stayed constant approximately 0.002V.

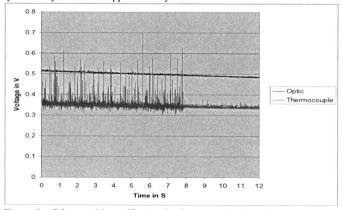

Figure 5.: Other machines effect on the thermocouple signal.

3.3.2. Grinding tests results.

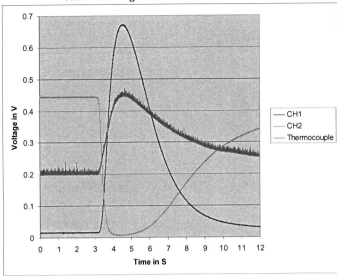

Figure 6.: Raw data for the DWDM and the thermocouple techniques.

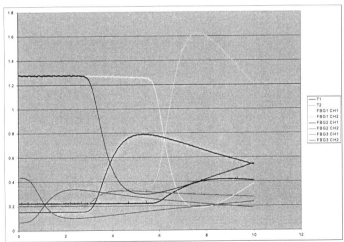

Figure 7.: Raw data for the distributed sensing interrogated by DWDM and thermocouples techniques.

The average sensitivity measured was 23.77mV/°C for the DWDM technique and a typical 10mV/°C for the K-type thermocouple. From the experiments results, it is possible to say that the DWDM technique was 2.2% faster than the thermocouple. However, further tests need to be done using a step input heat source to quantify the real values of the reaction time of the sensors.

4. Conclusion.

The thin film dense WDM technique is very sensitive and easy to install. Since the thin film dense WDM technique offers end-sensing capability, it is very easy to install.

This work has shown that it is possible to measure temperature accurately during harsh machining processes by using optical sensors based on fibre Bragg gratings. However the main drawback of the optical systems is the price. The equipment used to build an optical sensors based on fibre Bragg grating is more expensive than the equipment used for thermocouple based sensing. But overall, some optical techniques, such as the thin film dense WDM based sensors, proved to be more effective than normal k-type thermocouples for measuring temperature. The optical sensors developed, offer the following advantages: high sensitivity, fast response time, good repeatability, small signal noise levels and low sensitivity to externally generated electrical noise, ease of use, possible harsh environment capabilities where other conventional sensors would fail. The DWDM also offer a choice of a small number of different channels each covering a few nanometers; this property allows for easy multiplexing for either multi-points sensing or discrimination between measurands.

References.

1. D. F. McCormack, W. B. Rowe, M. N. Morgan, B. Mills and J. A. P. Pettit, "Prevention of Material Damage During Grinding", *Proc. 4th International Conference of Materials in Machining: Opportunities and Prospects for Improved Operations*, (1998), pp 238-247.

2. D. F. McCormack, W. B. Rowe, X. Chen, A. Bouzina, M. E. Fitzpatrick and L. Edward, "Characterising the Onset of Tensile Residual Stresses in Ground Components", *Proc. 6th International Conference on Residual Stresses (ICRS-6)*, Oxford University, (2000), pp 225-232.

3. S. C. E. Black, "The effect of abrasive properties on the surface integrity of ground ferrous materials", *Ph.D. Liverpool John Moores University Thesis* (1996).

4. Tan Jin, E. Carmona Diaz, A. Baldwin, J. Corbett, D. J. Stephenson, "A new grinding regime – thermal limitations to material removal by grinding", *Review of progress, School of industrial and manufacturing science, Cranfield University* (2002).

5. W. B. Rowe, B. Mills and S. C. E. Black, "Temperature Control in CBN Grinding", *The International Journal of Advanced Manufacturing Technology*, (1996), pp 387-392.

6. S. C. E. Black, W. B. Rowe, H. S. Qi and B. Mills, "Temperature Measurement in Grinding", *Proc. 31st International MATADOR Conference*, (1995), pp 409-413.

7. T. Ueda, A. Hosokawa and A. Yamamoto, "Studies of Temperature of Abrasive Grains in Grinding – Application of Infrared Radiation Pyrometer", *Trans. ASME, J. of Eng. for Ind., vol. 107*, (1985), pp 127-133.

8. T. Ueda, A. Hosokawa and A. Yamamoto, "Measurement of grinding temperature using infrared radiation pyrometer with optical fiber", *Trans. ASME, J. of Eng. for Ind., vol. 108* , (1986), pp 247-251.

9. Y. J. Rao, "In-fibre Bragg grating sensors", *Meas. Sci. Technol. 8*, (1997), pp 355-375.

10. R. Kashyap, *Fiber Bragg gratings*, "Chapter 3 Fabrication of Bragg Gratings, Optic and photonics, Academic Press (1999).

11. R. Leiderman, C. J. S. Matos, A. M. D. Braga, W. Margulis and L. C. G. Valente, "Interrogation methods for fiber Bragg grating sensors", *SPIE Vol. 3666*, (1999), pp 554-560.

12. F. A. Bezombes, D. R. Allanson, D. R. Burton, M. J. Lalor, "High speed temperature measurements using novel optical fibre-based systems", SPIE 5145, (2003), pp 117-127.

13. F. A. Bezombes, "Fibre Bragg grating temperature sensors for high-speed machining applications", Ph.D. thesis, Liverpool John Moores university, (2004), pp 174-176.

A Case Study on Continuing Education by Short Courses in a Specialised Area of Manufacturing

T R A Pearce

Institute of Grinding Technology, RAMP Laboratory, University of the West of England, Bristol
Frenchay Campus, Coldharbour Lane, Bristol, BS16 1QY, UK

thomas.pearce@uwe.ac.uk

Abstract. Over a period of 14 years the Institute of Grinding Technology has developed a portfolio of short courses in abrasive technology. This case study illustrates how this can be achieved in a niche area that is not adequately covered by mainstream education. Issues that have been encountered include the need to encompass a variety of specialisms within what is already a limited and specialised field and the need to develop courses in line with increased employment of graduate engineers within manufacturing. There particularly needs to be an emphasis on increasing interaction with delegates in order to provide them with analytical tools that can then be transferred to the shop floor for resolving production problems.

Keywords: Technology transfer, continuing education, grinding.

Introduction

The process of technology transfer from academia to industry has long been considered to be an important outcome of academic research projects. This is seen as a justification for the use of public money to fund research programmes.

History

During the late 1970's and early 1980's, fundamental research was carried out into the grinding process at a number of UK universities in a major coordinated programme sponsored by SRC/SERC. Creep feed grinding was the main focus of the grinding research group at the University of Bristol. Research techniques, particularly thermal modelling, were applied to a known aerospace industrial problem of overheating during grinding of nickel alloy turbine blades [1,2]. Further research led to the development of the continuous dressing technique [2,3], which was implemented into industry with major improvements in productivity and consequent reductions in costs. While the findings from the fundamental research had been successfully transferred into industry, it was perceived that academic research techniques could be used in a research and development environment, which was directly focused onto industrial applications. This concept resulted in the formation of the Institute of Grinding Technology at the University of Bristol in 1986. As might be expected, the first major project was on creep feed grinding, with both aerospace and automotive applications. The Institute then expanded into other areas, particularly applications of cubic boron nitride (CBN) grinding wheels. In retrospect, this development may be considered as an interim step towards an ongoing programme of technology transfer. While the results from basic research and applied research projects can be transferred into industry, there are certain limitations. Firstly, the technology goes primarily to the industrial partners that have supported the research project. Secondly, the continued implementation of the technology, even within these partners, can be inhibited by a change of personnel within the company. Often, the key industrial contacts will move on either to a different company or a different area within the same company. It is not unusual for someone who has been involved over a two or three year period on a grinding project to be transferred to a completely different area of manufacturing within the same company. Such moves are understandable as they are usually linked to the development of the individual's career path, where a broad knowledge of a number of areas is particularly useful for later positions at managerial and director levels. To overcome the above limitations, there was a need to develop a mechanism for continuous technology transfer. To meet this need, the Institute initiated training programmes in the form of short courses.

Development of Courses

The first courses were in the core expertise of the Institute, which was creep feed grinding, and were developed for one company and aimed at operators, setters and engineers. The logical progression was then to extend this to grinding processes in general and to have an open course which could be attended by personnel from any company involved in grinding. This evolved into a three day course entitled General Grinding Principles. There is no doubt that the initial success of these programmes was helped by the lack of equivalent training at apprentice level. College courses tend to concentrate on metal cutting processes, particularly turning, milling and drilling, with only a minor reference to grinding, usually at a tool room level of surface grinding only. Certainly, there would be no reference to specialised grinding processes such as cam grinding and creep feed grinding. The General Grinding Principles course was thus able to occupy a niche area.

Within 2 years of starting the General course, a need for an Advanced Grinding Principles course was perceived. This concentrated on more in-depth measurement and analysis of the grinding process and on CBN (cubic boron nitride) grinding wheels. This latter area was still a key emerging technology, even though this abrasive had been first developed some 40 years earlier.

	General	Advanced
Year started	1992	1994
Total no. of courses	43	17
Total attendees	437	189
Average attendance	10	11
Maximum atttendance	29	22
Minimum attendance	3	6

Table 1 An analysis of the General and Advanced courses up until the end of 2005

Table 1 shows an analysis of the two courses from the time that they were started up until the end of 2005. A key figure is the average attendance, which is very similar for both courses. Experience has shown that a number around 10 is ideal for promoting interaction between presenters and delegates and between delegates themselves. Often experience can be transferred between delegates from different companies, since no presenter has a monopoly on information in such a complex subject area. While, the minimum attendance on the General course was 3 (on one occasion only), this was far from ideal, with 6 being a much more realistic minimum. For both courses, the maximum attendance was over 20. While this was over twice the ideal, any deterioration in quality of the course was marginal.

A Systems Approach

The approach within the General Grinding Principles course is to consider the grinding process as a system, made up of individual parts, as illustrated in Fig. 1.

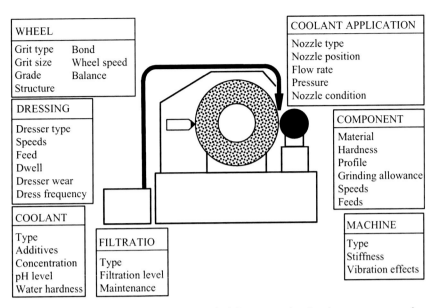

WHEEL		COOLANT APPLICATION

WHEEL

Grit type	Bond
Grit size	Wheel speed
Grade	Balance
Structure	

DRESSING

Dresser type
Speeds
Feed
Dwell
Dresser wear
Dress frequency

COOLANT

Type
Additives
Concentration
pH level
Water hardness

FILTRATIO

Type
Filtration level
Maintenance

COOLANT APPLICATION

Nozzle type
Nozzle position
Flow rate
Pressure
Nozzle condition

COMPONENT

Material
Hardness
Profile
Grinding allowance
Speeds
Feeds

MACHINE

Type
Stiffness
Vibration effects

Fig. 1 Structure of the General Grinding Principles course, showing the systems approach

There are seven main systems, which are dealt with in separate sessions. Within each system, there are a number of variables. Within a session, the influence of each of the variables on grinding performance is discussed. Thus an overall picture of what is a complex process is gradually built up in stages. The formal sessions on the various systems are complemented by looking at four of the most common grinding processes, which are cylindrical, surface, internal and centreless. It tends to be the three processes which produce cylindrical parts that are of the most common interest, so that surface grinding which is usually the only one taught at college level is of least interest. The main exception to this is the powerplant industry (aerospace and industrial) where creep feed grinding and, more recently, Viper grinding are key processes.

Problem Solving Strategies

The key to problem solving is to know what questions to ask. With abrasive processes, there is almost no limit. The variables in Fig. 1 provide a starting point and values should be obtained for each one. To this may be added the following:

- Standard measurements of the process – accuracy, integrity, finish, roundness, etc.
- Additional measurements of the process – power, forces, vibration, machine stiffness, vibration characteristics.
- Environment – location of machine.
- Place of grinding in the process chain and quality of incoming parts.

Within the General Grinding Principles course, individual problems are proposed first in which one system only is the main cause of the problem. This is done separately for wheel specification, dressing and coolant type. At the end of the course, the main problem solving session deals with a

237

process where there is more than one problem and the solutions can lie within any of the systems. Fig. 2 shows the procedure to be followed in analysing one of the problems.

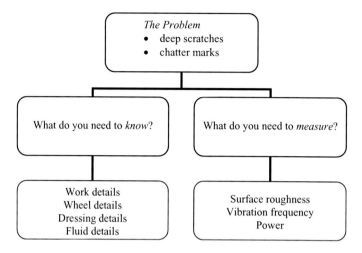

Fig. 2 Chart outlining the problem solving strategy

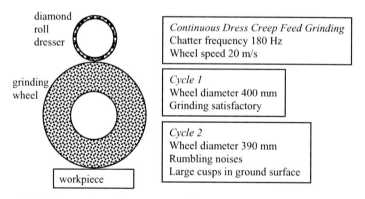

Fig. 3 Case study on the occurrence of chatter in continuous creep feed grinding

Case studies are a useful addition to the problem solving strategy, since they illustrate how the process can be analysed and sources of problems identified. An example is shown in Fig. 3, which is a case study that shows how a grinding process moves from a stable region to an unstable one, when a constant surface speed strategy results in spindle speed in rpm continuously changing with wheel diameter. Measurement is key to the analysis in this case study. A tap test was used to measure the vibration characteristics of the grinding system, which gave a value for the chatter frequency and for the system stiffness at that chatter frequency. The system stiffness confirmed that the process was close to the stability boundary and that changes in spindle rpm could cause the process to move across that boundary. Measurement of the vibration that occurred during Cycle 2 confirmed that the vibration was at the chatter frequency.

The Role of Modelling

In a research environment, modelling is an almost essential tool for examining a process. Indeed, a piece of research for which a PhD is to be awarded should by definition contain substantial modelling to show how well the candidate has understood the fundamentals of the process. Two examples of modelling used in the General Grinding Principles course involve simulation of the rounding mechanisms. One of these is for the centreless grinding process and shows how a roundness profile from the previous machining process is modified by a centreless machine and how this is influenced by throat angle and blade angle [4]. The other is for a plunge cylindrical grinding process and shows how the run-out of the grinding wheel generates roundness errors and how these errors are influenced by the ratio of wheel rpm to work rpm [5]. Example roundness profiles from this modelling are shown in Fig. 4. Thermal models also offer insights to temperature levels within the grinding process and these can be related to workpiece burn. The paper by Jaeger [6] on moving heat source theory is the fundamental work. Many other researchers have based their models on this work, for example Malkin [7] and Rowe [8]. While the real situation is often more complex, modelling does offer insights into the mechanisms involved in grinding processes.

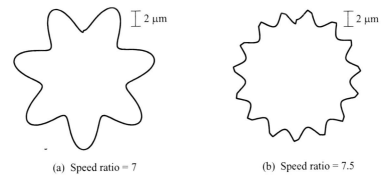

(a) Speed ratio = 7   (b) Speed ratio = 7.5

Fig. 4 Predictions of roundness profiles for a grinding wheel with 2 μm eccentricity

Conclusions

The following conclusions can be drawn and applied to other areas of manufacturing.
1. Ongoing technology transfer from academia to industry can be achieved by the use of specialised short courses.
2. Regular courses allow for the recruiting of new personnel within the customer base.
3. Courses need to be focused on problem solving strategies, so that delegates are equipped with tools for troubleshooting processes and improving efficiency.
4. Courses should include modelling tools that can be applied to production processes.
5. Where appropriate, a systems approach should be adopted.

References

[1]   G.R. Shafto: *Creep Feed Grinding* (Ph D Thesis, University of Bristol, 1975).

[2]   C. Andrew, T.D. Howes and T.R.A. Pearce: *Creep Feed Grinding* (Holt, Rinehart and Winston, UK 1985).

[3]   S.C. Salmon: *Creep Feed Surface Grinding* (Ph D Thesis, University of Bristol, 1979).

[4]   A J L Harrison and T R A Pearce: Proc I Mech E, Part B: J. Engineering Manufacture Vol. 216 (2002), pp 1201-1216.

[5]   D.C. Fricker, A. Speight and T.R.A. Pearce: *The modelling of roundness in cylindrical plunge grinding to incorporate waveshift and external vibration effects* (submitted to Proc I Mech E, Part B: J. Engineering Manufacture, 2005).

[6]   J.C. Jaeger: Proc. Royal Society of New South Wales, Vol. 76 (1942), pp 203-224.

[7]   S. Malkin: Trans. ASME, J. Eng. for Industry, Vol. 96 (1974), pp 1184-1191.

[8]   W.B. Rowe: Proc I Mech E, Part B: J. Engineering Manufacture Vol. 215 (2001), pp 473-491.

Innovative
Manufacturing Processes

The effect of process parameters on surface roughness in abrasive jet finishing with grinding wheel as restraint

G.Q. Cai[1], C.H. Li[2], J.F. Zhao[1]

[1]School of Mechanical Engineering & Automation, Northeastern University, Shenyang 110004 China;

[2]School of Mechanical Engineering, Qingdao Technological University, Qingdao, 266033, China

Abstract

The abrasive jet finishing process with wheel as restraint is a type of compound precision finishing process that combined with grinding and abrasive jet machining, in which inject slurry of abrasive and liquid solvent to grinding zone between grinding wheel and work surface under haven't cut-deep infeed condition when accomplished workpiece grinding. The abrasive particles are driven and energized by the rotating grinding wheel and liquid hydrodynamic pressure and increased slurry speed between grinding wheel and work surface to achieve micro removal machining. In the paper, the process technique on abrasive jet finishing process with wheel as restraint was investigated. The effects of different particle size, abrasive concentration, machining cycles, the velocity of grinding wheel and medium type on surface roughness were analyzed. Experiments were performed with plane grinder M7120 and workpiece material Q235A and 45# steel. The machined surface morphology was studied using SEM and microscope and microcosmic geometry parameters were measured with TALSYURF instrument. The experimental results under percentage 10 abrasive concentration, W7 Al2O3 particle and machining 20~30 circles showing the novelty process method, not only to attain higher surface form accuracy, to diminish grinding defects such as severely deformation, surface layer pollution and ground burnout, but also to can acquire efficiently free defects finishing surface with Ra0.15~1.6μm and finally achieve high efficiency, high precision and low roughness values, furthermore, Integrating grinding process and abrasive jet finishing process into one features.

Introduction

The conventional grinding makes surface defects such as micro-crack, tensile residual stresses and ground burnout because of high grinding zone temperatures. Such more grinding defects, if not well diminished, would effect the ground surface fatigue intensity, corroding resistance and contact rigidity. Accordingly, more important parts require micro removal finishing in order to reduce surface defects and diminish surface roughness values and ripple. However, this can increase machining procedures and extra equipment lead to increase costs [1].

According to above mentioned, authors invented a novel abrasive jet precision finishing method, which inject slurry of abrasive and liquid solvent to grinding zone under haven't depth of cut infeed condition when accomplished workpiece grinding. The abrasive particles with grinding wheel as restraint are driven and energized by the rotating grinding wheel and liquid hydrodynamic pressure and increased slurry speed between grinding wheel and work surface achieved micro removal finishing process. The method can either require high form accuracy or may attain free damage finishing surface. Hence, to study the effects of different process parameters (e.g. number of cycles, abrasive concentration, abrasive mesh size and media types) on surface microscopic morphology and surface roughness of Q235A and 45# steel, a setup of an abrasive jet machine with grinding wheel as restraint was designed and fabricated. Using this setup, experiments were conducted. The details of the experimental setup and the condition followed during experimentation are given below.

1. The finishing theorem

In abrasive finishing process, abrasive powders are mixed with a fluid carrier to form abrasive slurry that turned into the gaps between grinding wheel and workpiece. Since the gap between grinding wheel and work is smaller, in which slurry hydrodynamic pressure and speed field are bigger, showed in Fig.1, micro protrusion of ground surface was removed firstly which peak and micro protrusion were decreased due to abrasive attained more energy [2]. On the other hand, the fluid hydrodynamic pressure presenting sides direction decrease in the width of wheel lead to the lateral extrusion of abrasive fluid, the abrasive not only to wipe off work surface longitudinally, but also to polishing work surface transversely so as to homogenize and lower ripples, fluid hydrodynamic pressure vector profile figure showed in Fig.2. With machining progressing, the work surface micro protrusion was removed gradually and, longitudinal parameter values were diminished and surface form precision and ripple were improved to achieve finishing.

2. Experimental setup and conditions

The experimental setup diagram is showed in Fig.3. The machining system of the experiment is composed of a rotating grinding wheel and a work between which the slurry was filled in by the nozzle.

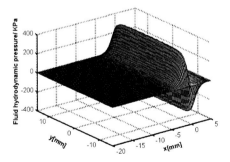

Fig. 1 Hydrodynamic pressure distributing profile

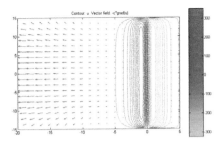

Fig. 2 Hydrodynamic pressure vector profile

The wheel type is WA60J8V, which has diameter 260mm and 30mm width. The grinding wheel main axis revolutions are 2880rpm. The media used for the present experimentation is a mixture of mineral lubricating oil or rustless emulsion and abrasive particles. The mixture of mineral lubricating oil or rustless emulsion is mixed with the abrasive particles of specified mesh size in a definite proportion to achieve the desired percentage concentration of abrasive particles by weight, which are the 5 %; 10%; 15%. The particle is W7 AI2O3 with primary mean grain size of 6.3 μ m. However, the common definition of the percentage abrasive concentration is given by: weight of abrasive particles´100/(weight of media). Before performing the actual experiments, the fresh media is mixed for 3–5 minutes with a pump, so as to get uniform mixing. Based on the conclusions from the preliminary experiments, four important variables are identified, namely the number of cycles, abrasive percentage concentration, abrasive mesh size, and media type. The workpiece material is 45# steel and Q235A has the surface roughness mean values of Ra=0.60 μ m after grinding. The machined surface morphology was studied using SEM and microcosmic and, geometry parameters were measured with TALSURF5 instrument, respectively [3].

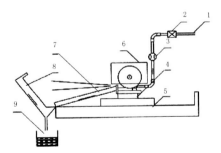

1-abrasive flow from pump 2-control valve 3-flowmeter 4-workpiece 5-worktable 6-grinding wheel cover 7-slide groove 8-flow baffle 9-flow box

Fig. 3 Schematic diagram of abrasive jet finishing process

3 Effect of process parameters on surface roughness Ra

3.1 Abrasive mesh size

Fig.4 shows that as the abrasive mesh size increases, the surface roughness values increase under other process parameters are kept constant. Further, as the number of cycles increases, the Ra value decreases. The surface roughness value obviously decreases before 10 cycles because of availability of peaks in early stages of machining, but as these peaks get machined, the roughness value in Ra slowly decreases after 15 cycles.

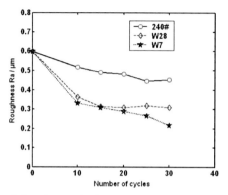

Fig. 4 Effect of abrasive mesh size on roughness Ra value

3.2 Abrasive concentration

With the number of cycles increase the Ra value decrease for the three abrasive concentrations. From the Fig.5, it can be induced that 15% abrasive concentration in roughness Ra value is larger than 10% abrasive concentration. With higher abrasive concentrations, more abrasive grains come into contact with the workpiece resulting in more abrasion, hence higher Ra value. The effectively active abrasive number is lower for 5% concentration of abrasive lead to smaller material removal. In the present machining condition, the machined surface roughness value for 10% concentration of abrasive is obviously diminished compared to other liquid concentration.

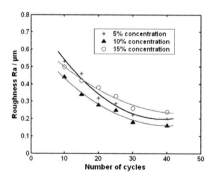

Fig. 5 Effect of abrasive concentration on roughness Ra value

3.3 Number of cycles

The workpiece surface micrographs change as Fig.6 showed. As might be expected, the work surface was found to be the most aggressive of the abrasives, in that it produced the greatest removal volumes and directionality groove which was machined by two-body lapping has the surface roughness values of Ra=0.46 μ m (Fig.6a) at machining circles is 10. When the machining circles increased to 20, the finished surface not only produced uniformity groove, but with very little sign of random pits. As the discussed in [3], the machining modes are mixed of two-body lapping and three-body polishing (Fig.6b). When machining to 30 circles, the surface produced randomly discontinuous micro-pit absolutely (Fig.6c) and the phenomenon is defined as three-body polishing machining. Consequently, the surface roughness for abrasive jet finishing was improved due to micro protrusion and peak removed.

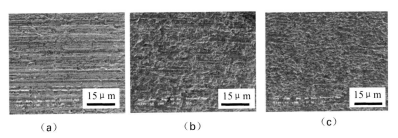

（a）　　　　　　　　　（b）　　　　　　　　　（c）

Fig.6 SEM images change with machining circles

3.4 Media type

The experiments were performed with two types of media, mineral lubricating oil and rustless emulsion. To study the effects of different media types, experiments are carried out at constant process parameters, showed as in Fig.7. The machined surface roughness value with lubricating oil as machining fluid is lower compare to machining surface with rustless emulsion as fluid media. But as these peaks get machined the surface roughness in Ra values slowly decreases after 30 cycles for two media types.

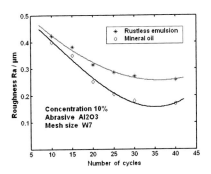

Fig.7 Effect of media types on roughness Ra value

4. Conclusion

The effect of process parameters on surface roughness and morphology was investigated by experiment. The experimental results showing, surface roughness value in Ra decrease with the increase in number of cycles, but the roughness improvement is obviously before 20 cycles. The roughness value in Ra gradually diminished after 20 cycles. Further, the micrograph showed, the machined surface from directionally continuous micro-groove to random pits transition with machining progressing. Experimental results were agreement with theoretical analysis and the process method validity was verified.

References

1. Li Chang-he, Cai Guang-qi and Li Qi. (2005), Generating mechanism of surface morphology finished by abrasive jet with grinding wheel as restraint, Journal of Northeastern University (natural science), vol. 26(6), pp.578-581.
2. C. H. Li, G. Q. Cai and S. C. Xiu. (2006), Material removal model and experimental verification for abrasive jet precision finishing with wheel as restraint, Key Engineering Materials, vols. 304-305, pp. 555–559.
3. Li Changhe, Cai Guangqi and Yuan Suoxian. (2005), Material removal model for abrasive jet precision finishing restricted by abrasive wheel, Transactions of the Chinese Society for Agricultural Machinery, vol. 36 (11), pp.132-135.
4. Li Changhe, Cai Guangqi, Li Qi, et al. (2005), Investigation on material removal mechanism for abrasive jet precision finishing with grinding wheel as restraint, China Mechanical Engineering, vol. 16 (23), pp.2116-2119

ASSESSMENT OF SOME DYNAMIC PARAMETERS IN ULTRASONIC MACHINING OF TITANIUM

Jatinder Kumar
Department of Mechanical Engineering, AKGEC, Ghaziabad, India
E-mail: jatin_thaparian@yahoo.co.in

ABSTRACT

Ultrasonic Machining is one of the most specifically used non-traditional machining methods these days. Unlike any other machining process; USM does not damage the work surface thermally leading to a stress free and very fine machined surface. The process has been applied exclusively for machining of quite brittle and fragile materials that possess poor machinability with traditional machining methods because of large cutting forces involved. The application of USM for the machining of relatively tough materials is still required to be explored.

This paper presents an investigation into the machining characteristics-Material removal rate (MRR), tool wear rate (TWR) and surface roughness of pure titanium; considered as a tough material using ultrasonic machining. The effect of two process variables-machine power rating and avg. slurry temperature has been studied on these performance indices of USM while machining titanium. The experiments have been conducted at three levels of power rating as well as slurry temperature. It has been concluded that Titanium is fairly machinable with USM process. Also the surface finish obtained is far better than other traditional and non-traditional machining methods. The optimum values of MRR and TWR have been achieved at a slurry temperature of 27 C whereas the surface roughness has been found to be least at slurry temperature of 10 C. The photomicrography of the machined surface reveals considerable refinement of grains on work surface leading to better surface finish.

Keywords: Ultrasonic machining, Tool wear, Slurry temperature, titanium

1 INTRODUCTION

Ultrasonic Machining is a non-conventional mechanical material removal process used for machining both electrically conductive and non-metallic materials; preferably those with low ductility [3,10] and a hardness above 40 HRC [4-6] e.g. inorganic glasses, ceramics and nickel alloys etc. The process came into existence in 1945 when L. Balamuth was granted the fist patent for the process. USM has been variously termed ultrasonic drilling; ultrasonic cutting; ultrasonic abrasive machining and slurry drilling.

In USM, high frequency electrical energy is converted into mechanical vibrations via a transducer/booster combination which are then transmitted to an energy focusing as well as amplifying device: horn/tool assembly. This causes the tool to vibrate along its longitudinal axis at high frequency (usually >20 kHz) with amplitude of 12-50 μm [7-8]. The power ratings range from 50-3000 W and a controlled static load is applied to the tool. Abrasive slurry, which is a mixture of abrasive material; e.g. silicon carbide, boron carbide or aluminium oxide suspended in water or some suitable carrier medium is continuously pumped across the gap between the tool and work (25-60 μm). The vibration of the tool causes the abrasive particles held in the slurry to impact the work

249

surface leading to material removal by micro chipping [9]. A typical USM set up uses a megnetostrictive/piezoelectric transducer (fig. 1).

Variations of this basic configuration include:

1. Rotary Ultrasonic Machining (RUM). In this process, tool vibrates and rotates simultaneously thereby improving the Material removal rate and reducing the geometric inaccuracies; e.g. oversize and out of roundness etc. [5].
2. USM combined with electrical discharge machining (EDM) [2].
3. Ultrasonic assisted cutting /machining. Ultrasonic assisted turning is the most common process in this category.
4. Other applications such as coating, cleaning, welding.

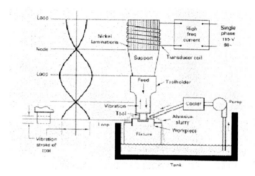

Figure 1: USM set up

2. SELECTION OF PARAMETERS

During the entire experimentation, two of the process parameters-power rating and slurry temperature were varied at three levels. The other parameters such as slurry concentration, Slurry flow rate, slurry type, grit Size of abrasive, amplitude of vibration and static load were held constant.

The following performance indices have been explored:

1. Material removal rate (MRR)
2. Tool Wear rate (TWR)
3. Surface roughness

3. METHODOLOGY

The experiments were conducted in three sets. In the firs set, the experiments were carried out with slurry maintained at room temperature of 27 C to see the effect of input process parameters on MRR, TWR and surface roughness. The power setting used in the first set was 30% of the maximum possible value (500 W). The initial weight of the work piece was recorded. Then the machine was allowed to drill for a fixed depth of cut (01 mm) with constant slurry flow. Similarly the experiments were carried out at 60% and 90% of the machine power rating i.e. 300 W and 450 W respectively.

In the second set up, the slurry temperature was maintained at 60 C by heating the water surrounding the slurry tank. In the same manner as in first set up, MRR and TWR were recorded. In the third set up, the slurry was kept at a temperature of 10 C and the experiments were repeated again to observe MRR and TWR. All experiments were repeated thrice to minimize the probability of error introduced due to noise factors. Average values of the performance indices were recorded for each set up as depicted in table 1.

The surface of each hole was divided into three sections micrographs were taken for each section with the help of image analyzer. All the photomicrographs were taken with same magnification (X100). For measuring surface roughness, a digital perthometer was used. The sampling length of 1.5 mm was selected for each cavity.

4 RESULTS AND DISCUSSION

The graphical representations of these calculated average values of MRR, TWR and surface roughness are depicted in fig 2, fig 3 and fig 4 respectively. To correlate the surface roughness with microstructure of the machined surfaces, micrographs were taken for each cavity. Each cavity was divided into three zones. First zone corresponds to the center of the tool tip to ϕ 1.5 mm, second zone from ϕ 1.5 mm to 3.5 mm and third zone from ϕ 3.5 mm to ϕ 5 mm.

4.1 Surface roughness
As observed in fig 4, surface roughness increases with increase in power rating for all slurry temperatures. The increase in surface roughness is sharp at slurry temperature of 60 C, however for slurry temperatures of 10 C and 27 C the increment appears to be moderate. Further, at 10 C slurry temperature there is a fall in surface roughness at power rating of 450 W. The reason for increase in surface roughness with increase in power rating may be explained on the basis that momentum of abrasive particles increases and thus they make impact with work surface at greater velocities creating larger cavities and thereby resulting in increased surface roughness.

The sharp increase in surface roughness with increase in power rating at slurry temp. 60 C may be explained on the basis that the particle movement becomes less restricted due to fall in the viscosity of slurry at higher temperature. Therefore the flow ability of abrasive particles results in more number of impacts per unit time hence removing material at higher rates and increasing surface roughness. On increasing the ultrasonic power from 300W to 450 W at slurry temperature of 10 C, the surface roughness decreases or remains almost constant. This trend may be explained on the basis that at such a high power rating and low slurry temperature, the abrasive grains are closely packed resulting in more precise and controlled striking of particles on work surface which causes better surface finish.

From the micrographs of the machined surface of titanium (figures 5,6) it can be concluded that the grains are more uniformly packed with high density in first zone, followed by the grains in second and third zone respectively. This means that at the center of toll tip, more refined grains are located which are due to super imposing of ultrasonic waves at the center of the tool.

251

TABLE 1. Experimental Results

S. No.	Temp. (C)	Power rating (W)	Average MRR (gm/min)	Average TWR (gm/min)	Avg. SR (μm)
1	60	150	4.70×10^{-4}	8.09×10^{-4}	0.37
2	60	300	2.27×10^{-4}	5.06×10^{-4}	1.17
3	60	450	5.22×10^{-4}	$1.2.0 \times 10^{-4}$	2.57
4	27	150	9.14×10^{-4}	10.2×10^{-4}	0.43
5	27	300	27.1×10^{-4}	57.0×10^{-4}	0.80
6	27	450	18.2×10^{-4}	48.9×10^{-4}	1.01
7	10	150	1.21×10^{-4}	1.82×10^{-4}	0.74
8	10	300	3.17×10^{-4}	1.15×10^{-4}	1.09
9	10	450	9.28×10^{-4}	1.25×10^{-4}	1.05

4.2 Material removal rate

As observed in the fig 2, the material removal rate (MRR) at slurry temperature of 27 C is extremely better than slurry temperatures of 10 C and 60 C. Further, MRR increase with increase in power rating from 150 W to 300 W for slurry temperature of 27 C and decreases with further increase in power rating. For slurry temperature of 60 C, MRR decreases with increases in ultrasonic power from 150 W to 300 W and increases with increase in power rating thereafter. The behavior of MRR with regards to power rating at slurry temperature of 10 C is quite normal and unidirectional; it increase with any increment in power rating in the entire range of 150 W to 450 W.

The increase in MRR with increment in ultrasonic power can be explained on the basis that as the ultrasonic power input is increased the number of abrasive particles impinging on the work surface increases and moreover, these particles strike at a greater momentum resulting in higher MRR. However, the decrease in MRR in case of machining at slurry temperature of 60 C with the increase of ultrasonic power from 150 W to 300 W may be because of strain hardening of the work piece.

Upon increasing the ultrasonic power from 300 W to 450 W, the decrease in MRR in case of machining at 27 C may be because of the reason that number of particles that are coming under the tool miss the target on work surface; the reason being too much increment in the momentum of the particles thus resulting in uncontrollable hitting at the work surface.

4.3 Tool wear rate

As observed in fig 3, tool wear rate is maximum in event of machining with slurry at 27 C temperature at all values of ultrasonic power. TWR increases with increase in ultrasonic power from 150 W to 300 W in case of machining at slurry temperature 27 C and then decreases with further increase in ultrasonic power from 300 W to 450 W. . This may be explained on the basis that any increment in input energy in form of power rating leads to more MRR and hence TWR. However, the decrease in TWR while increasing power input from 300 W to 450 W is related to decrease in MRR in this range of power input.

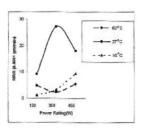

Figure 2 Effect of Slurry temp.
and power rating on MRR

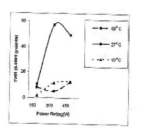

Figure 3 Effect of power rating
and slurry temp. on TWR

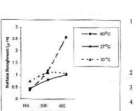

Figure 4. Effect of slurry temp.
and power rating on SR

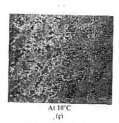

At 10°C
(ç)

At 27°C
(b)

Figures 5,6

At slurry temperature of 60 C, TWR increases with increment in power rating from 150 W to 450 W, i.e. in the entire range of power input, which is again in line with MRR phenomenon for this range. TWR remains unaffected while machining at slurry temperature of 10 C with increase in power input from 300 W to 450 W; the reason being strain hardening of the tool material and material deposition on the tool tip similar to the formation of built up edges in case of conventional machining. All these factors help in controlling Tool wear rate thus promoting the tool life. This observation is further entrusted from the deteriorated shapes of tool cross section, which required grinding before reuse.

5. CONCLUSIONS

1. As observed from the photomicrographs of the ultrasonically machined surfaces at various process conditions, it appears that Titanium is quite machinable with USM process employing a H.S.S. tool. There is no evidence of surface cracks on the work surface. Moreover, the mechanical motion of the abrasive particles caused considerable refinement of grains on work surface imparting it better mechanical properties.
2. The ultrasonic machining of commercially pure titanium shows better surface finish at slurry temperature of 10 C (low temp.) as compared to room temperature (27 C) and high temperature (60 C).
3. At high temperature (60 C) and low temperature (10 C) levels for slurry, there is significant decline in Material removal rate (MRR) and tool wear rate (TWR). Therefore for commercially pure titanium while machining with USM, machining with slurry maintained at room temperature (27 C) is recommended.
4. During the entire experimentation, H.S.S. tool did not experience any breakage. The extent of dish formation at tool face was also negligible.

6. REFERENCES

[1] Deng Jianxin and Lee Tiachiu, Ultrasonic machining of alumina based Ceramic Composites, Journal of European Ceramic Society, 32, 2002, pp. 1235-1241.
[2] Farago, F.T., Abrasive methods engineering, Industrial Press, 1980, 2, 480-481.
[3] Gilmore R., Ultrasonic Machining and orbital abrasion techniques, SME Technical Paper (series) AIR, NM89-419, 1989, pp. 1-20.
[4] Gilmore R., Ultrasonic machining of Ceramics, SME Paper, MS90-346, 1990, 12p.
[5] Gilmore, R., Ultrasonic machining-A case study, Journal of Material Processing Technology, 28, 1991, pp. 139-143.
[6] Haslehurst M., Manufacturing Technology, 1981, pp. 270-271.
[7] Kennedy, D.C. and Grieve, R.J., Ultrasonic machining-A review, The Production Engineer, 1975, 54(9), 481-486.
[8] Kremer, D., New developments on ultrasonic machining, SME Paper, MR91-522, 1991, 13p.
[9] Moreland M.A., Ultrasonic impact grinding: What it is: What it will do, Proceedings of 22nd Abrasive Engg. Conference: Abrasives and Hi-Technology, 1984, pp. 11-117.
[10] Moreland, M.A., Versatile performance of Ultrasonic machining, Ceramics Bulletin, 1988, 67(6), pp. 1045-1047.

A Laser Beam Diagnostic System for High Speed CO_2 Laser Cutting
Ivan Christy Arokiam, B.Eng., M.Sc (Eng.), Ph.D.[1]

Abstract

Beam analysis permits the investigation of the laser beam properties that are one of the factors determining the maximum speed in laser cutting. Enhancement of the beam positively contributes towards increasing the cutting speed and such enhancement can only be achieved if the beam properties are measured. For this purpose a pinhole based beam analysis system was developed and tested. The paper describes a new beam analyser that scans a pinhole across the beam in a raster pattern and measures the intensity transmitted through the pinhole using a semiconductor infrared detector. Results are reported from the measurement of the focussed beam produced using 50.8 and 63.5 mm focal length lenses. Good agreement is demonstrated with theoretical predictions of beam diameter. It is argued that the new analyser is a useful instrument for installation on a laser cutting table.

Key Words: Laser beam, pinhole, intensity, focal length, beam profile

Notation

d	Pinhole diameter (m)	W_F	Beam radius after lens (m)
f	Focal length of lens (m)	W_L	Radius of beam incident on lens (m)
h	Distance between the pinhole and the detector (m)	x, y, z	Beam position coordinates (m)
l	Detector active element length (m)	z_f	Distance from the lens (m)
M^2	Beam quality factor	α	Beam spread on exit via pinhole (rad)
$R(z)$	Radius of curvature (m)	λ	Laser wavelength (m)

Introduction

Laser cutting is an ideal candidate to replace punch press processing for cutting and perforating sheet steel components. The high set up costs and time involved in the manufacture of punch tools are avoided and a "just in time" approach to component manufacture is thus possible. However laser cutting cannot compete with punch processing unless a cutting speed approaching 1 ms^{-1} can be achieved.

The cutting speed is influenced by many factors including beam parameters within the focussed spot. It is the temporal variation in beam parameters within the focussed spot that currently represents one of the major limitations to improved cutting speed. Any attempt to improve the speed requires knowledge of the beam characteristics.

Determining the intensity distribution in the focussed spot is difficult. Firstly, the spot is small and many scanning systems have insufficient resolution to observe the fine detail within the spot. Furthermore, the intensity is much greater than in the raw beam and this can damage the scanning system. With the above issues in mind, the aim of the present work was to develop a beam analysis system capable of observing both the raw beam and the focussed spot with a spatial resolution of around 10 μm (10^{-5} m). The system developed uses a pinhole and detector fixed to the cutting system table. In the following sections this paper starts with previous work in this area and then goes on to discuss the system design, associated experimental results and ends with an overall summary. It is shown that the data measured in the focussed spot allow the determination of the beam quality factor M^2.

---

[1] The Agility Centre, University of Liverpool Management School, Chatham Street, Liverpool, L69 7ZH, ivan.arokiam@liverpool.ac.uk

Previous Work

Roundy [1] considered the reasons for variability in the raw beam and in the focussed spot. Because the cutting speed is strongly dependent on the intensity and intensity distribution within the focussed spot, it is important to be able to characterise and measure the beam and spot properties. Many workers have considered how to characterise a beam. For example, [2] explains the use of M^2, and its measurement. Work carried out [3, 4] in looking at the spatial and temporal intensity distribution, concluded that it was useful to measure certain beam characteristics. Some of the qualitative techniques available is discussed in [5].

The first of the modern instruments was the Laser Beam Analyser (LBA) described by [6, 7]. A similar principle to the LBA is used in hollow needle analysers. In a review article [8], it was concluded that the distortion of the beam profile that could occur with a conventional LBA was avoided with the hollow needle system. The Prometec UFF 100, based on the hollow needle principle, is one of the two available commercial devices for carrying out high power beam diagnostics. An alternative mechanical scanning system is the Nipkov or scanning drum. A beam analysis system for a CO_2 laser based on such a drum is presented in [9]. Other mechanical systems such as apertures can be in the form of knife edges [10], slits or pin holes.

An alternative beam analysis technique is to directly image the attenuated beam using a charge coupled device (CCD) camera and modern CCD systems such as described in [11] are capable of very high resolution but can be relatively expensive.

Design of a Pinhole Beam Analyser

The pinhole is effectively an attenuator when placed on the beam path. The beam emerging through the pinhole is a beam sample at a coordinate (x,y) on the beam. The beam is scanned across the pinhole in the x and y and thus the temporal variation in energy passing through the pinhole represents the spatial distribution of intensity in the beam. This variation in energy can be used to plot the beam profile.

The sensor was designed to operate with spot power densities up to that produced by a 3.0 kW CO_2 laser with a 15mm diameter raw beam and a 50.8mm focal length lens. A 10 μm pinhole in a 127μm thickness gold plated copper sheet was used. The raw beam from a 3kW CO_2 laser was attenuated by a factor of 1000 using a silicon beam splitter prior to the focusing optics.

The sensor chosen for the study was an ELTEC 420-2, a germanium antireflection coated sensor for 10.6μm wavelength with a damage threshold of $5 \times 10^4 Wm^{-2}$ and a surface area of 2.5x2.5 mm². A cutting table with a resolution of 1 μm and capable of movement in x,y,z (z out of the plane of the pinhole sheet) was used in the scanning. Finally the data collection unit consisted of a two stage amplifier in conjunction with the UNIDEX 600 table CNC controller I/O card. The set-up was such that the pinhole/detector arrangement was located at a fixed point on the cutting bed and the beam was scanned in the x and y directions in discrete steps to map the beam profile.

The beam focus was found by moving the cutting head in small increments in z in both directions from the expected focus position. In order to cater for any minor misalignment in the beam path the head is also moved in x and y directions to make sure the intensity at the established focus point was the highest. Once this point was confirmed the cutting head was moved in the x and y directions, collecting the intensity data at the required locations.

The pinhole/detector arrangement must be such that the beam emerging from the pinhole fills the active area of the detector so as to avoid excessive intensity and hence damage to the detector. Calculations performed gave an intensity of 2.5×10^4 Wm^{-2} at the detector. This gave a factor of safety of 2.0 when compared to the detector damage threshold of 5.0×10^4 Wm^{-2}.

To ensure that the full surface of the detector is illuminated it is necessary to determine the divergence of the beam after the pinhole. The measurement of the raw beam was made close to the beam waist, that is, where the beam radius of curvature is effectively infinite. Similarly, the focused spot was estimated at the focal plane and thus again the radius of curvature is infinite. The Rayleigh distance given by equation (1) is of the order of 10 μm. As it would be impossible to mount the detector within this distance from the pinhole, the diffraction from the pinhole is clearly of Fraunhofer type. Hence Equation (2) allows the determination of the beam divergence and (3) the required detector distance. From this the angle of spread of the beam can be evaluated (Figure 1).

$$z_R = \frac{d^2}{\lambda} \quad (1)$$ Beam divergence is given by

$$\alpha = \frac{1.22\lambda}{d} \quad (2)$$ Hence

$$\tan\left(\frac{\alpha}{2}\right) = \frac{l/2}{h} \; \text{Which gives } h = \frac{1}{2\tan\left(\dfrac{\alpha}{2}\right)} \quad (3)$$

This is the angle at which the first zero point occurs.
Table 1 below summarises the beam divergence, α and the detector distance, h.

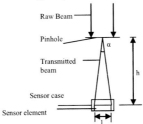

Figure 1: Beam transmission through a pinhole

Pinhole diameter (μm)	Angle of spread (rad)	Distance, h mm
100	0.13	19.3
50	0.26	9.60
10	1.29	1.70

Table 1 Beam transmission characteristics via varying pinhole size

From Table 1 it can be observed that the smaller the aperture the more rapid the divergence of the beam and hence small errors in the detector distance can result in damage to the detector. From the above, it was possible to locate the detector at the appropriate position.

Typical Beam Profile Results
The main objective was to measure the diameter and generate the profile of the spot formed by focusing the beam. The beam focus analysis was carried out for 63.5 mm and 50.8 mm focal length lenses as used for the cutting operation.
Figure 2 shows the beam profile at the beam focus when using a 50.8 mm focal length lens. This profile was taken over an area of 100 μm x 100 μm. The diameter was calculated by subtracting the background signal, summing the data from the beam outskirt until a ratio of 0.135 was formed compared to the total data. This definition of the beam diameter based on Hull and Stewart [12] is known as the $1/e^2$ diameter and is that enclosing 86.5% of the total beam energy. This gave a mean diameter of approximately 60 μm.

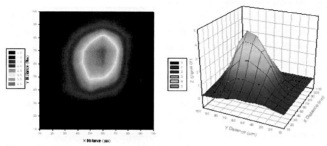

Figure 2: Plan and 3D view of the beam focus formed by a 50.8 mm focal length lens

The results obtained using the 63.5 mm focal length lens are shown in Figure 3. Calculating the spot diameter in a similar manner to that above gave a diameter of 80μm. It can be seen that a profile with good spatial resolution can be obtained. Furthermore the ISO standard [13] was also used to calculate this diameter. This diameter is a function of the second moments of area of power density distribution of the beam at a location along the z axis. From the beam profile result collected, the first moments was calculated to give the x and y centroids and then the second moments to obtain the respective diameters along both axes. This gave a mean diameter of approximately 87 μm which is close to the $1/e^2$ diameter of 80 μm.

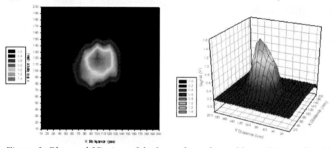

Figure 3: Plan and 3D view of the beam focus formed by a 63.5 mm focal length lens

In order to determine the beam propagation on either side of the beam focal plane, the beam diameters above and below the focus were measured. These were compared to theoretical values determined using Equation (4), derived from [14].

In Figure 4, the beam diameter is plotted against z movement when the beam is focused using 63.5 mm focal length lens. It can be seen that the theoretical curve and experimental data are in good agreement.

The theoretical curves were calculated using an M^2 of 1.52, obtained from the value of the focused beam diameter. The experimental point at the beam focus agrees closely with the theoretical value providing confirmation that the beam quality is approximately $M^2 = 1.52$ as used in the theoretical curve.

To provide comparative data the raw beam profile and diameter were measured using a Prometec UFF100 and the pinhole technique. These measurement were carried out simultaneously and the results shown in Figures 5 and 6. These figures display good agreement with one another. The calculation of the spot sizes on the two occasions revealed a discrepancy of approximately 7% between the two values.

$$W_F = \left\{ W_L^2 \left\langle \left[\left(1 - \frac{z_f}{f}\right) + \left(\frac{z_f}{R(z)}\right) \right]^2 + \left(\frac{z_f \lambda M^2}{\pi W_L^2}\right)^2 \right\rangle \right\}^{\frac{1}{2}} \qquad (4)$$

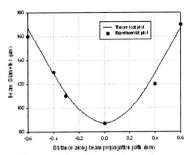

Figure 4 Experimental beam diameter data obtained using 63.5 mm

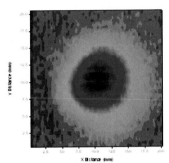

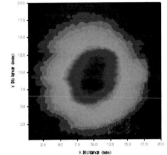

Figure 5 Raw beam profile generated by Prometec UFF 100

Figure 6 Beam profile generated by the pinhole arrangement

Summary

A pinhole method of beam analysis has been developed for the analysis of a CO_2 laser beam used for high speed cutting. It has been shown that the pinhole method of beam analysis is capable of analysing a high power beam with good spatial resolution. It would be possible to increase the resolution by decreasing the pinhole size. However a consequence of decreasing the pinhole size would be a reduction in signal strength and this would require modification of the signal processor.

The present method thus allows direct measurement of the focussed spot diameter and, through estimation of M^2, the determination of the depth of focus for a particular focal length lens. As the focussed spot diameter determines the laser intensity applied to the substrate and the depth of field influences the height control requirement to maintain the focus, this technique allows both the critical parameters in high laser cutting to be observed.

As the system allows the focussed spot profile to be determined at any position, the spot can thus be characterised to ISO standards using the second moment of area method. The spatial resolution of the system is limited by the time taken to make the large number of samples needed to achieve a high resolution. This does not represent a problem when using the system with a beam with good temporal stability. In the other situation this problem could be minimised by the use of a sensor with a shorter response time than the pyroelectric device used in the present study.

A pinhole based measurement system installed on a cutting table allows changes in the laser, mirrors or focussing optics to be detected. For example, minor damage to the lens will result in a greater focussed spot diameter than observed with a new, perfect, lens. Regular monitoring of the focussed spot thus allows preventative maintenance on the laser and optical system.

References

[1] C. B. Roundy. Maximising Laser Performance Using Laser Beam Diagnostics, SPIE Vol. 2426 (1995), pp. 528 – 539.

[2] T. F. Johnson (Jnr.). M^2 Concept Characterises Beam Quality, Laser Focus World, (1990), pp. 173 – 178.

[3] Gilse, J.V., Koczera, S. and Greby, D., "Direct Laser Beam Diagnostics", SPIE Vol. 1414, pp. 45 – 54, 1991.

[4] R. R. Prasad. and J. Schein. Time Resolved Beam profilers can Take the Heat, Laser Focus World, (2000), pp. 265 – 267.

[5] C. B. Roundy. Laser Beam Quality Characterisation, SPIE Vol. 3423 (1998), pp. 140 – 144.

[6] G. C. Lim and W. M. Steen. An Instrument for Instantaneous In-Situ Analysis of the Mode Structure of a High power Laser Beam, Journal of Physics, part E, vol. 17 (1984), pp. 999 – 1007.

[7] D. M. Hirak, D. C. Weckman and H. W. Kerr. Measuring the Spatial Intensity Distribution of High-Power Laser Beams using a Rotating Wire type Laser Beam Analyser. Parts I and II: Theory and Experimental Validation, Measurement Science and Technology, Vol. 5 (1994), pp. 1513 – 1532.

[8] J. F. Coutouly, P. Deprez, P. Vantomme and A. Deffontaine. Simple is Best for Real-Time Beam Analysis, OLE (1999), pp. 34 – 37.

[9] O. Gregersen and F. O. Olsen. Beam Analysing System for CO_2 Lasers, ICALEO (1990), Boston.

[10] Plass, W., Maestle, R., Wittig, K., Voss, A. and Giesen, A., ""High resolution Knife Edge Laser Beam profiling", Optics Communications, Vol. 134, pp. 21-24, 1997.

[11] D. MacCallum and G. A. Knorovsky. Spot Size Measurements for Ultra-Small Laser Welds, ICALEO (2002).

[12] D. Hull and A. F. Stewart. Laser Beam Profiles-Equipment and Techniques, Lasers and Applications (1985), pp. 71-76.

[13] International Standard Lasers and laser-Related Equipment- Test Methods for Laser Beam Parameters- Beam Widths, Divergence Angles and Beam Propagation Factor, ISO 11146, 1999.

[14] T. W. Silfvast. Laser Fundamentals, Cambridge University Press, UK, (1999).

[15] I. C. Arokiam. High Speed Laser Cutting with Control of Strategic System Parameters, ICMR (2006)

Acknowledgement

The work described in this paper was undertaken with the support of the EPSRC and numerous commercial sponsors. This support is gratefully acknowledged. The author was also supported by a University of Liverpool Scholarship.

260

Green Cutting using Supersonic Air Jets as Coolant and Lubricant during Turning

Andrea Bareggi, Trinity College Dublin, Ireland
e-mail: bareggia@tcd.ie

Prof. Andrew Torrance, Trinity College Dublin, Ireland
e-mail: atorrnce@tcd.ie

Garret O'Donnell, Trinity College Dublin, Ireland
e-mail: odonnege@tcd.ie

Abstract. Advanced materials such as aero-engine alloys and hardened steels provide serious challenges for cutting tool materials due to the high temperatures and stresses generated during machining, consequently accelerating tool wear and increasing manufacturing cost. A change in environmental awareness and increasing cost pressures on industrial enterprises have led to a critical consideration of conventional cooling lubricants used in most machining processes. Extensive Minimum Quantity Lubricant (MQL) research has been carried out, but Minimum Quantity Cooling (MQC), such as high pressure air jets, has until now, been seldom used, and therefore largely unexplored.

The focus of the research presented in this paper is to investigate the use of supersonic air jets as alternatives to mineral oil coolant, and examine the benefit on the cutting process from a thermodynamic and mechanical point of view. The potential benefits of this research are very important for many industrial machining processes as well. Initial results indicate the use of supersonic air jets leads to a reduced temperature in the cutting zone, reduced cutting forces and a modified chip shape.

Keywords: high performance cutting, aerospace alloys, MQCL, supersonic air jet

Introduction. As the temperature of a cutting tool may reach a high value, in particular when a heavy cut is taken at high speed, coolant is necessary to prevent thermal damage and tool wear. In machining fundamental studies on heat transfer are quite rare, most workers relying on empirical work. So, in most machining processes cooling is achieved using oil-based fluids. Oil is used for its high specific heat capacity and lubrication qualities. The cutting fluid, although reused several times, must eventually be replaced. During a recent CIRP conference about High Performance Cutting (HPC) in 2004, a number of presentations were based on Minimum Quantity Lubrication (MQL) and dry cutting [1], indicating both the active research and industrial interest in green cutting. The motivations for using air jets are not only environmental and economic considerations, but this approach also has technological benefits. In contrast to minimum quantity lubrication (MQL), minimum quantity cooling (MQC) has until now, been seldom used, and therefore remains a largely unexplored component of the MQCL technique among industrial users.

However, the minimum quantity cooling technique can make a major contribution to the solution of thermal problems affecting the tool and/or the part in dry machining operations [2]. These techniques include high pressure air jets, water vapour [3] and chilled air [4]. Current research shows impinging gas jets have a much greater potential for cooling than previously suspected. By using a supersonic nozzle, it has been possible to obtain benefits in machining comparable with conventional liquid coolants. The purpose of this research is to investigate the use of supersonic air jets in turning. Gas jets can be used in many situations where liquid cannot. Furthermore there are environmental and safety benefits, as liquid coolants are traditionally mineral oil based, and they represent a hazard to the environment and are toxic for the operator. The feasibility of using supersonic air jets as a suitable alternative to liquid coolant on a lathe has been investigated. Cutting forces, chip shape and workpiece temperature have been predicted by 3D finite element model using the commercial software Deform-3D™.

Experimental setup. A supersonic nozzle has been designed to direct the air jet on the chip formed by a Tungsten Carbide (WC) tool turning a steel workpiece (AISI 1020) in a lathe. The following cutting condition and references were used:

- Cutting speed: 270 m/min
- Depth of cut: 0.5 mm
- Feed: 0.095 mm/rev
- Insert nose radius: 0.4 mm
- Rake angle: 5°
- Air jet pressure (nozzle inlet): 6 bar
- Insert material: WC
- Workpiece material: AISI 1020 steel

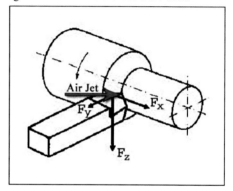

Fig. 1 – Reference System

Fig. 2 is a view of the nozzle placed on the tool. A nozzle holder has been designed to provide a range of positions for directing the air jet at the tool workpiece interface. The cutting forces on the tool have been monitored with a 3-component Kistler toolpost dynamometer. A Hommel surface roughness tester has been used for roughness test. A Finite Element Model has been developed using the commercial software Deform-3D™ and Comsol FEMLAB™.

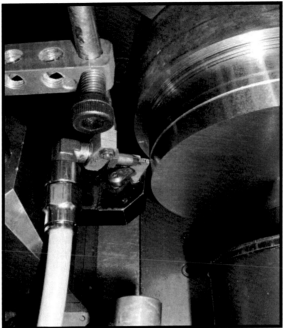

Fig. 2 – Supersonic nozzle placed in the cutting area

FEM prediction. The commercial FE software Deform-3D™ has been used to simulate the machining process. The power of this software is the Arbitrary Lagrangian-Eulerian (ALE) formulation and the ability to perform frequent automatic remeshing. The FE model was used to predict chip shape and workpiece temperature in an incremental analysis (Fig. 3). The figure shows a chip temperature up to 700°C in the shear zone, the model results were found to be in agreement with the work of Sales and Guimara [5]. The results from the FE model have been validated by the experimental investigations (see Fig. 6).

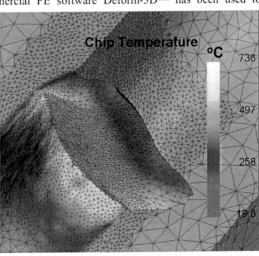

Fig. 3 – Workpiece temperature simulated by Deform

Since Deform-3D™ does not model heat transfer to the tool very well, the commercial FE software Femlab has been used to investigate the gradient of temperature in the insert, considering in particular the chip-tool interface area (Fig. 4).

The model uses the frictional power on the rake face calculated from the Deform-3D™ model as an input, and partitions it between the tool and the chip by assuming that the

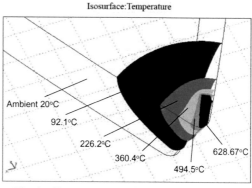

Fig. 4 – Temperature gradient inside WC insert

average temperature of the contact area of both is the same. The results of this simulation show that the temperature falls from a maximum value of 628 °C to 226 °C within a distance of 2.7 mm. This analysis provides support in choosing the most appropriate temperature measurement system for measuring tool temperatures during the experimental investigations.

Preliminary experimental investigations.

The temperature of the cutting tool has been monitored by an infrared camera. Fig. 5 shows the effect of supersonic jet during machining. Two cutting conditions have been considered: with air jet cooling (on the left side), and without air jet cooling (on the right side). Since the resolution of the infrared camera is poor, relative to the chip-tool interface area, this visualization provides only an average value of the temperature, but also shows the ability of the air jet to cool the cutting area.

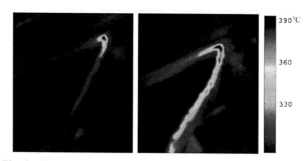

Fig. 5 – Temperature around cutting area with and without air jet

To estimate the benefits of the air jet on finishing, the roughness has been measured with a Hommel surface roughness tester. The results indicate a modest improvement in surface finish with the air jet:

R_a = 0.76 μm with air jet
R_a = 0.84 μm without air jet

The cutting forces on the tool have been monitored with a 3-component Kistler toolpost dynamometer and are shown in Fig. 6. The results clearly show a step change in cutting force when air jet cooling is used. The cutting force (Z-axis) predicted by the FE model has been compared to the experimental results and the results validate the model developed with Deform-3D.

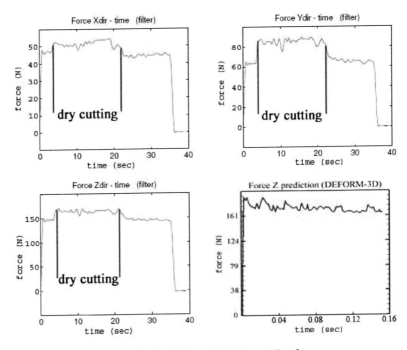

Fig. 6 – Effect of air jet on cutting forces

Present research. Current efforts focus on thermal analysis of the chip-tool interface. Considering the results of FEM carried out with Femlab and Deform, different types of temperature measuring devices are under consideration:

- Spot radiometer, pointing the lens as close as possible to the chip-tool interface
- Standard thermocouple placed inside the insert, drilled using spark-erosive method
- Non-Standard thermocouple using insert and workpiece material

Improvements in the Deform finite element model are also under development: a pressure is applied on chip back face in order to simulate the effect of the air jet and investigating the mechanical effect of the jet on chip shape, since the bending moment should change the shear plane angle, with significant savings in the power required for cutting.

Conclusions and further research. The initial results from the simulations and the experimental investigations undertaken are encouraging. The finite element model predicts measured forces well, and gives a good indication of the temperatures recorded by thermography. Significant benefits in terms of finish and forces have already been developed, but there are several questions still to be answered. Further work is needed to investigate how the ability of air jet to penetrate the chip-tool interface relates to the temperature of the tip of the tool. Quick stop tests are needed to investigate chip shape changes when the supersonic air jet is used; and to optimize the effect of the air jet, a fluid-dynamic FE model will be developed with Femlab. Once these preliminaries are complete, the process will be applied to aero-engine alloys to check the cooling ability of supersonic air jets when machining difficult to cut materials.

References

[1] Byrne. G., History of high performance cutting in CIRP, Proceedings of the CIRP International Conference on High Performance Cutting, Aachen, Germany, 19-20 October 2004.

[2] Weinert, K., Dry machining and minimum quantity lubrication (MQL), Proceedings of the CIRP International Conference on High Performance Cutting, Aachen, Germany, 19-20 October 2004.

[3] Han, R., Liu, J., Sun, Y., Research on experimentation of green cutting with water vapor as coolant and lubricant, Industrial Lubrication and Tribology, Vol. 57, No. 5, (2005), pp. 187–192.

[4] Rahman, M., Senthil Kumar, A., Manzoor-Ul-Salam, Ling, M.S., Effect of chilled air on machining performance in end milling, International Journal of Advanced Manufacturing Technology, Vol. 21, (2003), pp. 787–795.

[5] Sales, W.F., Guimara, G., Machado, A.R., Ezugwu, E.O., Cooling ability of cutting fluids and measurement of the chip-tool interface temperatures, Industrial Lubrication and Tribology, Vol. 54, No. 2, (2002), pp. 57–68.

[6] Dahlman, P., Escursell, M., High-pressure jet-assisted cooling: a new possibility for near net shape turning of decarburized steel, International Journal of Machine Tools & Manufacture, Vol. 44, (2004), pp. 109–115.

[7] Dawson, T.G., Kurfess, T.R., Tool life, wear rates and surface quality in hard turning, Proceedings of the NAMRC XXIX, Gainseville, Florida, 22-29 May, 2001.

[8] Klocke, F., Essel, I., Basics of HPC and mechanical and thermal characteristics, Proceedings of the CIRP International Conference on High Performance Cutting, Aachen, Germany, 19-20 October 2004.

[9] Fischer, C.E., Mylavaram, N.K.R., Design and simulation of cutting tools, Proceedings of the CIRP International Conference on High Performance Cutting, Aachen, Germany, 19-20 October 2004.

[10] Konig, W., Berktold, A., and Kock, K. F., Turning versus grinding—A comparison of surface integrity aspects and attainable accuracies, Annals of the CIRP, Vol. 42, (1993), pp. 39-43.

Dry Ice Blasting - Cleaning Control and Power Electronics without Downtime

E. Uhlmann[1, a], R. Veit[1, b]

[1]Institute for Machine Tools and Factory Management, Technical University Berlin, Department of Manufacturing Technology, Pascalstrasse 8 - 9, 10587 Berlin, Germany

[a]uhlmann@iwf.tu-berlin.de, [b]veit@iwf.tu-berlin.de

Abstract. The servicing and maintenance of production lines cost time and money. Especially the cleaning of control and power electronics requires a shut-down of machines or entire production areas. A possibility to avoid losses of production is Dry Ice Blasting, a blasting technology that uses solid carbon dioxide - so called dry ice - as a one way blasting medium. In atmospheric pressure dry ice has a temperature of -78.5 °C and sublimes immediately as it hits the surface of the parts to be cleaned. Only the removed contaminations have to be disposed. Dry ice is not inflammable, chemical inert, non toxic and electrical nonconductive and in principle applicable for the cleaning of electronic machine components. However, there is the danger that ambient humidity will condense on these components and may cause a flashover. Furthermore usual blasting nozzles are not suitable for the wide range of materials in electrical systems.

In collaboration with the Fraunhofer-Institute for Production Systems and Design Technology in Berlin and the Brandenburg Technical University Cottbus the Institute for Machine Tools and Factory Management of the Technical University Berlin has developed a cleaning device based on Dry Ice Blasting that allows live maintenance of production lines without any danger to men or machine. The voltage level can range from low voltage in micro electronics to 30,000 Volts in power electronics.

Keywords: Dry Ice Blasting, cleaning technology, live maintenance, carbon dioxide

Introduction

Cleaning technology has steadily gained significance in the past years and today represents an important part of the value chain. Whereas in manufacturing processes cleaning is seen as an integral step to reach product quality, it is still considered as an unwanted expense factor in maintenance and service. Down time of machines and facilities, because of disassembling, cleaning and assembling, causes loss of production and thereby high costs.

The European industry is forced to change current cleaning processes not only due to technical and economical aspects, but especially because of new ecological circumstances. The main reasons are increased environmental awareness, new environmental legislation, rising waste disposal costs, and increased sewage taxes [1]. More and more established cleaning technologies have to be substituted and so new technologies like *Dry Ice Blasting* gain in importance.

Dry Ice Blasting

Dry Ice Blasting is a compressed air process that uses solid carbon dioxide - so called dry ice - in form of pellets as a one way blasting medium [2]. In atmospheric pressure solid carbon dioxide has a temperature of -78. °C. Accelerated by compressed air the dry ice particles sublime immediately as they touch the surface of the part to be cleaned. Only the removed contamination has to be disposed. Compared to blasting technologies with solid blasting media which are based on the mechanical impact of the abrasives, Dry Ice Blasting is based on three different active mechanisms, the thermal effect, the mechanical effect and the sublimation effect (Fig. 1) [3, 4, 5].

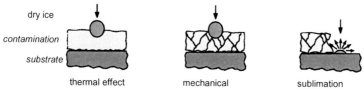

Figure 1: Active mechanisms of Dry Ice Blasting

First the low temperature of the dry ice particles leads to a local cooling of the part and contamination. As a result, the elasticity of the contamination is reduced and it gets embrittled and shrinks while forming cracks. Due to the different thermal expansion coefficients of the contamination and the substrate, the bond with the substrate dissolves when the adhesive energy is exceeded. The second active mechanism, the kinetic impact of the dry ice particles causes the contamination to chip of. The third effect, the sudden increase in volume resulting from the sublimation of the dry ice, supports the process. The removal of contaminations is hence based on a combined thermo-mechanical effect.

Dry Ice blasting is very flexible with reference to materials and contaminations. It can be used for the cleaning of very sensitive structures as well as for the removal of paint or thermal sprayed coatings. It is used e. g. in aviation to clean sensitive body parts of aircrafts before coating [6]. Dry ice is not inflammable, chemical inert, non toxic and electrical nonconductive and in principle applicable for the cleaning of electronic machine components.

Barriers for Dry Ice Blasting of electronic equipment

The hardness of solid carbon dioxide is comparable with the hardness of gypsum. Therefore Dry Ice blasting is a non abrasive process. Low blasting pressures in combination with well-adjusted blasting nozzles allow even the cleaning of mounted printed circuit boards [7]. Unfortunately usual blasting nozzles are not suitable for the wide range of materials in electrical systems. Especially plastics and cable insulations showed high sensitivity to the process (Fig. 2).

Figure 2: Damage on cables depending on the blasting pressure

Although Dry Ice Blasting is a dry process, ambient humidity can condense on the cleaned components because of the cooled surfaces. Measurements showed surface temperatures down to -7 °C. This affects the insulating resistance of the cleaned device directly, shown in figure 3 considering a low voltage distribution box as example. Immediately after the blasting process the insulating resistance breaks down and recovers first after 25 minutes. Working in live conditions this would cause leakage currents. In power electronics even flashover could occur, a great danger to men and machine.

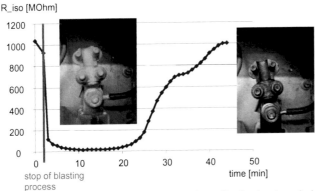

Figure 3: Insulating resistance of a low voltage distribution box during and after the blasting process

Also the surface of usual blasting nozzles can reach temperatures below 0 °C. Ambient humidity condenses in any case and forms conductive layers on the blasting nozzle, even if the nozzle is made of insulating material. Furthermore the dry ice particles rub against the inner wall of nozzle and hose and produce electrostatic charges. This may not harm the cleaning personnel directly, but electrostatic discharges may cause them to make uncontrolled moves. The consequences in electrical environments are unpredictable. On this account the grounding of nozzle and hose has to be assured.

Technological Concept

In the beginning of the research project the requirements towards the new cleaning technology had to be defined. Information about the target market had to be gathered. A market analysis was carried out, giving detailed information about devices and material which have to be cleaned, about typical contaminations in electrical equipment, about the relevant voltage level and about the expected market size.

There is no industrial standard or directive for the construction of equipment for Dry Ice Blasting in live working conditions. Nevertheless there are several standards for related technologies that can be adapted like the DIN VDE 0105 "Operation of electrical installations" [8], VDE 0682-130 "Live working - Minimum requirements for the utilization of tools, devices and equipment" [9] and DIN VDE 0682-621 "Live working - Suction device for the cleaning of live parts with rated voltages above 1 kV up to 36 kV" [10]. According to these standards, the technological concept of the cleaning device was developed.

Figure 4 shows the technical concept of the blasting lance. The dry ice particles are fed with compressed air through the hose (1). The handle (2) has to be designed for an optimum balance of the whole lance. The limiting shield (3) prevents the user from touching the insulating area (4). The

269

insulating area is the most important part of the lance and has to get in contact neither with the user nor with an electric device. Its length depends on the voltage level. A red ring (5) marks the end of the insulating area. The extension (6) as well as the nozzle (7) can be adapted in length and geometry according to the cleaning task. Apart from the handle all parts have to be made out of insulating material. Furthermore it has to be assured that these parts are kept dry during the cleaning process.

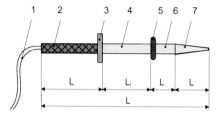

1 hose
2 handle (length L_h)
3 limiting shield
4 insulating area (length L_i)
5 end of insulating area
6 extension (length L_e)
7 blasting nozzle (length L_n)
L_t total length

Figure 4: Technological Concept of the blasting lance

Development of blasting nozzles

As described before, there are a lot of different materials in electrical devices. Metals, ceramics and plastics and not to forget labels and stickers must remain undamaged. The blasting process and especially the blasting nozzles have to be adapted to this wide range of materials. Blasting technologies can only applied to visible surfaces. Undercuts and surfaces that can not be reached directly by the jet can not be processed. To be able to clean surfaces on the side or the back of electrical devices, angular nozzles had to be developed.

All nozzles were produced with Selective Laser Sintering giving high flexibility for the geometrical definition of the nozzles. Also the used material polyamide is nonconductive and therefore applicable in electrical devices.

The goal for the development of the nozzles was to reach the maximum cleaning capacity depending on compressed air and dry ice consumption. Different models were realized: a linear nozzle, a 90 ° rectangular nozzle (Fig. 5) and a 135 ° rectangular nozzle.

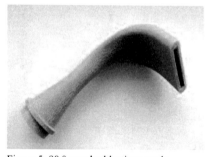

Figure 5: 90 ° angular blasting nozzle

Avoiding humidity on nozzles an cleaned devices

To avoid the cooling of cleaned surfaces and the blasting nozzle the use of heated compressed air was considered. Compressors produce a lot of waste heat that could be regained by heat exchanging devices. Investigations with heated compressed air showed that neither the surface temperature of the cleaned parts, nor the surface temperature of the nozzle could be increased considerably. It became apparent that the heated air had to be channelled separately through the nozzle onto the cleaned part.

The problem was solved by creating a dual-trace nozzle (Fig. 6). In the inner tube the dry ice is conveyed by compressed air and in an outer circular tube warm dry air is guided. The concept was also used for the entire blasting lance. The surface-temperature of nozzle and lance could be kept above the ambient temperature, avoiding any condensation of humidity.

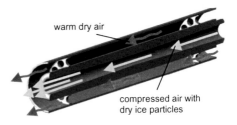

warm dry air

compressed air with
dry ice particles

Figure 6: Dual-trace nozzle

In the impact zone of the dry ice particles the cleaned part still cools down. But insulated from the ambient air by the circular warm and dry air stream, no ambient humidity can reach this zone. Passing over the cleaned area, the warm air reheats the part immediately.

Safety and field tests

To assure the safety of the new cleaning system in live working conditions comprehensive tests were done in a climatic chamber at the Brandenburg Technical University. Experience has shown that the major difficulties to pass the tests occur at high temperature and high humidity. From the applicable European Standards the leakage current test and the bridging test were chosen to assure that the insulating tube and the nozzle are suitable for live working. At the maximum humidity of 80 % the equipment passed all tests without problem. The system proved its applicability for live working up to 36 kV.

Still the suitability for daily use had to be investigated. Field test were carried out in a 36 kV substation were control and power electronics had to be cleaned. To assure repeatable conditions a test contamination was requested, which was produced with different earths, unburned carbon, grease, oil and other ingredients in an aqueous solution. This reference contamination allowed not only the measurement of the cleaning efficiency of the new technology, but also a comparison to established cleaning technologies.

The field test showd, that Dry Ice Blasting is a very effective cleaning technology for electrical components, especially for electrical devices used

Figure 7: Cleaning control electronics with the new Dry Ice Blasting equipment

in rough conditions. Hard sticking contaminations can be removed fast without harming the cleaned material.

Summary and Outlook

Dry Ice Blasting is an environmentally friendly technology with a wide range of applications. To clean control and power electronics in live working conditions a completely new machine concept was developed. The activities included the development of new nozzles and an insulation blasting lance. In this context, the problem of condensing ambient humidity, which is typical for Dry Ice Blasting, could be solved for the first time. The safety of the system was proved in various measurements in a climatic chamber. The efficiency of the technology was tested in real working conditions in a 36 kV substation.

Before the commercialisation of the cleaning technology an automatic monitoring system has to be developed to assure the safety of the worker. This system has to monitor e. g. the temperature on the surface of the blasting lance, the humidity of the compressed air and the grounding of the handle. Another aspect according to workers safety is the high sound pressure level of Dry Ice Blasting which has to be reduced considerably.

Acknowledgements

We would like to thank the Federal Ministry of Economics and Technology for the funding of the project.

References

[1]   E. Uhlmann, A. El Mernissi, J. Dittberner: Blasting Techniques for Disassembly and Remanufacturing. Global Conference on Sustainable Product Development and Life Cycle Engineering (Berlin, FRG 2004), pp. 217-223.

[2]   E. Rice, C. Franklin: Method for the removal of unwanted portions of an article by spraying with high velocity dry ice particles, Patent US 3,702,519, Chemotronics International Inc. (Michigan, USA 1971).

[3]   G. Spur, E. Uhlmann, F. Elbing: Experimental Research on Cleaning with Dry ice Blasting, Proceedings of the the international Conference on Water Jet Machining WJM `98 (Krakow, Poland 1998), pp. 37-45.

[4]   E. Uhlmann, B. Axmann, F. Elbing: Cleaning and Decoating in Disassembly, Proceedings of the 4th World Congress R `99 - Recovery, Recycling, Re-integration (Geneva, Switzerland 1999).

[5]   E. Uhlmann, F. Elbing, A. El Mernissi: Applications for Eco-Efficient Surface Machining with Dry Ice Blasting, Proceedings of the 1st International Conference on Design and Manufacture for Sustainable Development (Liverpool, UK 2002), pp. 195-2008.

[6]   C. Fong: Sandblasting with pellets of material capable of sublimation, Patent US 4,038,786, Lockheed Aircraft Corp. (California, USA 1975).

[7]   E. Uhlmann, F. Elbing: The Eco-Efficient Cleaning Technology of Dry-Ice Blasting for the Reuse of Electronic Components of Mounted Printed-Circuit Boards, Proceeding of the International Symposium on Sustainable Manufacturing Conference `99 (Shanghai, China 1999), pp. 193-199.

[8]   DIN VDE 0105: Operation of electrical installations (FRG 2005).

[9]   VDE 0682-130: Live working - Minimum requirements for the utilization of tools, devices and equipment (FRG 2003).

[10]   DIN VDE 0682-621: Live working - Suction device for the cleaning of live parts with rated voltages above 1 kV up to 36 kV (FRG 2004).

High Speed Laser Cutting with Control of Strategic System Parameters

Ivan Christy Arokiam, B.Eng., M.Sc (Eng.), Ph.D.[1]

Abstract

When compared to punch press cutting, laser cutting is attractive to many industries due to lower set up costs. However current laser cutting technology fails to compete with other processes in terms of speed. Despite a considerable volume of research there still exist potential areas for refinement which can help push cutting speed limits further. This work concentrates on the speed improvements achievable in CO_2 laser cutting using short focal length duplet lenses, accurate control of focal position, choice of gas type and pressure. Finally the paper examines the use of zoom beam expander prior to the focussing optics to increase the achievable cutting speed. The work demonstrates that a considerable improvement in cutting speed can be achieved by optimisation of the main process parameters.

Key Words: Laser cutting, focal length, depth of focus, lens, gas species

Introduction

Over the years laser cutting has been exploited by industries due to the nature of its flexibility. The most common application of industrial lasers in the world today is laser cutting [1, 2]. It is widely used due to the unique cut quality and process characteristics it offers [3]. Though laser cutting is preferred by most industries due to the mentioned characteristics it fails to compete with punch process operation in terms of speed. On the other hand, punch process operation, although superior in terms of speed to that of the existing laser cutting system require different shape press tools for different shape/dimension being cut. This incurs a high tooling as well as setup cost. A concurrent need for speed and flexibility in manufacturing industries is the driving force behind this work. The progression of laser cutting could be regarded as conventional, optimised and finally high speed laser cutting. Optimised laser cutting is channelled towards the achievement of high speeds by the use of more efficient hardware. In terms of process dynamics optimised laser cutting could be effectively imagined as the conventional laser cutting. Fanuc Ltd. (Oshino-mura, Japan) has carried out work in this area and outlined in [4]. Some major industrial suppliers use high power lasers in the 6 kW range, linear motors and beam conditioning unit to achieve high speeds[5],[6]. The linear motors can achieve accelerations of up to 7g, however this is reduced to 2g to maintain a vibration free system[7]. When the required speed could be achieved through process control with minimal hardware changes, it could be thought as a waste of resources from the economic point of view to simply use high power and precision equipment which may not necessarily be needed to achieve the required goal. High speed cutting is mainly different to the other two in that, instead of the formation of a semi-cylindrical cutting front, a closed keyhole with subsequent melt film ejection is produced[8],[9]. Some of the main factors that affect the cutting speed include power density, blow out gas type and pressure, nozzle alignment and beam polarization direction. In the following sections, this paper discusses along with experimental illustrations the effects of gas species, variation of focal length, gas pressure and the effect of using a zoom beam expander.

---

[1] The Agility Centre, University of Liverpool Management School, Chatham Street, Liverpool, L69 7ZH,
ivan.arokiam@liverpool.ac.uk

273

Effect of Gas Type

A number of different gases can be used to blow out the melt through the kerf. For the purpose of this investigation nitrogen and oxygen were selected. This experiment was carried out with the use of a 63.5 mm focal length meniscus lens, making sure that the effect of depth of focus was also observable. Due to the dependence of one factor on the other it is important to carry out the experiments such that these effects are revealed through the results. Tests were conducted by varying the distance between the lens and the work piece whilst keeping the nozzle stand off constant at 0.5 mm. Two speeds were determined: the "best maximum cutting speed" that guarantees separation of the two sides of the cut and the upper limit of cutting speed that does not necessarily provide a successful cut on every attempt. Figure 1 shows the cutting speed as a function of the distance from the optimum focus for nitrogen whereas Figure 2 shows the corresponding data for oxygen. In each of these series of tests the work piece was 0.9 mm thickness mild steel sheet. It can be seen from Figure 1 and Figure 2 that oxygen cutting was much faster when compared that of nitrogen. The best maximum cutting speed at optimum focus was approximately 33 metres per minute with oxygen compared to 24 metres per minute with nitrogen.

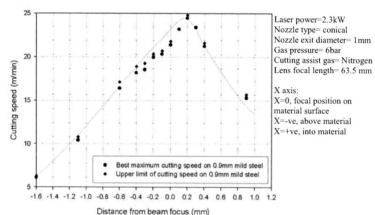

Figure 1: Nitrogen assisted laser cutting with 63.5 mm focal length lens

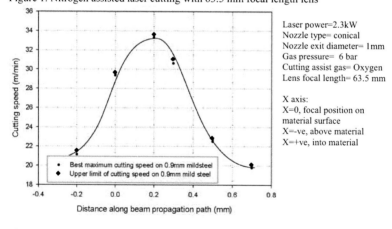

Figure 2: Oxygen assisted laser cutting with 63.5 mm focal length lens

274

It can be seen that the maximum cutting speed is achieved when the beam focus is set lower than the material surface by about 20% of its thickness. Also the observation of the cut edge quality of the samples revealed that oxygen produced a better sample set than that of nitrogen.

Cutting Using a Short Focal Length Lens
The Power density of the focused spot has significant effect on the cutting speed. In order to investigate this effect the experiments above were repeated using a 50.8 mm achromatic doublet focal length lens. This provided results that could be used to compare the change in performance when switching from a 63.5mm to 50.8mm focusing lens. The change in the focal length had a corresponding focus spot size change from 80 to 64μm. This in theory would deliver an increase in the power density by a factor of 1.56. At the time of conducting the experiment, the laser power had dropped from 2.3 to 2.1kW (change in cavity performance) and this in effect made the expected increase in power density a factor of 1.40. Figures 3 and 4 show the experiments conducted using nitrogen and oxygen as blow out gases respectively.

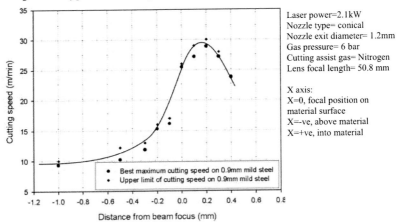

Figure 3: Nitrogen assisted laser cutting with 50.8 mm focal length lens

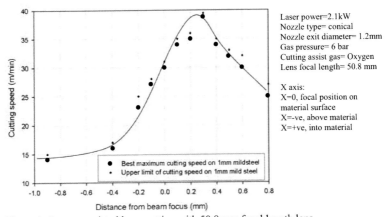

Figure 4: Oxygen assisted laser cutting with 50.8 mm focal length lens

In Figure 3, it can be seen that the best maximum cutting speed has increased from approximately 24 metres per minute for the 63.5 mm focal length lens to 29 metres per minute for the 50.8 mm focal length lens; a factor of 1.21. The speed thus did not increase by the same factor (i.e. 1.40) as the power density. This could be due to the effect of the narrower kerf, reflected by the spot size, beam quality, sensitivity of the depth of focus or other external factors.

Again in the case of oxygen blow out gas assisted cutting, the factor of speed increase was approximately 1.2, which could be due to any one or combination of the above mentioned problems. It is clear from the figures that the experimental depth of focus changes with the lens focal length and apparently with the assist gas species. A detailed work has been presented in [10] that covers investigation on the effects of depth of focus.

The critical feature is not the formal definition of depth of focus but the precision with which the lens height, and thus the focus, must be controlled. In Table 1 the effect on cutting speed of height errors of ± 100 μm and ±200 μm are shown. This data was obtained from Figures 1-4. It can be seen that a height error band of ± 200 μm results in an unacceptable speed reduction of up to 24.6% (50.8 mm focal length, Nitrogen assist gas). However if the height error can be maintained within ± 100 μm, the cutting speed is maintained within a maximum of 8.5%.

Change in distance (μm)	63.5 mm focal length lens		50.8 mm focal length lens	
	O$_2$ assisted (% speed drop)	N$_2$ assisted (% speed drop)	O$_2$ assisted (% speed drop)	N$_2$ assisted (% speed drop)
100	3.4	4.0	5.5	8.5
200	14.2	8.7	13.2	24.6

Table 1: Variation in cutting performance based on focus shift through a fixed distance

It was also observed in all except in one case that nitrogen assisted cutting was more sensitive to focal position than its counter part. This could be as a result of the fact that oxygen assisted cutting involves an exothermic reaction, heat input arises from both the laser source and the reaction. It is believed that the additional heat input reduces the sensitivity of the cutting speed to spot power density and thus to focus position. However in nitrogen assisted cutting, the cutting speed change is purely a consequence of change in beam focus position. From this work, it can be concluded that, there certainly is an advantage using shorter focal length lenses as long as a height sensor that is capable of keeping the spot within the short depth of focus is incorporated.

Gas Assist Pressure
Gas assist pressure is an important parameter that determines the cutting speed. In fact the above experiments were carried out at the optimum cutting pressure determined after undertaking an initial investigation. The results of this investigation are discussed below. Cutting was carried out at various gas pressures using a 50.8mm focal length lens. Figure 5 and Figure 6 shows the change in cutting speed with pressure when using nitrogen and oxygen gas respectively.

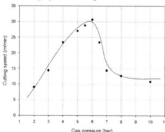

Figure 5: Nitrogen assisted cutting at various pressures

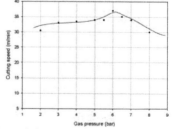

Figure 6: Oxygen assisted cutting at various pressures

In both cases it can be observed that the cutting speed increases with pressure until the pressure reaches approximately six bar. This is not due to the gas species as both figures display the same trend although the change in cutting speed is more pronounced in nitrogen assisted cutting. Oxygen forms a reactive part during the cutting process and hence makes, to an extent, the effect of pressure insensitive. So what is the reason for a high cutting speed at six bar. This may be due to the deformation of the focusing arrangement with the change in pressure which in turn shifts the focus position. Another reason can be that after a certain pressure, the gas cools the metal thereby affecting the material interaction process which in turn conveys diminishing returns on the cutting speed. It was confirmed by further experimentation that the shift in focus position did not occur with increase in cutting pressure. The assist gas velocity also changes with pressure and this change in velocity may also influence the cutting performance. Therefore these experiments prove that the gas assist pressure should be approximately around 6 bar to achieve the maximum cutting performance.

Use of Zoom Beam Expander

Theoretical prediction showed that the use of a zoom beam expander had the potential to further increase the cutting speed. The larger the raw beam, the smaller the achievable focussed spot size. The zoom beam expander is capable of delivering this feature and therefore investigation was carried out to verify if there was any increase in speed through expanding the raw beam. The expander had a capability of providing a maximum magnification of just over twice the laser raw beam diameter. For the case under consideration the use of a zoom beam expander at 2X magnification will decrease the focused spot diameter from approximately 64 μm to 32 μm when used with a 50.8 mm focal length lens. This will increase the power density by a factor of 4 compared to that generated by the 64 μm spot size. This should result in an increase in cutting speed. To demonstrate this a series of cutting trials were carried out, with the aid of the zoom beam expander, at different beam diameters (1.2, 1.4, 1.6 and 2X the original raw beam size). The experiments consisted of both oxygen and nitrogen assisted cutting using a 50.8 mm focal length lens, 2.3kW power and a zoom beam expander on a 0.9 mm thick mild steel. From the results it is evident that there is a speed increase as predicted. The power density also increased as expected. The speed only increased by 20% for oxygen assisted cutting (Figure 7) and a similar trend was observed when the nitrogen assisted cutting was carried out (Figure 8).

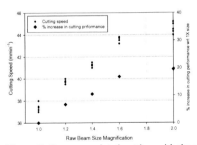 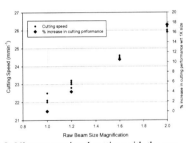

Figure 7: Oxygen assisted cutting with the use of zoom beam expander

Figure 8: Nitrogen assisted cutting with the use of zoom beam expander

Some of the reasons for not achieving the predicted increase would be due to or combination of the following.
(1) The material thickness could have been greater to get the full benefit of the system. This is because the depth of focus is much smaller and the actual focus may only be in contact with the material surface for a very short time. On the other hand if the thickness was much smaller, the short contact time would be sufficient to penetrate the material under consideration.

(2) At the point when the beam focus located at approximately 20% of the material thickness, due to the short depth of focus, the spot size on the surface of the work piece is larger than that conducted with the 50.8 mm lens in absence of the zoom beam expander.

The beam quality was evaluated during the course of this work to avoid unnecessary loss of performance [11]. The expander delivers a 20% increase in cutting speed without affecting the cut edge quality. In its own right this figure can be considered a substantial increase in speed that will enable laser cutting to deliver comparable, if not superior speeds to other manufacturing methods.

Summary
This paper has described some factors that are responsible for determining speed in laser cutting. The effect of some of these strategic parameters has been investigated to infer the optimal figure that will deliver the best possible result. Through integrated work in these areas a 45m/min cutting speed on 0.9 mm mild steel has been achieved with a 2.1 kW laser and a 50.8 mm focal length lens. This represents a substantial speed increase compared to existing systems and will help directly compete with alternative manufacturing methods. The following conclusions can be made from this work. Best cutting performance was achieved by operating the system with a gas assist pressure of 6 bar and good quality short focal length lens. Oxygen presents to be a better of the two gases for the work conducted. From the work carried out it is also evident that the use of a beam expander will further aid increase the cutting speed. It is believed that the effect of adding a beam expander will be more pronounced with decrease in material thickness. In effect this work has provided a set of optimal parameters towards some of the key strategic factors that affect the cutting speed. The current achievement itself is sufficient for manufacturing companies to move towards laser cutting systems due to the competitive nature of the advantages it offers in comparison to rival techniques.

References

[1] P. A. Hilton. The Early Days of Laser Cutting, SPIE Vol. 3097 (1997) pp. 10-16.
[2] W. M. Steen. Current Trends in Laser Material Processing, SPIE. 3097 (1997) pp. 2-7.
[3] W. M. Steen. Laser Material Processing, Springer-Verlag, (2003) UK.
[4] N. Karube, E. Yamazki, Y. Nakata, A. Mori and K. Suzuki. Fast Contour Cutting using Linear Motors" Industrial Laser Review, (1997) pp. 7-10.
[5] Alabama Laser Technologies – Machining Solutions Application Brief (1999).
http://www.gefanuc.com/literature/pdf/gef_appbriefAlabamaLaser.pdf
[6] Cincinnati Incorporated Publication: Success Stories (1999).
[7] W. M. Steen. Laser Material Processing- An Overview (2003) Journal of Optics A, Vol. 5, pp. S3-S7.
[8] K. Preibig, D. Petring and G. Herziger. High Speed Cutting of Thin Metal Sheets, SPIE Vol. 2207 (1997), pp. 96-110
[9] F. Schneider, D. Petring and R. Poprawe. Increasing Laser Beam Cutting Speeds, ICALEO'99, (1999), pp. 132-141.
[10] I. C. Arokiam, D. J. Brookfield, M. Sparkes and W. O'Neill. Beam Focus Control in Rapid Laser Cutting (ICALEO 2003, Jacksonville, USA)
[11] I. C. Arokiam. A Laser Beam Diagnostic System for High Speed CO_2 Laser Cutting, ICMR (2006).

Acknowledgements
The work described in this paper was undertaken with the support of the EPSRC and numerous commercial sponsors. This support is gratefully acknowledged. The author was also supported by a University of Liverpool Scholarship.

Materials Processing Technology

Optimisation of Dual Purpose Age-Creep Forming Tools

Gerard Chauveau, Manufacturing Systems Engineering, Airbus UK, Broughton

Dr. Lars Krog, Advanced Numerical Simulation, Airbus UK, Bristol

Gerard.Chauveau@Airbus.Com; Lars.Krog@Airbus.Com

Abstract

Age-creep forming is successfully used to form large wing skin panels for the Airbus A380 passenger aircraft. The process, which serves both to enhance the mechanical properties of the wing skin alloy and to generate the required aerodynamic shape, produces forming with very high accuracy. A significant contributor to the achieved forming accuracy is the optimisation of tools via a numerical optimisation process guided by non-linear finite element simulation of the forming process.

In order to accommodate the A380 freighter aircraft within the existing production facility, a development programme for both the existing numerical optimisation process and the production tooling was undertaken which realised the development of dual-purpose age creep forming tools that would allow forming of both A380 passenger and A380 freighter wing skin panels in a common tool. This development produced significant cost and leadtime benefits including the deletion of an additional set of tooling for the A380 freighter aircraft.

Keywords: *Age-Creep Forming, Dual Optimisation, Compromise Tool, Spring-back*

Introduction

Age-creep forming is used for forming large aluminium components such as aircraft wing skins. A *flat* wing skin is initially drawn into a *curved* form tool under vacuum and given a specific heat treatment in an oven or autoclave. Under the combined influence of temperature and stress the component material undergoes age hardening and permanent deformations are generated via age shrinkage and material creep. Once the vacuum is released, partial *spring-back* is exhibited, with permanent form being evident in the component.

The permanent shrinkage of an aluminium alloy during age hardening is one of two forming mechanisms used in age-creep forming. When designing an age-creep forming tool, the problem lies in predicting the complex interaction between age shrinkage and material creep. Both effects produce double curvature and it is the correct balance between these two effects that produces the desired shape after spring back.

The complex interaction between age shrinkage and material creep during age-creep forming is best modelled in a visco-elastic age-creep simulation, that should extend to include thermal dependant material elasticity and material plasticity and part/tool interaction effects via friction. A correct modelling of each of these effects and a correct modelling of their interaction in a non-linear finite element analysis, allows us

281

to accurately simulate the age-creep forming process and to accurately predict the partial spring back after forming, and therefore the formed shape.

Single Purpose Optimisation. For the first time, on the Airbus A380 passenger aircraft, wing skin age-creep forming tools were optimised through an entirely numerically based process. The efficiency and accuracy of this process, of which material characterisation during heat treatment was key, meant that tool surfaces could be developed very quickly and late in the development program.

Constitutive equations capable of describing the time dependent evolution of strain under the combined influence of temperature and stress in the component material were developed in close collaboration between Airbus and Qinetiq. Developments included both methods for accurate characterisation of alloy behaviour and materials models for integration into the non-linear finite element analysis of the forming process. Without such developments, achieving accurate simulations would not have been possible.

This technology was successfully validated and used for numerical optimisation of single-purpose age-creep forming tools for forming of each of four A380 passenger aircraft top skin panels.

Fig. 1: An A380 passenger age-creep forming tool after loading of a panel and after vacuum bagging and a formed piece of wing skin on a check fixture.

Dual Purpose Optimisation. The A380 freighter aircraft wing skins are made from a different material and have a different thickness distribution to that of the A380 passenger aircraft. However, the required outer formed shape is common. To avoid the significant additional cost associated with an additional set of tooling for the A380 freighter aircraft, a compromise tooling approach has been adopted, whereby the proven A380 passenger aircraft tools have been modified to enable accurate forming of both passenger and freighter wing skins in the same tool. This has been achieved by further development of the single purpose numerical simulation capabilities, to complete a dual purpose optimisation.

The design of the A380 age creep forming tools enables rapid tool shape modifications without expensive total replacement [1]. As a result of this, the exercise of modifying the A380 passenger aircraft form tools to a new dual purpose standard was achieved for 10% of the cost of a new tool set and in a fraction of the time, with minimal disruption to production.

Age-creep Forming Simulation and Tool Surface Optimisation

Tools used for age-creep forming of the A380 passenger aircraft wing skin panels were developed in an iterative optimisation process, guided by non-linear finite element analysis of the age-creep forming process. Fig. 2 provides a schematic view of steps performed during an iteration of age-creep forming simulation and tool surface optimisation. A flat panel is loaded into a form tool and forced by pressure against a double curved tool. The panel is held in a deformed state and heat treated, introducing permanent straining of the material via ageing and creep. The formed panel is moved onto a check fixture and allowed to spring back. If the panel is not perfectly formed, gaps will be seen between the formed panel and the check fixture. These forming errors are used to improve the tool surface in a heuristic tool surface growth scheme. The described tool surface optimisation scheme generally converges to an acceptable tool surface, producing near *zero* forming errors, in 5-8 iterations.

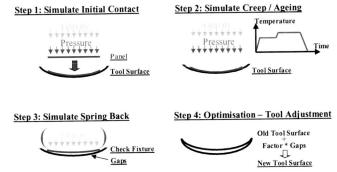

Fig. 2: Age-creep forming simulation and tool surface optimisation process.

For speed of computations during tool surface optimisation, an approximate age-creep forming simulation has been developed. This ABAQUS/Standard finite element analysis, assumes full contact between the panel and the tool surface during the age-creep forming simulation, and involves four finite element analysis steps:

Step 1. The panel is brought into full contact with the tool using forced displacements to achieve an *infinite pressure/zero friction* condition.
Step 2. Simulation of age-creep forming heat treatment in a visco-elastic age-creep analysis, with the panel held in full contact with the tool surface.
Step 3 Transfer of the formed panel onto a check surface, using a forced displacement technique, and application of gravity loads.
Step 4. Release of forced displacements and simulation of spingback against applied the gravity loading.

After an acceptable tool surface was generated using the approximate analysis, a more detailed finite element simulation was carried out to validate the surface accuracy.

Building on the developments for single-purpose tool surface optimisation, already applied and validated for optimisation of A380 passenger aircraft age-creep forming tools, it was a small extension to develop an optimisation scheme for multi-purpose and dual-purpose age-creep forming tool surface optimisation.

A developed dual-purpose tool surface optimisation capability, initially uses the tool surface optimisation updates suggested from the first iteration of two single-purpose optimisation runs, performed for an A380 passenger aircraft panel (P1) and for an A380 freighter aircraft panel (P2), respectively, to construct three new tool surfaces. The surface updates are essentially suggested changes in z co-ordinates of the tool surface grid points.

Tool Surface 1. Existing tool + full passenger aircraft update
Tool Surface 2. Existing tool + average of passenger and freighter aircraft updates from Tool Surfaces 1 and 2.
Tool Surface 3. Existing tool + full freighter aircraft update

The forming accuracy for each of these tools can be assessed running forming simulations for both the A380 passenger aircraft panel and for the A380 freighter aircraft panel, i.e. in total six individual forming simulations. Based on the forming errors observed in each of these runs it is possible to determine a factor deciding the optimum *blend* of tool updates for a best compromise solution. Fig.3. indicates runs 1-3 and 4-6 relating to passenger and freighter respectively, in tools surfaces 1-3 as above, where β=1, 0.5 and 0 has a bias towards tool surfaces 1,2 and 3 respectively. By solving for the intersection of two second order polynomials through points for runs 1-3 and 4-6 with the relative bias, the optimum bias factor can be determined. Finally, the common tool surface can be updated using an optimum blend of single-purpose tool updates.

This way of performing dual-purpose tool surface optimisation was implemented with minimum coding requirements, reusing all existing functionalities of the single-purpose age-creep forming tool surface optimisation capability. Numerical efficiency of the overall scheme was achieved by use of distributed computing. Fig. 3 shows a schematic view of the runs performed in a single iteration of dual-purpose tool surface optimisation and also the determination of an *optimum* tool surface update factor.

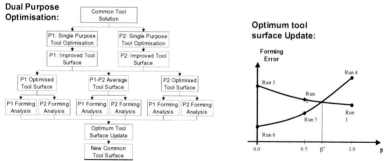

Fig. 3: Calculations performed in single iteration of dual-purpose tool optimisation and determination of optimum tool surface update.

Developments of Compromise Tools in Manufacturing

Tool Modifications. The validated dual-purpose age-creep forming tool surfaces, were compared to the original passenger tool surfaces. This offered a further cost-saving opportunity as it was identified that large regions of the original tooling could be preserved. CAD surfaces created from the dual purpose finite element tool surfaces were compared to the original passenger tool CAD surfaces. Regions of surface that fell within an allowable tolerance were unmodified. Those areas falling outside this limit were replaced by the compromise surface, and a blend region between new and old created. The hybrid tool surfaces were then validated via numerical analysis to confirm accuracy, and re-visited if necessary.

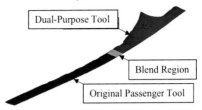

Fig 4: Definition of compromise tool with blend region between the dual-purpose tool solution and the original passenger tool surface.

Results

The dual-purpose optimisation scheme generally converged to an acceptable forming error in 5-8 iterations. The distribution of forming errors for both passenger and freighter panels after forming against an optimised dual-purpose age-creep forming tool could then be predicted, see Figure 5.

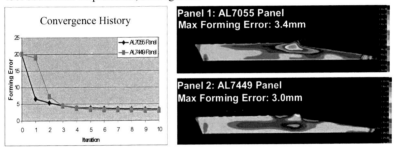

Fig 5: Convergence history showing reduction of maximum forming error for two panels during dual-purpose tool optimisation, and distribution of forming errors in the two panels after forming against an optimised tool

From experience of the single-purpose optimisations and successful forming of the A380 passenger panels, the predicted forming deviations indicated in Fig. 5 were considered acceptable. Modifications were made to the numerically optimised tools and simulations were made to validate that a successful blending had been performed between original A380 passenger tools and new dual-purpose tools as per Fig. 4.

Every A380 top skin panel processed through age-creep forming is measured on a check fixture that reflects the desired aerodynamic form. The panel is only loaded under gravity when form measurements are carried out. The deviations of the panel from the check fixture in a number of prescribed points are recorded. Fig 6 shows measured forming errors for an A380 Freighter panel after forming in a compromise tool .

285

Fig.5. Freighter Panel 1 Top, Measured Forming Errors

Discussion and Conclusions

Fig. 6 indicates the achieved forming accuracy of a freighter and a passenger panel under gravity alone after forming in the compromise tool. Upon assembly of the panel to the wing structure, *light* pressure is allowed, to deflect the panel into position. This pressure is simulated, by attaching weights to the panel in the check fixture, after which, a deviation of 1 mm is permissible. Measurements as indicated are typical of the process, where the majority of the panel form has less than 3mm deviation. Areas where the threshold is exceeded, easily pull-down to form with the addition of a permissible number of bag weights.

In assessing the success of the compromise tool, it is necessary to understand all of the influencing factors. The panel is machined prior to age-creep forming and exhibits some deformation due to the release of residual stresses. Therefore, the panel is not completely flat prior to the age-creep form treatment. Once the panel has been placed upon the check fixture post-treatment, there may still be some residual deviations from the machining process. There is obviously room for advancement in billet manufacture and machining philosophy. However, in light of these challenges, the single and dual optimised tools have still proven to be extremely capable.

Conclusion: All passenger and freighter panel first articles from the compromise tools have proven to be within specification. This further re-enforces the success of the original single purpose optimisation, and indicates that a dual optimisation tool is a viable solution, giving the desired accuracy and repeatability. It also utilises the flexibility of the original tool design to accommodate change, for comparatively low cost and effort. The process may be further extended to a larger number of panel materials of differing thickness if necessary, with a high degree of confidence.

Acknowledgements

We wish to acknowledge MG Bennett & Associates for their effort and support.

References

1. Patent No. US2006042347: Aircraft Component Manufacturing Tool and Method.
2. Hambrick, D M: Age Creep Forming Aluminum Aircraft Skins: 1st International SAMPE Metals and Metals Processing Conference. Vol. 1 (1987), pp. 135-143.
3. K C Ho, J Lin and T A Dean: Integrated Numerical Procedures for Simulating Springback in Creep Forming Using Abaqus: Abaqus UK Users Group Conference (2001)
4. Levers, A; Tanner, A; Al-Khalil, M; Platts, M J: Development of integrated decision support system for Creep Age Forming: Multidisciplinary design and optimisation Conference (1998), pp. 16.1-16-6.

WARM FORGING OF LONG FLAT PIECES

Steffen Reinsch[1, a], Achim Schott[1, b], Axel Specker[1, c]

[1] Institut für Integrierte Produktion Hannover gGmbH., Hollerithallee 6, 30419 Hannover, Germany

[a] Reinsch@iph-hannover.de, [b] Schott@iph-hannover.de, [c] Specker@iph-hannover.de

Abstract. Semi-hot or warm forging is an economical alternative to the conventional forging technology common for rotation-symmetric parts. It offers several advantages like reduced energy input, no scale, better surface quality and narrower tolerances. The main obstacle adopting the technology to the forming of long flat pieces is the increased number of forming operations and all the connected problems to keep the narrow temperature tolerances. In a cooperative effort within a European consortium of scientific institutes and forging companies, forming sequences for a warm forging process of a steering link and a connecting rod have been developed. Analyses of diverse processes have been performed by the use of FEM-simulations and experiments. Two promising forging sequences have been selected for testing. According to the resulting requirements, the equipment for the entire process chain has been chosen and is currently installed at the work shop of a partner of the consortium. In the next stage of the project, the simulation results are verified during the try out of the dies and the obtainable work piece properties are analyzed and documented. Finally, tool wear and process limits of the new process are tested and specifications for quality assurance and process control are defined.

Keywords: Bulk forming, Semi-hot forging, Steel forming, Warm forging

Introduction

Forged parts are used in areas in which high quality and excellent mechanical properties combined with the production of large quantities are required. These are mainly highly stressed automobile components, e.g. for motor, transmission, power train and chassis. Standards for these parts are permanently increasing, thus also the products and processes in massive forming have to meet rising demands. Characteristics of the changing conditions are the increasing complexity of products, growing number of product variations, lightweight construction, application of materials with great strength and a tendency of substituting bulk formed steel products with non-ferrous metal parts. Those changing circumstances constitute a serious problem for the forging industry in their long-standing competition with alternative technologies. Warm forging is expected to be a way to strengthen the economical competitiveness of the forging branch. Compared to the conventional hot forging technology warm forming offers several advantages that contribute to economic and environmental issues. These are reduced energy input, reduced scale formation, better surface quality and narrower tolerances. Compared to cold forging the spectrum of forgeable geometries and materials is increased and the process chains can be shortened. [1,2]

Those advantages lead to the development and introduction of the warm forging technology first in Asian and up to now also in European forging companies.

Figure 1 – Samples of warm formed components [1]

Nonetheless the warm forging technology has not yet been adapted to long flat pieces. Beside the problems to keep the narrow temperature tolerances during the warm forging process, no reinforcements can be applied to increase the durability of the tools like for rotation-symmetric work pieces. In this project warm forming sequences for a steering link of Kovarna "VIVA" Zlin (Czech Republic) and a connecting rod of Omtas Steel Forging (Turkey) have been developed.

Warm forging of steel

There are various definitions for warm forging of steel. All of them have in common that the temperature range is considered to be approximately 600 °C to 900 °C except for austenitic stainless steels which are forged between 200 °C and 300 °C [1,2,3,4]. In Figure 2 the impact of the temperature on the flow stress, the fracture strain and scale formation are shown for different steels. The lower range of the temperature is defined by an increase of the flow stress and a decrease of the formability of the material. This behaviour is represented by the fracture strain curves in Figure 2. The upper bound is defined by an increase of scale formation and decarburization which has a negative impact on the final work piece surfaces and the component quality. In some cases the phase transformation which occurs in this temperature range is deployed to improve the product quality by thermomechanical processing. To avail those transformation processes a very precise prediction and control of the material conditions temperature and pressure during the process is required.

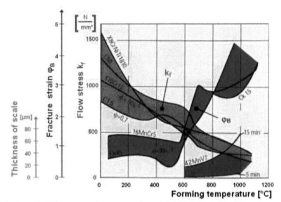

Figure 2 – Flow stress, fracture strain and development of scale depending of the temperature [2]

The warm forging technology is predominantly utilized by companies dealing with cold forging. This originates from the compatibility of the two technologies. A warm forged component can initially be preformed or finally be coined by cold forming almost without any investments in additional equipment. Figure 3 shows a process sequence which starts with two preliminary cold forging operations followed by three warm forging operations. The only additional investment for a cold forging company to introduce such a process sequence is an induction furnace to heat the intermediate part. Additionally a pregraphitation system can be bought but this is not mandatory. Another advantage for cold forging companies is their expertise in the use of reinforcements. Although the stresses for warm forging processes are lower than for a comparable cold forging operation, the tool stresses are still much higher than for conventional hot forging operations.

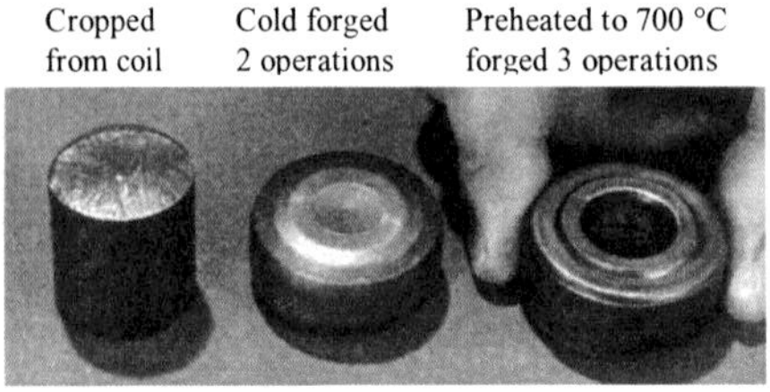

Cropped from coil | Cold forged 2 operations | Preheated to 700 °C forged 3 operations

Figure 3 – Cold-warm forged pinion gear blank [1]

In many cases the use of reinforcements is inevitable to reduce the number of forming operations and thus to avoid an intermediate heating operation. Of course the temperature induced stresses need to be considered during the dimensioning of the reinforcements.

To combine hot forging and warm forging processes an intermediate shot blasting and washing of the work pieces is necessary to remove the scale caused by hot forging. Despite this, the specific advantages of the combination of hot and warm forging processes compared to a combination of hot and cold forging processes are not apparent. The obtainable precision which can be achieved by a final cold forming operation is higher compared to a final warm forging operation as shown in Table 1. The obtainable strains are for both process combinations the same. In both cases, the determining factor for the obtainable strain is the hot forging process which has no limit to strain. In contrast to this, the introduction of warm forging processes constitutes an extension of the forgeable geometries and materials for the cold forging technology. It is especially applicable for geometries and materials that can not be produced by cold forging or only at uneconomic expenses. The combination of a warm forging process with a final cold coining operation increases the obtainable IT-quality up to IT 9 and in special cases of even IT 8 is expected to be reached [5].

Characteristic	Hot forging	Warm forging	Cold forging
Shape spectrum	arbitrary	preferably symmetric	mainly rotationally symmetric
Steel qualities	arbitrary	C arbitrary; other alloying additions < 10%	low-alloy steel; C < 0.5%, other alloying additions < 3%
Initial treatment of slugs	generally none	none or a graphite coating	annealing, phosphating, lathering
Intermediate treatments	none	generally none	annealing, renewed surface treatment
Achievable accuracy	IT 16 to IT 12	IT 12 to IT 9	IT 11 to IT 7
Economic lot size	Over 500 pieces	over 10000 pieces	over 3000 pieces
Die life	5000 – 10000 pieces	10000 – 20000 pieces	20000 – 50000 pieces
Material utilisation	60 to 80 %	generally about 85%	85-90 %
Energy required	460-490 J/kg	400-420 J/kg	400-420 J/kg

Table 1 - Process characteristics of hot, cold and warm forging [1,4]

In Table 1 some of the characteristics of the three competing forming technologies hot, warm and cold forging are displayed. None of the technologies is generally superior to the others but depending on the requirements of the forging geometry, material, production quantity and required accuracy the optimum technology can be chosen.

For the description of the shape spectrum which can be produced by utilizing warm forging processes in Table 1, it needs to be added that most of the geometries currently warm forged are rotational symmetric or at least the geometry allows for the use of reinforcements. It is the aim of this project to develop processes to overcome this limitation of warm forging and to show hot forging companies a way to introduce the warm forging technology in their shop floors. Since the forging line is set up at a hot forging company, the necessary investments for a small or medium sized hot forging company can easily be derived. Additionally, the problems encountered during the design of the process are documented and function as a guideline for hot forging companies.

Specifics of warm forging of long flat pieces

Initially two work piece geometries were chosen representing best the standard requirements of long flat work pieces currently hot forged. The two work piece geometries, a connecting rod and a steering link, were evaluated regarding their requirements towards a forging process. One of the boundary conditions of warm forging is to avoid any initial rolling or bending operation to distribute the material. To estimate the length of the necessary flow paths, the required strain and finally to choose the raw part diameter, diagrams of the volume distribution and the centre of area of the cross section along the longitudinal axis have been prepared.

For the connecting rod the longitudinal axis is straight so that a bending operation is not necessary. Therefore the material needs to be moved along the longitudinal axis. Figure 4 shows the distribution of the volume along the longitudinal axis which is not symmetric and shows strong variations. While the volume in the region of the web is comparably small, there is a distinctive mass concentration at the main lug. To achieve an acceptable material utilisation great amounts of material have to be redistributed along the main axis. The comparable conventional hot forging process consists of two forging steps. A warm forging process to manufacture this connecting rod needs more operations because of the increased flow resistance of the material. Starting from a two step forging process, the process sequence depicted in Figure 5 has been developed. The main problem which was encountered during the development of the tools

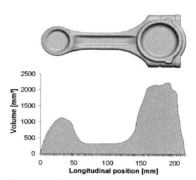

Figure 4 - Volume distribution along the longitudinal axis of the connecting rod forging geometry

is caused by high tool stresses and the connected tool deformation. During simulations runs, the temperature of the work piece remained comparably stable throughout the process sequence due to the energy introduced by the deformations. Hence, the depicted four step forging process with comparably low tool stresses and a material utilization of approximately 80 % has been developed.

After the cutting to length of the raw part the mass distribution is realized during the first preforming operation. In the upsetting operation, the geometry is flattened which is beneficial for the mass distribution and the positioning in the following forming step. The third operation is a preforming operation followed by the final forging. All process steps are realized in one mechanical forging press to avoid the cooling of the work piece and thus an additional intermediate heating operation. After the forging sequence the work pieces are clipped, pierced and calibrated on another press.

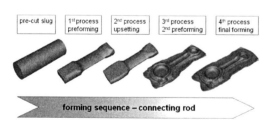

Figure 5 - Warm forging sequence of the connecting rod

Figure 6 shows the volume distribution of the steering link along the longitudinal axis for the final forging geometry and the deviation of its centre of area of the cross section along the longitudinal axis. The forging geometry is symmetric concerning the volume distribution, thus no forces in the direction of the longitudinal axis are induced in the press guidance. Also the volume variations along the longitudinal axis are rather negligible compared to those of the connecting rod shown in Figure 4. The difficulty concerning the warm forging sequence of this geometry is, that the longitudinal axis is not straight but bended. This can be shown best by a diagram of the position of the centre of area along the longitudinal axis of the work piece as displayed in Figure 6. Because of this, not only a mass distribution along the longitudinal axis is necessary but additionally the mass at the ends needs to be pushed in an orthogonal direction. Starting from a two step forging process, the process sequence depicted in Figure 7 has been developed. The main objective for the developed process was to improve the material utilization. The achieved reduction of raw material amounts to more then 25 % compared to a conventional hot forging

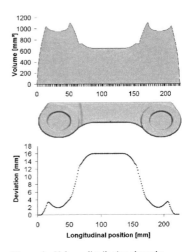

Figure 6 – Volume distribution along the longitudinal axis of the steering link forging geometry, deviation of the centre of area of the cross section along the longitudinal axis of the steering link

process. According to the simulations the tool stresses are more then 15 % higher for this process than for the warm forging process developed for the connecting rod. Since the assumed initial raw part temperature is only 800 °C the flow stresses can be reduced by increasing the forging temperature.

After the cutting to length the round raw part is bended in the die. In the following forming operation the intermediate geometry is preformed before the forming sequence ends with the final forging operation. The bended intermediate geometry can not be positioned in a defined way in the lower die of the second forming step. To avoid the production of scrap, additional simulations with the intermediate geometry in extreme positions have been performed. For all positions of the bended part form filling has been achieved in the final forging step. Again the forging sequence is performed on one press and the following clipping, punching and calibrating operations are performed on an additional press.

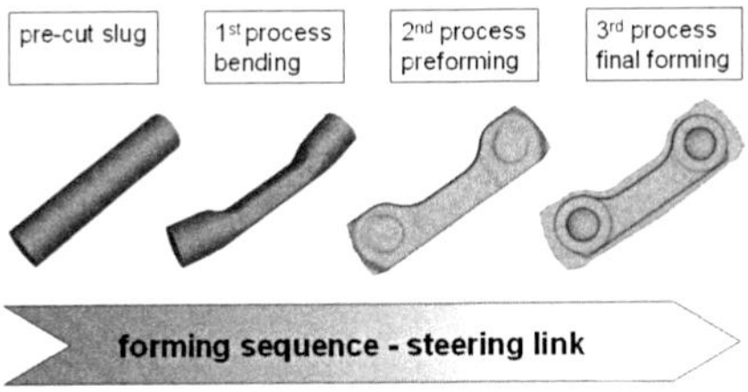

Figure 7 - Warm forging sequence of the steering link

Summary

Two representative long flat geometries, a connecting rod and a steering link, were chosen and evaluated regarding their requirements towards a production by warm forging. In an iterative way, forming tools have been designed; forging processes have been simulated and based upon the results the forming sequences have been adjusted. To increase the reliability of the simulations the press characteristics have been considered, friction tests have been performed, flow curves have been recorded and the simulations were performed in parallel with the simulation software Deform and Forge3. For the connecting rod a four step warm forging process and for the steering link a three step forging sequence have been developed. The equipment for the process has been chosen and is currently installed. Following, the line is put into operation and an experimental plan, varying the process relevant parameters is conducted. The process data is recorded and diagnosed and the most suitable parameter combination is determined. Finally the achievable accuracy and the resulting tool wear are documented. It is the aim of this project to warm forge long flat pieces with higher precision compared to hot forging. The increased precision causes a reduction of the subsequent machining operations, a save on material and energy and thus reduces the production costs.

We would like to express our gratitude towards our consortium partners for their support and work and the EC for the funding of this project in the sixth framework programme.

References

[1]   International Cold Forging Group, ICFG Document No. 12/01: *Warm Forging of Steels* (Erlangen, Ger 2001).

[2]   R. Neugebauer, M. Geiger: *Prozessgrundlagen für die Halbwarmumformung wellenförmiger Teile mit weit auskragenden Formelementen,* Forschungsbericht P 452 (Studiengesellschaft Stahlanwendung, Düsseldorf, Ger 2003).

[3]   P. Hustedt, J. Kohlstette: *Präzisionsschmieden von Langteilen – jetzt auch im Halbwarmbereich,* SCHMIEDE-JOURNAL MÄRZ 2003 (Hagen, Ger 2003), pp. 25-26.

[4]   T. Neumaier: *Zur Optimierung der Verfahrensauswahl von Kalt-, Halbwarm- und Warmmassivumformverfahren* (Fortschritt-Berichte VDI, Düsseldorf, Ger, 2003).

[5]   *Halbwarmumformung, Merkmale und Einsatzvorteile,* Fertigungstechnik 2, 5/1990 (Ger 1990), pp. 54-55.

DIMENSIONAL MANAGEMENT IN THE MANUFACTURE OF SCREW COMPRESSORS

J. Sai Deepak

Final Year Mechanical Engineering,
PCET, NH47, Kaniyur, Coimbatore-641659,
Tamil Nadu, India.

saimohan.ram@gmail.com

Abstract. This paper is dedicated to the exposition and application of a prevalent Concept termed Dimensional Management in the Manufacture of Oil Flooded Screw Compressors. Its leitmotif is to quantify, predict, control and reduce the deviations in critical dimensions, geometric features and Clearances. The primary clearances encountered in a screw compressor are (1) Axial, (2) Radial and (3) Interlobe clearances. These clearances are arranged in increasing order of their impact on the efficiency of the compressor as 1<2<3.The magnitude of these clearances depends upon the capacity of the compressors and is inversely related to their efficiency. A Probabilistic Method such as the Worst Case Method has been used to establish explicit relationships between the various mechanical parts and their cumulative effect on the efficiency of the rotor. The choice of this method has been justified on the basis of the sample which is less than 1000.

Consequently, a high amount of precision is required in their manufacture, which implies that the rejection rate in mass production is bound to be significant due to variations that might have crept in during manufacture. In order to increase the acceptance rate, a compromise has to be struck between the tolerances and rate of production. The whole idea is to establish the exact number of acceptable parts that would be manufactured from the given design drawings and to give a tangible shape to the risks involved.

Keywords: Dimensional Management, Oil Flooded Screw Compressors, Critical Parameters, Worst Case Method

1. Introduction:

Dimensional Management has its own terminology and assorted Symbology which is dealt in a restrained fashion in this project; as its application in the context of Manufacture of Oil Flooded Screw Compressors is the subject of its attention.

Note:

Henceforth in this Paper, the word Compressor refers to Oil Flooded Screw Compressor

The construction of a compressor primarily consists of the following parts:

1. Rotors
2. Cylindrical Rotor Bearings
3. Rotor Housing (RH) and Bearing Housing (BH)
4. Dowel Pins (Two each on RH and BH)

2. Definition of the Problem:

➤ When the rotors mate a certain amount of Clearance is formed between them which, is inversely related to the efficiency of the compressor. Nevertheless, it has to be maintained in order to avoid undercutting and to compensate for any machining errors that might have occurred.

➤ These clearances are of the order of few tens of microns and are allowed a certain variation which depends on the size of the compressor. For smaller machines, it is approximately 50 micron and for larger machines, it is 100 micron.

➤ The clearances encountered in a compressor are classified based on their position as (1) Axial, (2) Radial and (3) Interlobe Clearances. Axial clearance is the clearance between the rotors and the housing in the lateral direction. Radial Clearance is between the rotors and the housing in the longitudinal direction. Interlobe clearance is between the two rotors. These are arranged in increasing order of their impact on the efficiency of the compressor as 1<2<3.

➤ Here, we shall concentrate on the quantification of dowel pin position movement, for it affects critically the mating of the rotors and hence the Interlobe and Radial clearances

3. Project Objectives:

Broad Objectives:

➤ To achieve optimal clearance distribution and operating clearances. To improve performance characteristics of AIRENDS.

➤ Relaxing manufacturing tolerances to lower production time and cost.

➤ Arrive at a better specification of geometric and positional tolerances in design drawings.

3.1 Rotor Housing:

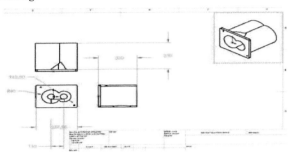

1. Rotor bore has to be perpendicular to the face of the discharge end.

2. The bore of the rotor bearing on the suction side has to be concentric with respect to the rotor bore.

3. The positional tolerances of the dowels with respect to the rotor bores have to be restricted. Perpendicularity of the dowels with respect to (wrt) the face of the discharge end has to be maintained.

3.2 Bearing Housing:

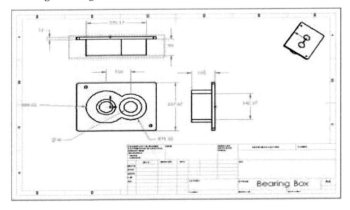

1. Perpendicularity of the bearing bore wrt to the face of discharge end.
2. Positional Tolerance of the dowels wrt the bores of the rotor bearing.
3. Positional Tolerance of the rotor bearing bores (suction side) wrt each other.
4. Perpendicularity of the dowel wrt discharge end face.

3.3 Rotors:

1. Lead Tolerance on the male and female rotors.
2. Runout on the rotors.
3. Form & Profile Error.

4. Analysis of the Critical Parameters:

4.1 Dowel Pin Position: The movement of the dowel pins within its positional tolerance zone affects the proper alignment of the Rotor and Bearing Housings and the thickness of Radial Clearance.

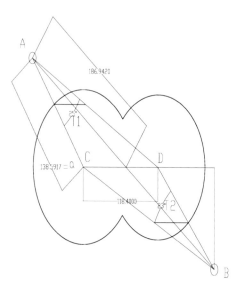

➤ It is imperative on our part to quantify the combined movement of both the dowel points with respect to each other as it would be of no consequence to us to consider them individually. The above diagram ABCDA has achieved this to largely successful extent.

- The subjects of our attention are the angles CAD and DBC given by T_1=24.68deg=0.4307rad and T_2=22.66deg=0.3954rad. Let AB = a= 138.51mm, AC = b=229.17mm, BC = e=118.4mm, BD = c=233.34mm, CD = d=138.28mm, angles ABC = T_3=126.08deg, ACB = T_4=29.24deg, DBC = T_5=26.74deg, DCB = T_6=130.6deg.

- Applying the Sine Rule to Triangle ABC, we get

  e/Sin T_1=b/Sin T_3=a/Sin T_4=K_1

  Implying e=K_1 Sin T_1------------------------------- (1)

- Applying the Sine Rule to Triangle BCD, we get

  e/Sin T_2=d/Sin T_5=c/Sin T_6=K_2-------------------- (2)

  Implying e=K_2SinT_2

  Equating (1) & (2), we get K1Sin T_1- K_2SinT_2=0----------------- (3)

- This implies that in an ideal situation equation (3) should be zero and any change in the dowels due to change in any of the others quantities which define it, would be reflected in it.

- The calculations for the above case considering uniform distributions are illustrated are in result 2.

☑ **Definition of input dimensions**

Table of input dimensions | | | | | | | | | **Clear table**

Label	Component name	Angle		Component size				Distribution
			Nominal	Tolerance	Minimum	Maximum	Mean	
A	K1	☐ [mm]	283.000	+0.20000 -0.20000	282.80000	283.20000	283.00000	Uniform ▼
B	K2	☐ [mm]	307.000	+0.00400 -0.00400	306.99600	307.00400	307.00000	Uniform ▼
C	angle BAC	☑ [deg]	0.431	+0.00034 -0.00034	0.43036	0.43104	0.43070	Uniform ▼
D	angle BDC	☑ [deg]	0.395	+0.00034 -0.00034	0.39506	0.39574	0.39540	Uniform ▼

Table of resulting dimensions | | **Clear table**

Component name	Nominal size	Required limit sizes [mm]	
		Lower limit	Upper limit
eqn	0.00873	0.00685	0.01210

Z1 ▼

Detailed description of resulting dimension

Required limit sizes

Lower limit	LL	0.006850	[mm]
Upper limit	UL	0.012100	[mm]
Mean		0.009475	[mm]

"Worst case" method

Mean	μ	0.008730	[mm]
Tolerance	±T	0.005032	[mm]
Minimum size	Z_{min}	0.003698	[mm]
Maximum size	Z_{max}	0.013762	[mm]

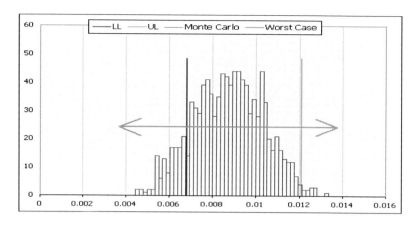

5. Conclusion:

The whole idea is to establish the exact number of acceptable parts that would be manufactured from the given design drawings and to give a tangible shape to the risks involved. Once the probability of an unwanted dimension has been calculated, the exact cost of that occurrence must be calculated. Tangible Factors such as repair, scrap, tool damage should be included. The results of this analysis have to be compared with the post production cost-benefit analysis. This sort of a formal approach to fixing tolerances, rather than opening them up randomly for the ease of manufacture, ensures that Conformance quality is achieved within the given economic constraints. In a nutshell; it encourages documentation of formal tolerance studies and leads to robust designs.

6. References:

[1] Journal of Manufacturing Science & Engineering (Vol.127, Issue 4, 10-768-772) issued in Nov'05.

[2] Peck Harry, *Geometric Tolerancing.*

[3] Curtis.A.Mark, *Geometric Dimensioning.*

[4] Morris Hamburg, *Statistical Analysis in Decision Making.*

[5] Comparison between DLM and Monte Carlo Methods, Chase, Gao & Magleby 1995a, Chase, Gao & Magleby 1995b

Development of automatic machine for filling of cement and embossing on cap for lighting industry

Vishal S Sharma[1, a], Hardip Singh[2, b]
[1]Department of Industrial Engineering, National Institute of Technology, Jalandhar,INDIA
[2]Department of Industrial Engineering, National Institute of Technology, Jalandhar,INDIA
[a]sharmavs@nitj.ac.in, [b]bainsgroup@vsnl.net

Abstract: Automation is the key word for the success of any organization. In this paper a machine developed for lighting industry has been discussed. The machine is used for automatically filling cement in the cap and embossing on the cap. The machine developed is manufactured, tested and installed. This paper contains 3D drawings of the machine and subassemblies. The working of machine and each subassembly is also discussed.

Keywords: automation, lighting industry

Introduction

Industrial competition is today truly global with fragmented markets and customers expecting to get the best product at the best price with immediate availability. Success in manufacturing requires continuous development and improvement of how the products are developed and produced. Several studies have indicated that some 70 – 80% of the final cost is committed before the detail design phase [1, 2]. Much of the productivity of a production process is dependent on the product design. In this pursuit the machine was developed for a lighting industry. The project was funded by M/s B.M.T. Corporation (Village Chearu, GT Road, Phagwara, India) which deals with manufacturing of automatic machinery for lighting industry. There are many approaches to design like original design, adaptive design, variant design and redesign [3, 4]. The development of the proposed machine is an adaptive design.

Development of machine

As such not much literature is available on this work. So mostly we had to rely upon the knowledge of the experts in the industry for short comings in the existing setup. Conventional machines were ratchet driven, due to which it was not possible to get accurate alignment with the cement drum. This resulted in the damage of the aluminum caps. High speed operations on these machines were not possible. Loading and unloading of the caps was done manually on the turret. There was no sensing unit for recognizing the presence of caps before injecting cement. These machines were not flexible.

The development activity of the machine is divided into various stages i.e. acquiring requirements of the machine; preparing rough sketches; preparing 3D models; Manufacturing, testing and installation of the machine.

The Cement and embossing machine is a vital component of Lamp industry which is used to fill bonding cement inside the aluminum cap which holds the cap and the sealed lamp glass. It also carries out embossing operation. This machine is fitted with indexing cam which is driven by worm and worm wheel fitted inside the oil housing. The indexing cam used is made of non corrosive hardened En36 material. The rollers used on the indexing plate are hardened and grinded so there is almost nil wear and tear of the rollers. This leads to driving the machine at high speed with accuracy. The loading and unloading of the caps is done automatically on this machine. This machine is quite flexible and it can accommodate different sizes of caps for cement filling operation. This machine is divided into six subassemblies as shown in figure 1.

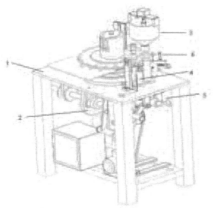

1. Table Assembly Unit   3. Cement Container Assembly   5. Automatic Unloading Unit
2. Index-Cam Assembly   4. Embossing Unit   6. Sensor Unit

Figure 1: Assembled machine

Working: - Loading of the caps is done automatically at station 1 of Turret Ring through vibrators (refer Figure 3). Caps are moving from one station to another station with the help of Indexing cam (refer figure 1 and 2). Adjusting Plate will align the caps in the appropriate slots at stations 5 and 6 of Turret Ring. Cap reaches for the embossing at station 7. Support shaft fits into the cap from top side before Embossing starts. Embossing is carried out on the outer portion of the cap at station 7. At stations 8 and 9 no operation is being done. The cap indexes to cement filling station 10. Before cement filling the sensor unit will sense the cap and send signal to pneumatic cylinder which operates the cement filling plunger. After cement filling at station 10 caps moves further to 18, 19 and 20 stations for automatic unloading.

Table assembly unit
Various parts of the table assembly unit are shown in figure 2.

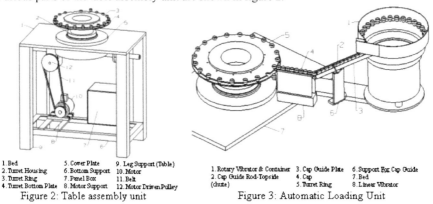

1. Bed	5. Cover Plate	9. Leg Support (Table)
2. Turret Housing	6. Bottom Support	10. Motor
3. Turret Ring	7. Panel Box	11. Belt
4. Turret Bottom Plate	8. Motor Support	12. Motor Driven Pulley

Figure 2: Table assembly unit

1. Rotary Vibrator & Container	3. Cap Guide Plate	6. Support For Cap Guide
2. Cap Guide Rod-Topside	4. Cap	7. Bed
(chute)	5. Turret Ring	8. Linear Vibrator

Figure 3: Automatic Loading Unit

Bed is casted using cast iron. After casting, the bed is all over machined and different markings are done. Then boring and tapping operations are carried out. Turret housing is also cast iron part which is all over machined. Turret ring is a mild steel part which is machined

300

and then fitted on the turret housing. The turret ring is provided with 20 slots to hold the caps. Turret bottom plate is mild steel part which is used to support the cap and is fitted on the turret housing below the turret ring. Cover plate is casted and then machined. Bottom support is an angle made of mild steel and bolted to the four legs of the machine. Panel box is made of mild steel sheet and powder coated, this is used for installing electrical accessories like contactors, relays, MCB's and electrical circuit. Motor support is mild steel flats bolted on the angle of bottom support. Leg support is a mild steel stand fabricated by welding two channels. Motor is used to provide drive to the machine. Belt is used to transmit power from the motor to the gear box. Motor driven pulley is made of cast iron and fixed on the worm shaft of the gear box.

Automatic Loading Unit
This unit automatically loads the cap from the vibrator container to turret ring. Various parts of the automatic loading unit are shown in figure 3. Rotary vibrator and container is basically aluminum casted part in which spiral grooves are provided inside the bowl. The bowl is fitted on mild steel plate by spring steel strips. The directions of strips play a vital role in providing proper direction to the caps in the bowl. Cap guide rod-topside is made of two mild steel rods welded to a cap guide plate so as to direct the caps from the rotary vibrator to the linear vibrator. Near to the exit of the bowl two arrangements are provided for proper orientation of the caps. All the oriented caps then ride down the chute. All the caps in the chute are gravity fed. The caps are then transferred to linear vibrator. Linear vibrator is provided to feed the caps on the turret in horizontal direction so that there is no overlapping of caps.
Working: The caps are dumped into the hopper of the vibrator (refer figure 3). Caps are oriented at the outlet of the vibrator. Caps slide down along the guide way (3) which is made by two guide plates to carry the caps. The cap guide rod (2) restricts the cap from jumping out of guide plate. Caps are then transferred to linear vibrator (8). Linear vibrator (8) in turn transfers the cap to Turret ring (5).

Indexing-cam Assembly
This Indexing cam unit is used for the indexing of the stations starting from 1 to 20. The various parts of the indexing cam assembly are shown in figure 4.

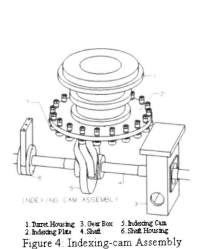

1. Turret Housing 3. Gear Box 5. Indexing Cam
2. Indexing Plate 4. Shaft 6. Shaft Housing
Figure 4: Indexing-cam Assembly

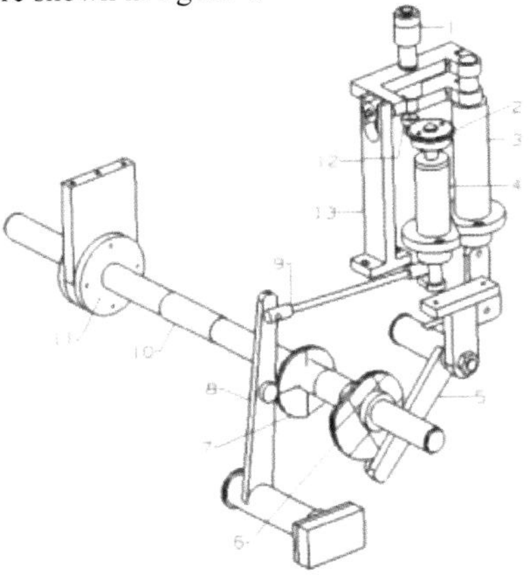

1. Embossing Support Shaft 5. Shaft Up-Down Lever 9. Tie-Rod
2. Emboss(tool) 6. Cam for Shaft Up-Down 10. Gear-Box Shaft
3. Support Shaft Housing 7. Emboss Rotating Cam 11. Shaft Housing
4. Emboss Housing 8. Emboss Rotating Lever
Figure 5: Embossing Unit

301

Indexing plate is a cast iron part, all over machined. After this 20 holes are drilled and bored. In these holes indexing pins are tight fitted and then pins are tightened by nuts. In the center of the plate indexing clamp is fitted which holds the indexing plate and turret housing. Gear box is casted and then machined which holds worm and worm wheel. This is oil fitted gear box in which worm wheel is made of gun metal and worm of En24. The ball bearing and thrust bearing are used to guide the worm wheel shaft. Taper bearing is used to support the worm shaft. Shaft is made of En24 material, machined and grinded from bars. Indexing cam made out of En 31 material. Shaft housing is made of mild steel plate on which self aligning bearing is fitted.

Working: - Power to the reduction gear box is coming from motor and belt drive shown in table assembly unit (refer figure 2). The Indexing plate (2) is fitted on Turret Housing (1) (refer figure 4). This indexing plate is divided into 20 stations and at each station one roller is fitted. The reduction gear box is used to reduce the revolutions of the shaft. The reduction gear box drives shaft and the indexing cam. When the indexing cam takes one revolution the slot guides the roller to make 18° of revolution.

Embossing Unit
The unit is used for embossing the caps. Various parts of this unit are shown in figure 5. Embossing support shaft is made of hardened En31 then all over grinded. Shaft is fitted inside the housing guided by linear bearing. The main purpose of the shaft is to guide the caps when emboss rotates. Emboss is made of die steel. After hardening the emboss tool is all over grinded. Marking for brand name and date is done on emboss by etching process. Support shaft housing is made of cast iron material. This shaft is all over machined and then bushes are fitted inside the bore. After this the housing is fitted on the main table of the machine. Emboss housing is also made of cast iron. Instead of bushes needle bearings are fitted inside the housing. Shaft up down lever is made of mild steel. First mild steel bush is machined and then operation of boring is done. Inside this bush cast iron bushes are fitted and on this bush mild steel strips are welded. On one side of the strip CAM follower is fitted and on the other side tie rod is fitted which moves the emboss shaft. CAM for shaft updown and emboss rotation is made of En31 material. These cams are two piece cams. First cam blank is machined, and then marking is done. Later it is machined and then hardened. Then after hardening the cam is grinded. Emboss rotating lever is made of mild steel. The process of manufacturing is same as that of Shaft Up down lever. On the Mild steel bush only single strip is welded. On this strip both cam followers as well as tie rod are bolted. Tie rod is mild steel rod on whose both ends threading is done. On one side right hand thread and on the other left hand thread. On these threads ball joints are tightened. These ball joints are tightened on one side of the lever and the other side on the clamp which moves the emboss shaft.

Working: - Cap reaches the station (7) for embossing (refer figure 5). With the help of Up-Down Lever (5) and Cam (6) the Embossing Support shaft (1) fits into the cap from top side before embossing starts. This support shaft gives the cylindrical shape to the deformed caps and gives support to the caps when embossing takes place. Embossing is carried out on the outer portion of the cap at station (7) by rotating Emboss tool (2). The Emboss tool (2) is rotated with the help of Cam (7), Lever (8) and Tie-Rod (9).

Sensor Unit
The Sensor Unit detects the presence or absence of each cap. Before cement filling the sensor will sense the cap and send signal to pneumatic cylinder which operates the cement filling plunger. Various parts of the sensor unit are shown in figure 6.

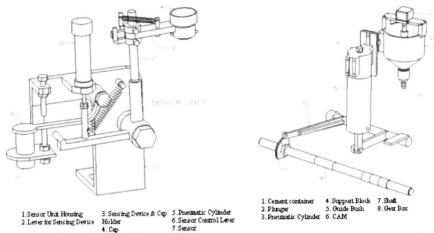

1.Sensor Unit Housing   3.Sensing Device & Cap   5.Pneumatic Cylinder
2.Lever for Sensing Device Holder   6.Sensor Control Lever
                            4.Cap   7.Sensor

1.Cement container   4.Support Block   7.Shaft
2.Plunger   5.Guide Bush   8.Gear Box
3.Pneumatic Cylinder 6.CAM

Figure 6: Sensor Unit   Figure 7: Cement container Assembly

Sensor unit housing is fabricated from mild steel plate. It is first welded and then all over machined. After this process boring is done. Lever for sensing device is made of mild steel. First the bushes are prepared. On one side of bush mild steel strip is welded and on the other side a rod is welded vertically. Sensing device and cap holder is used to give signal to the top pneumatic cylinder fixed on the cement drum. It is made of mild steel bush on which strip is welded which holds the cap during the process of cement feeding. Pneumatic cylinder is fitted on the sensor unit housing. The purpose of cylinder is to give motion to the lever for sensing device. Sensor control lever is fabricated from mild steel strip and round bar. Sensor used here is proximity type.

Working: - The Pneumatic cylinder (5) and the springs controls the rotation of sensing device lever (2) (refer figure 6). The sensing device (3) is fitted on the lever (2). The sensor control lever (5) is controlled by the Sensing device lever (2). When the Pneumatic cylinder (5) moves upwards the spring tries to come to its original position. Because of this spring force lever (2) and sensing device (3) tilts to make contact with the cap at station 10. If the cap is present at station 10 this device cannot swing further so the sensor control lever is kept at minimum distance from sensor (7) which sends the signal to pneumatic cylinder to operate the cement filling plunger. In absence of cap at station 10 lever (2) and sensing device (3) swings further, so the other end of lever lifts the sensor control lever (5) to keep maximum distance from the sensor (7) to prevent it from sending the signal to pneumatic cylinder.

Cement container Assembly

This unit carries the cement to be filled in the cap. Various parts of this unit are shown in figure 7. This unit is used for filling cement in the caps at station 10 of Turret ring. Up-down Motion to this unit is given with the help of cam and lever arrangement. At this station the sensor unit is installed which detects the presence or absence of each cap. This sensor in-turn operates the cylinder mounted on the container unit which fills the cement on the cap. Cement container is aluminium casted. After casting it is all over machined . Then the process of drilling and slotting is done. Plunger is made of stainless steel rod. On one side of the rod internal threading is done to which shaft of the cylinder is tightened and on the other side external threading is done and tightened. The purpose of cylinder is to give motion to the plunger when sensing unit recognizes the cap on the turret. Support block is made of cast iron.

First it is machined on the lathe then slots are made on the milling machine for holding the cement container. Guide bush is made of cast iron. After machining lever is fitted to give vertical motion. CAM used is two piece made of mild steel (EN31). After making required profile it is hardened, grinded and then tightened on the shaft.

Working: - Gear Box (8) drives shaft (7) (refer figure 7). On Shaft (7) Cam (6) is mounted. Cam (6) is connected to Up-Down lever (5). Up-Down lever (5) carries the support block (4). On the support block (4) container (1) is mounted which also contains the Pneumatic cylinder (3) and Plunger (2).

Automatic Unloading Unit

This unit automatically unloads the cap from the machine and sends to capping machine through belt conveyor. Various parts of this unit are shown in figure 8.

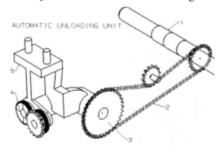

1. Gear Box Shaft 3. Gear Drive for Belt 5. Housing
2. Chain Drive   4. Conveyer

Figure 8: Automatic Unloading Unit

Working: Gear box shaft (1) drives the sprocket which is fitted on it (refer figure 8). This sprocket is connected with two other sprockets to make a chain drive (2). This Chain-Sprocket unit (2) drives the bevel gear unit which is fitted on the housing to transmit the power to Spur gear (3) used by Belt Conveyor. The caps are transmitted from this machine to capping machine through belt conveyor.

Summary

The machine is developed, manufactured, tested and finally installed in the production shop. The machine has automatic loading and unloading system. The machine can carry out two operations i.e. filling of the cap and embossing of the cap successfully. It was also possible to control the quantity of the cement to be filled in the caps. The machine can accommodate various sizes of caps by changing the turret only. The machine can produce 4000 pieces per hour.

References

[1] V. Krishnan and Karl T. Ulrich: Management Science, Volume 47, Number 1, pp 1-21, 2001.

[2] Robert P Smith: IEEE Transactions on Engineering Management, Volume 44, Number 1, pages 67-78, 1997.

[3] R.S Bharaj and Vishal S. Sharma: (CODEC2001), February 21-23, 2001, Dr.B.R.Ambedkar Regional Engineering-Jalandhar, India

[4] Vishal S Sharma., A. Bhardwaj and R. Bharj: XVI National convention of Production Engineers , January 19-20, 2002, IT, BHU Varanasi, India.

Advanced Manufacturing Technology: Cutting

New Prediction Method of Instantaneous Cutting Force in Finish Machining with consideration of Cutting Edge Roundness

Jun'ichi KANEKO[1, a], Koji TERAMOTO[2, b], Kenichiro HORIO[3, c] and Yoshimi TAKEUCHI[4, d]

[1]Saitama University, 255 Shimo-Okubo, Sakura-Ku, Saitama City, Saitama, Japan

[2]Muroran Institute of Technology, 27-1,Mizuoto-cho, Muroran City, Hokkaido, Japan

[3]Saitama University, 255 Shimo-Okubo, Sakura-Ku, Saitama City, Saitama, Japan

[4]Osaka University, 2-1,Yamadaoka, Suita City, Osaka, Japan

[a]jkaneko@mech.saitama-u.ac.jp, [b]teramoto@mmm.muroran-it.ac.jp, [c]horiken@mech.saitama-u.ac.jp, [d]takeuchi@mech.eng.osaka-u.ac.jp

Abstract. This study deals with prediction method of instantaneous cutting force in finish machining with ball end-mill. In finish machining process, accuracy of generated surface is one of the most important factors that influences success of machining process. In order to estimate cutting error caused by elastic deformation on cutting tool, spindle and machine tool, it is required to predict quantitatively accurate instantaneous cutting force at the moment when objective part of workpiece surface is generated. In this study, we propose a new prediction method, which can cope with cutting condition using minute feed rate. The proposed prediction method consists of following new simulation models. One is the workpiece removal model, which is designed to consider influences of cutting edge roundness about cutting force and spring back. Another is the geometric description model of machined workpiece shape, which is designed to be able to estimate a reproduction of cutting error by trochoidal movement of cutting edges. In order to evaluate the effectiveness of introduced models, we develop a prototype simulation system and conduct experimental cutting using ball end-mill with throwaway chip. The measured cutting force in the experiment shows a good qualitative agreement with the predicted force

Keywords: Instantaneous cutting force, prediction, ball end-mill, computer simulation, tool deflection

Introduction

In recent years, technology of machining tools has been improved. In finish machining process, high-speed spindle puts both the ball end-mill with small radius and cutting conditions with quite small feed rate to practical use, without reducing machining efficiency. Because cutter mark on machined surface is mainly influenced by tool radius and feed rate, it is expected that these new cutting conditions can achieve high quality finishing for curved workpiece surface. However, it is known that usage of small diameter end-mill causes some problems about accuracy on the finished surface. For example, such cutting tool usually has low rigidity. So, cutting tool is deformed by loaded cutting force and finished surface is distorted.

In conventional studies [1], in order to satisfy both accuracy and safety of machining process, evaluation methods of NC program based on *instantaneous cutting force* prediction have been proposed. Instantaneous cutting force is an idea of the load applied to cutting tool at each moment. By predicting the instantaneous cutting force when objective part of workpiece surface is generated, we can estimate the deflection of end-mill and cutting tools. Then, assuming that displacement of cutting edge is transcribed as cutting error on workpiece surface, it is expected that we can estimated the cutting error on generated surface caused by the instantaneous cutting force.

In the conventional instantaneous force prediction methods, following are assumed.

1. Uncut chip thickness on each part of cutting edge can be estimated only from geometrical relation between trochoidal trajectory of cutting edge movement and workpiece shape.
2. During rotation of end-mill, all part of workpiece volume is removed intersect the cutting edge.
3. Curved cutting edge consists of a set of finite straight flute. Then, the instantaneous cutting force can be estimated by summing of local force loaded on each finite flute as shown in Fig 1(a).
4. The cutting force loaded on the finite flute can be estimated independently by coefficient model. In the coefficient model, it is regarded that a liner relation exists between the uncut chip thickness and the local cutting force as shown in Fig. 1(b).

Fundamentally, these assumptions have been introduced on condition that the uncut chip thickness is large enough like rough machining process and it is not necessary to consider an effect of cutting edge roundness explicitly. However, it is clear that a cutting edge is always worn out. Then, it is known that small part of workpiece in contact with only the cutting edge roundness is not removed.

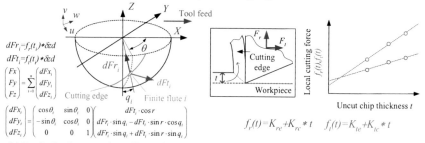

$$dFr_i = f_r(t_i) * \delta zd$$
$$dFt_i = f_t(t_i) * \delta zd$$
$$\begin{pmatrix} Fx \\ Fy \\ Fz \end{pmatrix} = \sum_{i=0}^{} \begin{pmatrix} dFx_i \\ dFy_i \\ dFz_i \end{pmatrix}$$
$$\begin{pmatrix} dFx_i \\ dFy_i \\ dFz_i \end{pmatrix} = \begin{pmatrix} \cos\theta_i & \sin\theta_i & 0 \\ -\sin\theta_i & \cos\theta_i & 0 \\ 0 & 0 & 1 \end{pmatrix} \begin{pmatrix} dFt_i \cdot \cos r \\ dFr_i \cdot \sin q_i - dFt_i \cdot \sin r \cdot \cos q_i \\ dFr_i \cdot \sin q_i + dFt_i \cdot \sin r \cdot \sin q_i \end{pmatrix}$$

$$f_r(t) = K_{re} + K_{rc} * t \qquad f_t(t) = K_{te} + K_{tc} * t$$

(a) Prediction by summing of local forces   (b) Coefficient model of the local cutting force

Figure 1 Conventional prediction method of the instantaneous cutting force

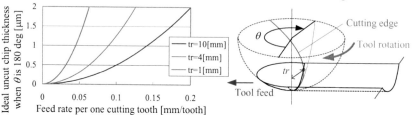

Figure 2 Relation between the uncut chip thickness and feed rate of cutting tool

Fig. 2 shows relations between the uncut chip thickness at the generating moment and feed rate. *tr* is radius of end-mill where cutting edge exists. It is estimated result by geometric simulation. In the recent finishing process, cutting conditions with quite small feed rate is often adopted. In such case, radius of cutting edge roundness is often larger than the uncut chip thickness. These situations of workpiece removal contradict the assumptions in the conventional prediction model. So, in order to realize accurate prediction, it is required to develop a new prediction method can adopt minute uncut chip thickness and take into consideration of an effect of cutting edge roundness explicitly. In the following sections, we propose new prediction method based on improvements of the conventional coefficient model, which is designed to adopt the finish machining by ball end-mill.

Improved coefficient model considering effects of cutting edge roundness

Cutting phases according to the uncut chip thickness. In order to reflect the effect of cutting edge roundness to prediction models, we introduce a new idea about removal situations of workpiece shape. In the proposed models, situation of workpiece removal is classified into three phases according to the uncut chip thickness, as shown in Figure 3. In phase(a), it is regarded that a part of workpiece in contact with the cutting edge is elastically deformed and the workpiece surface recovers after the cutting edge leaves. As result, the shape of workpiece is not changed by tool passing. In phase(b), a part of workpiece is plastically deformed and seems to vanish. This phenomenon has been reported as "ploughing" [2]. The new surface is generated by the cutting edge and it includes error by elastic recovery. In phase(c), the part of workpiece in contact with the part of the cutting edge which has roundness is vanish similarly to phase(b). The other part of workpiece is removed as chip. The new surface includes the error like phase(b).

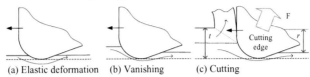

(a) Elastic deformation   (b) Vanishing   (c) Cutting

Figure 3 Phases of workpiece removal by cutting edge roundness

In the paper, the cutting phase(a) is called as "Elastic deformation", phase(b) as "Vanishing" and phase(c) as "Cutting". In the previous researches [3], it was reported that change of the cutting phase changes according to a ratio of the uncut chip thickness to the radius of cutting edge roundness. In Fig. 3, t is actual depth of cut, which is the uncut chip thickness determined by both the workpiece surface and the cutting edge location with consideration of error on workpiece surface and tool deformation. r is actual depth of removal, which is the depth of workpiece removed by the cutting edge passing. Moreover, we introduce two kinds of constants, e and p. e is the actual depth of cut at the moment when the cutting phase changes "Elastic deformation" from "Vanishing". Similarly, p is the actual depth of cut at the change "Vanishing" from "Cutting".

Prediction model for the actual removal depth.
As above mentioned, workpiece surface generated by cutting edge with roundness includes the error considered as elastic recovery as a cause. Therefore, t is not identical with r, t is always bigger than r. When the situation of workpiece removal is "Elastic deformation" phase, it is clear that r is always 0. Moreover, when it is "Cutting" phase, it is known that the contact length of the roundness on cutting edge and workpiece surface will not change. From this tendency, we can assume that the result of subtracting r from a in "Cutting" phase does not change and it is not related to the change of a. So, we propose a linear interpolation and estimation model of r as following equation:

$$r = \begin{cases} 0 & (t < e) \\ (t-e)/(p-e) \cdot q & (e \le t < p) \\ t-(p-q) & (p \le t) \end{cases} \tag{1}$$

where, q is the actual depth of removal when cutting phase changes to "Vanishing" from "Cutting".

Prediction model for cutting force. It is known that cutting force ratio to the actual depth of cut increases with decreasing the actual depth of cut when the actual depth of cut is smaller than the size of cutting edge roundness. This tendency is regarded as the influence of "ploughing force". In this study, we introduce following empirical assumptions about the instantaneous cutting force of end milling.
1. The ratio to the actual depth of cut does not change as long as cutting phase does not change.
2. The cutting force changes continuously when cutting phase changes.

Then, we introduce a simple prediction model to estimate cutting force from the actual depth of cut. In the model, the cutting force is calculated as following equation:

$$dF_j = \begin{cases} Ke_j \cdot t & (t < e) \\ \left(Ke_j \cdot e + Kp_j \cdot (t-e)\right) & (e \le t < p) \\ \left(Ke_j \cdot e + Kp_j \cdot (p-e) + Kc_j \cdot (t-p)\right) & (p \le t) \end{cases} \tag{2}$$

where δd is a width of cutting area in each finite flute. dF, Ke, Kp and Kc are vectors, which can be divided into tangential and radial components. dF is the local cutting force loaded on a finite flute. Ke, Kp and Kc are the coefficients in the improved prediction model according to each cutting phase.

It is thought that these constants are influenced by the ratio of the uncut chip thickness to the radius of cutting edge roundness. Then, it is quite difficult to estimate the radius of cutting edge roundness, because the cutting edge is always worn out and the shape of cutting edge is not a certain form. So, we introduce the idea of the adaptive prediction approach. In this approach, model parameters are gradually refined. In this study, we measure the instantaneous cutting force in only one case of cutting condition and determine model parameters. By combining the improved empirical simulation models and parameter tuning the previous machining process, it is expected that more accurate prediction can be realized.

Prediction algorithm with accurate estimation for the actual depth of cut

In cutting force estimation of end milling, it is required to estimate the actual depth of cut. The actual depth of cut is determined by the location of the cutting edge and the workpiece shape. The location of cutting edge is obviously influenced by the tool deflection. Then, the tool deflection is determined by cutting force. As a result, the cutting force, the actual depth of cut and the tool deflection interacts each other. So, a calculation method is required without such mutual contradiction. On the other hand, the workpiece surface usually has the error generated by previous tool revolutions. It is thought that this error is mainly determined by two kinds of phenomena, the elastic recovery and the displacement of cutting edge. Because the information of workpiece shape is required in order to determine the actual depth of cut, a method to refer the error on workpiece surface is required.

In this study, we propose an estimation procedure of cutting force in order to introduce the proposed coefficient model to the instantaneous cutting force prediction. A configuration of the proposed cutting force estimation system is shown in Figure 4. In the procedure, in order to simulate finite flute movement on a trochoidal trajectory, both tool revolution angle and location of spindle are renewed in each moment of cutting force prediction.

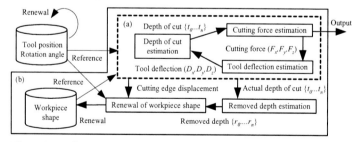

Figure 4 Configuration of the proposed cutting force simulation algorithm

Then, the cutting force and the actual depth of cut in each flute are calculated to satisfy all estimation models in the box(a) in Figure 4. In these calculations, shape of workpiece surface evaluated in a previous estimation is referred, and the calculation process is continued until the estimated results are mutually satisfied. Secondly, the actual depth of removal at each finite flute is calculated and the workpiece shape is renewed. This process is equivalent to the box(b) in Figure 4. In the proposed estimation method, the procedure of calculations is repeated for several tool revolutions. The proposed procedure consists of some estimation models about workpiece shape or cutting process. In the follows, let us mention the detail of these models.

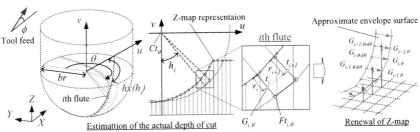

Figure 5 Geometrical estimation for the actual depth of cut and renewal of workpiece shape

Representation model of removal on workpiece surface. In order to estimate the actual depth of cut accurately, precise description and renewal algorithm of workpiece shape are required. So, we introduce the Z-map representation model to describe the machined workpiece shape. Figure 5 shows the idea of the introduced model. Workpiece shape is described a set of height information in Z direction arrayed in a lattice on XY plane. From the relative position among center of cutting edge Ct_θ, the finite flute i $Ft_{i,\theta}$ and the workpiece surface approximated with polyhedron, we can estimate the actual depth of cut t_i. In this case, $Ft_{i,\theta}(Xt_{i,\theta}, Yt_{i,\theta}, Zt_{i,\theta})$ are defined following equations.

$$\begin{pmatrix} Xt_{i,\theta} \\ Yt_{i,\theta} \\ Zt_{i,\theta} \end{pmatrix} = \begin{pmatrix} fd_x \\ fd_y \\ fd_z \end{pmatrix} + \begin{pmatrix} D_x \\ D_y \\ D_z \end{pmatrix} + br \cdot \begin{pmatrix} \sinh_i \cdot \sin(\theta - hx(h_i)) \\ \sinh_i \cdot \cos(\theta - hx(h_i)) \\ -\cosh_i \end{pmatrix} \tag{3}$$

where, fd is the location of end-mill center and D is the displacement caused by the cutting force. Since the generated surface is influenced by the cutting edge roundness, the actual depth of removal r_i is smaller than the actual depth of cut t_i. So, we assume an approximate envelope surface as shown in Figure 5 and renew the height of Z-map for each tool rotation. The approximate envelope surface is the polyhedron constituted by generated points $G_{i,\theta}$ $(X_{i,\theta}, Y_{i,\theta}, Z_{i,\theta})$ and $G_{i,\theta-d\theta}$

$$\begin{pmatrix} X_{i,\theta} \\ Y_{i,\theta} \\ Z_{i,\theta} \end{pmatrix} = \begin{pmatrix} fd_x \\ fd_y \\ fd_z \end{pmatrix} + \begin{pmatrix} D_x \\ D_y \\ D_z \end{pmatrix} + (br - r_i + t_i) \cdot \begin{pmatrix} \sinh_i \cdot \sin(\theta - hx(h_i)) \\ \sinh_i \cdot \cos(\theta - hx(h_i)) \\ -\cosh_i \end{pmatrix} \tag{4}$$

Evaluation of the proposed method

In order to evaluate the proposed method, we conduct an experimental machining with ball end-mill and compare the predicted result with measured force. Table 1 lists the experimental conditions. The experimental apparatus are illustrated in Figure 6 (a). The ball end-mill is fed to fabricate a slot shape on slope of workpiece. The experiments are performed with the same apparatus without dismantling it during experiments in order to avoid the change of experimental conditions.

Table 1 Cutting conditions

Workpiece material	S50C
Tool radius br	8.0[mm]
Number of cutting edge	1
Inserts material	Carbide(P)
Inderts placed angle ε	7.0[deg]
Type of cut	Slot
Depth of slot	1.0[mm]
Tool rotation speed	2000[rpm]
Feed rate f	0.1,0.3[mm/rev]
Slope angle ϕ	-10.0,0.0,10.0[deg]

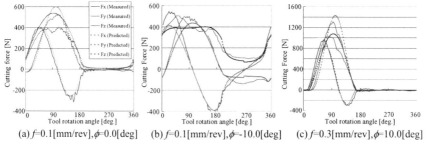

Figure 6 Experimental apparatus and result of teaching experiment

(a) f=0.1[mm/rev], ϕ=0.0[deg]   (b) f=0.1[mm/rev], ϕ=-10.0[deg]   (c) f=0.3[mm/rev], ϕ=10.0[deg]

Figure 7 Comparisons between the predicted cutting force and the measured cutting force

As the first step, we execute the experimental machining to fabricate the slot on the slope of 10.0 degree with feed rate of 0.1mm per one revolution. From the measured cutting force, we determined the coefficients in the proposed models. Figure 6 (b) shows the measured cutting force and the predicted force in teaching experiment. The result shows good agreement. Secondary, we conduct the experimental machining with another cutting conditions. Comparisons between the predicted cutting forces and the experimental results are shown in Figure 7. The predicted forces are calculated using the same coefficients from the first experiment. Every measured result by the proposed method shows good qualitative agreement. And, it is thought that an accuracy of the proposed method is enough to estimate the tool deflection.

Conclusion

In this paper, we proposed a new estimation method to predict the accurate instantaneous cutting force with consideration of the influences from cutting edge roundness. We introduce the prediction models about cutting force and the cutting depth of removal. Furthermore, a procedure for the actual depth of cut estimation is proposed, which can evaluate the error on workpiece surface machined in previous tool revolutions. From the results of evaluation, it is thought that the proposed method can quantitatively predict the instantaneous cutting force of finish machining by ball end-mill.

References

[1]   S.Takata, M.D.Tsai, M.Inui and T.Sata: Annals of the CIRP, Vol. 39 (1989), pp. 417-420.

[2]   P.Albrecht: Trans. ASME, J. Eng. Ind., Vol. 82-4, No.11(1960), pp. 348-358.

[3]   Y.Uno and H.Tsuwa: Bulletin of The Japan Soc. of Precision Eng. (in Japanese), Vol.42-5(1976), pp. 358-363.

Computer Modelling of an XY Table

Francisco J Lopez-Jaquez[1,a] , Bernard Hon[2,b]

[1]Universidad Autonoma de Ciudad Juarez, Av. Del Charro 450 Norte, C.P. 32310, Mexico

[2]Department of Engineering, University of Liverpool, L69 3GH, UK

[a]frlopez@uacj.mx, [b]hon@liv.ac.uk

Abstract

This paper is concerned with the kinematics simulation of the functionality of an XY table for plasma cutting of sheet metal. The Y axis is mounted on the X axis and a plasma torch holder is mounted on the Y axis. A graphical environment was created using OpenGL and Visual C++ under the Microsoft Windows platform. The trajectory is read from a graphic bitmap file and converted into xy set of points for the tool holder to follow the trajectory. Each movement is accomplished using a trapezoidal profile. Validation of the process of data input from a bitmap file and trajectory data generation is performed by a computer simulation model. At the end of running the model, the trajectory is converted into a sequence of commands that can be up loaded to the hardware, using software that is part of the intelligent microstepping motor driver LS-146.

Keywords: XY Table, Computer Simulation, Move Profile, Velocity Control.

Introduction

The background of this investigation is based on two previous projects, one related to 3D general purpose software modeling and other for trajectory generation from a bitmap file. This project is concerned with the integration of automation equipment via the construction of an XY table for sheet metal processing using a plasma cutter. Instead of moving directly to make a real prototype, a computer model of the XY table was proposed. This paper discusses the velocity control implemented in the computer simulation application.

Different algorithms and table configurations have been proposed. Velocity control is an issue for CNC machining centres and rapid prototyping systems, specially those require coordinate movement of multiple axes. Complex control schemes to minimize errors during path traverse considering different forces involved have been proposed. In this paper, a simple approach is used just to cover the kinematics of a two axes model [1, 2].

XY Table Configuration

The XY table model includes a module to process data in graphical form. In the application, this begins when the load trajectory button is clicked, the user needs to specify a valid input file, a bitmap file 256 colors type, previously created using a third party software. The raw data is converted into a list of (X,Y) data points. In case where a straight line is detected, intermediate points are eliminated. The tool is moved to the first position in the trajectory list. There are two lead screws, one for each axis. A tool holder for the plasma torch is mounted on Y axis and when the motor rotates, the rotational movement is converted into a linear movement through a lead screw, resulting into a displacement of the tool. The Y axis is mounted on X axis and coordinated movement of two axes, if necessary, will move the tool over the desired trajectory, reproducing the input trajectory in graphical form. Figure 1 shows a typical working cycle, positive velocity indicates a positive linear movement (forward) on the axis and negative velocity will result into negative movement (reverse). The movement from point to point follows a trapezoidal profile.

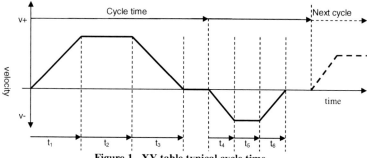

Figure 1. XY table typical cycle time.

Motor drivers are set to 1600 pulses per revolution and both lead screws have 6 threads per inch. If the lead screw rotates six revolutions then the base coupled to it will be displaced lineally by 25.4 mm. If the driver sends only one pulse, the linear displacement must be 2.65 μm, (25.4/9600). This is the minimum linear displacement that can be achieved with this driver where the motor is directly connected to the lead screw, neglecting external forces or backtracking due to the mechanical coupling between motor/lead screw and lead screw/base.

Computer Environment and Application Description

A computer model was developed using Visual C++ and the OpenGL graphics library under Windows XP environment running on a 2.6 GHz computer with a GeForce4 4200 Go Dell mobile graphics card. When the simulation software is loaded, a window appears showing the XY machine model in perspective. The arrow keys may be used to move around the model. The point of view may be moved up or down using the Page Up and Page Dn keys and the camera angle is modified if D or F keys are pressed. The model of the table was generated previously with an extension of the software that incorporates options to draw primitive objects but the main focus of this paper is the simulation of the machine kinematics for reproducing a trajectory from a bitmap file, the motion control of the machine.

There is a button to load a trajectory. If this is the case, a typical file open window appears where the user selects or inputs the file name that contains the desired trajectory. After clicking the OK button the selected file is loaded into memory and converted into a trajectory list. The file contains raw data in bitmap format. This is a map of the pixel information of a drawing, along with a header part that contains general information of the bitmap drawing, like bitmap type. There are different types of bitmaps, in this application the bitmap type must be eight bits 256 colors bitmap. Figure 1 shows the initial view of the model.

There is an execute button that sets the machine in simulation mode, clicking this button again will stop the simulation and reset the machine position to 'Home' at maximum speed. If a trajectory has been loaded already, the tool will start to move over the trajectory. The auxiliary fields at the top of the modeling area will show the current and go to X,Y positions. It is possible to move around the model during the simulation. The lead screws will rotate according to the move profile and the tip, used to model the plasma torch, will traverse over the trajectory and drawing the trajectory over the working surface to simulate the cutting profile. There is also a save model button for storing the current model parameters so that when the application is loaded again, it will start from the current view point.

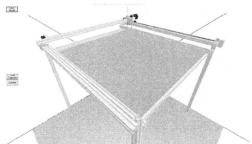

Figure 2. XY table model displayed after loading the simulation application.

Velocity Control Considerations

This section explains the strategy used to accomplish movement of the plasma torch. Friction and other external forces are not considered, it is supposed that this forces are overcome by the motor torque. Axes can move at same time and they are coupled, i.e., the Y axis is mounted over the X axis. A straight line is assumed for moving from point to point. Axes movements are based on a trapezoidal profile but this can have different parameters in order to accomplish the straight line objective when the distance to go is different on each axis. There is a maximum velocity limit of 1250 steps per second for each motor and motor drives respond to position profile move (PPM) commands, other strategies have been proposed to accomplish the desired movement [3].

Move Profile Parameters Estimation

It is assumed that the XY table starts from the home position. The first x,y data point in the trajectory list already loaded is used to make the first move for the tool to go to that position. The distance to go for each axis is converted into required steps. If the first co-ordinate is 120 and 163 mm, they are converted to 45354, 61606 steps for X and Y axes respectively using Eq. 1. This model is based on simple physics rather than strict mathematical modeling [4].

$$NS = (9600/25.4)d_{tot} \tag{1}$$

where:
NS = Number of motor steps.
d_{tot} = Distance to go in mm, diference beween the current and go to position.
$9600/25.4$ = Ratio defined by the motor driver and lead screw combination, the driver mode is 1600 steps per revolution and the lead screw has 6 threads per inch.

Moving to a point is considered to be relative. When the tool reaches a particular position, the difference between the current and the next go to position is the distance to go. The total time (t_{tot}) required to go to the next position at maximum velocity of 1250 steps per second is calculated using the greatest distance to go for both XY axes. The maximum velocity of 1250 steps/second is used because the threshold is 3750 steps. In this example, the Y axis requires 61606 steps while the X axis only requires 45354. The total time is calculated from Eq. 2, resolving for t_{tot} and substituting we get $t_{tot}=1.5(61606/1250)=73.9272$ seconds. If a standard trapezoidal move profile is used, one third of t_{tot}

315

will be used to go from zero to maximum velocity at a constant acceleration. Another third of the time will be used to move at the maximum velocity and the final third of the time will be used to reduce from the maximum to zero velocity at constant deceleration.

The maximum velocity for the X axis is calculated using Eq. 2. In this case $v_{max}=1.5(45354/73.9272)=920.2432$ steps/second. To traverse 45354 steps at the same time as the Y axis, the X axis needs to reduce its velocity.

$$v_{max} = 1.5(NS/t_{tot}) \tag{2}$$

where:
$v_{max} =$ Profile move maximum velocity.
$t_{tot} =$ Total time to move to go position.

In this example acceleration can be calculated using Eq. 3, substituting we get a=50.7256 and 37.3439 steps/second^2 for Y and X axes respectively.

$$a = 4.5(NS/t_{tot}^2) \tag{3}$$

where:
$a =$ Acceleration or deceleration, in steps/second^2.

Algorithm for Move Profile Simulation Description

Two main functions of the algorithm are the load point and rendering functions. Once a trajectory is loaded into memory and the simulation option is activated, move profile parameters for both axes are estimated in the load point function for the first segment of the trajectory. The time counter is reset to zero to signal the starting point of the move profile. The rendering function will run until the move profile time counter reaches the total time required to accomplish the move.

A condition is used in the rendering section to trigger the load point function. There is also a condition to verify the end of the trajectory, in such case, the total time is set to zero and the rendering function will avoid going through the velocity and position modification in the rendering function.

The time step can be modified during simulation to slow or speed up the simulation. During the rendering function the time step variable is monitored, if it is modified, the current value is used to increase the time counter.

During simulation, the relevant segment of the trajectory is displayed to show the required distance of the move profile and the required trajectory can be visualized and compared with the one generated by the rendering function.

In the rendering section, a segment of the move profile is determined based on elapsed time and the current velocity. Consequently, the traverse distance during the time step can be found. This distance is used to update the tool position and all associated elements. If there is a distance displacement on the X axis, all the elements of Y axis need to move. Traverse distance during step time is converted to angular displacement to rotate the lead screws and simulate rotation of the axes.

Converting Trajectory into Sequence of Motor Drive Commands

Presently, the simulation software is not able to send the commands directly to the motor drivers. However, it generates a file with the required sequence of commands that can be used to reproduce the simulated trajectory. When a move has been simulated, the move sequence commands for motor drivers are stored in a file that can be read by the motor drive software. Typically, the sequence begins specifying holding and running current limits supported by the motor drives, the holding current cannot be higher than running current, these parameters affect the peak and average current delivery to the motors independently of power supply and motor speed. Also, requires commands to turn on the motors, setting minimum working velocity and acceleration before sending a move command.

Both motor drivers are able to handle different commands to accomplish a required movement. In this case the position profile move, PPM, command is used. This command requires information on the go to position, maximum velocity and acceleration. In a relative movement strategy, a command is issued before the PPM to set the current position to zero. PPM commands are issued to the associated motor drive and a GO command will start the movement. After the move is accomplished, the sequence for the next move is issued and this process will continue till the end of the file.

A trajectory sequence for a rectangle of 260x246 millimeters, with starting point at 28,27 millimeters will be converted into commands including operation parameters setting for both motor drives, position of X axis set to zero, POS A1=0, and first move command sets X axis to go to position 10582, starting position of the rectangle, at maximum velocity 1250 and acceleration 4. Velocity and acceleration need to be coded in scale 1 is 25. Here, 10582 are the initial 28 millimeters in steps. 50 is the equivalent velocity of 1250, coded 50 times 25, and 12 is the code for acceleration 150. Y axis position is set to zero, POS A2=0 and move command is set to 10204 steps at maximum velocity of 49 and acceleration 12. To complete the trajectory same process is performed for each of the data points in the trajectory list. Commands are specific to motor drive LS-146. It is a single axis controller and works with two-phase stepper motors. It can be integrated into a distribute motion control network over an RS-485 using standard RJ-45 connectors.

Examples and Input File Considerations

Table 1 lists 6 trajectories and general information of the input file and trajectory. Bitmap sketches are considered to be generated with a line width of one pixel at any point of the trajectory. If two points are at the same distance from the previous point, the first one encountered during bitmap mapping is selected.

Table 1. Sample trajectories for simulation.

Input file bmp sketch	Bitmap size [pixels]	Total number of segments	Trajectory length [mm]
	512x512	4	1085.54
	128x128	55	311.20
	128x128	141	399.73
	128x128	139	418.83
	64x64	44	445.45
	1024x1024	1411	4635.32

However, the final trajectory will depend more on trajectory generator process where a sorting algorithm is used to produce the trajectory. All points in the input file will be considered for the trajectory but if it does not comply with the line width rule, then there is a chance that extra segments are introduced because the algorithm will try to accommodate all points in the sketch to produce a trajectory. The trajectory length includes moving from/to 'Home' position.

Conclusions

The tests using the computer simulation indicates that the algorithm is working as expected in trajectory generation, move profile simulation and command sequence generation. Although a prototype XY table has not been constructed yet, a network including the power supply, motor drives and step motors was set up. Using a third party software sequence of commands, the motors could be activated.

Initially this project was conceived based on specifications of existing hardware, step motors, motor drives and lead screws. The computer model allows modifications of elements of the table or even a complete redesign. Use of computer simulation has helped to foresee aspects of design and issues related to control and trajectory generation.

Further work includes construction of a XY table prototype to conduct tests on linear and circular contour and evaluate trajectories generated with the simulation software. Development of other strategies for path generation and move profiles will also be considered. New options will be added to the software to allow users to try different move strategy.

References

[1]   Y. Guoxng, D. Yucheng, L. Dichen, and T. Yiping: A low cost cutter-based paper lamination rapid prototyping system. Int. J. Machine Tools & Manufacture, Vol. 43, (2003), 1079-1086.

[2]   D. Renton and M.A. Elbestawi: Motion control for linear motor feed drives in advanced machine tools. Int. J. Machine Tools & Manufacture, Vol. 41, (2001), 479-507.

[3]   Y.T. Shih, C.S. Chen and A.C. Lee: A novel cross-coupling control design for Bi-axis motion. Int. J. Machine Tools & Manufacture, Vol. 42, (2002), 1539-1548.

[4]   M.S. Kim and S.C. Chung: A systematic approach to design high-performance feed drive systems. Int. J. Machine Tools & Manufacture, Vol. 45, (2005), 1421-1435.

A new approach for measuring tool wear volume in single point diamond turning of silicon

X. Luo[1a], P. Shore[1b], I. Durazo-Cardenas[1c], A. Heaume[1d] and T. Jacklin[2e]

[1]School of Industrial & Manufacturing Science, Cranfield University, Bedfordshire MK43 0AL, UK

[2] Qioptiq, Glascoed Road, St Asaph, Denbighshire LL17 0LL, UK

[a]x.luo@cranfield.ac.uk [b]paul.shore@cranfield.ac.uk [c]i. s. durazocardenas@cranfield.ac.uk

[d] a.m.heaume@cranfield.ac.uk [e]tony.jacklin@uk.qioptiq.com

Abstract: Diamond tool wear is a common problem in single point diamond turning of single crystal silicon. Effectively quantifying tool wear in the cutting process becomes an important issue in the study of tool wear. This paper reports a new technique for recording and measuring the wear behaviour of diamond tools during single point diamond turning of silicon. A 60 mm diameter copper piece was mounted on the vacuum chuck of an ultra precision diamond turning machine and a diamond tool is indented into the copper piece to copy the recession of the diamond tool. Surface optical profilers have been applied to measure the micro indentation. Sectional analysis is carried out to measure the flank tool wear land (VB) value as well as the tool recession on the tool rake face. Tool wear volume is finally obtained based on the results of sectional analysis of the micro indentations.

Keywords: Diamond turning, tool wear, tool flank wear, wear volume, micro indentation

Introduction

Single crystal silicon is a favourite material for manufacturing high added value components, e.g. IR optics, X ray optics, X ray interferometers, etc by diamond turning due to its low cost and light weight. However the sub-micrometer level form accuracy of diamond turned large silicon optics (typically a diameter larger than 100 mm) is still unachievable due to excessive tool wear encountered during the machining process. Therefore, efforts should be made to investigate the tool wear behaviour and its affecting factors so as to defer the tool wear [1].

Currently diamond tool wear has been characterised by either tool flank wear land (VB) or tool tip profile recession through direct measuring method. The direct measuring method is to measure the diamond tool after cutting tests using a microscope. Scanning electron microscope (SEM) is the measuring device widely used. Early measurements of the cutting edge radius of diamond tool have been performed by Asai et al. [2] using a SEM which has a pair of secondary electron detectors. SEM was also used to characterize tool flank wear by Sharif Uddin et al. [3], in which the average value of VB and VB_{max} were obtained. One of the limitations of SEM measurement is that the tool has to be removed from the tool post for measurement and the cutting test will therefore be interrupted. Born and Goodman evaluated the recession of the radius of the tool tip by an LVDT probe after diamond turning of silicon optics [4]. However, these methods are limited to a two-dimensional assessment. It would be of great interest if the wear behaviour of the diamond tool during the machining process can be presented by a three-dimensional characterization method. Recently Li et al have copied the diamond tool cutting edge profile by indenting the tool cutting edge into the surface of a copper piece. The copied cutting edge profile was measured using an Atomic Force Microscope (AFM) [5]. This work is of interest and provides a basis for an indirect approach of measuring diamond tool wear without interrupting the cutting test.

The paper presents a new technique to characterize the three-dimensional diamond tool wear in single point diamond turning of silicon by applying indentation test on a copper piece. The flank tool wear, tool recession on rake face and tool wear volume are then obtained by sectional analysis of the indentations and by geometrical calculations.

Characteristics of diamond tool wear in single point diamond turning of silicon

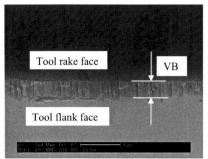

Fig. 1 SEM picture of a worn diamond tool (after cutting distance of 16 km).

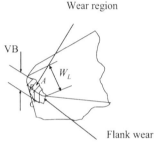

Fig. 2 Illustration of wear region.

Fig. 1 shows a SEM picture of a worn diamond tool after a cutting distance of 16 km in a single point diamond turning of silicon test. It clearly illustrates that the loss of tool material mainly happens on both the rake face and the flank face around the cutting edge. Therefore, the diamond tool wear can be characterised as the length of tool recession on rake face and the width of wear land between tool rake face and flank face, which is illustrated in Fig. 2. The whole wear region can be divided into a series of wear sections along the wear length W_L. The average length of AC is defined as flank wear land (VB). The length of AB is the length of tool recession on rake face. The tool wear volume can be described as:

$$W_v = \int_0^{W_L} S_{ABC} dL \qquad (1)$$

where S_{ABC} is the area of $\triangle ABC$ and dL is the notation for the variable (wear length) of integration. The value of length of AB, VB and the relative angles are essential to calculate tool wear. As long as they can be measured quantitatively, the whole three-dimensional wear region of the diamond tool can then be characterised. The following part of this paper will describe a new technique which plunge the diamond tool into a copper surface so as to copy the tool wear region onto the copper surface.

Indentation test for tool wear measurement

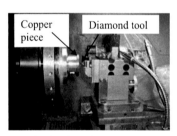

Fig. 3 Indentation test setup.

The indentation test is carried out on an ultra-precision diamond turning machine (Nanotech® 350UPL). The experimental setup is shown in Fig. 3. A copper piece (diameter 60 mm, thickness 6 mm) is installed on the vacuum chuck on the machine spindle. The copper piece has been diamond turned by a new diamond tool before the indentation test as the tool has to be plunged into a smooth and flat surface in the indentation test. The surface finish Ra value and form accuracy of the copper surfaces has been measured as 1.2 nm and 0.13 μm respectively. A worn diamond tool (after a cutting distance of 31.77 km) is mounted on the tool holder. Machine "C" axis mode is selected to eliminate movement in the spindle during the plunging process. The indentations are made on the copper piece by feeding the tool with a speed of 0.012mm/min. The indentation depth is set at 10 μm. The indent is measured using optical surface profilers including Wyko NT3300, Talysurf CCI 6000 and Zygo NewView 6300.

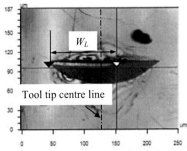

Fig. 4 Intensity image of an indent.

Measurement results and analysis

Fig. 4 shows the intensity image of one indent measured by Wyko NT3300. The centre line of the indent is the tool tip centre line. The whole indentation width is 168.2 μm. As the left side of the tool is on the approaching side, so the bright area in the upper left of the indent is the wear region. The wear length can be directly measured as 108.8 μm. The flank tool wear VB can be measured by sectional analysis of the wear region. Fig. 5 shows two sectional profiles in X and Y directions. The X profile can give information on the distance of Y profile to tool tip centre line. In this case it is 168.2/2-54.8= 29.3 μm. The Y profile shows the profile of rake face and flank face as Y direction is parallel to the cutting direction. The width of flat part at the bottom of the Y profile is VB. In summary this sectional analysis along X and Y directions shows the VB value is 3.9 μm at a position 29.3 μm from the tool tip centre line.

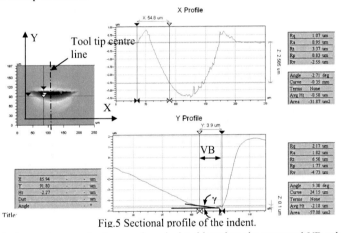

Fig.5 Sectional profile of the indent.

The tool recession on rake face can be calculated based on the measured VB value and the tool geometries, which is illustrated in Fig. 6. It can be described as:

$$AB = \frac{VB \cdot \sin \angle ACB}{\sin \angle ABC} = \frac{VB \cdot \sin(\beta - \gamma)}{\sin(90° + \alpha - \beta)} \qquad (2)$$

Where α and β are the absolute value of rake angle and clearance angle respectively. The angle γ can be obtained from the result of Y profile analysis data as shown in Fig.5.

By repeating the sectional analysis along the whole wear length, the three-dimensional wear behaviours will be illustrated. Fig. 7 shows the variation of VB value and tool recession on rake face AB value at different position on the tool, from the approaching cut edge side. The measurement results by the three surface optical profilers are consistent. It can be seen that values of VB and AB both approach their maximum values at the tool tip. This suggests that the stress level at the tool tip needs to be investigated in order to understand the wear mechanism of the diamond tool.

321

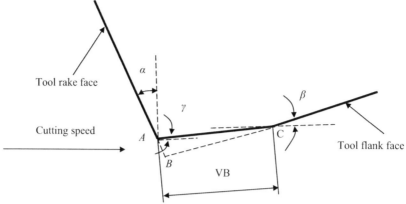

Fig. 6 Illustration of the tool wear section.

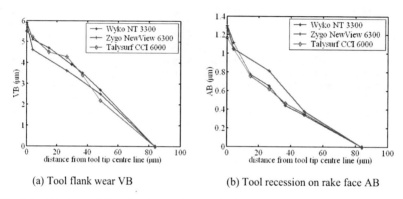

(a) Tool flank wear VB   (b) Tool recession on rake face AB

Fig. 7 Tool flank wear VB and tool recession on rake face AB at difference position on cutting edge side.

The tool wear volume can be obtained by digital approximation of Eq. 1. It is expressed as:

$$W_v = \sum_{i=1}^{N} S_{iABC} = \sum_{i=1}^{N} \frac{1}{2} AB_i \cdot VB_i \cdot \sin(90° - \alpha + \gamma) \tag{3}$$

Based on Eq. 3 the tool wear volume for this tool is calculated as 546.16 μm³.

Conclusions

The paper presents an indentation approach and associated sectional analysis method for measuring three-dimensional tool wear in single point diamond turning of silicon. The indentation approach has proved to be very effective to record the characteristics of tool wear on a copper piece. With the sectional analysis method, the tool flank wear and tool recession on tool rake face along the wear region can be acquired at the same time. By using these values the tool wear volume may also be obtained. This approach provides an effective measure for acquiring progressive tool wear behaviour during the cutting process by carrying out the indentation at defined times within the cutting period. There is no need to interrupt the cutting test by removing the tool from the machine for SEM assessment between each cut.

Acknowledgements

The authors would like to thank Mr. Dave Price of Qioptiq Ltd., Mr. Andrew Cox of Contour Fine Tooling Ltd., Dr. Drew Murray, Dr. Alex Winkel and Mr. Freek Pasop of Veeco Group, Mr. Joe Armstrong of Taylor Hobson Ltd, Mr. Dean Edward and Mr. Graeme Gibbons of Lambda photonics for their support and assistance during this research.

References:

[1] I. Durazo-Cardenas, P. Shore, X. Luo, T. Jacklin and S. Impey: Proc. 1st International Industrial Diamond Conference. (Barcelona, Spain 2006).
[2] S. Asai, Y. Taguchi, K. Horio, T. Kasai and A. Kobayashi: Annals of the CIRP, Vol. 39 (1990), pp. 85-88.
[3] M. Sharif Uddin, K. H. W. Seah, X. P. Li M. Rahman and K. Liu: wear, Vol. 257 (2004), pp. 751-659.
[4] D. Krulewich Born and W. A. Goodman: Precision Engineering, Vol. 25 (2001), pp. 247-257.
[5] X. P. Li, M. Rahman, K. Liu, K. S. Neo, and C.C. Chan: Journal of Materials processing technology, Vol. 140 (2003), pp. 358-362.

Super High Strength and Weak Rigidity Aluminum Alloy Workpiece Materials: Experimental Research on Cutting

H. N. Zhou[1, a], L. Han[1,b] and B. Lin[1, c]

The State Education Ministry Key Laboratory of Advanced Ceramics & Machining Technology, Tianjin University, Tianjin, China

[a]zhouhuina99@eyou.com, [b]hanlei@eyou.com, [c]linbinph@tju.edu.cn,

Keywords: precise turning, optimization, finite element, super high strength aluminum alloy

Abstract. This work reports on a series of experimental tests and theoretical analyses of super high strength, weak rigidity aluminum alloy workpiece material. A cutting force model is developed from an analysis of measured cutting forces. The extent of cutting deformation is estimated based on the finite element analysis and it is shown how the cutting parameters can be optimized. A new workpiece clamping method is described. The investigation demonstrates that the cutting precision and efficiency of the super high strength and weak rigidity aluminum alloy workpieces can be greatly improved if the recommendations from this study are applied.

1. INTRODUCTION

An important and increasingly popular engineering material: super high strength aluminum alloy, is widely used in many fields including aerospace, automotive and other industrial fields. Many countries attach high importance to the research of super high strength aluminum alloy and the machining of this material has received much recent attention [1– 3].

In this study, a very shallow cutting depth was selected for the precise processing of an aluminum alloy. However, the effect of cutting depth and cutting forces on the achievable precision could not be neglected due to the low rigidity of the workpiece material. It is known [4,5] that the magnitude of cutting forces directly or indirectly affect the accuracy of workpiece dimensions and shape, workpiece surface roughness, degenerated layer and tool life. It is also known that low workpiece rigidity results in large deformations and these are undesirable for precise machining operations. The effects of deformation can be reduced by reducing cutting forces. However, cutting depth must be correspondingly very small and under these conditions the process would not be cost efficient. Optimization of cutting parameters provides potential for a more cost effective solution. This paper reports on an investigation concerned with this approach.

2. EXPERIMENTAL TESTS

The lathe used in the experiments was the type CL—20 which has a high rigidity, precise transverse and longitudinal drives, and a minimum resolution of 0.001mm. The workpieces material was super high strength aluminum alloy - elastic modulus of $71KN/mm^2$, Poisson's ratio of 0.31, the density was $2680Kg/m^3$, HBS was 1.4GPa and intensifying factor was 0.36. The experimental tools were polycrystalline diamond tool with orthogonal rake of 0°, tool cutting edge angle of 117.5°, tool orthogonal clearance angle of 7° and tool cutting edge inclination angle of 0° or 6°. The cutting parameters are listed in Table 3. A high accuracy force-measuring system was employed. The experiment arrangement, shown schematically in Figure 1, is composed of: YDC— OOS type piezoelectric force-measuring apparatus, YE5850A type charge amplifiers (three suits), four channels dynamic data-logger, and the software. Prior to the actual experiments, the force-measuring apparatus was calibrated. The on-line measurement system is shown in Figure 2.

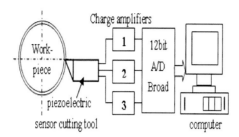

Figure 1 System Schematic

The cutting component forces were measured by the apparatus for a range of cutting parameters. Cutting parameter values are given in Table 1. In the experiment, two different groups of edge inclination angles datum were chosen, and the tool wear effect was neglected.

Table 1 The correspondence table of cutting parameters and cutting component forces

Cutting speed (m/min)	Cutting depth (mm)	Feed speed (mm/r)	Edge inclination angle λ=0°			Edge inclination angle λ=6°		
			Fx (N)	Fy (N)	Fz (N)	Fx (N)	Fy (N)	Fz (N)
400	0.05	0.1	1.4	2.9	6.4	1.9	3.0	6.0
	0.08		2.5	4.0	9.6	3.3	5.4	8.5
	0.12		3.4	6.0	14.5	4.7	6.8	13.5
	0.16		4.3	6.8	19.0	5.6	7.2	18.1
	0.20		5.4	7.0	23.7	6.3	7.6	22.0
	0.24		6.4	7.2	29.0	6.8	8.0	27.1
400	0.1	0.05	1.4	2.5	7.2	2.0	2.8	6.4
		0.08	2.0	4.4	10.9	3.5	5.3	9.6
		0.12	3.0	6.0	14.9	4.5	6.7	13.6
		0.16	3.8	6.4	18.8	5.2	7.0	17.1
		0.20	4.2	6.9	22.5	5.9	7.5	21.0
300	0.1	0.1	2.8	5.2	12.8	4.2	6.3	11.3
400			2.7	5.0	12.8	4.0	6.2	11.2
500			2.6	5.1	12.8	4.0	6.1	11.2
600			2.7	5.1	12.7	4.1	6.0	11.2
700			2.6	5.0	12.6	4.1	6.0	11.1
800			2.5	5.1	12.7	4.0	6.1	11.2

Figure 2 On-line measurement

3. EVALUATION OF RESULTS.

The cutting speed strongly affected the cutting force. When a_p=0.1mm and f=0.1mm/r, a correlation formula between cutting speed and cutting force was obtained through linear fitting of results.

When the edge inclination angle λ_s= 0°:

$$F_x = 2.9\text{-}0.0005*v \qquad F_y = 5.2\text{-}0.0001*v \qquad F_z = 12.9\text{-}0.0003*v$$

When the edge inclination angle λ_s= 6°:

$$F_x = 4.2\text{-}0.0002*v \qquad F_y = 6.4\text{-}0.0005*v \qquad F_z = 11.3\text{-}0.0002*v$$

The cutting depth and feed speed affected the cutting force greatly. Based on the dualistic regression [6, 7] analysis of the experiential formula ($F = C \bullet f^{X} a_p^{Y}$), adding the effect of cutting speed, the formulas for the three components of the cutting forces were obtained.

When the edge inclination angle λ_s = 0°:

$$F_x = 155.4*f^{0.83}* a_p^{0.94} *K_{vx1}$$

$$F_y = 100.1* f^{0.72}*a_p^{0.61} *K_{vy1}$$

$$F_z = 754.5*f^{0.82} * a_p^{0.96} *K_{vz1}$$

When the edge inclination angle λs= 6°:

$$F_x = 146.1*f^{0.78}* a_p^{0.81} *K_{vx2}$$

$$F_y = 100.2* f^{0.68}*a_p^{0.60} *K_{vy2}$$

$$F_z = 772.5*f^{0.85} * a_p^{0.98} *K_{vz2}$$

Where K_v was the factor of speed that equalled the ratio of the cutting force at the speed of v to the cutting force at the speed of 400m/min, as follows:

$$K_{vz1} = \frac{F_{VZ1}}{F_{VZ1400}} = \frac{12.9 - 0.0003 \bullet v}{12.8}$$

Using the equipment above and the edge inclination angle $\lambda_s = 6°$, the precision turning experiment was undertaken, at the same time the cutting forces, given in Table 2, were recorded. Data was then compared with theoretical values for a cutting speed of 500 m/min, cutting depth of 0.03mm and feed of 0.08mm/r.

Table 2 The measure values and the values from theory

	Fx	Fy	Fz
Measured values	1.1 N	2.4 N	3.1 N
Theory values	1.189 N	2.194 N	2.905 N
errors	7.5%	9.4%	6.7%

Through the finite element software, the workpiece static model (Figure 3(a)) was developed. The model adopted the SOLID45 (3D Structural Solid) which is defined by eight nodes having three degrees of freedom of each node and have the capabilities of enduring plasticity, creep, swelling, stress stiffening, large deflection, and large strain. The entire constraints were put on the torus beside the hole, which were the same to those in the real machining operation. The loads in Table 2 were computed from the cutting force model. The analytical results show that the maximum deformation (0.031mm) occured at the outer round (Figure 3(b)). The deformation was very large, so the method of clamping the workpiece was amended though adding assistant constraint on the inner round. In this way the workpiece rigidity was strengthened, the maximum deformation (0.003mm) fell greatly (Figure 3(c)), and the precision was also greatly enhanced.

The finite element software can compute the deformation according to the cutting forces, while the forces can be computed by the given deformation and the force model. In a certain range, the deformation and the force take on a function relation [8]. Using the improved model and the given deformation (0.01mm), the cutting forces F_x=3.3N, F_y=6.7N, F_z=10.2N can be determined. Then using the cutting force formulae, the cutting parameters a_p= 0.08mm, f= 0.1mm/r, v = 500m/min can be distributed rationally. In this way, not only the machining quality was guaranteed, but also the efficiency was improved greatly.

  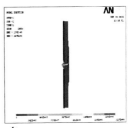

Figure 3   Finite element analysis results

(a) Workpiece static FM model (b) deformation before amending (c) deformation after amending

4. Conclusions

A series of precise turning experimental results of a super high strength aluminum alloy showed that the experimental model of the cutting force of the super high strength aluminum alloy was similar to that of the ferrous metal, so cutting force models were built, which were available for optimizing the cutting parameters. On the other hand, experimental results indicated that the primary cutting force when the edge inclination angle of the diamond tool is 6° was smaller than that of the tool edge inclination angle of 0°, and the cutting surface quality of workpiece of super high strength aluminum alloy become better. Based on the finite element software analyzing the deformation, it was found that the machining accuracy and efficiency were improved notably through changing the way of clamping the workpiece and choosing more rational cutting parameters.

References

[1] Hu Jiaguo, Yang Zhigang, Li Ying, Research of Aluminum Alloy Cutting Force while high-speed Milling, Tool Engineering, No. 11 (2003), pp. 33

[2] Wang Hongxiang, Sun Tao Zhang, Longjiang, Experimental Research on Cutting Force in Ultra-precise Turning, Tool Engineering, No. 5 (2003), pp. 10

[3] Yan Ping, Li Jianrong. Research about Super-high Strength Aluminium Alloy Pipe Structure and Property, Light Alloy Manufacturing Technology, Vol. 31, No. 12 (2003), pp. 23

[4] Zhou Zehua, Theory of metal cutting (ShangHai Science and Technology Publishing House, China 1993).

[5] Su Yilin, *Mechanics of materials* (Higher Education Publishing House, China 1987-1988).

[6] Wang Xiumei, The application of computer in unary regression analysis, Journal of Shangqiu Teachers College, Vol. 17, No. 4 (2001), pp 58

[7] Hong Yongcheng, Application of Binary Linear Regression Method to turning forces Test, Journal of Hubei Automotive Industries Institute, Vol. 16, No. 1 (2002), pp 10

[8] Wang Lijie, Fang Ziliang, The Cutting Edge Inclination Affecting to Working Angle of Cutter, Journal of NanJing Forestry University, Vol. 24, No. 6 (2000), pp. 51

An Evaluation of Flow Stress Material Models of AISI 1045 for High Speed Machining

S A Iqbal [a], P T Mativenga [b] and M A Sheikh [c]

School of Mechanical, Aerospace and Civil Engineering, University of Manchester, Sackville Street Building, Sackville Street, M60 1QD Manchester, UK

[a]amir.syed@postgrad.manchester.ac.uk, [b]P.Mativenga@manchester.ac.uk, [c]mohammad.a.sheikh@manchester.ac.uk

Abstract. This paper evaluates existing flow stress models for the simulations of metal cutting processes with regards to their accuracy over a wide range of cutting speeds. The predictive capability of flow stress models is first tested against published high strain rate experimental results from Split Hopkinson Pressure Bar (SHPB) method. The models are then assessed using FE simulations over a range of cutting speeds in orthogonal turning. Due to high cutting speeds, temperature dependent properties of the tool and the workpiece materials are utilised. The assessment of the models is carried out for their accuracy in predicting the shear angle. The paper presents a benchmark of appropriate flow stress models for different cutting speed regimes.

Keywords: Flow Stress Models, High Speed Machining (HSM), Finite Element Modelling, Shear Angle.

Introduction

Finite Element Modelling (FEM) of metal cutting can be considered as a promising approach to study the process, allowing a reduction in experimental costs. It was pointed out that flow stress data and friction conditions are the two most important inputs for the accurate modelling and simulation of the cutting process [1]. The driver for this work is to evaluate the accuracy of existing flow stress models for AISI 1045 in predicting flow stress and shear angle in both conventional and high speed cutting regimes.

The criteria for classification of high speed machining are highly dependent on the type of workpiece material. Due to this strong dependence on the workpiece material machinability, no exact definition of high speed machining is yet available. Schulz and Moriwaki [2] have developed a classification for high speed machining as shown in the Fig. 1.

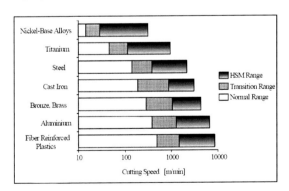

Fig. 1 Regimes of High Speed Machining [2]

The most cited flow stress σ, material models available in literature for AISI 1045 are summarized in Table 1.

Flow stress material models for AISI 1045

Material model	Equation	Material constants
Oxley [3]	$\sigma = \sigma_1 \varepsilon^n$	σ_1 = flow strss at $\varepsilon = 1.0$, n = strain hardening index
Maekawa et al [4]	$\sigma = B\left[\dfrac{\dot{\varepsilon}}{1000}\right]^M e^{aT}\left[\dfrac{\dot{\varepsilon}}{1000}\right]^m \left\{\displaystyle\int_{strain\ path} e^{-aT/N}\left[\dfrac{\dot{\varepsilon}}{1000}\right]^{-m/N} d\varepsilon\right\}^N$	B, M, N, m, a material constants
Zerilli-Armstrong [5]	$\sigma = C_o + C_1 \exp(-C_3 T + C_4 T \ln \dot{\varepsilon}^*) + C_2 \varepsilon^n$	$C_0, C_1, C_2, C_3, C_4, n$ material constants
Johnson-Cook [6]	$\sigma = \left(A + B\varepsilon^n\right)\left(1 + C \ln \dot{\varepsilon}^*\right)(1 - T^{*m})$	A, B, C, m, n material constants
El-Magd et al [7]	$\sigma_o = f(\varepsilon, \dot{\varepsilon}, T), \sigma = f(\sigma_o, \dot{\varepsilon})$ $\Delta\sigma_{steel-CK45} = f(T, \dot{\varepsilon}), \sigma_{steel} = \sigma + \Delta\sigma_{steel-CK45}$	$A^*, T^*, \dot{\varepsilon}^*, \varepsilon_o, \xi, \nu, \eta, m,$ n, K, T_1, T_2

Table 1 Material flow stress models for AISI 1045 steel

Benchmarking

In this study, the evaluation of the flow stress models, presented in Table 1, is carried out with reference to published flow stress test results reported by El-Magd et al for AISI 1045 [7]. These results cover wide ranges of temperature, strain and strain rates of up to 1000°C, 0.5 and 5000 s^{-1} respectively. It is widely accepted that in orthogonal turning, interface temperature increases with cutting speeds. Therefore flow stress data evaluated at high temperature could shed light on the HSM process. Fig. 2 shows the percentage variation in flow stress predicted by the reviewed models compared to El-Magd et al's data.

In Fig. 2, the high strain end of the graph is more relevant to the scenario encountered in metal cutting. At 500°C, more realistic for conventional cutting speeds, Maekawa et al's model is the best for predicting flow stress with an error of only around 7 %. The next best models are Johnson-Cook and Oxley with around 13% and 15% deviations respectively.

At 800°C, for higher strains of 0.5, Oxley's model shows a minor variation of 0.5% in predicting flow stress. This model also shows a trend of increasing accuracy for higher strains. This is relevant, as higher strains (> 0.5) are more likely to be encountered in metal cutting. At this test temperature, models by Maekawa et al, El-Magd et al and Johnson-Cook are very close in their predictive capability.

For the highest temperature which can be induced by high cutting speeds, of 1000°C, typical of high speed turning, Johnson-Cook's model makes the best prediction with only 5% error. Oxley model is the second best at 15%, while Maekawa et al and El-Magd et al show an almost equal performance with 21% error. However, the overall trend in percentage variation with strain shows that Johnson-Cook's model gives an increasing accuracy trend followed by a deterioration at the higher strain.

From this preliminary benchmarking of flow stress models, it appears that Oxley and Johnson-Cook models have the potential to be the representative of the (medium to high temperature scenarios) transition and the high speed machining regimes.

The next part of the investigation involved high speed turning experiments and the evaluation of the capability of flow stress models to predict the shear angle. The shear angle was selected here in this investigation, because this parameter is highly dependent on the workpiece material properties.

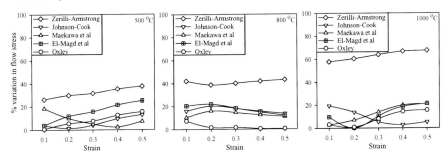

Fig. 2 Comparison of flow stress variation at T = 500 °C, 800 °C and 1000 °C, $\dot{\varepsilon}$ =5000 s^{-1} to El-Magd et al's experimental data for different material models

Cutting tests and Simulation Results

Orthogonal cutting tests were performed at cutting speeds of 197, 396, 624, and 874 m/min. To minimize the variation in material properties, which can result from the drawing process, a tube was machined from a solid steel bar. The feed rate was set at 0.1 mm/rev and the depth of cut fixed to the tube thickness of 2.5 mm. Commercially available tungsten-based flat triangular uncoated cemented carbide inserts (Sandvik TCMW 16T304 grade 5015) were used in the tests. A three component piezoelectric dynamometer (Kistler 3 Component type 9263) was used to measure the cutting forces. The shear angle (ϕ) was estimated from the chip compression ratio (λ) and rake angle (α) using Eq. 1.

$$\phi = \tan^{-1}\left[\frac{\cos\alpha}{\lambda - \sin\alpha}\right] \tag{1}$$

In metal cutting, strain can be approximated by the chip compression ratio. Fig. 3 shows the variation of chip compression ratio for different cutting speeds.

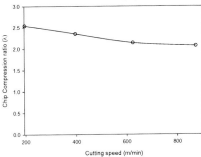

Fig. 3. Chip compression ratio vs. cutting speed.

The contact shear stress was estimated using Eq. 2.

$$\tau_F = \frac{F_f}{A_C}$$ (2)

where F_f is feed force and A_C is contact area. The tool chip contact area was measured using a CCD camera and digital image processing software. The influence of friction was examined using a friction model proposed by Wanheim and Bay [8] , given by Eq. 3.

$$\tau_F = mk \quad \therefore 0 < m < 1.$$ (3)

where τ_F is the frictional shear stress, m is shear friction factor, k is the shear flow stress in the primary shear zone, given by Eq. 4 [9].

$$k = \frac{F_v \cos\phi \sin\phi - F_f \sin^2\phi}{f\, a_p}$$ (4)

where F_v is cutting force, ϕ is shear angle, a_p is chip width and f is undeformed chip thickness.

For FEM simulations, an updated Lagrangian software DEFORM 2D^{TM} was used. It is based on an updated Lagrangian formulation that employs implicit integration method, designed for large deformation simulations. This implicit Lagrangian code offers very stable remeshing routines, which can handle large gradient of strain , strain rate and temperature. A dense mesh can be easily defined around the workpiece tool interface. This mesh is adapted as the tool advances and simulation of continuous chip formation is achieved. All the simulations in this study used a shear friction factor value 'm' for all flow stress models calculated according to Eq. 3, for the different cutting speeds tested. The simulations were run on cutting parameters identical to the cutting tests. Due to anticipated high temperature during cutting process, temperature dependent properties of workpiece and tool material cited in literature [10-12], were used as inputs to the simulation software.

Discussion

Fig. 4 shows the simulation results of shear angle at different cutting speeds, for all flow stress material models listed in Table 1. Among the material models cited, Zerilli-Armstrong and El-Magd et al's models are based on physics of deformation process. While Oxley, Johnson-Cook and Maekawa et al's models are empirical models fitted to experimental data.

For Zerilli-Armstrong and Johnson-Cook models, material constants were reported by Jaspers and Dautzenberg [13] for the test conditions of $\varepsilon = 0.3$, $\dot{\varepsilon} = 7500$ sec^{-1} and $T = 600$ °C based on SHPB test The material constants for Maekawa et al's models were reported by Childs [1], test conditions not specified. Oxley fitted the data of high speed compression test with $\dot{\varepsilon} = 450$ sec^{-1} with specimen preheated between room temperature to 1100 °C, to the given relation. El-Magd et al's estimated material constants from its reported results based on SHPB test. El-Magd et al also defined a separate relation to incorporate the dynamic strain hardening effect.

The main reason for highest variation shown by Zerilli-Armstrong model is that the exponential term (containing strain rate and temperature term) flattens the flow stress curve as the temperature increases. Whereas for constant strain and varying strain rates, flow stress decreases with increasing temperature [7]. This is shown by Fig. 1 that, with increasing temperature, the percentage variation in flow stress also increases for Zerilli-Armstrong model. For Maekawa et al's model, constant strain rate and temperature paths were assumed for simplifying the relation. This assumption might not be true for high cutting temperatures.

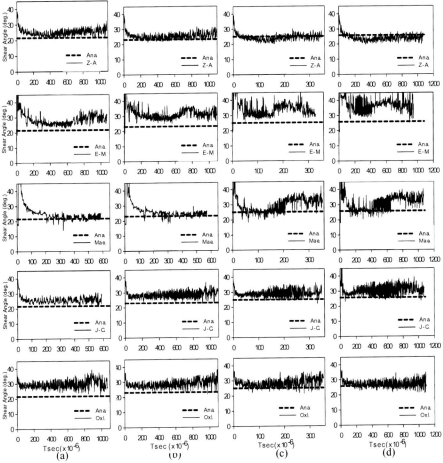

Fig. 4 Analytical and simulated shear angle for material models at different cutting speeds [(a) 197 (b) 396 (c) 624 (d) 876 m/min]

[Ana = Analytical, Z-A = Zerilli-Armstrong, E-M = El-Magd et al, Mae = Maekawa et al, J-C = Johnson-Cook, Oxl = Oxley model]

Maekawa et al's model represents a very good approximation of the shear angle in the steady state conditions at 197 and 396 m/min. It may be noted here that the benchmark discussed before, also indicated that Maekawa et al's model was the best for the low cutting temperature. Surprisingly Zerilli-Armstrong's, model which shows the highest variation in the flow stress prediction, as reported earlier, shows a fair approximation of shear angle in this instance.

At high cutting speeds of 624 and 896 m/min, Oxley's model gives the best prediction for the shear angle as shown in Fig. 4 (c) and (d). Johnson-Cook's model also gives a reasonable prediction but overestimates the shear angle by a couple of degrees. It is noted that both Oxley and Johnson-Cook models show a fairly consistent shear angle trend over the machining time. Zerilli-Armstrong's model again shows a reasonable prediction but underestimates the shear angle. It appears that Johnson-Cook and Oxley models are quite robust for application to high speed cutting regime and should be considered in the FEM simulations of high speed cutting of AISI 1045 using carbide tools.

Conclusions

Workpiece material flow stress data is an important input to the FE Models of the metal cutting processes. A number of flow stress material models are available in literature for this purpose. For the models reported and cutting conditions, the orthogonal machining tests and FE simulations support the superiority of Oxley and Johnson-Cook models for high temperature deformation and high cutting speed (624 - 876 m/min), whilst Maekawa's model was representative for lower cutting speed (197 - 396 m/min)

Although the test conditions reported in terms of strain, strain rate and temperature, for the estimation of material constants for Johnson-Cook and Oxley models are lower than El-Magd et al, it could be that their good extrapolating capability makes them accurate in predicting flow stress beyond the test operating conditions.

In conclusion the experimental tests and simulation result show that for modelling of a metal cutting process, a robust material model is required.

References

[1]   T.H.C. Childs: Machining Science and Technology Vol. 2(2) (1998), pp. 303-306.
[2]   H. Schulz and T. Moriwaki: Annals of CIRP Vol. 41(2) (1992), pp. 637-643.
[3]   P.L.B. Oxley: *Mechanics of Machining: An analytical approach to assessing machinability*, (Ellis Horwood, London 1989).
[4]   K. Maekawa, T. Shirakashi and E. Usui: Bulletin of Japan Society of Precision Engineering, Vol. 17(3) (1983), pp.167-172.
[5]   F.J. Zerilli and R.W. Armstrong: Journal of Applied Physics Vol. 61(6) (1987), pp. 1816-1825.
[6]   G.R. Johnson and W.H. Cook: Proc: Seventh International symposium on Ballistics, (The Hague 1983), pp 541-547.
[7]   E. El-Magd, C. Treppmann and M. Korthäuer: Journal De Physique (2003), pp. 141-146.
[8]   T. Wanheim, and N. Bay. Annals of CIRP Vol. 27(1) (1978), pp. 189-194.
[9]   W.R. DeVries: *Analysis of Material Removal Processes*, (Springer Verlag, New York 1992).
[10]   V. Kalhori, M. Lundblad and L.E. Lindgren: ASME International Mechanical Engineering Congress and exposition, MED, Manufacturing Science and Engineering, (Dallas, Texas. 16-21 Nov.1997).
[11]   ASM Handbook Committee: *Metals Handbook: Properties and Selection: Iron and steels*, (American Society for Metals., Metals park, Ohio 1989).
[12]   T.H.C. Childs, K. Maekawa, T. Obikawa, and Y. Yamane: *Metal Machining: Theory and Application*, (Arnold, London 2000).
[13]   S.P.F.C. Jaspers and J.H. Dautzenberg: Journal of Materials Processing Technology Vol. 122(2-3) (2002), pp. 322–330.

Production Systems
and Process Optimisation

Mix Flexibility: A Question of Capability, Capacity and Efficiency

Shellyanne Wilson[1, a] and Ken Platts[1, b]

[1]Department of Engineering

University of Cambridge

Mill Lane

Cambridge, CB2 1RZ

United Kingdom

[a]snw24@cam.ac.uk, [b]kwp@eng.cam.ac.uk

Abstract. Although manufacturing flexibility, the ability to change or to adapt to change, has been widely research, there remains a lack of complete understanding of the way in which flexibility is achieved. This paper aims at making a contribution to this research gap. It reports a case study that is part of an ongoing investigation of the process that leads to the achievement of one type of flexibility: mix flexibility, in the flour milling industry. The case is analysed from a resource-based perspective. It examines how resource configurations are developed in relation to the company's changing mix flexibility requirements. The empirical analysis shows that three factors: capability, capacity and efficiency, contribute to the actions taken in developing resource configurations to achieve mix flexibility.

Keywords: mix flexibility, resources, flour milling industry

Introduction

Flexibility, cost, quality and delivery are the four manufacturing objectives identified in the manufacturing strategy literature to be pursued by manufacturing companies in order to achieve success [1,2].

Despite the contentious debate between researchers who supported the concept of manufacturing objective tradeoffs versus researchers who argued that a firm can excel simultaneously at all four objectives [3], past research shows that, over time, manufacturers have altered their focus on the various objectives. Whereas cost and quality were considered to be top competitive priorities in the 1980s, manufacturers switched their focus to flexibility in the 1990s [4]. This led to flexibility being labeled as one of the most important dimensions of a successful manufacturing strategy [5,6].

Notwithstanding the important role flexibility plays in the manufacturing strategy of companies, there still remains a lack of complete understanding of the way in which flexibility is achieved [7]. This is evident in the difficulties encountered by manufacturing managers when they attempt to implement flexibility in their operations [8]. Although early research in manufacturing flexibility identified flexible resources: flexible manpower, technology and infrastructure, as the sources of flexibility [9], the way in which these resources are coordinated to achieve flexibility remains unclear. Resources, in this study, are defined as assets, knowledge, capabilities and organisational processes that enable a company to create and implement the company's strategies [10] and can be classified as physical capital resources, human capital resources and organisational capital resources [11].

It is this gap in the manufacturing flexibility literature that this research paper addresses. The paper reports on an ongoing research project which investigates the processes that lead to the achievement of one type of flexibility: mix flexibility, in the flour milling industry. Specifically, the research examines how resource combinations are developed to achieve mix flexibility. A case study methodology approach is taken, where an in-depth case study was conducted at a Caribbean flour milling company. The case study reviewed the history of the company's product mix changes and the resource configuration changes made to the company's milling and packaging departments.

This research paper is structured as follows. Firstly, a brief review of the role of mix flexibility in the flour milling industry is presented. Secondly, a summary of the case study is reviewed. The final section presents the paper's conclusion.

Mix Flexibility and the Flour Milling Industry

Mix Flexibility. Mix flexibility is one of the most common manufacturing flexibility types discussed in the literature. It is defined as the ability to change between current products [12] and is referred to by a number of other names, including process flexibility and product flexibility. Mix flexibility can be analyzed by considering its dimensions: range and response. Mix range flexibility considers the number of products manufactured by the company, while mix response flexibility considers the ease of changing among the different products.

A company's need for mix flexibility is dependent on a number of factors. Firstly, there is the nature of the company's product mix. This considers the number of products offered, the degree of differences between the products and the ease of changing among the different products. Secondly, there is the nature of the demand for the products, both with respect to demand variability and demand correlation among the products [13]. Thirdly, there is the manner in which the company chooses to manage its need for mix flexibility, in terms of the mixed use of controls, such as excess capacity, long quoted lead times and inventory [14] and the use of flexible resources.

The Flour Milling Industry. This project focuses on wheat flour, which is produced via a repetitive process of grinding and separating the three wheat grain components: endosperm, germ and bran. There are three main categories of flour types: white flour, brown flour and whole-meal flour. White flour is composed only of endosperm, while brown flour is composed of endosperm and a proportion of the bran and germ components of the wheat grain. Whole-meal flour, however, is composed of all the endosperm, germ and bran of the wheat grain.

Another major characteristic used to differentiate the various flour types is their protein content, since it is the protein content of the flour which determines the way in which the flour will behave during baking. Generally, high protein flours are used to produce items such as breads, bagels and pizzas, while low protein flours are used in the baking of goods such as cakes and biscuits.

Flour type variety is achieved via the milling process and the use of various types of wheat. Further flour type variety is achieved through additional processing steps, such as heat treatment or via the addition of ingredients such as malted grains. The finished flour type is then sold in various sizes, ranging from small packs for household to large sacks for industrial users.

Case Study Report

Case Study Background. The case study was conducted at a manufacturing company located in the Caribbean. The company began operations in 1966, and is involved in flour, rice, feed and edible oil production. This research, however, concentrated only on the flour milling and packaging operations.

The company produces ten different flour types: Bakers, Special Bakers, Hi-Gluten Bakers, All Purpose, Hibiscus, Cracker, Palms, Special Palms, Cake Flour and Whole-wheat. The range of flour types are achieved via the use of three different wheat types, the use of wheat blending and base flour blending. The finished flour is packaged into six pack sizes: 45kg, 10kg, 2kg, 1kg, 2lbs and 1lb. Flour is also sold in 1-ton sacks and in bulk, via the filling of bulk flour tankers. Additional variety results from the packaging of flour under an assortment of brand names. The company also manufactures baking powder, which has flour as one of its main ingredients. Table 1 gives a summary of the packaging lines used to package the various flour products.

Packaging Lines used in the Production of the Flour Package Sizes

Packaging Line	Product Size
Buhler	45kg
Fawema	10kg
SIG	2kg
Hayssen	1kg, 2lbs, 1lb
Hayssen Flour Station	1 ton
Bulk Transfer System	Bulk

Table 1

The study was guided by the research objective 'To investigate the process that leads to the achievement of mix flexibility in the flour milling industry'. A preliminary framework, developed from a literature review and an exploratory case study, was used to direct the case study. The preliminary framework, shown in Fig.1, is composed of three interrelated themes:
1. How much mix flexibility is needed?
2. What strategies are used to manage the need for mix flexibility?
3. Resource management:
   a. What are the company's current resources?
   b. How does the company configure and reconfigure its resource configurations?

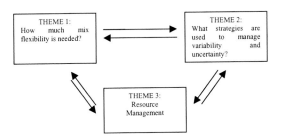

Fig.1: Preliminary Framework Used To Guide Case Study

Data was collected from twelve semi-structured interviews with the company employees, including the production manager, mill manager, shift superintendents, production planner, machine operators and process operators. Information was also gathered from the company's website, intranet, production and marketing reports, ISO documents, production log books and magazine and newspaper articles.

Case Study Results. This paper focuses on the third theme of the preliminary framework: resource management. It reports on resource management decisions, in terms of triggers and the actions taken by the company in response to these triggers. Triggers refer to the stimuli that could potentially influence an action to be taken that would affect the current resource configuration.

The triggers can be classified into four broad categories:

- o Environmental Triggers
- o Organizational Triggers
- o Market Triggers
- o Operational Triggers

Environmental triggers refer to the social, political and cultural environment in which the company operates. Organizational triggers include stimuli related to changes in the company's ownership structure, strategy, management and degree of control. Market triggers include stimuli relating to competitors, customers and company's product-market strategy. Operational triggers relate to stimuli that directly affect the manufacturing system.

The actions taken in response to the triggers outlined above include:

- o Retention of the current resource configuration
- o Acquisition of new resources
- o Modification of the current resource configuration (Temporarily / Permanently):
  - - Improvement to current resources
  - - Replacement of resources
  - - Rearrangement of resources
  - - Addition of resources
  - - Removal of resources

Regardless of the trigger, all of the above actions taken can be related to three features of the manufacturing system: capability, capacity and efficiency. The capability aspect considered the ability of the system to produce the company's product mix. For example, the case study investigated product mix decisions to expand the company's product range. In instances where the manufacturing system had the existing capability to produce the new product, the initial resource configuration was retained. However, where such capability did not exist, the findings of the case study showed that the company modified the existing system by adding the required equipment.

With respect to capacity, resource configuration actions followed this trend. When additional capacity was required, if the manufacturing system had spare capacity, the resource configuration was modified to exploit that slack capacity. Where the extra demand was short term, the resource configuration modification was temporary, as in the use of overtime. Where the extra demand was long term, the resource modification was more permanent, as in the addition of a second shift. In situations where slack capacity did not exist, additional capacity was acquired through the addition of resources.

The efficiency aspect included performance issues such as speed, cost effectiveness, quality and accuracy. When the company wished to improve performance, resource configuration actions included resource replacements and additions to the existing resource configuration.

Summary

The objective of this research project is to increase the understanding of the processes involved in the achievement of one type of manufacturing flexibility: mix flexibility. Using a case study methodology, a Caribbean flour milling company was investigated. The case study was guided by a preliminary framework, which is composed of three interrelated themes: the need for flexibility, the strategies used to manage the need for flexibility and resource management.

This research paper focused on the third theme: resource management, and investigated how environmental, organizational, market and operational triggers led the company to take specific actions that affected the resource configuration. The main findings coming out of the case study was that regardless of the trigger, all the actions taken could be related to three properties of the manufacturing system: capability, capacity and efficiency.

This research project continued with four additional cases in the Caribbean flour milling industry. The additional cases allowed for cross case analysis to investigate both the classification of the triggers and the scope of actions taken that affected the resource configuration. Preliminary analysis of the findings of the additional cases does confirm the reasoning behind both the classification of the triggers and the scope of actions taken. But, more importantly, the additional cases highlight the important role played by the environmental, market, organizational and operational contexts in which each of the companies operate. The ocntexts determine both the effect the trigger would have on the organization and the response the company will make to the trigger. Figure 2 summarizes the framework development coming out of the findings of the additional cases.

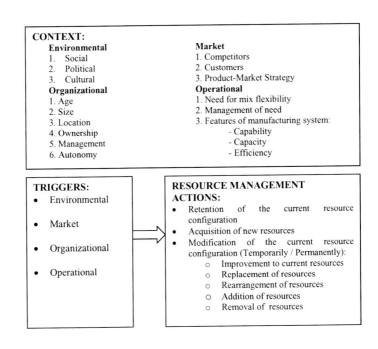

Fig. 2: Framework Development Incorporating Context, Triggers and Actions Related to Resource Management in the Achievement of Mix Flexibility

The next steps of the research project will further analyse the relationship between the four categories of triggers that stimulate resource management actions.

References

[1]   W. Skinner: *Manufacturing in the Corporate Strategy* (Wiley, New York 1978).

[2]   S.C. Wheelwright: *Reflecting Corporate Strategy in Manufacturing Decisions*. Business Horizons Vol. 21 No. 1 (1978), pp. 57 – 66.

[3]   J. Mills, K. Platts and M. Gregory: *A Framework for the Design of Manufacturing Strategy Processes - A Contingency Approach.* International Journal of Operations & Production Management Vol.15 No.4 (1995), pp. 17 – 49.

[4]   K. Ferdows and W. Skinner: *The Sweeping Revolution in Manufacturing.* Journal of Business Strategy Vol.8 No.2 (1987), pp. 64 - 69.

[5]   R. Beach, A.P. Muhlemann, D.H.R. Price, A. Paterson and J.A. Sharp: *A Review of Manufacturing Flexibility.* European Journal of Operational Research Vol 122, No.1 (2000), pp.41 – 57.

[6]   X. deGroote: *The Flexibility of Production Processes: A General Framework.* Management Science Vol. 40, No.7 (1994), pp. 933 – 945.

[7]   D.E. D'Souza: *Toward an Understanding of How Organizations Create Manufacturing Flexibility.* Journal of Managerial Issues Vol.XIV No.4 (2002), pp. 470 – 485.

[8]   D.M. Upton: *What Really Makes Factories Flexible?* Harvard Business Review July – August (1995), pp.74 - 84.

[9]   N. Slack: *The Flexibility of Manufacturing Systems.* International Journal of Operations & Production Management Vol.7 No. 4 (1987), pp. 35 – 45.

[10] K.E. Marino: *Developing Consensus on Firm Competencies and Capabilities.* Academy of Management Executive Vol.10 No.3 (1996), pp.40 – 51.

[11] J. Barney: *Firm Resources and Sustained Competitive Advantage.* Journal of Management Vol.17 No.1 (1991), pp.99 – 120.

[12] N. Bateman, D.J. Stockton and P. Lawrence: *Measuring the Mix Response Flexibility of Manufacturing Systems.* International Journal of Production Research Vol.37 No.4 (1999), pp.871 – 880.

[13] J. Bengtsson and J. Olhager: *The Impact of the Product Mix on the Value of Flexibility.* The International Journal of Management Science Vol.30 (2002), pp.265 – 273.

[14] W.R. Newman, M. Hanna and M.J. Maffei: *Dealing with the Uncertainties of Manufacturing: Flexibility, Buffers and Integration.* International Journal of Operations & Production Management Vol.13 No.1 (1993), pp.19 – 34.

Optimal Process Targeting of Multi-Components Multi-Characteristics Products

Moustafa Elshafei[1,a], Atiq W. Siddiqui[2,b], Salih O. Duffuaa[3,c]

King Fahd university of Petroleum and Minerals, Dhahran, 31261, Saudi Arabia.
[a]elshafei@ccse.kfupm.edu.sa , [b]atique@ccse.kfupm.edu.sa, [c]duffuaa@ccse.kfupm.edu.sa

Abstract. In this paper a process targeting model for multi-components multi-characteristic products is developed. The cost function is based on a multivariable Taguchi type quadratic loss function for product uniformity, and a quadratic term for the cost of components. Closed form expressions for the optimal process targets are derived. We provided an illustrative example, and discussed the effect of the weights in the quadratic cost on the tradeoffs between the product quality and the production cost. Further extension of the work is also discussed.

Keywords: Targeting, filling processes, optimization, manufacturing, quality

1. Introduction

In a manufacturing environment, a product has to go across a number of processes, undergoing diverse operations before obtaining a final form. Due to the natural and technological inconsistencies, especially systems of mechanical and chemical in nature, it is bound to have some variations in the final product. In order to minimize this variation, and to improve the overall characteristics of the product, quality control became an essential part of manufacturing. Process Targeting is one of the areas in economics of quality control, which has received a lot of interest from the researchers in the recent times.

The Targeting problem was initiated by Springer [1] for the canning problem. The objective was to minimize the expected cost. Kartha [2] presented a similar model, for the case of maximization of profit, where under filled cans are sold in a secondary market. Bisgaard et al [3] extended the above case where the under filled cans are sold at a price proportional to the can fill. In Golhar [4], the model presented is for the case where the under filled cans are reprocessed at a fixed cost. Golhar and Pollock in [5] considered the case where the fill in expensive and an artificial upper limit is also determined alongside the process mean. Golhar and Pollock [6] studied the effect of variance reduction on the profit. Arcelus [7] introduced the product uniformity via a Taguchi quadratic loss function. In Min and Jang [8] a situation where inspection is based on three class screening is considered.

Several other directions of research have evolved e.g., use of various sampling plans instead of full inspection in Carlsson [9], Boucher and Jafari [10] and Sultan [11]. Others have considered problems having production processes with linear drift e.g., Rahim and Banerjee [12], Sultan and Pulak [13]. In this paper we present a unified process targeting model for multi-components multi-characteristic products, and propose a multivariable quadratic cost for both product uniformity, and components cost. This frame work leads to simple closed-form expressions for the optimal process targets.

[14] and [15] presented model for multi-class screening target problem with Taguchi quadratic loss function to introduce a penalty for uniformity and incorporation of unbiased error in measurement.

The paper is organized as follows. In the next section 2, the model developed in this paper is described. In Section 3, an illustrative example is presented. A brief summary of the sensitivity analysis is discussed in Section 4. Finally, extensions and conclusions are outlined in Section 5.

2. The Model

In this section, an economic targeting model is developed for a production process having multi-components and/or process parameters as inputs, and a product with multi-characteristics as an input. In this model, a Taguchi quadratic penalty, to infuse the uniformity count, and a quadratic components cost are incorporated. The object of this model is to find out the input settings for the process that minimizes the cost while also trying to achieve the target characteristics of the finished products. Model assumptions are as follows:

Consider a production system (Fig. 1) for instance a process plant (examples include: a food processing, a petrochemical process, or a pharmaceutical plant etc.), where in order to produce a product n components/processes are required, represented as $x_1, x_2, ... x_n$. These components/process parameters may represent a direct ingredient or a process variable such as temperature or a process mixing/heating time, or any other related factor. The ideal target values to be used in the Taguchi quadratic loss function are represented as $\hat{y}_1, \hat{y}_2, ... \hat{y}_m$.

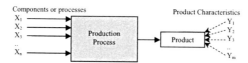

Fig. 1. A production process with n components/processes and a product with n characters.

The product quality is determined by the measurement of m characteristics $y_1, y_2, ... y_m$, e.g., weight, density, color, pH number, viscosity, etc. Ideal target values of the characteristics are represented as $\hat{y}_1, \hat{y}_2, ... \hat{y}_m$. If any characteristic is off target a quadratic (Taguchi) penalty is to be paid for it (see Fig.2).

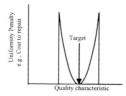

Fig. 2. Taguchi quadratic penalty for non-uniformity of a product

We assume that the measurement is related to the process components by the relation:

$$Y = CX + W \tag{1}$$

Where C is an m x n relational matrix (contribution factor of each x on y), and W is a vector of m normally distributed random noises with zero mean and covariance matrix Π_w. The dispensed components are described by the relation:

$$X = \mu + V \tag{2}$$

Where $\mu = (\mu_1, \mu_2, ..., \mu_n)$ the process set point vector, and V is is a vector of n normally distributed random variables with zero mean and covariance matrix Π_v representing natural variance of the production process. We further assume that W and V are independent.

It is now desired to find the optimal set point vector which minimizes the loss function given as:

$$J = E\{(Y - \hat{Y})^T Q(Y - \hat{Y}) + X^T RX\}\tag{3}$$

Where the weighting matrix Q reflects the cost of product non-uniformity, and R is the cost matrix of the product components/processes. Both Q an R are symmetric, and R is positive definite.

2.1 Solution To The Problem. For simplicity, let us assume that there is no measurement noise, i.e. $W=0$; Expanding Eq. 3

$$J = E\{(C\mu + CV - \hat{Y})^T Q(C\mu + CV - \hat{Y}) + (\mu + V)^T R(\mu + V)\}$$
$$J = E\{\mu^T C^T QC\mu + V^T C^T QCV + \hat{Y}^T Q\hat{Y} + \mu^T C^T QCV - \mu^T C^T Q\hat{Y} + V^T C^T QC\mu -\tag{4}$$
$$V^T C^T Q\hat{Y} - \hat{Y}^T QC\mu - \hat{Y}^T QCV + \mu^T R\mu + \mu^T RV + V^T R\mu + V^T RV\}$$

As V is a zero mean random vector, Eq. 3 can be simplified to

$$J = E\{\mu^T C^T QC\mu + V^T C^T QCV + \hat{Y}^T Q\hat{Y} - \mu^T C^T Q\hat{Y}$$
$$- \hat{Y}^T QC\mu + \mu^T R\mu + V^T R\mu + V^T RV\}\tag{5}$$
$$J = E\{\mu^T (C^T QC + R)\mu + V^T (C^T QC + R)V + \hat{Y}^T Q\hat{Y} - \mu^T C^T Q\hat{Y} - \hat{Y}^T QC\mu + V^T R\mu\}$$

Differentiating Eq. 5 with respect to μ and equating to zero

$$(C^T QC + R)\mu - C^T Q\hat{Y} = 0$$
$$\mu_{opt} = (C^T QC + R)^{-1} C^T Q\hat{Y}\tag{6}$$

Eq. 6 gives the optimal process set points for the input components/processes vector X. When W is not equal to zero, it can be shown that the expression for optimal set points is still given by Eq. 6, however the expression for the expected value of the minimum cost is given by:

$$J_{min} = \hat{y}^T Q\hat{y} - \mu_{opt}^T C^T Q\hat{y} + Tra((C^T QC + R)\Pi_v) + Tra(Q\Pi_w)\tag{7}$$

Eqs. 6 and 7 show that the optimal process targets does not depend on the characteristic of the process uncertainty and the measurement noise. However, the minimum quadratic cost is directly affected by the covariance matrices of the process uncertainty and the measurement noise.

3. Illustrative Example

In this section, an illustrative example is presented. The problem is as follows: Consider a carbonated cocktail juice which is to be manufactured to a target volume of 900 ml and a target calorific level of 150 calories. The juice is made up of: 1. the orange juice concentrate 2. the apple juice concentrate 3. the peach juice concentrate and 4. the carbonated water. The cost per ml of each of the component is assumed to be 0.004, 0.0042, 0.006, and 0.002 units respectively, The input settings are to be found so that cost is minimized while achieving these target values. In Case I, both volume and calorific values are considered equally important. The weights of their values are set high to reduce the deviation from the target requirement. While in Case II the target values are considered to be equal but of very low importance as compared to the cost of production. In case III and IV individual target weights are considered.

CASE I and II: Taguchi penalty factor, in Case I, is assumed to be set at 50 each when target values are more important than cost of production, while in case II it is set at 0.1 each so as to represent a situation where achieving targets is of low concern as compared to the cost of production. The optimal solution was found using Eq. 6 as in Table 1.

Table 1. Solution of the Illustrative example for case I and II

Taguchi Pen. fac. (Vol. – Cal.)	Optimal mean set points of inputs				Mean Output		Price
	Juice Conc. orange [ml]	Juice Conc. apple [ml]	Juice Conc. Peach [ml]	Carb. water. [ml]	Volume [ml]	Calories [Kcal]	Per 900 ml bottle
50 – 50	122.72	96.00	110.73	570.53	900.0	150.0	2.70
0.1-0.1	124.32	99.43	111.21	526.76	861.7	152.3	2.64

In Case I, Vector representing Target values, the Taguchi penalty matrix Q, the product cost matrix R and the input/output factors relationship matrix are given in equation 8

$$\hat{Y} = \begin{bmatrix} 900 \\ 150 \end{bmatrix}, \quad Q = \begin{bmatrix} 50 & 0 \\ 0 & 50 \end{bmatrix}, \quad R = \begin{bmatrix} 0.004 & 0 & 0 & 0 \\ 0 & 0.0042 & 0 & 0 \\ 0 & 0 & 0.006 & 0 \\ 0 & 0 & 0 & 0.002 \end{bmatrix}, \quad C = \begin{bmatrix} 1 & 1 & 1 & 1 \\ 0.43 & 0.55 & 0.35 & 0.01 \end{bmatrix} \tag{8}$$

Therefore the optimal target mean output matrix solution can be calculated as (as shown in Eq. 9:)
$\mu =$

$$\mu = \left(\begin{bmatrix} 1 & 1 & 1 & 1 \\ 0.43 & 0.55 & 0.35 & 0.01 \end{bmatrix}^T \begin{bmatrix} 50 & 0 \\ 0 & 50 \end{bmatrix} \begin{bmatrix} 1 & 1 & 1 & 1 \\ 0.43 & 0.55 & 0.35 & 0.01 \end{bmatrix} + \begin{bmatrix} 0.004 & 0 & 0 & 0 \\ 0 & 0.0042 & 0 & 0 \\ 0 & 0 & 0.006 & 0 \\ 0 & 0 & 0 & 0.002 \end{bmatrix} \right)^{+} \begin{bmatrix} 1 & 1 & 1 & 1 \\ 0.43 & 0.55 & 0.35 & 0.01 \end{bmatrix}^T \begin{bmatrix} 50 & 0 \\ 0 & 50 \end{bmatrix} \begin{bmatrix} 900 \\ 150 \end{bmatrix} = \begin{bmatrix} 122.72 \\ 96.0 \\ 110.73 \\ 570.53 \end{bmatrix} \tag{9}$$

Case II is similar to Case I except for Matrix Q with updated penalties of 0.1, 0.1 to deemphasize the target values as compared to the cost of production.

For the Cases III and IV where one of the characteristics is far more important i.e., assuming penalty to be set to zero for the non important while keeping the other at 50, the results are as follows in Table 2:

Table 2. Solution of the Illustrative example for case III and IV

Taguchi Pen. fac. (Vol. – Cal.)	Optimal mean set points of inputs				Mean Output		Price
	Juice Conc. orange [ml]	Juice Conc. apple [ml]	Juice Conc. Peach [ml]	Carb. water. [ml]	Volume [ml]	Calories [Kcal]	Per 900 ml bottle
50 – 0	194.84	185.56	129.90	389.68	900.0	235.2	3.12
0 – 50	116.23	141.59	63.07	5.41	326.3	150.0	1.45

It can be seen clearly that the model is giving optimal values from economic stand point while taking care of the uniformity of the product according to the given target values and the weight of the target values to be achieved as compared to the cost of production.

4. Sensitivity Analysis

In this section, sensitivity analysis is presented. Here two important issues were considered. Firstly, the effect of price on the optimal target input means were assessed. Secondly, the effects of quadratic uniformity penalties on the output values, for which the target is set, were evaluated.

The results are presented in Table 3. Similar case, as presented in the section 3 (Illustrated example) was taken for sensitivity analysis. Target Volume was taken to be fixed at 900 ml. While two levels (High=250 cal and Low=150 cal) of target calorific values were studied. Various levels of 'price factors' were taken to evaluate the effect of cost on optimal input settings. Various combinations of Taguchi penalties are also taken to asses the effect on output target values. The combination were taken to evaluate various levels of Taguchi penalties as well as the effects on target output if one or both are important with higher or lower penalties as compared to the costs at the same time.

The model performed as expected and following behavior was observed. Higher values of the Taguchi penalty factors as compared to the price factors forces mean optimal output to be very close to the target values. The model shows sensitivity to the price factor as well, i.e., showing variation in mean optimal input values with the variation in price factor. One important aspect evident from the result is that the higher values of Taguchi penalty factors as compared to price factors are required and these penalties cannot be set to zero. This is because the optimal settings will tend towards zero as the Taguchi penalty factor tends towards zero. This behavior is obvious as the model does not have any constraints to limit optimal mean settings within some predefined acceptable limits. As can be seen from the results, the model will also provide the optimal target input means settings that will always give mean optimal output values less (or approximately equal, in case of very high penalty factors) than the target values.

Table 3. Results of sensitivity analysis

Target *volume* is set at 900 ml and *calorific values* levels at 1=150 calories and 2=250 calories

Target Cal. [cal]	Price of concentrates				Tag. Penalties		Mean Output		Price $/900 ml
	Conc. orange	Conc. apple	Conc. Peach	Carbonated water	Vol.	Cal.	Vol. [ml]	Cal. [cal]	
1	0.004	0.0042	0.006	0.002	50	0	900.0	235.2	3.12
1	0.004	0.0042	0.006	0.002	0	50	326.3	150.0	1.45
1	0.004	0.0042	0.006	0.002	10	10	899.9	150.1	2.70
1	0.004	0.0042	0.006	0.002	10	1	899.9	151.4	2.70
1	0.004	0.0042	0.006	0.002	1	10	898.9	150.1	2.70
1	0.004	0.0042	0.006	0.002	1	1	898.9	151.4	2.70
1	0.004	0.0042	0.006	0.002	1	0.5	898.9	152.7	2.71
1	0.004	0.0042	0.006	0.002	0.5	1	897.7	152.7	2.71
1	0.004	0.0042	0.006	0.002	10	10	758.9	187.2	2.57
2	0.004	0.0042	0.006	0.002	10	1	899.9	250.0	3.19
2	0.004	0.0042	0.006	0.002	1	10	899.9	249.8	3.19
2	0.004	0.0045	0.006	0.002	10	10	899.3	250.0	3.19
2	0.004	0.0045	0.006	0.002	10	1	899.9	250.0	3.20
2	0.004	0.0045	0.006	0.002	1	10	899.9	249.7	3.20
2	0.0045	0.004	0.006	0.002	10	10	899.3	250.0	3.20
2	0.0045	0.004	0.006	0.002	10	1	899.9	250.0	3.19
2	0.0045	0.004	0.006	0.002	1	10	899.9	249.7	3.19
2	0.004	0.0042	0.006	0.002	50	0	899.3	250.0	3.19
2	0.004	0.0042	0.006	0.002	0	50	775.3	213.5	2.74

5. Conclusion and Suggestions

The paper presented a model and a quadratic cost criterion for solving the multi-characteristic process targeting problem. One key advantage of this model is its simplicity where a closed form solution is obtained. Previous approaches to this problem are mathematically complex and require search algorithm to solve. However, in order to use this model effectively careful estimation of the Taguchi penalty factors are required to achieve the best compromise between the process quality and production cost. The model can be applied to a wide spectrum of applications in process industry such as food, beverages, petrochemicals, pharmaceuticals, cement, paints, chemicals industry etc. Various extensions to this work are possible. An immediate extension is to include constraints on the acceptable limits for output values. Other possible extensions include systems having more complex relations between the quality characteristics and the process variables.

6. Acknowledgement

The authors would like to acknowledge King Fahd University of Petroleum and Minerals for its support in conducting this research.

7. References

[1]   Springer, C.: A Method for Determining the Most Economic Position of a Process Mean. Industrial Quality Control, Vol. 8, No. 1, July 1951, 36 - 39
[2]   Hunter W., and Kartha, C.: Determining the Most Profitable Target Value for a Production Process. Journal of Quality Technology, Vol. 9, No. 4, Oct. 1977, 176 - 181
[3]   Bisgaard, S., Hunter, W. and Pallensen, L.: Economic Selection of Quality of Manufacturing Product. Technometrics, Vol. 26, 1984, 9 - 18
[4]   Golhar, D..: Determining of the Best Mean Contents for a Canning Problem. Journal of Quality Technology, Vol. 19, No. 2, April 1987, 82 - 84
[5]   Golhar, D., and Pollock, S.: Determining of the Optimal Process Mean and the Upper Limit for a Canning Problem. Journal of Quality Technology, Vol. 20, No. 3, July 1988, 188 - 1992
[6]   Golhar, D., and Pollock, S. Cost Saving Due to Variance Reduction in a Canning Problem. IIE Transactions.
[7]   Arcelus, F. J.: Uniformity of the Production Vs. Conformance to Specifications in the Canning Problem. Optimization in Quality Control, 1996
[8]   Lee, M., and Jang, J.: The Optimal Target Values for a Production Process with Three Class Screening. International Journal of Productions Economics, Vol. 49, 1997, 91 - 99
[9]   Carlsson, O.: Economic Selection of a Process Level under Acceptance Sampling Variables. Engineering Costs and Production Economics, Vol. 16, No. 2, 1989, 69 – 78
[10] Boucher, T., and Jafari, M.: The Optimum Target Value for Single Filling Operations with Quality Sampling Plans. Journal of Quality Technology, Vol. 23, No. 1, 1991, 44 - 47
[11] Al-Sultan, K. S.: An Algorithm for the Determining of the Optimum Target Value for Two Machines in Series with Quality Sampling Plans. International Journal of Productions Research, Vol. 32, No. 1, 1994, 37 - 45
[12] Rahim, M. A., and Banerjee, P. K.: Optimal Production Run for a Process with Random Linear Drift. OMEGA, Vol. 16, No. 4, 1988, 347 - 351
[13] Al-Sultan, K. S., and Pulak, M. F.: Process Improvement by Variance Reduction for A Single Filling Operation with Rectifying Inspection. Production Planning and Control, Vol. 8, No. 5, 1997, 431 – 436.
[14] Duffuaa S.O. and Siddiqui A.W.: Integrated Process targeting and Product uniformity model for three-class screening, special issue of Journal of Quality reliability and Safety Engineering, Vol. 9, No. 3 (2002) 261-274.
[15] Duffuaa S.O. and Siddiqui A.W.: Process Targeting with Multi-Class Screening and Measurement Error. International Journal of Production Research, Volume 41, Number 7, 10 May 2003.

Integrating Production System Performances in the DFMA Methodology

Antonio C. Caputo[a], Pacifico M. Pelagagge[b]

Department of Mechanical, Energy and Management Engineering, University of L'Aquila, Monteluco, 67040, L'Aquila, Italy

[a] caputo@ing.univaq.it, [b] pelmar@ing.univaq.it

Abstract. A novel methodology is proposed to supplement traditional Design for Manufacture and Assembly techniques in order to evaluate the impact that design solutions may have of the overall performances of the manufacturing system. The method is based on a number of different performance indices giving a multicriteria assessment of the suitability of a product design which extends beyond the sole evaluation of manufacturing costs and assembly difficulty.

Keywords: Design for Production, Design for Manufacturing and Assembly, Concurrent Engineering, Manufacturing System Perfomances, Product Design.

Introduction

Traditional sequential design approaches are being gradually superseded by the concurrent engineering paradigm which advocates to carry out simultaneously the product and process designs with the aim of minimizing the product life cycle cost [1]. In this framework specific Design for Manufacturing and Assembly (DFMA) techniques have been developed and are widely employed [2,3,4]. However, the DFMA approach essentially focuses on obtaining a product with a high level of manufacturability, i.e. minimizing production cost through simplification of product structure mainly resorting to a reduction of parts count, proper selection of the best combination of materials, geometry and cost-effective manufacturing methods for all parts, and simplification of manual assembly tasks. This implies that most DFMA techniques rate a product design on the basis solely of direct manufacturing and assembly costs, with no further reference to the overall impact that the manufacturing tasks have on the performances of the entire production system, including planning and control issues [5,6]. It is thus clear that a product design solution may obtain a good DFMA rating if it is composed of a few parts, which may be manufactured at low cost, and assembled easily in a short time, regardless on the overall side effects on the entire manufacturing system performances. This is quite a limitation as many product design variables, such as tolerance levels, assembly tasks sequence constraints, utilization of bottleneck resources, degree of variability of materials flows and process times etc., significantly affect design, operation and management of the manufacturing system, with direct consequences on WIP levels, lead times and machines utilization. All these factors bear a cost as well as an adverse effect on system performances, which traditional DFMA techniques fail to account.

In order to contribute to a solution of this problem, in this paper an innovative Design for Production (DFP) methodology is proposed which allows to carry out a more exhaustive comparative ranking of design alternatives based on manufacturing system performances as affected by product features, and which can be also utilized to supplement and extend traditional DFMA ranking techniques.

The paper is organized as follows. At first, the proposed approach is described. This includes a discussion of the relevant product design factors as well as the main production systems performance measures with their driving factors, also discussing the underlying cause and effects relationships. Then the set of new rating indices are described and, finally, a new DFP index is defined.

An Innovative Design for Production Methodology

The proposed methodology is based on the following steps.

- Selection of a set of relevant product design features (PDF) able to affect the manufacturing system.
- Definition of a set of production system performances (PSP) and their drivers.
- Analysis of the functional relationships between the above mentioned sets based on either theoretical approaches, industrial best practices and intuition. This kind of analysis enables to highlight which PDF affects which PSP, to what extent and why.
- Introduction of specific indices to quantify the expected impact of each PDF choice on the PSPs.

351

- Superposition of effects through a multicriteria rating approach incorporating the values of the indices previously computed for each PDF.

In the following, the above conceptual steps are briefly described and the proposed rating indices are detailed.

Product Design Features. A number of PDFs decided at the design stage may directly affect the performances of the manufacturing system. Relevant PDFs may be related to the components specification, the process plan and the product complexity level. The component-related features most affecting the PSPs are the specified design tolerances. Tolerances affect the manufacturing cost, the duration and variability of manufacturing and assembly tasks as well as all quality related costs. When tolerances are not consistent with the available process capability significant scraps and reworks also result leading to excess resource utilization and high flow variability. The process plan specifies the sequence of processing operations and selects the resources which will perform the operations. This defines the routing through the manufacturing system and affects utilization level and saturation of the resources involved. This, in turn, defines processing times, manufacturing costs, delay times due to set up and other causes, WIP levels and flow time.

The product complexity is dictated by the absolute number of components in a product, by the number of manufacturing or assembly operations, as well as by the interactions among manufacturing and processing tasks which may impose precedence constraints preventing an effective utilization of the resources. Assembly processes, moreover, complicate the flows in production systems because involve matching. In a matching operation, processing can not start unless all the necessary components are present, and shortage of any one of the components may disrupt the fabrication process [7]. Furthermore, product complexity increases the costs of supporting production. These costs, according to Ulrich and Eppinger [8], are related to the number of new parts, new vendors, new custom parts, new major tools (e.g. molds and dies) and production processes introduced in the manufacturing system, while standardization of components has long been recognized as the simplest way of reducing variety and, consequently, the logistic effort [9,10].

Production System Performances. Several well known rules describing manufacturing systems behaviour may be utilized to gain insights about the effects of design choices on PSPs [7]. The basic rule is the Little's Law relating WIP to system throughput (TH) and cycle time (CT), i.e.

$$\text{WIP} = \text{TH CT}. \tag{1}$$

Cycle time, also called manufacturing lead time, flow time or throughput time, is the sum of the times the entities spend at the stations making up the manufacturing process (less any overlap). At any given station it can be expressed as the sum of the actual process time and delay times:

$$\text{CT} = \text{process time} + \text{move time} + \text{queue time} + \text{set up time} + \text{wait-to-batch time} + \text{wait-in-batch time} + \text{wait-to-match time} + \text{wait-to move time}. \tag{2}$$

In turn, delay times may be related to process and flow variability and resource utilization level resorting to Kingman's equation [7]

$$\text{Queue delay} = \left(\frac{CV_a^2 + CV_e^2}{2} \right)\left(\frac{u}{1-u} \right)T \,, \tag{3}$$

where CV_a and CV_e are the coefficient of variation of arrival times and effective process times, while u is the resource utilization computed as the ratio of arrival rates of the entities at a station to the effective production rate and T is the nominal processing time. Eq (3) clearly states that CT is a highly non linear increasing function of the utilization (i.e is affected by bottlenecks and their saturation level) and depends from the sum of squares of the variability components. As a consequence, any PDF that determines high variability and high utilization is a cause of WIP accumulation and CT increase, eventually penalizing the performances of the manufacturing system. In this work the following PSPs have been identified as the most relevant to this application.

Throughput. This is limited by the resources capacity and availability but, for a given manufacturing system, is also determined by the process times. Traditional DFMA techniques already help in selecting design solution characterized by minimum parts count and low processing and assembly times. Therefore, this PSP will not be dealt with explicitly in this method.

Resource utilization. A high level of resource utilization means that there is not enough spare capacity to accomodate for peaks of manufacturing flows or resource downtime, which will inevitably cause queues and WIP accumulation.

WIP. Accumulation of work in process beyond the minimum level required to obtain the desired throughput, apart from space utilization, severely affects the system performances. WIP has a cost as inflates the capital immobilization and, owing to Little's law, increases cycle time, thus making the system less responsive.

Cycle time. It is important to both costs and revenues. Shorter cycle time means reduced costs (owing to less WIP, better quality, better forecasting and less scrap) and increased revenues (thanks to better responsiveness). According to Little's and Kingman's equations, cycle time is inflated by WIP, flow and process variability, high utilization levels.

Quality. This PSP measure is a complex characteristic of the product, the process and the customer. However, in its most basic meaning can be expressed as the fraction of parts that are made correctly the first time through the manufacturing system. Quality problems result from an incorrect matching between design tolerancing choices and the machine process capability, from out-of-control processes, as well as from an ineffective quality control which enables the flow of defective parts through further processing stages before being either reworked or scrapped (go-round scrap). Defective parts, however, heavily penalize the performances of the manufacturing system. Apart from the consequences of a poor-quality finite goods being passed to the customer, defective parts are either scrapped or reworked. This implies flow and process times variability and increased resources utilization which affects WIP and cycle time.

Customer service. It may be defined as the fraction of demand satisfied on time, but is a complex function of all others PSP. Therefore, it will not be dealt with explicitly here because it is a consequence of the values of its drivers.

Manufacturing cost. Manufacturing cost is the sum of direct resource-related processing costs, and indirect costs related to the inefficiency of the manufacturing system, such as costs related to quality and scraps, WIP and cycle time. Traditional DFMA techniques already help in selecting the lowest cost process options, while indirect costs are a consequence of the above discussed PSP. Therefore, this issue will not be explicitly dealt with in this paper.

Rating Indices
In order to assess the overall impact level that the PDFs characterizing a given design solution have on the considered PSP measures, a number of separate indices have been introduced in this work. The indices have the unit value as a lower bound, meaning that the higher the score the worst is the expected impact of the designer's choice on the affected PSP. Since the actual performances depend on the details of the production system structure and the planning and control decisions made, which may not be known in advance by designers, the indices are formulated in a simplified manner. This enables a relative comparison among competing alternative designs, requiring only a minor knowledge of the status and characteristics of the manufacturing system, including for example average resources utilization level, process capabilities etc. In fact, an accurate knowledge of such parameters is often not available at the design stage, and is difficult to obtain as many of the production systems parameters are time varying and depend from production planning and control decisions which may have not been already taken when the design decisions are finalized (i.e. production mix and volumes, actual routings etc.). Therefore, estimated average values may be utilized as well, when only a relative judgment is required to compare on the same basis several design alternatives. The proposed indices are summarized in Table 1 and briefly described below.

Resource utilization index (I_1). This index accounts for the number of resources which show a high level of utilization. It is defined as Eq. (4) in Table 1, where $f_U^{0.8}$ is the fraction of highly utilized resources, computed as the ratio of the number of resources in the process plan with an utilization level greater than 80% to the overall number of resources included in the process plan. The latter term in Eq. (4) is a penalty factor computed as the average value of the capacity increase ratings CIR_i of the high utilization resources, being n the number of high-utilization resources. For a generic resource, the CIR may assume value 1, 2 or 3 according to whether it is easy and low cost, or not, to increase the resource capacity in order to reduce its utilization level. The index penalizes the products which more extensively resort in their process plan to highly utilized resources, because this implies the likely occurrence of bottlenecks and queues with WIP accumulation and flow time increase. However, the score is further increased if it is not feasible a capacity increase.

Process tasks duration index (I_2). The index (Eq. 5 in Table 1) is the ratio of the total production tasks duration (i.e. the sum of nominal duration t_i of the tasks making up the production cycle) to the reference duration T_{REF}. T_{REF} is the minimal total tasks duration among the alternative design options available. In this case the index compares the total task duration of a given design solution to the best performing one. If a single design is evaluated, then $T_{REF} = 1$ and the index has an absolute numerical value in time units representing the minimum theorical cycle time. The greater the value of the index the worst, because long tasks duration involves higher resource saturation and increased throughput times.

Standardization index (I_3). The index (Eq. 6 in Table 1) accounts for the standardization of both components and processes. Selection of standard components in a design solution implies reduced logistic efforts and higher service level, while adoption of standard processes implies possibility of enjoying learning effects, resulting in lower variability of effective process tasks duration, lower scraps or reworks, and less delays (shorter setup etc.) thus reducing variability causes. In Eq. (6) f_{C-ST} is the percentage of standard components adopted in the examined product design, while f_{P-ST} is the fraction of standard processes specified in the process plan.

Process time variability Index (I_4). This index (Eq. 7 in Table 1) rates the variability in the duration of the production tasks. On the basis of expert opinion or historical data the value of the coefficient of variation CV (ratio of the average process task duration to the standard deviation) for each task is estimated. The tasks are then broadly classified as small variability (CV<1), medium variability (CV≈1) or high variability (CV>1) and the ratio f_{t-HV} of the number of high variability process tasks to the total number of process tasks is computed. The index penalizes design alternatives utilizing a high percentage of high variability tasks as this increases the queueing delay.

Setup Index (I_5). This index (Eq. 8 in Table 1) rates the set up efficiency of the proposed process plan and resource selection, when shared resources are utilized such as in job shop settings. The set up time for each operation on the selected resources is evaluated and classified as having short, medium or long duration. Then the ratio f_{t-HSU} of the number of operations having high setup times to the total number of process operations is computed. The index penalizes design alternatives utilizing a high percentage of resources with high setup times as this reduces the effective capacity of the resources thus increasing their saturation and utilization level.

Table 1. Summary of partial rating indices

Index	(Eq.)	Index	(Eq.)	Index	(Eq.)
$I_1 = \left(1+f_U^{0.8}\right)\left(\dfrac{\sum_i CIR_i}{n}\right)$	(4)	$I_2 = \dfrac{\sum_i t_i}{T_{REF}}$	(5)	$I_3 = \left[1+\left(1-f_{C-ST}\right)\right]\left[1+\left(1-f_{P-ST}\right)\right]$	(6)
	(7)		(8)		(9)
$I_7 = \left[1+\left(1-f_{ACQ}\right)\right]$	(10)	$I_8 = \dfrac{NO_j}{NO_{REF}}\dfrac{NC_j}{NC_{REF}}$	(11)	$I_9 = 1+\dfrac{1}{\sqrt[K]{NR}}$	(12)
$I_{10} = 1+f_{SR}$	(13)	$I_{11} = 1+\dfrac{T_M}{T_0}$	(14)	$I_{12} = 1+\dfrac{T_M}{T_{MAX}}$	(15)
$I_{13} = 1+\dfrac{1}{PI-1}$	(16)	$PI = \dfrac{1}{N}\sum_{i=1}^{N}\dfrac{L_i+U_i}{2}$	(17)	$RI = \sum_i \alpha_i I_i^{\beta_i}$	(18)

Process quality index (I_6). This is an index characterizing the likelihood of scrap and rework problems resulting from the designer specifying tolerances non consistent with the existing capabilities of the processes (Eq. 9 in Table 1). Let us define for each resource and process the process capability index $C_{pk} = [\min (X_M - LSL, USL - X_M)]/3\sigma$ being X_M and σ the process mean and standard deviation respectively, USL the upper specification limit and LSL the lower specification limit. Then the analyst can evaluate which process is to be considered as capable (when for instance $C_{pk} > 1.33$, or any other specified value) and which not, according to the specified tolerance levels. Then the ratio f_{p-C} of the number of capable processes to the total number of operations to be performed in the process plan is computed. The index penalizes design alternatives utilizing a high percentage of not capable resources as this increases effective process time variability and rework necessity, increasing resources utilization as well as flow variability and queueing delays.

Go-round scrap index (I_7). This is an index characterizing the capability of the process organization to early identify quality problems thus preventing that defective items undergo further value adding processes before being scrapped or reworked (Eq. 10 in Table 1). This in fact, would increase resource utilization, manufacturing costs and flow variability. Processes and resources are classified as either quality-accurate or not according to whether at each process step an accurate quality control is available or feasible. Then the ratio f_{ACQ} of the number of accurately quality controlled processes to the total number of process operations to be performed in the process plan is computed. The index penalizes design alternatives utilizing process plans where an accurate quality control can not be implemented as this may imply a high amount of go-round scrap with negative impact on costs, resource utilization and variability.

Product complexity index (I_8). This index (Eq. 11 in Table 1) penalizes design solutions having a high number of components or requiring many different operations, which is assumed as representative of a high level of product complexity. With reference to the *j-th* design solution, in Eq. (11) of Table 1, NO_j is the number of operations characterizing design solution j, NC_j the number of components, while NO_{REF} and NC_{REF} are respectively the number of operations and components of the alternative design solutions having the lowest number of operations and components. There is no need to assess the absolute value of NC_j or NO_j as this is already included in the standard DFMA methods.

Routing flexibility index (I_9). This index (Eq. 12 in Table 1) evaluates the possibility of implementing the process plan through multiple alternative routings thanks to the existence of redundant resources in the departments or the availability of flexible machines. The flexibility of the manufacturing system, in fact may improve the process performances when single resources become saturated or are unavailable [11]. The number of possible routings is computed as

$$NR = \prod_k N_{Rk}$$ where N_{Rk} is the number of parallel resources available to perform the *k-th* process

operation. In Eq. (12) K is the number of process steps where multiple resources are available. This index penalizes design solution for which there are few alternative routings owing to a small value of the average number of resources available at each process step.

Resource sharing index (I_{10}). This index (Eq. 13 in Table 1) accounts for the number of resources selected by the process plan which are shared among different products, where f_{SR} is the ratio of the number of shared resources to the total number of resources selected by the process plan. A high number of shared resources implies a high saturation due to frequent set ups and likelihood of large WIP and cycle times owing to the increasing of delays.

Station saturation index (I_{11}). This index (Eq. 14 in Table 1) compares the average duration T_M of the tasks assigned to a station in an assembly or manufacturing line, to the total time (takt time) allowed for each station T_0. T_M is computed as the average of single tasks times t_i, while T_0 is the reciprocal of the line production rate (which has to be estimated at the design time). While it is strictly $T_M < T_0$, the lower is T_M, the lower will be the duration of the generic task assigned to a station respect the maximum allowed time. This enables to have less saturated stations, i.e. fewer bottlenecks, or the possibility of better balancing the stations workload.

Process times variation index (I_{12}). This index (Eq. 15 in Table 1) relates the range of average process tasks duration to the average task duration T_M by comparing the duration of the longest task

T_{MAX} to T_M. If $T_{MAX} \gg T_M$ then the minimum task duration would be $T_{MIN} \ll T_M$ and there will be a high variability of the nominal duration of process tasks. This may have a positive effect because it would be easier to obtain an effective line balance.

Precedence constraints index (I_{13}). This index (Eq. 16 in Table 1) accounts for the average number of degrees of freedom (dof) available in the assignment of a task to a station given the precedence relationships existing among the tasks. The higher the dof the better because a more effective line balancing is possible. The average number of dof is computed resorting to the parallelism index PI introduced by Portioli and Singh [12] and shown in Table 1 as Equation (17), where N is the number of operations and U_i the number of dof at step i when the assembly sequence is built by selecting at each step the operation that yields the largest number of dof, while L_i is the number of dof at step i when the sequence is built by selecting at each step the operation that yields the smallest number of dof. PI is therefore the average number of possible task choices at each step. Referring to the graph of precedence constraints, a serial graph has PI = 1, while an entirely parallel graph has PI = (N+1)/2, being the actual PI within those two extremes. When PI >1 the index is computed as indicated in Eq. (16) of Table 1, while if PI = 1 then I_{13} = 3 to avoid an indefinite value. The index penalizes the design solutions characterized by strong precedence constraints among tasks.

The overall DFP rating index RI is then computed for any given design solution as a weighed average of its partial indices I_i as indicated by Eq. (18) in Table 1, with α_i being the relative weights associated the partial indices (where $\Sigma_i \ \alpha_i = 1$) and β_i some constants utilizable to modify the dynamic range of the partial indices in order to homogenize their numerical values. Usually $\beta_i = 1$. RI enables to assess the impact of each design solution on the overall performances of the manufacturing system. The lower the RI, the better a design solution is suited to minimize adverse impacts on the manufacturing system performances. This rating index may be thus utilized to supplement the rating obtained from traditional DFMA techniques which usually include only an evaluation of the components manufacturing and assembly costs.

Conclusions

In this paper a novel Design for Production methodology was proposed to supplement the traditional concurrent engineering techniques. The method was based on the identification of relevant product design features as well as production system performances and the identification of the relationship between such groups of parameters. Based on this analysis it was possible to identify which product feature had a potential of negative impact on the overall performances of the manufacturing system. As a consequence, a number of specific indices were introduced to empirically but quantitatively assess the expected impact of design choices on the management and operation of the manufacturing system. The proposed system appears easy to use, requires only a minimal knowledge of the manufacturing system details, and enables to compare competing design alternatives on the basis of a multicriteria approach. The method is intended to supplement traditional DFMA techniques which are focused on the minimization of components manufacturing and assembly costs but not at optimizing the interactions between product design and production system.

References

[1]   B. Prasad: *Concurrent Engineering Fundamentals: Integrated Product and Process Organization* (Prentice Hall, 1996).
[2]   G. Boothroyd, P. Dewhurst, W. Knight: *Product Design for Manufacture and Assembly* (Dekker, Inc., 1994).
[3]   S.K. Gupta et al.: Research in Engineering Design Vol. 9 No. 3 (1997), pp. 168-190.
[4]   J.G. Bralla (Ed.): *Design for Manufacturability Handbook* (McGraw-Hill, New York, 1999).
[5]   D. Corti, A. Portioli-Staudacher: Robotics and Computer-Integrated Manufacturing Vol. 20 (2004), pp. 265-280.
[6]   D.G. Bramall, K.R. McKay, B.C. Rogers, P. Chapman, W.M. Cheung, P.G.. Maropoulos: Int. J. Computer Integrated Manufacturing Vol. 16 No. 7-8 (2003), pp. 501-508.
[7]   W.J. Hopp, M.L. Spearman: *Factory Physics* (McGraw-Hill, 2001).
[8]   K.T. Ulrich, S.D. Eppinger: *Product Design and Development* (McGraw-Hill/Irwin, 2004).
[9]   K.R. Baker, M.J. Magazine, H. Nuttle: Management Science, Vol. 32, (1986) pp. 982-988.
[10]   H.L. Lee, C.S. Tang: Management Science, Vol. 43 (1997), pp. 40-53.
[11]   S.K. Das, P. Nagendra: Int. J. of Production Research, Vol. 31 (1993), pp. 2337-2354.
[12]   A. Portioli: Proc. Int. Conf. on Industrial Engineering and Production Management (Glasgow, UK 1999) Vol. 1, pp. 342-349.

Productive Area Utilisation – Towards Measuring the Effectiveness of Facilities Layout

Dhamodharan Raman[1] and Sev V Nagalingam[2]

Centre for Advanced Manufacturing Research, University of South Australia,
Mawson Lakes Boulevard, Mawson Lakes SA 5095, Australia.
Dhamodharan.Raman@postgrads.unisa.edu.au[1] and Sev.Nagalingam@unisa.edu.au[2]

Abstract. In order to improve the effectiveness of a facilities layout, it is necessary to measure the effectiveness of the existing layout. Since, available layout measurement methods are only suitable for construction type layout problem, it is necessary to have an appropriate measurement method to determine the effectiveness of an existing layout by considering all significant factors. Hence, a set of three layout effectiveness factors and their measurement methods are developed in our research. The proposed method will enable the decision-maker of a manufacturing enterprise to analyse their existing layout in three different aspects to decide whether the layout is to be re-designed for productivity improvement or maintained as it is. Due to the depth of analysis involved in evaluating the factors, this paper, mainly discusses about measurement of single factor, productive area utilisation, which is developed in respect to the objective of improving the effectiveness of utilised area.

Keywords: Area utilisation, Effectiveness, Facilities Layout, Analytic Hierarchy Process.

Introduction

A manufacturing enterprise's facilities layout is one of the key areas which have a significant contribution towards manufacturing productivity in terms of cost and time. Tompkins [1] stated that 10 - 30% of the material handling cost (MHC) can be reduced by having an effective facilities layout. Benjaafar [2] argued that a layout has a direct impact on the operational performance, as measured by manufacturing lead time, throughput rate, and work-in-process. Thus it is evident that improving effectiveness of a layout is critical for productivity improvement in a manufacturing enterprise.

Oxford dictionary (2006) describes efficiency as "working productively with minimum wasted effort or expense", while effectiveness as "producing a desired or intended result". In other words, the efficiency is about doing the things right, whereas the effectiveness is about doing the right things. However, being efficient at a wrong thing is unproductive. Hence, it is clear that providing an enterprise with an effective layout (right thing) will act as a foundation upon which the enterprise can perform the production activities efficiently (doing the things right). When these terms are applied to the facilities layout, effectiveness can be defined as the capability of achieving the objectives of a layout and such objectives are [3]: Minimising MHC, Improving flexibility for arrangement and operation, Utilising the available area most effectively, Minimising investment in equipment, and Minimising overall production time.

Several methods [4-6] are available to measure the layout effectiveness. However, these methods help measure the effectiveness relatively with respect to alternate solutions and select an effective layout among these solutions for a construction type layout problem. Generally, in a construction type layout problem, where new layouts are considered, decision-makers evaluate a set of layout proposals and select one layout as effective with respect to particular factors. However, no one has attempted to measure the effectiveness of an existing layout (improvement type layout problem), which is essential to decide whether there is a need to re-design the existing layout for effectiveness improvement. Although factors like empty travel of material handling equipment, layout flexibility and area utilisation have a significant impact on the effectiveness of a layout, most of the existing methods considered only the MHC as the effectiveness factor. Therefore, there is a necessity to develop an appropriate measurement method to determine the effectiveness level of an existing layout taking into consideration the key factors that significantly impact on a layout design. Consequently, we identified three factors that can be used to assess a layout's effectiveness with respect to the objectives of a layout, which were outlined in the previous paragraph. The identified factors are: Facilities Layout Flexibility, Closeness Gap and Productive Area Utilisation (PAU). The 'closeness gap' considers the objectives of minimising the MHC and the total production time. The 'facilities layout flexibility' considers the objective of improving flexibility for arrangement and operation. Whereas, improving the effectiveness of utilised area is considered in developing the PAU. As we focus on the existing layout, the objective of minimising the investment in equipment is not considered in our effectiveness measurement. The methods to measure these factors are then developed in our research which will enable the decision-makers to analyse their existing layout in three different aspects; based on which a decision-maker of an enterprise can decide whether the layout has to be re-designed or the current layout is acceptable. However, in this paper we discuss about the measurement method of PAU. A detailed information on 'facilities layout flexibility' has been addressed by Raman *et al*. [7] and a research journal paper on 'closeness gap' is under review for publication.

Background on Productive Area Utilisation

Designing facilities layout involves allocating the area required at appropriate location for various needed production activities and administration activities. The production activities are related to the production at the shop floor and these are executed and supported by various elements such as machines, material handling equipment, material storage and others in a shop floor. Hence, the area utilised for these elements are defined as the productive area. In general, area utilisation level is measured only in terms of available free area [8]. Correspondingly, Lin and Sharp [9] used two measures to calculate the area utilisation: free area-ratio, which is free area available divided by total area available; and free area distribution within the shop floor. However, these two measures can lead to wrong conclusion that larger the area occupied, higher the area utilisation and these measures do not provide adequate insight into the utilisation effectiveness as they focused only on characteristics of available free area rather than the characteristics of utilised area. This is regardless of the fact that the characteristics of utilised area are crucial to measure the utilisation effectiveness; as all utilised areas might not add value to the enterprise. Moreover, calculating the available free area and its concentration help assess the possibility for future expansion but not the area utilisation. Thus, a true measurement of utilisation can be achieved only by measuring the effectiveness with which the area is utilised for various elements. As a result, in our research, the factor PAU is developed and it is measured similar to the lean manufacturing concept of waste minimisation. In lean manufacturing concept, activities performed in an enterprise are grouped either as value adding or non-value adding activity and through appropriate actions, the non-value adding activities are eliminated in order to minimise the waste. Similarly in our method to measure PAU, the area utilised for various activities are measured as either value adding or non-value adding areas in order to minimise the area utilised for non-value adding activities/ elements.

Measurement of Productive Area Utilisation

While measuring the total area required for a production system, the layout designers first measure the area required for individual workstation [1]. Secondly, the area required for departments are calculated, which includes the area required for all workstations in that department and relevant service requirements. Thirdly, the area required for inter and intra-functional material flow is assessed. Based on the above procedure, the area required for different purposes are categorised as in Table 1 along with the elements that contribute to each group.

Table 1: The purpose groups and their elements of productive area

Purpose groups	Elements of purpose group
	Space utilised for:
Machine area	(i) Machines , (ii) Clearance between machines, (iii) Machine access and (iv) Operator
Tool area	(i) Machine tools and (ii) Jigs and fixtures
Material storage area	(i) Raw material, (ii) Work-in-process material, (iii) Finished material and (iv) Scrap material
Material transportation area	(i) Material handling equipment and (ii) Material handling (Aisle)
Quality inspection area	(i) Quality inspection and its equipment and (ii) Reworking
Inactive area	(i) Inactive machines/ material handling equipment and others

The total productive area considering these purposes/elements are then categorised into value adding area and non-value adding area. A ratio of the total value adding area to the total utilised productive area gives a value for PAU. The obtained PAU value provides a measure of the layout effectiveness in terms of area utilisation.

Thus, higher the PAU value, higher the layout effectiveness.

PAU = Total value adding area / Total utilised productive area   (1)

Where;

Total utilised productive area = Total value adding area + Total non-value adding area (1a)

The total utilised productive area does not include the available free area, as in our approach it is considered when computing the other factor 'facilities layout flexibility'. However, there are two major issues to be considered when the above categorisation is used for calculating the PAU:

1. Although quantitative data may be obtained for the purpose groups in an enterpriser, it is very difficult to get the quantitative data individually for the elements of these groups. Therefore, a qualitative measurement is needed to measure the PAU.
2. Area utilised for any purpose group cannot be absolutely concluded either as value or non-value adding area. Because, area utilised for each element contains both value and non-value adding area with certain proportion, which varies with the purpose. Even for the same purpose, different enterprise will have different proportion. Therefore, a quantitative measurement of such varying proportion is very difficult. In lean manufacturing, material handling is considered as a non-value adding activity. Based on that, the entire transportation area could have been concluded as non-value adding. However, material transportation is necessary in an enterprise; therefore, a distinction has to be made on these decisions.

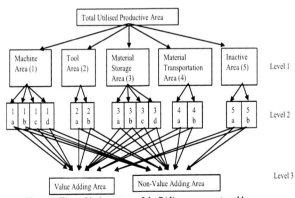

Figure 1: Hierarchical structure of the PAU measurement problem

These two critical issues can be overcome by using the analytic hierarchy process (AHP), as it is a well known and proven method to quantify the qualitative measures [10].

Application of AHP for PAU measurement. Application of AHP in our approach includes three steps: Structuring the hierarchy, Calculating the relative area utilisation for groups and its elements, and

Table 2: Relative area utilisation measurement scale

Verbal judgment of relative area utilisation measurement, when the area utilised for the purpose:	Comparison Value
PG_i is **equal** to the purpose PG_j	1
PG_i **slightly more than** the purpose PG_j	3
PG_i **notably more than** the purpose PG_j	5
PG_i **much more than** the purpose PG_j	7
PG_i **extremely more than** the purpose PG_j	9
Intermediate values between two adjacent judgments, to provide additional levels of discrimination	2, 4, 6, 8

Calculating the area utilised for value and non-value adding activities.

Step 1: Structuring the hierarchy. The hierarchical structure of the measurement problem is depicted in Fig.1. Level 0 represents overall objective of the measurement problem. At the first level, the purposes groups that contribute to the total utilised area are considered, while the second level details the individual elements that contribute to each group. The last level of the hierarchy identifies each element as either value adding or non-value adding area. This typical hierarchy is structured using the data obtained from an existing layout of a medium sized manufacturing enterprise. However, the number of groups and/ or elements involved may differ among enterprises. Because, data for same set of elements may not be available in all enterprises. Certain elements might have been combined or further classified by some of the enterprises. However, the AHP provides flexibility to change the contents of the hierarchy as deemed by the decision-maker.

Step 2: Calculating the relative area utilisation for groups and its elements. Once the hierarchy is structured, the decision-maker determines the relative weights of elements in Level 1 and Level 2 using a pair wise comparison. A relative measurement scale, which is given in Table 2, provides a guideline for the decision-maker to perform the pair wise evaluation [10]. Saaty's eigenvector method is then applied to get a priority weight for both groups and their elements. In addition the consistency ratio is computed to make sure that the ratio is less than or equal to 0.1, in order to have a satisfactory pair-wise comparison. The priority weights of the groups at Level 1 show their contribution, in terms of area, towards the total utilised productive area. Similarly, the priority weights of the elements at Level 2 express their importance in contributing to their corresponding purpose groups. However, if quantitative values for the groups at Level 1 are available, the priority weight for this level is obtained by normalising the available values. If it is not available, the AHP pair wise comparison is used.

Step 3: Calculating the area utilised for value and non-value adding activities. The priority weight for value and non-value adding purposes, in regards to each individual element at Level 2, are then calculated using the AHP. The individual priority weight of value adding and non-value adding purposes are then computed using Equations 2 and 3.

$$(ValueAdding)_{pg} = \sum_{ge=1}^{npg} W_{pg} * VAA_{ge} * U_{ge}$$

(2)

$$(Non-ValueAdding)_{pg} = \sum_{ge=1}^{npg} W_{pg} * NVAA_{ge} * U_{ge}$$

(3)

These values are then calculated for each purpose group and then combined to get the total value adding area and non-value adding area for the enterprise by using Equations 4 and 5.

Total Value adding area $= \sum_{pg=1}^{AG} (ValueAdding)_{pg}$

(4)

Total Non - value adding area $= \sum_{pg=1}^{AG} (Non - ValueAdding)_{pg}$ 　　　　　　　(5)

Where;

AG	Total number of Purpose Groups
npg	Total number of Group Elements in the Purpose Group 'pg'
$NVAA_{ge}$	Priority weight for non-value adding area in regards of a group element 'ge' at Level 2 of AHP
VAA_{ge}	Priority weight for value adding area in regards of a group element 'ge' at Level 2 of AHP
$(ValueAdding)_{pg}$	Proportion of value adding area in the Purpose Group 'pg'
$(Non-ValueAdding)_{pg}$	Proportion of non-value adding area in the Purpose Group 'pg'
U_{ge}	Priority weight for a group element 'ge' at Level 2 of AHP
W_{pg}	Priority weight for an AHP group 'ag' at Level 1 of AHP

The obtained values for value adding and non-value adding areas are then used in Equation 1 in order to calculate the PAU.

Case Study
A particular functional unit of an existing facilities layout in a medium sized manufacturing enterprise, which is located in South Australia, Australia, is used to validate the proposed PAU measurement method. The value adding and non-value adding areas are calculated according to the three steps described earlier. The priority weights for groups at Level 1 are calculated from the measurements obtained from the existing layout. However, the calculation at Levels 2 and 3 are performed using the pair wise comparison method. As an example, the pair wise comparison for the elements of machine area and material storage area groups are given in Tables 3 and 4 respectively. Thus obtained values are then applied in the Equations 2 and 3. Considering the purpose group 'machine area':

Value Adding 　　　= [0.44*0.49*0.99] + [0.44*0.05*0.88] + [0.44*0.10*0.86] + [0.44*0.36*0.89] = 0.415

Non-Value Adding = [0.44*0.49*0.10] + [0.44*0.05*0.12] + [0.44*0.10*0.14] + [0.44*0.36*0.11] = 0.0478

Table 3: Pair wise comparison for elements of machine area group

Pair wise comparison (A)					Weight (B)	(C)= A*B	(D) = C / B
MACHINE AREA	MACHINES	CLEARENCE	ACCESS	OPERATOR			
MACHINES	*1.00*	8.00	5.00	2.00	0.49	2.10	4.27
CLEARENCE	0.13	*1.00*	0.33	0.17	0.05	0.20	4.10
ACCESS	0.20	3.00	*1.00*	0.14	0.1	0.40	4.04
OPERATOR	0.50	6.00	7.14	*1.00*	0.36	1.61	4.46
Max Eigen Value (λmax)	= (∑D) / 4 = 4.22			Consistency Index (CI)	= (λmax - 4) / 3 = 0.07		
Random Index (RI) = 0.90				Consistency Ratio (CR) = CI / RI = 0.08			

Similarly, the above values are calculated for all other purpose groups. Then by applying Equations 4 and 5: *Total value adding area* = 0.4154+0.0528+0.305+0.0176+0.0030 = 0.5193 and *Total non-value adding area* = 0.0478+0.0127+0.2695+0.1424+0.0270= 0.4994.
Thus obtained values show that 49.94 % of the total utilised productive area is allocated for non-value adding purposes with the PAU value of 51.93%. Moreover, the proposed method can assesses the non-value adding contribution of each individual element at Level 2. From these individual

values, the decision-maker is able to identify the elements whose area allocation has to be minimised in order to minimise the non-value adding area.

Table 4: Pair wise comparison for elements of material storage

MATERIAL STORAGE AREA	RM	WIP	FINISHED	SCRAP		Weight
RM	1.00	0.14	5.00	2.00		0.17
WIP	7.01	1.00	9.00	8.00		0.68
FINISHED	0.20	0.11	1.00	0.33		0.05
SCRAP	0.50	0.13	3.00	1.00		0.1
CI = 0.07			CR = 0.08			

For an example, if work-in-process (WIP) consumes more area, the decision-makers will re-evaluate their production planning to reduce the total area required for WIP. At the same time the layout also has to be redesigned, because Benjaafar [2] argued that poor layout is a contributing factor that leads to a higher amount of WIP in the shopfloor. Consequently, the increase in WIP increases the proportion of non-value adding area.

Conclusion

Measuring the current effectiveness level will enable the decision-makers in a manufacturing enterprise to analyse and decide whether the existing layout is to be re-designed for productivity improvement or the current layout is still economically viable. However, from the review of related literature, it is apparent that the factors used in the existing measurement methods for layout effectiveness are more suitable for construction type layouts rather than improvement type. Besides, available methods considered only the MHC as the factor to determine the effectiveness, although other factors like empty travel, layout flexibility and area utilisation have a significant impact on the effectiveness. Hence, in order to measure the effectiveness of an existing facility layout and to overcome the identified drawbacks, we proposed three factors such as Facilities Layout Flexibility, Closeness Gap and Productive Area Utilisation (PAU).

In general, the area utilisation is measured only with respect to free area availability and its characteristics, which does not reflect on measuring the effectiveness of area utilisation but leads to the wrong conclusion that the higher the area occupied, higher the area of utilisation. Moreover, calculating the free area and its concentration help calculate the possibility of future expansion but not the effectiveness of the area utilisation. However, PAU factor helps the decision makers overcome that shortcoming in measuring the occupied areas for various production purposes in terms of either value adding and non-value adding. Currently, we are in the process of integrating these three factors into a decision support system, which is being developed using the Visual Basic.Net, to evaluate the overall effectiveness of an existing layout.

References

[1]   Tompkins, J.A., et al., *Facilities Planning*. Third ed. 2003, New Jersey: John Wiley & Sons.

[2]   Benjaafar, S., Modeling and Analysis of Congestion in the design of Facility Layouts. *Management Science*, 2002, **48**(5): p. 679-704.

[3]   Francis, R.L., McGinis, L.F., and White, J.A., *Facility layout and location - An analytical approach*. 1992, Englewood Cliffs, NJ: Prentice Hall.

[4]   Lin, L.C. and Sharp, G.P., Application of the integrated framework for the plant layout evaluation problem, *European journal of operational research*, 1999. **116**: p. 118-138.

[5]   Raoot, A.D. and Rakshit, A., A fuzzy approach to facilities lay-out planning. *International Journal of Production Research*, 1991, **29**(4): p. 835-857.

[6]   Yaman, R., Gethin, D.T., and Clarke, M.J., An effective sorting method for facility layout construction. *International Journal of Production Research*, 1993, **31**(2): p. 413-427.

[7]   Raman, D., Nagalingam, S., and Chiu, M. A Fuzzy Rule Based System to Measure Facility Layout Flexibility, in *18th International Conference on Production Research*. 2005. Fisciano (SA), Italy: University of Salerno.

[8]   Hu, M.H. and Wang, M.J., Using genetic algorithms on facilities layout problems. *International Journal of Advanced Manufacturing Technology*, 2004, **23**: p. 301-310.

[9]   Lin, L.C. and Sharp, G.P., Quantitative and qualitative indices for the plant layout evaluation problem. *European journal of operational research*, 1997, **116**: p. 100-117.

[10]   Saaty, T.L., *The Analytic Hierarchy Process*. 1980, New York: McGraw-Hill.

Intelligent Design
and Simulation

An approach for modelling and simulation of variable structure manufacturing systems

Olaf Hagendorf[1,2,a], Thorsten Pawletta[2,b], Sven Pawletta[2,c], Gary Colquhoun[1,d]

[1]Liverpool John Moores University, School of Engineering, UK

[2]Wismar University, RG Computational Engineering and Automation, Germany

[a]enrohage@livjm.ac.uk, [b]pawel@mb.hs-wismar.de, [c]s.pawletta@et.hs-wismar.de,
[d]G.J.Colquhoun@ljmu.ac.uk

Abstract. Discrete Event Simulation (DES) is an established method for manufacturing system analysis. The development of complex DES models requires a modular modelling and simulation approach. Modularity supports clear model structures, provides high model reusability and enables independent development and testing of components. A comprehensive theory of modular hierarchical modelling and accompanying simulator algorithms was introduced by Zeigler with the Discrete Event Specified System (DEVS) formalism. A disadvantage of the classical DEVS theory is the lack of capability to formulate complex structure variability. This paper provides a brief summary of the classical DEVS theory and introduces extensions to give comprehensive support to modelling and simulation of complex structural changes in modular hierarchical systems. The paper concludes by discussing the advantages of the variable structure modelling approach using an application in the photo-finishing industry.

Keywords: variable structure systems, discrete event simulation, DEVS, DSDEVS.

1 Introduction

Many real systems change their structure during lifetime. These can be technical systems [1] such as manufacturing, computing or communication systems, digital controllers [2] or natural systems such as in biology and ecology [3]. In a manufacturing environment structure changes can occur at different levels. At the management level shop floors can be opened or closed, at the shop floor level different production sections can be used to produce the same product and at the production level different operation sequences can be performed to produce a specific product or machines and operators can be replaced or moved to another production cell.

Traditional modelling and simulation systems provide only support for static structure models [4] [5]. That means, they offer modelling methods to specify modules or components with a behavioural dynamic and aggregation methods to compose them to complex structures. But the composition structure itself cannot be changed during model execution. Of course with these systems it is also possible to emulate structural system dynamics. But the specification has to be transformed to the behavioural modelling level. Sometimes it is hard to describe complex structural dynamic such as the various production possibilities in manufacturing systems on the behavioural modelling level. Furthermore, this procedure often leads to complex model components and reduces the component generality that results in reduced component reusability.

The goal of this paper is to introduce a structure dynamic modelling approach based on Zeigler's Discrete Event Specified System (DEVS) formalism. Chapter 2 briefly summarizes general aspects of the classical DEVS theory and its accompanying simulation approach. In chapter 3 the extension of the classic DEVS concept to a Dynamic Structure DEVS (DSDEVS) approach is introduced and the advanced modelling possibilities are discussed. After that the dynamic structure modelling approach is demonstrated using a complex photo-finishing laboratory application in chapter 4.

2 Discrete Event Simulation

General View. Discrete event systems are characterized by a continuous time base and discrete state changes [4]. In Discrete Event Simulation (DES) practice there are four dominant modelling techniques, called modelling worldviews [5]. These are process-interaction method, event scheduling method, activity scanning and the three phase method. A specific, material oriented view of the process-interaction method is often called transaction oriented. Each of the modelling worldviews has specific advantages and disadvantages and makes certain forms of model description more naturally expressible than others. In manufacturing simulation the process-interaction method is widely used. In modern simulation tools it is often combined with component-oriented approaches. The DEVS theory is able to handle all four above mentioned worldviews [4]. One of the most general and powerful features of the DEVS formalism is the modular, hierarchical model construction.

DEVS. Every DEVS system is described by two different types of entities, atomic and coupled models. Each model type has a clearly defined input and output interface and the internal structure is completely encapsulated. An atomic model describes the behaviour of a non- decomposable entity via event driven state transition functions. A coupled model describes the structure of a more complex model through the aggregation of several entities and their couplings. These entities can be atomic models as well as coupled models. All this together allows the modular and hierarchical construction of complex systems.

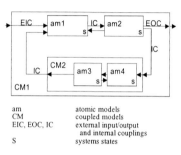

am	atomic models
CM	coupled models
EIC, EOC, IC	external input/output and internal couplings
S	systems states

Fig. 1 Example DEVS model

Figure 1 shows a simple DEVS model, a production cell with integrated queues, a server with quality checker and a rework server. The complete cell is depicted by the coupled model *CM1*. The model has an external interface with one input and one output port to receive and send work pieces. It contains two atomic models and one coupled model, the queue *am1*, the server *am2* and the rework facility *CM2*. The coupled model *CM2* consists of two further atomic models the queue *am3* and the rework server *am4*. When *CM1* receives a message (a work piece) at its input port it is forwarded over the external input coupling to queue *am1*. When *CM2* generates an output message at its output port, a reworked work piece is forwarded to the second input port of *am1* over an internal coupling.

The DEVS theory in [4] defines a simulator concept for the computation of modular-hierarchical DEVS models. Figure 2 shows the computational model structure of the model example from figure 1 according to the DEVS simulator concept. Each atomic model is connected to a *simulator* entity. This entity handles messages like 'initialisation', 'compute next state' or 'get time of next event'. Each coupled model is connected to a *coordinator* entity. It has the same interface as a *simulator*. But the *coordinator* entity handles messages, not itself, but forwards them to its subordinated *coordinators* or *simulators*. On top of the hierarchy the *root coordinator* initiates, controls and ends a simulation cycle. With this

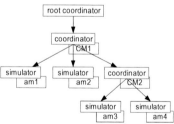

Fig. 2 Hierarchical simulator structure of the example DEVS model in fig.1

366

concept the modular hierarchical structure of the model remains a part of the computational model during simulation runtime in contrast to a transformation of the modular model to a monolithic computer implemented model.

Formal Concept of DEVS Theory. The description of an atomic model is a 7- tuple [4]:

$$AM = (X, Y, S, \delta_{ext}, \delta_{int}, \lambda, ta) \tag{1}$$

X, Y and S specify the sets of discrete inputs, outputs and states. The δ_{ext} function handles external input events. It can induce an internal state change by generating an internal state event. An internal state event can induce an output event and is handled by the state transition function δ_{int}. Output events are generated using the output function λ. After external and internal events the internal events are rescheduled with the time advance function ta.

The description of a coupled model is a 9-tuple [4]:

$$CM = (d_n, X_N, Y_N, D, \{M_d \mid d \in D\}, EIC, EOC, IC, select) \tag{2}$$

d_n represents the name of the coupled model, X_N and Y_N are the sets of inputs and outputs, D specifies the name set of subsystems, M_d represents a subsystem, EIC, EOC and IC are the external input, external output and internal couplings and finally the *select* function prioritize concurrent internal events of the subsystems.

The classic DEVS approach only supports the specification of a behavioural system dynamic in atomic systems and the specification of a component aggregation in coupled systems. It is not possible to describe a structural system dynamic, such as the deletion or creation of components or couplings, at the coupled system level, although all necessary structural information is available during runtime. The only possibility to realise a structure dynamic is to specify it with logical constructs at the atomic model level. This abolishes the advantages of reusability and model clarity and increases modelling complexity.

3 Dynamic Structure Devs

Several approaches extend the classic DEVS to Dynamic Structure DEVS (DSDEVS). Barros [2] [6] and Pawletta [1] [7] use an extension of the coupled system definition while the atomic model definition remains unchanged. Uhrmacher [3] and others introduce an agent based approach. They define extensions for both atomic and coupled systems. But in general all extensions allow nearly the same possibilities to specify structural dynamics at coupled system level such as creation, destroying, cloning and replacement of subsystems, movement to other coupled systems, and changes in the couplings and interface definition of subsystems.

This research is based on the approach of Pawletta, where a coupled model is defined by the following 6-tuple:

$$CM_{dyn} = (\{d_n\}, S_N, \delta_{x\&s}, \delta_{int}, \lambda, ta) \tag{3}$$

with

$$S_N = X_N \times Y_N \times H_N \times D \times \{M_d \mid d \in D\} \times EIC \times EOC \times IC \times select \tag{4}$$

The current structure of a coupled model is interpreted as a structure state $s \in S_N$. The additional introduced set H_N defines specific structure related state variables. Structure changes can be induced by external, internal or external events of subordinated components. In analogy to the dynamic of atomic systems internal structure events are scheduled by a time advance function ta

and their proposed structure changes are specified with a structure state transition function δ_{int}. Output events caused by internal events are generated using the output function λ. Structure state changes induced by external events or output events of subcomponents are handled by the transition function $\delta_{x\&s}$. However it is unreasonable to make changes in the subsystem set or coupling relations by this function directly. This could lead to ambiguous event handling because external events could influence simultaneously the dynamic of subcomponents and the structure state. That's why the $\delta_{x\&s}$ function is only allowed to modify structure related state variables in the set H_N to trigger an internal structure state event at the same time. Simultaneous internal events of sub-models and of the coupled model itself are controlled by the *select* function.

The structure variable modelling approach and its accompanying simulation algorithms were developed as a Matlab toolbox using Matlab's object oriented programming features. The theoretical *simulator* and *coordinator* definitions are directly mapped to software classes. User specified models have to be derived from these predefined classes. Matlab as a common scientific and technical programming environment offers a large amount of computation methods and toolboxes, e.g. for optimisation and parallel computing. With the implementation of the DSDEVS approach as a Matlab toolbox it is possible to use these toolboxes within the DSDEVS simulator [7] [8].

4 Application Example

Photo-finishing laboratories specialise in high volume production of some thousands to millions of pictures per day. As a consequence of the significant changes in the photography market during recent years they use a mixture of analogue and digital production facilities. Because of the growing complexity of these systems it is no longer possible to organise production manually in an optimal way as was usual some years ago. To analyse the system, optimise throughput and costs it is necessary to simulate the production process.

Figure 3 shows the product flow through the different departments of a laboratory. It depicts only an overview of the high volume product flow. The material arrives over several channels at the login department. After logging in and sorting the product mixtures, the single orders are combined to batches, depending on the order type (e.g. analogue or digital), the film type (e.g. 135

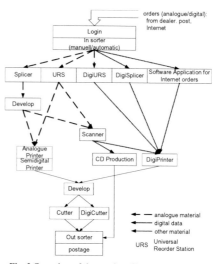

Fig. 3 Overview of the product flow and the departments of a photo-finishing laboratory

or APS) and the end product (e.g. paper width). It is done with different machine types: *(i)* a splicer combines undeveloped film rolls, *(ii)* a universal reorder station (URS) combines analogue reorders to a roll of film strips, *(iii)* a digital URS scans the analogue reorders and produce a digital batch, *(iv)* a digital splicer handles data carriers (CDs, flash cards etc.) and *(v)* software applications combine digital images received over the internet. Undeveloped analogue batches have to be developed and analogue material can be scanned. Next steps are printing, paper development and cutting. Finally all items are packed into a customer envelope.

Figure 4 shows the overview of a variable structure model for a photo-finishing process. It specifies *(i)* alternative ways to handle incoming material, *(ii)* some ways can be used in a different

368

sequence but with the same result, *(iii)* the number of operators is less then necessary to handle all machines at the same time and so they have to move between departments and *(iv)* machines can be removed from or put back into production.

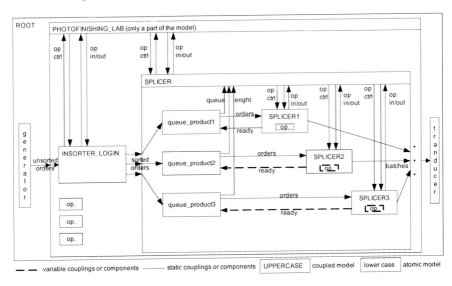

Fig. 4 Part of a photofinishing lab DSDEVS model

Because of the complexity of the complete system figure 4 shows only a fragment of the complete DSDEVS model, mainly the splicer department. The atomic model *generator* generates unsorted orders of different types as input events of the production process model *PHOTFINISHING_LAB*. The coupled model *INSORTER_LOGIN* implements the manual and automatic order login and sorting operations. The coupled model *SPLICER* depicts the splicer department. It needs a minimum limit of sorted orders in its input queues to work smoothly. The outputs of this model go to next sub-models which are not represented in figure 4. An operator is depicted by an atomic model *op*. The operator handling, requesting them from or sending to other departments, is implemented at a general level for the complete laboratory in the *PHOTFINISHING_LAB* model and at a lower level in the department sub-models such as *INSORTER_LOGIN* and *SPLICER*. Control messages for operator handling are sent over the *op ctrl* couplings and the operator sub-models *op* themselves over the *op in/out* couplings. At production start there is not enough material available in the splicer queues. Consequently operators have to be moved to the *INSORTER_LOGIN* model to increase the sorting throughput. *SPLICER2* and *SPLICER3* models are deactivated and the appropriate connections are deleted. When the length of *queue_product2* and/or *queue_product3* is long enough the coupled model *SPLICER* requests one or two *op* models from the parent model *PHOTOFINISHING_LAB*, adds them to the *SPLICER X* sub-model, activates the *SPLICER X* sub-model and creates the necessary couplings. When the length of the *queue_productX* model falls below a defined limit the *op* model will be released to the parent model, the *SPLICER X* sub-model will be deactivated and the internal coupling to the *queue_productX* sub-model will be disconnected.

In contrast to traditional modeling concepts the DSDEVS approach maps the real system structure one to one in the model. Not only the behavioural system dynamics of machines and products are directly depicted in the model but also the structural system dynamics of the production management and the movement of shared resources are comprehensible. The entire model structure and individual components reflect system reality in a more natural manner. Thereby independent component development, testing and reuse are improved.

5 Conclusions

The DEVS formalism with the extensions to DSDEVS by Pawletta was briefly introduced and the advantages of the variable structure, hierarchical modelling approach were shown using a manufacturing application. The real system structure with its structural and behavioural system dynamics maps one to one onto the model. Modules can be developed and tested independently of other parts in the complete system which eases the model development process and supports extensive model reuse. They can form a model library to ease the creation of further manufacturing systems. The modelling approach and its necessary simulation algorithms are implemented as a Matlab toolbox. Due to homogeneous integration in Matlab it can be combined with all other Matlab computation methods. The next step in this research programme is the development of optimisation methods in combination with the structure variable modelling and simulation approach to investigate structure optimisations of complex modular, hierarchical systems.

References

[1]   Pawletta T., Lampe B., Pawletta S., Drewelow, W. (2002) *A DEVS-Based Approach for Modeling and Simulation of Hybrid Variable Structure Systems.* In: Modeling, Anlysis, and Design of Hybrid Systems. Engel S., Frehse G., Schnieder E. (Ed.), Lecture Notes in Control and Information Sciences 279, Springer, pages 107-129

[2]   Barros F.J. (2004) *Modeling and Simulation of Digital Controllers for Hybrid Dynamic Structure Systems.* In: Proc. of CSM2004 - Conference on Conceptual Modeling and Simulation, Part of the Mediterranean Modelling Multiconference (I3M), Genova, Italy, October 28-31, 2004, Vol.1, pages 296-302

[3]   Uhrmacher A.M., Arnold R. (1994) *Distributing and maintaining knowledge: Agents in variable structure environment.* In 5th Annual Conference on AI, Simulation and Planning of High Autonomy Systems, pages 178-194

[4]   Zeigler B.P., Praehofer H., Tim T.G. (2000) *Theory of Modelling and Simulation.* Academic Press

[5]   Banks J., Carson II J.S., Nelson B.L., Nicol D.M. (2003) *Discrete-Event System Simulation.* Prentice Hall

[6]   Barros F. J. (1996) *Modeling and Simulation of Dynamic Structure Discrete Event Systems: A General Systems Theory Approach.* PhD thesis, University of Coimbra

[7]   Pawletta T., Deatcu C., Hagendorf O., Pawletta S., Colquhoun G. (2006) *DEVS-Based Modeling and Simulation in Scientific and Technical Computing Environments.* In: Proc. of DEVS Integrative M&S Symposium (DEVS'06) - Part of SpringSim'06, Huntsville/AL, USA, April 2-6, 2006, pages 151-158

[8]   Hagendorf O., Colquhoun G., Pawletta T., Pawletta S. (2005) *A DEVS – Approach to ARGESIM Comparison C16 'Restaurant Business Dynamics' using MatlabDEVS.* Simulation News Europe, no.44/45, (December)

A new TRIZ-based approach to design concept generation

D.T.Pham[1] and H.Liu[1, a]

[1]Manufacturing Engineering Centre, Cardiff University, Cardiff CF24 3AA, UK

[a]liuh@cf.ac.uk

Abstract. This paper presents a novel approach to producing creative designs of mechanical products during the conceptual design phase. The approach employs a knowledge base comprising rules that implement a Behaviour-Entity-Constraint (BEC) representation of modified TRIZ inventive principles. The BEC representation enables the generation of innovative solutions based on TRIZ knowledge. The objective is to retrieve existing inventive principles automatically as solutions according to design requirements.

Keywords: Conceptual Design, Creative Design, TRIZ.

Introduction

Conceptual design plays a very important role in the early stages of design. Conceptual design involves generating ideas or solutions, evaluating the outputs generated and exploring the best alternatives. The generation of solutions is where engineers require creativity and imagination to achieve the design objectives while satisfying the constraints [1]. This step is one of the most critical in conceptual design. Many tools and techniques developed by researchers to date have focused on solution generation, including computer-aided techniques and human-oriented creative thinking tools. This paper presents a new TRIZ-based methodology that integrates both computer-aided and human-oriented approaches to help designers solve invention problems and generate new design solutions.

Creative design with TRIZ

As mentioned above, previous research in innovative design can be classified into two areas: human-oriented and computer-aided approaches. A human-oriented approach would focus on assisting designers to improve their creativity and ability to solve problems, while a computer-oriented approach would concentrate on design optimisation. For example, a computer-aided creative design technique has been developed called evolutionary design [2]. This technique employs optimisation algorithms such as the genetic algorithm (GA) for evolving optimum design solutions. Human-oriented software tools include "Invention Machine" from TRIZ and "Visual Mind" from Mind Mapping. Both tools are used in industry but are somewhat limited as research tools due to their "closed" structures. On the other hand, there is a variety of techniques to help people to generate new design ideas, such as Morphological Analysis, Brainstorming, Lateral Thinking, Attribute Listing, Checklisting, Synectics etc. [3, 4]. This large collection of techniques can be classified into two groups: disciplined thinking and 'out-of-the-box' or divergent thinking. Disciplined thinking relies on logical or structured ways of creating a new product or service. Examples of this approach are Morphological Analysis and Reframing. One of the well-known 'out of the box' thinking methods is lateral thinking [5], which can be used to break out of patterned ways of thinking.

However, each type of approach has its strengths and weaknesses. Logical, disciplined thinking is very effective in making products and services better. However, it can only achieve so much before all practical improvements have been carried out. Divergent thinking can generate completely new concepts and ideas, and create exceptional improvements to existing systems. In the wrong place, however, it can be sterile or unnecessarily disruptive. TRIZ [6] is the acronym for "Theory of Inventive Problem Solving," in Russian. TRIZ integrates the advantages of disciplined and divergent thinking. For example, a contradiction matrix (CM) provides a structured way of solving technical problems while the Ideal Final Result (IFR) visioning method is a divergent thinking technique based on the philosophy of "breaking psychological inertia". Although TRIZ provides a number of tools for helping people generate new ideas, it has its limits. For example, tools encapsulated in TRIZ are difficult for people to understand and apply in practice. However, compared to other creative thinking tools, TRIZ is still one of the most powerful tools for generating ideas during conceptual design.

Behaviour-Entity-Constraint (BEC) representation

Modification of TRIZ inventive principles based on Behaviour-Entity (BE) representation
Among the comprehensive array of TRIZ tools, the set of 40 Inventive Principles is a useful creativity tool for a variety of problem solving situations. However, they are often criticised for their illogical sequencing, their level of overlap, the gaps that they contain, and most of all, the difficulty people experience in remembering them all. A systematic structure of modified inventive principles has been proposed in [7] to address this issue. Each principle is a method for solving problems. This normally consists of a behaviour and an entity or an attribute, expressed by two sets of relations between predicates and objects respectively. The expressions are arranged in a two-dimensional matrix, the Inventive Principles Matrix (IPM), according to the predicates and the objects that they contain. This symbolic Behaviour-Entity representation is able not only to reduce the amount of repeated information in the inventive principles, but also to facilitate the evolution of current inventive principles by integrating other TRIZ or TRIZ-derived tools [7].

Functional objectives and contradiction constraints in BEC representation
In a TRIZ matrix of contradictions, see Figure 1, the rows indicate system features that the designer typically wants to improve. Columns refer to undesired effects arising from improvements to a row parameter. Normally, the functional objective of a design is specified independently as a function of the design. The task is to investigate solutions that meet this individual objective. The links between objective and principles are shown in the CM.

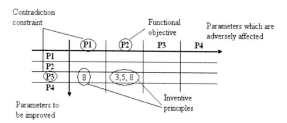

Figure 1. Segment of Contradiction Matrix (CM)

A contradiction is a pair of parameters in conflict with each other. Each matrix cell points to principles most frequently used in patents to resolve a contradiction. There are links to principles in the CM so that the principles can be retrieved according to the corresponding contradiction. Therefore, a contradiction is a constraint on a principle, called contradiction constraint. In addition, there is a second kind of constraint not involving contradictions. These constraints are functional objectives specified by the designer and represented along the first row and first column of the CM.

Behaviour, entity and constraint constitute a complete representation of an inventive principle in the form of a rule in the knowledge base. The new principle does not only contain information on a solution, but also information on constraints on the solution.

Modified list of functional objectives

The latest version of the CM is "Matrix 2003" [8], which offers forty-eight system features assembled into six groups and their mapping relationships with principles. Pahl and Beitz [9] also present a different category of design objectives and constraints. The list of system features from Matrix 2003 and the design objectives and constraints from Pahl and Beitz are integrated to make the list of functional objectives more comprehensive. These integrated objectives are used as parameters in an improved contradiction matrix (ICM). The list of functional objectives is shown in Table 1.

Table 1. List of functional objectives (adapted from Matrix 2003 [8] and Pahl and Beitz [9])

Physical parameters	1. Weight of Moving Object 2. Weight of Stationary Object 3. Length of Moving Object 4. Length of Stationary Object 5. Area of Moving Object 6. Area of Stationary Object	7. Volume of Moving Object 8. Volume of Stationary Object 9. Shape 10. Amount of Substance 11. Amount of Information
Performance-related parameters	12. Duration of Action - Moving Object 13. Duration of Action - Stationary Object 14. Speed 15. Force/Torque 16. Use of Energy by Moving Object 17. Use of Energy by Stationary Object	18. Power 19. Stress/Pressure 20. Strength 21. Stability 22. Temperature 23. Illumination Intensity
Efficiency-related parameters	24. Function Efficiency 25. Loss of Substance 26. Loss of Time 27. Loss of Energy	28. Loss of Information 29. Noise 30. Harmful Emissions 31. Object Generated Side Effects
Maintenance-related parameters	32. Adaptability/Versatility 33. Compatibility/Connectability 34. Ease of Operation 35. *Maintenance* 36. Reliability	37. Repairability 38. Security 39. Safety/Vulnerability 40. Aesthetics/*Ergonomics* 41. Object Affected Harmful Effects
Manufacture/ cost-reduction parameters	42. Manufacturability 43. Accuracy of Manufacturing 44. Automation 45. Productivity *46. Transport*	*47. Assembly* *48. Expenditure* 49. System Complexity 50. Control Complexity
Quality control-related parameters	51. Ability to Detect/Measure 52. Measurement Precision	*53. Quality Control*

Note: Underlined words indicate the objectives and constraints from Pahl and Beitz

TRIZ-based design concept generation

Compared with text, the BEC representation of inventive principles offers a more precise and systematic way to retrieve information because it stores keywords of a solution without any redundant information. Boolean search is selected as the search strategy. This technique retrieves those expressions that are true for a query expressed in terms of keywords and logical connections. A conceptual design problem is translated into a set of queries stating the entities of the design problem and constraints on the solution. The standard format of a query is Q = (e$_1$ OR e$_2$...OR...e$_j$)

AND (c_1 OR c_2 ...OR... c_i). This query will retrieve any principles of which the symbolic expression comprises (e_1 OR e_2...OR...e_j) in the set of entities and (c_1 OR c_2 ...OR...c_i) in the set of constraints.

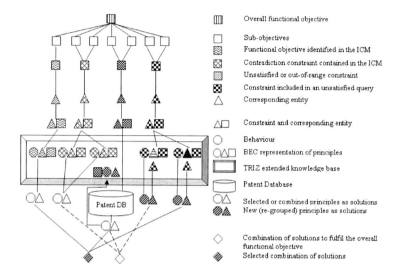

Figure 2. Flow diagram of the TRIZ-based design concept generation process

Figure 2 shows the flow of the proposed TRIZ-based design concept generation procedure. The process starts with analysing the overall functional objective of a design. That objective is then divided into several sub-objectives. Some sub-objectives may conflict with one another. These contradiction constraints or single sub-objectives together with the corresponding entities comprise the query to be presented to the TRIZ knowledge base. The knowledge base consists of BEC representations of modified TRIZ inventive principles in the form of rules. The results are those combinations of BE-represented principles that can satisfy the query. Four different situations may occur. The first two situations happen when the query can be satisfied and correspond to the two kinds of constraint. The third situation arises when constraints are not contained in the ICM or corresponding principles cannot be found to satisfy constraints in that matrix. The fourth situation occurs when queries cannot be satisfied. These four situations (illustrated in Figure 2) are discussed below:

Situation 1: Satisfied Queries --- Functional objectives identified in the ICM. This situation is when a sub-objective identified in the ICM is specified and no negative effects can be found. In this situation, principles can be obtained from the TRIZ knowledge base according to the query. This takes place commonly in conventional design because it is relatively simple for designers to work out what they wish to improve. The only problem is that many principles may be generated. The decision concerning the most suitable solution is left to the designer.

Situation 2: Satisfied Queries --- Contradiction constraints contained in the ICM. This situation happens when two of the sub-objectives in the ICM are conflicting. In this case, corresponding principles can be retrieved from the TRIZ database. The designer will generate the most suitable solution by selecting and combining principles from the database. This is a situation where innovative concepts will emerge.

Situation 3: Unsatisfied or Out-of-Range Constraints. In some cases, the objective or constraint that has been specified could not be matched with any of the general parameters defined in the ICM. Alternatively, certain principles used to solve design problems are not included in the ICM. A blank cell in the matrix shows that there are no principles to satisfy the corresponding contradiction.

As the original CM and inventive principles were derived from the patent database, the latter could be added to the system as a secondary database. A query for this database would still be a combination of design constraints and corresponding entities. The result would be a patent that might offer a suitable solution to the design problem. This new BE-represented solution and the original contradiction constraint form a rule that can be stored into the TRIZ knowledge base for future use.

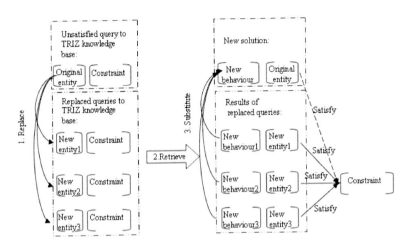

Figure 3. Generation of new design solutions based on BEC representation

Situation 4: Unsatisfied Queries. In this case, there is no matching principle that can be found to satisfy both the constraints and entities at the same time. The new TRIZ-based approach is applied to generate feasible solutions by re-organising the three elements in the BEC representation (Figure 3). The hierarchical structure of the list of entities has been explained in [7]. If a query is not satisfied, each original unmatched entity is replaced with its neighbour (entity at the same level) or its parent (entity at a higher level) until a matching solution is found. The aim of this step is to find similar solutions that could resolve the same contradiction. Combining a new behaviour with the original entity may make up an effective solution to the required constraint. Like many other creative thinking techniques, this process may not be sufficient for completely solving a design problem, but it does help the designer to generate new potential solutions

The final solution to the given design problem is obtained by combining the solutions generated in all the situations applicable to the problem.

Conclusion

This paper has proposed a TRIZ-based approach to retrieve inventive principles as solutions to a design problem automatically. The TRIZ Contradiction Matrix (CM) and inventive principles are used to develop this TRIZ-based concept generation approach by adding constraints to the standard Behaviour-Entity representation of TRIZ. The original TRIZ CM has limitations, including its inadequate number of row or column parameters and its lack of inventive principles to resolve contradictions or solve design problems. These limitations have been overcome by modifying the existing TRIZ inventive principles, enlarging the CM and applying the improved CM as the core of an expandable and customised TRIZ knowledge base. Future work will focus on integrating the method presented in this paper with concept evaluation and design collaboration.

Acknowledgement

The authors are members of the EU-funded FP6 Network of Excellence for Innovative Production Machines and Systems (I*PROMS). The work was partly supported by the ERDF Objective 1 SUPERMAN project and the EPSRC Innovative Manufacturing Research Centre at Cardiff University.

References

[1]   B. Hyman: *Fundamentals of Engineering Design*. (Prentice-Hall: Englewood Cliffs, New Jersey 1998).

[2]   J. Vancza: Artificial intelligence support in design: a survey. Keynote paper at the *1999 International CIRP Design Seminar*, http://www.sztaki.hu/~vancza/papers/AIsurvey1.pdf (Enschede, The Netherlands 1999)

[3]   C-C. Wei; P-H. Liu; C-B Chen: An automated system for product specification and design, *Assembly Automation*, Vol. 20, No. 3, July 2000, pp. 225-233(9)

[4]   Proctor T: New development in computer assisted creative problem solving, *Creativity and Innovation Management*, Vol. 6, No. 2, June 1997, pp. 94-98(5)

[5]   E. De Bono: *Lateral Thinking: Creativity Step by Step*. (Harper and Row Publishers, New York 1970)

[6]   G. Altshuller: Translated by A. Williams. *Creativity as an Exact Science*. (Gordon and Breach, New York 1988)

[7]   D.T. Pham, H. Liu: I-Ching-TRIZ inspired tool for retrieving conceptual design solutions. Proc. *2nd Virtual International Conference on Intelligent Production Machines and Systems*, http://conference.iproms.org (July 2006)

[8]   D. L. Mann, S. Dewulf, B. Zlotin, A. Zusman: *Matrix 2003: Updating the TRIZ Contradiction Matrix*. (CREAX Press, Belgium 2003)

[9]   G. Pahl, W. Beitz: *Engineering Design: A Systematic Approach*. (Springer, London 1995)

A model-based robot programming approach in the MATLAB/Simulink environment

Gunnar Maletzki[1, a], Thorsten Pawletta[1, b], Sven Pawletta[1, c], Bernhard Lampe[2, d]

[1]Wismar University of Technology, Business & Design, PF 1210, 23952 Wismar, Germany

[2]University of Rostock, Inst. of Automation, 18119 Rostock, Germany

[a]g.maletzki@et.hs-wismar.de, [b]pawel@mb.hs-wismar.de, [c]s.pawletta@et.hs-wismar.de, [d]bernhard.lampe@uni-rostock.de

Abstract. Based on the traditional off-line robot programming approaches, this paper presents a concept for a simulation model-based robot control. The practical use is demonstrated by applying this approach to an industrial robot cell.

Keywords: process control, task oriented programming, discrete event simulation, model re-use, robot programming

Introduction

Progressive robotics research opens up new application fields incessantly. Hence, demands on the development of robot controls are increasing. Easy programming and integration of different external hardware are of particular importance. In this context it is desirable to offer a task oriented robot programming environment. That means programming should be facilitated using task oriented procedures instead of writing single commands. The aim of every control implementation is to realise easy, safe, fast and cost-effective design and commissioning of robot applications. Therefore, it is essential to avoid re-implementations in the entire development process.

Different methods are available for the programming of robot controls. According to [1] these are divided in *on-line* and *off-line* methods. In contrast to on-line methods where the robot is required, off-line methods support the development of controls without a robot. Online-methods include: *(i)* programming with examples and *(ii)* programming via training, while *(iii)* robot oriented programming and *(iv)* task oriented programming are basic off-line methods. The simulation model-based development of controls belong to the off-line methods.

Robot oriented programming is based on the imperative programming model. It specifies explicit movement commands. *Task based programming* is based on a declarative description of complex tasks. Efficient design algorithms have to be available, because there are no path trajectories, action sequences etc. described in a task based specification. The execution of a declarative task specification is realised by a transformation algorithm. Thus a robot oriented control programm is generated or single control sequences are transmitted directly to a robot controller. Today different computer science concepts are used for the development and realisation of task oriented robot programming approaches [2, 3, 4]. First simulation model-based control concepts are demonstrated in [5, 6, 7]. They focus on the pure realisation of controls. Objects of this research are *(i)* the prevention of re-implementations, *(ii)* the development of a task oriented programming approach, *(iii)* methods for an easy integration of different hardware and *(iv)* concepts for the combination with complex analysis algorithms.

Section two of this paper summarises important off-line methods for robot programming including simulation model-based control. Afterwards, section three introduces a prototype development for the simulation model-based robot control concept and section four presents its usage by a material-related placement problem.

377

Important off-line methods for robot control programming

Traditional robot oriented control development. Realisation of simple robot controls starts with a specification of the control tasks. Afterwards the specification is implemented in a manufacturer specific programming language. Before commisioning, the implementation is tested using special robot simulation environments. In contrast to that, the realisation of complex controls demands the usage of additional discrete event oriented simulation models in the design phase. Subsequently the implemented strategies are specified in a formal and textual way. These workings are often made by design engineers, while control implementation and robot commissioning is done by control specialists. Fig. 1 shows the basic development cycle.

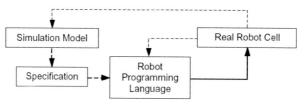

Fig. 1 Simulation & traditional robot programming

The described procedure for complex controls is partially problematic. On the one hand there are often problems caused by communication between design engineer and control specialist. On the other hand there is an extraordinary effort of programming. In the design phase, the control strategies are detailed implemented by means of simulation tools. Afterwards, this strategies are re-implemented using a special robot programming language. The integration of different external hardware and complex computation algorithms is another problem. The robot programming languages normally support only the integration of hardware, that is offered by the manufacturer.

Model-based control design with automatic code generation. With scope to embedded systems the model-based design of controls with automatic code generation is established in a large field of applications. The basic principle is shown in Fig. 2.

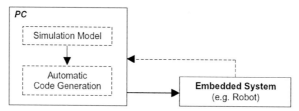

Fig. 2 Basic principle of the model-based design
with automatic code generation

Model-based design of controls uses abstract methods for specification such as petri nets or state machines and it supports an extensive off-line test. After testing, the executable target-code for the embedded system is generated by using special compilers. Generally the target-code of embedded systems enables a communication with the host-system. This chain of development is timesaving and it faciliates a high quality of the control software through an intensive test on the model level. A basic problem is the verification of the automatic generated code.

378

In the first instance, model-based design with automatic code generation offers advantages concerning the reduction of re-implementations. In regard to the robot programming it also could be a good base for a task oriented programming. For a mobile robot with embedded controller, a first prototype implementation of this approach is presented in [8]. Nevertheless this attempt seems to be problematic in general robotics. The implementation and verification of powerful code generators is enormous labour-intensive. Probably that is the reason why no code generators are avialable for common robotic systems.

Simulation model-based robot control. The concept of simulation model-based robot control is developed to negotiate the disadvantages of traditional robot programming and automatic code generation. Simulation models developed in the design phase are structured in a way, that it is possible to extend them stepwise to control programs. Important prerequisites are *(i)* the strict separation of material flow and information flow and *(ii)* a consequential component oriented modeling. The structure of a simulation model-based control program is shown in Fig. 3.

Each real process element, e.g. buffer, robot, server etc. is modeled as a separate component in the material flow modul. These components represent the states and the time behaviour of the real process elements. The control modul includes the control strategy and it analyses control relevant *state values* of the material flow components and sends *control values* back. To realise the extension of a simulation model to a control program it is essential to implement a process interface and a Real-Time synchronisation. A more detailed description of the simulation model-based control approach is presented in [9].

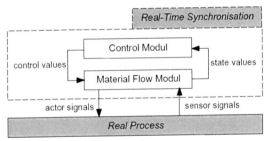

Fig. 3 Structure of a simulation model-based control program

Prototype-Development

Test and validation of the model-based robot control concept is carried out through a prototype-development basing on a KR3 robot from KUKA. For robot programming, KUKA offers a special imperative programming language (KRL[1]). The KRL is similar to the programming language C, however with less functionality. The possibility of generating visualisations or to execute an effective debugging is not supported in the KRL environment. Furthermore, the integration of additional hardware is limited on KUKA products. According to Fig. 4, the robot cell was extended by adding an PC including the software environment Matlab/Stateflow for two reasons. First, to compensate the mentioned disadvantages above and second to realise simulation model-based control approaches.

---

[1]KUKA Robot Language

379

The KUKA controller is connected with the PC via serial interface. Subsequently, an interpreter was implemented in KRL to realise a bi-directional communication. The interpreter runs on the KUKA controller and is responsible for the identification and execution of commands that are transmitted by the PC. The control program is developed using Matlab or Stateflow. Hence it runs on the PC. It is feasible to implement task based statechart libraries and complex controls can be implemented using predefined statecharts according to Fig. 6. The realisation of controls applying Matlab/Stateflow enables a varied integration of external hardware and complex analysis algorithms. As example, the integration of a radio camera is described in the subsequent chapter.

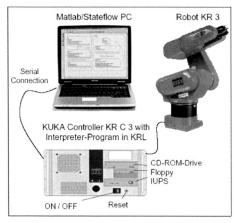 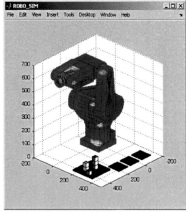

Fig. 4 Integration of Matlab/Stateflow PC,   Fig. 5 Visualisation of the KR3
            KRL Controller and robot   robot cell

Summarizing, there are the following important advantages: *(i)* a continuous homogeneous software basis from the early design to operation phase, *(ii)* an interactive and graphical development of controls with comfortable debugging, *(iii)* a comprehensive test of control strategies using simulation, *(iv)* perpetuation of security given by the KRL through workspace supervision, checking the final position switches of every robot axis etc. *(v)* the possibility of using Matlab-toolboxes from design to the operation. The limited communiction performance via serial interface could be a practical problem of the described prototype-development. A possible answer to this dilemma is the usage of the USB interface. But the existing applications did not show any runtime problems up to now.

To facilitate the development and test of simulation model-based controls, a visualisation toolbox was created. Thus, it is possible to visualise a robot cell including all movement actions. Fig. 5 exemplifies a visualisation of the KR3 robot cell. The robot control commands available in the visualisation environment have the same semantics as the commands transmitted to the real robot cell via serial interface. Thereby, the control programs can be developed and tested independently from hardware for different process scenarios.

Application example

The described control concept is validated by different application examples for a prototype robot cell. Subsequently, a material-related placement problem is presented. According to Fig. 5, the robot cell consists of an input buffer with different transport units and three output buffer. The robot has to sort the transport units according to given characteristics, e.g. the colour, in the three output buffer. Therefore, a picture-taken sensor is used to identify the transport units in the input buffer. The sensor is represented by a radio camera, which is mounted on the TCP[2] of the robot. The software-technical integration of the camera is realised by a Matlab-Mex-Function. Hence, important picture informations are interpreted with the Image Processing Toolbox. A switchable electromagnet, that is also mounted on the TCP, is used to pick and place the transport units.

The simulation model-based control program of the robot cell consists according to Fig. 3 of a control modul, which contains the task oriented control logic and a material flow modul. The material flow modul is configured in a component-oriented way. According to the real elements of the robot cell it contains one input buffer, one robot and three output buffer. Each material flow element consists of a High-Level Part and a process interface. The proces interface implements the gateway to the real process object. The High-Level Part saves state informations of the real process object and it communicates with other material flow elements as well as with the control modul. The control modul generates control informations (*control values*) on the base of the available state informations (*state values*). The *control values* are transmitted to the High-Level Parts of the material flow modul. The process interfaces generate the real actor signals.

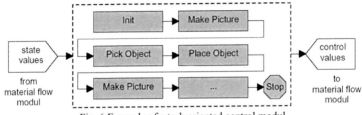

Fig. 6 Example of a task oriented control modul

The control modul, illustrated in Fig. 6, shows in extracts the task oriented control logic of the robot cell. Each task modul can poll state information and return control information. The complete task consits of parametrisable subtasks, which are executed sequentially in this case. Task moduls are pre-implemented in a statechart-library. The parametrisation is processed by graphical masks. The subtask *Init* is necessary for the initialisation of the robot cell. The task sequence *Make Picture*, *Pick Object* and *Place Object* describes the identification of one transport unit and its transport to a specific output buffer. The type of the transport unit and the address of the output buffer are specified by the parametrisation of each subtask. Finally, the subtask *Stop* represents the end of a complete placement task.

An important advantage of the described environment is the possibility to formulate control tasks, which consist of sequential and parallel subtasks, because finite state machines in Stateflow allow usage of parallel states. So it is possible to execute a collision detection simultaneously to the characterised placement task.

---

[2]Tool Center Point

Summary

Stepwise enlargement of simulation models from the design phase to robot control software allows design and commissioning of complex robot controls in an easier, cost-effective and faster way. Furthermore, the simulation model-based control approach supports a complex simulative control test. The introduced prototype development demonstrates that advantages of manufacturer specific robot programming languages such as workspace supervision and final position checking of robot axis are not lost. An essential advantage opposite to the model-based development with automatic code generation is, that no complex code generators have to be created. Simply a relative straightforward interpreter has to be developed. But the control of hard real-time processes can be problematic. The whole concept is based on a close coupling between robot controller and host-PC and particularly the communication link can form a performance bottleneck. However, all examined applications did not cause any runtime problems.

The simulation model-based control approach offers an excellent basis for advanced task oriented robot applications. Since the entire control program is implemented within a simulation environment, powerful planning algorithms can be realised using predictive simulation and optimisation models. This should be investigated in the further research phase. On more focus is put on speech control of robots, which is of particular importance for service robots. Within this research, an interface to connect a speech analysis system with the prototype robot cell was developed [10].

References

[1] H.-J. Siegert, S. Bocionek: Robotics: Programming Intelligent Robots, Springer Pub., 1996. (in german)

[2] K. Diethers et al.: A New Framework for Task Oriented Sensor Based Robot Programming and Verification, IEEE Int. Conf. on Advanced Robotics, pp. 1208-1214, Portugal, 2003.

[3] G. Kronreif, M. Fürst: TCP-based Communication for Task Oriented Programming and Control of Heterogenous Multi-Robot-Systems, Proc. of the 32 [th] Int. Symp. on Robotics, pp. 90-95, Korea, 2001.

[4] R. Simmons, D. Apfelbaum: A Task Description Language for Robot Control, Proc. of the Conference on Intelligent Robotics and Systems, 7 pages, 1998.

[5] H. Praehofer, G. Jahn, W. Jacak, G. Haider: Supervising manufacturing system operation by DEVS-based intelligent control, IEEE Computer Society Press, pp. 221-228, 1994.

[6] F. Gonzales: Intelligent control of flexible manufacturing systems using a distributed architecture, Proc. of the 17th International Conf. on Production Research, 12 pages, 2003.

[7] M. Kremp, T. Pawletta, S. Pawletta, G. Colquhoun: Investigation of different strategies for simulation-based control of material flow systems, Frontiers in Simulation - Simulationstechnik 17. Symp., SCS Publishing House, pp. 373-378, Ghent, 2003. (in german)

[8] Robot Car: An Embedded Target Example, The MathWorks, 2002 http://www.mathworks.com/products/rtwembedded/demos.html.

[9] M. Kremp, T. Pawletta, G. Colquhoun: Simulation-model-based process control of discontinuous production processes, In: Proc. of 4th Int. Conf. on Manuf. Research, Liverpool, UK, September 05-07, 2006, (submitted for publication, 2006/03, 6 pages).

[10] M. Reppenhagen: Integration of audio technologies in engineering-environments and technical applications, Diploma Thesis, Hochschule Wismar, 2006. (in german)

Combining knowledge-based engineering and case-based reasoning for design and manufacturing iteration

Marcus Sandberg[1, a] and Michael M. Marefat[2, b]

[1]Luleå University of Technology
Polhem Laboratory
SE-971 87 Luleå
Sweden

[2]The University of Arizona
Intelligent Systems Laboratory
1230 E. Speedway Boulevard
Tucson, AZ
United States of America

[a]marsan@ltu.se, [b]marefat@ece.arizona.edu

Abstract. Design has a major impact on downstream manufacturing activities, therefore computer and knowledge-based design support in early product development are crucial for long-term success in the manufacturing industry. Work on knowledge-based design and manufacturing exists, though too little supports iteration systematically. The aim of this paper is to provide a systematic approach for computer-based design and manufacturing iteration. This paper presents a way to combine the strengths of case-based reasoning (CBR) and knowledge-based engineering (KBE) to enable true design and manufacturing iteration in a CAD-environment. A KBE module generates a geometry definition. A CBR module then retrieves recent manufacturing plans, adapts the most feasible plan and evaluates the manufacturability. If manufacturing is not feasible, redesign suggestions are automatically generated for the designer. When a manufacturing plan is accepted, KBE enables a swift "what-if" analysis of the geometry to enhance the plan further. This method contributes by combining the strengths of CBR and KBE in a CAD-environment. An example case study of sheet metal products at a Swedish automotive industry demonstrates the potential for industry implementation. Using the proposed method, the designer can optimize the geometry for manufacturing activities and thereby reduce development cost.

Keywords: Design support, design and manufacturing iteration, knowledge-based engineering, case-based reasoning.

Introduction

The success of manufacturing companies depends on their ability to use computer-based design support and proper decision-making in the early stages of product development [1]. Iteration cycles between design and manufacturing are crucial to avoid costly design flaws, though, paradoxically, time to market needs to continuously decrease. Traditional computer-based design and manufacturing iteration using CAD/CAM often suffer from too many time demanding and repetitive steps. The functionality of CAD/CAM tools is continuously developing thanks to today's hi-tech computers, but the methods to use these tools have not developed at the same speed. Therefore, the research community has focused on new design support methods for several decades. Relevant research on design support for early design and manufacturing evaluation exists [2-4], but few have focused on design and manufacturing iteration. Therefore, this paper focuses on iteration by combining the swift "what-if" synthesis and analysis of KBE with the systematic and plan-based analysis of CBR. An approach to use KBE and CBR to conduct several different design and manufacturing iterations is proposed. A case study investigates the proposed approach in cooperation with a Swedish automotive manufacturer. As several iterations (automatic, plan-based, "what-if") take place, the possibilities of finding all opportunities to enhance the design for manufacturability exist.

Literature Review

This section focuses on research for computer-based design support for design and manufacturing activities in early product development.

Work for holistic design support methods exists, e.g. [1], and it is up to researchers to define the method details by means of industry close research. Shehab and Abdalla present a design support system for machining cost assessment, where inexperienced users can generate a design and evaluate manufacturing cost [2]. This system supports automated iteration, since redesign is suggested if the cost is deemed too high. Sandberg et al. describe a system for design, manufacturing, performance and maintenance evaluation based on the KBE "what-if" analysis, i.e. a geometry change can directly be evaluated by means of parametric rules [3]. This work enables iterations to be performed in each discipline and manufacturing iteration is supported by an automated "what-if" analysis. Both [2; 3] lack plan-based manufacturing iteration. Sharma and Gao present a rule- and plan-based approach to support the early design stages of machined components coupled to a PDM-system [4]. Even though this approach may enable automated iteration (both plan-based and "what-if"), their paper does not focus on iteration.

Therefore, iteration focused approaches are still needed.

Combining KBE and CBR

This section describes the proposed approach and neighbouring subjects to use KBE and CBR for design and manufacturing iteration. The fundamentals of KBE and CBR are outlined, followed by the presentation of the proposed approach. Lastly, the case study at a Swedish automotive manufacturer is explained.

Short Introduction to KBE and CBR.

KBE. The Concentra Corporation founded the embryo of knowledge-based engineering in 1984, while releasing one of the first commercial CAD-systems with a closely integrated rule base module [5]. In KBE, an object-oriented approach is used to code rules that can automate repetitive CAD-tasks. This is for the designer to make visible manufacturability effects due to design in the CAD-environment and also reduce loss of knowledge due to staff turnover, as knowledge is acquired and formalised in the KBE system. One challenge is to make the code easy to maintain.

CBR. Case-based reasoning is based on ideas from manual development where recent solutions (cases) are often modified to fit new requirements. By implementing algorithms to retrieve recent cases and adapt the best to the new requirements [6], areas such as manufacturing planning have benefited from CBR research. One challenge is to integrate CBR techniques in the industry, as CBR-algorithms are often research lab centric stand-alone modules.

Proposed Approach. This section describes the proposed approach for design and manufacturing iteration. A flowchart of KBE, CBR and manual activities is depicted in Fig. 1. The flowchart consists of three phases: *KBE synthesis and routine analysis*, *CBR* and *KBE "what-if" analysis*.

KBE Synthesis and Routine Analysis. This phase starts with "Specify Input Requirements" and ends with assessment of "Routine Verification". The user initially gives input to the system, typically geometric properties (e.g. dimensions and tolerances) and manufacturing constraints (e.g. acceptable cost) through a graphical user interface (GUI). Based on these inputs a geometry is generated. If errors are found due to general design for manufacturing (DFM) guidelines, e.g. a hole is too close to a bend line to comply with given form tolerances, an error message is generated explaining which rules are violated and how to change the input to resolve the problem, *automated iteration*. The next step is "Routine Verification", where automated and semi-automated (contains automated and manual steps) manufacturing assessment are based on manual calculations or applications that, for example, take the geometry as input and assess its manufacturability. Routine verification can also be automated verification through applications based on methods in FEA, CFD or modal analysis that are controlled by the KBE system. If the user finds the results from the routine verification to be non-satisfactory, iteration is started and the user must do a redesign, *manual iteration*, otherwise the CBR phase is entered.

CBR. The CBR module takes the design definition parameters from the KBE module as input and retrieves the manufacturing plans for similar cases (designs). If no other plan is adequately similar, an arbitrary plan is retrieved. The arbitrary plan then needs to be manually modified to suit the new design features. The "Adapter" then chooses the most similar plan according to a similarity metric and adapts the plan. If the adapter fails to adapt, feedback is given to the retriever to help avoid retrieval of non-manufacturable plans, and the "Design Definition Change Proposal" algorithm is triggered, *automatic iteration*.

KBE "what-if" analysis. The final phase visualises the retrieved and adapted manufacturing plan as well as the geometry for the user who can do swift manufacturing "what-if" analysis by changing the last design features in the feature-history and directly see the resulting change in the plan. If the user finds the plan unsatisfactory, new fundamental design (the first features in the feature tree) inputs can be altered, *manual iteration*. If the plan is deemed satisfactory the user can decide if the plan is unique enough to be saved in the "Manufacturing Plan Case Base" and continue to the next design phase.

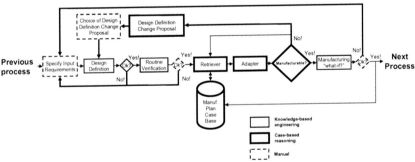

Figure 1. Proposed approach process flowchart for KBE, CBR and manual activities. Arrows that describe start of iteration are in boldface.

Case Study. A case study at a Swedish automobile manufacturer was preformed to initially investigate the potential of the proposed approach. Brackets are common components in an automotive structure; hence, bracket design was to be supported in the case study. Knowledge

385

acquisition was performed through interviews with industry staff within design and manufacturing along with studying product specifications containing requirements for the brackets and the components to fasten to the bracket (e.g. the signal horn and circuit breakers). The acquired knowledge was then formalised to suit the KBE-module *UGS NX Knowledge Fusion* [7], and *Python* for the CBR algorithms [8]. A GUI was developed using the *UI styler* application in UGS NX; see Fig. 2. In Fig. 2, the user has received a partly adapted plan, since the "Total manufacturing cost" is higher than the "Maximum allowed manufacturing cost". The system suggests redesign proposals that the user can accept or start from scratch.

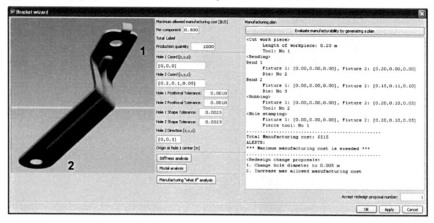

Figure 2. GUI for case study example.

Discussion

This section discusses the capabilities of the proposed approach by addressing iteration, system maintenance, industry potential and generic issues.

Iteration. The proposed approach enables four iterations, viz. two manual iterations triggered by the "Routine Verification" and the "Manufacturing what-if" activity and two automatic iterations triggered by the "Design Definition" and the plan-based iteration triggered by the "Adapter". Since four iterations are possible, the probability of finding a design property that can be enhanced in a manufacturing point of view may increase, and costs can be saved. As these iterations are performed both automatically and manually in a four-step dialog with the user, the user may trust the system more rather than if all four iterations were conducted automatically in one step. The black-box feeling may then increase and the level of trust may be reduced. Although the focus is to move forward in the product development process, more iteration may save further costs if costly design flaws are found and avoided. It may also be possible to increase the number of iterations and reduce the development time. Further refining the iteration at the KBE "what-if" analysis would permit altering design changes more freely than just choosing between the suggested redesign proposals or starting from the beginning with new inputs (start of phase 1).

System Maintenance. It is important to separate the design support knowledge into *application logic* and *analysis logic* as described in [4], where the analysis logic needs to be updated more likely than the fundamental logic governing the generic information flow of the application. As all geometric features are defined in the KBE module, feature recognition for the CBR module is facilitated. Feature recognition for CBR can otherwise be time demanding to code.

Industry Potential. Because KBE-systems often are integrated with a CAD-system, industry implementation of the proposed approach is facilitated, as no new software needs to be introduced. KF was used in the case study, but the choice of KBE system may need to be adapted to other industry CAD-environments. If the CAD-system lacks a KBE-module, API or Macro programming can be used instead, even though this may increase the programming burden. Python is suggested for implementation of the CBR algorithms and because Python is freeware even for commercial products, cost issues of investing in software may not hinder industry implementation.

Research Issues. This approach is suitable for manufacturing industries that have timely and repetitive phases in their product developing process and develop products that require several years of experience to evaluate the manufacturability. There may otherwise not be time saved in automating the process. The proposed approach has been informally validated through the case study, though to be able to state that the proposed approach can improve product development in the industry, a comprehensive validation needs to be conducted. In such a comprehensive validation, a measure such as time or cost needs to be stated and used to compare the work process with and without the proposed approach.

Conclusion

This paper presents an approach for computer-based support for design and manufacturing iteration in early design by combining KBE and CBR. A case study at a Swedish automotive manufacturer was performed to initially validate the proposed approach. The main contributions from the work are the following:

- Because several automated and manual iterations are available, the possibility of finding potentials for design enhancements to reduce the manufacturing cost may increase compared to doing fewer iterations.
- Since the iterations are divided into several steps in automatic and manual dialogs with the user, the user may trust the design support more than if all iterations are conducted in one step.
- As the proposed approach uses KBE, which often is integrated in CAD-environments, industry implementation may be facilitated.

A comprehensive validation where a measure is identified and used to clarify the impact of the proposed approach on the product development process needs to be done.

Acknowledgement

This research was funded by VINNOVA (Swedish Agency for Innovation Systems) via TIPS (Tillverkningsindustrins produktframtagning) and by partner companies in the Polhem Laboratory. The support of these organizations is hereby gratefully acknowledged. The authors also wish to thank Saab Automobile AB for making the necessary information available. This information has been altered to protect company specific data. Master's thesis student Mr. Mohammed Golkar is also acknowledged for his work with the bracket wizard at Saab Automobile AB.

References

[1]   B. Prasad *Concurrent engineering fundamentals: Integrated product development, Vol. II*, (Prentice and Hall, Saddle River, New Jersey 1997).

[2]   E. M. Shehab, and H. S. Abdalla, Robotics and Computer-Integrated Manufacturing, Vol. 17, (2001), pp. 341-353.

[3]   M. Sandberg, P. Boart, and T. Larsson, Concurrent Engineering: Research and Applications, Vol. 13, (2005), pp. 331-342.

[4]   R. Sharma, and J. X. Gao, Computers in Industry, Vol. 47, (2002), pp. 155.

[5]   L. W. Rosenfeld, 1995. *Solid Modeling and Knowledge-Based Engineering*, Handbook of Solid Modeling, LaCourse, D. E., ed., McGraw-Hill, Inc., New York.

[6]   J. Britanik, and M. Marefat, Computational Intelligence, Vol. 20, (2004), pp. 405-443.

[7]   UGS, www.ugs.com, Last accessed: May 2 2006

[8]   Python, www.python.org, Last accessed: May 2 2006

Keynote Paper

Issues facing the UK Automotive Industry
Professor Neil Barlow, Northwest Automotive Alliance,
c/o MI Technology Group, Aston Way, Leyland, UK

389

Keynote Lecture
International Conference on Manufacturing Research 2006 (ICMR 2006)
Liverpool John Moores University
England, United Kingdom

Issues facing the UK Automotive Industry

Professor Neil Barlow

Northwest Automotive Alliance, c/o mi Technology Group, Aston Way, Leyland, UK

N.Barlow@nwautoalliance.com

Abstract.

The world's leading vehicle and automotive component companies have long seen the UK as being an important location for manufacturing. Currently Ford, General Motors, BMW, Volkswagen, Honda, Nissan, Toyota and Peugeot build cars in the UK. In 2005 UK vehicle assembly plants produced some 1,600,000 cars and 200,000 commercial vehicles, contributing around £8.4bn added value to the economy and accounting for 1.1% of GDP, 5.8% of manufacturing value-added and 9.5% of total UK exports. Some 237,000 people are employed in the design and manufacture of vehicles and components. UK based automotive companies are leaders in global best practice in many areas of manufacturing and provide a key source of improvement for the UK manufacturing sector. The UK industry as a whole needs to make up ground in terms of productivity but the productivity record of the best firms here show that UK based operations can match and exceed the best of their rivals. The presentation outlines the strength and diversity of the sector in the UK and the issues/challenges it faces in competing in what is a truly global market.

Invited Speaker
from Industry

● **Paper to be confirmed**
Rahul Sharma, Infosys Technologies Limited, India.

Micro Manufacturing

Heat Transfer in Injection Molding for Reproduction of Sub-micron Sized Features

M. Nakao[1, a], K. Tsuchiya[2,b], T. Sadamitsu[1, c], Y. Ichikohara[1, d], T. Ohba[1, e], T. Ooi[1, f]

[1] Department of Engineering Synthesis, The University of Tokyo, Hongo 7-3-1, Bunkyo-ku, Tokyo 113-8656, Japan

[2] Institute of Industrial Science, The University of Tokyo, Komaba 4-6-1, Meguro-ku, Tokyo 153-8505, Japan

[a]nakao@hnl.t.u-tokyo.ac.jp, [b]tsu@iis.u-tokyo.ac.jp, [c]sadamitu@hnl.t.u-tokyo.ac.jp

[d]ichiko@hnl.t.u-tokyo.ac.jp, [e]ohba@hnl.t.u-tokyo.ac.jp, [f]ooi@hnl.t.u-tokyo.ac.jp

Abstract. Heat transfer in injection molding was quantitatively measured with micro heat-flux sensors. The 0.1-10 microns wide micro-grooves with aspect ratios of 0.5-1.0 were etched by focus ion beam on a Ni plated mold. During the short time just after injecting, heat-flux in the mold was maximized to 10-50 W/cm^2, and heat transfer coefficient between plastic and mold was 0.27 $W/(cm^2K)$ with PMMA and 0.085 $W/(cm^2K)$ with PS. The maximum mold surface temperature just after injecting should be above glass transition temperature of plastic, then reproducing sub-micron wide micro-ridges.

Keywords: Injection, Micromachining, Plastic

Introduction

Injection molding is widely used in reproducing 3D shapes. Compared to hot pressing, injection molding has a shorter process cycle time of several seconds and suits mass production. It injects a pressurized plastic softened with high temperature into a cooled metal mold, and lets the plastic harden quickly. Experienced engineers qualitatively know that the thermal condition in the short period of 1 second or less just after injecting is dominant for precise reproduction. Especially, when micro-features on the plastic surface are reproduced, heat transfer in this period will be the most important process variable. But few measured data about heat flux, surface temperature or heat transfer coefficient were precisely reported, causing a miscalculation in computer aided engineering (CAE). Conventional researches on injection molding have measured pressure in cavity and temperature inside the mold, to prevent the hardened plastic from depressing or deforming. When the injection pressure is low, the process fails pushing enough molecules into the cavity, and the cooled and shrunk plastic has several micron deep depressions. Effective ways of preventing these depressions are time control of in-cavity pressure [1-3]. When cooling of the cavity is uneven, partially hardened plastic deforms due to residual stress. Spatially controlling the cooling in the mold can effectively prevent such deformation [3].

Reproduction of sub-micron sized features on plastic is catching attention of industries. Nanoimprinting, that is a kind of hot pressing, is an alternative process to optical lithography for producing quantum device patterns with widths of sub-100nm. This process produces: for example, on a 1 micron thick spin-coated plastic film under hot pressing pressure of 5 MPa for pressing/heating time of 4 minutes at mold temperature of glass transition temperature (Tg) + 80 °C [4]. Industries other than semiconductors, e.g., optics, electronics or bioengineering, have also been interested in sub-micron sized features on surfaces [5], but the hot pressing is not for mass production due to the long process cycle time of several minutes.

The purpose of this paper is to reproduce sub-micron sized features with injection molding. Of course, higher mold temperature and higher injection pressures work better; however, the process cycle time takes ten minutes or more and the product may stick to the mold to make the releasing difficult. The authors ran some preliminary tests, and found that precise reproduction of 100 nm wide line pattern requires high relatively temperature of the mold, only just after injecting, but that not necessarily high pressure. This paper quantitatively formulates this empirical rule of injection molding, measuring heat transfer in cooling using micro heat flux sensors.

Experiment method

The paper has two experiments: (1) the heat transfer measurement with heat-flux sensors and (2) the reproduction test of sub-micron sized features. The latter experiment used a smaller heat capacity mold than the former's one to quick control heat transfer, and injected plastic of PMMA (poly methyl-methacrylate), instead of the former's PS (poly styrene), to compare the reproductivity with hot pressed PMMA. The molecular weight of PMMA pellets were several 100,000, and its Tg was about 100 °C.

Figure 1 shows the conventional small-sized mold for (1) the heat transfer measurement with heat-flux sensors. The mold is a cubic with sides of about 100 mm, weight of 8 kg; its material is the stainless steel. Near the interface between the plastic cavity and the mold core, two heat-flux sensors were installed inside the cavity and inside the core. The cavity heat-flux sensor sticks two thermocouples out at 0.2 mm and 0.4 mm high from the surface. The thermocouples were welded by YAG laser with two wires of diameter 25 microns; were cut to a cone shape by femtosecond laser to prevent a releasing trouble after injection molding; and were insulated except its tips by cashew resin. Some conventional micro thermocouple sensors, e.g., a metal layers pattern on a polyimide substrate, have been developed using micromachining technology. But even the 50 microns thick substrate has volumes of heat capacity; the sensible heat flows along the substrate or thermocouple's metal wires, falsely measuring a larger heat flux by 1-10 W/cm^2 [5]; Figure 6 shows a small false peak of 0.5 W/cm^2 just after injecting on the high injection temperature data. The difference of temperatures measured divided by distance of 0.2 mm and multiplied by heat conductivity of 0.10 W/(m·K) of PS make the heat-flux per area (W/cm^2) through the plastic. The mold core heat-flux sensor embedded bare thermocouple wires with diameter 30 microns at the mold depths of 0.3 mm and 0.6 mm from the surface, and welded their tips on the mold [3]. In the same way, the difference of temperatures divided by distance of 0.3 mm and multiplied by heat conductivity of 16 W/(m·K) of stainless steel make the heat-flux per area through the mold. Electric heater attached on the outside surface heated the mold; a natural convection air cooled it. Hydraulic cylinders inject the plastic and clamp the mold with 50 kN (JUKEN, JMW-015S-5t).

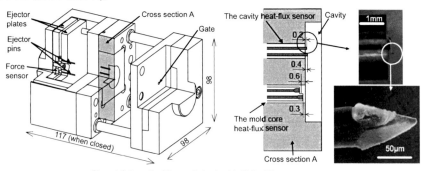

Figure 1:Schematic of the small-sized mold with heat flux sensors.

Figure 2 shows the miniature mold for (2) the reproduction test of micro-structures. Its size of diameter 30 mm, weight of 0.3 kg, and material of beryllium copper keep its heat capacity small. The mold heat-flux sensor was installed in the stainless steel mold core; the thermocouples were at the depth 0.3 mm and 0.5 mm. A piezoelectric pressure sensor installed on the 4 ejector pins measured the in-cavity pressure. A halogen lamp heated the mold and a natural convection air cooled it. Electric motors inject the plastic and clamp the mold with 50 kN (FANUC, Roboshot S-2000 i5A).

Figure 3 shows the typical measured data in heat-flux, mold surface temperature, and in-cavity pressure during 1 process cycle using the miniature mold. Just after injecting, the pressure rose to its maximum of 40 MPa and gradually decreased as the plastic shrank. A pin side gate of diameter 0.8 mm made the large pressure drop of 60 MPa between sprue and cavity. The pressure was hold at 10 MPa for 15 seconds, but the thin gate might be closed due to plastic solidification quickly within 1 second. The heat-flux and surface temperature respectively increased to 35 W/cm^2 and 170 °C immediately upon the start of injection, and after reaching their maximum values, they decreased gradually. The maximum heat-flux, as shown in the figure, cancelled the heat-flux value when injecting no plastic, namely, that of natural cooling from the heated mold.

Figure 4 shows the micro-grooves produced on the miniature mold surface. They were made by lapping the mold surface to a mirror quality, electroless plating of nickel, and etching the surface with gallium focused ion beam (FIB). The process conditions for thin grooves were an electrical current of 0.02 nA, accelerated voltage of 30 kV and process time of 1 hour per groove. Figure 4 shows 16 microns long shallow grooves with widths 0.1, 0.3 and 1 microns and aspect ratios between 0.5 and 1.0, in directions parallel and perpendicular to the injection direction; while, thick grooves of 32 microns long and 3, 5 and 10 microns wide were processed at 0.02 nA, 30 kV and 0.3 hrs. The figure displays the parallel grooves only.

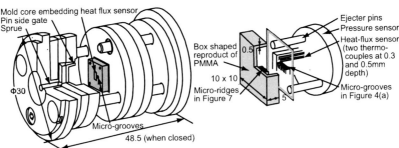

Figure 2: Schematic of the miniature mold with heat flux sensors and micro-grooves.

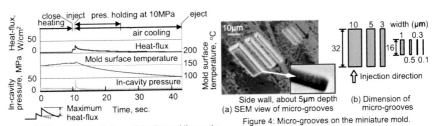

Figure 3: Measured data during an injection molding cycle with the miniature mold.

Figure 4: Micro-grooves on the miniature mold.

(a) SEM view of micro-grooves

(b) Dimension of micro-grooves

Experiment results

Figure 5 shows the measured data, using the set-up shown in Figure 1, of temperatures (a) using four thermocouples of the heat-flux sensors, and of heat flux (b) in the plastic cavity and in the mold core. Both the figures indicated the sharp peaks just after injecting; they reduced drastically. When the injection temperature was 220 °C, the maximum heat flux in the mold was 15 W/(cm^2), but in the cavity 2 W/(cm^2). At 2 seconds later, both heat fluxes reduced to 1 W/(cm^2) or less. The mold had higher heat flux, because the plastic skin layer from the surface to 0.2 mm high in cavity was hardened just after injecting, and its sensible heat of 4 J/(cm^2) flowed into the mold. These could be analysis reveal that the large heat flux just after injecting was caused by the quick generation of a thin skin layer hardened. The injection was repeated to 370th shot for 18.5 hours without releasing troubles, and the temperature and heat flux kept stable from 10th shot to the end. The heat flux values are reasonable; e.g., the heat flux of cooling for a CPU in computer devices is 5-15 W/(cm^2) with a forced air cooling.

Figure 6 shows heat flux when the injection plastic temperature was varied from 180 to 260 °C. Heat transfer coefficient W/(cm^{2}K) is, as shown in Figure 9 (a), heat flux per area (W/cm^2) divided by the difference of mold surface temperatures (K) and injection plastic temperature (K). Regardless of injection plastic temperature, the coefficient was constant to 0.083±0.002 W/(cm^{2}K). The value is similar to 0.03-0.5 W/(cm^{2}K) of a cooling surface with flowing water.

Figure 7 shows the SEM images of the micro-structures reproduced by injection molding set-up as shown in Figure 2. Samples of (A), (B) and (C) are represented in Figure 8 and 10 depicted later. The complete reproduction (A) demonstrates that the reproduced product had equally high ridges with the grooves. On side walls, beam removal marks of the mold in Figure 4 were precisely replicated. The incomplete one (B), reproduced with ridge heights about half of the groove depths, shows a smooth micro-depression at the whole area except the short edges of the ridge. The no reproduction (C) has large explosion-like micro-depressions in the ridges.

Figure 8 displays the reproduced features when the initial mold temperature and the injection velocity were varied. The horizontal axis of the diagram is the maximum mold surface temperature and the vertical axis the maximum in-cavity pressure. The symbols of circles, triangles and crosses respectively indicate complete, incomplete and no reproduction. From the figure, the maximum mold surface temperature to Tg of 100 °C or above succeeded in reproducing all the 10, 1 and 0.1 microns wide micro-ridges. The figure indicates only the 0.1 microns results. The micro heat flux sensors reveal that reproduction of micro-structures is decided by the maximum mold temperature in the short period just after injecting. Within the first 1 second, the 0.1-0.2 mm thick skin of the plastic is hardened with micro-structures on the plastic surface [5]. Of course, pressure is also one of the important parameters; low pressure like 10 MPa makes the micro-depression as shown in Figure 7 (B) (C). Moreover, the injection direction did not affect the results as shown in the left and right images of Figure 7.

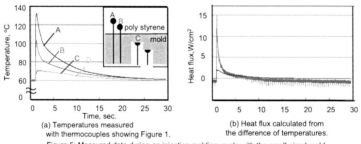

(a) Temperatures measured with thermocouples showing Figure 1.

(b) Heat flux calculated from the difference of temperatures.

Figure 5: Measured data during an injection molding cycle with the small-sized mold.

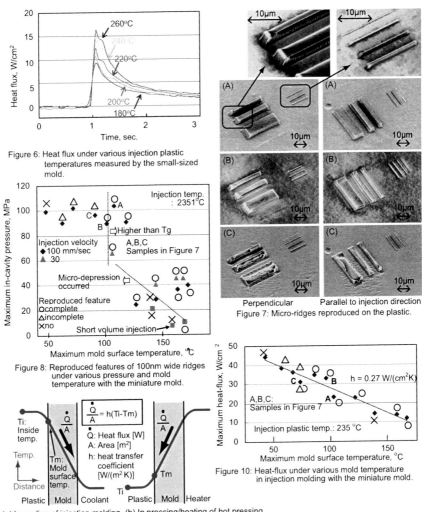

Figure 6: Heat flux under various injection plastic temperatures measured by the small-sized mold.

Figure 7: Micro-ridges reproduced on the plastic.

Perpendicular   Parallel to injection direction

Figure 8: Reproduced features of 100nm wide ridges under various pressure and mold temperature with the miniature mold.

$$\frac{\overset{\bullet}{Q}}{A} = h(Ti-Tm)$$

Q: Heat flux [W]
A: Area [m²]
h: heat transfer coefficient [W/(m² K)]

(a) In cooling of injection molding (b) In pressing/heating of hot pressing

Figure 9: Schematic of temperature change.

Figure 10: Heat-flux under various mold temperature in injection molding with the miniature mold.

Figure 9 shows temperature change along the plastic, mold and coolant in injection molding. Heat transfer coefficient between plastic and mold will be calculated if plastic inside temperature is the same as injection temperature of 235 °C. Heating due to large friction of the plastic flow through the pin gate, however, may increase the inside temperature by 10-30 °C.

Figure 10 rearranges the resulting reproduced features of Figure 8, with the maximum mold surface temperature in the horizontal axis and the maximum heat flux in the vertical. The heat flux was dependent on the mold temperature. It is because heat capacity of the miniature mold was still so large that heat-flux just after injecting could not quickly control with any conventional coolant/heater. Even a hydro-fluoro-carbon (HFC) spray cooling of 80 W/cm^2 on the outside surface of the mold could not increase the heat flux on the inside surface. The gradient of the line indicates the heat transfer coefficient of 0.27 W/(cm^{2}K). From these heat transfer data, we can design the process for reproduction of sub-micron sized features. The cooling method decides maximum heat flux just after injecting; plastic material, injection pressure, mold surface roughness, etc. decide heat transfer coefficient; in result, the maximum heat flux, the heat transfer coefficient and injection plastic temperature decide maximum mold surface temperature; finally, if the maximum mold surface temperature is larger than glass transition temperature, the micro-structures can be reproduced.

Discussion

In this chapter, the difference between injection molding and hot pressing is discussed; the following data imply that injection molding may replace hot pressing. Hot pressing reproduced the micro-structures just at the start of pressing/heating as shown in Figure 9 (b). Heat flow is in the reverse direction of injection molding. Heat transfer coefficient could be calculated like Figure 10; the coefficient was 0.46 W/(cm^{2}K). Press pressure in hot pressing made higher coefficient than that of injection molding. In hot pressing, the mold surface temperature and pressing pressure could be easily controlled. Then, the reproduction was checked as in Figure 8. When the mold temperature was 120 °C or above, the micro-structures irrespective of the pressure; the reproduction was succeeded above Tg. The same result was revealed in both injection molding and hot pressing.

Conclusion

The sub-micron wide micro-grooves on the mold etched by focus ion beam could be precisely reproduced into plastic surface with injection molding. Then, the plastic temperature at the first time of mold contact, that is, for a short period just after injecting should be set raising to glass transition temperature (Tg) of plastic. In this time, the new micro heat flux sensors measured the temperature and heat flux near the interface between plastic and metal mold. In the experiments, the maximum heat-flux in the mold just after injecting was 10-50 W/cm^2, and heat transfer coefficient between the plastic and the mold surface was 0.27 W/(cm^{2}K) with PMMA and 0.085 W/(cm^{2}K) with PS.

References

[1] Yan, C., Nakao. M., Go, T., Matsumoto, K., Hatamura, Y., 2003, Injection Molding for Micro Structures Controlling Mold-Core Extrusion and Cavity Heat-Flux, Microsystem Technologies 9, 188-199.

[2] Wang, K. K., Zhou, J., 2000, A Concurrent Engineering Approach Toward the Online Adaptive Control of Injection Molding Process, Annals of the CIRP, 49/1:379-382.

[3] Nakao, M., Yoda, M., Nagao, T., 2003, Locally Controlling Heat Flux for Preventing Micrometre-order Deformation with Injection Molding of Miniature Products, Annals of the CIRP, 52/1:451-454.

[4] Guo, L. J., 2004, Recent Progress in Nanoimprint Technology and Its Application, J. Phys. D: Appl. Phys. 37(2004), R123-R141.

[5] Tsuchiya, K., Nakao, M., 2005, Micro Thermocouple Array for Measuring Resin Temperature in an Injection Mold, Journal of Japan Society for Precision engineering, 71/10, 1255-1259

Design Requirements of an Advanced Micromilling Setup

P. Li[1,a], R.S. Blom[1,b], J.A.J. Oosterling[2,c], M. Achtsnick[1,d]

[1] Laboratory for Precision Manufacturing and Assembly, Delft University of Technology, Mekelweg 2, 2628 CD Delft, The Netherlands

[2] TNO Industrial Technology, De Rondom 1, 5600 HE Eindhoven, The Netherlands

[a]P.Li@tudelft.nl, [b]R.S.Blom@tudelft.nl, [c]Han.Oosterling@tno.nl, [d]M.Achtsnick@tudelft.nl

Abstract. This paper presents the experimental results of micromilling on a commercial state of the art milling machine. This study was performed to establish the limitations of using such machine tools for micromilling. It was observed that the tool runout has a big influence on the cutting process, tool wear and workpiece quality. The runout was studied by analyzing the cutting force data and the machined features. For further process investigations, an ultra-precision experimental setup was designed. A high speed spindle with Active Magnetic Bearings (AMB) and a linear motor X-Y stage are used to achieve high machining performance and process monitoring and control possibilities.

Keywords: Micromilling, machine tool design, AMB spindle

Introduction

With the increasing demand for miniature components, which are of a few microns to a few millimetres with high accurate 3-dimensional geometries, a flexible fabrication method is becoming more and more important. Attempts have been made to manufacture these products by mechanical machining processes with micro tools, e.g. micromilling [1,2].

Currently, most of the micromilling activities were done on conventional machine tools. Although micro components can be produced, there remain some issues that should be dealt with because of the special characteristics of the micromilling process. First, due to the decreased cutting diameters of the micro endmills, high speed spindles are required to achieve the recommended cutting speeds by high speed machining. Micromilling could benefit from high speed machining in that lower cutting force, better workpiece quality, and higher material removal rates are achieved, which are verified in conventional machining [3]. Second, a high positioning accuracy is required to realize the high relative accuracy (tolerance-to-feature size), which is in the range of 10^{-3} to 10^{-5} for miniaturized applications [4]. Third, measures should be taken to eliminate or compensate the influence of vibrations and thermal fluctuations on the machine tool structure. In [5] it was found that the spindle axial depth error is a major source of inaccuracy when using conventional machine tools. Fourth, innovative process monitoring methods should be designed because the process signals in micromilling are too small to be detected by conventional methods [6]. Finally, the tool clamping system and micro part fixturing bring new challenges.

In this paper, an initial study of micromilling on a commercial state of the art milling machine is addressed. Hardened tool steel was milled by micro endmills. According to the experimental observations, an advanced micromilling setup has been designed to fulfil the requirements of further investigations on micromilling.

Experimental setup

Experiments have been conducted on a 5-axis milling machine (Fehlmann Picomax 60-HSC) with a spindle speed range from 50 to 36000 rpm. The resolution of the direct measuring system is 1μm. After calibration, the positioning accuracy is 3μm; the repetition accuracy is 2μm. The maximum radial runout at the end of the spindle shaft is 4μm. An HSK 50E tool clamping system with a shrink fit toolholder is used. The machine is equipped with a Heidenhain CNC continuous path control iTNC 530. For the tool setting, a BLUM Laser Control System is employed which is capable to measure endmills bigger than 0.3mm in diameter with a repeatability precision of 1-2 microns. This machine tool is located in a temperature controlled environment (22°C±2°C).

The micro endmills used in this research are two-fluted 0.1mm and 0.5mm square endmills with TiAlN coating. The workpiece material is tool steel (SAE H11) with different hardness of 44, 52, and 56HRC. The cutting force has been measured by using a Kistler (MiniDyn 9256C2). The tool conditions and the quality of the milled workpiece were checked by Keyence microscope (VHX/VH Series) and FEI Quanta 600 Scanning Electron Microscope.

Results and Discussions

Tool runout effect. During the micromilling tests, tool runout was commonly observed, resulting in severe tool wear, poor surface quality, and dimensional error. The effect of the tool runout was studied qualitatively through the cutting force profile. Fig. 1 gives two examples of the cutting force plots in micromilling. Because of the runout, the cutting forces exerted on two cutting edges of the endmill are different, as shown in Fig. 1(a). The maximum cutting force in this example is 7.2N, while the difference of the cutting forces on the two cutting edges is 4.1N. This means that only one edge performed the cutting operation; the other edge cut much less or did not even cut at all. Fig. 1(b) shows the maximum cutting forces on both cutting edges of the micro endmill in a complete tool life cycle. The difference between the force magnitudes on the two edges presents the change of the runout effect during the micromilling process. It is clear that runout exists in the whole milling process; while the magnitude of the tool runout is not constant, which is decided by the combination effect of the several runout sources.

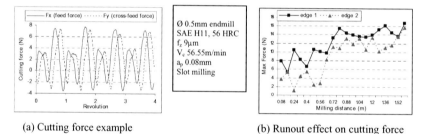

    (a) Cutting force example   (b) Runout effect on cutting force

Fig. 1 Cutting force plot in micromilling

During experiments, several sources for tool runout were identified, namely spindle bearings, the tool clamping interface, the toolholder, asymmetric tool geometry, and the vibration of the micro-tools during machining. If these sources have a negative combined effect, the resultant tool runout can be relatively high. It was observed that after reloading the toolholder, the difference of the maximum cutting forces on the two cutting edges changed from 0.1N to 9.4N in one case, as shown in Fig. 1(b).

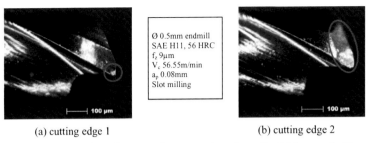

(a) cutting edge 1   (b) cutting edge 2

Fig. 2 Asymmetric tool wear on the two cutting edges of a Ø 0.5mm endmill

The asymmetric cutting forces lead to asymmetric tool wear on both cutting edges, as shown in Fig. 2, and, therefore, the tool life is largely shortened. Also, the tool runout results in a larger machined feature. This effect was used to evaluate the tool runout in this research. Measurement results showed that the tool runout was between 1% and 24% of the tool diameter for a Ø 0.5mm endmill under the current setting.

Spindle speed. During experiments, it was observed that cutting speed has an influence on the burr formation. The burr size was largely reduced when the cutting speed changed from 15.7m/min to 47.1m/min, as shown in Fig. 3. This is because the workpiece material is more plastically deformed than cut by shearing under low cutting speeds. As a result, micro burrs are formed when the tool exits from the workpiece. Micro burrs are difficult to be removed for micro components, therefore measures should be taken to control the burr size while machining. Experimental results showed that the burr size can be controlled by optimizing the cutting conditions, such as the cutting speed.

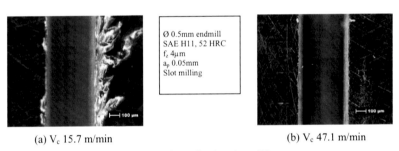

(a) V_c 15.7 m/min   (b) V_c 47.1 m/min

Fig. 3 Burr formation in micromilling.

Tool setting system. Ø 0.5mm endmills were measured by the laser tool setting system to test its capability. The repetition precision of the laser system is 1-2 microns. The measurement results showed that the absolute accuracy of the tool setting system is largely influenced by the spindle conditions, such as thermal fluctuations and spindle speed. For a Ø 0.488mm endmill, the diameter measured with the tool setting system was 0.4716mm when the spindle was cool, while the measured data was 0.4984mm when the spindle was warm. Fig. 4 illustrates the influence of spindle speed on the tool setting system. With the increase of the spindle speed, the measured tool diameter was also increased. The possible reasons for this error are the spindle runout, tool change error, and lengthening effect of the spindle shaft because of thermal influence. Tests also showed that for smaller endmills, e.g. Ø 0.1mm endmills, the tool setting error can be up to 40%. Therefore in order to achieve the tight tolerance of the miniature product and avoid premature tool failures, special methods should be taken to improve the accuracy of tool presetting.

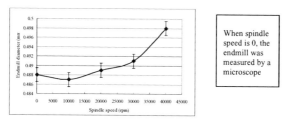

When spindle speed is 0, the endmill was measured by a microscope

Fig. 4 Accuracy of the laser tool setting system

Design of the Micromilling Setup

For further research, an experimental setup was designed based on the observations in the preliminary experimental study. Special considerations were given to control the tool runout in order to achieve high machining accuracy. Fig. 5(a) is the schematic drawing of the experimental setup.

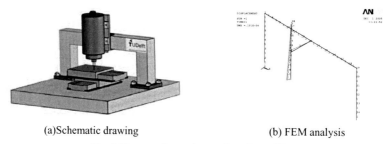

(a)Schematic drawing   (b) FEM analysis

Fig. 5 The experimental setup for micromilling

A high speed spindle of 120000rpm with Active Magnetic Bearings has been selected for its unique features. First, the position of the spindle shaft can be tilled through the control of the bearings which gives the possibility to compensate tool runout in a certain range. Second, the machining forces can be measured by built-in position sensors; this will give a chance to monitor the process and adapt process variables. Third, the damping and stiffness of the spindle can be adjusted by the control system. The generated heat in the spindle is removed by constant cooling water; therefore the axial depth error can be controlled. A high precision X-Y linear stacked stage is used. The positioning accuracy is about 1μm, and the repetition accuracy is 0.5μm. The setup will be mounted on a granite base with damping components and located in a temperature-controlled environment.

The mechanical properties of the design were evaluated by Finite Element Analysis. For the experimental setup it is required that deflections due to static forces and vibrations stay within 1μm. The results showed that this design can fulfil this requirement. No generated frequency coincides with the natural frequencies of the bridge, and the stiffness of the bridge is about 198N/μm, as shown in Fig. 5(b).

406

Conclusions and Outlook

Micromilling experiments were conducted on a commercial milling machine. According to the observations, the design requirements for an ultra-precision setup were derived. A high speed AMB spindle with digital control and an X-Y stage with air bearings were used in order to achieve high machining performance and maximum process monitoring and control possibilities.

Because of the dominant effect of tool runout, it should be considered when modelling the micromilling process. In [4], several current mechanistic models for micromilling were reviewed; however they all excluded the tool runout factor. In order to accurately predict cutting forces in micromilling, new models with tool runout effect will be developed in future work.

References

[1]   H.Weule, V.Huntrup and H.Tritschler: Annals of CIRP, Vol. 50 (2001), pp. 61–64.

[2]   M.Takacs, B.Veroe and I.Meszaros: Journal of Materials Processing Technology, Vol. 138 (2003), pp. 152-155.

[3]   P.Fallböhmer, C.A.Rodríguez, T.Özel and T.Altan: Journal of Materials Processing Technology, Vol. 98 (2000), pp. 104-115.

[4]   X.Liu, R.E.DeVor, S.G.Kapoor and K.F.Ehmann: Journal of Manufacturing Science Engineering, Vol. 126 (2004), pp. 666–678.

[5]   G.Bissacco, H.N.Hansen and L.De Chiffre: Proceedings of the Fourth Euspen International Conference (Glasgow, Scotland, UK, 2004), pp. 386-387.

[6]   W.Bao and I.N.Tansel: International Journal of Machine Tools and Manufacture, Vol. 40, Issue 15 (2000), pp. 2155-2173.

Manufacturing of Polymer Micro- and Nano-Structures

Ioannis S. Chronakis [a], Pernilla Walkenström [b] and Bengt Hagström [c]

IFP Research, Swedish Institute for Fiber and Polymer Research, Box 104, SE-431 22 Mölndal, Sweden,

[a] ioannis.chronakis@ifp.se, [b] pernilla.walkenstrom@ifp.se, [c] bengt.hagstrom@ifp.se

Abstract. Nanostructures such as nanofibres and nanotubes based on polymers (synthetic and natural) can be processed by electrospinning. Electrospun nanostructures are an exciting class of novel materials due to several unique characteristics, including their nanometer diameter, the extremely high surface area per unit mass, the very small pore size, and their tunable surface properties. To this may be added their cost effectiveness. Significant progress has been made in this field in the past few years, and the resultant nanostructures may serve as a highly versatile platform for a broad range of applications in areas such as medicine, pharmacy, sensors, catalysis, filter, composites, ceramics, electronics, and photonics. Some latest developments in the processing of nano-structured polymers by electrospinning are presented.

Keywords: Micro – and Nano-Structures, Nanofibres, Electrospinning, Polymers,

Processing of Polymer Micro- and Nano-Structures by Electrospinning

Electrospinning is being used to an increasing extent to produce ultra-thin fibres from a wide range of polymer materials [1-5]. This non-mechanical, electrostatic technique involves the use of a high-voltage electrostatic field to charge the surface of a polymer solution droplet, thereby inducing the ejection of a liquid jet through a spinneret. In a typical process, an electrical potential is applied between a droplet of a polymer solution held at the end of a capillary tube and a grounded target. When the electric field applied overcomes the surface tension of the droplet, a charged jet of polymer solution is ejected. On the way to the collector the jet will be subjected to forces, allowing it to stretch immensely. Simultaneously, the jet will partially or fully solidify through solvent evaporation or cooling, and an electrically charged fibre will remain, which can be directed or accelerated by electrical forces and then collected in sheets or other useful shapes. A characteristic feature of the electrospinning process is the extremely rapid formation of the nanofibre structure, which is on a millisecond scale [2]. Other notable features of electrospinning are a huge material elongation rate in the order of 1000 s^{-1}, and a cross-sectional area reduction in the order of 10^5 to 10^6, which have been shown to affect the orientation of the structural elements within the fibre [2].

 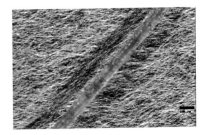

Figure 1. a) SEM image of PET nanofibre mats. The PET nanofibre was electrospun from a 10% PET solution (wt) in a 1:1 (v/v) mixture of TFA and DCM. The diameter of the fibres is about 200 nm. b) PET nanofibre mats - Comparison with human hair. [6]

To control the electrospinning process and to tailor the structures of fibres, the traditional set-up for electrospinning has been modified in a number of ways in recent years. A number of set-ups that allow *control of the orientation of fibres* have recently been developed (Fig. 2). A large part of the set-ups is based on rotating collection devices [7]. The driving force for orientation of fibres in a structure is the large influence on mechanical, electrical and optical properties of the web. Furthermore, the orientation is also crucial for application purposes and paves the way for new opportunities for the manufacture of yarn, nanowire devices, etc.

Figure 2. SEM image of aligned PA6 nanofibres electrospun from a solution of 12.5 % wt in formic acid (unpublished results). The scale bar is 10μm.

Set-ups for electrospinning involving a dual syringe spinneret that enables spinning of highly functional nanofibres such as *hollow nanofibres, nanotubes and fibres with a core/sheet structure* have also been developed [8]. In this case, a high voltage is applied to a pair of concentric needles used to inject two immiscible liquids, leading to the formation of a two-component liquid cone, which elongates into coaxial liquid jets and forms hollow nanofibres or nanotubes.

Characteristics of Polymer Nanofibres

Polymer nanofibres have a diameter that ranges from an order of a few nanometres to several micrometers and are remarkable for their very high surface area per unit mass, their small pore size and very high porosity, and a low basis weight. The electrospinning process parameters (applied potential, electric field lines, spinning distance, flow rate) and fluid parameters (conductivity, viscosity, surface tension, dielectric constant) can be adjusted to tune and optimise micro- and nanofibre morphologies and characteristics [3,5].

Moreover, this process is highly versatile and allows not only the processing of many different polymers into polymeric nanofibres but also the co-processing of polymer mixtures and mixtures of polymers and low-molecular-weight nonvolatile materials. This is done simply by using ternary solutions of the components for electrospinning to form a combination of nanofibre functionalities [3,5]. Polymer blends, core-sheet structures and side-by-side bicomponent electrospinning are growing research areas connected with electrospinning of multicomponent systems. The targets are either to create nanofibres of an "un-spinnable" material or to adjust the fibre morphology and characteristics. The electrospinning technique can also be applied to lace together different types of nanoparticles or (carbon) nanotubes and other structural entities to be encapsulated into an electrospun nanofibre matrix (Fig. 3). Another interesting aspect of nanofibre processing is that it is feasible to modify not only their morphology and their (internal-bulk) content but also their surface structure to carry various chemically reactive functionalities, Thus, nanofibres can be easily post-synthetically functionalised, for example, by using plasma modification and physical or chemical vapour deposition (PVD, CVD).

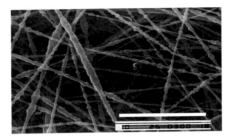

Figure 3. Encapsulation of nanoparticles within a nanofibre structure (unpublished results). The scale bar is 10μm.

Polymer Nanofibres for Nano-Electronic Applications

Electrically conductive polymers have attracted much interest in the past 20 years because they simultaneously display the physical and chemical properties of organic polymers and the electrical characteristics of metals. Fabrication of nanofibres made of conductive electronic polymers has recently been demonstrated in the design and construction of nanoelectronic devices [9]. Conductive polypyrrole nanofibres can be obtained using polyethylene oxide (PEO) as the carrier through electrospinning of aqueous solutions (Fig. 4). The electrospun PPy/PEO nanofibres exhibited a cylindrical morphology and were randomly distributed in a fibrous mat with very uniform and dense structures that adhered to each other. The average diameter of the nanofibres was in the range of about 200 to 300 nm and increased with increasing PPy concentration [10].

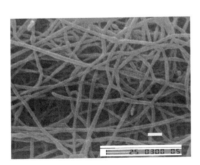
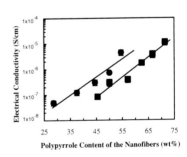

Figure 4. a) SEM micrograph of electrospun nanofibres from aqueous solutions of 1.5 wt% PEO as carrier The PPy content of the nanofibres is 45.5 wt%. The scale bar is 1μm. (b) Electrical conductivity of PPy/PEO nanofibre webs as a function of their polypyrrole content. Solutions of PPy with 2.5 wt% PEO (●) and 1.5 wt% PEO (■) as carrier were used (lines are visual guides) [10]

The electrical conductivity of these nanofibre structures can be varied by controlling the ratio of PPy/PEO. As illustrated in Fig. 4, the conductivity through the thickness of the electrospun PPy/PEO nanofibres increased by two orders of magnitude from the lowest to the highest concentration of PPy and ranged from about 4.9×10^{-8} to 1.2×10^{-5} S/cm.

We have also prepared pure (without carrier) polypyrrole conductive nanofibres by electrospinning organic solvent-soluble polypyrrole using the functional doping agent di(2-ethylhexyl) sulphosuccinate sodium salt (NaDEHS). Pure (without carrier) polypyrrole nanofibres with an average diameter of approximately 70nm were formed using $[(PPy3)^+ (DEHS)^-]_x$ dissolved in DMF (Fig. 5). This low average nanofibre diameter probably results from the relatively low molecular weight of the conducting polymer. The cylindrical nanofibres obtained are primarily randomly orientated, composed of many smaller fibres adhered to each other and are much thinner than PPy/PEO nanofibres. To the best of our knowledge, this is the first conducting polymer with such a small average nanofibre diameter that has been electrospun without the use of a carrier.

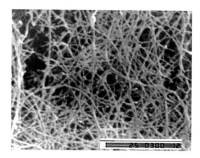

Figure 5. SEM micrograph of electrospun nanofibres from 7.5wt% $[(PPy3)^+ (DEHS)^-]_x$ solution in DMF. The scale bar is 1μm. [10]

The electrical conductivity of the pure $[(PPy3)^+ (DEHS)^-]_x$ nanofibre web was about 2.7×10^{-2} S/cm,
which is about four orders of magnitude higher than that of the PPy/PEO nanofibres. This can obviously be explained by both the high initial polymer conductivity and the molecular orientation of conducting domains induced during electrospinning. Overall, our results show that the following factors facilitate the formation of electrical conduction paths throughout the electrospun nanofibre segments: (i) both the nature of the polymer solutions (compatibility in solution) of the conducting/carrier polymer blends prior to solidification and the extremely rapid structure formation of polymer nanofibres diminish the formation of phase-separated domains between conductive polymer molecules along the length of the nanofibres, (ii) the conductive polymer/carrier polymer ratio, which controls the fraction of conductive molecules that remain connected to one another to form continuous conduction paths, (iii) the stretching of fibres in the electrospinning process, which may orientate conductive polymer molecules along the longitudinal direction of fibres, potentially increasing their charge-carrier mobility.

Polymer Nanofibres for Biomedical Applications

The use of polymer nanofibres for biomedical applications is an active research area. Drug delivery, wound healing, tissue engineering and regeneration are the main applications concerned. Biopolymers show attractive biocompatibility properties in addition to renewability and are often used within this field. Fabrication of nanofibres based on biopolymers has attracted much interest in recent years [11]. The electrospinning technology opens up new opportunities for processing these types of materials, in particular polysaccharides, which cannot be melted and therefore cannot processed by more traditional means such as melt spinning, extrusion etc.

Chitosan is a cationic polysaccharide that shows attractive biological properties. Its cationic properties facilitate cell attachment and thus open many potential new applications as scaffolds for tissue engineering, wound healing materials and drug delivery devices. Chitosan and its acetylated form, chitin, have been successfully electrospun [12-13], and fibres with diameters down to 40nm have been reported. A detailed investigation of the effect of the solvent and the chitosan concentration on the morphology of the resulting nonwoven fabrics has been conducted by Ohkawa et al [13]. The morphology changed from spherical beads to interconnected fibrous networks as the chitosan concentration increased. The solvent was shown to influence the homogeneity of the electrospun chitosan fibre.

Initial studies by the present authors focus on electrospinning of chitosan/PEO (poly ethylene oxide) mixed systems with the aim to create different morphologies on the nanofibres. Chemical parameters such as molecular weight and chitosan/PEO-ratio were varied, resulting in nanofibres with different morphologies. The results are summarised in the SEM images below, which show fibres with a broad diameter distribution and nanofibres with a smooth surface and with an irregular surface, the latter built up of fused nanobeads on the surface.

Figure 6. SEM micrographs of electrospun nanofibres from 6.5wt% Chitosan/PEO solution in 2% acetic acid (unpublished results).

Electrospinning of polymer blends is an increasing research area that opens up possibilities for creating nanofibres of an "un-spinnable" material or experimenting with fibre morphology, and thereby characteristics such as surface structure, by means of natural phase separation phenomena in polymer blends. Bognitzki et al utilised the natural phase separation between poly(lactic acid) (PLA) and polyvinylpyrrolidone to design the structures of electrospun fibres on the nano scale [14]. Co-continuous phase morphologies were reported, and selective removal of one of the components resulted in specific surface topologies and fine pores [14].

413

CMC (carboxy methyl cellulose) has been successfully electrospun together with PEO (polyethylene oxide). Upon removal of PEO, the fibre diameter shrank to some extent but was otherwise more or less unaffected by the extraction. This behaviour suggests that the two polymers are highly compatible. In the SEM images (Fig 7), nanofibres of CMC/PEO and of PEO-extracted fibres are shown.

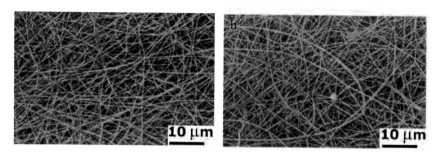

Figure 7. SEM micrographs of electrospun nanofibres from water solutions of a.) CMC/PEO and b.) CMC by extraction of PEO (www.ifp.se).

Summary

Electrospinning is a very simple and versatile method of creating polymer-based high functional and high performance nanofibers that can revolutionize the world of structural materials. The process is versatile in that there is a wide range of materials that can be spun. At the same time electrospun nanofibers possess unique and interesting features. This assembly approach can also be expanded into a hierarchical assembly of produced nanofibers in other well-defined functional nanostructures.

References

[1]   D.H. Reneker, I. Chun, Nanotechnology, 7 (1996) 216-223.

[2]   D. H. Reneker, A. L. Yarin, H. Fong, S. J. Koombhonge, Appl. Phys., 87 (2000) 4531-4547.

[3]   A. Frenot, I. S. Chronakis, Current Opinion in Colloid & Interface Science, 2003; 8: 64-75.

[4]   Y. Dzenis, Science, 304 (2004) 1917-1919.

[5]   D. Li, Y. Xia Advanced Materials, 16 (2004) 1151-1170.

[6]   I. S. Chronakis, B. Milosevic, A. Frenot, L. Ye Macromolecules, 39 (2006) 357-362.

[7]   B. Sundaray, et al., App Phys Letters, 84 (2004)1222-1224.

[8]   Z. Sun, et al., Advanced Materials, 15 (2003) 1929-1932.

[9]   I. D. Norris, et al.,, Synthetic Metals. 114 (2000) 109-114.

[10]   I. S. Chronakis, S. Grapenson, A. Jakob Polymer, 47 (2006) 1597-1603.

[11]   A. Frenot, and P. Walkenström, IFP-report nr. 05-010 (2005)

[12]   N.-M. Min, et al., Polymer, 45 (2004) 7137-7142.

[13]   K. Ohkawa, et al., Macromol Rapid Commun, 25 (2004) 1600-1605.

[14]   M. Bognitzki, et al., Polym Eng and Sci, 41 (2001) 982-989.

Machining of Micro Tools by Electrical Discharge Machining

Eckart Uhlmann[1, a], Sascha Piltz[1, b] and Markus Röhner[1, c]

[1] Fraunhofer Institute for Production Systems and Design Technology (IPK), Pascalstrasse 8-9,

Berlin 10587, Germany

[a] eckart.uhlmann@ipk.fraunhofer.de,

[b] sascha.piltz@ipk.fraunhofer.de,

[c] Corresponding author Tel.: +49 (0)30 6392 5105; fax : +49 (0)30 6392 3962 E-mail address:
markus.roehner-projekt@ipk.fraunhofer.de

Abstract. Mass production of micro or miniature parts is increasingly based on replication technologies, such as hot embossing, micro-injection moulding, and bulk forming. These technologies rely on the application of high thermal and mechanical loads on the forming tool and especially on the integrated microstructures. To achieve sufficient tool life, functional tool materials with high strength and hardness like steel or cemented carbide are used. The mechanical properties of these materials are a strong limitation to the variety of structuring technologies which can be applied. Due to the non-contact thermal removal mechanism, electrical discharge machining (EDM) is a manufacturing technology which allows an almost process force free machining. It is used in many micro-technological applications. EDM offers a suitable alternative to conventional mould-and-die-making in terms of obtainable structure dimensions and accuracy. In combination with a wide range of geometric complexity and high accuracy, electrical discharge machining is able to process functional materials with precision of few micrometers. Since micro-electrical discharge machining can be used economically small series production, next to primary structuring of micro parts, it is predestined for the machining of micro tools. This paper presents a comparison of various micro-electrical discharge machining technologies and strategies for application in the field of micro tool manufacturing.

Keywords: Micro Manufacturing, Micro Electrical Discharge Machining, Die and Mould Making

Introduction

According to the NEXUS III market report, the world market for products based on MEMS shows a doubling over the next five years from approximately 12 billion US$ in the year 2004 to 25 billion US$ in 2009. Micro technical components with a part volume of less than 1 mm³ or structure dimensions in the range of micrometers are applied in various industrial products such as inkjets, gyroscopes or micro fluidics chips. The common manufacturing technologies for the production of these components originated from semiconductor industry but cutting and non-conventional processes are increasingly applied due to the technological and economical limitation of the semiconductor processes like material properties and batch size. Micro cutting, laser machining, LIGA-technology and electrical discharge machining (EDM) are manufacturing technologies, which are nowadays applied in many micro technological process chains. Because of the thermal material removal mechanism, EDM allows an almost process force free machining which operates independently from the mechanical properties of the processed material. In combination with the opportunity to produce complex geometries with high accuracy, electrical discharge machining can process functional materials like hardened steel, cemented carbide and electrically conductive ceramics to precision levels of just a few microns. Since EDM can be used economically in the single and small batch production, next to primary structuring of micro parts, it is predestined for the production of micro forming tools [1, 2, 3].

Technology of Micro Electrical Discharge Machining

Micro electrical discharge machining (μ-EDM) is the application of electrical discharge machining technologies for the manufacturing of micro and miniature parts and structures. It means the adoption of process technologies and machine tools to the requirements of micro production [4, 5, 6]. Therefore different aspects like miniaturized tool electrodes, reduced discharge energy and composition of the machined materials have to be considered. Compared to conventional EDM with discharge energies about 100 μJ the μ-EDM operates, depending on the type of generator, at discharge energies from 5 μJ to 0.1 μJ per single discharge. Modern ED machining tools use static impulse generators which are able to produce rectangular impulses with discharge currents down to 1 A and discharge durations of 0.2 μs. That means a minimum discharge energy of about $W_e = 5 \mu$J which is limited due to the electrical components and their switching rates. Another common used generator type is the relaxation generator which is able to produce impulse durations of 40 ns and discharge currents of 100 mA. This results in extremely small gap widths of $s_L = 1.5 \mu$m to $s_L = 5$ μm and very small material removal rates due to the minimum discharge energies of $W_e = 0.1 \mu$J. To achieve an economic process it is necessary to increase the material removal rate. Therefore spark generators which are able to produce extremely high impulse frequencies f_p of up to 10 MHz [7] are used for machining of micro parts and structures. Another important aspect of micro electrical discharge machining is the polarity of the electrode. In conventional EDM, with long impulse durations, the tool electrode is usually charged anodic to increase the material removal rate and to reduce electrode wear due to the polarity effect. This effect turns around at short pulse durations used in micro EDM due to the limited thermal and mechanical stability of the micro structures. On this account the tool electrode in micro electrical discharge machining is charged as cathode. Another aspect which has to be considered in all micro machining technologies is the composition of the machined material. Due to the thermal removal mechanism of EDM, micro structures of the material can be negatively affected by decomposition or transition processes and in certain cases influence the mechanical stability of the work piece. Furthermore, residual stresses resulting from melting and re-solidification of the material can plastically deform the micro structures by exceeding the yield stress of the supporting cross section [8].

Depending on the named aspects and the geometry of the work piece, different process variants have been developed in the micro electrical discharge machining. The following sections will give an overview of the possibilities and the limitations of the different EDM technologies.

Micro Wire Electrical Discharge Machining

Micro electrical discharge machining (μ-WEDM) is commonly used for the production of micromechanical devices and micro stamping tools (Fig. 1). Due to the requirements to micro structures like smallest slit widths and small inner corner radii, thin wire electrodes with diameters of $d_w = 0.1$ mm to $d_w = 0.01$ mm are used. The wire electrode material is usually tungsten or coated steel with tensile strength of more than 2000 N/mm², to guarantee sufficient thermal and mechanical stability. Still, the thermal and mechanical stability of the wire electrode limits the EDM process regarding the machinable structure height, i.e. a wire electrode with a diameter of d_w = 0.03 mm allows a maximum work piece height of approximately 5 mm. The limited mechanical pre-tensioning of the wire electrode, due to their mechanical stability, leads to wire vibration and causes a loss of machining accuracy or surface quality. On this account coaxial flushing of the gap is reduced or even totally avoided.

Figure 1: Micro wire-eroded components of a stamping tool

Nowadays, high precision machining systems with super finishing spark generators obtain a minimum slit width of 0.04 mm at machining accuracies in the range of ± 0.001 mm and achieve aspect ratios of more than 100. Furthermore, it is possible to machine reproducibly structures with a width of 15 μm by micro wire electrical discharge machining. In order to obtain a surface roughness of less than Ra = 0.1 μm, the usage of super-finishing technologies, applying one main cut and several trim cuts with reduced discharge energy, is necessary.

Micro Die Sinking

Micro die sinking is mainly used for the manufacturing of replication tools as used in micro injection moulding or hot embossing, to produce micromechanical parts in large numbers. Micro die sinking uses micro structured form electrodes to manufacture defined structures and work pieces.

Figure 2: Rotational form electrode (right) manufactured by micro-WEDG with wire-electrodes with a diameter of d = 50 μm, minimum structure size 30 μm (left)

The obtainable structure size is limited by the erosion process and by the design and the different micro structuring technologies to produce the form electrodes as μ-WEDM, micro-wire electrical discharge grinding (micro-WEDG) (Fig. 2), micro milling and electro forming. Due to the polarity effect, relative wear in micro die sinking is up to 30 % higher than in conventional sinking EDM. For compensation, high wear resistant composites, based on refractory materials like tungsten copper or cemented carbides, are used as electrode material for micro die sinking EDM although they are more complicated to machine. Another important aspect of micro die sinking is the flushing of the gap, since flushing through the electrodes is not possible due to their small dimensions. The poor flushing conditions and the small gap width result in high requirements to the feed control and the mechanical properties of the positioning system.

Micro Electrical Discharge Drilling

Micro electrical discharge drilling is a special application of micro die sinking industrially used in the manufacturing injection nozzles and starting holes for wire EDM. It uses rotating pin electrodes to manufacture rotationally symmetrical bores and through holes. There are special demands on the electrode production, electrode handling and electrode positioning due to minimum electrode diameters of less than 25 μm. Deployed electrode materials are cemented carbide, tungsten or tungsten copper due to the high requirements in respect to mechanical stability and wear resistance. To improve the flushing of the gap and therewith the roundness accuracy of the bore hole, rotation spindles with a rotational speed of up to 2000 min^{-1} are applied. Experimental results and numerical simulations by computational fluid dynamics (CFD) have shown that rotating electrodes and therewith flushing of the gap can only improve the process stability to a certain level. To improve removing of debris out of the gap moreover it is necessary to use an additional translatory vibration, which is superposed to the feed movement of the electrode. Boreholes with an aspect ratio of 50 can be machined with this technology.

Micro Electrical Discharge Contouring

Due to the limitation of wire EDM, like limited thermal and mechanical stability of the wire electrode, or the limitations in die sinking EDM, in respect to the overall dimensions of the work piece that permit the use of shaped die sinking electrodes because of the process instabilities caused by the poor flushing conditions and large active electrode surface, micro electrical discharge contouring (EDC) is an alternative machining technology. Micro EDC uses a path-controlled multi axis feed motion between work piece and the rotating tool electrode, which is generally geometrically simple in order to reduce effort and costs for electrode production. Due to the similarity to electrical discharge drilling wear resistant materials are used for the tool electrodes. They are either commercially available or machined on fly by electrical discharge dressing. Furthermore, the electrode wear can be compensated during the machining by implementing technology-dependent correction algorithms in the path-controlled motion. The flushing of the gap and therewith the removal of the debris is less critical compared to electrical discharge drilling due to the relative movement of the electrode and the open contour of the work piece. Due to the overcoming of the above mentioned limitations regarding micro wire and micro die sinking EDM, the obtainable complexity of contours is higher, but the achievable surface quality is lower because of the non-existence of process regimes for roughing and finishing technologies.

Micro electrical discharge contouring can be classified into two process variants namely micro electrical discharge grinding (μ-EDG) and micro electrical discharge milling. Micro electrical discharge grinding uses the path controlled movement of a rotating disk electrode superimposed by the feed of the EDM process to machine straight channels. The channel cross section results from the profile of the disk electrode. Minimum channel width of 50 μm can be machined with an aspect ratio of 15. Technological investigations concentrate on the series production stability especially for the manufacture of forming tools with micro channels as used in micro fluidic applications [9, 10]. Micro electrical discharge milling uses a rotating pin electrode for the machining of the work piece contour. It can be used to produce almost any kind of three-dimensional structures [11]. The achievable minimum structure dimensions depend on the diameter of the pin electrodes and the gap width. Nowadays pin electrodes machined by electrical discharge dressing with a minimum diameter of 0.1 mm are used in micro electrical discharge milling. Due to the importance of the process strategy on the machining results, the development of appropriate path-control algorithms, feed control strategies, and wear compensation techniques are in the focus of investigation [12, 13].

Micro Electrical Discharge Dressing

The availability of geometrically defined electrodes is a requirement for the micro electrical discharge drilling and milling. To avoid deviations in true running accuracy due to the electrode clamping and the filigree form, the electrodes are mainly manufactured directly using electrical discharge dressing technologies. This can be done using a block electrode of cemented carbide and applying an inverse polarity causing over proportional wear on the rotating electrode. Due to the large contact area on a block electrode and the relatively high transferable discharge energy it is possible to achieve a high erode volume and therewith a short dressing time. The limitations of this technology regarding the machinable complexity of profiled electrodes can be overcome using micro wire electrical discharge grinding (μ-WEDG). μ-WEDG uses an unwinding wire electrode to machine a rotating electrode [14]. In comparison to electrical discharge dressing on a block electrode the transferable discharge energy and therewith the dressing rates are much lower due to the limited thermal and mechanical stability of the wire electrode. In order to achieve satisfying machining times multi-step dressing strategies are commonly used where in the first step a cemented carbide block electrode is used for roughing and afterwards the final electrode shape is machined by the unwinding wire electrode in μ-WEDG. With this dressing technologies pin electrodes with a diameter of 100 μm and an aspect ratio of 50 can be machined (Fig. 3). Similar technologies can also be used to manufacture micro structured cylindrical parts, which can serve as forming tools [15].

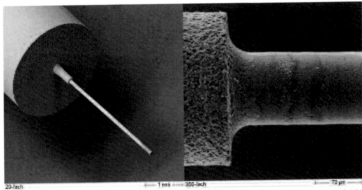

Figure 3: Rotational tool electrode manufactured by micro-WEDG with a diameter of 100 μm and a length of 5 mm

Conclusion

This paper presents a comparison of various micro-electrical discharge machining technologies and strategies for applications in the field of micro tool manufacturing. Due to the technology of

419

micro EDM, it has high potential as a structuring technology for the manufacturing of micro/miniature tools i.e. dies and moulds.

Acknowledgement

The work was carried out as a part of the European Integrated Project "Integration of manufacturing systems for mass-manufacture of miniature/micro products –MASMICRO", the DFG-research project (German Research Foundation) UH 100/40-1 "Electrical Discharge Microstructuring of Rotating Components of Hard Materials", the DFG-research project (German Research Foundation) UH 100/9 "Development of an EDM Machining Centre for Micro technology".

References

[1]   E.Uhlmann, U. Doll, 'Application of μ-EDM in the Machining of Micro Structured Forming Tools' 3rd Int. Machining & Grinding Conference, Cincinnati (USA), 1999 published as Technical Paper – Society of Manufacturing Engineers MR 99-285, pp.1-11.

[2]   F. Michel, W. Ehrfeld, O. Koch, H-P. Gruber, 'EDM for micro fabrication technology and applications', Proceedings International Seminar on Precision Engineering and Micro Technology, Aachen (Germany), 2000, pp.127- 139.

[3]   T. Masuzawa, 'State of the Art of Micromachining', CIRP Annals – Manufacturing Technology, Vol 49/2, 2000, pp. 473-488.

[4]   T. Masuzawa, 'Micro-EDM', Proceedings of the 13th International Symposium for Electromachining – ISEM XIII, Bilbao (Spain), 2001, pp. 3-19.

[5]   D. M. Allen, 'Microelectrodischarge Machining for MEMS Applications', IEE Seminar on Demonstrated Micromachining technologies for Industry, Ref. No. 2000/032, pp. 6/1-6/4.

[6]   D. T. Pham, S.S. Dimov, S. Bigot, A. Ivanov, K. Popov, 'Micro-EDM – recent developments and research issues', Journal of Materials Processing Technology, Vol. 149, 2004, pp. 50-57.

[7]   T. Masaki, et. al, 'Micro Electro-Discharge Machining', Proceedings of the 9th International Symposium for Electromachining – ISEM IX, Nagoya (Japan), 1989, pp. 26-29.

[8]   G. Spur, N. Daus, U. Doll, 'WEDM of microstructurd Component Parts – Heat Conduction Model', Int. Journal of Electrical Machining (IJEM), Vol. 4, 1999, pp. 41-46.

[9]   E.Uhlmann, U. Doll, S.Piltz, 'Electrical Discharge Grinding of Microstructures', Int. Journal of Electrical Machining (IJEM), Vol. 6, 2001, pp. 41-46.

[10] H.M. Chow, B.H. Fan, F.Y. Huang, 'Micro slit machining using electro discharge machining with a modified rotary disk electrode (RDE)', Journal of Materials Proceeding Technology, Vol. 91, 1999, pp. 161-166.

[11] W. Zhao, et. al., 'A CAD/CAM system for micro-ED-milling of small 3D freeform cavity', Journal of Materials Processing Technology, Vol. 149, 2004, pp. 573-578.

[12] Z.Y. Yu, T. Masuzawa, M. Fujino, 'Micro-EDM for Three-Dimensional Cavities – Development of Uniform Wear Method', CIRP Annals – Manufacturing Technology, Vol. 47/1, 1998, pp. 169-172.

[13] K.P. Rajurkar, Z.Y. Yu, '3D Micro-EDM Using CAD/CAM', CIRP Annals – Manufacturing Technology, Vol. 49/1, 2000, pp. 127-130.

[14] T. Masuzawa, M. Fujino, K. Kobayashi, 'Wire-Electro-Discharge Grinding for Micro-Machining', Annals of the CIRP, Vol.34/1, 1985, pp. 431-434

[15] E. Uhlmann, S. Piltz, S. Jerzembeck, 'Micro Machining of Cylindrical Parts by Electrical Discharge Grinding', Journal of Material Processing Technology, Vol. 160, 2005, pp. 15-23.

Knowledge Based Systems Support in Micro-Manufacturing

N. D. Mekras[1, a], N. A. Karbadakis[2, b], P. V. Kontovazenitis[3, c], N. M. Vaxevanidis[4, d]

[1, 2, 3, 4] ANTER Ltd.–Technology Development and Research Co, Feidippidou 22 Str., 11527 Athens, Greece

[a]anter@anter.gr, [a]nkmekras@otenet.gr, [b]nkarba@anter-net1.com, [c]pkonto@anter-net1.com,
[d]vaxev@ath.forthnet.gr

Abstract. The scope of this paper is to indicate how Knowledge Based Systems (KBS) can be applied to support manufacturing systems and especially activities concerning decision support on micro-manufacturing. Also an approach will be presented concerning the integration of the KBS with the rest IT applications of a manufacturing enterprise. Such an approach is already being implemented within the EU FP6 project MASMICRO, where a Knowledge Based Decision Support System is being developed to support micro-manufacturing. The paper includes: a) an introduction to Knowledge Based Systems, with a short presentation of the three main Knowledge Representation Structures (KRS) used in KBS and their relevant knowledge processing methods for reasoning and knowledge update, b) a list of possible Knowledge Bases (KB) examples to support applications within a manufacturing system, concerning processes, products, materials, machines and tools, and c) a presentation of an approach for the integration of the KBS support with the rest IT applications of a manufacturing enterprise.

Keywords: Artificial Intelligence, Knowledge Based Systems, Micro-manufacturing.

Introduction

In this paper a short presentation is given on how Knowledge Based Systems (KBS) technology can support manufacturing systems, and also a presentation of a methodological approach for the integration of the KBS with the rest IT applications in a manufacturing company. KBS have emerged as an Artificial Intelligence (AI) research field more than 20 years ago and provided useful methods and techniques for knowledge representation and processing, mainly for two basic categories of Knowledge Representation Structures (KRS) which are based on Rules and Object-Oriented structures. In the next sections of this paper, besides a short introduction on these knowledge representation and processing methods, a presentation will be included concerning possible KBS application examples, which can be used to support activities in manufacturing, together with a proposed approach for the integration of these applications with the rest Information System of an enterprise. The goal of this integration approach is to help the KBS developer, to develop KBS applications, which are part of the rest IT system of the enterprise, use common IT resources (like common production databases) and work as a supplement to the rest production software modules. Through this approach manufacturing knowledge and experience that can not be expressed algorithmically, can be represented, stored and processed through the KBS methods and techniques, and cooperate with the rest IT software in an integrated manner, increasing by this way the utilization, use and efficiency of the KBS in manufacturing. The software implementation of this approach is under development within the EU FP6 project MASMICRO, focusing on the development of KBS applications for micro-manufacturing systems.

Introduction to KBS. Since the 70's Artificial Intelligence (AI) researchers focused on efforts to represent knowledge and process it by computers trying to develop methods that resemble the way that the human mind stores and processes knowledge, besides algorithmic knowledge and mathematical procedures. From these efforts several methods have appeared for the representation and processing of Knowledge Bases of both rule-based type and object-oriented type (Semantic networks, Frames/Objects) [1,2,3], aiming mainly at the representation and processing of symbolic knowledge, that can also cooperate and work supplementary with algorithms and mathematical models. A short introduction on the three main Knowledge Representation Structures (Rules, Semantic Networks and Frames/Objects) used in KBS follows next:

One of the most common Knowledge Representation Structures used for the creation of knowledge bases are the *Rules* in the form of Horn clauses. Rules may also use and be supported by data, stored in simple predicates or in records in a conventional database. Creating and combining rules, knowledge bases can be created and processed with formalized techniques, like the techniques of forward and backward rule chaining. Processing the rules, inferences can be made and results can be obtained, that are based on the rules and data of the knowledge base.

Another form of Knowledge Representation Structures is the representation through the *Semantic Networks*. In this model entities are represented as the nodes of a graph structure, in which the links represent the relationships between entities. The links can represent functional relationships, class membership relationships, hierarchical relationships, etc. The semantic network reasoning process is based on the processing of the network aiming to establish whether two concepts can be related within a network. The most common processing method within a semantic net is the method of intersection search.

A third structure for representing knowledge are the *Frames* or *Objects*, which were developed originally by Minsky in 1968 at MIT. The main idea in frames/objects is that knowledge is organized in classes of entities (frames), which are related and classified in the knowledge base. Each frame contains information that is stored in specific information slots, which identify its basic structural properties and may include values, restrictions and methods. We may say that the frame/object structure resembles to the structure of complex networks, where on each node much more information is stored than the information stored on the nodes of a semantic net. Processing a frame system for reasoning purposes gives the possibility for obtaining inferences about existence of frames/entities, generic and default properties and methods' results. Also results of reasoning by analogy and checking for abnormal situations are possible. Object-oriented programming that is used widely nowadays originates from the frame systems and uses the basic principles of classification, inheritance, slot-filler knowledge representation and message passing between objects/frames.

KBS applications in micro-manufacturing

As it is already mentioned in previous paragraphs, KBS methods and tools are applied by the authors of this paper within the FP6 EU project MASMICRO, for the development of a KBS decision support tool for mass-micro-manufacturing. The aim of this tool is to support the representation, storage and processing of both symbolic and algorithmic knowledge concerning *processes*, *products*, *materials*, *machines* and *tools*. In the next paragraphs of this section a short introduction on KBS implementation and a listing of possible KBS examples for micro-manufacturing is presented for the above 5 main categories of production entities. The listing of the KBS examples is given in Table 1, which includes the Knowledge Representation Structures (KRS) for the Knowledge Bases (KB) content and examples of results that the knowledge processing mechanisms (inference engines) can provide for the several applications.

Note, that micro-manufacturing in the context of the present paper is considered to be the production of parts and components with at least two dimensions in the sub-millimeter range; see also [4,5].

422

Processes. Software applications for the representation, storage and processing of both symbolic and algorithmic manufacturing processes' knowledge, are of vital importance for a manufacturing enterprise since processes are considered the core elements of a manufacturing system. From the time that the industrial revolution started, until today, several approaches for the design and improvement of production systems are based on the concept of a well designed and efficient process that can be represented and re-engineered using methods for process mapping, calculations and measurements [6]. KBS methods, both rule-based and object-oriented (semantic networks, frames/objects) can be useful for the representation and the processing of processes' knowledge, to support their management and improvement [3,7,8]. A presentation of the available processes for the production of micro-components is beyond the scope of the paper; see [5,9] for an overview. However, it should be noted that three main production routes are followed: (a) the down-scaling of existing precision manufacturing processes, (b) the up-scaling of MEMS processes from the micro-electronics sector and (c) the development of entirely new technologies. Both up-scaling and down-scaling suffers, in most cases, from process stability and worsening of materials properties whilst on the other hand, entirely new processes have not yet reached the level of industrial use [4,9].

Products. The types of knowledge for describing and classifying micro-products and micro-components concern mainly symbolic knowledge structures of the object-oriented form for the representation of the product/component entities, their attributes and their relations [3,10]. On the other hand rule-based knowledge and algorithmic knowledge can be attached to these entities to express products' manufacturability, dimension limits and tolerances, conformance with quality standards, etc. Note, that in case of micro-products the geometry (dimensions and tolerances) affects significantly not only the possible manufacturing sequence but also the associated production support in terms of handling, assembly and metrology. Micro-products should possess a high degree of integration of functionalities and components and require an innovative product design methodology; see [9].

Materials. The structure of materials' knowledge needed for manufacturing usually describes certain attributes and specifications of the materials needed in a process for the production of a specific type of product. Usually the knowledge concerning materials information for manufacturing purposes is rather of a simple structure and can be stored in data tables of relational databases that can be used by both symbolic and algorithmic knowledge bases of processes and products. Also, apart from materials information in the form of data records, additional knowledge is often necessary, mainly for the relation of the materials attributes and properties to the processes and the products that need these materials. Since the origin of micro-manufacturing is the micro-electronics sector the use of semi-conducting materials (mainly silicon) is quite established. The specific properties of the more traditional materials (metals, ceramics, polymers) and the observed size effect, limit for the time being, their direct use in micro-products [4,9]. However, these "traditional" materials together with the corresponding manufacturing methods are well suited for mass production.

Machines and tools. Both object-oriented and rule-based knowledge structures can be used for the representation of machines' and tools' attributes & functionalities [3,7,10]. The object-oriented structures can be used for the classification of the machines and tools according to their general and more specific attributes, while the rules can express manufacturing size limits, sequence of tasks, tools' usage etc.

Examples of KBS content	Examples of Inference Engines' Results
a) PROCESSES (Forming / Machining / Thermal processes (micro-EDM, LBM), Assembly, Handling, Quality Control, Metrology, Operations Management)	
a1) *Rules* for selecting type of micro-fabrication process and material according to product type.	a1) Micro-fabrication process to be applied and material selection.
a2) *Rules* for relating the sequence of micro-fabrication tasks with product geometrical features.	a2) The sequence of micro-fabrication steps.
a3) *Rules* for relating the fabrication process parameters with material attributes.	a3) Operational parameters of micro-fabrication processing steps (e.g. punch force and speed, type of lubrication)
a4) *Rules* for selecting assembly method and the sequence of assembly steps according to material type, shape of components and product attributes.	a4) Assembly method (e.g. miniature nut and bolt fasteners, glue, snap fit, built-in approach) and sequence of assembly steps.
a5) *Rules* for selecting the type of micro-handling method and micro-handling parameters according to product attributes (e.g. product dimensions, fragility, etc.).	a5) Micro-handling method to be applied (e.g. using friction, electrostatic, cryogenic) and handling parameters (e.g. movement range, velocity, gripper dimensions, force).
a6) Object-Oriented structures (*Semantic Networks* or *Frames / Objects)* to classify and relate micro-production processes.	a6) Grouping of micro-production processes according to common attributes.
a7) *Rules* for relating values of quality variables with machinery status, raw material and other factors & parameters that influence quality.	a7) Causes for non-conformities.
a8) *Rules* for recognizing product features indicative to quality problems.	a8) Product features with quality problems.
a9) *Semantic networks* to represent and process cause / effect models to investigate quality problems (Ishikawa method).	a9) Causes for non-conformities.
a10) *Rules* for expressing availability constraints and precedence conditions for processes or for tasks within a process.	a10) Scheduling of processes.
b) PRODUCTS (Micro-pins, micro-gears, micro-cups, micro-valves, MEMS, implants, etc.)	
b1) Object-Oriented structures (*Semantic Networks* or *Frames / Objects)* to represent, classify hierarchically and relate product entities and their attributes.	b1) Grouping of products according to generic and more specific attributes.
b2) *Rules* for modifying existing products according to new specifications / needs.	b2) New product specifications.
c) MATERIALS (Metallic Alloys, Silicon, Ceramics, Polymers, etc.)	
c1) *Rules* for selecting the material according to product type and process needs & conditions.	c1) Selection of appropriate material.
c2) *Rules* for controlling material properties during process implementation.	c2) Process parameters that do not affect the material quality.
d) MACHINES / TOOLS (Forming, Machining, Micro-EDM, Micro-Assembly, Handling, Metrology & Inspection)	
d1) *Rules* for selecting machine set-up parameters and tools according to product specifications and process needs (e.g. product geometry, material).	d1) Machine set-up parameters.

Table 1. KBS application examples in micro-manufacturing

Integrating the KBS applications

The level of integration of the KBS methods and tools in the factory is an important factor for improved performance and better utilization of the KBS applications, which should work in a cooperative manner and as a supplement to the rest IT applications of a manufacturing enterprise. Considering the KBS applications as part of an integrated IT system, among others, the following main benefits appear:

- Use of common databases for both the KBS and the rest IT applications. Often such databases already exist and both rule-based and object-oriented knowledge bases can utilize the already existing information.
- KBS can solve problems that concern mainly symbolic processing of knowledge and can work in parallel and cooperatively with algorithmic applications, in cases that together with the implementation of mathematical formulas and procedures, human decision making takes place that needs symbolic processing of expert knowledge.
- KBS applications, as part of an integrated IT system, can be used by several people in the company, and will not be implemented as isolated applications on a personal computer of a specific staff member or for a single work center.

Anyway, the achievement of full integration of the KBS applications within a manufacturing company is a quite difficult task and almost in all cases the KBS applications that have appeared, were developed to support knowledge processing for a specific manufacturing activity (e.g. design). By this way, the later integration of the KBS with the rest IT applications (e.g. Bill of Materials, MRP, Process Planning, etc.) is difficult, if not impossible in most cases.

Within the EU FP6 project MASMICRO, in which the authors of this paper are working for the development of a KBDS (Knowledge Based Decision Support System), which in fact consists of a set of KBS applications to support micro-manufacturing processes, an approach is being followed, by which the core components of the whole production system are considered to be the *processes,* as these are described by the IDEF0 and ASME international standards for processes representation [6]. The several MASMICRO KBS applications are considered as part of these processes, by including rules and object-oriented structures to represent and process knowledge both of rule-based type and object-oriented type that are applicable and are needed for decision making during the process implementation. By this way the systemic approach for production systems representation is followed, considering that the whole production system consists of chains of *processes,* which are linked, interrelated and use common production databases, and on the other hand the KBS applications are developed as attached to and as part of these *processes,* by representing and processing knowledge that the processes need and can not be expressed through mathematical formulas or algorithms. KBS applications, that are supporting decision making for the other four main categories of production entities, which are: the *products,* the *materials,* the *machines* and the *tools,* are also considered tightly linked and are attached to the *processes,* considering that the products are the outputs of the manufacturing processes, the materials are the inputs and the machines and the tools are the means for the processes to be implemented.

The basic structure of the MASMICRO KBDS is given in the next Fig. 1.

425

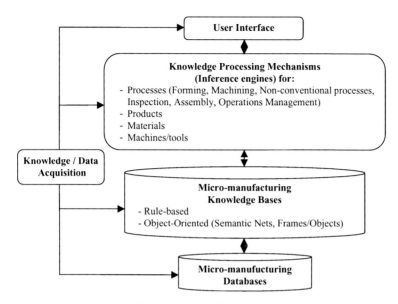

Fig. 1. Basic structure of the MASMICRO KBDS

References

[1] A. Frost: *Introduction to Knowledge Base Systems* (W. Collins & Sons Ltd., UK 1987).

[2] I. Malpas: *PROLOG: A relational language and its applications* (Prentice-Hall International, New Jersey, USA 1987).

[3] R. Kerr: *Knowledge-Based Manufacturing Management* (Addison-Wesley, Sydney 1991).

[4] U. Engel and R. Eckstein: Journal of Materials Processing Technology Vol.125-126 (2002), pp. 35-44.

[5] T. Masuzawa: Annals of the CIRP Vol. 49/2 (2000), pp. 473–488.

[6] J. Peppard and P. Rowland: *Redesigning processes,* in: *The essence of Business Process Re-engineering* (A. Buckley – Ed., Prentice Hall Europe, London, UK 1995).

[7] W. Meyer: *Expert Systems in Factory Management – Knowledge-Based CIM* (Publ. Ellis Horwood Ltd., UK 1990).

[8] N. Mekras: *Using Knowledge-Based Systems in Production Planning and Control Systems,* in conf. proceedings of IMS 2004 International Forum (Politecnico di Milano, Como, Italy 2004), pp. 650-657.

[9] L. Alting, F. Kimura, H.N. Hansen and G. Bissacco: Annals of the CIRP Vol. 52/2 (2003), pp. 635-657.

[10] S. Adiga: *Object-oriented Software for manufacturing Systems* (Chapman & Hall, New York, USA 1993).

A feasibility study of using rings of Shape Memory Alloy for forming-error compensation in micro-forming

Wenke Pan[1a], Yi Qin[1b]*, Fraser Law[1], Yanling Ma[1], Andrew Brockett[1] and Neal Juster[1]

[1]Centre for Micro-Technology, DMEM, University of Strathclyde, Glasgow G1 1XJ, UK
[a]email: *wenke.pan@strath.ac.uk;* [b]email: *qin.yi@strath.ac.uk*
* Corresponding author.

Abstract. Taking advantage of the special properties of Shape Memory Alloys (SMA), a concept of error compensation for micro-forming involving the use of SMA as an actuating element is proposed. Initial tests on tubular-cylinders with SMA enhancement wires have shown that the pressures created due to geometric changes of the SMA at temperatures above its transformation value can generate contraction of the cylinders of such magnitude as to indicate their possibility for application to error-compensation in micro-forming. A micro-forming tool design with an SMA enhanced ring structure is, therefore, proposed.

Keywords: Micro-forming, Tool design, Shape Memory Alloy, Forming-errors

1. Introduction

Due to variations of the forming conditions in precision forming, the accuracy of the formed part often varies from cycle to cycle [1]. Major efforts in tool design for forming-error compensation included the improvement of material flow, the reduction of forming pressure and tool-deflection, and the extension of tool-life. A tool configuration with internal pressure relief was used to form spur-gears [2]. Using relief-hole principles can also be found in the literature [3]. The "pressure-relief" concept was also used recently in the design of tools for the backward can-extrusion of cartridge-cases [4]. Another method used to reduce the forming pressure at the final stage of forming was to employ the so-called "divided flow" concept [5]. A retractable container, which was driven axially by an actuator while the billet was squeezed by the punch, was employed, to achieve the reduction of the forming pressure by using friction as an assistance to the material flow [6]. The non-linearity of the variation of component-form with the process parameters in precision forming suggests that it would be difficult to achieve error-compensation by the above-mentioned measures alone. "In-process error compensation" concepts were therefore proposed. A ring-shaped die [7] was designed to reduce errors in extrusion and drawing in which the die-orifice was reduced as the forming-pressure was increased. A truncated, conical-shell die was also designed to effect in-process error-compensation in which the extrusion pressure acted in such manner as to reduce the die-orifice to counteract its natural tendency to expand, a small rotation of the die being enforced by the increased forming pressure [8].

Considering the sizes of the formed parts, the precision to be achieved and scale of the forming processes in Micro-forming the above-mentioned methods may not applicable to Micro-forming. The latter renders challenges to forming-tool-fabrication not only from the reduced tool-sizes point of view but also from the requirements in respect of greater precision [9-12]. An intelligent forming-tool design concept was, therefore, proposed to target "in-process" forming-error compensation without applying excessive constraint onto the tool-fabrication. The design was to use Shape Memory Alloy as a tool actuating-element to effect die-deflections in a controlled manner and hence, to influence the dimensional variations of the workpiece. To validate the concept of using SMA as an actuating element for the forming tool, a test rig was developed to explore the possibility of using SMA wires in the design of the forming tool. For this purpose, a SMA enhanced tubular structure design was proposed. Two types of the tubular structures and two types of the

427

tubular materials were tested. Both theoretical analysis and experiment showed the feasibility of using the proposed tool-structure to achieve particular levels of error-compensation (from a few microns to ten microns for the tool-dimensions examined) with the SMA' actuation being in either a self-adapted or a controlled manner. The study conducted so far has laid down a solid foundation for the development of the design concept into a full forming-tool testing system. This paper reports the experiments and findings, as well as the proposed full tool-system for error-compensation for micro-bulk-forming.

2. Shape Memory Alloy (SMA)

Shape Memory Alloys (SMA) have a unique ability to 'remember' their original shapes, among these alloys the most widely used being Nickel and Titanium (Nitinol). At lower temperatures, the Nitinol structure is a highly twinned Martensitic structure, and its stress-strain curve resembles that of an elastomer, in which there is a plateau stress. At higher temperatures, its Austenite structure shows the characteristic stress-strain curve of most metals but the structure is much harder. The phase transformation temperature range can be between -50°C to 100°C. The elastic modulus for Martensite and Austenite are, typically, 28GPa and 83GPa respectively, and the initial yield stress about 70 MPa and 200MPa respectively. The ultimate tensile strength for Austenite is, however, much higher (about 900MPa). When Nitinol is heated to above the transformation temperature, it will recover its original shape. However, if it is constrained, it may generate sufficient force for forming-die applications.

3. Experimental Investigation of SMA-wire Enhanced Tubular-Cylinders

3.1 Brass cylinder and experimental procedure

A tubular brass cylinder with inner and outer diameters of 25 and 31mm respectively was prepared. A thread of 1mm depth and 2 mm pitch was machined on the outer surface. A shape memory wire of 1 mm diameter was embedded tightly into the thread (A steel jubilee clip was used for tightening the SMA wire). The head of a thermocouple was fixed onto the surface of the shape memory wire. An induction coil, connected to a power supply, was used to generate the required temperature.

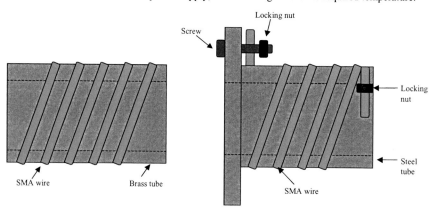

Figure 1 Illustration of the tubular brass cylinder enhanced with the SMA wire

Figure 2 Illustration of the tubular steel cylinder enhanced with the SMA wire

Three tests were performed. The tool used for the measurement of the inner diameter was a 'Micro-MAAG' with an accuracy of 2 to 3 microns. Fig. 1 shows the design of the tubular brass cylinder with the SMA wire. At room temperature, the inner diameter of the tubular cylinder was measured at selected locations and the average inner diameter was calculated. After the power supply had been switched on and the temperature in the SMA wire had increased to about 100°C, the inner diameter of the tube was measured again. Following this, the induction coil was removed, as also were the jubilee clip and the SMA wire. The jubilee clip was then re-placed onto the surface of the brass cylinder and re-tightened, and the inner diameter of the cylinder was measured again. The result was compared with that initially measured. If the average inner-diameter value was greater than that measured initially, the jubilee clip was tightened further and the process repeated until both measured values were close to each other. Otherwise, the jubilee clip was relaxed and the same procedure was then repeated. This was done with a view to eliminating the influence of the jubilee clip on the deflection of the cylinder when it was heated.

After the above operation, the power supply was switched on and the tube inner diameter was measured again when the temperature reached about 100°C. Figs. 3 and 4 show the measured inner diameter of the brass cylinder with and without the SMA wire being heated respectively, the average inner diameters being 25.033 and 25.046mm respectively. It can be seen that the inner diameter of the tube with the SMA wire being heated is smaller than that without being heated, the difference being about 13 microns, which indicates the contraction of the tube when the temperature reached 100°C.

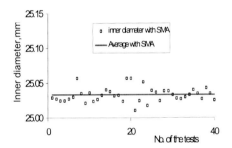

Figure 3 Measured inner diameter values at temperatures above the transformation temperature of the SMA

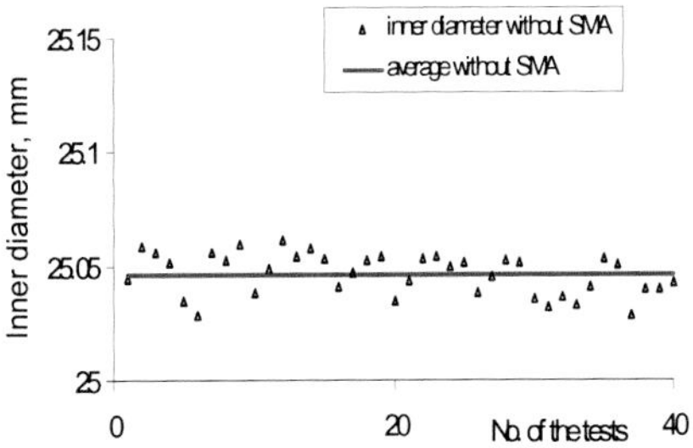

Figure 4 Measured inner diameter values at temperatures below the transformation temperature of the SMA

3.2 Steel cylinder

The average inner diameter of the tubular steel cylinder was 25.048mm and 25.044mm without and with the SMA wire being heated respectively, the difference being about 4 microns only. The compression force from the SMA wire was only able to reduce a small amount of the deflection of the cylinder, which may not be sufficient for meeting error-compensation requirements. SMA tubes or rings will have to be used for this purpose.

Two experiments showed that the SMA wire contracts when it was heated above its transformation temperature. This contraction may lead to sufficient reduction of the die-bore diameter when a ring-die structure is used. If the contraction of the die-bore is sufficient when the forming pressure is applied, it may be introduced into micro-forming tool design for error compensation where the compensation requirements are relatively low, compared to those for the forming of macro-components.

4. A Simplified Algorithm for SMA Wire/Ring Design

A model for a simplified analysis which considers a tubular cylinder with an embedded SMA wire is shown in Fig. 5, whilst Fig. 6 shows another model which considers a workpiece, a die and a shape memory ring (a compound die structure). The die material is assumed to be a tool steel with E=193GPa and v=0.3, and the Shape Memory Alloy ring to have properties of E=28GPa and v=0.3. Only elastic deflection of the die is considered. It is assumed that the temperature increases to 100°C from room temperature (20 °C). Two steps may be used for the prediction of the effect of the SMA wire/ring for forming-error compensation. The first step is to assume a required contraction from the SMA ring and then to determine how much pressure is needed to achieve this contraction, based on which the contraction of the die inner surface is then calculated. Assuming the inner and outer radius of the SMA ring to be r2 and r3 respectively (Fig. 5), the pressure P to cause 2.5% contraction of the outer surface, for example, can be calculated by means of the following equation:

$$P = \frac{E_2}{(1+v_2)}*(\frac{1}{r_2^2}-\frac{1}{r_3^2})*(\frac{1-v_2}{1+v_2}*\frac{1}{r_2^2}+\frac{1}{r_3^2})\frac{1}{r_3}*u_{cr} \qquad (1)$$

The second step is the analysis of the compound-ring die model. The die inner and outer surface radius is r1 and r2 respectively. The displacement may be calculated by means of the following equation:

$$u_{Ar} = \frac{r_1}{2(1-v_1)}*\frac{\alpha_1 P}{\alpha_2*\alpha_4+\alpha_3*\alpha_5} \qquad (2)$$

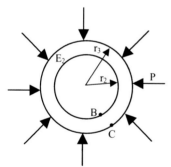

Figure 5 Model for the prediction of the contraction pressure induced by SMA phase transformation

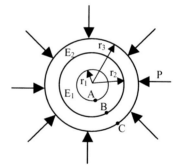

Figure 6 Model for the prediction of the contraction of the die inner surface

where α_1 to α_5 are function of the die and SMA material constants and structure geometrical parameters.

Fig. 7 shows the equivalent pressures induced by the contraction of the SMA ring for the radii examined. The contraction varies from 3.5 microns to 6.1 microns when the SMA ring diameter is 4mm. For a smaller radius of the SMA ring, e.g. 3mm, the contraction varies from 4.9 microns to 6.8 microns (Fig.8). Therefore, for the same thickness, the smaller inner radius can contract more.

430

The radius change of the die-insert with temperature can be calculated with $\Delta u = r * \alpha * \Delta T$. When the die-insert radius r is 0.5mm, $\alpha = 1.85 * 10^{-5}$ and $\Delta T = 80\,^{\circ}\text{C}$ (i.e. the transformation temperature is about 100 °C), die inner surface contraction will be less than 1 micron. Compared to the compensation possibly induced by the SMA ring, this change is insignificant.

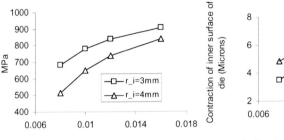

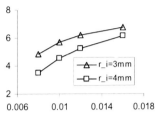

Figure 7 Equivalent pressures induced by the contraction of the SMA ring

Figure 8 Displacement of the die inner surface due to the contraction of the SMA ring

5. Micro-forming Tool-System Design

Based on the results of experiment and analysis, a forming tool system with error-compensation functions was proposed (Fig. 9). The forming-tool system consists of a punch, a die insert, a part-ejector, an SMA ring, a die support, an outer ring and a guidance cylinder. The insulated induction coils are wired around the outer ring and connected to a power supply. A thermocouple is embedded into the outer ring. During the forming process, the temperature in the die can be controlled and hence different levels of the die-contractions can be achieved. This system has been fabricated by an industrial company and a full-scale investigation on the error-compensation capability of the system has been started.

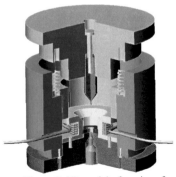

Figure 9 3D model of a micro-forming tool system with the SMA enhanced structure

6. Conclusions

From the tests on the SMA enhanced tubular cylinders and the theoretical prediction of the die-deflections, it can be seen that SMA enhanced tubular-structures may function well as actuating elements for micro-forming applications. A SMA ring may be combined with a die-insert to form an error-compensation unit. The test results show that successful error-compensation is achievable, of from a few microns to more than 10 microns, through properly controlling the temperature in the SMA and the appropriate design of the tools.

Acknowledgement

Financial support from the European Commission for conducting part of the research reported is acknowledged (MASMICRO Project, Contract No. EU-NMP-CT2-2004-500095).

References

[1]. Y. Qin and R. Balendra, "Analysis of temperature and component form-error variations during cold extrusion of engineering components in multi-cycle productions", J. Mats. Proc. Tech., 145 (2) (2004) 171-180.

[2] J. C. Choi and Y. Choi, "Precision forging of spur gears with inside relief", Int. J. Mach. Tools and Manufact., 39 (10) (1999) 1575-1588.

[3] K. Kondo, "Methods for improving accuracy in forging", in: Proc. JSTP Int. Seminar on Precision Forging, Osaka, 31 March – 1 April (1997), pp. 13-1 - 13-8.

[4] Y. Qin and R. Balendra, "FE simulation for development of process design considerations – An industry-case study", Int. J. Manufact. Sci. & Prod., 5 (1-2) (2003) 73 – 77.

[5] K. Kondo and K. Ohga, "Precision cold die forging of a ring gear by divided flow method", Int. J. Mach. Tools. & Manufact. 35 (8) (1995) 1105-1113.

[6] K. Osakada, X. Wang and S. Hanami, "Precision forging of spline by flashless die forging with axially driven die", CIRP Annals, 46 (1) (1997) 209-212.

[7] K. Osakada, "Precision cold forging with controlled elastic deformation of die", in: Report of the 27th ICFG Plenary Meeting, 19-23th Sept. Padova, Italy, 1994.

[8] T. Wanheim, R. Balendra and Y. Qin, "Extrusion die for in-process compensation of component-errors due to die-elasticity", J. Mats. Proc. Tech., 72 (2) (1997) 177-182.

[9] M.Geiger, M.Kleiner, R.Eckstein, N.Tiesler and U.Engel, "Microforming", Annals of CIRP, 50 (2) (2001) 445 – 462.

[10] U. Engel, R. Eckstein, "Microforming – from basic research to its realisation", J. Mats. Proc. Tech.,. 125/126 (2002) 35-44.

[11] F. Vollerston, Z. Hu, H. Schulze Niehoff and C. Theiler, "State of the art in microforming and investigations into micro-deep drawing", J. Mats. Proc. Tech.,. 151. (1-3), (2004) 70-79.

[12] Y. Qin, "Micro-forming and miniature manufacturing systems – Development needs and perspectives", Keynote paper of the 11th Int. Conf. of Metal Forming, Sept. Birmingham, J. Mats. Proc. Tech., in-press, 2006.

Intelligent
Manufacturing Systems

Business Benefit Analysis for Manufacturing Enterprise Projects: Towards Generic Tools

Sackett, P.J. [1], Tiwari, A. [1], Turner, C.J. [1], Salmon, R [2],

[1]*Manufacturing Department, School of Applied Sciences,*

Cranfield University, Cranfield, MK43 0AL, U.K.

Phone: +44 (0) 1234 754250

Fax: +44 (0) 1234 750852

e-mails : [p.j.sackett, a.tiwari, c.j.turner]@cranfield.ac.uk

[2]*BOC Edwards, Dolphin Road, Shoreham-By-Sea, West Sussex, BN43 6PY, U.K.*

Abstract

Many manufacturing enterprises rely on local, ad-hoc and simplistic investment appraisal tools in assessing the viability of business initiatives. The authors illustrate the gap between user requirements and current functionalities of available support tools. This paper details the design and construction of an interactive robust business benefit analysis tool specifically for use within a manufacturing enterprise setting. The application of the tool in generic cost reduction initiatives is illustrated through an industrial case study.

Keywords: Cost-benefit analysis; Sensitivity analysis; Computer based tool; Investment appraisal

1. Introduction

Typically within manufacturing enterprises there are multiple models and tools for investment appraisal; these may provide conflicting advice and are inappropriate for the integrated and global manufacturing environment. Existing methods often require users to make ad hoc changes to complex spreadsheet applications requiring significant specialist knowledge and expertise on the part of the user. These models and tools are rich in undocumented legacy assumptions and typically based on personal data sets that lack transparency and application across the enterprise. Tools rely heavily on local model developers and the users to tailor the decision support framework to multiple individual application instances. Traditionally business benefit analysis has been performed with classical financial analysis techniques. Financial analysis has been described by Sharpe and Alexander [1] as a way of analysing investment options for inclusion in a portfolio. Business benefit analysis in literature tends to point towards the use of the financial function within Microsoft Excel.

Cost Benefit Analysis has a wider application than financial analysis, creating a more holistic and long term view of an investment decision. Some Cost Benefit Analysis (CBA) tools are commercially available to carry out a subset of functionalities required for business benefit analysis. Where Cost Benefit Analysis is utilised it is usually tailored to particular tasks; such as the evaluation of specialised industrial processes or use within the public sector, such as simple pro-formas for evaluating environmental costs.

At present there is no industry standard support tool for assessing business benefits of initiatives within manufacturing enterprises. This paper details the development of a robust business benefit tool for the assessment and comparison of alternative business initiatives within manufacturing enterprises.

2. Literature review

In essence benefit analysis tools ask the users to input appropriate quantitative measures (usually financial) to costs and benefits algorithms and users are invited to only accept projects where the benefits are greater than costs [2].

Net Present Value (NPV) as a way of gauging the suitability of a capital investment proposal can offer a number of advantages. NPV assesses all of the cash flows involved with the project being assessed and it takes into account the time adjusted value of money [3]. While being a good indicator for project viability there is an assumption that the cash flows for a project occur at the year end only, and that the estimation of the cost of capital and the overall complexity of NPV calculations can lead to further difficulties in its use [4]. Ross [5] adds an important caveat with manufacturing projects '..undertake the project as long as doing so doesn't interfere with the ability to take on a competing project'. Like NPV Internal Rate of Return (IRR) calculations also recognise the future value of money and incorporate every cash flow for an investment project. IRR has been defined as 'the maximum rate of interest that a company can afford to pay without making a loss on the project', if a company can borrow money for less than the IRR then the project is worth investing in [4]. Fundamental to IRR is the establishment of a break-even rate of return for a project. In common with NPV, IRR calculations also suffer from the inclusion of irregular cash flows, and are complex to compute and understand [4].

The modelling of risk and uncertainty of projects can be reflected in a cost-benefit analysis. Often uncertainty about global manufacturing factors such as technology costs and labour rates can be quantified by calculating a project's NPV and then arriving at a set of what-if scenarios to test against the NPV. In doing this the sensitivity of the NPV to different scenarios can be calculated, in effect a sensitivity analysis calculation can be made [3].

Sensitivity analysis establishes the extent to which the outcome of the benefit-cost analysis is sensitive to the assumed values of the inputs used in the analysis' [3]. By changing the discount rate in an NPV calculation for a project the sensitivity of the NPV can be derived. It is possible that a project that is deemed to be a higher risk will be assigned a risk premium via the discount rate used when calculating its NPV value. This would normally lead to the project achieving a lower NPV and so making it less likely to pass the hurdle rate (the hurdle rate is the minimum rate of NPV that the company would judge to indicate that the project is worth pursuing).

Practical examples of optimisation, in relation to CBA, are limited. Though, examples limited to the examination of, primarily, NPV values do exist and have been examined and the most practical one is now described in more detail in the course of this section. The optimisation process will usually have to take into account any limiting factors, such as finite resources (a limited amount of capital available to fund new projects, for example) to draw valid conclusions from the given data [7]. Winston [6] provides a practical model for the optimisation of capital budgeting decisions. The template examines alternative projects based on their respective cash-flows and total NPV values. A constraint to the model is the introduction of yearly capital expenditure limits, in effect for an optimal project to be selected by this model it must 'live within its means' in terms of annual cost.

There is a high level of functionality available through the above techniques but it is not exploited due to lack of accessibility for the end users in the manufacturing domain and lack of clarity about the necessary functional capabilities.

3. Requirements capture

The end user functional requirements for the generic business benefit tools were captured within a high performance complex manufacturing environment. The industrial case study organisation was selected due to its diverse product ranges and multi-site operation. There was a need within the organisation for a generic purpose built tool that would replace the many disparate ad-hoc tools previously in use.

The requirements capture involved in depth semi-structured interviews with this group of staff members, consisting of a mix of senior managers and project controllers. Existing spreadsheet templates in use were examined in detail and their functionality discussed with relevant members of staff (including the template authors). Special note was given to the identification of key financial and operational functionality. The financial measures are detailed in Table 1 on the next page. These were filtered and summarised so a requirements document could be produced that detailed the key operational and financial measures to be included in the templates.

Table 1: Measures to be included in the business benefit analysis tool

User Requirement Description	Functionalities Offered		
	Financial Analysis	Cost-benefit analysis	Provision in business benefit analysis tool
Provide Net Present Value and Internal Rate of Return calculations	Limited use and recognition of Net Present Value though more use of Internal Rate of Return -	Net Present Value & Internal Rate of Return - Central to practice	Both measures to be provided
Accommodation of currency fluctuations	Any currency	Any Currency	User to enter new currencies and conversion rate
What-if functionality	Most models provide a way to change parameters quickly	Usually more difficult to change parameters	What – if multiplier to be provided to easily change model parameters
Holistic view of project place within organization	Usually concentrate on the detail of the project rather than its wider context	Recognises the wider place of the project in the organization and its environment	Must work with existing measurement systems in place at the organisation
Sensitivity analysis	Provided through discount rate of Net Present Value	Provided through discount rate of Net Present Value	The user to enter a discount rate for Net Present Value
Project comparison	It is normal to compare competing investment projects	Cost –benefit assessments are traditionally undertaken on an accept/reject basis	To provide a way of comparing projects via NPV value comparison
Risk calculations	Provided through combination of sensitivity and what-if analysis	Provided as an overall output of the process (time consuming to re-calculate for different scenarios)	To be provided through combination of sensitivity and what-if analysis
Entry of user defined calculations	Calculations are usually standard; customisation not normally allowed	Calculations are usually standard; customisation not normally allowed	To allow for user to enter a calculation for inclusion in the template as a parameter

437

It was clear from this research that a wider view of project analysis was required than that provided by standard Financial Analysis methods and software. Though, it was also noted that elements of cost-benefit analysis practice, as used in the public sector, would have to be translated into a more generic format pertinent to the needs of an industrial organisation.

4. Functionality Gap

From the research outlined in the literature review and the organisation based interviews:
- A flexible template resource is required that addresses a wider number of issues than Cost-Benefit Analysis or Financial Analysis can satisfy alone
- There are few examples of generic cost-benefit analysis tools in the manufacturing domain. Where examples do exist, their design lacks user friendliness and their implementation is fragmentary
- Approaches to template design are overly generic, and lack much of the functionality detail required by most manufacturing enterprises
- Literature on private sector cost-benefit analysis emphasises the hard measures such as Net Present Value (NPV) and Internal Rate of Return (IRR) but devotes little time to methods for comparing projects

5. Business Benefit Tool Description

The tool is comprised of the following functionalities:
- *Primary data screen.* This screen allows the entry of capital cost and savings items for a particular project. A multiplier column is provided in this screen to allow for sensitivity analysis.
- *Time phase screen.* The screen allows apportioning of cost and savings items over a user defined time period.
- *Quarter screen.* This screen displays the impact on operating capital, profit and loss and cash flow totals for the project.
- *Year by year breakdown screen.* This is the primary results screen, displaying the calculation totals by financial year. The NPV and IRR totals are also displayed for each financial year in the user defined time-period.
- *Scenario analyser screen.* Compares the NPV contributions for each project being considered and selects the best combination of projects to match user defined available yearly capital totals.

Fig. 1:

Primary data Screen

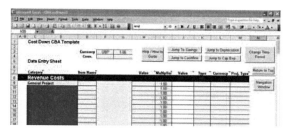

Fig. 1 shows the primary data screen. A colour code has been used on this screen with the data entry cells coloured yellow showing the user where data entry is possible.

438

Fig. 2:

Year-by-Year
Breakdown
Screen

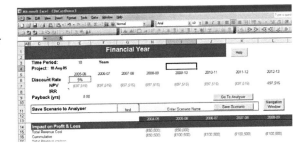

The screen shown in Fig. 2 is the year-by-year breakdown screen, showing yearly totals and the impact on the profit and loss and cash flow statements.

Fig. 3:

Tool
Navigation
Window

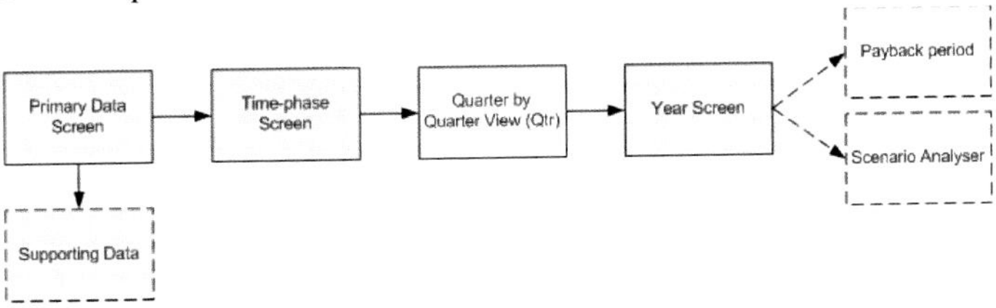

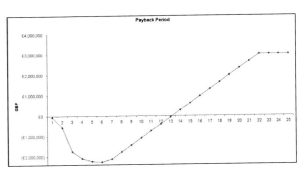

Fig.3 above shows the navigation window which may be launched from any screen within the application.

In addition to the main screens the tool provides three graphical displays:

Fig. 4:

Payback
Period
Graph

- Payback period: (shown above in Fig.4) based on the cash-flow totals from the year screen and displayed by financial quarter.
- Internal rate of Return
- Cash-flow and Net Present Value (comparison)

6. Tool Evaluation

Alternate case study scenarios were run through the tool and the results compared with expected outcomes. The tool succeeded in replacing the different tools previously employed in the case study enterprise. Staff members originally interviewed as part of the requirements gathering phase were involved in the evaluation of the tool and their comments and suggestions incorporated into a final development iteration of the tool.

The Analyser has been tested by creating several scenarios of one project. The scenarios were created by changing the multiplier value for certain line items within the template.

7. Conclusions

The key operational requirements focus on the ease of use, simplicity, security and error handling. These requirements illustrate that a wider view of project analysis was required than that provided by standard Financial Analysis methods and software. The tool also automates tasks that were previously manual (and in most cases quite time consuming). The time period and project start date functionality customises the entire tool to a user defined timeframe. The tool also benefits from the analyser project scenario choice optimiser. This is new functionality which has not been used in the case study organisation before. The ability to select projects based on NPV value will, in a limited way, further aid the decision maker's task when selecting between alternative project scenarios. The test users of this template, at the case study organisation, were impressed with the range of functionality offered. However it was suggested by the users that a more complex analyser function would be useful, for more detailed sensitivity analysis activities. This functionality, together with the functionality offered by the @Risk Excel add-in (used to provide more detailed risk analysis assessments) could be explored in more detail.

The cost reduction tool also benefits from the analyser project scenario choice optimiser. This is new functionality which has not been used in the case study organisation before. The ability to select projects based on NPV value will, in a limited way, further aid the decision maker's task when selecting between alternative project scenarios. There are a variety of tools available in the public domain providing leading edge functionalities. However, these tools are not popular in industry since the functionalities that they offer do not map to the immediate user requirements. This project has succeeded in addressing the fragmentary nature of current cost benefit analysis tool provision in the industrial sector. By repackaging existing functionality into a single generic tool industrial organisations now have a single integrated solution to address their business benefit analysis requirements.

References

[1] Sharpe, W.F. and Alexander, G.J., Investments, Fourth Edition, London, Prentice-Hall, 1990
[2] Layard, R. & Glaister, S. Cost-benefit analysis, Cambridge, Cambridge University Press, 1994.
[3] Campbell, H. F. & Brown, R. Benefit-cost analysis - financial and ecomomic appraisal using spreadsheets, Cambridge, Cambridge University Press, 2003.
[4] Jones, M. Accounting for non specialists, Chichester, Wiley, 2002.
[5] Ross, S. A. Uses, abuses and alternatives to the net present value rule. Financial management, 1995, 24, 3.
[6] Winston, W. L. Microsoft excel - data analysis and business modelling, Redmond, Microsoft Press, 2004.
[7] Lin, G. C.I. CIM justification and optimisation, New York, Taylor & Francis, 2000.

Techniques for Business Process Comparison and Conformance: State of the Art and Future Trends

A. Tiwari [1], C.J. Turner [1], B. Majeed [2]

[1] School of Applied Sciences, Cranfield University, Cranfield, Bedfordshire. MK43 0AL, UK.

[2] British Telecom, Computational Intelligence Group, IS Lab, BT Research and Venturing, Orion Building, Adastral Park, Martlesham, Ipswich, IP5 3RE, UK.

Abstract

The quantitative comparison of business processes is an area that has not received much attention from the process mining and automation community. This paper examines both qualitative and quantitative approaches to this issue and current research efforts to provide an automated method for measuring the conformance of a real process to a documented process. The paper also examines areas for further research with regard to process conformance issues.

Keywords: Business process; Process comparison; Process conformance; Process modelling.

Introduction

The automation of business processes within organisations is increasingly becoming common with the use of business process management software. Areas allied to business process management practice, such as process mining and modelling, are often augmented by the use of computers. However, one area of practice still needs to be developed into an automated technique that can be readily used by business. This area is business process comparison. This paper examines the current research into the practice of business process comparison and points out possible directions for future research.

1. Business Process: A definition

An examination and definition of the term 'business process', is required to fully understand the central subject of this paper. Havey [1] provides guidance on the meaning of the word process stating that it implies issues of work, movement and time; and suggesting that the actions of a process are performed over a time-period in order to journey towards or reach an objective. A generic definition of business process is given by Harmon [2] as 'any set of activities performed by a business that is initiated by an event, transforms information, materials, or business commitments, and produces an output'. Processes are usually comprised of multiple tasks (each with their own inputs and outputs); a process with only one task is not usually considered to be a process in its own right [3]. There is evidence that processes are often described at varying levels of abstraction; indeed many processes may be broken down into sub processes [4]. Lee [5] points out that the term process is often confused with practice. Lee defines process as codified routines carried out by individuals with explicit knowledge of those routines, whereas practice refers to tacit knowledge of individuals being used to carry out a routine without codified guidance. In essence Lee argues that practice requires heuristic knowledge of a routine.

2. Modelling Processes

When considering how to compare processes it is useful to represent the process as a graphical model. A wide variety of methods exist to model processes. Aguilar-Saven [6] describes a process model as the means to analysing and understanding a business process. Sadiq [7] also offers a useful definition of a process model stating that it orders and defines aspects of a process, such as resources, data and tasks. Process models are often called workflow models by some authors, and can take the form of a directed graph showing the individual tasks that make up a particular process. Aguilar-Saven [6] proposes a simple classification of business process models. Models are compared based on their ability to allow the model developer to make changes to a model as the process being modelled changes. A model that does not allow changes is said to be passive, one that does allow changes is said to be active.

Of the techniques outlined by Aguilar-Saven [6] it is the opinion of the author of this paper that the modelling techniques marked as active in the classification should be considered when producing dynamic models of business processes. This includes -

- Flow Chart Technique
- Data Flow Diagrams
- Role Activity Diagrams
- Role Interaction Diagrams
- Gantt Chart
- IDEF
- Coloured Petri Net
- Object Oriented Methods (including UML)
- Workflow Technique

This is due to the fact that any model(s) employed for documentation of such a dynamic system must be able to react or be modified to reflect real-time changes in processes.

3. Business Process Comparison

Sorumgard [8] provides a definition of process conformance as 'The degree of agreement between a process definition and the process that is actually carried out'. This author points out that there are three challenges that lead from this definition –

- Measuring the degree of agreement between two processes
- Arriving at a definition of process agreement
- Defining what is meant by a process definition

Sorumgard's work concerned the analysis of processes in the realm of software design. Manual observations were made of process designs; the observed process design and the recommended design were then compared with a deviation vector calculation. In general there are relatively few methods available for the comparison of processes. Van der Aalst [9] outlines two broad approaches that may be applied to this problem area, delta analysis and conformance testing. Delta analysis is the comparison of an actual process with a pre defined template. Node mapping techniques are popular in the task of delta analysis, checking for differences in the syntax used to describe individual nodes. However, such techniques do not examine processes in terms of their behaviour. Van der Aalst [9] recommends the use of inheritance techniques (an object-oriented approach) to examine behaviour differences. This approach aims to find a common super or subclass for two process models. An alternative way of comparing process behaviour is also possible though the calculation of change regions. This is achieved by comparing two processes and then examining the parts of both processes that have been affected by a difference in the models to determine a region of change. Van der Aalst recommends the use of Petri nets as the modelling notation for such delta analysis techniques.

Conformance testing involves the comparison of data within an event log with a process template. In the view of van der Aalst [9] this approach overcomes the problems encountered in delta analysis. One problem is that of insufficient events meaning that a process model cannot be constructed from known data. Additionally delta analysis cannot provide a quantitatively sound index of conformity between processes. There are, however, two broad problems encountered with conformance testing. It is possible that an event log may contain actions that are not allowed in the process template; in this case model under fitting is a problem. Conversely the problem of model over fitting is also possible where parts of the process template are not documented by the event log. In the opinion of van der Aalst [9] the situation of over fitting is preferred as it is easier to quantify.

One attempt at defining a conformity model for processes is provided by Breu et al. [11], who examines the measurement of conformity between software process models. Breu et al. [11] approach borrows much from the Capability Maturity Model (CMM) for software development. There are five levels of conformance that two processes may meet, ranging from level one non conformance to level five workflow conformance. Breu et al. [11] concentrate on qualitative measures of conformity between processes and does not provide a quantitative index.

In terms of business process conformance Juan & Ou-Yang [12] have put forward a process comparison approach based on benchmarking. A benchmarking project will normally start with the selection of processes and one or more benchmarking partners (usually partner processes are used as standards to compare against). It is also normal practice to gather wider process information in the form of key performance indicators or other types of quantitative process performance indicators. In terms of the analysis of the processes the following stages are employed by this benchmarking technique:
- Business process modelling phase
- Semantic analysis phase
- Business process gap analysis phase

This quantitative approach uses semantic similarity analysis to match entities in actual and best practice template processes to be compared. A semantic similarity degree calculation is made; this is a calculation based on process entity names and their properties. A semantic dictionary is used to store associations between entities to assist in the task of process comparison. The entities embedded in both processes are then examined in a similar semantic fashion. Process gaps are calculated from analysis of actual processes and best practice templates. This is achieved through the examination of entity and function pairs and the calculation of possible process execution paths that may be followed through both processes. Juan & Ou-Yang [13] also detail the use of process benchmarking for the comparison of processes from different organisations and detail a software interface they have developed to aid the task of process logic comparison [13].

Cook & Wolf [14] employ a different method in their comparison of software processes. The authors employ a string distance metric where the template and actual processes are represented as text strings (where each event of a process is represented by a character). The metric counts the number of insertions and deletions necessary to transform the actual process string into the template process string. Weighted values can be applied to the insertion and deletion operators to allow for fine tuning of the metric. An additional metric is put forward by Cook & Wolf [14], the non-linear string distance metric. It allows for a series of like activities to be recognised as a significant detour from normal operation. This metric replaces sequences of like operations on a string as one block. The block is then given a higher weighting, if over one insertion or deletion in length, to signal that a series of events has been changed. A table of references detailing process conformance is displayed below in Table 1.

Figure 1 (on the next page) shows the papers available in the area of process conformance (based on Table 1). It is interesting to note that a number of papers (37%) take an algorithmic approach to a largely qualitative subject as process conformance, though it must be noted that the approaches taken are broad in nature. There is a fairly even split between the number of papers that detail conformance in the business process and the software process areas. One paper has also adapted the popular software standard, the Capability Maturity Model (CMM), approach and applied it to the rating of processes [11].

Table 1: Process Conformance Papers in Literature

	Software Development Perspective	Algorithmic Approach	Benchmarking Practices Used	Based on CMM (the Capability Maturity Model)	Business Process Related
(Sorumgard, 1996)	x	x			
(Breu, Huber, and Schwerin, 2001)	x			x	
(Cook & Wolf, 1999)	x	x			
(Aalst, 2005)		x			x
(Juan & Ou-Yang, 2004)		x	x		x
(Juan & Ou-Yang, 2005)		x	x		x
(Briand, Differding, and Rombach, 1997)	x				
(Rozinat & van der Aalst, 2005)		x			x
(Aalst, de Beer, & van Dongen, 2005)		x			x

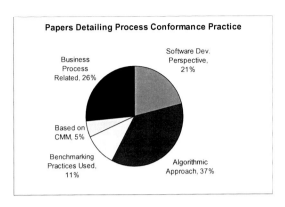

Figure 1: Papers Detailing Process Conformance Practice

4. Conclusions and Further Research

Process conformance practice is still largely qualitative in nature. Most of the literature concentrates on the conformance of software processes rather than business processes. The author of this paper is not aware of the existence of a mathematical conformity index for business processes. Only a few quantitative methods of process conformance exist at present. However, the string distance and benchmarking methods outlined by Cook & Wolf [14] and Juan & Ou-Yang [12], respectively, do offer a potential base for a more formal generic approach to process comparison and gap quantification. At this present time soft computing techniques have not been used in the practice of process conformance. Juan & Ou-Yang [12] propose an algorithmic method of identifying and quantifying process conformance gaps. In this technique they attempt to quantify qualitative information using a semantic similarity score (which is based on the work of Song et al. [15]).

It is possible that such a method of semantic similarity could be built into a more formal process conformance framework. By 'more formal', it is meant that the index of conformity would be generic within a particular sector of business allowing for like for like process comparison. The drawbacks of efficiency and accuracy experienced by Juan & Ou-Yang [12] may be addressed by the use of fuzzy logic in the semantic comparison phase allowing for a more accurate numerical representation of qualitative process entities. Cook & Wolf [14] with their string distance method of measuring process conformance, provide an alternative event based method of comparing processes. This method too could benefit from fuzzy logic, in the task of accurately allocating string tokens to represent events within a process. The automated identification of processes and their events in the string token allocation task is a necessary addition to this technique.

It is the opinion of the author of this paper that examination of a fuzzy logic approach to the design of a conformity index would be worthy of further investigation. The ability to quantify qualitative measures with fuzzy logic could provide a basis for a mathematical conformity index. The combination of existing process comparison and gap quantification techniques with fuzzy logic and a more formal mathematical index of process conformance could provide a generic solution applicable to an entire sector of the service and IT industry. It is in this direction, the author would advise, that further research efforts should be made.

Reference List

[1] Havey, M. *Essential Business Process Modelling*. Sebastapol, CA.: O'Reilly, 2005.

[2] Harmon, P. *Business Process Change: A Managers Guide to Improving, Redesigning, and Automating Processes*. San Francisco: Morgan Kaufmann, 2003.

[3] Amaravadi, C. S. and Lee, I. The dimensions of process knowledge. *Knowledge and Process Management*, 2005, 12: 1:65-76.

[4] Giaglis, G. M., Paul, R. J., and Doukidis, G. I. Simulation for Intra-Organisational Business process Modelling. Charnes, J. M., Morrice, D. T., Brunner, D. T., and Swain, J. J. *Proceedings of the 1996 Winter Simulation Conference* . New York: ACM Press; 1996, 1297-1304.

[5] Lee, L. L. Balancing business process with business practice for organisational advantage. *Journal of Knowledge Management*, 2005, 9: 1:29-41.

[6] Aguilar-Saven, R. S. Business process modelling: Review and framework. *International Journal of Production Economics*, 2004, 90:129-149.

[7] Sadiq, S. (2000). On capturing exceptions in workflow process models. *Proceedings of the 4th International Conference on Business Information Systems,* Heidelberg: Springer Verlag; 2000.

[8] Sorumgard, S. An empirical study of process conformance. *Proceedings of the Twenty-First Annual Software Engineering Workshop*, Norway, 1996.

[9] Aalst, W. M. P. (2005). Business Alignment: Using Process Mining as a Tool for Delta Analysis and Conformance Testing. *Requirements Engineering Journal*, 2005, 10: 3:198-211.

[10] Aalst, W. M. P., de Beer, H. T., and van Dongen, B. F. Process mining and verification of properties: An approach based on temporal logic. In Meersman, R. & Tari Z. *On the Move to Meaningful Internet Systems 2005.* Heidelberg: Springer Verlag, 2005.

[11] Breu, R., Huber, W., and Schwerin, W. (2001). A conformity model of software process. *Information and Software Technology*, 43:339-349.

[12] Juan, Y. C. and Ou-Yang, C. Systematic approach for the gap analysis of business processes. *International Journal of Production Research*, 2004, 42: 7.

[13] Juan, Y. C. and Ou-Yang, C. A process logic comparison approach to support business process benchmarking. *International Journal of Advanced Manufacturing Technology*, 2005, 26:191-210.

[14] Cook, J. E. and Wolf, A. L. Software process validation: quantitatively measuring the correspondence of a process to a model. *ACM Transactions on Software Engineering and Methodology,* 1999, 8: 2:147-176.

[15] Song, W. W., Johannesson, P. and Bubenko, J.J., Semantic similarity relations in schema integration. Data and Knowledge Engineering, 1996, 19:65-97.

[16] Briand, L. C., Differding, M., and Rombach, H. D. Practical guidelines for measurement-based process improvement. *Software Process Improvement and Practice Journal, 1997,* 2: 4.

[17] Rozinat, A. and van der Aalst, W. M. P. Conformance testing: measuring the alignment between event logs and process models. *Workshop on Business Process Intelligence, Business Process Management Conference 2005*, Nancy, France, 2005.

Author's Index

Authors' Index